ULTIMATE MARVEL

ULTIMATE MARVEL

Written by

Adam Bray Lorraine Cink Melanie Scott Stephen Wiacek

CONTENTS

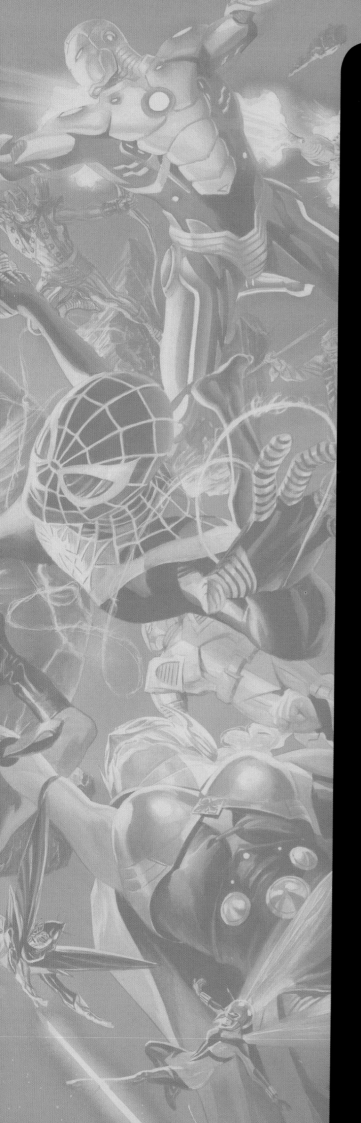

INTRODUCTION

Readers seeing a book titled *Ultimate Marvel* may wonder what it could contain—surely not *everything* in the Marvel comic book Multiverse! And, of course, without running to many volumes, that would be impossible.

So let's start by saying what *Ultimate Marvel* isn't: It's not a comprehensive encyclopedia of characters, or a history of the company. It's an in-world guide to the mainstream Marvel Universe, featuring, in chronological order of comic book appearance, as many Marvel characters, locations, vehicles, weapons and incredible artifacts that will fit into 320 pages.

Following a Timeline that details key events in the Marvel Universe, there are sections titled Super Heroes and Villains, Vehicles, Weapons and Technology, Cosmic Artifacts and Powers, Magical Artifacts, Planets and Realms, and Countries and Places.

One of the most intriguing features of *Ultimate Marvel* is the various character timelines. These function as a quick guide to a character's history and are organized by comic book era as follows: The Golden Age 1939-1950, The Atlas Age 1951-1959, The Marvel Age 1960-1969, The Bronze Age 1970-1985, The Modern Age 1986-1999), and The Heroic Age 2000-the present day.

Ultimate Marvel takes you on a fact and thrill-packed journey via the first major Marvel heroes, villains, cowboy stars, and comic characters of the 1940s and 1950s to the iconic Super Heroes and Super Villains of the 1960s and beyond, as well as delving into the secrets of their powers, technology, and bases.

Alastair Dougall, Senior Editor

FOREWORD

Being invited to write this brief preface to DK's humongous *Ultimate Marvel* is a treat for me. Because comic books have been a part of my life nearly as far back as I can remember—and Marvel Comics has been with me nearly as long. Long before I was lucky enough to be hired by Stan Lee in 1965 to write and edit for Marvel, and even got a chance to co-create new Marvel heroes such as the Vision, Iron Fist, Luke Cage, Havok, and Wolverine.

My mother always told me I discovered comics on my own, at age four, and cajoled her into buying me one. It probably starred Superman or Batman—but by the time I entered first grade, I was already cutting up copies of *Marvel Mystery Comics* so I could make up my own stories of the Human Torch, Sub-Mariner, and Captain America. When I dog-paddled around the local swimming pool, it was always Sub-Mariner I played at being, never that other underwater wannabe.

I know that, back in that era, the company only referred to itself as "Marvel Comics" for maybe a year…but that name stuck, as far as I was concerned.

When the Marvel Super Heroes, like most others, went AWOL by the late '40s, I grieved for them and couldn't understand why the rest of the world clearly didn't have the same innate good taste that I did. That feeling persisted in 1953-55, after Torch, Namor, and Cap were too briefly resuscitated.

So when I saw *Fantastic Four* #1 on sale at a Missouri newsstand, around the time I graduated college, I purchased it as eagerly as I would have any of its predecessors a decade or more earlier. And time has definitely proved me right: I did have better taste in heroic entertainment than much of the rest of the planet. Oh, it's caught up with me to some extent in recent years, but it'll never entirely overtake me.

I've had too much of a head start.

ROY THOMAS

A TIMELINE OF MARVEL UNIVERSE EVENTS

GOLDEN AGE | ATLAS AGE | MARVEL AGE | BRONZE AGE | MODERN AGE | HEROIC AGE

Born in the late 1930s, the Marvel Universe has developed into a multidimensional, interconnected arena of adventure, intrigue, and action. Each era of Marvel's history has had its landmark "crossover" events, involving a host of characters, both heroic and villainous. Here is a guide to many of Marvel's most epochal "in-world" epic storylines.

Namor battles the Human Torch (1940)
After nearly being electrocuted by land dwellers (despite trying to help them) Namor the Sub-Mariner runs amok in New York City. The Human Torch intercedes —beginning the first crossover event in Marvel history. Parts of the story were told in both Namor's and the Human Torch's storylines, marking the beginning of a shared Marvel Universe in which heroes and villains could cross into each other's titles.

THE GOLDEN AGE (1939–50)
When Timely Publications (Marvel Comics' original name) enters the burgeoning comic book market in 1939, they quickly distance themselves from competitors through one simple tactic. Whilst offering the standard range of cowboys, cops and troubleshooters, *Marvel Comics* #1 also introduces the concept of interconnected, realistic heroes. These Super Heroes soon join the patriotic effort against fascism, but begin to fade in popularity once World War II ends. By the end of the decade, the gaudy gladiators are nearly all gone and Westerns, spy, detective, and supernatural stories fill the company's pages. In addition, the public questions the effects comics may have on impressionable young minds.

Into the future...(1953)
The 1950s craze for science fiction finds comic book expression in characters such as Speed Carter, Spaceman. He hails from the late 21st century and captains the Space Sentinels, keeping the galaxy safe from alien threats such as the Blobs, the Saturnians, the Starmen, the Birdmen of Uranus, and many more.

Timely's first Super Hero team (1946)
For the first time, Timely's heroes come together to create a super-team. The All-Winners Squad is comprised of Captain America, Bucky, the Human Torch, Miss America, Namor the Sub-Mariner, Toro, and Whizzer. Together, they attempt to discover the identity of the mysterious Isbisa, who is trying to steal a nuclear bomb.

THE ATLAS AGE (1951-59)
With costumed crusaders out of fashion, the company—commonly known as Atlas—concentrates on genre favorites: Westerns, war, horror, science fiction, comedy, romance, and jungle tales, starring human-scale heroes such as the Two-Gun Kid, Combat Kelly, Jann of the Jungle and Millie the Model. Mid-decade, Atlas attempts to rekindle the nation's love of patriotic supermen when an anti-communist scare prompts a brief revival of Namor, Human Torch, and Captain America. An economic downturn reduces Atlas' output, but editor/writer Stan Lee and artist Jack Kirby turn the business around, offering a new kind of all-action, comic book experience.

MARVEL AGE (1960–69)

Super Heroes are back in fashion again, and Marvel Comics is born through a bold new concept: costumed champions with human foibles who would as soon argue with each other as battle Super Villains. The concept catches the imagination of a generation of readers who are further beguiled by the enhancement of a brilliant innovation: a consistent, interlinked, shared universe where these new heroes and villains can live and interact. Marvel expands its pantheon of stars, debuting Super Heroes that will soon become household names, such as the Fantastic Four, the Hulk, Spider-Man, Thor, Iron Man, and Doctor Strange. By the end of the decade, Marvel is the predominant publisher of comic books in the U.S.

The Avengers (1963)
A conflict with the mischievous Loki leads to the formation of the Avengers, one of the greatest super-teams of all time. The initial gathering—Thor, Iron Man, Hulk, Ant-Man, and the Wasp—remain together to fight foes no single hero can withstand.

X-Men: the strangest Super Heroes of all! (1963)
X-Men #1 sees the introduction of one of the most significant innovations in Marvel history—mutants, super-evolved human beings. Instead of gaining super-powers by scientific or magical means, mutants' remarkable abilities manifest in their teens. Feared by ordinary folks, the young mutants—X-Men—are protected in a special school by mutant telepath Charles Xavier (Professor X).

Reed Richards and Susan Storm's wedding (1965)
The Fantastic Four's Mister Fantastic and the Invisible Girl are about to walk down the aisle, but that doesn't mean the day will go off without a hitch. As the hour approaches and Marvel's greatest heroes fill the Baxter Building, a gang led by Doctor Doom attacks—leading to an epic brawl of heroes and villains! Luckily, heroes win the day, which ends happily, with Reed and Susan Richards tying the knot.

The birth of Franklin Richards (1968)
Following their spectacular wedding a few years earlier, Reed and Sue Richards of the Fantastic Four announce the birth of a son, Franklin Richards. At the time, few Super Heroes are depicted with children; Marvel helps to make family issues an important theme in comics.

THE BRONZE AGE (1970–1985)

Marvel diversified their offerings by creating genre-themed stars for war, Western, science fiction, kung fu and, especially, horror fans. All these seemingly incompatible champions and anti-heroes are scrupulously included in Marvel's ever-expanding shared continuity, which allows the Avengers to team up with cowboy champions and Spider-Man to battle Dracula. As the years pass, Super Heroes become the basis for Marvel's expansion into other areas: specifically movie and licensed property tie-ins. Boosted by TV adaptations, Spider-Man and the Hulk become global sensations. The mutant X-Men's incredible popularity paves the way for the next publishing breakthrough: vast crossover events that impact many titles at the same time.

The Korvac Saga (1978)

The cyborg Michael Korvac downloads data from the planet-devouring Galactus' starship into his computer and is imbued with the Power Cosmic. Turning himself into the humanoid form Michael, he sets sights on turning Earth into his own utopia. On Earth, Michael begins an unlikely romance with Carina, daughter of the cosmic Elder of the Universe the Collector. The Guardians of the Galaxy from the far future and the Avengers team up to stop Korvac's plans. Korvac slays many of them, but feeling Carina has lost faith in him, he commits suicide. The grief-stricken Carina then kills herself with Thor's hammer. Feeling penitent, the dying Korvac returns the heroes to life.

Contest of Champions (1982)

The Grandmaster, another Elder of the Universe, engages the lady Death in a game of strategy to win the resurrection of the Collector. Using two teams of Super Heroes as their pawns, they compete to find the four pieces of the Golden Globe of Life. Though Death ultimately concedes the victory, Grandmaster learns that to free the Collector from Death's realm, someone must take his place. Because he vowed to never again to use the Super Heroes of Earth, he agrees to take the Collector's place himself.

The Thanos War (1973–4)

Hungry for power and obsessed with the female embodiment of death, the Mad Titan Thanos hunts down the reality-altering Cosmic Cube and uses it to give himself godlike power. Captain Marvel—with the help of Drax the Destroyer, the Avengers, and Mantis—tracks down the cube and destroys it, returning Thanos to what he was before.

The Kree-Skrull War (1971–2)

An epic war of the worlds is waged between the alien Kree, the shape-shifting Skrulls, the heroes of Earth, the Inhumans, and the U.S. government, which has been infiltrated by a Skrull. When the Avengers' friend Rick Jones gets caught up in the fray, the Kree Supreme Intelligence unlocks Jones' full potential and triggers the powerful Destiny Force, which allows Jones to stop the war and make all well for the heroes of Earth.

The First Clone Saga (1975)

The Jackal clones Gwen Stacy and Peter Parker. Obsessed with Gwen and blaming Spider-Man for her recent death, he pits Spidey (whom he knows is Peter Parker) and his clone against each other, neither knowing who is the genuine article. The clone turns on his creator and fights alongside Peter. The clone and the Jackal apparently both die in an explosion, and the clone of Gwen Stacy leaves to find a new life.

Secret Wars (1984)

The omnipotent alien the Beyonder brings Earth's greatest heroes and villains to Battleworld to fight for his own research. While heroes and villains clash over and over again, Doctor Doom steals immense Power Cosmic from Galactus' homeship. Now with epic powers, he bests the Beyonder and steals his reality-shaping powers. Molecule Man, enjoying a new understanding of his powers, rips off a chunk of the planet and returns many of the villains to Earth. The heroes, meanwhile, battle Doom until the Beyonder reclaims his powers, and Mister Fantastic finds a way to send the heroes home, too.

THE MODERN AGE (1986–1999)

The era of the mega-crossover event sees armies of heroes unite against wave upon wave of cosmic threats, even as a new kind of lone wolf hero emerges in the Marvel Universe. Uncompromising vigilantes such as Punisher and Wolverine seize an eager readership's attention. In the early 1990s, Marvel releases collectible, limited-series comics, often featuring variant, gimmick covers, helping to lead to an investor boom and implosion. Eventually, Marvel decides to prune back its range of titles and focus on its core strengths: great storytelling and continuity-based Super Hero adventures.

The Infinity Gauntlet (1991)

Using his all-powerful Infinity Gauntlet, Thanos erases half of sentient life in the universe in a bid to win the affections of his lady Death. Killing more and more cosmic entities, Thanos transforms himself into an embodiment of the universe, allowing surviving Earth heroes, including Thanos' long-time enemy Adam Warlock, to take the Infinity Gauntlet from his vulnerable body, setting the universe back as it was.

Inferno (1988)

Demonic sorcerers N'astirh and S'ym seek to expand their power beyond their native Limbo (Otherplace) to conquer Earth. Planning the sacrifice of 13 mutant infants to open a portal to Earth, the demons also corrupt Madelyne Pryor—the clone of X-Man Jean Grey—but they are ultimately stopped by the X-Men, X-Factor, and the New Mutants.

Acts of Vengeance (1989–90)

A disguised Loki brings together the world's foremost Super Villain masterminds in a scheme to spread chaos and destroy the Avengers. However, internal squabbles and the Avengers' bravery eventually lead to the villains' defeat.

Operation Galactic Storm (1992)

Earth is caught in the middle of the Kree-Shi'ar War, and Earth's Mightiest Heroes must protect it. Discovering that the war is a plot by the Kree's Supreme Intelligence to decimate its own people and jumpstart the Kree's stagnant evolution, a group of rogue Avengers ignore their vow to not kill and execute the Supreme Intelligence after his manipulations result in a Nega-bomb's detonation and the death of millions.

The Evolutionary War (1988)

The High Evolutionary hopes to do what he does best—help humanity to reach their next level of evolution no matter the cost. The Avengers are called in to stop him and his Genetic Bomb. Using the High Evolutionary's own equipment, the Avengers power up Hercules to best the villain in battle.

Mutant Massacre (1986)

At the behest of mad geneticist Mister Sinister, the malicious assassins known as the Marauders set out to hunt down and kill the Morlocks, an underground society of mutants. Together, the X-Men and X-Factor attempt to protect them, but doing so has grave costs for all sides.

Fall of the Mutants (1987)

Anti-mutant sentiment grows and mutants are pressured to register with the government's Mutant Registration Act. Meanwhile, the X-Men take on the Adversary, X-Factor faces Apocalypse and his Four Horsemen, and the New Mutants fight off both the Ani-Mates and a faction of anti-mutant terrorists called the Right. Wars are won, but the battle for public acceptance for mutants continues.

Atlantis Attacks (1989)

The Deviant Lemurian Ghaur teams up with the sea-dwelling subversive Llyra and the Atlantean warlord Attuma to overthrow the surface world and resurrect the would-be conquering Elder God Set. However, their plans are foiled by the Avengers and Fantastic Four, with help from Namor the Sub-Mariner.

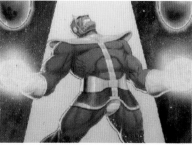

The Second Clone Saga (1994–6)

When Aunt May falls into a coma, Peter's clone returns alive and well, calling himself Ben Reilly. The Jackal is also revealed to be alive and Peter is confronted with yet more clones of himself, including the deformed Kaine and the insane Spidercide, causing great confusion. After Aunt May apparently dies, Peter is tricked into believing he was a clone and Ben was the original Peter Parker all along. Accepting this as fact, Peter decides to hand the mantle of Spider-Man to Ben, in order to focus on his relationship with his pregnant wife, Mary Jane. However, Ben dies saving Peter's life from Norman Osborn, who revealed that he has manipulated everyone the entire time. When Ben dies, he disintegrates, proving to Peter that he isn't a clone after all and once more becomes Spider-Man.

Onslaught (1996)

Magneto's negative emotions combine with Professor X's telepathic supermind, creating the ultra-powerful being Onslaught, who seeks to make Xavier's dream of utopia come true using Magneto's lethal means. Onslaught wreaks havoc, and Earth's Super Heroes set out to stop him. Onslaught mutates into a pure energy form, which members of the Avengers and Fantastic Four enter to deplete—leaving Onslaught vulnerable to the X-Men's attacks. Many heroes are believed to have died in the battle, but instead they are temporarily spirited away to a pocket dimension by Reed Richards' reality-manipulating son Franklin.

Thanos Quest (1990)

To win Death's love, Thanos embarks on a quest to gain the six vastly powerful Infinity Gems from the cosmic entities and beings that possess them. Using various stratagems, he gains five of the gems, completing the set by outwitting and killing the Grandmaster. Thanos sets the gems into a single artifact of immense power named the Infinity Gauntlet. He temporarily gains godlike status, but to his chagrin, Death's love continues to elude him.

THE HEROIC AGE (2000–PRESENT)

The new century sees Marvel embrace its many-layered Multiverse and introduce Ultimate Comics, a separate line of titles suitable for new readers seeking continuity-lite introductory versions of Marvel's core heroes, or older readers wanting a fresh and more mature take. Meanwhile, mainstream Marvel continuity becomes darker and more compelling, with across-the-board destruction and reinvention of many of Marvel's most treasured heroes, where even the most famous characters are no longer safe from radical alteration or sudden death. This darker, edgier milieu staggers from one planetary—and even cosmic—catastrophe to the next, culminating in the destruction of the entire continuity, before being gloriously reborn as a bold new Marvel Universe.

Dark Reign (2008–9)
Norman Osborn leverages his part in ending the Skrull invasion to replace Tony Stark as S.H.I.E.L.D. director. Renaming the organization H.A.M.M.E.R., Osborn uses it to enforce his rule with other Super Villain allies in an attempt to grab more and more power for himself.

Avengers Disassembled (2004–5)
When the Scarlet Witch learns that she has been manipulated into forgetting the existence of her own children, she turns the Avengers on each other in epic clashes. The Scarlet Witch is eventually stopped by Doctor Strange, but the team has already been pulled apart and their teammates Hawkeye, Ant-Man, and the Witch's own former husband Vision have each been killed.

World War Hulk (2007)
To protect Earth from his periodic rampages, well-intentioned heroes exile the Hulk into deep space. He ends up on the planet Sakaar, where he is forced to fight as a gladiator by the ruling Red King. Together with his Warbound allies, Hulk overturns the evil monarch and rules alongside his pregnant wife Caiera. The planet is devastated when Hulk's exile spaceship explodes, destroying Hulk's dream of happiness. Hulk returns to Earth with his Warbound to exact revenge against the heroes who turned on him, but he is eventually defeated.

War of Kings (2009)
The Inhumans, seeking retribution for the damage they suffered at the hands of the Skrulls, inadvertently attack a Shi'ar ship, resulting in an epic battle of alien alliances. The Shi'ar ultimately surrender after a hole is ripped in the fabric of space and time because of the war.

Annihilation (2006–7)
The villain Annihilus looks to extend his rule beyond the Negative Zone by conquering the positively charged universe with his army, the Annihilation Wave. Cosmic heroes and the peacekeeping Nova Corps face them in an intergalactic war that results in the gruesome death of Annihilus and countless victims across the universe.

Siege (2010)
Hungry for even more power, Norman Osborn ignores the orders of the U.S. President and attempts to lay siege to Asgard. With the blessing of the government, the Avengers reassemble and fight off Osborn and his Dark Avengers. They stop the villains, but not before Asgard is devastated.

House of M (2005)
The Scarlet Witch, driven mad by her reality-altering powers and manipulated by her brother Quicksilver, alters the fabric of reality so that mutants rule and humans serve. Seeing the error of her ways, she restores the Earth. But wanting to end the human/mutant tensions, she also strips the majority of mutantkind's abilities, in an event known as M-Day.

Decimation (2006)
After the decimation of M-Day, mutants deal with the near-extinction of their race. Desperate to protect the few remaining mutants, X-Men leader Cyclops resorts to violent means that some consider to be borderline villainous.

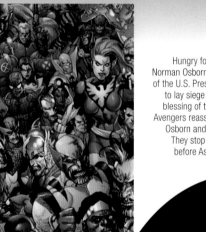

Secret Invasion (2008)
Shape-shifting alien Skrulls infiltrate the planet Earth replacing heroes and villains alike. Despite vast confusion and intense confrontations, Earth's heroes rally to root out the invasion, and eventually succeed in ridding Earth of alien Skrull doppelgangers.

Civil War (2006–7)
The government's Superhuman Registration Act forces heroes to unmask and submit to U.S. regulation. With Iron Man leading the pro-Registration faction, and Captain America the resistance, many other heroes are forced to choose a side. Captain America and his team go on the run, eventually facing their former allies in battle. Cap surrenders when on the verge of killing Tony Stark.

Shadowland (2010)

Possessed by the demonic Beast of the Hand, Daredevil becomes Hell's Kitchen's greatest dictator. Facing off against other heroes, he is eventually stopped by Iron Fist, who uses his chi to exorcise the demon, freeing Daredevil.

Fear Itself (2011)

The All-Father Odin's wicked brother, the Serpent, seeks the throne of Asgard and terrorizes Earth by sending forth a group of world-breakers named the Worthy to lay waste to Midgard with their enchanted hammers. The heroes of Earth take down this titanic team, whose hammers are melted down by Odin.

Age of Ultron (2013)

The robot Ultron takes over all technology on Earth and uses it to destroy civilization, killing many of his superhuman foes. Wolverine and the Invisible Woman travel back in time to alter the timeline of Ultron's creator, Hank Pym. When Wolverine kills Pym, this creates an even worse future, so Wolverine goes back in time again to stop himself from killing Pym and convince Pym to create a fail-safe virus in Ultron that enables his defeat.

Spider-Verse (2014)

Peter Parker leads an army of every spider-powered individual in every reality, universe, and time, to fight Morlun and his family of Spider-Totem-hunting Inheritors. The spider-powered heroes travel the Multiverse finding fellow Spider-Totems to recruit into their Spider-Army in order to protect them. Eventually, the Spider-Army converges on the Inheritors' Loomworld to directly confront them. The Inheritors are eventually defeated, and the surviving spider-powered beings return to their native realms.

Black Vortex (2015)

An ancient mirror-like Celestial artifact called the Black Vortex gives untold cosmic powers to those who submit to it. The Guardians of the Galaxy steal the mirror from Star-Lord's father J'Son to keep it safe from evil hands. Disguised as Mister Knife, J'Son seeks the artifact in his quest for power, allying with the terrifying Brood parasites in his quest. The Guardians recruit Earth's X-Men in opposing Mister Knife, some of the heroes gaining temporary cosmic powers from the Black Vortex.

Secret Wars (2015-16)

When the Earths of parallel dimensions begin crashing together, the entire reality of the Earths are destroyed. The shards of the remaining planets are patched together into Battleworld, ruled by a now cosmically powered Doctor Doom. The territories are brewing with civil unrest when Mister Fantastic and the Black Panther, in possession of the Infinity Gauntlet, eventually discover that Doctor Doom has caused the Multiversal destruction, using power stolen from the reality-altering Beyonders. In a moment of weakness, Doom agrees that Mister Fantastic would do better with these powers. Molecule Man moves the Beyonders' powers to Mister Fantastic who helps re-create reality.

Chaos War (2010-11)

Hercules builds a God Squad of titans to take down the embodiment of disorder and nothingness, the Chaos King, ultimately sealing him off into the void, away from Earth's reality.

Avengers Vs. X-Men (2012)

When the impending return of the Phoenix Force threatens the world as a powerful force of death and rebirth, the Avengers face off against the X-Men who welcome its power in hopes it could reignite the near-extinct mutant race. In a final epic battle, a Phoenix-possessed Cyclops kills his mentor Professor X. The heroes ultimately work together to restart mutantcy with the Phoenix Force.

AXIS (2014)

Red Skull steals the brain of the deceased Professor X to gain his telepathy, using it to spread hate across the globe and eventually become the vastly powerful Red Onslaught. While trying to bring Professor X's psyche to dominance with magic, Earth's heroes accidentally invert the characteristics of those present: heroes become villains and vice versa, causing global chaos, before magic wielders reverse the spell and restore normalcy.

Original Sin (2014)

All-seeing observer of the universe Uatu the Watcher is murdered, and his eyes, which contain many Marvel Universe secrets, are stolen. The crime is investigated by Nick Fury and the Avengers. One eye is traced to the villain Orb, who detonates the eye, creating a "truth bomb" that unlocks heroes and villains' secrets in its vicinity; however, Orb insists he is not Uatu's murderer. Uatu's second eye is in the possession of Nick Fury, who is revealed as the true culprit. Uatu had refused to tell him who had taken his first eye, so Fury ruthlessly killed him to find out. Fury then stopped the Orb and his accomplices exploiting Uatu's powerful armory.

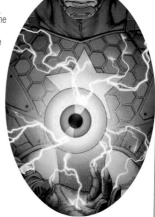

Infinity (2013) and Inhumanity (2014)

Thanos sets out with his ruthless Black Order to kill his every known descendant to please lady Death, including his Inhuman son Thane. Razing planet after planet, he sets sights on both the Earth and the Inhuman city of Attilan. Black Bolt and Maximus the Mad set off a Terrigen Bomb stopping Thanos, but it covers the Earth in Terrigen Mist, killing mutants and creating hundreds of new Inhumans, from humans that were unaware they carried the Inhuman genes. These "NuHumans" are the first wave in a greatly expanded Inhuman race.

Civil War II (2016)

When a NuHuman named Ulysses comes forward predicting coming attacks, Earth's Super Heroes become divided. After the death of her boyfriend War Machine at the hands of Thanos—predicted by Ulysses—Captain Marvel believes that they should use Ulysses' predictions to stop conflicts before they start. Iron Man is at the forefront of dissent and does not believe they can trust Ulysses' predictions because they only calculate events that could *possibly* occur, thereby finding people guilty before a crime has been committed. Both Super Heroes form alliances, ending in a major battle between Captain Marvel and Iron Man that leaves him on the verge of death. Captain Marvel gains greater power in the Super Hero community, and Ulysses leaves Earth to evolve to a higher plane of existence alongside the embodiment of Eternity.

SUPER HEROES AND VILLAINS

The Multiverse is bursting with life. Humans, Inhumans, mutants, aliens, monsters, beasts, androids, and celestial beings of immense power travel the galaxy and the portals between dimensions, waging battles for conquest—and freedom.

Earth is the center of activity in the universe. The planet's Super Heroes engage in perpetual struggles against evil forces, supported by their brave families, friends, and human allies, such as the agency S.H.I.E.L.D.

Some super-powered humans are mutants, born with extraordinary gifts, like Professor X and Scarlet Witch. Some are legendary gods, like Thor. Some experience transformation by Terrigenesis, like the Inhumans, scientific alteration, like Hulk, or bizarre accidents, like the Fantastic Four. Others, like the Guardians of the Galaxy or the Silver Surfer, come from the far reaches of the universe to aid Earth against threats from beyond. To face the gravest threats, or in special times of need, these champions form teams—the Avengers, the X-Men.

These brave heroes face off against super-powered villains as well—megalomaniac conquerors, psychotic killers, underworld crime lords, evil scientists. They, too, may band together in syndicates, such as the Sinister Six, the Masters of Evil, or the terror group Hydra, becoming even greater threats. Other Super Villains, like the Mad Titan Thanos, menace the entire universe. The balance between good and evil is always in flux. The world's greatest hero today may be corrupted into its worst villain tomorrow. The guardians of freedom must be ever vigilant.

NAMOR THE SUB-MARINER

FIRST APPEARANCE *Marvel Comics* #1 (October 1939) **BASE** Atlantis, New York City **AFFILIATIONS** Invaders, All-Winners Squad, Defenders, Avengers, Fantastic Four, The Cabal, Illuminati, The Order

Namor the Sub-Mariner is a man of two worlds, a being of immense power and towering passions. His story begins in the early 20th century, when American explorers set off test explosions in Antarctic waters and unknowingly destroy sections of Atlantis, far below the surface. Atlantean Princess Fen infiltrates the ship on behalf of her father, King Thakorr. She is captured, but falls in love with the expedition leader, Leonard McKenzie.

Seaborn fury
Although Namor despises all surface-dwellers, he reserves his most vicious acts of vengeance for the Nazis who attack Atlantis.

When rescued by Atlantean soldiers, Fen believes that Leonard has been killed and sadly returns to Atlantis carrying his unborn child. Months later, Namor—which means "Avenging Son"—is born. His skin is pink, not blue and, as he grows, he develops other traits denied his *Homo mermanus* kin. His strength, speed, and endurance are beyond belief, and his ankles sport tiny, feathered wings enabling him to fly. Crucially, he can survive indefinitely in air, although his strength decreases the longer he is out of water.

As a half-breed hybrid, Namor's upbringing is harsh, but he grows into a dutiful son of Atlantis. In 1939, the teenager swims to New York to declare war on the surface world. After initially terrorizing

the city he becomes an ally of the U.S. when Atlantis is attacked by Nazis. After serving with wartime super-team the Invaders, Namor battles crime with its successor, the All-Winners Squad, and alongside his cousin, Namora.

Namor is lost for years after telepath Paul Destine wipes his mind and leaves him an amnesiac hobo in New York City. He is restored to sanity by Human Torch Johnny Storm and rushes back to Atlantis, to find his people vanished and the city a radioactive ruin. Blaming surface-worlders, he begins a ruthless war against humanity, before reuniting with his subjects and rebuilding Atlantis.

Over the years, Namor behaves erratically: sometimes a savior, but often an enemy of mankind. This is explained when a human scientist reveals a biological imbalance has been responsible for Namor's lifelong mood swings.

Namor has teamed up with Super Hero teams the Defenders, Avengers, Fantastic Four and—following the decimation of Earth's mutant population—with the X-Men. He sees two wives die: Lady Dorma is murdered by archfoe Llyra of Lemuria and Namor has to kill his second wife, Marrina Smallwood, after she transforms into a gigantic predatory monster.

While a member of Super Hero brain trust the Illuminati, Namor causes the obliteration of many alternate Earths and for these crimes is executed by the Squadron Supreme. He is later resurrected through the misuse of his old rival Reed Richards' time machine.

Deep sea diplomacy
Even though he is a former Avenger, Namor insists on established ceremony and protocol whenever the heroes request his aid against surface threats.

"Imperius Rex!"
NAMOR

timeline

GOLDEN AGE   MARVEL AGE   BRONZE AGE   MODERN AGE   HEROIC AGE

The enemies of my enemies Namor suspends hostilities with Americans and joins other metahumans fighting the Axis powers.
Marvel Mystery Comics #3–5 (Jan.–Mar. 1940)

◄ **Imperius Rex** Namor invades the surface world. Mister Fantastic destroys the Atlanteans' breathing helmets, forcing them back beneath the sea.
Fantastic Four Annual #1 (July 1963)

Black suit Exposed to a nerve gas that sends his people into a coma, Namor loses the power to breathe air and adopts a moisture-sustaining suit designed by Reed Richards.
Sub-Mariner #67 (Nov. 1973)

▶ **Modern oracle** Namor learns to control his wild mood swings and becomes a player on the global financial stage.
Namor the Sub-Mariner #1–3 (Apr.–June 1990)

Widows and orphans Reed Richards is presumed dead; Namor joins the Fantastic Four and resumes his years-long courtship of Susan Richards.
Fantastic Four #386 (Mar. 1994)

▶ **Battle royal** A long-running war between Atlantis and Wakanda ends with both nations devastated and the undersea realm laid to waste.
New Avengers #4 (May 2013)

End of an era What remains of Atlantis and its people is destroyed by Hyperion and the Squadron Supreme.
Squadron Supreme #1 (Feb. 2016)

Immortal and imperious
Namor's execution by the Squadron Supreme fails to end his amazing story, after his killers, Hyperion and Doctor Spectrum, accidentally resurrect him with Reed Richards' time machine.

TORO

FIRST APPEARANCE *Human Torch* #2 (Fall 1940) **BASE** New York City, mobile **AFFILIATIONS** Invaders, Young Allies, Kid Commandos, Inhumans

In 1940, orphan Thomas Raymond is taken in by circus folk and performs as "Toro, the Fire-Eating Boy." When the Human Torch visits, the boy ignites into a youthful copy of the hero. Toro and the Torch confront crime and global tyranny together for years; when the Torch dies, Toro retires, marries, and settles down.

He is later brainwashed by the Mad Thinker and dies fighting Namor the Sub-Mariner. Toro is resurrected by his friend Bucky Barnes using a wish-granting Cosmic Cube. When Terrigen Mists blanket Earth, Toro transforms, revealing that his powers came not from mutation—as previously believed—but because he has recessive Inhuman genes.

Toro currently resides in New Attilan with his Inhuman extended family.

HUMAN TORCH

FIRST APPEARANCE *Marvel Comics* #1 (October 1939) **BASE** New York City, Los Angeles **AFFILIATIONS** Invaders, All-Winners Squad, Avengers, West Coast Avengers, Oracle Inc., Heroes for Hire, Secret Avengers

Professor Phineas Horton builds the Human Torch, an android that mimics all human functions. A defect of the power-supplying photoelectric "Horton Cells" covering its body makes the android spontaneously ignite in air, although its body mass never diminishes.

Due to public outcry, Horton entombs his creation in concrete, but it escapes and goes on a panicked rampage until snared by mobster Anthony Sardo. The criminal wants to use the Human Torch as a weapon, but its rapidly evolving mind refuses and—after discovering how to control his flames—the Human Torch inadvertently destroys Sardo.

Wanting to help mankind, the Torch creates the identity of Jim Hammond and joins the N.Y.P.D. His boss, Chief John Wilson, uses him to counter emergencies, such as the repeated attacks of the Sub-Mariner.

During World War II, the Torch and his teenage partner Toro divide their time between defending the U.S. and working in Britain with super-team the Invaders. Hammond's artificial blood is used to save the life of Lady Jacqueline Falsworth, triggering her transformation into the super-fast hero Spitfire.

The Torch and Toro continue their careers until 1949, when communist agents and American gangsters use a chemical weapon to plunge Hammond into a coma. He revives in 1953 after absorbing nuclear radiation and resumes crime-busting until his atomically supercharged powers overload.

Hammond becomes inert for years, but is revived by the Mad Thinker;

Immortus makes a chronal duplicate of Hammond, which becomes the basis of synthezoid hero the Vision.

Hammond has "died" and been resurrected many times. He has served as security chief for Oracle Incorporated in addition to working for Heroes for Hire. He has served with various Invaders and Avengers teams, and for S.H.I.E.L.D.

Battle buddies
The android hero finds true friendship in Cap, Bucky, and the Sub-Mariner, a.k.a. the Invaders.

THE ANGEL

FIRST APPEARANCE *Marvel Comics* #1 (October 1939) **BASE** New York City, Los Angeles, mobile **AFFILIATIONS** Penance Council, V-Battalion, the Scourges

Thomas Halloway is born in the late 1870s and raised by his prison warden father. From an early age, he learns the secrets of crime and crime-fighting from both guards and convicts. After the boy saves an inmate from electrocution, he is dubbed "the Angel." On reaching manhood, Halloway becomes a private detective.

In the 1940s, his cases become increasingly bizarre as he divides time between catching mortal crooks and spies and battling monsters and mad scientists. One case involves him saving a 4,000-year-old woman, who rewards him with the mystic Cape of Mercury. The garment allows him to fly, greatly extends his life span, and grants other enhancements; but he uses it sparingly, preferring to trust in his own strength, athletic abilities, and keen intellect.

When World War II ends, the Angel joins a group of heroes to create the clandestine Penance Council—operating secret army the V-Battalion to counter Cold War tensions and global dictatorship. He later founds vigilante group the Scourges to hunt and assassinate Super Villains and costumed criminals.

In Manhattan, an aged derelict claiming to be Halloway's brother Simon—and a second Angel active during the 1930s and 1940s—is killed by the villain Zeitgeist (Larry Ekler) while protecting homeless people. The truth of his heroic claim is never verified. In recent years, grown old and frail, Thomas Halloway becomes a recluse on his Los Angeles estate.

Avenging Angel
The caped Angel never met a thug, madman, or monster who could resist his blazing guns, brilliant mind or bludgeoning fists.

BETTY DEAN-PRENTISS

FIRST APPEARANCE *Marvel Mystery Comics* #3 (January 1940) **BASE** New York City **AFFILIATIONS** N.Y.P.D., Atlantis, Hydro-Men

Police Officer Betty Dean is the bait in a trap when the Sub-Mariner attacks New York City in 1939. Although easily overpowered, she reasons with Namor and convinces him to cease fighting.

When Namor battles the Human Torch, she again persuades the Sub-Mariner to stop. After the war, they adventure together, but when he returns to Atlantis, Betty marries Blake Prentiss and settles down. Years later, they meet again, and she becomes his confidante and a guardian for his teenaged cousin Namorita.

After Betty is mutated into an amphibian by the villainous scientist Doctor Hydro (Dr. Herman Frayne), she gives her life saving Namor from Tiger Shark (Todd Arliss), Attuma, and Doctor Dorcas.

"My life has been dedicated to the triumph of good over evil!"
CAPTAIN AMERICA

CAPTAIN AMERICA

Steve Rogers is supposed to be the first of many Super-Soldiers. But the U.S. Army's World War II program is sabotaged and, as Captain America, Rogers becomes the embodiment of American strength and bravery against the enemies of liberty.

FIRST APPEARANCE *Captain America Comics* #1 (March 1941) **BASE** Brooklyn, NYC; Avengers Tower **AFFILIATIONS** U.S. Army, S.H.I.E.L.D., Avengers, Secret Avengers

MEET CAPTAIN AMERICA

In the late 1930s, the U.S. high command decides to create a battalion of Super-Soldiers to combat the Nazi threat. The first test subject for Project: Rebirth, headed by Dr. Abraham Erskine, is a young artist named Steve Rogers, rejected by the army for being physically unfit (4-F). Rogers' body

doubles in size and is transformed into the absolute peak of athletic condition. Trained in combat, he is given an unbreakable shield and dubbed "Captain America." Alongside his intrepid sidekick Bucky Barnes, Cap is soon defeating all manner of Nazi threats, most notably the deadly plots of the agent Red Skull (Johann Schmidt). Sadly, in the war's final days, Cap seemingly falls to his death in the Arctic while trying to capture Nazi scientist Baron Zemo (Heinrich Zemo).

Super-Soldier serum
In a secret laboratory disguised as a curio shop, Steve Rogers is transformed in front of an audience of scientists, F.B.I. and army officials.

THE RISE AND FALL OF AN AVENGER

Decades later, Captain America is discovered frozen in the Arctic ice and revived by the Avengers. He becomes a vital member of the team, and also serves with government security agency S.H.I.E.L.D. However, Cap is strongly opposed to the Superhuman Registration Act, whereby Super Heroes have to register with the government and reveal their secret identities. He splits with

his friend Tony Stark (Iron Man) and forms a resistance movement. The resulting civil war tears the Super Hero community apart. Eventually realizing that his efforts are putting innocent lives at risk, Cap surrenders, despite being on the cusp of victory. Then, in a shocking turn of events, Steve Rogers is assassinated on his way to the New York City courthouse—seemingly shot by his brainwashed girlfriend and S.H.I.E.L.D. ally, Sharon Carter.

The "death" of Captain America
Even as he lies dying on the courthouse steps, Captain America is more concerned with the safety of people nearby, begging Sharon Carter to protect them.

CAP RESTORED

Captain America's assassination turns out to be a plot by Doctor Doom—not to kill Cap, but instead freeze him in a specific moment in time. However, through a scheme gone wrong perpetrated by Red Skull, Rogers is restored to the present as Captain America. Rogers finds that his pal Bucky Barnes has done a fine job filling in as Captain America in his absence, so the two share the title for a time. The U.S. President asks Rogers to rebuild the reputations of both S.H.I.E.L.D. and the Avengers after disgraced security chief Norman Osborn leaves both organizations in disarray. Cap then leads the Avengers into a major confrontation with the X-Men over the potential danger to humanity posed by the cosmic Phoenix Force.

The Phoenix Five
Cap and the Avengers try to stop Cyclops, Colossus, Emma Frost, Namor, Magik, and the X-Men.

ALL-NEW CAPTAIN AMERICA

During a battle with S.H.I.E.L.D. enemy Iron Nail (Ran Shen), the Super-Soldier serum in Steve Rogers' body is neutralized, causing him to age

rapidly. After an attack on New York City by evil biochemist Arnim Zola, Rogers realizes he is no longer strong enough to be Captain America and makes his friend Sam Wilson (Falcon) his successor. Later, while inspecting a secret S.H.I.E.L.D. prison run by a reality-altering sentient Cosmic Cube known as Kobik, Steve is nearly killed by the assassin Crossbones. With Rogers on the verge of death, Kobik intervenes and restores his youth, returning Cap to prime condition. At the urging of Sam Wilson, Steve Rogers takes up Captain America's shield once more.

Two Captain Americas
Sharon Carter helps Steve Rogers adjust to being young again, while Sam Wilson welcomes him to share their title.

A true Super-Soldier

In addition to his integrity and inspiring leadership, the Super-Soldier serum endows Steve Rogers with a peak physique, superhuman athletic abilities and drastically slows his aging. Combined with his additional combat training, this makes Captain America a soldier that surpasses all others.

timeline

GOLDEN AGE

◄ **Super-Soldier** Steve Rogers volunteers for Operation: Rebirth and is transformed by Dr. Erskine into a soldier of peak physical perfection. *Captain America Comics #1 (Mar. 1941)*

ATLAS AGE

Battling Soviet agents While attending a parade in New York City, Captain America and Bucky encounter a shocking new Russian agent named Electro. *Captain America Comics #78 (Sept. 1954)*

▼ **Joining the Avengers** The Avengers discover Cap frozen in a block of sea ice and offer him a place in their new team, which he accepts. *Avengers #4 (Mar. 1964)*

MARVEL AGE

Sleeper hit Captain America thwarts Red Skull's scheme to crash sleeper robots into the North Pole and explode the Earth's core. *Tales of Suspense #74 (Feb. 1966)*

Application rejected Steve Rogers recounts how he came to volunteer for Operation: Rebirth, revealing details about his past to S.H.I.E.L.D. Director Nick Fury. *Captain America #109 (Jan. 1969)*

▼ **Abandon ship** Rogers resigns as Captain America and becomes Nomad, "The Man Without a Country," when he discovers the U.S. President is a villain. *Captain America #180 (Dec. 1974)*

BRONZE AGE

The Captain Steve Rogers is ordered back into military service as a secret operative. He resigns as Captain America and assumes a new identity, "The Captain." *Captain America #337 (Jan. 1988)*

Murky memories Machinesmith uses Cap's memories to frame him for treason, then tries to assassinate the U.S. President and crash the S.H.I.E.L.D. Helicarrier. *Captain America #450-453 (Apr.–July 1996)*

MODERN AGE

◄ **Civil War** Captain America rebels against the Superhuman Registration Act and forms the Secret Avengers, which pits him against Tony Stark and many former friends and allies. *Civil War #1 (July 2006)*

Bucky takes charge Cap's best friend Bucky Barnes steps in as Captain America when Rogers is seemingly assassinated. Meanwhile, suspended in time, Rogers relives traumatic past events. *Captain America #34 (March 2008)*

▼ **Dimension Z** Stuck in Dimension Z, Cap raises Arnim Zola's son as his own. When he returns to the present, he finds that just a few minutes have gone by! *Captain America 1–10, Jan.–Oct. 2013)*

HEROIC AGE

Falcon flies in Rogers succumbs to old age and Sam Wilson takes up the Captain America mantle *Captain America: Sam Wilson #1 (Oct. 2015)*

Agent of Hydra Steve Rogers becomes a double agent inside the Hydra terrorist group. *Captain America: Steve Rogers #1 (July 2016)*

RED SKULL

FIRST APPEARANCE *Captain America Comics* #1
(March 1941) **BASE** Nazi Germany; later mobile
AFFILIATIONS Nazis, Hydra, A.I.M., Arnim Zola,
Sin, Crossbones, S-Men

Red Skull is Captain America and Bucky
Barnes' archenemy. His affiliations—and
even his body—may change, but his evil
core remains the same.

German-born Johann Schmidt has a
tragic start in life. His mother dies giving
birth to him. His father blames the child
and tries to drown baby Johann, before
committing suicide. The orphaned Schmidt
grows up on the streets, a thief
and vagabond.

One day Adolf Hitler walks into the very
hotel where young Schmidt is a bellboy.
Hitler sees something of himself in
Schmidt—the hatred and ambition—and
personally trains him as a Nazi agent,
giving him a red mask and the codename
Red Skull. Red Skull answers only to Hitler,
though even the Nazi dictator comes to
fear his protegé.

The U.S. Army develops a Super-Soldier
to combat Red Skull. Steve Rogers
becomes the villain's World War II nemesis
Captain America. During a showdown in
Adolf Hitler's own bunker, the roof
collapses and seemingly kills Red Skull.
However, an experimental gas keeps the
villain alive for decades in suspended
animation. Communist Albert Malik fills in
for Schmidt for a while, but the original
Red Skull is eventually revived. When old
age takes him, Schmidt's ally, Arnim Zola,
transfers Red Skull's mind into a clone of
Captain America. Physical perfection
doesn't last long, however. An accident
with Red Skull's own "dust of death"
mutilates Schmidt's face, giving him a
natural red, skull-like visage.

The Russian General Ludkin orders an
agent, the Winter Soldier (a brainwashed
Bucky Barnes), to assassinate Red Skull.
But before the Red Skull dies, he uses
a Cosmic Cube to transfer his
consciousness into Ludkin's body.

Red Skull's dreams seem to have
come true when, following the end of the
superhuman civil war, he teams up with
Doctor Faustus, Crossbones, and his own
evil daughter Sin to kill Captain America
on his way to the courthouse.

However, the whole plot is a ruse. Red
Skull actually traps Captain America at a
point in time instead, thanks to the
expertise of Doctor Faustus. Red Skull's
plan is to extract Captain America from this
point in time and transfer his own
consciousness into Cap's body—once
again with Arnim Zola's help. The plan
works—until Captain America's
consciousness returns and forces
Red Skull out of his body.
Red Skull ends up in a
robot body, which
Sharon Carter and the
Avengers destroy.
Despite this and other
setbacks, Red Skull
returns again and
again, thirsting for
vengeance against his
archfoe Captain
America.

Best fiend forever
Red Skull has been Captain America's
chief antagonist from the beginning.
No matter how many times Red Skull
dies, he always comes back for more!

Cosmic control
Red Skull is highly
intelligent but doesn't
have super-powers.
He relies on artifacts
like the Cosmic
Cube for his
megalomaniac
schemes.

timeline

▶ **The riddle of the Red Skull**
Captain America and sidekick
Bucky Barnes thwart Nazi spy
George Maxon, who poses as the
Red Skull. *Captain America
Comics* #1 (Mar. 1941)

Back from the dead Believing Captain America is
dead, Red Skull (Albert Malik) comes to America and
starts a crime syndicate. The communist villain takes
hostages in the U.N. building, but Cap and Bucky put
a stop to him. *Young Men Comics* #24 (Dec. 1953)

Origin story Red Skull (Johann Schmidt) tells Captain
America the story of his birth and how he came to be
a leader of Adolf Hitler's Nazi forces in World War II.
Tales of Suspense #66 (June 1965)

Trouble in the North Red Skull's plan to explode the
Earth's core by crashing sleeper robots into the North
Pole is foiled by Captain America. *Tales of Suspense*
#74 (Feb. 1966)

▼ **Das ende!** Age catches up with Captain America
when Red Skull infects him with a poison that brings
them both close to death. They fight in Red Skull's
bunker, but Cap refuses to deliver the killing blow—
Red Skull's aged body finally shuts down on its own.
Captain America #300 (Dec. 1984)

Turnabout Red Skull finds himself in his own
personal nightmare—as the lowly servant of
non-Aryans from all over the world.
Captain America #14 (Feb. 1999)

▶ **Mind-altering experience**
Red Skull steals Charles Xavier's
body and harvests his brain to
acquire Xavier's psychic powers.
The result is a psionic version
of Red Skull, known as Red
Onslaught. *Uncanny Avengers* #1
(Dec. 2012)

Always Hydra With Crossbones and daughter Sin,
Red Skull founds his own Hydra group and
brainwashes Steve Rogers into believing he has
always been a Hydra sleeper agent. *Captain America:
Steve Rogers* #1–4 (July–Oct. 2016)

Deadly dust
The Red Skull blows his "Dust of Death" onto
a victim's skin, causing the head to shrivel and
turn red. The hair falls out as the victim dies.

CITIZEN V

FIRST APPEARANCE *Daring Mystery Comics* #8 (January 1942)
BASE Mobile **AFFILIATIONS** V-Battalion, Thunderbolts

Several heroes have gone by the name of Citizen V (the "V" stands for "Victory"). The first Citizen V is Briton John Watkins who, as a member of V-Battalion, aids the French Resistance against the Nazis. He is killed in action by Baron Heinrich Zemo. Watkins' French lover, Paulette Brazee, flees to England. Once V-Battalion is reformed, she takes on the role of Citizen V and joins in their hunt for Nazi war criminals. Years later, Paulette Brazee's son, John "J.J." Watkins Jr., takes on the mantle of Citizen V from his mother.

When the Avengers and Fantastic Four are seemingly killed by Onslaught, Baron Helmut Zemo takes the name Citizen V (whom his father had killed) and converts his Masters of Evil into the new "Super Heroes" known as the Thunderbolts. His Thunderbolts turn against him, however, and the Avengers and Fantastic Four return to defeat Zemo, who is revealed as a villain. Dallas Riordan who had been dating Thunderbolt member Atlas) then joins V-Battalion and becomes Citizen V. She fights Baron Zemo and the Crimson Cowl, but is paralyzed in a fall off a bridge.

John Watkins III, grandson of the original Citizen V, takes on the hero identity as a member of V-Battalion, but is left in a coma after an accident. When Zemo dies, in an ironic twist, he becomes Citizen V once again, when his mind is transferred into Watkins' body by Techno (Norbert Ebersol). Watkins remains Citizen V, even when Zemo's mind is finally transferred out of his body.

Watkins the warrior
John Watkins helps Captain America stop Baron Zemo from releasing Particle X on Europe and aids the Avengers against Red Skull.

V-Battalion
Zemo sends an operative to infiltrate the Nazi-fighting V-Battalion, resulting in the deaths of all the original members.

CAPTAIN WONDER

FIRST APPEARANCE *Kids Komics* #1 (February 1943) **BASE** Mobile **AFFILIATIONS** The Twelve

Jeff Jordan is a chemistry teacher seeking to invent a formula—Wonder Fluid—to increase human strength. During class, one of his students, Tim Mulrooney, throws a ball, accidentally hitting Jordan on the back of his head. Tim is given detention, where he tries to help Jordan to perfect Wonder Fluid. Through a mishap, the serum actually works. Both Jordan and Mulrooney are endowed with superhuman strength, and Jordan—now Captain Wonder—also gains the ability to fly. Jordan joins the American forces toward the end of World War II. Captured by the Nazis, he is placed in suspended animation. More than 60 years later, he is revived with his fellow soldiers, dubbed The Twelve.

MISS AMERICA

FIRST APPEARANCE *Marvel Mystery Comics* #49 (November 1943)
BASE Mobile **AFFILIATIONS** Liberty Legion/All-Winners Squad

Washington D.C. heiress Madeline Joyce Frank is raised by her uncle, radio tycoon James Bennett. Her uncle is a benefactor of Professor Lawson, a scientist who claims to have gained super-powers from a device he invented. Madeline toys with this mysterious device during an electrical storm and gains amazing abilities: super endurance, levitation, and flight. She becomes costumed Super Hero Miss America and uses her gifts to serve her country along with her friend Whizzer (Robert Frank). They fight foreign spies and other enemies of the U.S. and join the Liberty Legion, together with Patriot, Red Raven, Tin Man, Jack Frost, Blue Diamond, and Bucky Barnes. When the U.S. enters World War II, they fight Nazis as members of the Invaders, along with Captain America, Bucky, Namor the Sub-Mariner, and their allies. When the war ends, the Invaders changes its name to the All-Winners Squad.

Miss America and Whizzer decide to leave the squad, return to civilian life, and marry. The couple eventually resume working for the U.S. government in 1949 as security agents at a secret nuclear project in New York City. The facility is sabotaged and the two are exposed to massive amounts of radiation. Sadly, Miss America is pregnant at the time and gives birth to a mutant son, Nuklo. The government takes Nuklo away and locks him in suspended animation until he can be cured of his propensity to release nuclear energy.

All-Winners Squad
The team faces villains like Isbisa, who turns the heroes against each other, and an android named Adam II, who tries to take out presidential hopeful, John F. Kennedy

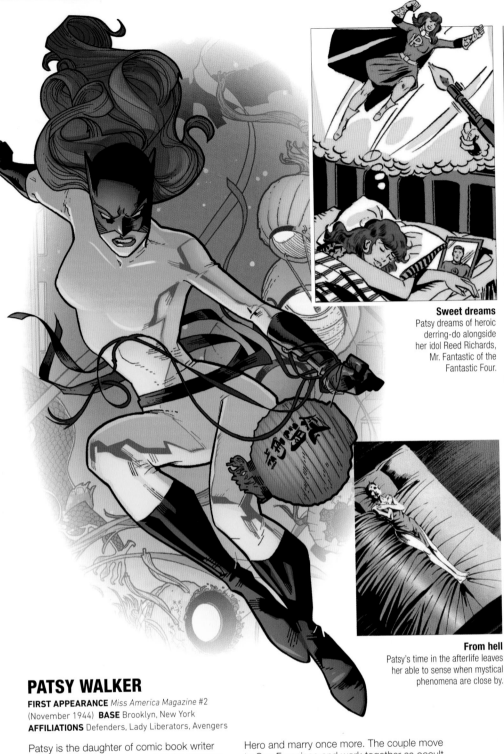

Sweet dreams
Patsy dreams of heroic derring-do alongside her idol Reed Richards, Mr. Fantastic of the Fantastic Four.

From hell
Patsy's time in the afterlife leaves her able to sense when mystical phenomena are close by.

PATSY WALKER

FIRST APPEARANCE *Miss America Magazine* #2 (November 1944) **BASE** Brooklyn, New York
AFFILIATIONS Defenders, Lady Liberators, Avengers

Patsy is the daughter of comic book writer Dorothy Walker, who makes her the teenage star of her very own title. Although Patsy dislikes having her life thrust into the spotlight, she loves comics and grows up idolizing Super Heroes, especially Reed Richards of the Fantastic Four. Patsy marries her childhood sweetheart, Robert "Buzz" Baxter, and a carefree life seems assured.

In time, Patsy comes into contact with Beast (Hank McCoy) of the X-Men, whom Buzz, now a security consultant (and much later the psychotic mutant Mad-Dog), is investigating. Starstruck, Patsy begs Hank to help her become a Super Hero. After her marriage to Buzz breaks down, Patsy transforms herself into the hero Hellcat. She travels to the planet Titan to hone her psionic potential and undergo martial arts training, with the aim of joining the Avengers but, on returning to Earth, opts to join the Defenders.

When expert in the occult Daimon Hellstrom (Son of Satan, later Hellstorm) also becomes a Defender, Patsy falls in love with him and decides to give up the life of a Super

Hero and marry once more. The couple move to San Francisco and work together as occult investigators, but tragedy strikes when Daimon's suppressed demonic side reasserts itself. Patsy is first driven insane and then to suicide. Her soul is trapped in Hell, in the realm of the demon Mephisto, but Patsy is freed and brought back to life when Hellstrom tricks the Avenger Hawkeye (Clint Barton) into believing that Patsy is his dead wife, Mockingbird (Barbara Morse).

Patsy takes up the Hellcat identity again and clashes with warlock Nicholas Scratch, Dormammu, and Yandroth the Magician. In order to defeat Yandroth, she reunites her old team, the Defenders. She is then recruited by She-Hulk (Jennifer Walters) to join a new version of the Lady Liberators team, assembled to take down Red Hulk (General Thaddeus E. "Thunderbolt" Ross). Later, Patsy decides to take a step back from being a Super Hero, finding alternative employment first as a private investigator for She-Hulk, then opening her own recruitment agency for Super Heroes.

MILLIE THE MODEL

FIRST APPEARANCE *Millie the Model* #1 (Winter 1945) **BASE** New York City
AFFILIATIONS None

Hailing from Sleepy Gap, Kansas, Millie Collins wants nothing more than to make it big in the glamorous world of fashion. Her family, amazed that she would rather wear chic dresses than sturdy overalls, decide to let her to go to New York City and find out for herself how horrible life in the Big Apple is. Despite the lack of hay bales and barn dances, Millie finds that she fits right in. Her dazzling beauty, coupled with her small-town innocence, has men falling at her feet, one of whom is photographer Clicker. Sweeping Millie into a taxi, he rushes her to the Hanover Modeling Agency, where she becomes their top model. This puts their previous top model's nose out of joint, and the fiery Miss Chili Storm becomes Millie's sharp-tongued rival.

Millie becomes a superstar, frequently followed by adoring fans desperate for her autograph. With the devoted Clicker by her side, and the loyalty of friends Toni and Daisy, Millie takes to the glamorous life of an elite model like a duck to water. She is even a celebrity guest at the wedding of the Fantastic Four's Reed Richards and Susan Storm. After a long career in front of the camera, Millie enters a new phase of her career when she opens her own modeling agency, mentoring aspiring young models like her niece, Misty. She even hires Alison Blaire (Dazzler), who helps foil a plot by a deranged fashion designer to kidnap models.

Feelin' groovy
Millie's jet-set lifestyle brings her into the orbit of top-rocking beat combo the Gears, with whom she performs as a dancer on several occasions.

TWO-GUN KID

FIRST APPEARANCE *Two-Gun Kid* #1 (March 1948)
BASE Tombstone, Texas **AFFILIATIONS** Avengers, Sunset Riders

Clay Harder is a legend of the West. It is said that he carried the two guns that inspire his nickname to remind him of the balance between good and evil—one gun being his dead father's and the other the weapon of the crook who killed him—but that may just be a tale put about by the Kid himself. Roaming the Wild West as the Two-Gun Kid, he foils unscrupulous sheriffs, prevents innocent landowners being forced off their property, and catches bandits red-handed…

Buttoned-down Harvard lawyer Matt Hawk stands out like a sore thumb in 1870s Tombstone—and he is in imminent danger of getting more than a sore thumb when the town loudmouths make him "dance" with their pistols. He is saved from being one more tombstone in the burial yard by Ben Dancer, a wise old gunslinger who teaches Hawk marksmanship and bare-knuckle fighting.

In order to continue practicing law and to keep the bad guys off his back, Matt adopts a mask and the identity of the Two-Gun Kid, inspired by Western stories starring the original Kid, Clay Harder. As the heir of the Two-Gun Kid identity, Matt Hawk's life is changed forever when, visited by the Avengers, he travels back in time to fight Kang the Conqueror. When Matt returns with them to their own time, he and Hawkeye go on a trip around the American West; however, the Two-Gun Kid pines for the Old West, and so returns home. He marries and has a child, but his family dies of an illness that would have been cured had they lived in modern times. Matt returns to fighting bad guys, forming a team called the Sunset Riders. He is killed trying to save the town of Wonderment, Montana, but resurrected when She-Hulk chooses him, as an Avenger from past history, to come to the modern era.

Matt carries on the good fight in the present day until age forces him to retire, and he returns to the past for the last time. Wishing to witness the dawn of the age of heroes, he relocates to New York City and meets the man who will become the Angel, before dying of old age.

Bushwhacked!
Clay Harder, the Two-Gun Kid, runs into an ambush by the Unlucky Thirteen Gang. Fortunately, his faithful horse, Thunder, "keeps ahead of every bullet."

Hawk and Hawkeye
The Two-Gun Kid strikes up a friendship with the Avenger Hawkeye, but the duo runs into trouble riding the range when they are attacked by the Purple Man.

VENUS

FIRST APPEARANCE *Venus* #1 (1948) **BASE** Atlas Foundation HQ, San Francisco, California **AFFILIATIONS** Agents of Atlas, God Squad

The origins of Venus are shrouded in mystery. At first, she believes herself to be the Goddess of Love, come down from Olympus to live among mortals and help them avoid violence. She is, in fact, a former siren, who once used her bewitching song to lure sailors to their deaths. Given a soul by a magician, Venus is horrified at the deaths she has caused, and takes herself off to a nunnery. Venus lives there many years, until she is forced to leave when her singing inflames a group of visiting clergymen.

Venus goes out into the world and tries to use her voice for good, to promote peace and suppress violence. As Victoria Starr, she joins the staff of *Beauty* magazine and has numerous adventures. Eventually, she becomes a Super Hero and joins the Agents of Atlas. She has suppressed memories of her past, but they come bursting to the surface during a mission, endangering her teammates, until one of them reminds Venus of all the good she has done since her siren days.

Her siren abilities then return, along with her memories, and she is once again able to bring people under her spell using her ethereal voice.

Venus later incurs the wrath of the goddess Aphrodite for daring to impersonate her, but the Olympian is so moved by Venus' song that she officially bestows on her the title Goddess of Love. Venus has since fought alongside the Silver Surfer, Thor, and Galactus against the shape-shifting alien Skrulls as part of the God Squad, a powerful team of immortals.

The Olympian Gods

Venus is not the only denizen of the divine realm of Olympus to interact with Earth's Super Heroes. Zeus, the king of the gods; his jealous queen Hera; his brothers Hades, God of the Underworld and Poseidon, God of the Sea; sisters Demeter and Hestia; and his children Ares, God of War; Athena, Goddess of Wisdom; Artemis, Goddess of the Hunt; Apollo, God of the Sun; Hephaestus, God of the Forge; and Hermes, the messenger, have all become involved in terrestrial matters at various times. However, the Olympian best known to Earth's Super Hero community is the super-strong demigod Hercules, who has served with the Avengers.

Gift from a goddess
As well as the power of her siren song, Venus can inspire feelings of love in people using her divine girdle, or Cestus, which was bequeathed to her by the goddess Aphrodite.

Elemental encounter
Fiery-tempered android hero the Human Torch is keenly
aware that, although the N.Y.P.D. need him, they neither
like nor trust him. That situation changes when he
valiantly battles Namor the Sub-Mariner to a standstill
and drives him away from the beleaguered city.

CLASH OF THE MARVELS

"Come back, water rat, and fight it out!" HUMAN TORCH

Android hero the Human Torch is asked by the New York Police Department to stop Atlantean invader Namor from wrecking the city.

Manhattan trembles in terror. The rampaging Sub-Mariner is tearing the town apart and freeing ferocious beasts from the city zoo. The Atlantean's one-man invasion is as terrible as any natural disaster and looks certain to continue until New York City is nothing but rubble. Suddenly the skies seem afire and there's a spark of hope. The Human Torch—so recently deemed a menace himself—is roaring to the rescue.

The android had been repairing train tracks damaged during Namor's reign of terror while policewoman Betty Dean tried to convince the Atlantean to use reason instead of force. That plea for peace ends as Sub-Mariner attacks again, tearing the mooring mast off the Empire State Building and throwing it into the streets below.

FIRE VS. WATER

Like a flaming star, the Torch hurtles to the rescue, cutting free trapped civilians before blazing off to recapture the escaped zoo animals. He is intercepted by Betty, who tells him that Namor is now shredding the George Washington Bridge.

Their first clash is short, savage and inconclusive. Caught by surprise, the Atlantean is driven off by the Torch's sizzling barrage of flaming fireballs, but swears to return and settle accounts.

Namor resurfaces, trapping the Torch while tearing up the colossal dynamos providing heat, light, and communications to the embattled citizens. Their second fight results in stalemate, only ending when Betty Dean finally convinces Namor to cease hostilities and leave.

No compromise
Despite Betty Dean's efforts to play peacemaker and avoid more destruction, Namor is resolved to punish mankind for its transgressions against Atlantis.

MARVEL BOY

FIRST APPEARANCE *Marvel Boy* #1 (December 1950) **BASE** Temple of Atlas, California **AFFILIATIONS** Agents of Atlas, Atlas Foundation

During the rise of Nazi Germany, Robert Grayson is brought to Uranus by rocketship and raised there by his scientist father. He mysteriously gains his Marvel Boy super-powers and telepathy from the Uranian people.

Grayson's father sends him back to Earth when a new continent rises from the sea. Marvel Boy saves the people of the new continent and stops villains taking it over. From that time on, traveling in his spacecraft named *Silver Bullet*, Marvel Boy works to protect the people of Earth from harming each other, often returning home to Uranus.

A young agent of S.H.I.E.L.D. named Wendell Vaughn (later known as Quasar) subsequently takes the codename Marvel Boy. The name is then taken up by a telekinesis-empowered mutant named Vance Astrovik, before he changes his name to Justice, whereupon he hands the moniker on to fellow mutant David Bank.

The latest hero possessing the mantle of Marvel Boy is Noh-Varr, a member of the Kree alien race, who works with the Young Avengers.

Punching pirates
Marvel Boy takes aim against the pirates and would-be usurpers of power who have set their sights on ruling a newly discovered continent.

COMBAT KELLY

FIRST APPEARANCE *Combat Kelly* #1 (November 1951) **BASE** Mobile, Korea **AFFILIATIONS** U.S. Army, Baker Company

Hank "Combat" Kelly becomes a legend in both World War II and the Korean War. A soldier in the U.S. Army, he is of Irish descent, with the ginger hair to prove it. This fearless, fire-bellied battle dynamo doesn't only love a fight, he also loves a good meal and a pretty lady. Kelly's closest friend is Cookie Novak, who often gets wrapped up in Kelly's reckless missions. Whether running headfirst into a North Korean camp or battling Nazis, Kelly always wins through.

The Kelly legend continues in the person of Michael "Combat" Kelly and his Deadly Dozen, a team of convicts with big personalities and nicknames such as Hoss, Ace, and Bullseye. Together Kelly and the boys, and their one female member, Laurie, take on missions too dangerous for the average soldier and are just crazy enough to pull them off.

RAWHIDE KID

FIRST APPEARANCE *Rawhide Kid* #1 (March 1955) **BASE** Rawhide, Texas **AFFILIATIONS** Kid Colt, Two-Gun Kid, Apache Kid

An unnamed cowboy hero known only as the Rawhide Kid—because of the rawhide shirt he wears—rights wrongs in the Wild West for a time before mysteriously riding off into the sunset.

Born in the 1850s, Johnny Clay becomes the second gunfighting hero to take the name. Orphaned by a Native American raid, he is adopted by Ben Bart, a Texas Ranger. Johnny learns to shoot from his "Uncle Ben." One day, making his way into town, a gunslinger named Brown, looking to make a name for himself, challenges Uncle Ben to a duel. Unbeknownst to Ben, the duel is rigged—a second man, Spade, fatally distracts him. Johnny finds his uncle's body and sets out to avenge his death, tracking down Brown and Spade and having them arrested.

Taking the name the Rawhide Kid, Johnny hunts down many more criminals, until his vigilantism catches up with him. Accused of killing an innocent man, who in reality is pulling a gun, the Rawhide Kid becomes an outlaw. For many years he is on the lam, hoping eventually to live on the right side of the law. The Kid goes up against all kinds of villains, including the supernatural Living Totem, and also has time-traveling encounters with Kang the Conqueror, the Avengers, and even a dinosaur.

Ride 'em cowboy!
Indestructible Hulk encounters Johnny Clay, the Rawhide Kid, *(above)* as he travels through time trying fix the past and to stop Tok Baltusar and his crew of ridable dinosaurs *(right)*.

BLACK KNIGHT

FIRST APPEARANCE *Black Knight* #1 (May 1955) **BASE** Mobile
AFFILIATIONS Knights of the Round Table (Sir Percy); Masters of Evil,
Legion of the Unliving (Nathan Garrett); MI-13, Avengers, New Excalibur (Dane Whitman)

Sir Percy of Scandia
Wielding the magical
Ebony Blade, the original
Black Knight, battles
villainy at the court of
King Arthur.

Nathan Garrett
Unworthy to wield the Ebony
Blade, villainous Black Knight
Nathan Garrett creates an
atomic Power Lance that
fires energy bolts.

Dane Whitman
Descended from Sir Percy,
Black Knight Dane Whitman
takes up the Ebony Blade
once more and proves his
worth as a Super Hero.

Pretending he has been ousted from his lands, Percy of
Scandia seeks sanctuary in King Arthur's court. In
reality, the wizard Merlin has sent for Percy to protect
Arthur against the King's evil illegitimate son Mordred
and his sorceress aunt, Morgan Le Fay. Percy poses
as a coward, only good for singing songs and playing
the lute; however, disguised as the Black Knight, he
protects the King from Mordred's schemes with his
magical Ebony Blade, a gift from Merlin.

Unable to prove Mordred's guilt without revealing
his secret identity, Percy suffers the constant insults
of his fellow knights, and worst of all, his beloved, Lady
Rosamund. In his final battle, both he and Mordred are
killed. Merlin casts a spell to ensure that if Mordred ever
rises again, so too shall the ghost of the Black Knight.

Sir Percy's Black Knight legacy passes on to many of
his descendants. One such, Professor Nathan Garrett,
is so infuriated to find that he is unworthy to wield the
Ebony Blade due to his evil tendencies that, armed with
an atomic-powered lance and mounted on a genetically engineered flying horse,
he goes on a crime spree. He then joins the Masters of Evil at the request of its
leader, Baron Zemo.

Garrett's nephew, Dane Whitman, restores honor to the Ebony Blade, taking
on the mantle of the Black Knight and working with the Avengers, Defenders,
and other Super Hero teams against ancient and arcane foes. While with New
Excalibur, he switches bodies with the original Black Knight, Percy of Scandia,
to save Arthur, with the help of Merlin.

MORGAN LE FAY

FIRST APPEARANCE *Black Knight* #1 (May 1955) **BASE** Weirdworld; formerly mobile
AFFILIATIONS Darkholders, Doctor Doom

The half-sister of King Arthur, Morgan
is granted immortality through her
faerie heritage. The aunt and ally of
the evil Mordred, who lusts after King
Arthur's throne, Morgan becomes
a force of dark magic after her
nephew's death. In addition to
her natural talent for magic, astral
projection, and ability to manipulate
mystical energies, she devotes many
lifetimes to studying the *Book of the
Darkhold*, which encompasses the dark arts
she uses to try to kill her brother Arthur, and
also to defeat the time-traveling Avengers.

She is so renowned as a sorceress that
Doctor Doom travels back in time to entreat
her to help him save his mother from Hell.
In return, Doom agrees to lead her undead
troops against Arthur. Luckily, Iron Man,
doing a little time travel of his own, puts a
stop to Morgan and Doom's plan.

Doctor Doom later meets Morgan again as
a lover and a student, hoping to learn how to
destroy the Avengers. Angered when Doom
disappears and offers her nothing for her
teachings, she travels to the future to destroy
him and any of the Dark Avengers that stand
in her way.

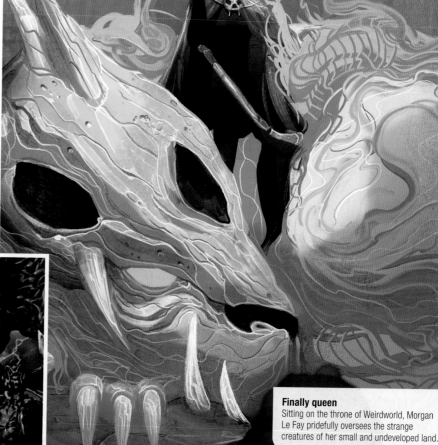

Monstrous victory
After conquering Doctor Doom,
Morgan Le Fay faces off against the
Dark Avengers, unleashing upon them
a horde of slavering monsters.

Finally queen
Sitting on the throne of Weirdworld, Morgan
Le Fay pridefully oversees the strange
creatures of her small and undeveloped land.

THIN MAN

FIRST APPEARANCE *Mystic Comics* #4
(August 1940)

Granted eternal youth, augmented physical resilience, and the ability to flatten his body by the ancient Kalahian civilization, explorer Dr. Bruce Dickson becomes costumed detective The Thin Man.

BLACK WIDOW (CLAIRE VOYANT)

FIRST APPEARANCE *Mystic Comics* #4
(August 1940)

Murdered medium Claire Voyant is chosen by Satan to return to Earth and hunt the wicked. She is immune to weapons and can kill with a single touch.

VISION (AARKUS)

FIRST APPEARANCE *Marvel Mystery Comics* #13 (November 1940)

Aarkus is a law officer from Smokeworld, invited to Earth by scientist Markham Erickson to battle evil with his flight, smoke-borne teleportation, illusion-casting, and temperature manipulation.

BLACK MARVEL

FIRST APPEARANCE *Mystic Comics* #5
(March 1941)

After passing the hallowed rites and deadly tests of the Blackfeet tribe, Dan Lyons wins the right to battle evil in the sacred costume of the Black Marvel.

THE BLUE DIAMOND

FIRST APPEARANCE *Daring Mystery Comics* #7
(April 1941)

An explosion embeds fragments of a mystic gem in the skin of archaeologist Elton T. Morrow, imbuing him with superhuman strength and invulnerability, which he thereafter employs to fight the Nazis on the battlefields of Europe.

YOUNG ALLIES

FIRST APPEARANCE *Young Allies* #1
(Summer 1941)

Costumed sidekicks Bucky and Toro team up with a gang of patriotic kids to battle monsters, zombies, and the Red Skull, as well as human terrors such as Hitler, Hirohito, and Mussolini.

MAJOR LIBERTY

FIRST APPEARANCE *U.S.A. Comics* #1
(August 1941)

History teacher John Liberty has the supernatural ability to summon the spirits of famous American patriots. When called, these heroes of the past join him in the battle against tyranny.

JACK FROST

FIRST APPEARANCE *U.S.A. Comics* #1
(August 1941)

A member of the Liberty Legion, Jack Frost is an Arctic elemental spirit of mysterious origins (possibly descended from Norse Frost Giants) who takes humanoid form, and uses his cryokinetic powers to defend the weak and fight evil.

ROCKMAN, UNDERGROUND SECRET AGENT

FIRST APPEARANCE
U.S.A. Comics #1
(August 1941)

Hailing from the depths beneath America, Rockman utilizes the technological marvels of the hidden city of Abysmia to crush tyranny and subversion targeting the U.S.A.

FATHER TIME

FIRST APPEARANCE *Captain America Comics* #6 (September 1941)

When Larry Scott's father is framed for murder, Larry clears his name just too late to prevent his execution. Heartbroken, he creates a time-themed costume and brings criminals and spies to justice.

THE DESTROYER

FIRST APPEARANCE *Mystic Comics* #6
(October 1941)

American concentration camp prisoner Keen Marlow is given experimental Super-Soldier serum by fellow prisoner Eric Schmitt, allowing Keen to escape and fight the Nazis on their home soil.

POWERHOUSE PEPPER

FIRST APPEARANCE
Joker Comics #1
(April 1942)

Pro boxer Powerhouse Pepper is big-hearted, ever-cheerful, super-strong, but dim-witted. His true talent is finding trouble and causing big slapstick laughs.

ZIGGY PIG AND SILLY SEAL

FIRST APPEARANCE *Krazy Komics* #1
(July 1942)

Funny animal bumpkins Ziggy and Silly get up to all kinds of surreal slapstick antics. Their adventures are soon spiced up by a mean interloper named Toughy Cat.

TESSIE THE TYPIST

FIRST APPEARANCE *Tessie the Typist* #1
(Summer 1944)

Ditzy working girl Tessie the Typist stumbles from office job to office job, romance to romance and, unfortunately, embarrassment to embarrassment, but she never lets life get her down.

GEORGIE

FIRST APPEARANCE *Georgie Comics* #1
(Spring 1945)

Lovable halfwit and typical teenaged New Yorker Georgie struggles with the universal adolescent problems of work, play, sports, school, and, especially, love.

NELLIE THE NURSE

FIRST APPEARANCE *Nellie the Nurse* #1
(December 1945)

Resourceful, fun-loving Nellie the Nurse saves lives, sets broken bones, turns heads, and breaks hearts. She doesn't mind letting medicine take a back seat while looking for romance.

BLONDE PHANTOM

FIRST APPEARANCE *All Select Comics* #11 (Fall 1946)

Secretary Louise Grant secretly helps her private-eye boss Mark Mason solve tough cases by donning an evening dress and domino mask and crushing criminals as the Blonde Phantom.

FUTURE MAN

FIRST APPEARANCE *All Winners Comics* #21 (Winter 1946)

Vanguard of an invasion from a dystopian tomorrow, Future Man tries to eradicate humanity to make room for his people, until stopped by the All-Winners Squad.

MADAME DEATH

FIRST APPEARANCE *All Winners Comics* #21 (Winter 1946)

Criminal mastermind Madame Death is happy to sell out humanity for profit, but pays the ultimate price when the All-Winners Squad strikes back.

NAMORA

FIRST APPEARANCE *Marvel Mystery Comics* #82 (May 1947)

Aquaria Nautica Neptunia, nicknamed Namora, is the Sub-Mariner's cousin, and, possessing similar powers, becomes an avenging crime-buster after her father is killed by loot-hungry surface dwellers.

ASBESTOS LADY

FIRST APPEARANCE *Human Torch Comics* #27 (Summer 1947)

Racketeer and arsonist Victoria Murdock uses her scientific expertise to create fireproof suits. She dons them to commit crimes and battle her archenemies Human Torch and Toro, whom she holds responsible for the execution of her twin brother.

HYENA

FIRST APPEARANCE *Human Torch Comics* #30 (May 1948)

Born with a birth defect that gives him a perpetual grin, Henry Mortonson is a Nazi-sympathizer who graduates from sabotaging U.S. military vehicles during the war to committing vicious crimes with his gang of scavengers.

KID COLT

FIRST APPEARANCE *Kid Colt, Hero of the West* #1 (August 1948)

Gunslinger Blaine Colt is branded an outlaw after he kills a corrupt sheriff and deputy responsible for the murder of his father. Thereafter, he roams the Wild West as Kid Colt, fighting injustice while trying to clear his name.

SUN GIRL

FIRST APPEARANCE *Sun Girl* #1 (August 1948)

Personal secretary to the Human Torch, Mary Mitchell falls for her boss and takes over as his crime-fighting assistant after Toro retires. She later becomes a solo crime fighter.

BLACK RIDER

FIRST APPEARANCE *All-Western Winners* #2 (Winter 1948)

Outlaw Matthew Masters reforms and becomes a physician, but when bandits strike he creates a masked disguise to face them; deciding that the world needs avengers as well as healers.

MARVEL BOY

FIRST APPEARANCE *Marvel Boy* #1 (December 1950)

Raised on Uranus by his scientist father, Robert Grayson returns to Earth to battle crime, evil, and supernatural terror with the super-science of the utopian alien race known as the Eternals.

APACHE KID

FIRST APPEARANCE *Two-Gun Western* #5 (December 1950)

There have been several Apache Kids. The original is Alan Krandal, who is adopted and raised by the Apache chief Red Hawk, after Alan's parents are killed in a battle with Red Hawk's warriors.

RINGO KID

FIRST APPEARANCE *Ringo Kid Western* #1 (August 1954)

The outlaw son of a white settler and Comanche princess, the Ringo Kid roams the plains of the Old West after his mother's murder, dispensing help to the needy and grim justice to the guilty.

OUTLAW KID

FIRST APPEARANCE *Outlaw Kid* #1 (September 1954)

After his father is blinded in a gun battle, lawyer Lance Temple dons a mask to conceal his face after promising his father to never use guns. He battles thieves and killers as the Western hero Outlaw Kid.

WYATT EARP

FIRST APPEARANCE *Wyatt Earp* #1 (November 1955)

Buffalo hunter Wyatt Earp starts hunting crooks and outgunning bad men as sheriff of Ellisworth, Kansas, after personally experiencing the evil and corruption of the city.

MORDRED

FIRST APPEARANCE *Black Knight* #1 (May 1955)

This craven usurper wants to destroy King Arthur and rule Camelot, unaware that his schemes are constantly foiled by foppish kinsman Percy of Scandia— secretly the mysterious Black Knight.

YELLOW CLAW

FIRST APPEARANCE *Yellow Claw* #1 (October 1956)

Immortal communist mastermind the Yellow Claw uses ancient lore and futuristic science to attack America, only to be foiled by his niece Suwan and her F.B.I. agent lover Jimmy Woo.

"Together we have more power than humans have ever possessed."

MISTER FANTASTIC

FANTASTIC FOUR

The first family of Super Heroes, the Fantastic Four are renowned across the globe. Shunning secret identities, Mister Fantastic, Invisible Woman, the Human Torch, and the Thing fight the good fight in the full glare of the spotlight.

FIRST APPEARANCE *The Fantastic Four* #1 (November 1961) **BASE** Baxter Building, New York City

MEET THE TEAM

Brilliant scientist Reed Richards, chasing his dream of interstellar flight, takes his best friend, pilot Ben Grimm, his fiancée Susan Storm, and her brother Johnny on a test run in a spacecraft he built himself. However, they are bombarded with cosmic radiation from a solar flare and physically changed forever. Reed discovers that he can stretch his body to fantastic limits, while Sue can become invisible. Johnny Storm can cover his body in flame and fly, and Ben Grimm develops a monstrous, rock-like body that gives him super-strength. They all agree that the only way forward is to use their newfound super-powers—further enhanced by the inventions and discoveries of Reed Richards—to help mankind as the Fantastic Four.

Technical hitch
The ship's shields fail to protect the crew from a burst of cosmic radiation.

FRIGHTFUL FOES

The Fantastic Four soon put their powers to good use in the battle against evil. First up is Mole Man (Harvey Elder), a villain living underground on Monster Isle with a menagerie of freakish beasts at his command. After leaving Mole Man buried in his tunnels, the FF face a host of terrible threats, both alien and human. Their most formidable foes are the powerful Molecule Man (Owen Reece), the extraterrestrial, shape-changing Skrulls, Negative Zone dweller Annihilus, planet-eater Galactus, and the FF's evil equivalents, the Frightful Four. Their most enduring enemy is Doctor Doom, whose diabolical sorcery is the polar opposite to Reed Richards' calm devotion to science.

Fateful meeting
Victor von Doom first meets his nemesis Reed Richards at State University. He blames Richards for the lab accident that left his face disfigured.

FAMILY AFFAIR

Theirs is not just a coalition of the strong—the Fantastic Four are truly held together by family ties. With a brother and sister in the team from the start, these connections are reinforced when Reed Richards marries Sue Storm. Reed and Sue's two children, Franklin and Valeria, carry on the family tradition of Super Heroism. Franklin is born a mutant with incredibly powerful psionic abilities, unfortunately making him a target for Super Villains everywhere. His sister Valeria has no superhuman powers, but has a genius-level intellect, just like her father.

Family first
As the family has grown, and Four become six, their spirit of adventure and discovery remains as strong as ever.

CREATORS OF THE MULTIVERSE

The Multiverse is almost entirely destroyed, leaving only Battleworld—created by Molecule Man from fragments of other realities and ruled by Doctor Doom, with Sue Storm Richards and daughter Valeria as his unwitting "family." When Reed Richards arrives, he and his old adversary clash, with Doom forced to admit that Reed would have made a better job of ruling Battleworld than he has. Molecule Man gives Richards all the Beyond power that Doom had had and restores reality. Reunited with his family, Reed decides that his time as a Super Hero is over for now. His family's new mission, with the help of Molecule Man, is to recreate all the worlds that disappeared from the Multiverse.

Reality-shapers
The first family of Super Heroes are turning their skills to the task of rebuilding the Multiverse.

Super explorers
While their super-powers are something special, what really makes the Fantastic Four tick is their close-knit family dynamic and thirst for discovery.

timeline

Space race Reed Richards launches his spaceship, but cosmic radiation gives he and his fellow travelers, Ben Grimm, Susan and Johnny Storm, strange powers. They become the Fantastic Four. *Fantastic Four* #1 (Nov. 1961)

▼ **Star-crossed lovers** Sue Storm and Reed Richards marry, although the wedding is disrupted by villains sent by Doctor Doom. *Fantastic Four Annual* #3 (Oct. 1965)

Surf's up The Fantastic Four cross paths with the Silver Surfer and the planet-eating Galactus. *Fantastic Four* #48 (Mar. 1966)

Let there be life The lives of Sue Storm Richards and her unborn child are put at risk by the cosmic radiation in her body. The rest of the FF travel to the Negative Zone to find a cure, and Franklin Richards is born safely. *Fantastic Four Annual* #6 (Nov. 1968)

New member Invisible Girl leaves the Fantastic Four and is replaced by the prehensile-haired Medusa, an Inhuman (an alien Kree/human hybrid) and former member of the Frightful Four. *Fantastic Four* #132 (Mar. 1973)

▼ **I, robot** To provide computer backup, Reed Richards builds a robot, Herbie, whose relationship with the skeptical Thing is instantly prickly. *Fantastic Four* #209 (Aug. 1979)

She-Hulk joins When the Thing chooses to remain on Battleworld after the Secret Wars, his place in the FF is taken by She-Hulk. *Fantastic Four* #265 (Apr. 1984)

Girl interrupted After a traumatic encounter with Psycho Man, Sue Storm Richards declares that Invisible Girl is dead and that she is now Invisible Woman. *Fantastic Four* #284 (Nov. 1985)

Holding a torch Johnny Storm marries Alicia Masters, the step-daughter of one of the FF's old adversaries—the Puppet Master. The villain plans to stop the wedding, but is moved by Alicia's happiness. *Fantastic Four* #300 (Mar. 1987)

Psi-Lord Franklin Richards is kidnapped and taken into the future by his grandfather Nathaniel. He returns almost instantly, as a teenager possessing great power and calling himself Psi-Lord. *Fantastic Four* #376 (May 1993)

◄ **Doctor in the house** Following a traumatic labor, baby Valeria Richards is delivered by an unlikely midwife: Doctor Doom! *Fantastic Four* #54 (June 2002)

Future Foundation Disillusioned with Earth's scientists, Reed Richards gathers a group of heroes and great minds to form the Future Foundation. *Fantastic Four* #579 (July 2010)

▼ **Torch extinguished** Johnny Storm is killed preventing an Annihilation Wave crossing over from the Negative Zone. It is later revealed that he has been resurrected by Annihilus. *Fantastic Four* #587 (Mar. 2011)

Rebuilding reality After prevailing over Doctor Doom on Battleworld, Reed Richards, his family, and the Future Foundation resolve to rebuild the Multiverse. *Secret Wars* #9 (Mar. 2016)

MARVEL AGE

BRONZE AGE

MODERN AGE

HEROIC AGE

GROOT

FIRST APPEARANCE *Tales to Astonish* #13 (November 1960) **BASE** Mobile **AFFILIATIONS** Guardians of the Galaxy

The tree-like entity Groot is a member of the species *Flora colossus*, originating from Planet X. Groot claims to be the rightful ruler of his homeworld, although that declaration appears to be false. Due to his wooden larynx, Groot is unable to communicate with most other beings, apparently saying nothing but "I am Groot," although telepaths and a select few can actually understand him. One such being is fellow Guardian Rocket Raccoon, who becomes Groot's closest friend.

When Groot first visits Earth he is a hostile extraterrestrial—he wants to abduct humans and experiment on them. However, this may well be a case of mistaken identity (all the other beings from his planet are tree-like entities who also say "I am Groot"). After being captured by the Collector and then cast into the Negative Zone, Groot is captured by Nick Fury's Howling Commandos. He decides to join up with the S.H.I.E.L.D.

supernatural unit, but eventually winds up in a Kree prison. It is here that he meets and joins up with the Guardians of the Galaxy.

Groot is naturally large and exceptionally strong and durable, but he has been close to being destroyed on a number of occasions—in battles against cybernetic telepaths the Phalanx and the Children of Tomorrow. Fortunately, Groot is able to regrow himself from a cutting and can rapidly increase his size if needed—he demonstrates this ability when he destroys Doctor Doom's castle on Battleworld during the Secret Wars.

Groot later takes his friend Rocket Raccoon hitchhiking across the galaxy. When Rocket Raccoon is captured by a space pirate, Groot assembles a ragtag band to rescue him. The pair then visit Earth, where Groot is reunited with Hannah, an old woman whom he had rescued as a child back on Planet X.

Hidden depths
When Jean Grey communicates telepathically with Groot, she discovers that he is, in fact, a complex, intelligent being.

FIN FANG FOOM

FIRST APPEARANCE *Strange Tales* #89 (October 1961) **BASE** Valley of the Sleeping Dragon, China **AFFILIATIONS** Dragon Lords of Kakaranthara, Fin Fang Four

A dragon-like alien from the planet Kakaranthara—also known as Maklu IV—Fin Fang Foom is shipwrecked on Earth along with his crew during a mission of conquest. While the other extraterrestrials take the form of humans, Fin Fang Foom is left in an artificially induced slumber guarding the crash site. There, the sleeping dragon enters local legend, and several times Fin Fang Foom is awakened to help an Earthling's scheme, nefarious or otherwise. Each time he has grown bigger, eventually reaching around 100 feet in height. Even when his vast body appears defeated, the spirit of Fin Fang Foom lives on and inhabits new vessels. Brought to New York, he adopts Buddhism and appears to change his ways, carving out a surprising new life as a chef in a Chinese restaurant in the Baxter Building. However, Foom does not remain small, or Earthbound—Drax encounters the huge beast on a distant moon trying to hatch dragon eggs, desperate to perpetuate his species.

DOCTOR DRUID

FIRST APPEARANCE *Amazing Adventures* #1 (June 1961) **BASE** Boston, Massachusetts **AFFILIATIONS** Monster Hunters, Avengers, Secret Defenders, Legion of the Unliving

Descended from the druids of ancient Britain, Anthony Ludgate has a fascination with the occult. He studies medicine at Harvard and becomes a psychiatrist. Ludgate later meets a mysterious Tibetan lama—the Ancient One in disguise—who puts him through a series of magical tests to determine his suitability as a disciple. Although the Ancient One chooses another as his Sorcerer Supreme, Ludgate decides to use his magic for good, firstly under the name Doctor Droom, and then Doctor Druid. After a period with the Monster Hunters, he is selected for Avengers membership, having been instrumental in evicting the Masters of Evil from the Avengers Mansion. Doctor Druid is killed by Hellstorm, and has since been seen serving with the Legion of the Unliving.

MOLE MAN

FIRST APPEARANCE *Fantastic Four* #1 (November 1961) **BASE** Monster Island, Subterranea **AFFILIATIONS** Outcasts

Harvey Elder, shunned and mocked all his life because of his strange appearance and extreme near-sightedness, decides to seek out a legendary land beneath the Earth's surface. Stowing away on board a plane carrying the Monster

Hunters, Harvey ends up abandoned on Monster Island, having lost his glasses. He stumbles upon the Valley of Diamonds and, dazzled by the glare from the priceless gems, is rendered virtually blind. From this moment on, Harvey refers to himself as Mole Man and declares himself the ruler of Subterranea—a vast network of caves and tunnels inhabited by yellow-skinned Moloids and a terrifying menagerie of monsters.

Mole Man hates the surface world that rejected him, and many of his schemes seek to punish or subjugate surface-dwellers. The first of these plots is foiled by the Fantastic Four, who travel to Monster Island and attempt to bury Harvey and his monstrous minions. Mole Man survives and unsuccessfully battles other costumed heroes. Retaining sympathy for unloved creatures,

he forms the Outcasts, and the Thing briefly becomes a member before he takes exception to Harvey's latest evil scheme. Mole Man's rule seemingly ends when he is overthrown by the Mole Monster, his son with Deviant Kyzerra Os.

Love quest
Mole Man is always looking for love and acceptance, and has often sought brides to live with him in Subterranea— even trying his luck with She-Hulk.

REED RICHARDS

FIRST APPEARANCE *Fantastic Four* #1 (November 1961) **BASE** Baxter Building, New York City **AFFILIATIONS** Fantastic Four, Future Foundation

Mister Fantastic, a.k.a. Reed Richards, is an awesome combination of superhuman elasticity and seemingly boundless intelligence. If he can defeat an enemy with his intellect, he will, but if fighting is needed, he's right in the thick of it.

Even before he acquires his superhuman abilities, Reed Richards possesses an intellect so impressive that it is virtually a superpower in itself. Attending college at just 14 years old, Reed is particularly outstanding in math and the sciences. Moving to New York to study at State University, he meets several people who will prove pivotal in his life: Susan Storm (later his wife and Fantastic Four teammate, Invisible Woman), Ben Grimm (later FF teammate Thing), and Victor von Doom (later FF archenemy Doctor Doom). Teenager Sue Storm is the niece of Reed's landlady, and the two young people immediately hit it off—and are soon engaged. On campus, Reed tries to befriend fellow science student Victor, but is met with hostility. Reed soon finds a more sociable roommate, football star Ben Grimm, and the two become lifelong friends. However, Reed's obsession with studying problems from every conceivable angle sometimes infuriates the more direct Ben.

Reed's dream is to design and build a spacecraft capable of interstellar flight and he pours all his resources into achieving this. Accompanied by Ben—who is now a test pilot—Sue, and her younger brother, Johnny, Reed makes his maiden flight—but disaster nearly strikes when the ship is pelted with cosmic radiation. Returning to Earth, Reed and his crew have all acquired strange powers—Reed is now super-elastic and can stretch his body into any shape. Calling himself Mister Fantastic, he and the others pledge to use their powers for good as the Fantastic Four.

Reed is the natural leader of the group, and it is his genius that both funds their activities and foils evil masterminds. His scientific expertise also leads other major Super Heroes to seek his advice in their own battles. Reed and Sue eventually marry and have two remarkable children: Franklin, a hugely powerful mutant who can manipulate reality, molecular energy and travel through time; and Valeria, who may be even cleverer than her father. The Fantastic Four are a close-knit family; however, they have their fallings out. For example, Reed sides with Tony Stark (Iron Man) during the clash over superhuman registration, which brings him into serious conflict with the other members of the FF, particularly his wife, Sue.

The FF faces many enemies, but their most persistent foe is Victor—now Doctor Doom—whose hatred for Reed still burns brightly. This comes to a head during the Secret Wars event, when all realities are reduced to tiny fragments and joined together to make Battleworld, ruled by Doom. Reed, saved from the disintegrating Earth, works with a version of himself from another reality to end Doom's reign and reboot the Multiverse. Putting aside his Super Hero career, Reed sets about recreating universes with his family at his side.

Council of Reeds
A freak accident leads to the Reed Richards from many different realities coming together in the space between universes. From here, the Reeds watch over the Multiverse, so that they can act against major threats.

timeline

▼ **College boy** Gifted student Reed Richards arrives in New York where he meets nemesis Victor von Doom, best friend Ben Grimm, and future wife Susan Storm. *Fantastic Four* #1 (Nov. 1961)

Kitted out Reed Richards invents the Fantasti-Car and Fantasti-Copter to help his team get around. *Fantastic Four* #3 (Mar. 1962)

Tough choices When his son Franklin's powers threaten to get out of control, Reed uses a device he has invented to shut down Franklin's mind, which horrifies the rest of the FF. *Fantastic Four* #141 (Dec. 1973)

On trial After refusing to kill the planet-eater Galactus, Reed Richards stands accused of being responsible for the deaths of seven billion Skrulls. He is found not guilty after the Watcher, Odin, Galactus, and Eternity speak in his defense. *Fantastic Four* #262 (Jan. 1984)

Fantastic Avengers Having left the Fantastic Four hoping to give Franklin a more normal life, Reed and Sue agree to become Avengers. A born leader, Reed cannot adjust to taking orders. *Avengers* #301 (Mar. 1989)

▼ **Onslaught** Reed and the rest of the FF apparently die while saving Franklin from the monstrous psionic entity Onslaught. In fact, Franklin saves them by using his reality-reshaping powers to create a pocket universe for them to shelter in. *Heroes Reborn: The Return* #4 (Dec. 1997)

Civil War In the battles triggered by the Superhuman Registration Act, Reed Richards is one of the most prominent heroes supporting the Act—in opposition to the other members of the FF. *Civil War* #1 (July 2006)

Secret Invasion Reed Richards is instrumental in defeating a Skrull invasion by inventing a device that forces the shape-shifting aliens to revert to their original forms. *Secret Invasion* #5 (Oct. 2008)

▼ **Doomsday** In what seems to be their final confrontation, Reed Richards asserts his superiority over Doctor Doom, then the ruler of Battleworld, before retiring as a Super Hero. *Secret Wars* #9 (Mar. 2016)

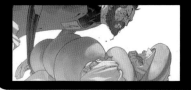

"There's no problem that can't be solved."
REED RICHARDS

Elastic fantastic
Mister Fantastic's body is super-malleable and can bend, stretch, compress, and expand—even encircling massive villains such as Galactus. He can also repel bullets and contain explosions unharmed.

HANK PYM

FIRST APPEARANCE *Tales to Astonish* #27 (January 1962) **BASE** Avengers Compound, California; mobile **AFFILIATIONS** Avengers

Hank Pym is a brilliant scientist with a troubled mind. His inventions are both a help and hindrance to the Avengers, and he has to overcome many personal difficulties before he can prove—to himself and others—that at heart he's a true hero.

Dr. Henry "Hank" Jonathan Pym discovers subatomic particles that allow him to shrink or grow at will. He first develops these "Pym Particles" into a serum, but finds a way to absorb them in gas form or in a capsule. Pym also develops a suit and a cybernetic helmet to communicate with ants and other insects, which he often calls on for aid.

Pym marries Janet van Dyne (Wasp) and they help to found the Avengers. However, frequent size changes cause stress to his body and mind, and marriage problems result. At times his personality fractures, leading to some of his various alter egos, which include Ant-Man, Giant Man, Goliath, Yellowjacket, and, in honor of Janet following her apparent death, Wasp. Pym's greatest mistake is creating the robot Ultron, based on his own brain patterns. The android rebels and repeatedly returns to terrorize, not only Pym and Janet, but the whole of humanity. The guilt of creating Ultron nearly destroys Hank Pym.

During Norman Osborn's Dark Reign, Pym forms his own team of renegade Avengers to work against the evil U.S. security chief. Afterward, Pym turns to teaching and founds Avengers Academy. During the Skrulls' Secret Invasion, Pym is impersonated by a Skrull who mimics his own genetic code. The Skrull has a son with the Avenger Tigra, who turns out to be genetically Pym's son, so Pym becomes his godfather.

Ultron emerges from enforced exile on Titan and attacks Earth. The Avengers try to subdue Ultron, but the robot tricks Pym and phases him inside his body. The two become merged and, locked in emotional and psychological conflict, drift off into space. Assuming Pym is dead, the Avengers hold a funeral for him. Ultron and Hank survive, however, terrorizing the galaxy as they travel from world to world and "purify" them in the name of the Avengers. Ultron then returns to Earth, claiming that Hank is in control. However, Ultron is really calling the shots, and the Avengers hurl him toward the sun. Ultron shrinks himself small enough to hitch a ride on a neutrino and he and Pym are blown away on solar winds.

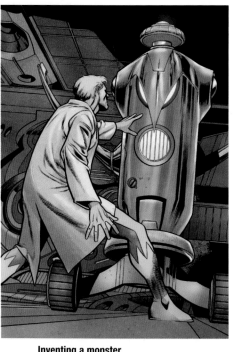

Inventing a monster
Hank Pym discovers that creating Ultron is a terrible error when the robot comes alive. Ironically, Pym has no immediate memory of the event and, when Ultron re-emerges, several upgrades later, his existence is a very disturbing and unpleasant surprise.

Pym Ult
Ultron causes Hank g▮ anguish and destroys his ▮ Hank's number-one probl▮ eventually consumes ▮ and the two beings—H▮ and Ultron—become c▮

timeline

MARVEL AGE

Pym Particles
Hank Pym invents two serums, one that will shrink him to the size of an ant, and another that will restore him to normal size. *Tales to Astonish* #27 (Jan. 1962)

Introducing the Wasp
Pym teams up with Janet Van Dyne as Ant-Man and Wasp. *Tales to Astonish* #44 (June 1963)

► **Mister Big**
Seeking more power, Pym becomes Giant-Man. *Avengers* #2 (Nov. 1963)

◄ **Identity issues**
Pym adopts a cool (in his opinion) new codename and look as Goliath. *Avengers* #28 (May 1966)

BRONZE AGE

► **All mixed up**
As his new alter ego Yellowjacket, Pym is brainwashed by Ultron into thinking he is Ant-Man again, leading to a big fight with the Avengers. *Avengers* #161–162 (July–Aug. 1977)

Back and gone again
Hank Pym rejoins the East Coast Avengers as Giant Man, and is seemingly killed, along with the rest of the team, battling psychic entity Onslaught. *Onslaught Marvel Universe* #1 (Oct. 1996)

MODERN AGE

Avengers Academy
In his Giant-Man persona, Pym founds Avengers Academy to help troubled teens, developing them into Super Heroes—before they can become Super Villains—making amends for his troubled past. *Avengers Academy* #1 (June 2010)

HEROIC AGE

► **Rage of Ultron**
Hank Pym and Ultron merge, two minds in one cyborg body. Ultron is fuelled by Pym's frustrations and insecurities—making for a dangerously unstable pairing. *Rage of Ultron* #1 (Apr. 2015),

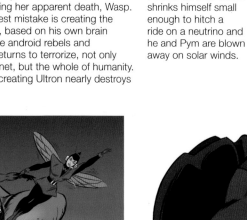

Tiny team
Pym reveals his secret identity to Janet van Dyne. the daughter of his murdered partner. They team up as Ant-Man and Wasp and battle the Creature from Kosmos, a rampaging, green, alien monster. The couple marry, but Pym's insecurities eventually wreck the relationship.

Pym power
With his Pym Particles, Hank can shrink to the size of an ant, or even smaller. He can also grow up to 100ft (30.5m) tall. He has taken on many identities over the years, including *(top to bottom)*: Ultron, Giant-Man, Yellowjacket, Goliath, himself, and Ant-Man.

SKRULLS

FIRST APPEARANCE *Fantastic Four* #2 (January 1962)
BASE Tarnax IV, Andromeda Galaxy

The Skrulls are reptilian, shape-shifting aliens from the Andromeda Galaxy. After building an interstellar empire, they are attacked by another alien race, the Kree, who steal their starship technology. War is declared between the Kree and Skrulls, one that lasts indefinitely.

The Skrulls create the first Cosmic Cube, which becomes self-aware and then obliterates the Skrull empire, becoming the entity known as Shaper of Worlds. However, the Skrulls eventually recover and establish a new capital on Tarnax IV.

The Skrulls begin looking to Earth for resources and conquest. They embed secret agents in Earth society, but the Fantastic Four root them out and defeat them. The Skrull Emperor Dorrek VII then develops a Super-Skrull (named Kl'rt) who is equipped with all the powers of the Fantastic Four. The Skrulls also develop the Warskrulls, a race who can assimilate the abilities of any Super Hero they mimic.

The Skrulls endure even more misfortune when Galactus devours their home planet and their empire is lost in civil war. The mad Skrull Zabyk then unleashes a hyper-wave bomb, which removes the Skrulls' shape-shifting abilities. The Super-Skrull escapes, however, and later restores the abilities of his people.

The Skrulls lose control of much of their empire when the Annihilation Wave moves through the galaxy. Its weapon, the Harvester of Sorrows, turns the Skrull's conquered worlds into fuel for the Annihilation fleet. The Super-Skrull destroys the Harvester, but is killed in the process.

The Skrulls make Veranke their queen and launch their Secret Invasion to turn Earth into their new homeworld. They are eventually defeated, but scattered Skrull groups secretly remain on Earth.

Illuminating secrets
The Illuminati Super-Skrull poses as Black Bolt but also has the powers of Mister Fantastic, Namor, Professor X, and Doctor Strange. He is the first of many Super-Skrulls.

Secret invaders
Wolverine, Captain America, and Venom battle the Skrull hordes. During their Secret Invasion, the Skrulls infiltrate all levels of human society, spreading confusion and paranoia among authentic humans. No super-powered team is safe from the incursions of these alien shape-shifters.

MIRACLE MAN

FIRST APPEARANCE *Fantastic Four* #3 (March 1962) **BASE** Mobile
AFFILIATIONS Hood's Crime Syndicate/gang

Joshua Ayers starts his devious career as a stage magician. He is likely a mutant, with the ability to mesmerize people and make them see incredible illusions. The Fantastic Four come to see one of his shows. When he spots them, Ayers begins taunting them, proclaiming that his powers are even greater than theirs. The Thing challenges him, but is humiliated on stage.

As the evil Miracle Man, Ayers perpetrates numerous diabolical schemes against the Fantastic Four. He is killed by an assassin, Scourge of the Underworld, but resurrected by crimelord the Hood, in order to kill the Punisher. Miracle Man evades this obligation, however, and continues to be a problem for the Fantastic Four.

"Hulk smash!"
HULK

THE HULK

He has been belittled as a mindless monster, but the gamma-powered giant has saved the world many times. The Hulk is unpredictable and full of contradictions, as his twin selves—a savage angry brute and a gentle, brilliant scientist—vie for control.

FIRST APPEARANCE *Incredible Hulk* #1 (May 1962) **BASE** Mobile **AFFILIATIONS** Avengers, Defenders, New Fantastic Four, S.H.I.E.L.D., Illuminati

FROM GREY TO GREEN
Physicist Robert Bruce Banner is overseeing the testing of his G-Bomb when teenager Rick Jones sneaks onto the U.S. Army test site. Banner rushes out to rescue the boy, ordering his assistant, Igor Starsky (real name Drenkov), to halt the countdown. A Soviet spy, Igor ignores the order and Banner is caught in the detonation before he can join Rick in a safety trench. At the base hospital, Banner's gamma radiation levels spike when the sun sets and he transforms into a monstrous brute that a terrified guard dubs "Hulk." The Hulk's grey skin color turns green as gamma radiation saturates his body's chemistry.

Twilight terrors
As darkness falls, Banner turns into an uncontrollable, super-strong brute; he becomes Banner again at sunrise. Before long, stress or anger make Banner change into Hulk at any time.

Jade juggernaut
Fueled by gamma radiation, the Hulk is the strongest mortal on Earth. His most frequent persona is short-tempered and childlike; his immeasurable strength increases the angrier he gets. Hulk's super-dense body repairs wounds and regenerates quickly from any injury. Hulk's transformations are triggered by stress, until Bruce Banner devises chemical and meditative methods of controlling his emotional state.

HERO OR ANTI-HERO?

Although Banner only wants to benefit mankind, the Hulk's hostile attitude brands him a menace in the eyes of the authorities, as represented by General "Thunderbolt" Ross, the irascible father of Banner's future wife, Betty. The old soldier's obsessive pursuit of the monster with virtually every weapon at the military's disposal leads the Green Goliath to clash with the Fantastic Four. Hulk is then framed for wrecking a train by Asgardian trickster Loki and, when Iron Man, Thor, Wasp, and Ant-Man gather to stop him, Hulk is instrumental in the formation of the Avengers. After Loki's defeat, Hulk joins the new hero team, but his bellicose nature alienates his comrades, and capturing Hulk becomes their most urgent priority.

Titanic tussle
Not even Asgardian god Thor can restrain the Hulk's fury.

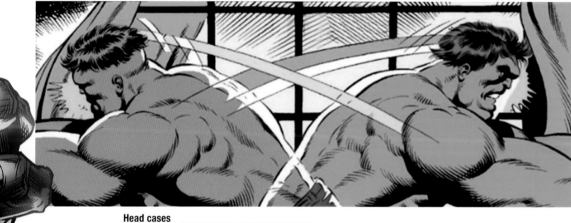

Head cases
The reintegration of Bruce Banner's splintered personality produces a superhuman powerhouse far greater than the sum of his parts. But for how long?

BETTER TOGETHER

Because of childhood abuse by his father, Bruce Banner suffers from Dissociative Identity Disorder, which manifests as physically different forms of the Hulk. These vary in size, intellect, emotional development, and even color. Thanks to the efforts of psychiatrist Leonard (Doc) Samson and hypnotic villain Ringmaster, after months of spontaneously switching between gamma-fueled alter egos—Banner, savage Green Hulk, cunning Grey Hulk Joe Fixit, clever Professor Hulk, and evil Devil Hulk—Hulk psychologically integrates into a new amalgamated version. For a while, Hulk has Bruce's intellect, Fixit's wily assertiveness and the unstoppable power of the original Hulk.

WORLD WAR HULK

To protect Earth, its smartest heroes, the Illuminati—Black Bolt, Iron Man, Professor X, Doctor Strange, Namor, and Mister Fantastic—exile the Hulk to outer space, but he lands on the wrong planet. Rising to be king of barbaric Sakaar, he marries its queen, Caiera, and (unknown to him) fathers twin sons, Skaar and Hiro-Kala. This idyll is shattered when the ship he arrived in explodes; millions die, the pregnant Caiera seemingly among them. Holding the Illuminati responsible, Hulk leads some of Sakaar's savage survivors, the Warbound, in a vengeful assault on Earth. However, his regard for human bravery and an intervention by Rick Jones rekindles Hulk's human feelings and he eventually surrenders.

Hulk's revenge
Hulk begins his mission of vengeance by confronting the Illuminati's Black Bolt and his consort Medusa on the moon.

timeline

Out of the fire Military scientist Bruce Banner is caught in a G-Bomb explosion while saving teenager Rick Jones. Bruce turns into a monster at sunset. *Incredible Hulk #1* (May 1962)

▼ **Secret service** Despite periodically becoming the Hulk, Banner remains an army scientist, using a gamma-ray projector to control his transformations. *Incredible Hulk #3–6* (Sept.1962–Mar. 1963)

The wanderer His secret exposed, Banner abandons true love Betty Ross and becomes a fugitive, avoiding capture while battling Super Villains. *Tales to Astonish #77* (Mar. 1966)

Titanic togetherness After aiding Doctor Strange against the Undying Ones, and helping Sub-Mariner and Silver Surfer destroy an atomic engine, the Hulk joins his new friends in the Defenders. *Marvel Feature #1* (Dec. 1971)

▼ **Love hurts** Betty Ross, believing that Bruce is dead, marries Colonel Glenn Talbot. *Incredible Hulk #158* (Dec. 1972)

Paradise lost Hulk rescues his new beloved, Princess Jarella, from a dying microworld, but she dies saving a child from robot bandit Crypto-Man. *Incredible Hulk #205* (Nov. 1976)

▼ **In the family** Banner's cousin, lawyer Jennifer Walters, is shot and Bruce's gamma-blood transfusion gives her the unwanted ability to turn into She-Hulk. *Savage She-Hulk #1* (Feb. 1979)

▼ **Banished** Hulk goes on an unstoppable rampage through Manhattan and is banished by Doctor Strange to the Crossroads between realities. *Incredible Hulk #299–300* (Sept.–Oct. 1984)

Deadly beloved Bruce finally marries Betty Ross, but the ceremony is disrupted by her father brandishing a gun. *Incredible Hulk #319* (May 1986)

What happens in Vegas… The Hulk is believed dead. In Las Vegas, a publicity-shy, grey super-thug calling himself Joe Fixit starts working for gangster Michael Berengetti. *Incredible Hulk #345–7* (Jul.–Sept. 1988)

▼ **Into the Pantheon** A super-smart Hulk takes charge of secret society the Pantheon and begins acting as a trouble-shooting power-broker on the world stage. *Incredible Hulk #379* (Mar. 1991)

Agent unknown Banner and the Hulk rejoin the Avengers and become a new, top-secret division of S.H.I.E.L.D. *Indestructible Hulk #1–3* (July–Sept. 2013)

A new Hulk Amadeus Cho removes Hulk from Bruce Banner's body and takes on the power himself to become the Totally Awesome Hulk. *Totally Awesome Hulk #4* (May 2016)

"I am Doom…Destroyer of worlds…What gods dare stand against me?"

DOCTOR DOOM

DOCTOR DOOM

FIRST APPEARANCE *Fantastic Four* #5 (July 1962) **BASE** Doomstadt, Latveria; Battleworld
AFFILIATIONS The Cabal, Future Foundation

With his inventive mind, tactical brilliance, and utter ruthlessness, Victor von Doom is the ultimate threat to freedom: a despot convinced that he is the rightful ruler of all he surveys. Victor is the son of a Romani healer and a witch dedicated to black magic, who soon dies. Raised by his tribe, Victor proves an outstanding inventor. As a teenager, he is approached by an American college recruiter who offers him a full scholarship to State University in New York. The educator is unaware that this prodigy has also been mastering magic since finding his mother's spell-books as a child.

At S.U., Victor clashes with freshman Reed Richards, instinctively realizing he is—at least—his intellectual equal. Victor uses college resources to build an inter-dimensional engine capable of warping space-time. He intends breaching Hell to rescue his mother's soul from Mephisto, but in his arrogance, rushes his calculations. When Reed points this out, Victor flies into a rage; later his machine malfunctions and explodes, scarring his handsome face.

Enraged, Victor leaves the U.S., journeying to Tibet, where mystic monks forge a metal mask and an armored suit to hide his disfigurement. Years later he resurfaces, blackmailing the Fantastic Four into time-traveling back to secure Merlin's eldritch gems for him. Outsmarted by Reed Richards, Doom swears eternal vengeance, dividing his time between plans for world domination with schemes to destroy his despised rival.

Doom's genius and cunning enables him to overthrow Latveria's ruler and make himself king of the small Balkan country. As undisputed monarch, he protects his realm from encroachment by larger countries and rules the people with an iron fist. From this secure base, he launches numerous attacks against U.S-based Super Heroes, cloaked from retribution by diplomatic immunity. Even after all his attempts to conquer the world, Doom avoids the political ramifications of his acts by cleverly playing other nations off against each other.

Doom is a master of strategic planning. After seemingly dying in battle against Terrax and the Silver Surfer, the despot's robotic duplicates enact a failsafe plan: imprinting schoolboy Kristoff Vernard with Doom's pre-recorded brain-patterns to recreate their master. In later years, the new Doom is challenged by the original, who had saved himself by transferring his consciousness into an innocent bystander. Eventually, the original is restored to full control of Latveria and Kristoff becomes his heir and ally in his incessant quest to subdue mankind.

Secret warrior
On Battleworld, Doom uses the Beyonder's power to destroy heroes, including Captain America. The Beyonder tricks him into reviving them.

timeline

The powers of Doom
Doctor Doom combines great scientific knowledge with mastery of magic. He can also transfer his mind into another person's body. His weaponized, armored battlesuit enhances his strength.

Doom doomed?
The Beyonder dramatically reclaims his power and blasts Doctor Doom. Once more overconfidence and hubris has brought about Doom's downfall. However, Earth's heroes have not seen the last of him…

GENERAL ROSS/ RED HULK

FIRST APPEARANCE *Incredible Hulk* #1 (May 1962) **BASE** Mobile **AFFILIATIONS** U.S. Air Force, Hulkbusters, Gamma Base, Avengers

General Thaddeus "Thunderbolt" Ross of the U.S. Air Force is appointed commander of the U.S.'s Gamma Bomb project at Desert Base, New Mexico. When physicist Bruce Banner is transformed into the Hulk, Ross leads military efforts to capture or destroy the monster with fanatical zeal, even though his daughter Betty is in love with the mutated scientist. Ross hunts the Hulk for years and the fruitless pursuit blights his career.

Ross eventually suffers a nervous breakdown and becomes a homeless wanderer. He is possessed by the electrical monster Zzzax, before sacrificing his life to save Betty from a marauding gamma mutant. He is later resurrected by the Leader, and returns to the U.S. Air Force, where he resumes hunting both Banner and the Hulk.

Some time later, Doc Samson, M.O.D.O.K., and the Intelligencia collude to turn Ross into the hyper-aggressive Red Hulk, as part of a new Super-Soldier program. Red Hulk becomes a rogue agent, battling both heroes and villains, until inducted into the Avengers.

Red Hulk forms his own Thunderbolts squad to rectify the problems he caused as General Ross, but is targeted by Bruce Banner who, as "Doc Green," is forcibly curing gamma mutates. Transformed from Red Hulk back to human form, Ross is interned in a military prison.

> ## "I'm going to end the menace of the Hulk once and for all!"
> **GENERAL THUNDERBOLT ROSS**

Driven by rage
His men did not nickname their commander "Thunderbolt" for nothing. But Ross' fury at anyone who defies him—the Hulk, his own daughter Betty—proves his undoing, and leads to him on a path to becoming the raging Red Hulk.

RICK JONES

FIRST APPEARANCE *Incredible Hulk* #1 (May 1962) **BASE** Mobile; formerly Los Angeles, California; New Mexico; New York City **AFFILIATIONS** Avengers, Teen Brigade, Captain Marvel, Incredible Hulks, the Loners

For a dare, orphaned teenager Richard Milhouse Jones breaks into an atomic test site and is saved from the blast of a G-Bomb by Bruce Banner. Gamma radiation mutates Banner into the Hulk. Feeling responsible, Rick befriends the Hulk.

When World War II legend Captain America joins the Avengers, Rick becomes the hero's sidekick until, sick of comparisons to Cap's previous partner, Bucky Barnes, he runs away.

Rick is then trapped in a symbiotic relationship with Kree warrior Captain Mar-Vell. Mar-Vell floats helplessly in the Negative Zone, only freed by trading atoms with Rick for short periods when Rick smashes his "Nega-Bands" together. Separated during the Kree-Skrull war, after Rick's psionic powers end the conflict, they are re-merged by the Kree Supreme Intelligence to save Rick's life. Following a clash with Thanos on Earth, Rick and Mar-Vell go on a galactic odyssey, which results in them becoming two separate individuals.

Jones' past constantly draws him into danger, with Banner and a new Captain Marvel both embroiling him in their crises. Rick writes a biography and marries, but his wife, Marlo, is killed and resurrected as an avatar of Death. Rick even briefly becomes a Hulk.

Years of gamma radiation exposure have altered Rick's genetic makeup and the Intelligencia transform him into A-Bomb, dull-witted but super-strong. Rick's mind recovers and he rebels. Bruce Banner removes his powers, which has the effect of increasing Rick's intelligence. He becomes crusading hacktivist the Whisperer, until caught by S.H.I.E.L.D. and drafted into their ranks.

Safety first
Bruce Banner saves Rick from a Gamma-bomb blast.

No puppet
Rick's inherent goodness helps him to overcome being turned into the monstrous A-Bomb.

ELIZABETH ROSS

INCREDIBLE HULK #1 (May 1962) **BASE** Gamma Base, New Mexico; Sunville, Florida; **AFFILIATIONS** Defenders, Incredible Hulks

Elizabeth "Betty" Ross is the daughter of General Thaddeus "Thunderbolt" Ross, and the long-time love interest of both Hulk's alter ego Bruce Banner and his rival, General Talbot. Banner's transformations into the Hulk alienate Betty. She marries Talbot, but still loves Bruce. A.I.M. villain M.O.D.O.K. exploits Betty's fragile mental state to turn her into the villainous Harpy, using the same kind of gamma radiation that created the Hulk. Bruce Banner saves Betty, reverting her to her human form. Realizing where her heart truly lies, Betty divorces Talbot and marries Bruce.

Hulk foe the Abomination later infuses Betty with his gamma-radiated blood, nearly killing her. She is declared dead, severing her marriage to Bruce; in reality, her father has preserved her in a cryogenic chamber.

Betty is resurrected by the same process that turned her father into the Red Hulk, transforming into the Red She-Hulk. Controlled by the Intelligencia, she is sent on a mission to kill her own father. Red She-Hulk's true identity is not revealed until she is stabbed by Hulk's son Skaar during the World War Hulk event and she becomes human once again. Betty later uses her Hulk form to heal and shake off her evil programming. Now on the right side of the law, she works with hero teams such as the Defenders and the Ancient Order of the Shield.

Seeing red
As Red She-Hulk, Betty is far more aggressive and violent. She is also stong enough to take down Lyra, the Savage She-Hulk from another reality.

"With great power comes great responsibility."

UNCLE BEN PARKER

SPIDER-MAN

He's "your friendly neighborhood Spider-Man," a wisecracking, wall-crawling, web-swinging protector of the innocent. Peter Parker's amazing powers utterly transforms his safe, secure life. But does a secret identity, fame, and the respect of the world's greatest Super Heroes prove a blessing—or a curse?

FIRST APPEARANCE *Amazing Fantasy* #15 (August 1962) **BASE** New York City **AFFILIATIONS** Avengers, Fantastic Four, New Fantastic Four, New Avengers

The fateful bite
At the science exhibit "Experiments in Radioactivity," a spider swings into the path of a particle accelerator, bites Peter, and changes his life.

DAY OF THE SPIDER

Orphan Peter Parker is raised by his kindly Aunt May and Uncle Ben. Shy, with a talent for science, Peter is a misfit at Midtown High. Then, during a visit to a science exhibit, a radioactive spider-bite gives him a range of amazing spider-related abilities. His confidence now soaring, Peter designs a colorful costume and web-shooters, calls himself Spider-Man, and becomes a TV star. But when he fails to use his powers to stop a burglar, who then kills Uncle Ben, Peter is overcome by grief and guilt. He vows henceforth to use his unique abilities to save lives and combat villainy.

DEATH OF GWEN STACY

Fuelled by his Goblin formula, Norman Osborn, the Green Goblin, develops an insane hatred for Spider-Man. He discovers Peter's identity, kidnaps Peter's college sweetheart, Gwen Stacy, and throws her off the Brooklyn Bridge. Peter's attempt to save her fails and he swears vengeance. In a rooftop showdown, the Green Goblin impales himself on his own glider and is seemingly killed. However, Peter's clashes with the Green Goblin and his successors are only just beginning.

Tragedy strikes
Riding his glider and armed with a pumpkin bomb, Green Goblin Norman Osborn sneaks up on Gwen Stacy *(left)*. Later, unable to save Gwen, Spider-Man swears vengeance on the Green Goblin *(above)*.

FIRST FOES

Needing a job, Peter joins the staff of the *Daily Bugle*. The paper's irascible owner, J. Jonah Jameson, is waging a campaign against vigilantes like Spider-Man and wants all the photos he can get. With the help of an automatic camera, Peter is happy to oblige. In his secret role as Spider-Man, Peter battles a gallery of bizarre villains, such as the appearance-altering Chameleon, flying criminal the Vulture, Doctor Octopus with his metal tentacles, master illusionist Mysterio, sand-manipulating Sandman, big-game hunter Kraven, and Electro who has limitless electrical powers.

The Sinister Six
Having failed to beat Spider-Man on their own, the Web-Swinger's foes try teamwork.

SAVING THE SPIDER-VERSE

Peter is caught up in a complex battle to preserve the "Spider-Verse"—the many male and female Spider-themed heroes who hail from alternate worlds and times. They are threatened by the Inheritors, led by Morlun. These universe-hopping vampire-like beings feed on "Spider-Totems" and aim to hunt down every one of them. Various Spider-heroes unite to battle this menace to their existence. One group is led by a time-displaced Otto Octavius masquerading as Peter in the guise of the Superior Spider-Man, ensuring additional trouble.

Fight for survival
Spider-heroes gather from every corner of the Multiverse to battle the Inheritors. To do so successfully, they must set aside squabbles and petty jealousies and work together.

Spider powers

Spider-Man possesses the proportionate strength, speed, agility, and reflexes of a spider, as well as the ability to move over any surface (wall-crawling) and instinctively sense danger (spider-sense). Wrist-mounted web-shooters fire an adhesive fluid that turns into super-strong swing-lines or webs.

timeline

Spider-Man swings! Spider-Man saves *Daily Bugle* editor J.J. Jameson's astronaut son, but is still villified by the paper. To get money and improve Spidey's image, Peter joins the *Daily Bugle* as a photographer. *Amazing Spider-Man* #1–2 (May 1963)

Super Villainy Spider-Man clashes with Norman Osborn, alias the Green Goblin. *Amazing Spider-Man* #14 (July 1964)

▼ **Hitting the jackpot** Aunt May arranges a blind date for Peter with her friend's niece, model Mary Jane Watson, beginning a long relationship. *Amazing Spider-Man* #42 (Nov. 1966)

Formula for a nightmare Peter's college sweetheart Gwen Stacy is killed by the Green Goblin, who dies during a battle with Spider-Man. *Amazing Spider-Man* #121 (June 1973)

Another Green Goblin Seeking revenge against Spider-Man for his father's death, Norman Osborn's son Harry, Peter Parker's best friend, becomes a new Green Goblin. *Amazing Spider-Man* #136 (Sept. 1974)

▼ **Venomized** Spider-Man acquires a new black suit—an alien symbiote. Eddie Brock is later possessed by it and becomes Venom. *Amazing Spider-Man* #299 (Apr. 1988)

Send in the clone Peter retires, handing his Spider-Man role to his clone, Ben Reilly. Ben sacrifices his life to save Peter from the Green Goblin and Peter becomes Spider-Man once more. *Web of Spider-Man* #118 (Nov. 1994)

Identity crisis Green Goblin frames Spider-Man for murder, causing Peter to take on four other identities: Ricochet, Hornet, Dusk, and Prodigy. *Amazing Spider-Man* #434 (May 1998)

▼ **Death and rebirth** Spider-Man is killed by Morlun, but is reborn with enhanced powers. *Amazing Spider-Man* #527 (Feb. 2006)

Iron Spider Tony Stark uses nanotech to give Spidey a new, armored, Iron Spider suit. *Amazing Spider-Man* #529 (Apr. 2006)

▼ **Spidey's secret revealed** With the passing of the Superhuman Registration Act, civil war breaks out among Super Heroes. Encouraged by Tony Stark, Peter reveals his Spider-Man identity. *Civil War* #1 (Aug. 2006)

The demon's bargain To save Aunt May's life, Peter makes a deal with the demon Mephisto to alter reality. As a result, Peter and MJ's relationship never happened. *Amazing Spider-Man* #545 (Jan. 2008)

Superior Spider-Man A dying Doc Ock uploads a copy of his mind into Parker's body and, believing himself better than the original, becomes the Superior Spider-Man. In time, Peter's consciousness regains control. *Amazing Spider-Man* #700 (Feb. 2013)

Parker Industries Peter becomes boss of Parker Industries. The tech company becomes a global conglomerate— and a target for Super Villains. *Amazing Spider-Man* #1 (Dec. 2015)

MARVEL AGE

BRONZE AGE

MODERN AGE

HEROIC AGE

FLASH THOMPSON

FIRST APPEARANCE *Amazing Fantasy* #15
(August 1962) **BASE** Queens, New York City
AFFILIATIONS Secret Avengers, Guardians of
the Galaxy

Eugene Thompson is nicknamed "Flash"
while attending Midtown High School,
thanks to his speed on the football pitch.
Popular and athletic, Flash bullies bookish
Peter Parker, although he eases up a little
after a spider-powered Parker "luckily"
beats him in a boxing match. Flash is a big
admirer of Spider-Man, even starting a fan
club; ironically he bans Peter, Spider-Man's
secret alter ego, from joining.

 After school, both Flash and Peter go
to Empire State University. Here their
animosity fades, thanks to their mutual
friend, Harry Osborn. Flash starts to
appreciate Peter's intelligence, and can't
help but admire the way he attracts
beautiful women like Gwen Stacy and Mary
Jane Watson. Flash joins the army straight
out of college and, during a tour of duty in

Iraq, loses both legs below the knee
rescuing a fallen comrade. His heroics
make him the ideal candidate, despite his
disability, for Project Rebirth 2.0, and Flash
is melded with the Venom symbiote. The
procedure generates new legs for him and,
almost as good in Flash's eyes, gives him
powers just like Spider-Man. Now
codenamed Agent Venom, he strikes
fear into the hearts of terrorists
everywhere. Spider-Man is famous for
not wanting to take a life, but Agent
Venom has a very different reputation.

 Flash can only be bonded to the
symbiote for a limited period of time before
it starts to take him over. He goes on a
number of government missions, but his
connection to the symbiote leads him to
split up with his longtime girlfriend, Betty
Brant. After working with the Avengers,
Flash is granted honorary membership
and implanted into the Guardians of the
Galaxy as the Avengers' representative.
While in space, Flash also becomes an
Agent of the Cosmos.

"Y'know, Parker, you really
ought to watch where you're
going. Imagine if that was an
iron lamppost, instead of
soft, cuddly me!"

FLASH THOMPSON

Agent Venom
His heroics in the military make
Flash the perfect candidate to
merge with the Venom symbiote
and become an anti-terror
government agent.

AUNT MAY PARKER

FIRST APPEARANCE: *Amazing Fantasy* #15 (August 1962)
BASE Queens, New York City **AFFILIATIONS** None

May Parker, née Reilly, has an unhappy childhood.
Her parents have financial difficulties, and her mother
makes the girl feel guilty about being an extra mouth
to feed when her father walks out on them. When May
meets Ben Parker, May at first resents his little brother
Richard hanging around them on their dates, but she grows
to love the boy. When the grown-up Richard and his wife

Mary die in a plane crash, May and Ben raise the couple's young
son, Peter. At first she fears that the child will put pressure on
her marriage, remembering the tension in her own family, but
May is soon won over by Peter's good heart and ends up loving
him as if he were her own son. When her beloved husband Ben is
killed by a burglar, May is devastated, but she and Peter stay
strong for each other.

 As Peter goes through college and tries to help her financially in
any way he can, May has no idea that he is leading a double life
as the amazing Spider-Man. But his secret leads her into
danger—she is kidnapped by Spidey foes, such as the Sinister
Six, the Beetle, and Norman Osborn, and even gets engaged
to Doctor Octopus! She later discovers Peter's torn Spider-Man
costume, and realizes his secret identity.

 When Peter unmasks himself during the superhuman civil war,
May is put at even greater risk from attack by Spider-Man's legion
of Super Villain enemies. However, there is more to this elderly
lady than meets the eye—she singlehandedly defeats the
Chameleon by feeding him drugged cookies. After May is terribly
wounded in an attack by a Kingpin assassin, Peter does a deal
with the demon Mephisto to save her, wiping his marriage to
Mary Jane Watson from reality, and his identity is secret once
more. May then meets and marries Jay Jameson, the father of
media mogul J. Jonah Jameson, but he later falls ill and dies,
leaving her a widow for a second time.

Stop the wedding!
Doctor Octopus devises a scheme to marry Aunt
May and get his tentacles on a nuclear facility she
has inherited, but the wedding is interrupted by
Doc Ock's enemy, the gangster Hammerhead.

UNCLE BEN PARKER

FIRST APPEARANCE *Amazing Fantasy* #15 (August 1962)
BASE Queens, New York City **AFFILIATIONS** U.S. Military Police

As a young man, Ben Parker works as a carnival barker at
Coney Island, trying to attract customers to the fairground rides.
But the person he wants to attract most of all is beautiful May
Reilly, who goes to his high school. Unfortunately, May is smitten
with Johnny Jerome, a flashy type who, Ben knows, is up to no
good. When Johnny shoots someone in a botched robbery and
a heartbroken May realizes she can never love a criminal, Ben
comforts her and they fall in love. They marry and live very happily,
although they are not blessed with children. But when Ben's
younger brother Richard and his wife are killed, Ben and May take
in their orphaned son, Peter.

Ben is an ideal father figure for the young boy—loving,
protective, and firm when he needs to be. He tries to bring Peter
up to do the right thing, and never to settle for less if he can reach

for more. But the life of this beloved uncle and husband is brought
to a cruel end when Ben is shot trying to protect his wife May
during a burglary. Peter, who has recently gained amazing powers
as Spider-Man, is devastated and wracked with guilt, for he had
the chance to capture the killer not long before and let him
escape. Ben's death has a profound effect on the young hero,
and he vows that no more innocent lives will be lost on account of
his failure to act. The death of Uncle Ben teaches Spider-Man that
with great power there must also come great responsibility.

> "My death is one
> of the greatest
> gifts the universe
> ever gave you."
>
> **UNCLE BEN TO PETER PARKER**

Magical reunion
A birthday present from Doctor Strange enables Peter to have
one more conversation with his loving Uncle Ben. In a vision,
Ben reassures Peter that he's on the right path.

CIRCUS OF CRIME

FIRST APPEARANCE *The Incredible Hulk* #3
(September 1962) **BASE** Mobile
AFFILIATIONS None

The nefarious organization known as the
Circus of Crime is a mobile gang of
showmen and thieves. Once a crowd has
gathered to watch their show, the group's
leader, Maynard Tiboldt, the Ringmaster,
uses a device on his hat to hypnotize
everybody. With the audience in a trance,
the performers roam through the crowd,
liberating them from their valuables.

Although the lineup changes, regular
members of the Circus of Crime are Zelda,
known as Princess Python, Crafty Clown,
a.k.a. Funny Man, a strong man known as
Bruto, the acrobatic Great Gambonnos,
and the Human Cannonball. Early in their
career they manage to get the Hulk under

their control, although with little idea of
the danger he poses. Luckily, Rick Jones
alerts the authorities before any real harm
is done.

The Ringmaster's hypnosis does not
work on everyone—notably when blind
attorney Matt Murdock is in the audience.
Realizing what is happening, Murdock
changes into his Daredevil costume and
takes on the crooks with the help of
Spider-Man, who is at first hypnotized but
then released by Daredevil. Seeing how
useful Super Heroes could be both to the
circus and robbery sides of their racket,
the Circus of Crime vainly tries to recruit
disaffected Avengers Hawkeye, Scarlet
Witch, and Quicksilver. She-Hulk is later
duped into joining the Circus of Crime as
the strongwoman Glamazonia, but once
her hypnotic trance is broken, she makes
short work of the crooks.

Wedding crashers
The Circus of Crime pose
as caterers to infiltrate the
wedding of the Wasp and
Yellowjacket, hoping to
wipe out a roomful of
Super Heroes, but the
Avengers prevail.

44

Will of iron
Trapped under tons of metal, Spider-Man seems beaten, doomed to die a miserable death. However, sheer determination not to let his loved ones down again helps him find strength he never knew he had.

SPIDER-MAN'S DESTINY

"I'll do it, Aunt May! I won't fail you!" SPIDER-MAN

Trapped in Doctor Octopus' underwater lair, Spider-Man thinks his time is up. Will his love for Aunt May give the web-swinger the strength to beat almost impossible odds?

Peter Parker is just starting college when his beloved Aunt May falls seriously ill. Worried about losing her, and under pressure to pay her medical bills, Peter is tired and distracted. Then comes devastating news: His own radioactive blood, given during a transfusion, has caused Aunt May's illness. Spider-Man goes to Dr. Curt Connors for help and discovers that there is a new serum that might save his aunt. Just as things seem to be looking up, the precious serum is stolen by a gang on the orders of Doctor Octopus. Spider-Man shakes down all the hoods he can find looking for Doc Ock's secret base. He locates it under one of New York City's rivers and fights his old enemy with such violence that the whole structure starts to collapse. Doc Ock escapes, but Spider-Man is trapped under an enormous chunk of iron weighing several tons. The only way to save his aunt is to lift the metal and escape, but after days of fighting street punks and going to college, and nights spent sleepless with worry or taking photos to make some money, Peter Parker is exhausted.

WHY HE FIGHTS

The stricken Spider-Man stares at the vial of serum, just out of reach, and phantom visions of Aunt May and Uncle Ben swim before his eyes. Guilt over his uncle's death still weighs heavy on the young man's shoulders, and the thought of Aunt May losing her life because of him is unbearable. Spider-Man desperately tries once again to lift the metal from his back—

and this time he succeeds. Rushing out of Doc Ock's base, sheer force of will enables him to defeat a horde of henchmen— Spidey lets them beat him up while he gathers his strength. He then takes the serum to Dr. Connors. After a successful test, Spider-Man races to the hospital with the formula and, following an anxious wait, Aunt May revives.

Ghostly memories
With the life-saving serum tantalizingly just out of reach, Spider-Man thinks of his family. Still haunted by guilt over the death of Uncle Ben, Spidey is determined not to fail Aunt May.

> "I am the God of Thunder, Lord of the Savage Lightning, the very skies must tremble when speaks the Mighty Thor!"
>
> **THOR**

THOR

The Mighty Thor is the Asgardian God of Thunder who, with the help of his trusty hammer Mjolnir, battles to protect Asgard and Earth alongside his allies, the Avengers.

FIRST APPEARANCE *Journey Into Mystery* #83 (August 1962) **BASE** Asgard; New York City **AFFILIATIONS** Asgardian gods, Avengers

AN EARTHLY BEGINNING

To teach Thor humility after being disobedient, his father Odin, king of the Asgardian Gods, sends him down to Earth in the form of a young medical student named Donald Blake. On vacation in Europe, Blake witnesses a landing of malevolent extraterrestrials and seeks to make his escape.

Using a wooden staff found on the ground of a cave, he tries to move a boulder blocking his way. When the staff hits the ground, Donald Blake transforms into the legendary Thor! Thus begins Thor's heroic journey as he switches back and forth between his human and godly forms, battling and defeating a host of otherworldly menaces.

Godly transformation
Mortal Donald Blake touches an enchanted wooden stick on the ground, transforming him into the Mighty Thor.

A FOUNDING AVENGER

After the Avengers unite for the first time to battle the likes of Thor's mischievous brother Loki, Thor goes on to aid the Avengers in many more battles, often against villains from otherworldly realms.

On one such occasion, Thor's brother Loki aids the villainous Dormammu to find a device called the Evil Eye, which would allow Earth to be swallowed into Dormammu's Dark Dimension. Dormammu would trick the Defenders into seeking the six pieces of the broken device. Loki, seeing that Dormammu could overtake Asgard next, tips off Thor and the Avengers, saying they must stop the Defenders: resulting in some of the most classic clashes of all times, including Thor's battle with Hulk in the middle of Los Angeles. Luckily, the Avengers and Defenders realize they must work together to stop Dormammu's evil plan.

Hulk vs. Thor
Among the rubble of a destroyed Los Angeles sidewalk, muscle-bound Hulk and the mighty Thor battle it out.

RAGNAROK AND THE CASKET OF ANCIENT WINTERS

Many times, Thor has confronted those who would bring about Ragnarok, the end of the world—as prophesied in Norse mythology. One such time, an evil Dark Elf from Svartalfheim, Malekith the Accursed, strikes a deal with Loki and the fire demon Surtur to unleash the Casket of Ancient Winters on Midgard (the Asgardian name for Earth) allowing Surtur to enter from the bowels of the fiery realm of Muspelheim. Surtur next moves to invade Asgard, and remove the legendary Twilight Sword, thereby ushering forth the end of all things. Unable to take on these great foes alone, Thor joins Odin and Loki—who, typically, has switched sides—to stop the prophecy.

A family affair
Thor's father Odin takes on Surtur in battle, as they race to stop Ragnarok from ending the world.

UNWORTHY

Suddenly Thor Odinson has become unworthy to wield his hammer, Mjolnir, whose inscription reads: "Whosoever holds this hammer, if he be worthy, shall possess the power of Thor." A mysterious woman finds the hammer and is imbued with the power of Thor. This new Thor is revealed to be Thor's Earthly love, Jane Foster. The world must be protected, but using the power of Thor is draining her already ailing human form—she is battling cancer—while fighting villains as Thor. Odinson, formerly Thor, now wields the ax Jarnbjorn, fighting villainy in all ten realms.

Thor no more
When Odinson becomes unworthy, he can no longer lift Mjolnir, and Jane Foster, in disguise, emerges as a new Thor.

timeline

Double life Donald Blake discovers his powers in the cave where Thor is born and begins to divide his time between being an ordinary human doctor and an immortal god. *Journey Into Mystery* #83 (Aug. 1962)

An Avenger In an effort to ward off Loki, Thor bands together with Iron Man, the Hulk, Ant-Man, and Wasp, creating one of the most powerful super teams of all time. *Avengers* #1 (Sept. 1963)

◄ **Dad doesn't approve** When Thor requests his father Odin's permission to marry the human Jane Foster, Odin requires her to prove her worth—by setting her tasks that are impossible for mortals. *Journey Into Mystery* #100 (Jan. 1964)

Godly rivals An encounter with the demigod Hercules results in a humbling defeat and an eventual team-up. Thor and Herc will be more-or-less friendly rivals for years to come. *Thor* #126 (Mar. 1966)

False king Evil monstrosity Mangog, disguised as Odin, takes over the throne of Asgard. He bests Thor and his allies the Warriors Three, but Thor breaks free from his shackles and defeats the unmasked villain. *Thor* #250 (Aug. 1976)

Backstory Thor's early years are revealed. He is born in Asgard to Odin and Jord (Gaea) and his stepmother Frigga. Proving himself in battle, Odin deems Thor worthy of Mjolnir. *Thor Annual* #11 (Nov. 1983)

Banished It is revealed that Odin banished Thor to Earth in the form of Dr. Donald Blake for being rowdy and pig-headed. *Thor Annual* #11 (Nov. 1983)

◄ **Thor meets his match** Following a head-to-head battle, alien Beta Ray Bill proves so evenly matched with Thor that Odin creates a second hammer for him as Thor's true equal. *Thor* #338 (Dec. 1983)

Surtur saga The Casket of Ancient Winters is unleashed on Earth to usher forth Surtur and Ragnarok, the end of the world. *Thor* #346–353 (Aug. 1984–Mar. 1985)

Thunderstrike To save the life of architect Eric Masterson, Odin fuses together Masterson and Thor. Eventually the two are separated, but Eric Masterson takes with him a new weapon and codename: Thunderstrike. *Thor* #408 (Oct. 1989)

► **Jake Olson** Thor fuses with another human, Jake Olson, but Jake ends up being less than worthy and his body is later taken over by Loki. *Thor* #1 (July 1998)

Only sleeping Thor is presumed dead, but is actually in deep hibernation after breaking the Ragnarok cycle by severing the tapestry of Asgardian existence from the gods of gods called Those Who Sit Above In Shadow. *Thor* #85 (Dec. 2004)

▲ **Cybernetic clone** During the superhuman civil war, Tony Stark uses one of Thor's hairs to clone a cyborg version of the god. However, the clone lacks Thor's moral sense. *Civil War* #3 (July 2006)

Return to Midgard Thor returns from the Void once more fused with his human host Donald Blake. *Thor* #1 (Sept. 2007)

All gods must die Gorr the God Butcher sets out to create a bomb to destroy the gods. Thor's younger self, current self, and future self band together with other gods and ancestors to foil Gorr's plot. *Thor: God of Thunder* #6–11 (May–Oct. 2013)

Worthy wielder Jane Foster takes over the mantle of Thor, when Odinson becomes unworthy of his hammer, Mjolnir. *Thor: God of Thunder* #25 (Nov. 2014)

The powers of Thor
The Asgardian god Thor possesses superhuman strength, durability, and an extremely long lifespan. As the God of Thunder, Thor uses magical artifacts, especially his magic hammer Mjolnir, to wield thunder and lightning, teleport, and crush his enemies. He is also a skilled tactician.

LOKI

FIRST APPEARANCE *Journey Into Mystery* #85
(October 1962) **BASE** Asgard **AFFILIATIONS** Asgardian
gods, Frost Giants

Loki, the God of Mischief, is one of the greatest magicians Asgard
has ever known, and the most malevolent. This trickster can never
resist the opportunity to cause trouble, seize power, or better yet,
torment his adoptive brother Thor.

Loki was hidden away by King Laufey, his Frost Giant father,
for being a runt, by giant standards. The god Odin found Loki as
an abandoned infant in Jotunheim after slaying Laufey.
Remembering his own father's words to never abandon a child
that you orphan, Odin and his wife Frigga raise Loki with their own
son, Thor. For many years, Loki is unaware that he is adopted, but
he keenly feels the difference in how he and his brother are treated
by his "father" Odin. As he grows, Loki becomes consumed
by jealousy and contempt.

Resentful toward his favored brother Thor, Loki sees fit to wreak
havoc on Earth (or Midgard, as it is called by Asgardians), when
Thor is sent there by Odin. In an early adventure, Loki uses his
crafty nature to free himself from imprisonment in a tree and project
himself down to Earth. There he tries to steal Thor's hammer,
turning Thor back into his mortal identity, Dr. Donald Blake, and
take control of Midgard for himself. Loki's antics cause such a
commotion that Thor enlists Iron Man, Hulk, Wasp, and Ant-Man
to stop him, creating one of the greatest Super Hero teams of all
time—the Avengers.

Not being a true son of Odin, Loki knows that the only way he
can seize Asgard's throne is by trickery. Luckily for Loki, Odin
requires long periods of hibernation—Odinsleeps—to recharge
his power. This gives the trickster ideal opportunities for power
grabs; however, his attempts to usurp Odin always end in
failure. Odin's powerful enemies, such as the monstorous
Mangog and the fire demon Surtur, also wish for Odin's power
and to bring about the end of time, known as Ragnarok.
However, Loki wants to rule Asgard and does not want to see it
completely destroyed.

Any magic-wielding god has to be good at shape-shifting, and
Loki is the king when it comes to impersonating others. Removing
his name from the book of Hel so that he may never die, Loki has
been born again several times. On one occasion, he is born with
the body of Thor's former lover Sif as Lady Loki, much to Thor's
confusion. On another, Loki is torn apart by the killer Void and
reincarnated as a child, Kid Loki, ready to turn over a new leaf.
However, Loki's prior life leaves a lot of trouble for Kid Loki to
navigate. Eventually, Loki seemingly reconciles his wicked former
self with his younger, better persona, and goes forward, hoping to
do good by joining the Young Avengers…but old habits die hard.

"I am the Lord of Chaos!"

LOKI

Ruled by ambition
Heavy is the head that
wears the horns…Loki
lusts for nothing more
than to sit upon his
father's throne.

timeline

▼ **Enter the trickster** Loki hypnotizes Thor and tries
to steal Mjolnir in a power grab for Midgard.
Journey Into Mystery #85 (Oct. 1962)

Avengers villain Loki causes so much trouble that
the Avengers assemble for the first time in order to
stop him. *Avengers* #1 (Sept. 1963)

An evil duo Loki and Dormammu of the Dark
Dimension team up to manipulate the Defenders and
Avengers. *Avengers* #118 (Dec. 1973)

Surtur saga Loki teams up with Surtur to usher forth
the end of time, Ragnarok. *Thor* #353 (Mar. 1985)

Frog of Thunder Loki causes mischief when he turns
Thor into a frog. *Thor* #364–366 (Feb.–Apr. 1986)

At death do we part Thor becomes one with his
hammer and draws out Loki's life force, killing
him—but not for long. *Thor* #432 (May 1991)

Origin revealed Hela allows Loki to look into his past
and, for the first time, Loki remembers his life as a
Frost Giant. *Thor* #12 (Jan. 2009)

Siege Loki convinces Norman Osborn, now U.S.
security chief, to help him lay siege to Asgard. Loki is
later killed by the Void. *Siege* #1–4 (Mar.–June 2010)

Reborn Loki is born anew and
joins the Young Avengers.
Journey Into Mystery #622–630
(June–Dec. 2011)

▶ **Loki for President** Loki
uses his silver tongue and
godly trickery to run for
President of the United
States! *Vote Loki* #1–4
(Aug.–Nov. 2016)

New tricks
A younger incarnation
of Loki uses his silver
tongue to try to win
over the new
incarnation of Thor
(Jane Foster).

BALDER

FIRST APPEARANCE *Journey Into Mystery* #85 (October 1962) **BASE** Asgard **AFFILIATIONS** Asgardian Gods, Avengers

Balder the Brave is an Asgardian God, the half-brother and close friend to Thor, and a true Prince of Asgard. A prophecy foretells that his death will usher forth the end of days known as Ragnarok, so Loki exploits Balder's one vulnerability: He arranges for the blind god Hoder to shoot him with an arrow tipped with mistletoe. Odin doesn't allow his son to die for long, but Balder is forever changed by his interlude in Hel.

As an adult, Balder fights alongside Thor in many battles, rules Asgard in his father's absence, and aids Thor while he rules Asgard. Balder dies in the final battle of Ragnarok, only to be later reborn anew.

ODIN

FIRST APPEARANCE *Journey Into Mystery* #85 (October 1962) **BASE** City of Asgard, Asgard **AFFILIATIONS** Council of Godheads

Odin Borson is the All-Father and ruler of the Asgardian Gods. In his younger years, he went on many adventures throughout the ten realms, one of which cost him an eye and another that brought him his adopted son, Loki. Odin serves not only as ruler of the Gods with his wife, Frigga, but as the ruler of Thor. Odin gives Thor his hammer, Mjolnir, with its powers of lightning and thunder. Sometimes Odin punishes Thor, casting him down to Earth; and sometimes Odin leaves the world vulnerable to attacks by the likes of Loki, Surtur, and many others when he takes his hibernation-like Odinsleep, necessary to restore the Odinforce that gives him his godly powers.

THE WIZARD

FIRST APPEARANCE *Strange Tales* #102 (November 1962) **BASE** Manhattan, New York City **AFFILIATIONS** Frightful Four

Bentley Wittman is a chess prodigy, genius inventor, and master escape artist who legally changes his name to his stage name, "The Wizard." He loses popularity with the emergence of Super Heroes like the Fantastic Four and seeks to recapture his former fame by taking down the most notable hero of the time—Johnny Storm, the Human Torch. Posing as a victim, the Wizard lures the Human Torch into his lair and locks him in. Impersonating the Human Torch, the Wizard goes on a crime spree, snapping photos along the way. Fortunately, Johnny defeats the Wizard, seizes the pictures, and turns him in.

No matter what the Wizard does, he is unable to best Johnny Storm on his own. So he brings together a villainous team—the Frightful Four—to take on the Fantastic Four. The Wizard, with Sandman, Paste-Pot Pete, and the amnesia-stricken Inhuman Queen Medusa, try to ruin Sue Storm and Reed Richards' engagement party, steal their super-powers, and send them into space on anti-gravity discs, but are foiled by Johnny Storm and the rest of the Fantastic Four. Over time, the Frightful Four changes its roster—especially when Medusa remembers who she is. However, even with the Wizard's big brain, the villains just can't beat the Fantastic Four.

Feeling the chill
The Wizard's technology is no match for Iceman's freezing mutant abilities.

PUPPET MASTER

FIRST APPEARANCE *Strange Tales* #102 (November 1962) **BASE** Manhattan, New York City **AFFILIATIONS** None

Born in the Balkan country of Transia, Philip Masters discovers that radioactive clay from Wundagore Mountain mind-controls anyone he makes clay sculptures of. Relocating to the U.S., Masters, now calling himself the Puppet Master, embarks on a career as a criminal mastermind. His attempts to rule New York are repeatedly foiled by the Fantastic Four. His loathing for the team deepens when his blind stepdaughter Alicia abandons him and starts a romantic relationship with the Thing.

Puppet Master's subsequent schemes, which sometimes involve partnerships with other villains, such as the Mad Thinker and Egghead, are foiled by the Fantastic Four and numerous other Super Heroes.

EGGHEAD

FIRST APPEARANCE *Tales to Astonish* #38 (December 1962) **BASE** New York City
AFFILIATIONS Emissaries of Evil, Masters of Evil, Intelligencia

Disgraced for trying to steal and sell U.S. government secrets, atomic scientist Elihas Starr was dubbed "Egghead" by the press because of his unfortunate appearance. Now unable to work for the government, Egghead is in demand among the criminal fraternity. To win their approval, he is tasked with defeating Ant-Man. After failing in this objective, Egghead becomes obsessed with Ant-Man, and later Hank Pym's other alter ego Giant-Man, and he also clashes with the Avengers and Spider-Man. Egghead seemingly dies after his ray gun is struck by one of Hawkeye's arrows, but it later transpires that he survives, thanks to his patented Rejuvetech serum. Egghead tries to cause havoc with robotic versions of the Avengers, but is thwarted by Hank Pym and Ant-Man Scott Lang.

TRAPSTER

FIRST APPEARANCE *Strange Tales* #104 (January 1963) **BASE** Various
AFFILIATIONS Frightful Four

Although he has made himself rich by devising an ultra-strong adhesive, Peter Petruski believes that he can make even more money if he uses his invention for crime. Adopting the moniker Paste-Pot Pete, he robs a bank with a glue gun. Upping the ante, Pete next tries to steal a missile from the U.S. military, but is foiled by the Human Torch. Wanting to get revenge on the young hero, he becomes one of the founding members of the Frightful Four, with the Wizard, Sandman, and Medusa. Pete changes his name to Trapster, hoping to sound more threatening, but his old name continues to embarrass him for the rest of his career. During a period as a solo villain, following a weapons upgrade, Trapster frequently clashes with Spider-Man, but his loyalty to the Wizard draws him back to a reunited Frightful Four. He then goes solo again, becoming a mercenary for hire.

IMPOSSIBLE MAN

FIRST APPEARANCE *Fantastic Four* #11 (February 1963) **BASE** Poppup
AFFILIATIONS None

The Impossible Man is a native of the planet Poppup. Poppupians possess a hive mind and have the ability to evolve rapidly into any form. Both these attributes develop as a response to the monster-infested environment of Poppup. Looking for another world to provide a diversion from Poppupian life, one of their number travels to Earth, where his curiosity and alien ways cause havoc in New York City. When the Fantastic Four arrive to rein in the mischievous extraterrestrial, the Thing calls him "impossible" and the name sticks. Eventually, Mister Fantastic decides that the only way to deal with the Impossible Man is to ignore his antics, and the alien gets bored and leaves. But visiting Earth has fascinated the Impossible Man, and several years later he returns, offering up Poppup to the World-Eater Galactus to save Counter-Earth. Interested in human relationships, the Impossible Man creates an Impossible Woman and many Impossible Kids—this large, unruly family causes upset across the universe.

Troubled soul
Chameleon, filled with regret about the way his life has turned out, opens his heart to Spider-Man before throwing himself off the Brooklyn Bridge.

CHAMELEON

FIRST APPEARANCE *Amazing Spider-Man* #1 (March 1963) **BASE** Mobile
AFFILIATIONS Sinister Twelve, Exterminators, M.O.D.O.K.'s Eleven, Sinister Six, Superior Six

With an uncanny knack for impersonating others, this master of disguise is one of the first villains Peter Parker fights after becoming Spider-Man. Born in Soviet Russia, Dmitri Smerdyakov is brought up with his half-brother, Sergei Kravinoff—the future Kraven the Hunter. Dmitri is bullied by his brother and grows up torn between the need to impress Sergei and outdo him. Leaving his home, Dmitri travels to America, where he decides to use his talent for deception to commit robberies as the Chameleon. It is not long before Sergei follows his brother to the U.S. and, after being bested by Spider-Man, the Chameleon encourages Sergei to join him in pursuing the Wall-Crawler. However, the Chameleon clashes with other heroes, too, including Iron Man, Hulk, Ant-Man, and Daredevil.

When his brother kills himself, the Chameleon's hatred for Spider-Man increases, as he holds the hero responsible for not preventing Sergei's death. The Chameleon ploughs all his ill-gotten wealth into developing a serum to make his face featureless and totally malleable, vastly increasing his capacity for impersonation. A holographic belt allows him to project the appearance of any person in his database. However, the Chameleon is hampered by his mental fragility. After tricking Spider-Man into believing his parents are still alive, Chameleon's childhood anguish bubbles to the surface. Suicidal, he lures Spider-Man to the Brooklyn Bridge, where Peter Parker's girlfriend Gwen Stacy died years before, and lays his soul bare before throwing himself off. He survives, but is incarcerated in an institution. After a spell in the Sinister Six, the Chameleon is bested by Spider-Man once more, this time by the Superior Spider-Man, Otto Octavius in Peter Parker's body. Chameleon later takes up an unusual role—executive producer for corpulent, other-dimensional, reality-TV mogul Mojo.

JOHN JAMESON

FIRST APPEARANCE *Amazing Spider-Man* #1
(March 1963) **BASE** Queens, New York City
AFFILIATIONS N.A.S.A., Avengers

John Jameson, son of publisher J. Jonah
Jameson, is a gifted test pilot for N.A.S.A.
His father holds him up as an example of
a real hero, in contrast to "costumed
menaces" like Spider-Man, but it is
Spider-Man who steps in to save John's
life when an orbital flight goes wrong.
John returns to space, however, but
brings back a mysterious gem that
causes him to turn into the bestial
Man-Wolf for three days every month. He
discovers the origin of the gem when he
travels through a portal to the Other-
Realm—it contains the essence of a being
called Stargod. When in this realm, John
retains his humanity as Man-Wolf, but
back on Earth he is unable to control the
beast. Although Jameson seems to rid
himself of the Man-Wolf persona several
times, it resurfaces, for example during his
stint with the Avengers as Captain
America's official pilot. Jameson marries
She-Hulk, although the couple's marriage
is later annulled.

J. JONAH JAMESON

FIRST APPEARANCE *The Amazing Spider-Man* #1 (March 1963)
BASE New York City **AFFILIATIONS** *Daily Bugle,* Fact Channel

Raised by a war veteran who beat his wife and son, J. Jonah
Jameson is all too aware that heroes cannot live up to their own
ideals all the time. This feeds into a distrust of costumed heroes,
although he is more tolerant toward those who don't wear a
mask. Jameson becomes a crusading journalist, whose pet
subjects are civil rights and organized crime. He is fearless in
uncovering the shady activities of gangsters like the Kingpin or
corrupt officials like Randolph Cherryh, which often leads him
into physical danger. Making his name as a reporter, including a
stint in a war zone, Jameson eventually buys the newspaper he
works for, the *Daily Bugle.*

As editor-in-chief, Jameson starts a new crusade—trying to
bring down and unmask Spider-Man, whom he sees as a
dangerous vigilante. However, pictures of Spidey sell papers, so
Jameson is happy to pay young photographer Peter Parker for
his uncannily excellent shots of the masked hero. As Jameson's
obsession with the wall-crawler grows, he employs increasingly
dubious methods to catch him. More often than not, the plans go
awry and Jameson can only appreciate the irony as Spider-Man
swings to his rescue.

After his time at the *Daily Bugle* comes to an end, Jameson
has a spell as Mayor of New York City. His tenure ends amid
accusations of wasting public funds pursuing Spider-Man and
allowing this obsession to take priority over protecting New
Yorkers against Norman Osborn's Goblin Nation. After leaving
office, Jameson returns to the media and establishes the
television news station Fact Channel.

> ## "The trouble with me is—I'm too sweet! …It's time I was roasting Spider-Man's hide in an editorial again!"
>
> **J. JONAH JAMESON**

The Scorpion stung
J. J. Jameson's plan to create the villain
Scorpion in order to catch Spider-Man
backfires when Scorpion attacks
Jameson in his office and Spider-Man
ends up coming to his rescue.

"Everything I've done, everything I'll do today, everything I'll ever do, I do to protect this world."

TONY STARK

IRON MAN

Scientific genius Tony Stark builds his first armored suit to save his life, but soon realizes his invention's even greater potential. He becomes Iron Man, a near-invincible protector of humanity.

FIRST APPEARANCE *Tales of Suspense* #1 (May 1962) **BASE** New York City **AFFILIATIONS** Avengers, New Avengers, Mighty Avengers, Guardians of the Galaxy, S.H.I.E.L.D., Illuminati

LIFE-SAVER

Arms manufacturer Anthony Stark oversees a battlefield test of his weapons but is caught in a booby trap and gravely injured.
He awakens a prisoner of rebel warlord Wong Chu and learns that he has shrapnel lodged near his heart. He is promised medical aid if he builds a super-weapon and is imprisoned in a lab with fellow hostage Professor Yinsen. Knowing they cannot trust their captors, the hostages construct an iron bodysuit to keep Stark's wounded heart beating, and equip it with weapons. Wearing this rough and ready armor, Stark defeats the bandit gang and makes his way back to the U.S.

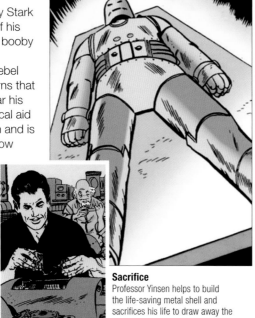

Sacrifice
Professor Yinsen helps to build the life-saving metal shell and sacrifices his life to draw away the guards, allowing Stark time to fully charge the iron suit.

GOING UNDER

After a life of playboy excess as Tony Stark and years of unrelenting pressure as Iron Man, the hero is framed for killing a diplomat and plunges into a web of diabolical intrigue woven by villainous rival industrialist Justin Hammer. The initial success of the scheme is aided by Stark himself, who refuses to acknowledge his growing dependence on alcohol. While countering the plot, Stark's drinking intensifies and he alienates friends and allies, until girlfriend Bethany Cabe forces him to confront his addiction.

Demon in a bottle
Iron Man's armor is hacked and under Hammer's control when Iron Man kills the Carnelian ambassador; however, Stark knows that his drinking is ultimately responsible for the tragedy.

ARMOR WARS

Top-secret Iron Man technology has been stolen by Spymaster and sold to the highest bidder by unscrupulous businessman Justin Hammer. Stark resolves to destroy all weaponry and battle-suits criminals have improved, thanks to his designs. Legal avenues prove ineffective, so Iron Man resorts to force. Unfortunately, his technology has also been used to augment U.S. military gear, such as Mandroids and Guardsmen. When Iron Man goes after them, he is declared an outlaw and kicked out of the West Coast Avengers. The military then try to crush Iron Man with their own armored suit, Firepower—and nearly succeed.

Death metal
Tony Stark believes he is responsible for every death or injury caused by his stolen plans, and will stop at nothing to end their threat.

SUPERIOR IRON MAN

His personality inverted by a mystic spell, Tony Stark moves to San Francisco and begins maximizing his fortune. His selfish, devious scheme panders to public shallowness through an Extremis app, which provides physical perfection and immortality but results in instant addiction. If the user wants to remain agony-free, he or she must pay Stark Industries a daily fee.

Stark begins drinking again and switches to remote-controlled, liquid-metal Endo-Sym armor. As he becomes increasingly unstable, he is challenged by his greatest friend, Pepper Potts. She is aided by Daredevil, She-Hulk, Teen Abomination, and a secret weapon built by Stark himself as a precaution against drastic personality change.

The enemy within
Personality change is Stark's greatest nightmare, which is why he has downloaded a spare normal personality in case he ever goes bad.

timeline

◀ **Will of iron** Tony Stark escapes captivity and death in his armored, mobile, life-support system. He resolves to use it to combat evil. *Tales of Suspense #39* (Mar. 1963)

Earth's Mightiest Heroes Iron Man realizes that many heroes are better than one and throws Stark Industries' resources into backing the Avengers. *Avengers #1–2* (Sept.–Nov. 1963)

Mark II Iron Man redesigns his cumbersome battle-suit, creating an outfit with more weapons and gadgets while reducing strain to his damaged heart. *Tales of Suspense #48* (Dec. 1964)

Enemy mine The Pentagon asks Iron Man to investigate the mysterious Mandarin, who becomes the hero's archfoe. *Tales of Suspense #50* (Feb. 1964)

▲ **Spy games** Stark is asked to renovate S.H.I.E.L.D.'s security systems and design cutting-edge weaponry for its agents. *Strange Tales #135* (Aug. 1965)

My friend, my enemy Tony's friend Kevin O'Brien dies battling Iron Man during a protest rally at Stark Industries. *Iron Man #46* (May 1972)

Clash of the titans Iron Man rescues Drax the Destroyer and battles Thanos for the first time. *Iron Man #55* (Feb. 1973)

◀ **Iron supplement** Obadiah Stane tries to take over Stark International; Tony slips back into drinking heavily and surrenders the Iron Man role to best friend Jim Rhodes. *Iron Man #167–70* (Feb.–May 1983)

Wages of sin Stark is shot by stalker Kathy Dare and loses the use of his legs. He still enjoys full range of movement as Iron Man. *Iron Man #242–3* (May–June 1989)

War Machine Stark "dies" and is placed in cryogenic suspension. Control of Stark Industries passes to James Rhodes, who receives the War Machine battle-suit. *Iron Man #284* (Sept 1992)

◀ **Agent of S.H.I.E.L.D.** Following the superhuman civil war, and with Iron Man's identity now public knowledge, Tony Stark is made Director of S.H.I.E.L.D. *Iron Man #15–16* (Apr.–May 2007)

Stark 2.0 Tony Stark's friends restore his mind with a digital copy created before the superhuman civil war. Tony cannot recall the terrible things he has done in the name of keeping the U.S. safe. *Invincible Iron Man #24* (May 2010)

◀ **Who are you?** Stark learns that he is not the son of Howard and Maria Stark, but secretly adopted while their true offspring, Arno, was raised in seclusion. *Iron Man #17* (Dec. 2013)

MARVEL AGE

BRONZE AGE

MODERN AGE

HEROIC AGE

Golden Avenger
Originally built to keep inventor Tony Stark alive, the Iron Man armor has undergone frequent revision and upgrading to keep it the most sophisticated and powerful battle-suit in the world. Providing physical and psionic protection, the suit also grants immense strength, speed, and flight, as well as housing a host of weapons systems.

RED GHOST

FIRST APPEARANCE *Fantastic Four* #13 (April 1963) **BASE** Soviet Russia, mobile **AFFILIATIONS** Intelligencia

Former Soviet scientist Ivan Kragoff duplicates the stellar accident that created the Fantastic Four, flying into space with three primates. He gains the power of intangibility while baboon Igor becomes a shape-shifter, orang-utan Peotor controls magnetic forces, and Miklho the gorilla becomes super-strong.

Red Ghost allies with villains such as Mole Man and the Unicorn, but meets humiliating defeats. His apes increase in power and briefly make a slave of their master. Kragoff bounces back and joins the Intelligencia—a coalition of mad scientists and Super Villains—but they are crushed by Red Hulk. Kragoff is later killed by Captain America (Steve Rogers), while Cap is mind-controlled by Hydra.

UATU THE WATCHER

FIRST APPEARANCE *Fantastic Four* #13 (April 1963) **BASE** Earth's moon **AFFILIATIONS** Watchers, Fantastic Four

Uatu the Watcher comes from an immortal race of immensely advanced beings who begin recording universal events soon after the birth of creation. The Watchers accidentally contribute to the doom of less-developed planet Prosilicus; thereafter, they adopt a strict code of non-interference. Stationed on the Moon, Uatu, however, is constantly tempted to intervene in the fate of humanity, such as warning of the coming of Galactus and imprisoning the Molecule Man.

As the Multiverse spirals towards total obliteration, Uatu is seemingly murdered by rogue super-spy Nick Fury for the limitless information stored in his eyes.

VULTURE

FIRST APPEARANCE *Amazing Spider-Man* #2 (May 1963) **BASE** New York City **AFFILIATIONS** Superior Six, Sinister Six

Aging engineer Adrian Toomes invents an electromagnetically-powered flight harness but is swindled by his business partner Gregory Bestman. The harness enables Toomes to fly and boosts his strength and vitality to superhuman levels, and he vengefully destroys the company before embarking on a new career of thievery as the Vulture. Able to overwhelm younger foes and plunder normally inaccessible venues, Toomes carries out daylight raids on New York's banks, jewelers, and even armored cars. He is then defeated by Spider-Man, who devises an anti-magnetic scrambler to neutralize the flying thief's power pack.

The Vulture unites with other Spider-Man foes as the Sinister Six, but again suffers defeat. While incarcerated, he is injured and tricked into sharing his scientific secrets with cellmate Blackie Drago. After Drago reveals that he caused Adrian's accident to steal the Vulture-suit's secrets, the old man escapes, determined to destroy his latest betrayer.

Toomes often returns for vengeance or to make a quick buck, but is always beaten by Spider-Man. Despondent, Adrian retires, but while in an old people's home, he meets May Parker's friend Nathan Lubensky. This old curmudgeon inadvertently inspires Toomes to reclaim his dignity and place in the world.

Despite the rejuvenating effects of his harness, Toomes retreats from active life. He becomes a Fagin-like figure, manipulating a gang of flying kids to steal for him. The scheme is broken up by Otto Octavius, the Superior Spider-Man, after which he coerces the Vulture into joining his gang, the Superior Six.

Bird of Prey
Although a swift and strong fighter, the Vulture's true calling was as a malevolent planner of crimes and manipulator of innocents.

BARON MORDO

FIRST APPEARANCE *Strange Tales* #111 (August 1963) **BASE** Castle Mordo, Transylvania **AFFILIATIONS** Dormammu

Baron Karl Amadeus Mordo is born into a family of sorcerers. Aged 18, he travels to Tibet to study magic under the Ancient One. When Mordo discovers the evil entity Dormammu, he defies his master and aligns himself with the demonic monster.

The Ancient One resolves to train a sorcerer strong enough to stand against Mordo—young surgeon Dr. Stephen Strange—and he and Mordo become bitter rivals. When Strange discovers that Mordo is attempting to poison the Ancient One, he battles Mordo in astral form and Strange saves the life of the wise sorcerer.

Mordo's use of black magic causes him to contract terminal cancer, and he repents his evil deeds. However, a past version of Mordo travels through time and kidnaps Cartier St. Croix, the father of Monet St. Croix (known as M), in an attempt to force her to cure his cancer. M tricks him, however, and rescues her father. The elder Mordo is later resurrected by Dormammu, who sends him on a mission to kill Strange.

Devil's disciple
Mordo has the knowledge and power to destroy rivals such as Doctor Strange, but lacks the confidence of a true mystic master.

NICK FURY

FIRST APPEARANCE *Sgt. Fury and His Howling Commandos* #1 (May 1963)
BASE Mobile, classified **AFFILIATIONS** U.S. Army, Howling Commandos,
C.I.A., S.H.I.E.L.D., Secret Warriors, Great Wheel of the Zodiac

Nicholas Joseph Fury fights for the little guy, overcoming impossible odds to ensure the world is safe from tyranny, even obliteration. The quintessential fighting man, he never deviates from his belief that ends justify means.

Fury grows up in depression-era Hell's Kitchen in New York City and when the U.S. joins World War II, quickly enlists. A born soldier, he triumphs in many "impossible" missions, encountering superhuman operatives such as Captain America, Canadian mutant Logan, and the Invaders.

Sergeant Fury achieves two kinds of immortality: firstly as the commander of the famous special operations unit "the Howling Commandos" and, in a more literal sense, after meeting Professor Berthold Sternberg in occupied France. The scientist inoculates Fury with Infinity Formula, a life-preserving, anti-aging super-serum, but makes Fury pay a high price for further treatments over the ensuing decades.

After the war, Fury serves with the C.I.A. between periods of military service in Korea and elsewhere. During the Cold War, Fury creates a team of Secret Avengers utilizing metahuman operatives for a mission in Cuba.

With Earth increasingly at the mercy of magical monsters and invading aliens, Fury inherits another dirty job—one he conceals from friends and foes alike. As "The Man on the Wall," he assassinates potential threats to humanity, using embargoed technology and gamma-irradiated bullets. Fury roams the Multiverse killing thousands of extraterrestrial and extra-dimensional beings so other heroes don't have to.

In the 1960s, he takes on his most high-profile role. As Director of the Supreme Headquarters, International Espionage Law-Enforcement Division (S.H.I.E.L.D.) he is tasked with smashing terrorist group Hydra and its many splinter organizations, such as Them, A.I.M., and the Secret Empire. Here he finally becomes adept—if not comfortable—with the task of sending operatives out to almost certain death for the greater good. Fury safeguards humanity for decades, countering international political threats, such as those posed by Soviet spy agency Leviathan, global events such as the invasion by Skrulls, anf home-grown menaces like corrupt U.S. security supremo Norman Osborn.

Ousted from S.H.I.E.L.D. for leading an unsanctioned black–ops operation in Latveria, Fury employs stolen resources and creates Secret Warriors squads to continue fighting his way.

Fury is exposed as the murderer of Uatu the Watcher, whom he ruthlessly killed for the secrets contained in Uatu's all-seeing eyes. For this crime, the Watchers transform him into the Unseen—a silent, powerless witness of events on Earth.

All-seeing eye
Even with the murdered Watcher's stolen eye and the world's secrets exposed, Fury could not hold at bay all the threats endangering mankind.

> ## "Ain't you heard? Nick Fury's got more lives than a cat!"
> **NICK FURY**

Dirty Work
Fury was a plain and simple man who knew his duty and never shirked or stinted in getting his hands dirty.

timeline

MARVEL AGE

▼ **Waa-hooo!** Fury's Howling Commandos disrupt the Axis war effort, meet Reed Richards and Captain America, and battle Nazi villains. *Sgt. Fury and His Howling Commandos* #1–13 (May 1963–Dec. 1964)

Fantastic adventure Fury recruits the Fantastic Four to invade a South American country and battle the menace of the Hate-Monger. *Fantastic Four* #21 (Dec. 1963)

Man on a mission Colonel Nicholas Fury is selected to run S.H.I.E.L.D. and end the menace of Hydra, A.I.M., and other threats to global security. *Strange Tales* #135 (Aug. 1965)

BRONZE AGE

▼ **Back to basics** Fury institutes a program of S.H.I.E.L.D. super-agents, but the project fails since half of his team are traitors: infiltrators from enemy organizations. *Captain America* #217 (Jan. 1978)

Inside man When S.H.I.E.L.D. agents are almost all replaced by corrupt Deltite Life Model Decoys, Fury has to destroy the agency he built and start all over again. *Nick Fury Vs. S.H.I.E.L.D.* #1 (June 1988)

Tear it up and start again A new S.H.I.E.L.D. is formed, with Fury training and commanding a small band of trusted human agents in the Strategic Hazard Intervention Espionage Logistics Directorate. *Nick Fury, Agent of S.H.I.E.L.D.* #1 (Sept. 1989)

MODERN AGE

Secret Warrior When the U.S. President prevents Fury from arresting Latverian leader Lucia von Bardas, Fury secretly enlists Super Heroes to bring the terrorist to justice. *Secret War* #1 (Apr. 2004)

▼ **Eye on the prize** After years of ceaseless toil, Fury discovers S.H.I.E.L.D. has been Hydra's puppet from the start and tasks his Secret Warriors with destroying both organizations. *Secret Warriors* #28 (July 2011)

HEROIC AGE

WASP

FIRST APPEARANCE *Tales to Astonish* #44
(June 1963) **BASE** New York City
AFFILIATIONS Avengers, Axis, Defenders,
Lady Liberators

As Wasp, Janet van Dyne may be small
and unassuming but she has tremendous
spirit and a big heart. She needs plentiful
quantities of both these attributes to
survive her stormy relationship with science
genius Henry "Hank" Pym.

When Dr. Vernon van Dyne is murdered
by Pilai, a monstrous alien from Kosmos,
his daughter Janet asks his scientist
partner, Hank Pym, for help. Pym already
has a role open for an assistant and
realizes that Janet is the perfect fit. Pym
possesses the secret of altering his own
size at will, and shares his "Pym Particles"
technology with Janet. Together they form
a Super Hero team: Hank Pym as Ant-Man
and Janet as the Wasp.

Wasp and Ant-Man battle foes such as
Egghead, Porcupine, Kang, and Ultron—
who, being programmed with Pym's
brain patterns, is obsessed with Janet—
and are founding members of the
Avengers. At first, the Wasp is a
fun-loving member of the team,
but she later develops into
one of the Avengers' most
important leaders.

Wasp takes a leave of absence when
she is injured by Count Nefaria, but, on her
return, takes a greater role in the Avengers.

She and Hank Pym marry, but the marriage
is stormy and his mental instability and
chronic insecurity eventually lead to Janet
divorcing him.

As Chairman of the Avengers, the Wasp
leads the team through the difficulties
caused by Baron Zemo's attack on
Avengers Mansion. Her life later takes a
tragic turn when, during the shape-shifting
Skrulls' Secret Invasion, a Skrull posing as
Hank Pym turns Wasp into a living bomb.
Thor is forced to kill Wasp to prevent a
disaster. Later, the Avengers discover a
mysterious message from her, and rescue
her from another dimension.

During the events of the second
superhuman civil
war, another
Wasp emerges—
Russian Nadia
Pym, the
daughter of Henry
Pym and his Hungarian
first wife, Maria Trovaya.
Nadia ends up sharing the
codename Wasp with her
stepmother, Janet.

Powering up
Hank Pym hooks Janet up to a machine
in his lab. A pinprick later, and the
"specialized cells"—Pym Particles—will
be in place and Janet will be able to shrink
to the size of a wasp, and grow wings and
tiny antennae.

timeline

Ant-Man and the Wasp Feeling lonely, Hank Pym
develops equipment for a future partner, then asks
Janet van Dyne to join him and help avenge her
father's murder. *Tales to Astonish* #44 (June 1963)

The coming of the Avengers After defeating Loki,
Ant-Man and Wasp suggest the assembled Super
Heroes form a team, which Wasp names the Avengers.
Avengers #1 (July/Sept. 1963)

Until death do us part Janet Van Dyne and Henry
Pym are finally married, though Pym takes his vows
as his wise-guy alternate personality, Yellowjacket.
Avengers #60 (Jan. 1969)

▼ **New beginnings** Newly divorced from Hank, Wasp
nominates herself to head the Avengers and wins the
role. *Avengers* #217 (Mar. 1982)

West coast hero Wasp joins the West Coast Avengers
when Iron Man leaves, and battles Yetrigar,
a cave monster. *West Coast Avengers* #32 (May 1988)

▼ **The new Wasp** Janet emerges from a healing
cocoon in a new, insect-like form, with antennae, long,
spindly fingers, and a new costume. *Avengers* #394
(Jan. 1996)

Back from inner space Believed dead after the
Skrulls' Secret Invasion, Janet emerges from the
Microverse, where she has been battling tyrant Lord
Gouzar. *Avengers* #32 (Dec. 2012)

The unstoppable Wasp Nadia Pym, daughter of Hank
Pym and his murdered first wife, Maria Trovaya,
creates a Pym Particle-powered suit to become the
new Wasp. *Free Comic Book Day 2016: Avengers*
(July 2016)

MARVEL AGE

BRONZE AGE

MODERN AGE

HEROIC AGE

Nadia Pym
Teenager Nadia Pym spends
most of her life locked up in the
Russian secret service training
facility known as the Red Room.
When she finally escapes, she
resolves to continue the heroic
legacy of her mother and father.

The sting of the Wasp
Thanks to Pym Particles, Wasp can grow as tall
as a building or shrink to insect size. At the latter size
she sprouts tiny wings and can fly at speeds
up to 40mph (64kph). She can also fire energy blasts
("wasp stings") from her hands.

"The Avengers are about giving
you a chance to start over."

WASP

> # "Now, watch me trap a spider in a web of my own—a web made of my new-found arms!"
>
> **DOCTOR OCTOPUS**

Mind over matter
Radiation from a lab accident causes Doctor Octopus' artificial arms to adhere to his body. Awaking in hospital, he finds they will obey his mental commands.

DOCTOR OCTOPUS

FIRST APPEARANCE *Amazing Spider-Man #3* (July 1963) **BASE** New York City **AFFILIATIONS** Sinister Six, Masters of Evil

Doctor Octopus is one of Peter Parker's greatest foes. He and his mechanical tentacles are intertwined in Spider-Man's fate from the beginning. For a time, he even becomes Peter Parker.

Dr. Otto Gunther Octavius is a nuclear scientist who uses a set of telescoping arms to handle nuclear material at the U.S. Atomic Research Center. A lab accident causes these mechanical arms to fuse with his body. Radiation exposure alters his mind, allowing him to control his new tentacles with his thoughts and increasing the scope of his ambitions.

As Doctor Octopus (nicknamed Doc Ock), he embarks upon a life of criminal conquest, repeatedly clashing with Spider-Man. He also assembles a criminal gang, the Sinister Six, to aid him in his battles against the web-slinger.

Doc Ock's body gradually deteriorates as both his tentacles and battle injuries severely affect his health. As a last resort, he uses his scientific genius to place his mind into the super-fit body of Peter Parker, in effect killing his long-time rival. Octavius then sets out to become an even greater hero, as the Superior Spider-Man. In time, however, he realizes that he cannot be the hero that Peter Parker is, and allows his mind to be erased so that Peter Parker may re-emerge in his own body and save the day.

An evil iteration of Doc Ock soon returns, however, one with scant regard for the valuable life lessons Otto previously learned as the Superior Spider-Man.

Armed and dangerous
Doctor Octopus has psychic control over four titanium tentacles that can reach up to 24ft (7.3m) long and lift up to three tons. The three pincers at the tip of each tentacle can squeeze with a pressure of 170lbs per sq. in. (11.95kg per sq. cm.)

Superior Spider-Man
Otto Octavius switches bodies with Peter Parker and watches his rival perish inside the deteriorating body of Doctor Octopus. Octavius sets out to be the better Spider-Man, but learns it's not so easy.

timeline

Spider-Man versus Doctor Octopus Spider-Man is beaten so badly during his first encounter with Doctor Octopus that he needs a pep talk from the Fantastic Four's Human Torch to face the Super Villain again. *Amazing Spider-Man #3 (July 1963)*

▼ **The Sinister Six** Doc Ock gathers Electro, Mysterio, Kraven, Vulture, and Sandman as the Sinister Six, and kidnaps Peter's girlfriend Betty Brant and Aunt May. *Amazing Spider-Man Annual #1 (Oct. 1964)*

The arms of Doctor Octopus Doc Ock demonstrates an amazing long-distance mental link with his mechanical arms, calling them at the museum from prison and commanding them to return. *Amazing Spider-Man #88 (Sept. 1970)*

▶ **Arachnophobia** Doctor Octopus develops a debilitating fear when he is badly beaten by Spider-Man. Later, Spider-Man loses a fight to save the city, which unfortunately restores Doc Ock's confidence. *Amazing Spider-Man #297 (Feb. 1988)*

Superior Spider-Man After switching bodies with Peter Parker, Otto Octavius crafts a new Spider-Man suit and begins a new life as the Superior Spider-Man. *Avenging Spider-Man #15.1 (Feb. 2013)*

◀ **Doc Ock's comeback** Doctor Octopus is restored to life once again when a digital copy of his consciousness is transferred into a cloned body. *Amazing Spider-Man #20 (Dec. 2016)*

MARVEL AGE

BRONZE AGE

MODERN AGE

HEROIC AGE

"But faith is my sword. Truth my shield. Knowledge my armor."

DOCTOR STRANGE

DOCTOR STRANGE

Doctor Stephen Strange is the Earth's Sorcerer Supreme, wielding powerful artifacts like the Eye of Agamotto, the Cloak of Levitation, and the Book of the Vishanti to protect the world against mystical foes and malevolent entities.

FIRST APPEARANCE *Strange Tales* #110 (July 1963) **BASE** Kamar-Taj, Tibet; Greenwich Village, New York City **AFFILIATIONS** Defenders, Avengers, Illuminati

MASTER OF THE MYSTIC ARTS

Skilled surgeon Dr. Stephen Strange suffers a crippling car accident that severely damages his hands. No longer able to perform surgery after unsuccessful treatment with Western medicine, his road to rehabilitation brings him East to Kamar-Taj in Tibet. Under the guidance of the Ancient One, Doctor Strange learns the mystical arts. Alongside a fellow student, the evil Mordo, Strange learns the limitless powers available to him and ways to heal himself while protecting the world.

Meeting the master
Doctor Stephen Strange first encounters his master, the Ancient One, on his road to learning the mystical arts.

THE SANCTUM SANCTORUM

At 177A Bleecker Street on the corner of Fenno Place, in New York City's Greenwich Village, is Doctor Strange's Sanctum Sanctorum where he works as a mystical consultant with faithful friend and fellow magician, Wong. Together, they take cases battling dark villains, such as the vampire Dracula, the other-dimensional Shadowqueen, and various hellish demons. One of the worst attacks on the Sanctum Sanctorum is perpetrated by the alien sorcerer Urthona, who spirits away Strange's entire collection of books, as well as Wong and their fellow sorcerer, Topaz.

Enchanting home
Though the Sanctum Sanctorum appears to be a lavish and larger-than-average brownstone home in Greenwich Village, it is even bigger on the inside.

TOMB OF DRACULA

Doctor Strange finds his magical companion Wong close to death from puncture wounds in his neck. After a little psychic investigation, the doctor discovers the attacker's identity: Dracula. Uncovering Dracula's lair and still hoping to save Wong's life, Strange battles the vampire in the psychic realm. However, in the material plane, Dracula bites Strange, turning him into a vampire. Eventually the mage is able to defeat Dracula with the help of various gods and his new vampiric powers. With the last of his mystical strength, Strange summons the wherewithal to cure himself, and also bring back Wong from near-death.

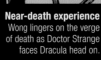

Near-death experience
Wong lingers on the verge of death as Doctor Strange faces Dracula head on.

THE DARK DIMENSION

At the request of the Ancient One, Doctor Strange ventures to face the dread Dormammu, ruler of the hellish Dark Dimension, who plans to take over the Earth. A young woman named Clea, Dormammu's niece, watches on as Doctor Strange faces a bevy of combatants on his way through the Dark Dimension. Worried for the fearless traveler, she tries to warn Doctor Strange of the dangers he will face, but he is undaunted.

Clea resolves to aid him in his journey, despite sealing her own doom. Strange finally bests Dormammu and returns to Earth. Clea remains in the Dark Dimension, but later reappears to help Doctor Strange against Dormammu and other foes. She eventually becomes his wife.

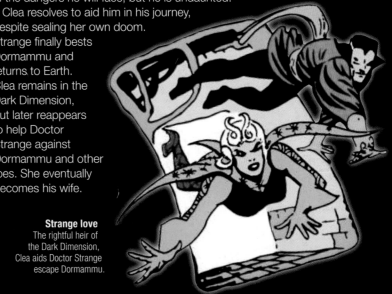

Strange love
The rightful heir of the Dark Dimension, Clea aids Doctor Strange escape Dormammu.

SORCERER SUPREME

Sorcerer Supreme The Ancient One, master to Doctor Strange, lays dying as Shuma-Gorath—the inverse embodiment of the Ancient One, composed of pure evil—leaches his energy in a bid to rule the universe. Using the Eye of Agamotto, Strange delves into the mind of the Ancient One where he battles his great foes Dormammu, Nightmare, and a now monstrous, tentacled Shuma-Gorath. Finally, Doctor Strange realizes that the only way to stop Shuma-Gorath is to kill the Ancient One, a fate his master knew must come to pass. This act vanquishes Shuma-Gorath, leaving Strange wracked with guilt. The Ancient One appears to him and says that Strange did as he wished, and names him Earth's new Sorcerer Supreme.

Death of a legend
The Ancient One lies at death's door as Doctor Strange makes the most difficult decision of his life—deciding whether or not to end his master's life to stop Shuma-Gorath.

Master magician
Doctor Strange has a natural ability for magic, but what truly sets him apart is his intensive study of manuscripts, books of the occult, and his vast collection of enchanted artifacts.

timeline

◄ **Fateful crash** A car accident sends the arrogant neurosurgeon Dr. Stephen Strange on a twisting path toward spiritual fulfilment. *Strange Tales* #115 (Dec. 1963)

Light in darkness Doctor Strange meets future wife Clea and his worst foe Dormammu in the Dark Dimension. *Strange Tales* #126 (Nov. 1964)

Defensive measures Doctor Strange brings together Namor, Silver Surfer, and the Hulk to defeat the apocalyptic nuclear threat of Omegatron, founding the Defenders hero team. *Marvel Feature: The Defenders* #1 (Dec. 1971)

Sorcerer Supreme Upon his death, the Ancient One passes down the title of Sorcerer Supreme to Doctor Strange. *Marvel Premiere* #10 (Sept. 1973)

◄ **Unlikely pair** Doctor Strange helps Doctor Doom rescue his mother from Hell. *Marvel Graphic Novel* #49 (July 1989)

Blood brother Stephen Strange resurrects his dead brother Victor, but accidentally uses a spell from the Vampiric Verses, turning him into vampire Baron Blood. *Doctor Strange, Sorcerer Supreme* #13-15 (Jan.-Mar. 1990)

Supreme no more Doctor Strange refuses to fight a war on behalf of the Vishanti and forfeits his title. *Doctor Strange: Sorcerer Supreme* #48–9 (Dec. 1992–Jan. 1993)

Soldier of the Vishanti After helping the Vishanti defeat the mystical threat of Salome, Strange is once more Sorcerer Supreme. *Doctor Strange: Sorcerer Supreme* #80 (Aug. 1995)

▲ **Secret brotherhood** Doctor Strange, Reed Richards, Charles Xavier, Black Bolt, Namor the Sub-Mariner, and Tony Stark come together in secret as Super Hero think tank the Illuminati. *New Avengers* #7 (July 2005)

Crushing defeat During a battle, the Hulk crushes Strange's hands, sending him reeling into dark magic. Defeated, conflicted, and ashamed, Strange forfeits the title of Sorcerer Supreme. *World War Hulk* #3 (Oct. 2007)

Supreme once more After the death of Doctor Voodoo (Daniel Drumm), Strange reclaims the mantle of Sorcerer Supreme. *New Avengers* #34 (Jan. 2013)

Possessed To save the life of a young girl, Doctor Strange becomes a host for a demon. *New Avengers Annual* #1 (Aug. 2014)

▲ **Death of Strange** During the second Secret Wars, Doctor Doom kills his Battleworld sheriff, Stephen Strange, when Strange claims that Doom is afraid of Reed Richards. *Secret Wars* #4 (Aug. 2015)

Resurrection After the events of Secret Wars, the Multiverse is reformed and Doctor Strange is brought back to life by Reed Richards, with his memories of Battleworld erased. *All-New, All-Different Marvel Universe* #1 (May 2016)

> "Each of us has a different power! If we combine forces, we could be almost unbeatable!"
>
> ANT-MAN

THE AVENGERS

The Avengers exist to protect Earth from threats that no other single Super Hero or military force can handle. The team's membership is ever-changing, as are the dire menaces it is their mission to defeat.

FIRST APPEARANCE *Avengers* #1 (September 1963) **BASE** Stark Tower, Avengers Mansion, Avengers Compound, Hydrobase
AFFILIATIONS Secret Avengers, West Coast Avengers, S.H.I.E.L.D., Fantastic Four

Stronger together
The Avengers' original founding members: the Hulk (Bruce Banner), Ant-Man (Hank Pym), Thor, Iron Man (Tony Stark) and the Wasp (Janet van Dyne).

AVENGERS ASSEMBLE!
In an elaborate scheme to take revenge on Thor, the Asgardian Loki manipulates the Hulk into causing a train wreck. The Hulk's friend, Rick Jones, sends out a call for help. Not only does Thor respond, but Ant-Man, Iron Man, and the Wasp come to his aid, too. While Thor captures Loki, the others try to subdue the Hulk. Learning that Hulk is innocent, Ant-Man suggests they form a team, and Wasp comes up with the team's new name, "the Avengers."

Tony Stark provides the Avengers with technology and weapons. He also donates his three-story home to use as their base, which they christen the Avengers Mansion. The Avengers' first foes include the likes of Baron Zemo and the Masters of Evil, Kang, Mole Man, Namor, and Space Phantom.

AVENGERS VS. ULTRON
Hank Pym aspires to build a highly intelligent robot, Ultron. After attaining consciousness, the robot attacks Pym and escapes from the lab. Following repeated clashes with the Avengers, Ultron upgrades himself several times, making himself more powerful with each incarnation

The robot's irrational hatred of his "father," Hank Pym, the Avengers, and all humanity drives Ultron to diabolical schemes that nearly obliterate them all. His evil deeds and obsession with Pym's wife, Janet (Wasp), are an ongoing source of anguish for Hank, leading to his mental breakdown,

Showdown with Ultron
After kidnapping the Wasp and tricking Ant-Man into helping him try to transfer Wasp's consciousness into a robot bride, Ultron battles the Avengers when they intervene.

divorce from Janet, and departure from the Avengers. Ironically, Ultron's own creations have a habit of turning against him. Both his synthezoid "son," Vision, and Jocasta, his first android "bride," go on to become Avengers.

AVENGERS DISASSEMBLED
Scarlet Witch (Wanda Maximoff) suffers a nervous breakdown and her sanity is completely shattered. A series of horrifying, epic events follows. First an undead Jack of Hearts—Jonathan Hart, who had died a year earlier—shows up at the Avengers Mansion and explodes, taking much of the building with him. Then Vision crash-lands a quinjet into the front yard, before hatching five copies of Ultron from his corpse; Captain Britain (Brian Braddock) is killed in the ensuing fight. Shortly after, the U.N. revokes the Avengers' charter and the Kree attack the heroes left at their mansion. Hawkeye (Clint Barton) sacrifices himself to save his friends from the Kree.

In the end, Doctor Strange reveals that the deluded Wanda—blaming the Avengers for the loss of her illusory children—used her reality-altering hex powers to cause these terrible events. Strange places Wanda into a coma using the Eye of Agamotto, ending the chaos. She is then taken away by her father, Magneto. Though the series of tragedies cause the Avengers to briefly split up, Captain America and Iron Man later reassemble the team.

Civil war fury
The forces of Captain America and Iron Man battle outside the Baxter Building. The Vision weakens Iron Man's armor and Captain America attacks with his shield.

Scarlet Witch's worst
Wanda's madness causes the temporary deaths of Ant-Man, Hawkeye, and the Vision, leaving Cap and her former teammates in shock.

AVENGERS DIVIDED
Congress passes the Superhuman Registration Act and requires all super-powered citizens to register their real names and disclose their secret identities. Both Iron Man and Mister Fantastic agree to enforce the law, but Captain America opposes it and forms a resistance movement.

The conflict that erupts results in the death of Goliath (Bill Foster) and a split between Susan and Reed Richards. Spider-Man, who initially cooperates and reveals his true identity to the public, has second thoughts and is nearly killed by the Thunderbolts (who work for the U.S. security organization S.H.I.E.L.D.), before switching to Cap's side. The fight culminates in a battle at the Negative Zone prison, 42, where Cap and his allies ultimately surrender. Dark times are still to come, yet the Avengers continue to reassemble in new incarnations, facing threats with their customary bravery.

Earth's Mightiest
The Avengers' roster is constantly changing. Some members come and go, or remain on reserve duty even if they aren't on active membership *(clockwise from top right)*: Iron Man, Spider-Woman (Jessica Drew), Wolverine (James Howlett a.k.a Logan), Captain America (Steve Rogers), Hawkeye (Clint Barton), Spider-Man (Peter Parker), and Thor.

Fragile new alliance Loki tries—and fails—to use the Hulk to bring down his brother, Thor, and the Avengers are born. *Avengers* #1 (Sept. 1963)

▼ **Return of Captain America** The Avengers discover missing World War II hero Captain America frozen in an Arctic ice floe. They thaw him out and offer him a spot on the team. *Avengers* #4 (Mar. 1964)

Cap's kooky quartet The founding Avengers take a break, leaving Captain America to form a new group with Hawkeye, Quicksilver, and Scarlet Witch. The team earns a good reputation after defeating villains such as the Masters of Evil. *Avengers* #16 (May 1965)

"The Avengers…dead!" Captain America invites the Black Panther to join the team, only to discover Hawkeye, Goliath, and Wasp seemingly killed by the Grim Reaper. *Avengers* #52 (May 1968)

Kree-Skrull war Kree warrior Ronan the Accuser comes to Earth, hoping to turn humans into cavemen and use the planet as a base to attack the Skrull Empire. A clash with Earth's Mightiest Heroes is inevitable. *Avengers* #89–97 (June 1971–Mar. 1972)

The bride of Ultron Ultron kidnaps Ant-Man and Wasp in a diabolical scheme to create a robot bride, Jocasta, using the likeness and brain patterns of his human "mother," Wasp. *Avengers* #162 (Aug. 1977)

▶ **Price of victory** Seeking revenge for the death of his father, Baron Zemo and his Masters of Evil nearly destroy Avengers Mansion, forcing the heroes to temporarily relocate to the Hydrobase, an island-like research station. *Avengers* #277 (Mar. 1987)

Onslaught The Avengers battle psychic entity Onslaught. The team is believed to be slain, but is saved by Franklin Richards, who sends the members to a pocket dimension named Counter-Earth. *Heroes Reborn* #½ (Sept. 1996)

◀ **This evil reborn** Ultron destroys the capital city of Slorenia, planning to use the site as a staging ground for a new world inhabited by copies of himself. His plot is thwarted by the android Jocasta, who destroys his near-invincible adamantium body with rare Antarctic Vibranium. *Avengers* #19 (Aug. 1999)

Chaos Scarlet Witch remembers her missing children—who no longer exist—loses her mind, and causes catastrophic events that bring an end to the Avengers. *Avengers* #500-503 (Sept.–Dec. 2004)

Civil war Explosive villain Nitro wipes out the population of Stamford, Connecticut. A public outcry against Super Heroes turns the Avengers against each other. *Civil War* #1 (July 2006)

◀ **All-new, all-different** Captain America, Iron Man, Spider-Man, Ms. Marvel, Thor, and Vision assemble to stop Warbringer invading Earth. Once he is vanquished, the heroes form a new Avengers. *All-New, All Different Avengers* #1–6 (Nov. 2015–Apr. 2016)

CAP JOINS THE AVENGERS

"Wait! Don't you recognize it?? It's the famous red, white, and blue garb of— Captain America!" WASP

Captain America hasn't been seen since the end of World War II. His bizarre discovery not only amazes the public, but also sets a new course for the Avengers!

Namor the Sub-Mariner and the Hulk are battling the Avengers, but when the Hulk suddenly leaves, Namor realized he is outmatched and retreats beneath the sea. Searching for his lost people, the Atlanteans, in the North Atlantic, Namor finds a group of Eskimos worshiping a figure trapped in a block of ice. Enraged and jealous, he threatens them and throws the frozen man into the sea. The ice block floats down the Gulf Stream, slowly melting. From the Avengers' submarine, Thor spots the figure drifting past. Giant-Man hauls him aboard and the Wasp immediately recognizes him as Captain America.

The hero suddenly awakes from suspended animation, calling out for his friend, Bucky Barnes. When he tells the Avengers that he is Captain America, they are suspicious because he hasn't aged a day since World War II. They test his mettle in a brawl, before the Wasp puts a stop to it, as she sees he is undeniably formidable.

Captain America then tells how he came to be frozen in the sea toward the end of the war. He and Bucky were trying to stop a drone plane carrying a bomb, when it blew up. Cap fell into the ocean off Newfoundland, and he believes Bucky died aboard the exploding plane. The Captain's body then froze in the cold northern sea.

The Avengers arrive back in New York. A mishap leaves Cap scrambling to find answers with the help of a new friend, Rick Jones. Following another struggle with Namor, the Avengers invite Captain America to join the team.

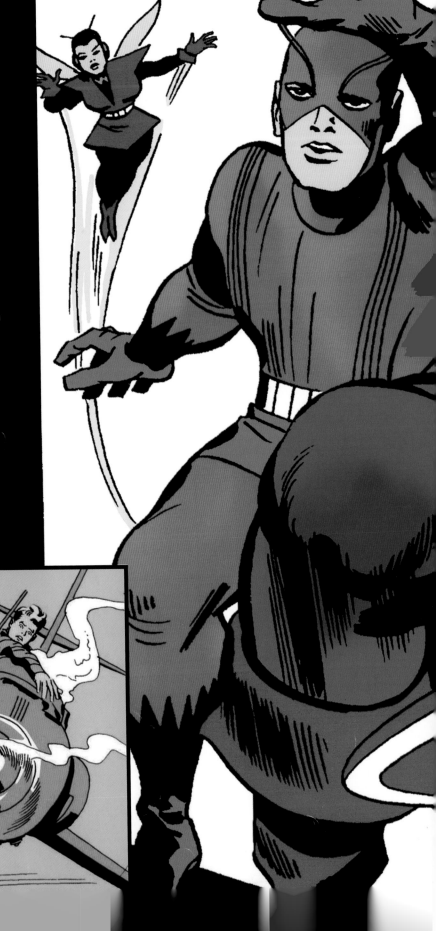

A heroic death and a long fall
Cap recounts to the Avengers the tragic moments when his partner Bucky was killed and he himself came to fall into the freezing waters of the North Atlantic.

Cap's back!
Captain America finds himself in the middle of the action from the beginning. His first challenge is helping the Avengers when they are turned to stone by an alien. Next, he aids them in battle against Namor the Sub-Mariner.

> ## "We…use our powers for the benefit of mankind."
>

X-MEN

Professor X brings together a group of young mutants with extraordinary abilities to form the uncanny, astonishing X-Men. Sworn to protect ordinary human beings, they are nevertheless feared for their mutant powers.

FIRST APPEARANCE *X-Men* #1 (September 1963) **BASE** Xavier Institute for Higher Learning, Westchester, New York; Utopia; Graymalkin Industries, San Francisco

GIFTED YOUNGSTERS

One of the first mutant pupils at Xavier's School for Gifted Youngsters is Scott Summers (Cyclops). Rescued by Professor X from a childhood blighted by the malign influence of Mister Sinister, Scott's eyes are capable of delivering powerful optic blasts. Cyclops is joined by the brilliant Hank McCoy, (Beast), who possesses extraordinary agility and reflexes, Warren Worthington III (the winged Angel), Bobby Drake (Iceman) and the powerful telepath Jean Grey (Marvel Girl). Under Professor X's tutelage, the young mutants, dubbed the X-Men due to their "extra" powers, are turned into a finely honed unit, trained to combat evil threats wherever they appear.

Mutant power
The X-Men quickly learn to trust each other's abilities when facing formidable enemies such as Professor X's former friend Magneto.

AGE OF APOCALYPSE

Xavier's psychotic son Legion (David Haller) travels back in time to kill Magneto, but accidentally murders his father instead, before he can found the X-Men. This act creates a dystopian alternate reality–the Age of Apocalypse—in which North America is conquered by the evil mutant Apocalypse. Moved by his friend's death, Magneto decides to pursue Xavier's dream of peaceful co-existence between mutants and humans and brings together the X-Men to battle Apocalypse's tyranny. The X-Men encounter the mutant Bishop, who has left his own future timeline. He reveals to them how Xavier's murder has disastrously changed the future. Having enabled Bishop to travel back in time to prevent Xavier's murder taking place, Magneto destroys Apocalypse with his immense magnetic powers.

The warlike Apocalypse
Even in the absence of Charles Xavier, the X-Men come together to fight back after Apocalypse declares war on humankind.

The ruling class
In the reality constructed by the Scarlet Witch, her family, the House of Magnus, rule a world dominated by mutants. She is also the mother of twin boys. Left to right: Pietro Magnus, Wanda Magnus, William Magnus, Thomas Magnus, King Erik Magnus, Lorna Magnus.

HOUSE OF M

The insane Wanda Maximoff, the Scarlet Witch, is being held in Genosha after her actions lead to the deaths of three Avengers. While a group of Avengers and X-Men wonder what to do about her destructive, reality-altering powers, the world turns to white… A new reality is born, one in which mutants are the dominant species on Earth and humans ("Sapiens") are a despised minority. Ruling over them is the House of M—Magneto and his children. The X-Men and Avengers all have different lives and no memory of what went before —except for Wolverine. With the help of a young mutant, Layla Miller, Wolverine forces the other heroes to remember the truth. They persuade the Scarlet Witch to give up her reality-bending illusion. When it transpires that it was not Magneto but Quicksilver who had instigated the House of M, Magneto attacks his son. Furious, the Scarlet Witch utters three words— "No more mutants"—and all but a couple of hundred mutants lose their powers. This moment is immortalized as M-Day.

Stand united
The X-Men feared and distrusted the Scarlet Witch; the Avengers felt the same about Hope Summers. However, the heroes unite to destroy the all-consuming Phoenix Force.

AVENGERS VS. X-MEN

The cosmic Phoenix Force is approaching Earth, with Hope Summers, the first mutant born since M-Day, as its intended host. The X-Men believe that this will herald the rebirth of the mutant species, but the Avengers fear that it will bring about the end of life on Earth. The two factions are on a collision course. After initial clashes on Utopia, island base of the X-Men and the mutant race, the two superteams go head to head across the globe. When the Phoenix Force reaches Hope Summers but is rejected, it possesses Cyclops, Emma Frost, Colossus, Namor, and Magik, who try to use their new power to achieve world peace. Ultimately Cyclops becomes the sole host of the Phoenix Force; it overwhelms him and he becomes Dark Phoenix, lashing out and killing his former mentor, Professor X. Only a team-up between Hope and the Scarlet Witch can prevent him from destroying Earth.

timeline

Mutant heroes The X-Men prove themselves to the public for the first time by stopping Magneto from taking over an army base. *X-Men* #1 (Sept. 1963)

Family villain The X-Men battle Juggernaut, (Professor X's step-brother Cain Marko). *X-Men* #12 (July 1965)

▼ **Robot foes** The X-Men encounter Sentinels, programmed to hunt mutants. *X-Men* #14 (Nov. 1965)

New recruits The X-Men change roster with new members Wolverine, Storm, Colossus, Nightcrawler, and Thunderbird. Cyclops is the only original member remaining. *Giant-Sized X-Men* #1 (May 1975)

From the ashes Jean Grey is reborn as Phoenix. *X-Men* #101 (Oct. 1976)

◄ **A terrible beauty** Jean Grey transforms into the Dark Phoenix and goes on a celestial rampage before she can be stopped. *X-Men* #129–138 (Jan.–Oct.1980)

▼ **Future shock** Kitty Pryde (Sprite) is possessed by her future self, who begs the X-Men to avert Senator Kelly's assassination, which led to the downfall of mutants. *Uncanny X-Men* #141–142 (Jan.–Feb.1981)

X-Factor Jean Grey returns and reunites the original X-Men under the name X-Factor. *X-Factor* #1 (Feb. 1986)

Morlock massacre The Marauders, mutant killers acting for Mister Sinister, massacre underground mutant group the Morlocks, although some are saved by the X-Men and X-Factor. *X-Factor* #10 (Nov. 1986)

A nightmare reality Legion's murder of Charles Xavier brings about the dominance of villainous mutant Apocalypse and a reality in which the X-Men are created by Magneto. *X-Men* #41 (Feb. 1995)

M-Day The Scarlet Witch's volatile powers first create a reality where mutants are Earth's dominant species, and then one in which only a handful survive. *House of M* #1–8 (June–Nov. 2005)

Hope or despair? The first mutant born after the Decimation, Hope Summers, is located. Opinion is divided as to whether she will be mutantkind's savior or destroyer. *X-Men* #205 (Jan. 2008)

With a bullet The X-Men must prevent a missile destroying Earth. Kitty Pryde makes the missile go straight through, but is trapped inside it. *Astonishing X-Men* #24 (Mar. 2008)

Breaking away After a schism in the X-Men, some members base themselves on Utopia with Cyclops while others go with Wolverine to the new Jean Grey School for Higher Learning in Westchester. *Wolverine and the X-Men* #1 (Dec. 2011)

▼ **Clash of the super-teams** The Phoenix Force sends the Super Hero community into disarray as the X-Men clash with the Avengers. Cyclops becomes Dark Phoenix and kills Charles Xavier. *AVX: VS* #1 (June 2012)

Classic inspiration The time-displaced original X-Men are brought to the present day to remind their present selves what had originally inspired and motivated them. *All-New X-Men* #1 (Jan. 2013)

In the genes

Mutants like the X-Men get their powers from the X-gene. Some believe them to be the next stage in human evolution, a subspecies known as *Homo superior*. This 2016 grouping comprises (top to bottom): Angel (Warren Worthington III); Cyclops (Scott Summers); Iceman (Bobby Drake); Oya (Idie Okonkwo); Wolverine (Laura Kinney); Beast (Hank McCoy).

PROFESSOR X

FIRST APPEARANCE *X-Men* #1 (September 1963) **BASE** Xavier's School for Gifted Youngsters, Westchester County, New York **AFFILIATIONS** X-Men, Starjammers, New Mutants

Powerful telepath Charles Francis Xavier spends his life working for peaceful co-existence between humans and mutants. As Professor X, he creates the X-Men to help make his dream a reality, but his good intentions lead him down some dark paths.

Despite being born into a life of privilege, Charles Xavier's childhood is not a happy one. His scientist father dies when Charles is very young, and his mother marries his father's colleague, Kurt Marko. He brings with him his son, Cain, who resents and bullies his new stepbrother. While still a child, Charles manifests the mutant power of telepathy, which enables him to discover Marko's mercenary reasons for marrying his mother.

After his mother dies, Xavier seizes the opportunity to escape his stepfamily—his brilliant mind is his passport to Oxford University in England. There, he meets his first love, future Nobel-prizewinning geneticist and mutant genome expert Moira Kinross (later MacTaggert); however, their relationship is interrupted when Xavier volunteers to fight in the Korean War.

As a telepath, a war zone proves almost unbearable: he is "plugged in" to the suffering of those around him. But Xavier's power is also useful, and he becomes renowned for his uncanny ability on search and rescue missions. Serving alongside him is his stepbrother Cain who, in a jungle temple, discovers a strange ruby—the Crimson Gem of Cyttorak—that turns him into the monstrous Juggernaut.

After the war, Xavier travels the world, becoming aware of more mutants, including Erik Lehnsherr (later Magneto), who has power over magnetism. They pair up to fight former Nazi Baron von Strucker, but later part company when it becomes clear that they have different views on mutant-human relations.

On his travels, Xavier encounters an alien named Lucifer. When Xavier foils Lucifer's invasion plans, Lucifer drops a block of stone on the telepath, crushing his legs and paralyzing him.

Xavier, styling himself Professor X, decides to gather together the good mutants on Earth to protect themselves and normal humans from external threats. He converts his family mansion into the Charles Xavier School for Gifted Youngsters and invents a mutant detection device called Cerebro to help him find pupils.

Professor X's phenomenal abilities are not solely Earthbound—they reach across space. His mind connects with Lilandra, a Shi'ar princess, and they marry. Life as a Shi'ar consort does not satisfy Professor X, however, and he returns to Earth. Later, he helps Lilandra win her throne back after a coup, but returns home as the unwitting host of an egg belonging to malignant alien insectoids the Brood. The hatching of the Brood egg almost kills Xavier, but his consciousness is transferred to a clone, enabling him to walk again. However, fate has other ideas, and Xavier is paralyzed once more during a fight with the demon Shadow King.

Professor X is single-minded in his pursuit of his dream of mutants living in harmony with humans. Even his loyal X-Men feel that he uses his powers invasively as a means to an end, and he and Cyclops (Scott Summers) often disagree about how the X-Men should function. Even so, the end is still shocking when it comes: Cyclops, taken over by the destructive Dark Phoenix force, lashes out and seemingly kills Xavier, his former mentor.

Psi power
Professor X is one of the world's most powerful telepaths. As well as being able to read people's thoughts and put ideas into their heads, he can also make them see illusions and even induce temporary paralysis.

First love
Xavier meets Moira Kinross at university. Although she breaks off their engagement, Moira helps Xavier set up his school and continues to take an interest in the mutant cause.

"The greatest power on Earth is…the power of the human brain!"

CHARLES XAVIER

timeline

School's in Wheelchair-bound Charles Xavier opens a school for training fellow mutants in his ancestral mansion. His students are dubbed the X-Men. *X-Men* #1 (Sept. 1963)

▶ **Changeling** Professor X apparently dies during a battle with Grotesk, but it turns out that he is in hiding and has been replaced by reformed villain and shape-shifter Changeling. *X-Men* #42 (Mar. 1968)

Alien bride Xavier, believing most of the X-Men are dead, leaves Earth with his royal Shi'ar lover, Lilandra. *X-Men* #118 (Feb. 1979)

Kidnapped Anti-mutant extremist Reverend William Stryker abducts Xavier and tries to force him to locate and kill other mutants. *God Loves, Man Kills* #5 (Jan. 1983)

Brood host Carrying an alien Brood egg, Xavier nearly dies when it hatches. His consciousness is transferred into a new body and he is able to walk for a time. *Uncanny X-Men* #167 (Mar. 1983)

Patricide Charles is accidentally killed by his disturbed, time-traveling son, Legion, before he can found the X-Men, bringing about the Age of Apocalypse. Magneto manages to defeat Apocalypse and restore the timelines. *X-Men* #41 (Feb. 1995)

Powerless Professor X is one of many mutants to lose his powers after the "House of M" event, but he regains the use of his legs. *X-Men: Deadly Genesis* #5 (May 2006)

▶ **Into ashes** Professor X is killed by his former star pupil Cyclops, who has been possessed by the Dark Phoenix. *Avengers vs. X-Men* #11 (Nov. 2012)

Friends like these

Xavier first meets Erik Lehnsherr in Israel, at a clinic specializing in treating Holocaust survivors. Charles is delighted that his new friend is so interested in his theories on human evolutionary mutation, but soon realizes they are poles apart when it comes to the future of human-mutant relations. While searching for Nazi gold, Hydra agents abduct a patient from the clinic. Charles and Erik mount a rescue mission, but Charles is dismayed to see Erik flying off with the loot. Their friendship turns to enmity, and Erik calls himself Magneto. Their paths are destined to cross many times.

MAGNETO

FIRST APPEARANCE *X-Men* #1 (September 1963)
BASE Asteroid M, Avalon **AFFILIATIONS**
Brotherhood of Evil Mutants, X-Men, Acolytes

As a child, Magneto witnesses the worst that humans are capable of during World War II, and becomes fanatical about protecting mutants from persecution. He believes that mutants—*Homo superior*—should inherit the Earth.

Magneto is born Max Eisenhardt to a German Jewish family and sent with them to the Warsaw Ghetto. During an escape attempt, his parents and sister are killed and Max finds himself in Auschwitz concentration camp. There, Max is reunited with his first love, a gypsy girl named Magda, and the two manage to escape during a prisoner revolt. Making their way to the city of Vinnitsa in the Soviet Union, Max and Magda marry and have a daughter, Anya. Max acquires forged documents that give him a new name: Erik Magnus Lehnsherr. When Erik first manifests his mutant power—magnetism—fearful locals set fire to his home, killing his daughter. Enraged with grief, Erik unleashes his powers, laying waste to Vinnitsa. Terrified, Magda slips away. For years Magneto believes that she later gives birth to twins, who become Scarlet Witch and Quicksilver (Wanda and Pietro Maximoff).

After the war, Erik tracks down war criminals for various secret-service organizations. While in Israel, he meets Charles Xavier (Professor X), and the two debate at length, and disagree strongly, about the place of mutants in the world. Around this time Erik starts calling himself Magneto, Master of Magnetism.

Magneto travels to the U.S. to attack the Cape Citadel military base. He is foiled by the X-Men, assembled by his former friend Professor X and on their first mission.

What drives Magneto is his fear that mutants will end up being hated and exterminated by *Homo sapiens*, just as the Jews and other minorities were by the Nazis. His ruthless determination to protect mutants leads to many human deaths. However, sometimes even Magneto feels he has overstepped a mark. When he almost kills Kitty Pryde—the kind of young mutant he wants to protect—he reassesses his behavior and is briefly on the same side as the X-Men. It has also dawned on the Master of Magnetism that his actions might actually make life worse for mutants, as anti-mutant sentiment among humans rises. But all too often, Magneto's instinct is to fight fire with fire.

> ## "You have no idea what true horror looks like."
> **MAGNETO**

Magnetic man
Magneto's powers over magnetism enable him to summon magnetic force fields to protect himself, and to shoot electromagnetic pulses of enormous power that can disable electronic devices and machinery the world over.

Mixed motives
Magneto brings Kitty Pryde, trapped in a giant bullet, back to Earth, but it is not altruism that drives him, but the need to win the X-Men's trust.

timeline

My gang Magneto assembles his own team, the Brotherhood of Evil Mutants. They frequently clash with his former friend Professor X's X-Men. *X-Men* #1 (Sept. 1963)

▼ **The Savage Land** Discovering a lost world of dinosaurs and prehistoric people in the Antarctic, Magneto creates new mutants from its inhabitants with the aim of taking over the world, before being thwarted by the X-Men. *X-Men* #63 (Dec. 1969)

Magneto on trial The Master of Magnetism is tried for crimes against humanity. After the trial breaks down, a stricken Xavier asks Magneto to take over his school as headmaster. *Uncanny X-Men* #200 (Dec. 1985)

Crossing a line Magneto uses his power to rip Wolverine's Adamantium skeleton from his body; Professor X retaliates by wiping Magneto's mind. *X-Men* #25 (Oct. 1993)

Apocalypse conquered During the rule of Apocalypse, Magneto manages not only to fix the timelines but also to rend the mighty Apocalypse in two with his power. *X-Men Omega* (June 1995)

Island paradise The United Nations grants Magneto the island of Genosha for him to rule, in exchange for not attacking other nations. *X-Men* #87 (Apr. 1999)

◄ **House of M** In a new reality brought about by Scarlet Witch, Magneto and his family are rulers of a mutant paradise. It ends in tragedy as Magneto attacks his son and loses his powers. *House of M* #7 (Nov. 2005)

JEAN GREY

FIRST APPEARANCE *X-Men* #1 (September 1963) **BASE** Xavier Institute, Salem Center; White Hot Room **AFFILIATIONS** X-Men, X-Factor

Jean Grey is one of the original members of the X-Men and in many ways the soul of the team. She steals the hearts of several of its members, but tragedy and sacrifice steal her away from the X-Men.

Jean Elaine Grey's mutant abilities are awakened by a childhood tragedy. Aged ten, she cradles her best friend, Annie Richardson, as she lies dying from a car accident. Her latent telepathic powers cause Grey to share her friend's experience on a psychic level, which traumatizes her. Charles Xavier helps young Jean by placing psychic barriers around her powers so she can't access them until she is older.

Grey later enrols in Xavier's School for Gifted Youngsters under the codename Marvel Girl, becoming the fifth mutant member. Scott Summers (Cyclops, one of the original members) and Jean Grey soon fall in love, but they don't reveal their mutual feelings for some time.

After much training, Xavier unlocks Grey's telepathic powers. When the X-Men are kidnapped by Sentinel robots and taken aboard a space station, she volunteers to pilot a shuttle from an unshielded section so that they can escape. As a result, she is exposed to a near-lethal dose of radiation. When the shuttle crash-lands in the sea, Jean Grey astonishes everyone by rising from the water and proclaiming herself to be the immensely powerful Phoenix.

In time, the villain Mastermind begins manipulating Jean's mind in an effort to prove his worth and join the Inner Circle of the Hellfire Club. He awakens Phoenix's evil tendencies and she becomes the Dark Queen of the Hellfire Club. Mastermind is unable to control her power; she spirals out of control and becomes the insane Dark Phoenix. Jean attacks the X-Men and destroys an entire world in the process, until, in a moment of clarity, she kills herself to protect her friends from her own destructive power.

When she dies, Jean Grey's life force returns to her original body, kept safe in a cocoon at the bottom of Jamaica Bay where she is discovered and released. The X-Men learn that, when their shuttle crashed long ago, the Phoenix Force came to her aid and put her in the cocoon to heal, creating a duplicate body containing a portion of her consciousness within. It was this copy that became the Phoenix.

Jean Grey returns to the X-Men and marries Scott Summers, but her troubles are far from over. She continues to wrestle with the Phoenix Force for control of her own identity. This carries on even after she dies at the hands of the traitorous mutant Xorn, and is transferred to the White Hot Room—a pocket universe where she must reassemble the lost fragments of the Phoenix Force. Here, she becomes the White Phoenix of the Crown.

Mighty mutant
Marvel Girl Jean Grey's natural powers of telepathy and telekenesis are magnified to almost unlimited levels when she is at one with the Phoenix Force.

A Super Hero romance
Life in the X-Men is very tough on relationships. Jean Grey and Scott Summers, who have experienced the longest-running, most troubled of love affairs, can testify to that.

timeline

Marvel Girl Jean joins Charles Xavier's School for Gifted Youngsters and, as Marvel Girl, begins a fantastic life battling mutants, villains, and monsters. *X-Men* #1 (Sept. 1963)

▶ **Full power** With Charles Xavier seemingly dying, he reactivates Jean's telepathic abilities to augment her telekinetic prowess. *X-Men* #42–43 (Mar.–Apr. 1968)

Phoenix rising Jean Grey sacrifices herself, flying the X-Men to safety while she is exposed to lethal radiation. Instead of dying, however, she rises again as Phoenix. *X-Men* #100-101 (Aug.–Oct. 1976)

Into the dark Power corrupts the new Jean Grey. As Dark Phoenix, she becomes an enormous threat to the X-Men. Again, she sacrifices herself to save everyone. *X-Men* #129-138 (Jan.–Oct. 1980)

Like a phoenix… The Fantastic Four discover the real Jean Grey is locked inside an underwater cocoon they recover from the bottom of Jamaica Bay. *Fantastic Four* #286 (Jan. 1986)

At last! Jean Grey and Cyclops are finally married, surrounded by all of their friends. Even Wolverine and Sabretooth watch peacefully from a nearby hilltop. *X-Men* #30 (Mar. 1994)

▶ **Death of Jean Grey** Xorn traps Wolverine and Jean Grey on Asteroid M, headed for the Sun. Wolverine impales her with his claws to spare her more suffering, which releases her Phoenix Force and saves them both—for the moment. *New X-Men* #150 (Feb. 2004)

▶ **Future leader?** A teenage Jean Grey, along with the other X-Men founding members, finds herself transported through time to the present-day by Beast. *All-New X-Men* #3 (Feb. 2013)

Ashes to ashes
In her Phoenix form, Jean Grey has seemingly limitless powers. Though her intentions are good, her power is incredibly destructive and threatens to consume everyone around her.

MARVEL AGE

BRONZE AGE

MODERN AGE

HEROIC AGE

SANDMAN

FIRST APPEARANCE *Amazing Spider-Man #4* (September 1963) **BASE** Brooklyn, New York City **AFFILIATIONS** Frightful Four, Sinister Six, Avengers, Jackal

William Baker has a difficult childhood. He grows up in a poor, single-parent home and gets caught up in crime. Thrown out of high school, Baker, using the alias Flint Marko, becomes entangled in New York's criminal underworld. After spending time in prison, he heads south.

In Georgia, Marko is on a beach when a nuclear reactor explodes and knocks him unconscious. When he comes to, he finds his body now behaves like sand. He can suddenly reshape his body into any form, disperse himself, or solidify parts of his body into powerful weapons. He takes up the alias Sandman and goes on a crime spree, clashing with the likes of Spider-Man, Fantastic Four, and the Avengers. He also has spells in the Wizard's Frightful Four gang and Doctor Octopus' Sinister Six.

Sandman teams up with Hydro-Man (Morris Bench), but they accidentally combine into a new creature, dubbed the Mud-Thing. When Sandman breaks free, he tries to reform and becomes a reserve member of the Avengers. His hero days prove fleeting when Wizard brainwashes him into re-joining the Sinister Six.

Sandman discovers he can create duplicates of himself, each with a distinct identity. He begins spending time with Alma Alvarado and her daughter Keemia. Marko and Keemia bond as father and daughter. Unbeknownst to him, however, his Sandman copies murder Keemia's mother, Alma, and Keemia subsequently ends up in foster care. Henceforth, Sandman's main motivation becomes gaining custody of his "daughter," or at least caring for her from a distance as best he can.

Keemia's castle
Sandman develops the ability to make copies of himself and thus is able to capture Spider-Man—putting Keemia in danger.

LIZARD

FIRST APPEARANCE *Amazing Spider-Man #6* (November 1963) **BASE** New York City **AFFILIATIONS** Sinister Six, Sinister Twelve

Army surgeon Dr. Curtis Connors loses an arm while on military service. Leaving the army, he researches the ability of reptiles to regrow lost limbs. Connors develops a serum to do just that, but with devastating results—he turns into a ferocious, humanoid lizard. Connors' friend Spider-Man (Peter Parker) cures him—but only for a short time. He relapses into the Lizard again and again, and proves a frequent danger to Spider-Man. Spidey is careful not to hurt his friend, if he can help it. Connors is also a help to Peter Parker in scientific matters.

The longer Connors remains the Lizard, however, the more of his human identity is lost to his reptilian side. The Lizard hates all mammals—chief among them humans —and hopes to rid the world of them so that reptiles can reign once more.

Tragically, the Lizard kills Connors' own son, Billy, devastating Curtis, who turns into a feral reptilian monster known as Shed. In his new state, he can reduce the minds of other humans to reptilian levels. Dr. Michael Morbius (the Living Vampire) restores Connors' human form, but his Lizard mind remains.

Later, while in custody at the Raft prison, Connors finds his condition reversed, with a human mind trapped in the Lizard's body. Wracked with guilt, Connors believes he is receiving the punishment he deserves. Later, the Jackal (Miles Warren) visits Connors in the Andry Correction Facility and persuades him to escape—but only after the Jackal reveals he has Connors' wife Martha and son Billy—both of whom he thought had died.

Face-to-face with…the Lizard!
J. Jonah Jameson issues a challenge to Spider-Man to capture the Lizard, and Peter Parker heads to Florida and meets Dr. Curtis Connors.

BLIZZARD

FIRST APPEARANCE *Tales of Suspense #45* (September 1963) **BASE** New York City **AFFILIATIONS** Masters of Evil, Thunderbolts, Fifty-State Initiative

Blizzard is an alter ego assumed by several people. None initially have super-powers. Instead, they use a suit that draws on air humidity to generate ice, snow and freezing effects. Dr. Gregor Shapanak is an employee of Tony Stark, fired for stealing. He develops the original battle suit, first under the name Jack Frost and later Blizzard. After he is killed by Arno Stark (Iron Man from the future), the role is taken over by Donny Gill.

Gill transforms from villain to hero and back again, with an upgraded suit, thanks to Mandarin. Using one of Gill's spare suits, Randy Macklin takes on the role, and reforms, with help from Tony Stark.

BARON VON STRUCKER

FIRST APPEARANCE *Sgt. Fury and His Howling Commandos* #5 (January 1964) **BASE** Mobile; formerly Strucker Castle, Bavaria, Germany; Hydra Island **AFFILIATIONS** Death's Head Squadron, Blitzkrieg Squad, Hydra, THEM, Great Wheel of the Zodiac

Nazi aristocrat Baron Wolfgang von Strucker is dispatched to Southeast Asia early in World War II, where he makes contact with the Yakuza and the Hand. He also clashes with time-travelers such as Excalibur and X-Force. He is then hand-picked by Adolf Hitler to destroy Nick Fury and his Howling Commandos; failing to achieve this, he creates a Blitzkrieg Squad in an attempt to match the Allies' flamboyant international unit.

Following numerous humiliating failures against Fury and the Invaders, the Baron loses Hitler's confidence and, on the advice of top Nazi agent Red Skull, flees for his life. He resurfaces in the Pacific, joining Japanese deserters and black marketeers to create a criminal secret society he calls Hydra. By 1961, von Strucker has become a key member of international espionage elite the Great Wheel of the Zodiac. By double-dealing, he ensures splinter organizations of S.H.I.E.L.D., Leviathan, and the Zodiac crime cartel are in the pocket of Hydra.

When his archenemy Nick Fury is appointed chief of S.H.I.E.L.D., von Strucker attempts to destroy him, but is killed on Hydra Island. Although Life Model Decoys of Strucker remain at large to attack heroes like Captain America, the real Baron is eventually resurrected by Hydra mystics, who sacrifice themselves to restore their leader, enabling him to reunite Hydra's factions into a force capable of conquering the world.

This time von Strucker's plans seem perfect, until Nick Fury—now a fugitive from S.H.I.E.L.D. and running his own squad the Secret Warriors—hunts him down and kills him.

Strucker is active once again, but it is unknown whether this is the real Baron or another doppelgänger.

Satan claw
The Baron attacks Nick Fury and Hydra-agent-turned-ally Laura Brown with his Satan Claw, which enhances strength and delivers powerful electric shocks.

Constant craving
Perpetual defeat and even death cannot quell Strucker's insatiable hunger for conquest and domination.

ELECTRO

FIRST APPEARANCE *Amazing Spider-Man* #9 (February 1964) **BASE** New York City **AFFILIATIONS** Sinister Six, Emissaries of Evil, Frightful Four, Sinister Twelve, Superior Six, Defenders, Legion Accursed, Exterminators

Telephone lineman Max Dillon gains the power to absorb and control electricity after being struck by lightning, and turns to crime.

Repeatedly bested by heroes such as Spider-Man and Daredevil, he becomes obsessed with proving his status as a major villain. Defeats by minor foes such as Omega the Unknown undermine his confidence and compel him to ally with other Super Villains in teams such as the Sinister Six, Emissaries of Evil, and the Frightful Four.

Despite being potentially one of the most powerful beings on Earth, Dillon's meagre intellect means he can be easily manipulated by more cunning villains like the Kingpin or Wizard, while his arrogance and impetuous temper frequently cause his downfall and imprisonment. However, Electro eventually learns to curtail his flamboyant attention-seeking and begins using his powers in a more covert manner. He accepts a power upgrade sponsored by underworld mastermind the Rose (Jacob Conover) but again meets defeat before he rejoins a new Sinister Six team.

Electro's most successful exploit is when he is hired by Brainchild to clandestinely disrupt the power at supermax Super Villain prison the Raft, enabling an army of America's worst metahuman menaces to break out.

After a troubled alliance with Black Cat (Felicia Hardy), Dillon is captured and deprived of his electrical abilities through technology invented by Parker Industries. Surprisingly, he is happy to stay ordinary, but is kidnapped by the Rhino, Lizard, and Jackal, who forcibly attempt to restore his powers. When this process fails, Dillon is inadvertently killed by Francine Frye—a former accomplice who, thanks to the Jackal's scientific machinations, absorbs Dillon's dormant electrical energies and becomes a new Electro.

Shock treatment
Despite possessing incredible power and utter ruthlessness, Electro never understands why he keeps losing to relative non-entities who prefer brain over brawn.

A brighter spark
After taking Max Dillon's powers, Francine Frye tries to prove herself a better Electro, but soon becomes just another pawn of true master villains.

MANDARIN

FIRST APPEARANCE *Tales of Suspense* #50 (February 1964) **BASE** Mandarin City; Dragon of Heaven; Palace of the Star Dragon, Valley of Spirits, China **AFFILIATIONS** Prometheus Gentech Inc., M.O.D.O.K.'s 11, the Hand

The living embodiment of autocratic tyranny, the Mandarin combines ancient lore with modern technology and employs ten rings of incredible extraterrestrial power to further his plans for world domination.

Born in China and tracing his lineage back to Genghis Khan, the haughty Mandarin grows up poor, proud, but despised by his family and countrymen. This brilliant outcast wanders the country until he reaches the remote, shunned Valley of Spirits and stumbles upon an immensely old, crashed spaceship from the dragon planet Maklu-4.

After years spent mastering its alien technology, he takes possession of ten mighty energy-generating rings and, defying the Communist authorities, begins carving out his own kingdom within the People's Republic. Soon, the increasingly nervous Chinese government cannily trick the Mandarin into attacking Iron Man.

After a humiliating defeat by the Armored Avenger, the Mandarin becomes obsessed with destroying Iron Man, while repeatedly attacking the "decadent" West.

After years of striving to restore the glory of Imperial China—with himself as emperor—the Mandarin is killed by a rival with the same goals: the mastermind Yellow Claw. However, the victor's servant, Loc Do, appropriates the discarded power rings and is possessed by Mandarin's consciousness. With a matter-arranger, Loc Do's body is transformed into a younger, fitter version of the Mandarin, dreaming once more of world conquest.

After further defeats, Mandarin reinvents himself as a ruthless businessman in the new, capitalism-embracing China; however, he is still wedded to the Imperial past. After acquiring the magical Heart of Darkness, he recreates a land of feudal serfdom, but is again foiled by Iron Man and his allies.

Mandarin claws his way back to dominance under the name Tem Borjigin, a ruthless businessman whose Prometheus Corporation provides bioweapons for terrorists.

"I pity you, Iron Man! For though you do not even suspect my existence, you head the list of those the Mandarin has vowed to destroy! And the Mandarin never fails!"

MANDARIN

East meets West
Whatever advantage Iron Man's technological ingenuity provides is always offset by the Mandarin's brilliant mind, alien weaponry, and ancient mystic lore.

timeline

▼ **China crisis** The Mandarin seeks to prove his superiority to the Communist regime by destroying its greatest enemies: Tony Stark and Iron Man. *Tales of Suspense* #50 (Feb. 1964)

Celestial intervention The Mandarin recruits an army of Super Villains to attack the Avengers as a way of masking his plans to cover Earth with his space-based hate-ray. *Avengers Annual* #1 (Sept. 1967)

Jade tiger The Mandarin attempts to enslave the Hulk and foment war between Russia and America, but his scheming is useless against Hulk's fury. *Incredible Hulk* #107-108 (Sept.–Oct. 1968)

◀ **Undying evil** Yellow Claw kills the Mandarin, but the villain's rapidly fading consciousness possesses Yellow Claw's servant and the Mandarin lives on. *Iron Man* #70 (Sept. 1974)

▼ **Dragon seed** Mandarin returns to assail Iron Man, controlling ten ancient alien dragons, each connected to one of his mighty power rings. *Iron Man* #270-275 (July–Dec. 1991)

Heart of darkness Using a mystic gem to turn back time, Mandarin battles Iron Man, War Machine, and Force Works. *Iron Man* #311–312 (Dec. 1994–Jan. 1995)

◀ **Secret invader** The Mandarin inserts himself into Tony Stark's mind and believes he has finally made his greatest enemy his slave. *Invincible Iron Man* #520 (Sept. 2012)

> "There is no defense against the Scarlet Witch's HEX!"
>
> SCARLET WITCH

SCARLET WITCH

A magical mutant of sometimes fragile sanity, Wanda Maximoff—a.k.a. the Scarlet Witch—has cultivated her hex powers to become an extremely powerful reality-altering sorcerer of Chaos Magic alongside the Avengers.

FIRST APPEARANCE *X-Men* #4 (March 1964) **BASE** Mobile; Avengers Tower **AFFILIATIONS** Brotherhood of Evil Mutants, Avengers, Avengers West Coast, Force Works, Uncanny Avengers

BROTHERHOOD OF EVIL MUTANTS

Raised in Europe and of Roma descent, Wanda and her twin brother Pietro (Quicksilver) become servants of Magneto after he saves Wanda from being burned as a witch by superstitious villagers who do not understand her mutant powers. Joining Magneto's Brotherhood of Evil Mutants, along with Mastermind (Jason Wyngarde) and Toad (Mortimer Toynbee), the twins clash with the X-Men in New York. After putting themselves in harm's way one too many times, however, Wanda and Pietro decide that their debt to Magneto is paid and plan their return home to Europe.

Thwarting the X-Men
Feeling indebted to Magneto, Wanda and her brother Quicksilver reluctantly agree to fight their fellow mutants.

A STRANGE ROMANCE

The object of Wanda's affections is, to say the least, unusual—the synthezoid (synthetic human android) Vision. Vision learns human emotions by sensing Wanda's love for her brother and feeling compassion for her when Quicksilver goes missing. These emotions flower as the two work together as Avengers, despite objections from her other suitor Hawkeye and teammates. However, after a tussle with Dormammu, who has kidnapped Wanda, Vision saves her, and then…she saves him right back. Vision knows that no other woman could entice him because no other woman could understand their work as Avengers. He proposes and they soon marry.

Double wedding
Immortus marries Scarlet Witch to the synthezoid Vision in front of their Avengers teammates in a dual wedding ceremony shared with Mantis and Swordsman.

Cap's kooky quartet
Captain America announces to the public his new team of Avengers with Scarlet Witch, Quicksilver, and the archer, Hawkeye.

TURNING OVER A NEW LEAF

Hidden away in a chalet in Switzerland, the twins read in the newspaper that the Avengers are considering replacements, including another hero with a shady past, Hawkeye. This could be their chance to finally be on the right side of a fight! They write of their desire to join, and head to the U.S., where they are received by the dashing Tony Stark. Unbeknownst to the world, Stark is the Invincible Iron Man, who is preparing to exit the Avengers with Giant-Man and the Wasp. Captain America accepts the twins and Hawkeye to create a new Avengers lineup; they also seek out Hulk to add some much-needed muscle. Wanda goes on to fight for the Avengers for decades to come.

TEARING APART A UNIVERSE

Wanda's magical power grows thanks to years of training with the witch Agatha Harkness, developing her reality-warping abilities to omega levels. But after her relationship with Vision falls apart and her children (whom she conjured into existence) are lost, Wanda loses her grip on reality. In a moment of mental lapse, she creates a reality in which she and Vision are able to have twins once more. When Professor X confronts Wanda, asking her to return the universe to what it was, she uses her Chaos Magic to create a history where mutants rule humanity (House of M). Finding out that Quicksilver convinced Wanda to create this reality, Magneto kills him. Now hating mutants, Wanda uses her powers, saying, "No more mutants," and the world reverts back, but with many mutants bereft of their powers.

"No more mutants"
After uttering these words, Scarlet Witch creates a white flash that returns the world to its former state—but with many fewer mutants.

Endless possibilities

Using powerful Chaos Magic, Wanda warps reality itself to her will. A skilled tactician, Scarlet Witch employs her signature hex bolts to manipulate energies which she directs at her opponents. She can teleport, use telekinesis, and is well versed in traditional magic and sorcery.

timeline

Magneto's servant The Scarlet Witch and brother Quicksilver join the Brotherhood of Evil Mutants to confront the X-Men. *X-Men* #4 (Mar. 1964)

Quick exit Only a couple of months after their first appearance, the Scarlet Witch and Quicksilver escape Magneto's Brotherhood of Evil Mutants to return to Europe. *X-Men* #11 (May 1965)

Rightful return Hearing that the Avengers are seeking new team members, Wanda and her brother Pietro come out of hiding to join the team. *Avengers* #16 (May 1965)

Falls for Vision Feelings between Wanda and Vision develop when she leans on him during Pietro's disappearance. *Avengers* #109 (Mar. 1973)

Marrying Vision After a harrowing confrontation with the Dread Dormammu, the Vision proposes to the Scarlet Witch and they are married. *Giant-Sized Avengers* #4 (June 1975)

▼ **Twin joys** The Scarlet Witch magically makes herself pregnant, and gives birth to twin sons Billy and Tommy. *Vision and the Scarlet Witch* #12 (Sept. 1986)

Loveless marriage Wanda and Vision join the West Coast Avengers, but Immortus (Nathaniel Richards, Earth-6311) persuades the government to dismantle Vision. He is reassembled, but without emotions, so his relationship with Wanda suffers. *West Coast Avengers* #45 (June 1989)

Unreal children The witch Agatha Harkness tells Wanda that her children are not real but magical constructs of fragments of the demon Mephisto's soul. *Avengers: West Coast* #51–2 (Nov.–Dec. 1989)

▼ **Back from the dead** The West Coast Avengers are renamed Force Works. Estranged from Vision, Wanda falls for Wonder Man, whose brain patterns helped form Vision's mind. Devastated when Wonder Man is killed on the first Force Works mission, she uses her hex powers to resurrect him. *Avengers* #3 (Apr. 1998)

▼ **Avengers' chaos** Wanda, finding out that memories of her lost children were removed by her former teacher, Agatha Harkness, becomes enraged. With her chaos magic, she sets out to destroy the Avengers. *Avengers Disassembled* #1–4 (Sept.–Dec. 2004)

House of M In severe mental distress, Wanda tears apart reality to give mutants rule over humans. When she eventually returns the universe back to how it was, she depowers many mutants. *House of M* #1–8 (Aug.–Dec. 2005)

Children's crusade The Scarlet Witch's reincarnated twins, Young Avengers Wiccan (Billy Kaplan) and Speed (Tommy Shepherd) set out to save their mother from marrying the manipulative Doctor Doom. *Avengers: The Children's Crusade* #3 (Jan. 2011)

▼ **Avengers vs. X-Men** As the two great teams war over the use of the Phoenix Force, the Scarlet Witch works with Hope Summers to end the conflict. *Avengers Vs. X-Men* #6 (Aug. 2012)

Magical mystery Wanda sets out to protect the mystical forces of the world when a mysterious foe tries to destroy all magic in the Multiverse. *Scarlet Witch* #1 (Feb. 2016)

MARVEL AGE

BRONZE AGE

MODERN AGE

HEROIC AGE

QUICKSILVER

FIRST APPEARANCE *X-Men* #4 (March 1964)
BASE Mobile **AFFILIATIONS** Brotherhood of Evil Mutants, Avengers, Inhuman royal family, X-Factor, Avengers Unity Division, Avengers Academy, West Coast Avengers

Super-fast speedster Pietro and his twin sister Wanda (Scarlet Witch) are raised in the Balkan country of Transia by Romani puppeteer Django Maximoff after his own children are stolen. As their powers manifest away from prying eyes, Pietro's devotion to his sister begins to express itself as obsessive over-protectiveness.

As teenagers, they are attacked by a mob and rescued by Magneto. He believes that Pietro and Wanda are mutants like himself and convinces them to join his Brotherhood of Evil Mutants as Quicksilver and Scarlet Witch.

Essentially a good person, Pietro despises this arrangement. Eventually, they quit the Brotherhood, and he and Wanda relocate to the U.S., where they establish themselves as true Super Heroes with the Avengers.

Over time, Wanda's increasing independence drives a wedge between them, exacerbated when Pietro marries Inhuman princess Crystal but objects to his sister's marriage to the android Vision.

Perhaps because of his super-fast thought processes, Quicksilver is frequently over-emotional and prone to mood swings bordering on sociopathy. Quicksilver has acted with great heroism and compassion in teams like the Avengers, X-Factor and the X-Men but also as a villain, ruthlessly pursuing Magneto's murderous goals; he also triggers his sister Scarlet Witch's de-powering of most of Earth's mutant population on "M-Day."

After years of confusion, Pietro reconciles with Wanda and seeks to redeem himself by returning to a life of heroism. He goes on to work with the Avengers Unity Division.

The twins' origins remain confused and obscure for years. Initially, 1940s hero the Whizzer claims to be their father but later revelations seem to prove Magneto is their father: a deception all involved believe for years. Eventually, Quicksilver discovers that he and his sister are not mutants but products of genetic experimentation. As babies, Anna and Mateo Maximoff were stolen by the High Evolutionary and transformed by his biological tampering.

Gangway!
Pietro often seems brusque and impatient—a result of living in a world where everybody else appears to be moving in slow motion.

Big bad band
Members of the Brotherhood pose with young X-Men student Evan Sabahnur (Genesis) at the front and the dead body of Fantomex at the back *(clockwise from left)*: Shadow King, Omega White, Omega Red, Omega Black, Blob, Sabretooth, Mystique, Daken, and Skinless Man.

BROTHERHOOD OF EVIL MUTANTS/FREEDOM FORCE

FIRST APPEARANCE *X-Men* #4 (March 1964)
BASE Mobile

Founded by Magneto, the Brotherhood of Evil Mutants is a terrorist cell dedicated to the domination of humanity by *Homo superior*. Its stated agenda is to subjugate or eradicate mankind and inherit the Earth. When teleporting mutant Astra quits and vanishes, Magneto treats his remaining recruits—Toad, Mastermind, Quicksilver, and the Scarlet Witch—as servants in a political struggle against oppression.

The Brotherhood's first triumph is the conquest of South American nation Santo Marco, but after being routed by the X-Men, the group retreats to orbiting Asteroid M. Magneto recruits more members, including the Blob and Unus the Untouchable, but has less luck in his attempts to sign up Namor the Sub-Mariner and Thor.

When Magneto and Toad are captured by the Stranger and taken off-world, the Brotherhood dissolves. On his return, Magneto again assumes control, and, with Savage Land mutate Lorelei, attempts to create a world-conquering artificial mutant, "Alpha." Instead, "Alpha" attacks them, and turns them into babies.

On recovering, Magneto forms another Brotherhood (Burner, Lifter, Peeper, Shocker, and Slither). When they are defeated by Captain America, Magneto leaves them to their fate. They eventually evolve into Mutant Force (later the Resistants).

While Magneto abandons the Brotherhood concept, it is taken up by other mutant leaders, including Toad, Havok, Xorn, Exodus, Sunspot, and Professor X. The most successful and dangerous iteration is assembled by the shape-shifter Mystique, who convenes four different teams over the years.

When the most effective of these groups is finally captured, the U.S. government offers them a deal. As federal team Freedom Force they tackle mutant problems and even arrest Magneto, while pursuing Mystique's personal agenda.

Magneto's gang
The original Brotherhood seem to have the X-Men at their mercy *(left to right)*: Toad, Mastermind, Magneto, Scarlet Witch, and Quicksilver.

ENCHANTRESS

FIRST APPEARANCE *Journey Into Mystery* #103 (April 1964) **BASE** Asgard, Asgardia, Earth (mobile) **AFFILIATIONS** Dark Council, Astonishing Avengers, The Sisterhood, Masters of Evil, Lady Liberators

The sorceress Amora, alias Enchantress, is a powerful Asgardian deity. Beautiful, spiteful, and proud, she is tricked by Loki into seducing heroic Thor and becomes the hero's sworn enemy when the Thunder God rejects her for mortal Jane Foster.

Enchantress and her besotted occasional companion Skurge the Executioner are stripped of most of their powers and banished to Earth, where they ally with Baron Zemo as the Masters of Evil in repeated attacks against the Avengers.

After Zemo dies, Enchantress abandons Skurge and seeks out fresh puppets, creating Power Man and beguiling Olympian god Hercules to win her revenge. She also seeks ways to restore her full power, and continues her vendetta against Earth's Mightiest Heroes. Turning the Black Knight to stone with a poisoned kiss triggers war

between the Avengers and Defenders.

Enchantress finally seduces Thor just before Onslaught devastates Earth's heroes. In the aftermath, her fellow Asgardians also vanish, and Enchantress takes on the task of finding and restoring them, battling Egyptian death god Seth and subsequently earning Thor's forgiveness and love.

Enchantress is killed by Loki during the Asgardian doom cycle of Ragnarok, but later resurrected when Thor recreates Asgardia on Earth. Although restored Amora remains wilful, self-serving, and capricious, attacking Asgardia and Yggdrasil the World-Tree, she also saves Thor from Death Goddess Hela.

Learning from the master
Amora considered herself to be wicked beyond redemption, until she encountered true evil in the form of Thor's adopted brother Loki.

Mistress of the Hulk
Amora possesses enough mystic might to conquer Amadeus Cho's Totally Awesome Hulk. She is determined to discover what makes him tick.

MYSTERIO

FIRST APPEARANCE *Amazing Spider-Man* #13 (June 1964) **BASE** New York City **AFFILIATIONS** Sinister Six, Sinister Seven

Sidelined by filmmakers and critics, Hollywood stuntman and special-effects wizard Quentin Beck creates a costumed identity with fake powers and seeks notoriety by framing and then capturing Spider-Man. He joins the Tinkerer's gang to better study his enemy, as well as potential competitors.

When this scheme fails, Mysterio seeks vengeance as part of Doctor Octopus' Sinister Six team; he also institutes further psychological attacks by creating the persona of psychiatrist Dr. Ludwig Rinehart and creating illusions to convince Spider-Man that he is going mad.

Beck passes on his illusionist skills to his prison cellmate Daniel Berkhart. The two even work together briefly, sharing the identity of Jack O'Lantern, a.k.a. Mad Jack. Berkhart also adopts the Mysterio identity when Beck seemingly dies.

After numerous failures, Beck decides to commit crimes away from the public eye. He opens a nursing home to swindle elderly clients, but still clashes with the Wall-Crawler after May Parker is admitted. Beck fakes his death at the behest of his partner—the burglar who killed Ben Parker—but is brought to justice once more by a fighting-mad web-slinger.

Beck also trains his cousin Maguire Beck in many of his techniques, enabling his pupil to become costumed mercenary Jack O'Lantern. Years of dabbling with hallucinogenic chemicals and effects result in Quentin Beck developing cancer. The dying Super Villain determines to go out in style, trying to trick Daredevil into killing a child. When the plot fails and the Man Without Fear also refuses to kill Mysterio, the weary illusionist takes his own life.

Mutant Francis Klum then attempts to usurp the role of Mysterio, but Beck seemingly returns from Hell to challenge him and Berkhart, who has resumed

The power of illusion
Even the amazing Wall-Crawler's spider sense was initially fooled by the astounding gimmicks and theatrics of the seemingly supernatural Mysterio.

the mantle. Months later, Beck is once more operating as Mysterio, partaking in such schemes as Doc Ock's attempt to kill almost everyone on Earth. However, Mysterio's most audacious exploits are his attempts to gain wealth and power in the Ultimate Universe (Earth-1610). After finding a way to access Earth-1610, Beck sends an android to that dimension and begins committing various crimes. After being defeated by Peter Parker and Miles Morales, Beck is imprisoned in the Ultimate Universe, warning its residents when Galactus comes to devour it. Following the destruction and restoration of the Multiverse, Beck returns to the Marvel Universe, where he targets Peter Parker and Parker Industries on behalf of the enigmatic Patient Zero.

Blowing smoke
More than money or power, Mysterio is driven by a hunger for acclaim and a desire to humiliate his enemies.

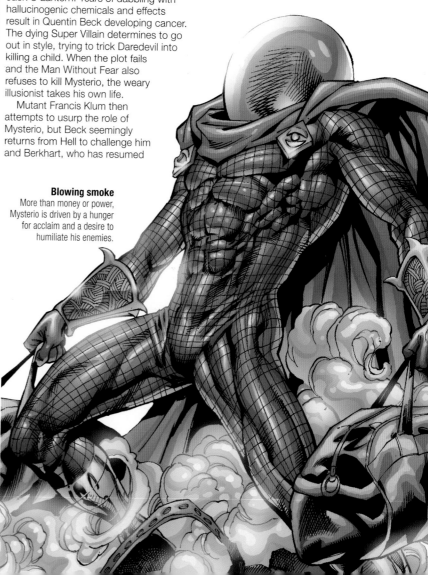

> "I can do anything a man with eyesight can…and do it better!"
>
> **DAREDEVIL**

DAREDEVIL

Lawyer Matt Murdock loses his sight, but that doesn't stop him taking to the streets of Hell's Kitchen as Daredevil, a crusader for justice feared by mobsters everywhere. The Man Without Fear keeps his identity a secret to protect those he loves.

FIRST APPEARANCE *Daredevil* #1 (April 1964)   **BASE** Hell's Kitchen, New York City   **AFFILIATIONS** New Avengers, the Hand, the Chaste, Defenders

SUPER SENSES

Matt Murdock was born in New York City, the son of boxer 'Battling' Jack Murdock. His father wanted Matt to use his brain to get ahead and made sure he studied hard, but the boy secretly trained at Jack Murdock's gym, honing his muscles and mastering fighting techniques. Matt's life changes forever when he saves a blind man from being hit by a truck carrying radioactive material—some of the truck's cargo falls on Matt and he is left permanently blind. However, the accident has another effect: It heightens his senses to superhuman levels, compensating for his lost sight. Matt can now sense his surroundings so accurately it is as if he possesses inbuilt radar.

Life saver
His bravery in saving a man from being hit by a truck is just the start of Matt Murdock's Super Hero career.

LAW MAN

In keeping with his father's wishes, Matt Murdock goes to Columbia University to study law. Here he meets Franklin "Foggy" Nelson, who will become his closest friend and business partner. Just before his son's graduation, however, Jack Murdock is murdered by a mobster after refusing to fix a fight. Matt embarks upon a mission of vengeance in costume as Daredevil, keeping his identity secret while at the same time starting out in his day job as a lawyer. Soon Matt and Foggy open their own law firm, Nelson & Murdock, and hire beautiful heiress Karen Page to be their secretary. Karen will become Matt's on-off girlfriend for years.

Dual role
His law firm enables Matt Murdock to bring criminals to justice…but for those that evade it, there is always Daredevil.

FRIENDS AND ENEMIES

Insane vendetta
Failure to get the better of Daredevil eventually drives the assassin Bullseye insane.

While Matt Murdock has Foggy Nelson and Karen Page, Daredevil usually prefers to work alone. However, he has occasionally accepted outside help—both human and superhuman. *Daily Bugle* reporter Ben Urich is a loyal supporter of The Man Without Fear and has helped him track down criminals and defend Matt's good name. Daredevil has also made lasting alliances with local heroes Spider-Man, Luke Cage, Iron Fist, White Tiger, and Jessica Jones, as well as teaming up both professionally and romantically with Black Widow. Although he has fought a vast array of villains, the most persistent of Daredevil's enemies are Kingpin, Bullseye and ninja assassins the Hand.

LAID LOW

Daredevil takes great pains to keep his identity secret, knowing that this knowledge will put the people he loves in grave danger. However, when gang boss the Kingpin receives documents revealing that the Man Without Fear is in fact blind lawyer Matt Murdock, he decides to destroy Murdock, using his considerable influence and contacts to take his life apart piece by piece. Broke, homeless, and ostracized by friends and society, Matt fights the Kingpin—and loses. The villain stages his enemy's death by drowning, but against all the odds Daredevil escapes. Rescued by a mysterious nun, he regains his strength and is finally able to clear his name, thanks to journalist Ben Urich.

Knockout punch
A down-on-his-luck Matt Murdock is no match for the monstrous Kingpin, who observes that a man without hope is truly a man without fear.

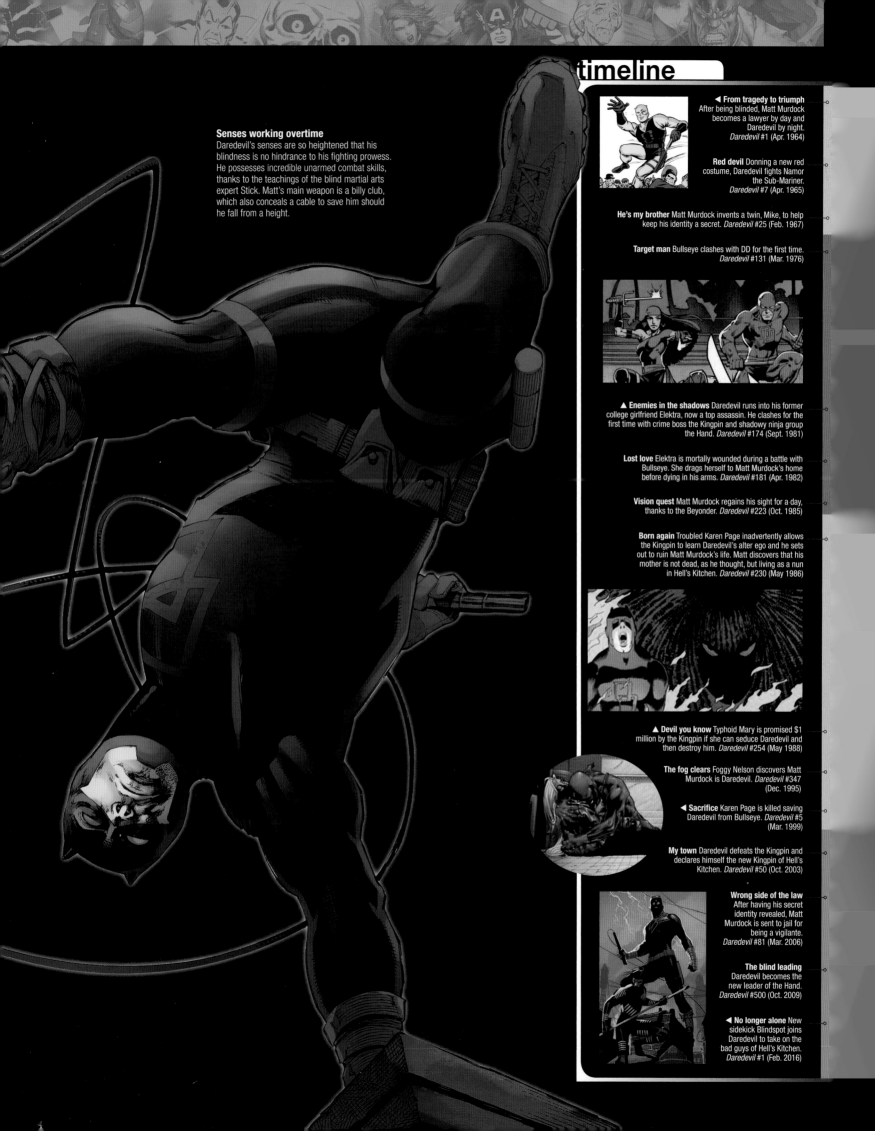

Senses working overtime
Daredevil's senses are so heightened that his blindness is no hindrance to his fighting prowess. He possesses incredible unarmed combat skills, thanks to the teachings of the blind martial arts expert Stick. Matt's main weapon is a billy club, which also conceals a cable to save him should he fall from a height.

◄ **From tragedy to triumph**
After being blinded, Matt Murdock becomes a lawyer by day and Daredevil by night. *Daredevil* #1 (Apr. 1964)

Red devil Donning a new red costume, Daredevil fights Namor the Sub-Mariner. *Daredevil* #7 (Apr. 1965)

He's my brother Matt Murdock invents a twin, Mike, to help keep his identity a secret. *Daredevil* #25 (Feb. 1967)

Target man Bullseye clashes with DD for the first time. *Daredevil* #131 (Mar. 1976)

▲ **Enemies in the shadows** Daredevil runs into his former college girlfriend Elektra, now a top assassin. He clashes for the first time with crime boss the Kingpin and shadowy ninja group the Hand. *Daredevil* #174 (Sept. 1981)

Lost love Elektra is mortally wounded during a battle with Bullseye. She drags herself to Matt Murdock's home before dying in his arms. *Daredevil* #181 (Apr. 1982)

Vision quest Matt Murdock regains his sight for a day, thanks to the Beyonder. *Daredevil* #223 (Oct. 1985)

Born again Troubled Karen Page inadvertently allows the Kingpin to learn Daredevil's alter ego and he sets out to ruin Matt Murdock's life. Matt discovers that his mother is not dead, as he thought, but living as a nun in Hell's Kitchen. *Daredevil* #230 (May 1986)

▲ **Devil you know** Typhoid Mary is promised $1 million by the Kingpin if she can seduce Daredevil and then destroy him. *Daredevil* #254 (May 1988)

The fog clears Foggy Nelson discovers Matt Murdock is Daredevil. *Daredevil* #347 (Dec. 1995)

◄ **Sacrifice** Karen Page is killed saving Daredevil from Bullseye. *Daredevil* #5 (Mar. 1999)

My town Daredevil defeats the Kingpin and declares himself the new Kingpin of Hell's Kitchen. *Daredevil* #50 (Oct. 2003)

Wrong side of the law After having his secret identity revealed, Matt Murdock is sent to jail for being a vigilante. *Daredevil* #81 (Mar. 2006)

The blind leading Daredevil becomes the new leader of the Hand. *Daredevil* #500 (Oct. 2009)

◄ **No longer alone** New sidekick Blindspot joins Daredevil to take on the bad guys of Hell's Kitchen. *Daredevil* #1 (Feb. 2016)

"I'm my own woman—first, last—and always!"

BLACK WIDOW

BLACK WIDOW

Natasha Romanova is a Russian double agent who defects to work for S.H.I.E.L.D. and the Avengers. She lacks traditional superpowers, but her gymnastic prowess and lethal weapons make all foes fear Black Widow's bite.

FIRST APPEARANCE *Tales of Suspense* #52 (April 1964) **BASE** New York City **AFFILIATIONS** K.G.B., Avengers, S.H.I.E.L.D.

Boris and Natasha
Natasha is dressed to the nines and ready to distract ladies' man Tony Stark.

SPY GAMES

Posing as a science teacher and his sister, K.G.B. agents Boris Turgenov and Black Widow are on a mission to track down a former Russian defector, Professor Vanko. They infiltrate the labs of Iron Man and Avenger Tony Stark. Tony, being quite the ladies' man, takes Natasha on a tour and later for a romantic dinner while Boris searches for Professor Vanko.

Boris dons Vanko's Crimson Dynamo armor and begins smashing up the place. Iron Man enters to save the day, with Natasha in tow. She tries to distract Iron Man by playing the victim, but Stark soon sees her true colors. Vanko heroically vanquishes Boris by destroying the armor and them both with it. Defeated and alone, the Black Widow retreats, but she is destined to face the Avengers again.

DAREDEVIL TEAM-UP

Natasha first encounters the hero Daredevil by saving him from the flying villain Owl. Returning the favor, Daredevil saves her from an attack by the Scorpion (Mac Gargan), but the villain then falls to his death.

Accused of Scorpion's murder, Natasha is arrested by Daredevil, though he promises her that the D.A. (Foggy Nelson, best friend of Daredevil's alter ego Matt Murdock) won't press charges. Nevertheless, a trial ensues and Natasha is castigated for her spy past. Eventually, with a little goading from Matt, Nelson drops the case.

Natasha and Matt work together again and again and they fall in love, eventually moving to San Francisco to start a new life together. Their on-again, off-again romance becomes one of Natasha's most long-lasting relationships.

Love bites
Battling Super Villains helps to ignite a spark of romance between Black Widow and Daredevil.

AGENT OF S.H.I.E.L.D.

After besting the alien Ixar for the Avengers, Black Widow hopes to be accepted into their ranks. However, she is intercepted by Nick Fury who sends her on a double-agent mission for S.H.I.E.L.D. Telling no one, not even Hawkeye—her lover at the time—she infiltrates a communist group, posing as their ally against the U.S. Not trusting her, she is jailed by the mysterious Red Guardian and the communists use their nightmare-inducing Psychotron to brainwash her. The communists then force her to take a polygraph lie-detector test to prove her allegiance, which she passes due to her brainwashing.

Meeting the Director
Nick Fury gives Black Widow the chance to prove herself as a S.H.I.E.L.D. agent.

The Avengers, following Hawkeye, attack the base. In the presence of her beau, the Red Guardian reveals that he is Natasha's husband, Alexei, who was presumed dead. Alexei seemingly dies in the ensuing fight and Natasha shakes off her brainwashing and dismantles the Psychotron. She destroys the base, completing her mission and proving herself an ally to S.H.I.E.L.D.

AVENGING HER PAST

Black Widow's lifelong ally and father figure, Ivan Petrovich, is murdered and his brain is mined for memories. Near his body, she finds a threat declaring that everyone she has ever loved will soon die. Natasha must follow a trail into her past to save the people she cares about, since they have been infected with nanites. Natasha recalls the death of her parents, and training with Wolverine (the nanites' attack barely gives him a headache). She remembers training, first as a ballerina, then as a K.G.B. agent in the mysterious Red Room. Then the Black Widow recalls being coerced into marrying Soviet test pilot Alexei, despite her romantic involvement with the Winter Soldier.

Natasha seeks out everyone close to her, starting with Alexei, then Iron Man, Hawkeye, the Winter Soldier, Hercules, and Daredevil. With a little help from Natasha, they can all look after themselves; however, "regular" folks, like her former teacher and her paperboy, are not so lucky. The trail finally leads her back to Ivan, who has been upgraded into a metal Soviet Guardian. He sent her on this journey, hoping she would finally come to love him. Realizing that Ivan is now far removed from the person she once knew, Natasha is forced to kill him, and so move on from her past.

Looking back
Natasha must scour her memories for the clue that unlocks the identity of a murderer before anyone else is hurt—or killed.

timeline

Villainous beginnings Working as a Russian spy, Black Widow and fellow Soviet agent Boris infiltrate Tony Stark's private lab, but are foiled by Iron Man. *Tales of Suspense* #52 (Apr. 1964)

▼ **Aim for the heart** Natasha beguiles criminal archer Hawkeye into joining her in thwarting Tony Stark's plans and occasionally those of his compatriots, the Avengers. *Tales of Suspense* #60 (Dec. 1964)

Agent of S.H.I.E.L.D. When Hawkeye goes legit by joining the Avengers, he encourages Natasha to do the same, and she is recruited as a double agent for S.H.I.E.L.D. *Avengers* #38–44 (Mar.–Sept. 1967)

New look Bored by civilian life and inactivity, Natasha dons her iconic black jumpsuit for the first time, hoping to get back into the Super Hero game and impress the jet-set crowd. *Amazing Adventures* #1 (Aug. 1970)

Daredevil Natasha teams up with Matt Murdock both as heroes, and romantically. Together they move west to San Francisco and she pursues a daytime career as a fashion designer. *Daredevil* #88 (June 1972)

The Avenger Natasha joins the Avengers when Hawkeye comes looking for her, and decides to officially join the team in order to take a break from her relationship with Matt. Natasha would work on and off with the team for the rest of her career. *Avengers* #111 (May 1973)

◀ **We are the Champions** After breaking up with the Avengers and with Matt, Natasha moves to L.A. where she joins the Champions, alongside Angel, Iceman, Ghost Rider, and her sometimes lover Hercules. *Champions* #1-3 (Oct. 1975– Feb. 1976)

Widow's bite Black Widow spiders are known for their venom, but Natasha nearly dies from poison, courtesy of the Hand's ninjas. Luckily, Daredevil's martial arts mentor, Stick, and his student, Stone, save her life. *Daredevil* #188-9 (Nov.–Dec. 1982)

Past unveiled Wolverine reveals that Natasha was protected by him as a child and taught fighting skills before being kidnapped by Hydra. There, she trained as a Soviet spy and fell in love with the Winter Soldier. *Uncanny X-Men* #268 (Sept. 1990)

▼ **Another Black Widow** Natasha discovers that there is another Black Widow—Yelena Belova—also a product of the K.G.B.'s Black Widow program. These formidable opponents face off to find Nick Fury's anti-aging Infinity Formula super-serum. *Black Widow* #1 (June 1999)

Face swap On a mission for S.H.I.E.L.D., Natasha surgically swaps faces with her rival Black Widow, Yelena Belova, in order to infiltrate the K.G.B. After teaching Yelena a life-changing lesson, Natasha agrees to return Yelena's face to her. *Black Widow* #1 (Jan. 2001)

▼ **Winter Soldier** Natasha's past is revealed as the Winter Soldier attacks S.H.I.E.L.D., and Natasha is shocked to see her former lover still in service with the K.G.B. *Captain America* #27 (Aug. 2007)

A dark reign After a clandestine Skrull invasion of Earth, the devious Norman Osborn wins control of U.S. security. Natasha poses as Yelena Belova on his Thunderbolts team, while secretly working for Nick Fury in hopes of ousting Osborn. *Thunderbolts* #134 (Sept. 2009)

Making things right Now an Avengers mainstay and powerful assassin, Natasha takes on solo missions, hoping to avenge past trespasses and wipe out "the red in her ledger." *Black Widow* #1 (Mar. 2014)

Widow's weapons
Natasha is a highly trained secret agent with minor bio-enhancements accounting for her long lifespan, but she is not a super-powered hero. Her most notable weapons are her Widow's Bites. These gauntlets provide a shock of up to 30,000 volts.

MARVEL AGE

BRONZE AGE

MODERN AGE

MASTERS OF EVIL

FIRST APPEARANCE *Avengers* #6 (July 1964)
BASE Various

Baron Heinrich Zemo is horrified to find that his nemesis Captain America is not dead, as he thought, but revived and fighting with the Avengers. The villain assembles a team designed to take out Earth's Mightiest Heroes so Zemo can get to Cap. The other members are Black Knight, Radioactive Man, and Melter—all villains who have proved tricky foes for a particular Avenger in the past.

After the defeat of these self-styled Masters of Evil, new versions of the team are put together by Ultron-5 and then Egghead, but these too are thwarted. The next iteration is the brainchild of Zemo's son, Baron Helmut Zemo. He decides to leave nothing to chance and gathers a veritable army of villains that lays waste to Avengers Mansion. Zemo tortures Jarvis and gets hold of Captain America's shield before the Avengers can take control of the situation. Facing off against Captain America on the roof of the Mansion, Zemo falls and is badly injured.

After another Masters of Evil team has come and gone under Doctor Octopus, Helmut Zemo returns with another lineup, also known as the Thunderbolts. Zemo is furious when yet another Masters of Evil group, led by a mysterious woman called Crimson Cowl, faces off against his Thunderbolts.

Meeting their match
The Masters of Evil are originally assembled so that each member targets a particular Avenger. Earth's Mightiest Heroes defeat this strategy by switching to fight each other's foes.

Later, the Masters of Evil return under the leadership of Max Fury, but after his death Helmut Zemo takes over again. This time the Masters are based on the island of Bagalia, and perhaps are the most dangerous iteration yet, with ties to demons and dark sorcery.

Evil army
Max Fury leads the Masters of Evil, including Carrion, Pink Pearl, Taskmaster, Vengeance, and Lady Stilt-Man, against the Secret Avengers.

KRAVEN THE HUNTER

FIRST APPEARANCE *Amazing Spider-Man* #15 (August 1964)
BASE Kravinoff Estate, New York, Savage Land
AFFILIATIONS Avengers of the 1950s, Sinister Six

Originally of aristocratic Russian stock, Sergei Kravinoff's family are forced to flee their country in the wake of the Revolution. Kravinoff becomes a legendary big-game hunter, who prefers to finish off targets with his bare hands rather than using weapons.

While in Africa Kravinoff consumes a serum that gives him enhanced strength and slows his aging. In the 1950s, he fights with Nick Fury's Avengers as Kraven, but leaves, obsessed with proving himself the world's greatest hunter. Eventually, he comes to believe that to do this he must take down the ultimate target: Spider-Man. However, the Web-Slinger proves even trickier than Kraven expects.

Kraven finally hatches a monstrous plan. He drugs Spider-Man and buries him alive, before going onto the streets of New York in a Spider-Man costume and doing Spidey's job the way he thinks it should be done: with brutal force. When Spider-Man wakes and digs himself free he confronts Kraven, who declares himself the victor. Satisfied, he allows Spider-Man to go free before killing himself with a shotgun.

This is not the end of Kraven's story, however, as his family later seek to reanimate him using the blood of various Spider Totems. The Kravinoffs lure Spider-Man to a graveyard and slay him—and Kraven rises from the tomb. However, the Spider-Man who dies is not Peter Parker but Kaine, his clone, and so the ritual is corrupted. The real Spider-Man, consumed with rage at the attacks on his kind, comes for the Kravinoffs. Although he intends to kill Kraven, he stops at the last second, realizing that it goes against everything he stands for. Kraven takes what is left of his family and travels to the Savage Land. He later goes on to face Venom, Hulk, and a resurrected Kaine before being imprisoned by S.H.I.E.L.D. He escapes from custody with the aid of

Back from the grave
After a blood ritual involving the slaughter of Spider-Man, Kraven is brought back from the dead, but does this former suicide really want to be alive again?

NORMAN OSBORN

FIRST APPEARANCE *Amazing Spider-Man* #18 (July 1964) **BASE** New York City **AFFILIATIONS** Oscorp, Brotherhood of Scriers, Goblin Nation, H.A.M.M.E.R., Thunderbolts, Dark Avengers, The Cabal, Enforcers

Since childhood, Norman Osborn has been fundamentally driven by a thirst for power, no matter who he has to hurt to get it. He builds a successful business, Oscorp, with his partner Mendel Stromm, but his wife's death makes him more twisted and he grows neglectful and abusive towards his son, Harry. He also looks for a way to take Stromm out of the picture, framing his partner for financial irregularities. Now in total control of Oscorp, he discovers the Goblin Formula, created by Stromm, which is supposed to greatly increase strength and intelligence. Osborn makes the formula, but it explodes in his face. Afterward, he is indeed stronger and more intelligent, but the formula has also removed any remaining moral inhibitions. Deciding that the quickest path to great wealth and power is through criminality rather than legitimate business, Osborn adopts the costumed identity of the Green Goblin and devises a range of explosives—Pumpkin Bombs—as well as a powered glider to ride upon. Determined to make his mark on the New York underworld, Green Goblin makes the fateful decision to attack Spider-Man. The two will clash many times over the years, their destinies linked in a cycle of pain and tragic loss. This is only accentuated by the fact that their alter egos are also linked—Peter Parker is close friends with Harry Osborn. On one occasion, Spider-Man discovers that Norman Osborn is the Green Goblin and hides the costume, trying to protect Harry from the terrible truth.

Osborn's Green Goblin alter ego leads him to lure the web-slinger out for a showdown by kidnapping Peter's girlfriend Gwen Stacy and throwing her off Brooklyn Bridge. Spider-Man tries to save Gwen but she dies. Enraged, he pursues the Goblin, who is apparently killed, accidentally

impaled by his own glider. However, the Goblin Formula has given Osborn remarkable healing powers; he survives and travels to Europe and continues to meddle in Spider-Man's life from afar. This comes to a head when he convinces Peter Parker that Peter's clone, Ben Reilly, is the real Spider-Man, and causes the loss of Peter and Mary Jane's baby.

After killing a *Daily Bugle* reporter, Osborn is publicly revealed to be the Green Goblin by the paper's Jessica Jones. He goes to prison but is freed when he makes a deal with S.H.I.E.L.D. to take medication to suppress his manic Green Goblin alter ego and support the Superhuman Registration Act. Osborn assembles a team called the Thunderbolts to search for super-powered individuals refusing to register. He plays a key role in defeating the Skrull invasion and is given control of the Avengers Initiative, as well as license to replace S.H.I.E.L.D. with his own H.A.M.M.E.R. paramilitaries. Osborn leads from the front in the armor of the Iron Patriot. However, he is disgraced when he engineers an attack on Asgard.

When Otto Octavius becomes the Superior Spider-Man, Osborn proclaims himself the Goblin King to oppose him, planning to rule New York City's underworld. Due to Otto's hubris and less-than-heroic tactics as Spider-Man, Osborn is able to amass a large criminal organization. Dubbing this group the Goblin Nation, Osborn's forces run riot. When Octavius finally allows Peter Parker to resume control of his own body, Peter defeats the Green Goblin and gives him an antidote to the Goblin Formula, removing his powers.

Osborn later resurfaces selling his Goblin weapons to warlords in the African nation of Nadua. However, he also has his sights set on Peter's new tech company, Parker Industries…

The Cabal
Following the defeat of the Skrull's Secret Invasion, Norman Osborn is fortuitously selected by the President to become chief of U.S. security. Osborn soon becomes part of a Super Villain alliance known as The Cabal *(left to right)*: Namor, Emma Frost, Doctor Doom, Osborn himself, and Loki.

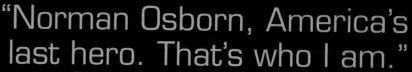

"Norman Osborn, America's last hero. That's who I am."

NORMAN OSBORN

Green machine
After taking the Goblin formula, Norman Osborn has enhanced strength and intellectual prowess. He uses his intelligence to invent gadgets and weapons to further his evil schemes.

American hero?
Norman Osborn's Iron Patriot armor combines the strength of Iron Man with the inspiring colors of Captain America's uniform.

timeline

◄ **The lure of stardom** The Green Goblin targets Spider-Man by luring him into the desert to film a Hollywood movie. *Amazing Spider-Man* #14 (July 1964)

The secret is out Green Goblin discovers that Spider-Man is Peter Parker and reveals himself to be Norman Osborn. Luckily, an electro-chemical blast causes Osborn to lose his memory. *Amazing Spider-Man* #39–40 (Aug.–Sept. 1966)

▼ **Death by glider?** Spider-Man confronts Green Goblin after Gwen Stacy's death. The villain accidentally impales himself on his own glider and is apparently killed. *Amazing Spider-Man* #122 (July 1973)

Resurrection Osborn returns as Green Goblin, revealing that he has been manipulating Peter Parker's life, including making Peter believe he is a clone. *Spider-Man* #75 (Dec. 1996)

Exposed Norman Osborn is publicly revealed as the Green Goblin. *The Pulse* #5 (Nov. 2004)

Secret Invasion Osborn kills the Skrull queen. Thanks to public gratitude, he takes control of the Avengers Initiative. *Secret Invasion* #8 (Jan. 2009)

Iron Patriot Osborn unveils his very own Dark Avengers team, with himself leading as Iron Patriot. *Dark Avengers* #1 (Mar. 2009)

◄ **Goblin King** Assembling a crime family to oppose the Superior Spider-Man, Osborn proclaims himself the Goblin King. *Superior Spider-Man* #10 (July 2013)

Tangled up
Influenced by Black Widow, Hawkeye defeats Iron Man's repulsor tech with one of his special trick arrows.

In and out of love
Hawkeye and Mockingbird marry, divorce, date, and then break up again. While together, they team up to track down criminal Jaime Slade (a.k.a. Phantom Rider) and Hawkeye's nemesis, Crossfire.

> "If I miss, it means I'm just another dude with a bow… And that's why I never miss."
>
> **HAWKEYE**

HAWKEYE

FIRST APPEARANCE *Tales of Suspense* #57 [July 1964]
BASE New York City, Los Angeles **AFFILIATIONS** Avengers, West Coast Avengers, Secret Avengers, Defenders

Hawkeye is an unlikely Avenger who begins on the wrong side. But with the faith and support of his new teammates, he becomes one of the Avengers' most valuable members, even bringing Black Widow into the fold.

At age 14, Clint Barton joins Carson's Carnival of Traveling Wonders, where his matchless skill with a bow and arrow earns him the title Hawkeye the Marksman. Hawkeye is inspired by Iron Man to fight bad guys, but falls for manipulative Russian spy Black Widow and becomes her partner in crime. However, he soon reforms and joins the Avengers.

Hawkeye remains an important member of the Avengers team for a long time, taking short breaks to join the Defenders and lead the West Coast Avengers. For a time, he even takes Pym Particles to become the new Goliath. Hawkeye marries Mockingbird (Bobbie Morse) but when she is apparently killed, the West Coast Avengers are shut down and Hawkeye rejoins the main team. During the Scarlet Witch's mental breakdown, when the Avengers are disassembled, he sacrifices his life to stop an invading Kree warship; after the M-Day event, Scarlet Witch restores him to life.

Hawkeye then temporarily assumes the role of the swordsman, Ronin. During Norman Osborn's Dark Reign, the assassin Bullseye commandeers his identity as Hawkeye in Osborn's Dark Avengers team. When things return to "normal," Hawkeye resumes membership in the Avengers and trains Kate Bishop (now also known as Hawkeye) as his protégée. After he is severely burned trying to save Scarlet Witch from Emma Frost, Hawkeye begins taking life more seriously. At the close of the second superhuman civil war, he switches his focus from fighting Super Villains to campaigning for socio-political issues.

Always on target
Hawkeye lacks super-powers but is a superb acrobat and exceptional marksman. He is armed with a quiver full of trick arrows to both defeat and embarrass his opponents. His sarcastic wit is as sharp as his arrows.

timeline

The marksman Hawkeye teams up with Black Widow against Iron Man. Hawkeye shoots Iron Man but ends up hitting Black Widow instead. *Tales of Suspense* #57 (Sept. 1964)

▲ **The old order changeth!** There is a shake-up at the Avengers as Thor, Iron Man, Giant-Man, and Wasp all leave. Led by Captain America, the new team adds Hawkeye, Quicksilver, and Scarlet Witch. *Avengers* #16 (May 1965)

Listen to the Mockingbird Hawkeye encounters Mockingbird for the first time. They start with a fight, but she convinces him that his current girlfriend has a treacherous secret. *Hawkeye* #1 (Sept. 1983)

Earth's mightiest marksman Hawkeye falls into a trap set by Taskmaster and his team of Albino (scientist Augusta Seger), Batroc, Machete, Zaran, and Oddball. With the help of Justice and Firestar, he thwarts the villains. *Hawkeye: Earth's Mightiest Marksman* #1 (Oct. 1998)

Secret Avengers Captain America turns over leadership of the Secret Avengers to Hawkeye. He assembles Venom, Captain Britain, Giant-Man, and the original Human Torch to his team. *Secret Avengers* #21.1–25 (Mar.–June 2012)

▶ **The death of the Hulk** Hawkeye kills Bruce Banner, but is acquitted of murder when he reveals that Banner asked Hawkeye to kill him if he Hulked-out again. *Civil War II* (Sept. 2016)

KANG THE CONQUEROR

FIRST APPEARANCE *Avengers* #8 (September 1964)
BASE Mobile; Ancient Egypt **AFFILIATIONS** Chronos Corps, Anachronauts, Council of Kangs

Kang has many identities and even alternate versions of himself from other timelines. This time-traveler from the future creates havoc with the timestream in an attempt to both conquer Earth and rewrite his own history.

Nathaniel Richards is born in the 30th century of an alternate timeline. Some data suggests he is a descendant of Reed Richards, but he may also be a descendant of Doctor Doom—or perhaps they are even the same person. At age 16, Nathaniel Richards' future self (Kang the Conqueror) attempts to disrupt his timeline, causing him to become Iron Lad and then Kid Immortus.

Nathaniel Richards discovers time-traveling technology created by Doctor Doom and appears in ancient Egypt. He becomes the Pharaoh Rama-Tut, until his reign is toppled by the Fantastic Four. An encounter with Doctor Doom persuades Richards to try out a new villain identity, the Scarlet Centurion; in this guise, he is vanquished by the Avengers.

Richards resumes his identity as Rama-Tut but attempts a return to his own time. Instead, he accidentally arrives in the 40th century. There, he becomes Kang the Conqueror and subjugates not only Earth, but other planets and celestial empires, such as the Badoon. Back in the 20th century, Kang is driven by an obsession to marry a powerful being known as the Celestial Madonna. The Avengers continually thwart this and his other megalomaniac schemes to gain power, resulting in an ongoing, bitter conflict.

Young Avenger
Nathaniel Richards (young Kang) tries to convince the older heroes of the Young Avengers' legitimacy. Meanwhile, the villainous Kang the Conqueror arrives from the future.

Prisoners of the Pharoah
Pharoah Rama-Tut (Kang), a time-traveler from the year 3000, captures the Fantastic Four, enslaves them, and makes Invisible Woman Sue Storm his queen.

"The twentieth century belongs to Kang!"

KANG

timeline

◄ **The conqueror** Kang arrives to conquer the Earth. He captures most of the Avengers, leaving only the Wasp and Rick Jones free to defeat him. *Avengers* #8 (Sept. 1964)

▼ **One of three** Kang kidnaps Scarlet Witch, Mantis, and Agatha Harkness, hoping one of them will give birth to a child of extraordinary power. *Avengers* #129–135 (Nov. 1974–May 1975)

The rise of Apocalypse Nathaniel Richards travels to Ancient Egypt to become Pharaoh Rama-Tut and claim the mutant destined to become Apocalypse as his heir. *Rise of Apocalypse* #1 (Oct. 1996)

Immortus The Time-Keepers try to force Kang's transformation into his future self, Immortus. They fail, resulting in a possible separation of the two identities into two different beings. *Avengers Forever* #12 (Feb. 2000)

Iron Lad Kang attempts to hasten his original rise to power but his teenage self rebels and joins the Young Avengers as Iron Lad. *Young Avengers* #2–6 (May–Sept. 2005)

▲ **Mr. Gryphon** A flaw in the timestream causes Kang to split into different versions of himself, including the diabolical CEO of nefarious organization Qeng Enterprises. *All-New, All-Different Avengers* #1–6 (Jan.–Apr. 2016)

All-time menace
Time-traveling Kang has a vast knowledge of history, warfare, physics, and engineering. His futuristic battle armor boosts his strength and allows him to project holograms, energy blasts, and force fields.

WONDER MAN

FIRST APPEARANCE *Avengers* #9 (October 1964)
BASE New York City, Los Angeles **AFFILIATIONS**
Avengers, Avengers West Coast, Force Works,
Crazy Eight

Simon Williams reluctantly inherits the
family business, but is caught embezzling
funds and sent to jail. Freed by villain
Baron Zemo and the Masters of Evil,
Williams is transformed into Wonder Man,
an ionically powered superhuman, and
blackmailed into infiltrating the Avengers.
After initially betraying them to save his life,
Wonder Man has a change of heart and
dies saving them.

After years in the grave—during which
time his recorded brain patterns are used
to give the android Vision a human
personality—Simon is revived, his body
transmuted into ionic energy by the
vengeance-crazed Grim Reaper (Eric
Williams, his own brother) and the
voodoo priest Black Talon.

Wonder Man joins the Avengers a
second time, determined to redeem his
wasted life and serves with distinction with
the East and West Coast branches while
pursuing a career as an actor. He later
follows the Scarlet Witch into new
super-team Force Works, but apparently
perishes on their first mission, saving Earth
from a Kree invasion.

Some time later, Scarlet Witch
accidentally resurrects Wonder Man as
a blazing ionic energy-being and in the
months that follow restores him to full
physical life. Their romantic affair ends
badly and Williams leaves. Coerced into
joining S.H.I.E.L.D., he reluctantly enforces
the Superhuman Registration Act and is

Hard choices
Coerced by the Masters of Evil, Simon
Williams becomes an unwilling villain
and, later, a somewhat reluctant hero.

press-ganged into joining Iron Man's
Mighty Avengers.

This treatment leads him to become a
vigorous public advocate for outlawing all
Super Hero activity. He remains inactive
when Norman Osborn institutes his Dark
Reign and, after his overthrow, seeks to
violently prevent Steve Rogers reforming
the Avengers for a new Heroic Age.

Thanks to his feelings for the Scarlet
Witch, Simon is later recruited by the
Avengers Unity Squad; however,
he refuses to fight and operates in
a strictly non-combat role.

PURPLE MAN

FIRST APPEARANCE *Daredevil* #4 (October
1964) **BASE** Mobile **AFFILIATIONS** Electro,
Thunderbolts

Yugoslavian spy Zebediah Killgrave is
affected by a nerve gas he steals from a
U.S. Army base. It dyes his skin and
enables him to control minds with spoken
suggestions. As Purple Man, Killgrave
becomes a criminal, driven by his need for
pleasure and luxuries, but is bested by
Daredevil, whose willpower enables him to
resist Purple Man's commands. Preferring
to indulge his desires in the shadows,
Killgrave enslaves young hero Jewel
(Jessica Jones) for eight months. He
attacks her again years later, but this time
finds Jessica a much tougher proposition
and is badly beaten up. Frequently
defeated, Killgrave is often a pawn of even
more manipulative
monsters, such as
Doctor Doom and
Baron Zemo.

DORMAMMU

FIRST APPEARANCE *Strange Tales* #126
(November 1964) **BASE** Dark Dimension
AFFILIATIONS The Faltine

A being of overwhelming power with
an unquenchable thirst for conquest,
Dormammu rules the hellish Dark
Dimension. Eons before, Dormammu and
his sister Umar—energy beings of the
Faltine race—slay their progenitor Sinifer
and are driven from their home dimension.
Acquiring material forms, they explore
many realms before settling in the Dark
Dimension, where Dormammu ingratiates

himself with ruler King Olnar, before seizing
the wizard leader's throne.

As his empire expands, Dormammu
merges with the fundamental magic of the
Dark Dimension and reverts to a primarily
energy-based form. Dormammu adheres
to a strict ethical code; where he cannot
conquer, the Dark Lord negotiates. After
allying with Odin and an embodiment of
Eternity to imprison chaotic occult
berserker Zom in a mystic amphora,
Dormammu respects the treaties
established and turns his attentions
away from the Nine Realms and
towards other prospects.

Dormammu is especially drawn to Earth,
observing it for millennia and participating
in the creation of Earthly demon-lord
Satannish. Dormammu's incursions,
however, are repulsed by Agamotto,
the first Sorcerer Supreme.

Dormammu renews his efforts over
the centuries but is always beaten by
Agamotto's successors, such as the
Mystic, who forces him back to his home
plane in the year 1666, using the Sorcerer
Supreme's weapons the Eye of Agamotto
and the Staff of One.

The Mystic—later known as the Ancient
One—passes his mantle on to Doctor
Stephen Strange, who, along with the
Avengers, Defenders, and Guardians of
the Galaxy, foils Dormammu's continuing
attempts to conquer Earth.

Fires of fury
Dormammu's arrogance and hunger for
conquest always drives him into making
self-defeating errors, such as attacking Eternity.

EDWIN JARVIS

FIRST APPEARANCE *Tales of Suspense* #59 (November 1964) **BASE** New York City **AFFILIATIONS** Avengers, Stark Industries, Stark family, Canadian Air Force

Edwin Jarvis begins a life of service by leaving the U.S. during World War II to join the Canadian Air Force and fight the Nazis. When hostilities end, he enters the household of Howard Stark, remaining to raise young heir Anthony when the wealthy industrialist and inventor dies.

With Tony Stark bankrolling the Avengers, Jarvis becomes head of domestic affairs at the Avengers Mansion in Manhattan, New York City. As a crucial component of the team's support structure, Jarvis also doubles as security chief and is harassed and injured many times in the line of duty. When Norman Osborn takes over the team, he retires from active life.

THE LEADER

FIRST APPEARANCE *Tales to Astonish* #62 (December 1964) **BASE** Mobile **AFFILIATIONS** Freehold, the Alliance, Intelligencia

Dull-witted manual worker Samuel Sterns is deeply jealous of his scientist brother and, after accidental exposure to gamma-irradiated waste, develops a vast hunger for knowledge and a super-brain. As the Leader, he begins a carefully calculated plan to conquer Earth, using human agents and a variety of purpose-built humanoids. His plans are regularly foiled by the Hulk, and the intellectual colossus becomes obsessed with destroying his gamma-powered, green-colored archenemy.

After years of employing super-powered minions such as the Rhino or Arsenal, the Leader creates gamma-spawned servants and works with other super-intelligent criminal masterminds; however, he is increasingly distracted by longings for redemption and forgiveness.

IMMORTUS

FIRST APPEARANCE *Avengers* #10 (November 1964) **BASE** Limbo **AFFILIATIONS** Infinity Watch, Time-Keepers, Avengers, Fantastic Four

Immortus is Nathaniel Richards, a 30th-century human and inveterate time-meddler. He becomes intertwined in the fabric of history, battling iterations of himself in a quest to control time. His stated goal is to stop earlier incarnations of himself threatening humanity and untangling the temporal anomalies his own intrusions have caused.

Among his other identities are Young Avenger Iron Lad and villainous incarnations Kid Immortus, Rama-Tut, Scarlet Centurion, and Kang the Conqueror. Even he is unsure of his actual origins after his constant interventions in his own timeline, employing increasingly complex stratagems and going so far as to even edit his own memories.

After brief stints as Iron Lad and Kid Immortus—possibly caused by the manipulations of his own older selves—Richards eschews time travel until adulthood, at which time he journeys to ancient Egypt.

As Pharaoh Rama-Tut, Immortus is driven off by the Fantastic Four and encounters Doctor Doom—whom he believes to be an ancient ancestor—in a time-storm. This accidentally creates a divergent timeline where he almost conquers the 20th century as the Scarlet Centurion.

Defeated by the Avengers, Richards becomes Kang and conquers most of the 40th century before returning to attack the Avengers at the start of their career. Beaten again, he becomes obsessed with destroying them and controlling their time era. After decades of failure and frustration, the aging tyrant abandons his Kang identity. Moving to the timeless Limbo realm, he toils to reclaim his wasted years. This only succeeds in creating a more intransigent Kang, numerous divergent timelines, and constant chronal chaos. Eventually, Immortus apparently retires to the year 9999 to live out his final years in peace and isolation.

Forever war Throughout all the ages of time and alternate realities, Immortus never faces a more stubborn or deadly foe than his younger self.

ATTUMA

FIRST APPEARANCE *Fantastic Four* #33 (December 1964) **BASE** Skarka, Atlantic Ocean; mobile **AFFILIATIONS** Barbarian Horde, the Worthy.

Attuma is born to the barbarous nomads at the fringes of Atlantean civilization. Far stronger than most of his people, Attuma becomes their leader, driven by an ancient prophecy declaring that a conqueror will one day rule Atlantis.

His frequent attempts to seize the city are thwarted by Namor the Sub-Mariner, so, spreading his net wider, Attuma begins attacking the surface world. He is thwarted by Iron Man, Giant-Man, the Avengers, and the Fantastic Four, among other heroes.

As Namor's connections to the surface-world increasingly anger his subjects, the Sub-Mariner is forced to abdicate and Attuma is invited to replace him. Sometime later, Attuma allies with Namor to defend Atlantis against the Squadron Supreme.

SCORPION

FIRST APPEARANCE *Amazing Spider-Man* #20 (January 1965) **BASE** New York City **AFFILIATIONS** Masters of Evil, Sinister Twelve, Thunderbolts, Dark Avengers

J. Jonah Jameson discovers that Dr. Farley Stillwell has invented a way to transfer the abilities of animals to humans and asks the doctor to test the process on a private investigator named Mac Gargan. After Gargan is mutated by the serum, he gains the strength and agility of a scorpion. However, his scorpion abilities come at a high cost: his sanity. To complement his new abilities, Gargan dons a cybernetic battle-suit with a mechanical tail that can fire blasts, sting enemies, or spring Gargan into the air. Calling himself Scorpion, Gargan is often contracted to take out Spider-Man, but fails time after time.

Gargan also becomes a host for the Venom symbiote and joins Norman Osborn's Sinister Twelve. While a member of Osborn's Dark Avengers, he assumes the role of a fake Spider-Man. Unfortunately for Gargan, he loses the symbiote at the end of Osborn's Dark Reign as U.S. security chief and is sent to prison. With neither the symbiote nor his Scorpion suit to keep his mutations in check, Gargan suffers serious health problems.

In the hopes of teaming up for revenge against J. Jonah Jameson, scientific genius Alistair Smythe breaks Gargan out of jail and fits him with a new Scorpion suit. Gargan uses the suit to battle the violent Superior Spider-Man (Otto Octavius), but suffers a seemingly lethal jaw-break. Scorpion is revived, however, and—re-fitted with another new suit by Smythe—is ready for revenge once more.

Scorpion vs. Spider-Man
Spider-Man's only defense against the Scorpion's tail is to dodge it! It is fixed to the base of the villain's spine.

COUNT NEFARIA

FIRST APPEARANCE *Avengers* #13 (February 1965) **BASE** Castle in the New Jersey Palisades (relocated from Italy) **AFFILIATIONS** Nefaria "family" of the Maggia, Legion of the Unliving, Lethal Legion

Italian nobleman Count Luchino Nefaria is believed by many to be an upstanding citizen. Contrary to public perception, he uses his immense fortune to become the leader of the Maggia crime syndicate. While giving them a tour of his castle, Nefaria frames the Avengers for treason, in revenge for the team's opposition to the Maggia. Nefaria accomplishes this by trapping them in his "time-transcender beams" and essentially creating holograms of the Avengers, which he manipulates to dishonor their reputations. When they are eventually cleared of all charges, Nefaria is exposed as a criminal.

Nefaria renews his battle with the Avengers, powered by the abilities of Whirlwind (speed), Living Laser (energy projection), and Power Man (strength). He is bestowed these new powers—which are increased a thousand-fold—by Baron Zemo's scientist, Professor Kenneth Sturdy. Nefaria pays a terrible price for these gifts: accelerated aging.

Nefaria's daughter, Giulietta, grows up in the U.S. under the alias Whitney Frost. She eventually becomes the leader of the Maggia, and goes by the name Madame Masque. Thinking that scientific genius Tony Stark might have the answer to his aging problem, Nefaria uses Stark's trust in his daughter to ambush him.

The resulting scuffle between Nefaria and Stark (as Iron Man) leaves the aging count seemingly dead, but he later returns as an ionic-energy-powered Super Villain. His superpowers now include the ability to drain energy from other ionic beings, regenerate, fly, and project lasers from his eyes. Count Nefaria is now more formidable than ever!

> "Accept your master —Nefaria!"
>
> **COUNT NEFARIA**

Seemingly invincible
On their own, Captain America and Hawkeye are no match for the immense powers of Count Nefaria.

KA-ZAR

FIRST APPEARANCE *Uncanny X-Men* #10 (March 1965) **BASE** Savage Land **AFFILIATIONS** Avengers

British nobleman and explorer Lord Robert Plunder discovers a deposit of the invaluable, energy-manipulating ore Vibranium in Antarctica. When Plunder returns to England, he takes some of the Vibranium (locking the rest away) and fashions it into a medallion. He splits this in two, and gives each half to his sons, Kevin and Parnival, as their inheritance.

When news of Robert Plunder's discovery leaks out, secret agents attempt to learn the whereabouts of his Vibranium by force. Plunder escapes and sends his son Parnival with his butler, Willis, while he flees with Kevin to the Savage Land, beneath Antarctica.

Robert Plunder is murdered there by Maa-Gor and his tribe of Neanderthal-like Man-Apes, but his son, Kevin, is saved and raised by an intelligent sabertooth tiger named Zabu (later a member of the Pet Avengers). Kevin grows up in the lost Savage Land, where he is known as Ka-Zar ("Son of the Tiger" in the language of the Man-Apes). He learns to survive against such threats as the Man-Apes, dinosaurs, Savage Land Mutates, and his jealous, crime-lord brother, Parnival the Plunderer. Ka-Zar marries ecologist Super Hero Shanna the She-Devil and together they raise a son, Matthew.

Ka-Zar is a normal human with exceptional athletic and hunting skills, and an empathy for wild animals that helps him communicate with them. He fights effectively with primitive weapons such as a spear, sling, and bow and arrow. Ka-Zar goes on to team up with the Avengers to defeat the Skrulls.

Formidable opponent
Ka-Zar's strength and athletic abilities alone make him the equal of many superpowered beings. He is also extremely skilful with his bowie knife.

Enemies and friends
When they first meet, Ka-Zar and Spider-Man fight, but they become friends and later team up against the Skrull's Secret Invasion.

> "The time is come for them to face…the wrath of Ka-Zar! For none may break the jungle law!"
>
> **KA-ZAR**

ABSORBING MAN

FIRST APPEARANCE *Journey into Mystery* #114 (March 1965) **BASE** Mobile **AFFILIATIONS** Wrecking Crew

Crusher Creel—Absorbing Man—is an ex-boxer (and felon) who gains the power to draw strength and unique abilities from any material he touches. Thanks to a potion given to him by the Asgardian trickster god Loki, Absorbing Man can assimilate the properties of nearly any substance, including wood, metal, rock, gas, liquid, or energy. Some substances also allow him to change his size. For a time, he can even control minds.

Loki uses Creel as a pawn against his brother, Thor. In their first clash, Thor fears that Creel might gain the powers of Mjolnir, and is almost defeated. Absorbing Man overreaches himself by trying to absorb the power of the Earth itself. He explodes—but Loki reassembles him to fight once again.

FRIGHTFUL FOUR

FIRST APPEARANCE *Fantastic Four* #36 (March 1965) **BASE** HQ beneath Manhattan, NYC

Bentley Wittman is a highly praised scientist—until his fame is eclipsed by the even-more-talented Reed Richards of the Super Hero team the Fantastic Four. In an effort to get back on top, Wittman forms a team of Super Villains—the Frightful Four—to destroy Reed and his allies. The original members are the Wizard (Wittman), Sandman, Paste-Pot Pete, (who have already been working together due to their mutual hatred for the Fantastic Four's Human Torch), and Medusa. Wizard frequently changes the team roster in an effort to gain the upper hand against the Fantastic Four. Other team members have included Absorbing Man, Beetle, Brute, Deadpool, Electro, Klaw, Living Laser, Mister Hyde, Red Ghost, and Taskmaster.

Villainous foursome
The roster of the Frightful Four often changes, but the villains never triumph for long *(left to right)*: She-Thing, Sandman, Wizard, and Thundra.

MEDUSA

FIRST APPEARANCE *Fantastic Four* #36 (March 1965) **BASE** Attilan, Baxter Building, New Attilan **AFFILIATIONS** Frightful Four, Lady Liberators, Fantastic Four

Medusa is a member of the royal family of Inhumans, a species descended from a group of prehistoric humans who underwent DNA splicing experiments by the alien Kree. Cutting themselves off from *Homo sapiens*, the Inhumans end up creating their own, technologically advanced society, albeit one paralyzed by a caste system. Each individual is assigned his or her caste after exposure to the Terrigen Mists, which confers a super-power; Medusa's power is that her long, long hair can move independently and grasp objects.

Medusa falls to Earth during an uprising by the downtrodden Alpha Primitive caste. Having lost her memory, she is recruited into the Frightful Four by the Wizard. She performs well in battle against the Fantastic Four, although she fails to fully defeat them.

Her Inhuman family, alerted to her presence, come to claim her. It includes Black Bolt, the rightful king of the Inhumans and Medusa's true love, and his mad brother Maximus, who wants the crown—and Medusa—for himself. After marrying Black Bolt and becoming queen of the Inhumans, Medusa and Black Bolt have a son, Ahura, who becomes very powerful but dangerously unstable.

Medusa tries to foster good relations between her species and Earth's humans. She even takes up membership of the Fantastic Four for a time when Invisible Woman takes a leave of absence.

The Inhumans are drawn into the shape-shifting alien Skrulls' Secret Invasion of Earth when it emerges that Black Bolt has been replaced by a Skrull. The Inhumans draw on their ancient connections with the Kree to rescue the real Black Bolt from Skrull captivity. Tragedy strikes when Black Bolt is killed during a clash with the warlike, alien Shi'ar, and Medusa must then reign alone.

Voice of a nation
Black Bolt does not speak as his voice has destructive power, so one of Medusa's main roles as queen-consort is to interpret his wishes and communicate them to their subjects.

JUGGERNAUT

FIRST APPEARANCE *X-Men* #12 (July 1965) **BASE** Xavier Institute, Crimson Cosmos **AFFILIATIONS** Exiles, X-Men, Excalibur, Thunderbolts

When Cain Marko's father marries Charles Xavier's mother, Cain makes his new stepbrother's life a misery. Following the deaths of both parents, the boys end up in the military, serving in Asia together. Cain tries to escape the dangers of the battlefield by hiding in the lost Temple of Cyttorak, where he finds a mysterious red stone, the Crimson Gem of Cyttorak. Grabbing it, he is transformed into the Juggernaut, a monstrous being that crushes anything in its path. Buried under the collapsing temple, it is some time before Juggernaut can dig his way out and return to the U.S., still driven by hatred of his stepbrother.

When Juggernaut faces Xavier's X-Men for the first time, he seems unstoppable —especially as he wears a psionic helmet to protect him from Xavier's mental attacks. Xavier manages to deploy his X-Men—and the Human Torch—to remove Juggernaut's helmet, so that he can finally take the Super Villain down with the power of his mind.

Juggernaut goes on to fight the X-Men and other heroes many times. However, it seems that Cain's humanity is not irretrievably lost, and he has a spell in the X-Men and then the Thunderbolts. After losing his powers, he is selected by the mystical entity Cyttorak to become Juggernaut a second time, and is filled with rage against the X-Man Cyclops (Scott Summers) over the killing of Charles Xavier.

MARY JANE WATSON

FIRST APPEARANCE *Amazing Spider-Man* #25 (June 1965) **BASE** Chicago, New York City **AFFILIATIONS** Stark Industries

Peter Parker wishes his Aunt May would stop nagging him about going out with her best friend's niece—until he meets her. Mary Jane Watson is a beautiful redhead and an aspiring actress and model with a carefree attitude. Peter is captivated, then he reminds himself that he should be focusing on making some money to pay Aunt May's bills.

Mary Jane, known as MJ, becomes part of Peter's circle of college friends and begins dating Harry Osborn, while Peter ends up going out with Gwen Stacy. But when Gwen is captured by the Green Goblin and killed, MJ comforts the heartbroken Peter. Her support gives their friendship new depth and, after a couple of years, the two become an item. Their relationship is rocky, however, as MJ is loath to give up her party lifestyle, while Peter is often mysteriously absent, owing to his double life as Spider-Man.

Eventually, MJ reveals that she has known for some time about Peter's heroic alter ego, but has kept the secret. The couple marry, and she continues modeling and acting. She then falls pregnant, but tragically loses the baby, a girl, thanks to an evil plot by Norman Osborn. MJ is then kidnapped and believed dead for a while, after which she and Peter have a trial separation so she can get her head straight. She moves to Los Angeles, but misses Peter as much as he does her.

Back together, MJ and Peter, plus Aunt May, move into the security of Stark Tower at Tony Stark's invitation after both their homes are burned down. The reconciliation comes to a tragic end when Peter and MJ make a deal with the demon Mephisto to save Aunt May's life. As part of Mephisto's price, their marriage is erased from history. The couple are still friends, however, and seem to be getting closer, until Otto Octavius takes over Peter Parker's body as the Superior Spider-Man. Mary Jane decides that being near Peter is too much of a risk for both of them, and relocates to Chicago, where she

opens a nightclub named the Jackpot. After this is destroyed during a violent clash between Iron Man, Madame Masque, and Doctor Doom, MJ accepts a job at Stark Industries.

For better or for worse
Mary Jane Watson marries Peter Parker in front of friends, family, and J. Jonah Jameson.

S.H.I.E.L.D.

FIRST APPEARANCE *Strange Tales* #135 (August 1965) **BASE** Helicarrier, Triskelion, New York City

U.S. government agency S.H.I.E.L.D. deals with threats too extraordinary to fall under the remit of regular law enforcement. But its greatest enemies are often to be found within its own ranks.

Officially S.H.I.E.L.D. is founded in response to the growing threat from technologically advanced terrorist groups after World War II, particularly Hydra. Its first director is Rick Stoner, but he succumbs to a Hydra bullet and is replaced by Colonel Nicholas Fury. Any S.H.I.E.L.D. director is answerable to the Executive Board, a group of 12 people whose identities the director does not know. Below the director are seven other high-ranking agents, while thousands of others report to them.

As director, Fury surrounds himself with trusted cronies he fought alongside in the war—first among these is "Dum-Dum" Dugan, his right-hand man. The agency deploys a number of cutting-edge vehicles, such as the Helicarrier, a flying aircraft carrier and mobile headquarters. Added to S.H.I.E.L.D.'s futuristic fleet is an incredible array of espionage gadgets, including a device causing temporary invisibility and another that wipes the last two hours of a person's memory. The man behind these weird and wonderful inventions is Sidney Levine, better known as the Gaffer. His most brilliant—and dangerous—creation is the Life Model Decoy (L.M.D.). Using a piece of replicating technology dating back to the Renaissance, the Gaffer manages to build robots that can duplicate existing people. Their credibility is proven when Hydra agents assassinate a Nick Fury L.M.D. by mistake. However, this futuristic technology comes back to bite S.H.I.E.L.D. when an L.M.D. of Nick Fury's brother, Jake, becomes the Super Villain Scorpio.

The secretive nature and powerful reach of S.H.I.E.L.D. makes it a prime target for infiltration by enemies. Nick Fury uncovers a web of corruption running right through the organization, including members of the controlling board, and has to go rogue in order to root out the traitors and determine whom he can trust.

Fury's habit of ignoring protocol if he feels the end justifies the means goes too far when he organizes a clandestine group of Super Heroes to assassinate the corrupt Latverian prime minister Lucia von Bardas. Fury is replaced by Maria Hill, an agent chosen for being suspicious of costumed heroes and outside Fury's close circle. She oversees a period in which S.H.I.E.L.D. helps to round up rebel Super Heroes who have refused to sign the Superhuman Registration Act. Hill's reign is followed by two unlikely S.H.I.E.L.D. directors, Tony Stark and Norman Osborn, who dismantles the organization in favor of his own, named H.A.M.M.E.R. After Osborn is sacked, Hill is put back in charge.

In the shadows
The Director of S.H.I.E.L.D. answers to its board members, a group of 12 people whose identities are never revealed.

Layers upon layers
The vast, labyrinthine S.H.I.E.L.D. headquarters in New York City speaks volumes about the complexity of the organization.

Agents of Stark
As Director of S.H.I.E.L.D., Tony Stark makes some sweeping changes that do not sit well with old-school military veterans like Dum-Dum Dugan.

timeline

Fury leads S.H.I.E.L.D. appoint Nick Fury as the organization's director. He proves his worth by foiling a Hydra booby trap on the Helicarrier. *Strange Tales* #135 (Aug. 1965)

Germ warfare Hydra threatens to unleash a germ bomb on the world, but S.H.I.E.L.D. prevents catastrophe thanks to Nick Fury, who smuggles himself onto Hydra Island to stop the plot. *Strange Tales* #156 (May 1967)

▼ **Scorpio rising** S.H.I.E.L.D. is attacked by the villain Scorpio, who turns out to be a Life Model Decoy of Nick Fury's brother, Jake. *Nick Fury, Agent of S.H.I.E.L.D.* #1 (June 1968)

Forever young Nick Fury is blackmailed by a crook in possession of the Infinity Formula that keeps the S.H.I.E.L.D. Director youthful. Agent Valentina Allegra de Fontaine saves the day. *Marvel Spotlight* #31 (Dec. 1976)

▼ **Enemy within** S.H.I.E.L.D. is infiltrated by L.M.D.s imitating its top agents. Fury goes rogue to root out the enemy within. *Nick Fury Vs. S.H.I.E.L.D.* #6 (Nov. 1988)

Director Hill After Nick Fury takes a group of Super Heroes on an off-the-books mission to Latveria, Agent Maria Hill is appointed S.H.I.E.L.D. Director. *Secret War* #5 (Dec. 2005)

▼ **New world order** S.H.I.E.L.D. is disbanded after failing to prevent the Skrulls' Secret Invasion. It is replaced by new U.S. security chief Norman Osborn's H.A.M.M.E.R. *Secret Invasion* #8 (Jan. 2009)

Pleasant Hill S.H.I.E.L.D. has a new way to reform imprisoned Super Villains: convincing them they are upright citizens in a perfect little town. *Avengers Standoff: Welcome to Pleasant Hill* #1 (Apr. 2016)

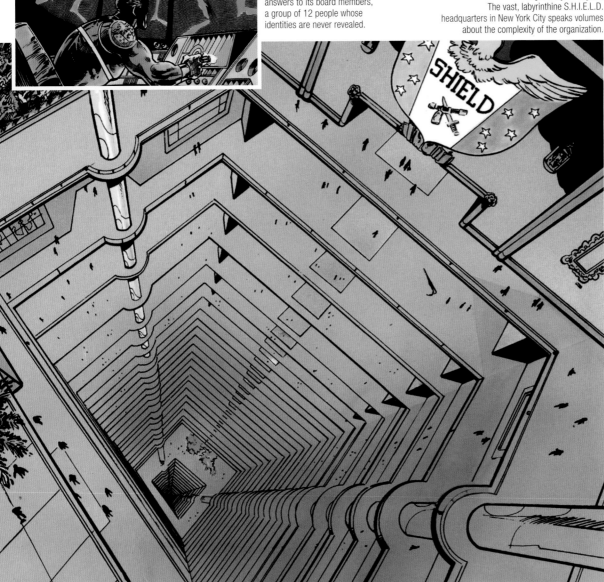

MARVEL AGE

BRONZE AGE

MODERN AGE

HEROIC AGE

Hail Hydra!
The masked figures of Hydra gather together to celebrate their latest evil scheme—replicating the Super Heroes Thor, Iron Man, Captain America, and Hawkeye and sending them to wreak havoc in New York City.

HYDRA

FIRST APPEARANCE *Strange Tales* #135 (August 1965) **BASE** Germany; mobile
AFFILIATIONS A.I.M., Secret Empire, THEM, Nazi party

Hydra has come close to dominating the world many times. This cult-like group's first known modern mission is to capture Director of S.H.I.E.L.D., Nick Fury. Although Hydra fails, it is not defeated: Their mantra is, "Cut off one head and two more shall take its place."

First documented during the third dynasty in ancient Egypt, Hydra rises to infamy working with the Axis powers during World War II in the Far East, when it is taken over by Nazi officer Baron Wolfgang von Strucker. After the war, it survives in the shadows.

Hydra is known to have a great deal of hidden political and military influence—as is revealed by Nick Fury and the Secret Warriors, who lay bare Hydra's comprehensive infiltration of S.H.I.E.L.D., and the U.S. government. However, Hydra isn't only concerned with espionage. The group has also bred subsidiaries, such as the scientific terror organization Advanced Idea Mechanics (A.I.M.), the diversionary organization the Secret Empire, and von Strucker's inner council, known simply as THEM, in addition to its own powerful pharmaceutical and capital management companies.

Sign of Fear
The red and black emblem depicting a skull and octopus-like arms is the calling card of Hydra, symbolizing their deadly, tentacular reach.

MOLTEN MAN

FIRST APPEARANCE *Amazing Spider-Man* #28 (September 1965) **BASE** New York City **AFFILIATIONS** Osborn Industries, Exterminators, Alchemax

Mark Raxton, the stepbrother of Spider-Man's former high-school crush Liz Allan, accidentally absorbs an experimental alloy he was trying to steal from Professor Spencer Smythe's lab. Turning Raxton's skin to slick metal, it bestows super-strength, and he becomes a Super Villain named Molten Man. However, Molten Man's skin also generates burning heat and flames, and only Spider-Man's intervention saves Raxton's life. Eventually Raxton takes a job as a security guard at Osborn Industries. When he begins to melt again, the company's CEO, Harry Osborn (Liz's husband), discovers a cure. Molten Man occasionally helps out Spider-Man and his friends, until he is brainwashed by the Green Goblin. He is later forced to join Chameleon's Exterminators gang. Only when Liz Allan becomes CEO of Alchemax is a lasting cure found for her troubled stepbrother's condition.

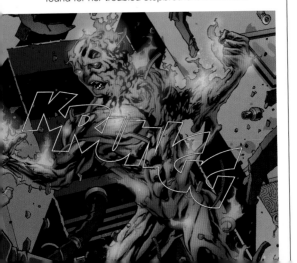

HERCULES

FIRST APPEARANCE *Journey Into Mystery Annual* #1 (October 1965) **BASE** Olympus, New York City
AFFILIATIONS Avengers, Champions, Heroes for Hire, New Warriors

The son of Zeus, Hercules becomes a worthy opponent of Thor when the God of Thunder falls through a portal onto Mount Olympus. The two sons of gods are sometimes rivals, sometimes allies.

Hercules becomes a Super Hero when he is banished to Earth by Zeus. He is an early member of the Avengers, taking on numerous villains, including the titan Typhon, who aims to usurp Zeus' Olympian throne. With the Avengers' help, Hercules defeats Typhon and frees his father and the other Olympian gods —a feat for which his father gladly welcomes him back to Mount Olympus.

Love hurts
Thor and Hercules' competitive rivalry intensifies when Herc takes a fancy to Thor's mortal lady love, Jane Foster.

However, Hercules is soon back on Earth, landing in Los Angeles to lead the Champions hero team. He courts Black Widow and becomes quite a ladies' man, often using his charm to not only woo, but somehow save the day. He rejoins the Avengers, teaming up with Thor, then moves to the Heroes for Hire, hoping to find the Avengers (who have gone missing), before serving with the New Warriors.

During the Chaos War event, Amadeus Cho gifts Hercules with omnipotent power, which he uses to defeat the Multiversal threat of the Chaos King, Mikaboshi.

SENTINELS

FIRST APPEARANCE *X-Men* #14 (November 1965)
BASE Sentinel HQ, New York City **AFFILIATIONS**
U.S. government, Trask Industries

These mutant-hunting machines are first developed by Dr. Bolivar Trask of Trask Industries. Fearing that mutants will use their superior abilities to enslave the human race, he designs his Sentinel robots to overpower mutants. However, during a demonstration in a televised debate with Professor X, they become sentient, turn on their creator and take him prisoner.

The Sentinels take Trask to their factory and, set on enslaving humankind, insist that he make more of them. The prime Sentinel, known as the Master Mold, leads the revolt, forcing Trask to use a mind probe on the now-captured Beast of the X-Men. Through this probe, Trask realizes that the X-Men hope only to protect humans, not enslave them. Trask sees the error of his ways and, with the help of the X-Men, destroys the Sentinel factory, sacrificing himself to stop his creations enslaving mankind.

Though Trask perishes, the Sentinels live on. They are recreated by Trask's son Larry, who blames mutants for the death of his father, but is unknowingly a mutant himself. Other versions are developed by Shaw Industries, founded by Sebastian Shaw of the Hellfire Club, by other Trask family members, and even Stark Industries. It seems as long as there are mutants, there will be those that fear their powers.

Nowhere to run, nowhere to hide
Sentinel robots vary in scale from human-sized to several stories tall. They can fly, shoot projectiles, and fire energy blasts.

The silent king
Black Bolt sits on the throne in Attilan, relocated from the ocean to the Himalayas.

BLACK BOLT

FIRST APPEARANCE *Fantastic Four* #45 (December 1965) **BASE** Attilan, New Attilan **AFFILIATIONS** Inhumans, Illuminati

The Inhumans are a race of human beings genetically evolved by the Kree alien race. Their king is named Blackagar Boltagon—more commonly known as Black Bolt. He possesses superhuman strength, durability and stamina, and also a quasi-sonic scream, capable of leveling cities and splitting continents. He relies on his queen, the prehensile-haired Medusa, to read his body language and translate for him.

Together with the weakness-exploiting Magister Karnak, the element-manipulating Crystal, the Earth-shaking Gorgon, the aquatic Triton, and Lockjaw the teleporting bulldog, Black Bolt protects the Inhuman people from attacks by human renegades, and other threats. Black Bolt's archenemy is his brother Maximus the Magnificent (also known as Maximus the Mad), who seeks time and again to usurp the throne, heedless of the cost to the Inhumans.

Black Bolt's rule becomes more complicated when he and Medusa conceive their first child. All Inhuman children must face the scrutiny of the Genetic Council, who proceed to use the child against Black Bolt, resulting in internal conflict and Black Bolt abdicating. He returns to the throne, but Maximus once more attempts a coup.

During the Infinity event, the Mad Titan Thanos comes to the Inhumans' floating capital city, Attilan, and, hoping to destroy his estranged Inhuman son, demands that Black Bolt kill every young Inhuman. Thanos finds Attilan virtually deserted. During the ensuing battle with Thanos, Black Bolt's screams destroy the city and he detonates an enormous Terrigen Bomb. Black Bolt is presumed dead from the explosion, which spreads Terrigen Mists across Earth, creating thousands of new Inhumans. However, Black Bolt mysteriously returns, this time with help from his brother Maximus.

Total destruction
Thanos tells Black Bolt to give up Thane, or face the death of all Inhuman-kind. Black Bolt unleashes his lethal reply, "Noooo!" The intense sound waves detonate a Terrigen Bomb. By destroying Attilan, Black Bolt hopes to destroy Thanos as well.

JACKAL

FIRST APPEARANCE *Amazing Spider-Man* #31
(December 1965) **BASE** New U Headquarters,
San Francisco; New York City **AFFILIATIONS**
Spider-Man clones, Spider-Queens, Miles Warren
clones, New U Technologies

Biochemist Miles Warren studies with the
High Evolutionary at Wundagore Mountain
but is expelled after his man-jackal creation
kills his own family, and for concentrating
on cloning duplicates rather than seeking
ways to evolve subjects.

Returning to the U.S., Warren teaches
at Empire State University and becomes
infatuated with one of his students, Gwen
Stacy. When she is killed, Warren creates
duplicates of Gwen and her boyfriend,
Peter Parker. During this process, Warren
realizes Parker must be Spider-Man, whom
he now blames for Gwen's death. His first
Parker clone, Kaine, is mentally unstable
and malformed. After some time, Warren
manages to create clones who do not
mutate, rapidly age, or succumb to
the necrotic Carrion Virus.

When his lab assistant
Anthony Serba threatens to
inform the authorities, Warren
kills him and becomes
psychotic. As the Jackal,
Warren sends a wave of
villains and the Punisher to
kill Spider-Man, before using
Peter clone Ben Reilly in a plot
which leaves both the clone
and Peter unsure who is the
original Spider-Man and who
is the copy.

Warren has made many
clones of himself, ensuring
that he can bedevil Spider-
Man through a host of plots
involving genetic monstrosities
and "reanimations" of many
of the Wall-Crawler's old foes.
He also releases a virus that
gives everyone in Manhattan
spider-powers.

Rage of the Jackal
Placid Miles Warren's bestial alter ego
combines insane fury with ruthless
cunning and brilliant biological invention.

GWEN STACY

FIRST APPEARANCE *Amazing Spider-Man* #31
(December 1965) **BASE** New York City
AFFILIATIONS None

Gwen Stacy meets Peter Parker when
both are students at Empire State
University. She is also a science major and
instinctively drawn to the studious loner,
but due to his troubled double life, Peter
rebuffs her. Eventually, Peter and Gwen fall
in love, and his secret life as Spider-Man
starts to impact on hers. When her
policeman father, Captain George Stacy,
is killed as Spider-Man battles Doctor
Octopus, Gwen has a breakdown and
flees to England. On her return, Gwen
cannot bear any mention of the Wall-
Crawler, crushing Peter's plans to share
his secret with her.

Her life ends when Norman Osborn, the
Green Goblin—who knows Spider-Man's
secret identity—hurls her from the Brooklyn
Bridge to torment his greatest enemy.
Unknown to Peter, Osborn fathered two
children with Gwen while she was in
Europe, and wants her dead so he can
raise the siblings himself.

Gwen is cloned many times by
deranged geneticist Miles Warren (Jackal),
who developed an obsession with her at
Empire State University. One Gwen clone
is used by Jackal to torture Peter Parker,
while another becomes Carrion-Virus-
infected superhuman Abby-L.

Miles Warren later resurfaces with yet
another Gwen Stacy that he claims is the
original and not a clone. His ruse is quickly
exposed by Spider-Man and the Parker
clone Kaine, who reveal her to be the
Spider-Woman of Earth-65, a.k.a.
"Spider-Gwen."

The perils of Gwen
Spider-Man prevents
Gwen getting mixed up
in a campaign by
J. Jonah Jameson and
lawyer Sam Bullitt to
bring down Spider-Man.
Unfortunately, he cannot
stop her becoming the
target of Super Villains
and criminals.

Academic interest
Despite herself, Gwen
is attracted to shy but
brilliant student Peter
Parker, even though he
barely acknowledges her.

HARRY OSBORN

FIRST APPEARANCE *Amazing Spider-Man #31* (December 1965) **BASE** Parker Industries, Manhattan, New York City; formerly Seattle, Washington **AFFILIATIONS** Parker Industries; formerly Osborn Industries, Dark Avengers

Harry Osborn's early life is a troubled one. His wealthy, domineering father alternately neglects or micro-manages his son. While at college, Harry slips into drug abuse when his girlfriend, Mary Jane Watson, ends their relationship.

Harry only learns his father is the Green Goblin after the maniac murders Gwen Stacy and dies battling Spider-Man. Simultaneously, Harry discovers his best friend Peter Parker is the Web-Slinger. Using his father's serums and weaponry,

Harry becomes a new Green Goblin, launching attacks on Spider-Man, until the Wall-Crawler reluctantly defeats him.

Treated by psychiatrist Bart Hamilton, Harry is abducted by the doctor, who steals his secrets to become a third Green Goblin. When Harry escapes and captures Hamilton, the catharsis seemingly ends his mental troubles. He marries Liz Allan, settles down to run the Osborn businesses and they have a son, Normie. This joyous time ends when Harry's father returns. Norman has been hiding in Europe and pulling strings from afar, running the U.S. government's Thunderbolts Super Villain brigade. When the alien shape-shifting Skrulls invade Earth, Norman executes their leader and is made head of U.S. metahuman security.

Instituting a Dark Reign of terror, Norman dons confiscated Stark armor to become Iron Patriot and manipulates Harry into becoming the armored hero American Son. His ultimate plan is to stage-manage Harry's death in order to secure public sympathy.

Transformed once more into a mentally unstable,

reluctant adventurer, Harry eventually discovers his father's secret agenda and helps Spider-Man thwart Norman's plans. Harry has since changed his name to Harold Lyman and works for his good friend Peter Parker at Parker Industries.

Goblin unmasked
Spider-Man exposes troubled Harry Osborn as the Green Goblin. When police and medics arrive, Harry tells them that Peter Parker is Spider-Man. Fortunately, they don't believe him.

INHUMANS

FIRST APPEARANCE *Fantastic Four #45* (December 1965) **BASE** Attilan, the Himalayas, the Moon, above New York City **AFFILIATIONS** Fantastic Four, Avengers, Fantastic Force, Kree Empire

Inhumans are a genetically distinct subspecies of *Homo sapiens* changed in prehistory by biologists belonging to the alien Kree. At war with the Skrulls and also seeking ways to escape their own evolutionary cul-de-sac, the Kree mold some early humans' DNA to create advanced, potentially super-powered cannon-fodder. They then abandon the research when a prophecy foretells that their subjects will one day destroy Kree ruler the Supreme Intelligence.

On Earth, the modified humans prosper, achieving a high level of technological sophistication. They remove themselves from contact with lesser humanity to live in a mobile city named Attilan. Around 25,000 years ago, the Inhuman king and geneticist Randac develops Terrigen Mists, which accelerate the mental and physical powers of his people.

Although ruled by a hereditary monarchy, personified by King Black Bolt and the royal family, true power lies with the Genetic Council who control the Terrigen Mists and dictate who may marry or have children.

Lost tribes of Inhumans have hidden amongst ordinary humanity for millennia and become heroes and villains such as Ransak the Reject, Daisy Johnson, and the animalistic hero known as Yeti.

Following Thanos' invasion of Earth, Black Bolt releases Terrigen into the Earth's atmosphere, triggering uncountable

transformations among those of the human population with latent Inhuman genes. These new super-beings are termed NuHumans. The mists also have an unexpected and tragic side-effect: anyone with the mutant X-gene is susceptible to toxic shock from Terrigen exposure. As NuHumans proliferate, mutants all over Earth begin to die.

Evolve or die
Randac's forced evolution and incredible Inhuman power proves the Kree's concerns about their human genetic guinea pigs are well-founded.

GALACTUS

FIRST APPEARANCE *Fantastic Four* #48 (March 1966) **BASE** Worldship *Taa II*
AFFILIATIONS God Squad

The Devourer of Worlds is feared throughout the universe. The implacable hunger of Galactus has left a trail of destruction all the way back to the creation of Earth.

In the unmaking of one universe and the creation of another in the Big Bang, one being survives. Galan of Taa merges with the Sentience of the Universe to become Galactus, but at first this mighty being can only drift inside his incubator ship, waiting until the young universe supports enough life for him to feed on. For Galactus is a devourer of worlds, surviving by consuming the energies that sustain life. He builds armor for himself, and a home —the worldship he calls *Taa II*, in memory of his former life.

At first Galactus only consumes uninhabited worlds, and manages to go long periods without feeding. But his appetite grows, and the gaps between meals get smaller. Soon, his hunger can only be satisfied by planets teeming with life. To find suitable worlds, Galactus uses a series of heralds, beings who speed ahead of him and carry out reconnaissance. Once the world-eater himself arrives at the unfortunate planetary target, he assembles a machine on that world's surface that transforms it into energy he can draw into himself.

Saving the world-eater
Refusing to countenance allowing a living being to die, even one that consumes entire worlds, Reed Richards assembles a machine to heal the stricken Galactus.

timeline

First failure Galactus is prevented from consuming Earth when Reed Richards threatens him with the Ultimate Nullifier weapon. *Fantastic Four* #50 (May 1966)

▶ **Serious indigestion**
The High Evolutionary reduces Galactus to a giant brain when he is rendered mortally ill after consuming the planet Poppup. *Fantastic Four* #175 (Oct. 1976)

Galactus saved When Galactus becomes so low on energy that he is close to death, Reed Richards uses his scientific genius to save him, an act for which he is later brought to trial. *Fantastic Four* #244 (July 1982)

Star witness Galactus speaks in defense of Reed Richards at his trial. Mister Fantastic is accused of causing the deaths of seven billion Skrulls by failing to kill Galactus. *Fantastic Four* #262 (Jan. 1984)

I hunger His appetites having changed so that only consuming life force will do, Galactus returns to Earth. Despite many of Earth's heroes teaming up against him, only the Silver Surfer can stop Galactus eating his fill. *Galactus the Devourer* #3 (Nov. 1999)

▶ **The fury of Galactus**
After being captured and used as a weapon by Annihilus, Galactus brings about the end of the Annihilation War by unleashing a wave of destruction. *Annihilation* #6 (Mar. 2007)

Galactus seed The Devourer of Worlds clashes with Odin the All-Father when he comes looking for the Worldheart, a piece of the Tree of Life that has the potential to satiate him for good. *Mighty Thor* #5 (Oct. 2011)

Lifebringer The Ultimates Super Hero team uses Galactus' long-abandoned incubator to re-make him as a bringer of life rather than a destroyer. *The Ultimates* #2 (Feb. 2016)

> "I am power which is beyond power, knowledge which is beyond thought."

GALACTUS

Power Cosmic
As a wielder of the Power Cosmic, Galactus has almost unlimited powers, but despite this is in many ways a slave—to his hunger.

Eventually, a herald of Galactus, the Silver Surfer, chances upon planet Earth as a suitable repast for his master. However, the Surfer is moved by humanity and helps the Fantastic Four stop Galactus from devouring the planet. While the inhabitants of the worlds he consumes are usually not worthy of his notice, Galactus ends up almost respecting Mister Fantastic Reed Richards, after the super scientist prevents his death.

Later, the homeworld of the Skrull Empire falls victim to Galactus and Reed Richards is put on trial for his part in the deaths of seven billion Skrulls. The World-eater speaks on behalf of Mister Fantastic and when Eternity reveals Galactus' true role in the universe to the jury that Richards is acquitted.

Although Galactus has promised not to return to Earth, he is led back there by his herald Terrax. The Silver Surfer tricks Galactus into going instead to the Shi'ar homeworld, where Galactus is seemingly destroyed and turns into a star. But the Devourer of Worlds returns after Reed Richards is forced to use the Ultimate Nullifier weapon to reset reality. However, the problem of Galactus' destructive hunger later seems to be solved when the Super Hero team the Ultimates remake him in the incubator ship in which he survived the Big Bang. The Devourer of Worlds emerged anew as the creator of worlds, renamed the Lifebringer. Galactus' first task was to restore the very first planet he had consumed—Archaeopia.

Death of Galactus
Defeated by a coalition of forces from across the galaxy, Galactus is laid low by his former herald the Silver Surfer and becomes a star lighting the Shi'ar homeworld.

SILVER SURFER

FIRST APPEARANCE *Fantastic Four* #48 (March 1966) **BASE** Mobile
AFFILIATIONS Titans Three, Defenders, God Squad, Annihilators

Roaming infinity on his cosmic-powered surfboard, the Silver Surfer seems aloof and emotionless, but is in fact capable of great compassion and empathy. He is also one of the most powerful beings in the universe.

The being known as Norrin Radd comes from the planet Zenn-La, a world so advanced that its people no longer feel the need to explore space or make technological discoveries. But Norrin is restless and longs to travel from his homeworld. When the Devourer of Worlds Galactus comes to Zenn-La, Norrin offers himself as his herald, in exchange for sparing Zenn-La. Galactus grants Norrin a portion of the Power Cosmic; he becomes silver and roams the universe on a surfboard-like craft, searching for suitable worlds for his master to consume. The Silver Surfer's powers are immense and almost limitless. He can shape matter and harness energy, phase through solids, and move safely through all sorts of celestial phenomena, such as black holes and supernovas. His metallic body is near invulnerable and he does not need to eat, breathe, or sleep.

The Silver Surfer tries to seek out worlds for Galactus that are uninhabited, but this is not always possible, and he seems to accept the necessity that many beings must die so that his master may live. It is later revealed that Galactus has made a small adjustment to the Silver Surfer's soul to enable him to carry out his duties without being overwhelmed by guilt.

When he arrives on Earth, the Surfer is struck by the nature of humanity and its capacity for good. This is personified by blind sculptor Alicia Masters, who tries to help him, even though he is a stranger. This act awakens the Silver Surfer's empathy, and he rebels against Galactus and helps to drive him off. As a punishment, the World-Eater imprisons the Silver Surfer on Earth.

Although the Silver Surfer has great respect for humans, he becomes frustrated by their ignorance and self-destructive tendencies. Thinking that people would become more noble if they had to unite against a common enemy, the Surfer begins a campaign of destruction, before realizing his mistake.

The Silver Surfer eventually regains the ability to leave Earth and travel the universe, but retains his affection for the little, blue-green planet and returns in times of need. He even agrees to become the herald of Galactus again to protect Earth. Later, he acquires a companion from Earth, Dawn Greenwood, who travels with him on his endless voyages.

Carnage Cosmic
The Silver Surfer's capacity for compassion is tested when the Carnage symbiote attempts to bond with him. However, he decides to return the symbiote to its previous host, Cletus Kasady, to save his life.

timeline

MARVEL AGE

Earthbound After fighting Galactus to prevent him consuming Earth, the Silver Surfer is trapped on the planet, prevented from roaming space and time as he had before. *Fantastic Four* #50 (May 1966)

◄ **The Surfer attacks** Frustrated by the inhumanity he sees on Earth, the Silver Surfer carries out a series of attacks to force people to come together against a common threat. *Fantastic Four* #72 (Mar. 1968)

BRONZE AGE

Titans Three The Silver Surfer teams up with Namor the Sub-Mariner and Hulk to stop humans imperilling the Earth. *Sub-Mariner* #34 (Feb. 1971)

Free at last Following a suggestion from the Thing, the Silver Surfer leaves his board behind and manages to break through the barrier preventing him leaving Earth. *Silver Surfer* #1 (July 1987)

MODERN AGE

Stuck in the middle The Silver Surfer is caught up in a battle between the demonic Mephisto and Galactus, and the former herald helps the World-Eater triumph. *Marvel Graphic Novel* #38 (Oct. 1988)

Battle of the Heralds The Silver Surfer leads a team of former heralds of Galactus, looking to take down the evil and powerful Morg, the World-Eater's current herald. *Silver Surfer* #75 (Dec. 1992)

HEROIC AGE

◄ **Citizen of Earth** After destroying the culture of his homeworld to save Earth, the Silver Surfer is the first alien being to become an official citizen of Earth, in recognition of his heroism. *Silver Surfer* #3 (June 2016)

Sentinel of the skyways
The Power Cosmic enables the Silver Surfer to travel throughout the universe at light speed on his board, and has made him one of the most powerful beings in the universe.

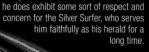

Faithful servant
Although Galactus is incapable of emotion, he does exhibit some sort of respect and concern for the Silver Surfer, who serves him faithfully as his herald for a long time.

A host of heralds
Silver Surfer and other heralds gather to fight Morg when he displeases Galactus.

Heralds of Galactus
The heralds of Galactus are very different beings, although their function is always the same—to seek out worlds suitable for their ravenous master to consume. The best known and most powerful of Galactus' heralds is the Silver Surfer, but others include Air-Walker, Firelord, Terrax the Tamer, and the amoral Morg. Another herald comes from Earth —Frankie Raye, a.k.a. Nova. She, like the Silver Surfer before her, tries to steer the Devourer of Worlds toward planets that have no sentient life forms. She and the Surfer even have a romantic relationship for a time.

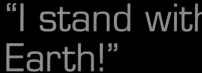

"I stand with Earth!"
SILVER SURFER

BLACK PANTHER

FIRST APPEARANCE *Fantastic Four* #52 (July 1966) **BASE** Wakanda
AFFILIATIONS Avengers, Defenders, Fantastic Four, Illuminati

Father and son
Young T'Challa stands proudly at his father T'Chaka's side. Soon tragedy will strike when the monarch of Wakanda is murdered.

"The Black Panther" is a title granted to the reigning monarch of the African nation of Wakanda. T'Challa is just a boy when his father, T'Chaka, the Black Panther and King of Wakanda, is murdered by criminal scientist Ulysses Klaw. The King's brother, S'Yan, temporarily becomes the new Black Panther while T'Challa attends the best schools in the West. When he returns to Wakanda, T'Challa undergoes a series of tests to prove his worthiness, and he successfully challenges his uncle (who gladly steps down and remains T'Challa's trusted advisor until his death) for the title of Black Panther and the throne of Wakanda.

Black Panther is an ally of the Avengers and the Fantastic Four, but the safety of his kingdom, with its invaluable deposits of the metal Vibranium, always comes first. He marries his childhood love, Ororo Monroe (Storm), and together they fend off a Skrull invasion of Wakanda. When Black Panther is critically wounded by Doctor Doom, his sister, Shuri, assumes the throne, and the Black Panther title. T'Challa regains his powers—and more—later, becoming King of the Dead. Conflict between the X-Men and Avengers results in a divorce from his wife, Storm (Ororo Munroe) and he operates from the U.S.A. for a time. However, the destruction of the Multiverse finds him ruling over Wakanda once more.

"We are Wakanda.
We will not be terrorized.
We are terror itself."
BLACK PANTHER

Storm warning
With her mutant power to manipulate weather, Storm is revered as a goddess of rain. Sadly, her marriage to Black Panther proves as troubled as her name implies.

Power of the Panther
The Black Panther appellation is passed down many generations. T'Challa takes the title and gains his special powers from a rare heart-shaped herb native to Wakanda. It grants him a range of superhuman abilities, including speed, strength, endurance, agility, keen senses, and elevated intelligence.

timeline

▼ **Welcome to Wakanda** Black Panther invites the Fantastic Four to Wakanda. When they arrive, he tests each one in combat—and wins. *Fantastic Four* #52 (July 1966)

Death calls Black Panther visits Avengers Mansion and finds the team apparently murdered. At first he is blamed; after he is cleared of the crime, he joins the Avengers. *Avengers* #52 (May 1968)

▼ **Invasion** Black Panther returns to Wakanda in order to stop Doctor Doom tunnelling from Latveria and stealing Wakanda's deposits of Vibranium. *Astonishing Tales* #6 (June 1971)

Panther's prey Villainous metamorph Solomon Prey rises against the Black Panther while drug lords threaten T'Challa's rule in Wakanda. *Black Panther: Panther's Prey* #1 (Sept. 1990)

Manhattan beat Black Panther becomes the protector of Hell's Kitchen under the alias Mr. Mokonkwo, supposedly a Congolese immigrant and diner owner.

▶ **A Wakandan uprising** The Midnight Angels and the People lead a revolution in Wakanda while Black Panther struggles to maintain order.

MARVEL AGE

BRONZE AGE

MODERN AGE

HEROIC AGE

THE COLLECTOR

FIRST APPEARANCE *Avengers* #28 (June 1966)
BASE Mobile **AFFILIATIONS** Elders of the Universe

The Collector (Taneleer Tivan) hails from the dawn of the universe. His powers are sourced from cosmic energy and he is almost indestructible. The Collector can foresee possible future scenarios and believes that Thanos will destroy the universe. As an immortal Elder, he feels he has a duty to preserve not the universe itself, but the best specimens and artifacts it has to offer. He uses a Temporal Assimilator to jump through time and gather whatever he desires for his personal collection. Unfortunately for the Avengers, he aims to add each of them to his collection. His conservation efforts are intended to repopulate the universe later, but his methods are utterly ruthless. The Collector unleashes an alien life form known as the Brethren on Earth in an attempt to cull the population so he can collect the strongest survivors.

The balance shifts when the Collector believes the seemingly omnipotent cyborg Korvac may be an even greater threat to the universe than Thanos. He asks his daughter, Carina, to spy on Korvac. She falls in love with Korvac instead and betrays her father. As a result, Korvac kills the Collector. However, the Collector's fellow Elder, the Grandmaster, revives him after winning a contest with Death. The Collector later reciprocates the favor for the Grandmaster.

When the Multiverse ends following the events of Secret Wars, the Elders compete over a new substance known as Iso-8, concentrated as an Iso-Sphere. This unique substance is the priceless remains of Battleworld, locked within a broken dimension. The Collector and Grandmaster select Maestro and the Punisher to fight for them in a competition for the substance, but they are outsmarted by Maestro, who gains control of the Iso-Sphere and then forces the two Elders from the dimension.

BOOMERANG

FIRST APPEARANCE *Tales to Astonish* #81 (July 1966) **BASE** Mobile **AFFILIATIONS** Sinister Six, Sinister Twelve, Sinister Syndicate, Masters of Evil, Heavy Hitters, Hood's Gang, Thunderbolts

Originally from Australia, Frederick Meyers is a Major League baseball pitcher with incredible aim. He turns to crime after he is suspended for taking bribes. The Secret Empire (an organization of red-robed terrorists bent on conquering the U.S.) provides him with gear and the codename Boomerang. Meyers is a frequent thorn in the side for Super Heroes such as Daredevil, Spider-Man, and the agents of S.H.I.E.L.D.

During the Fifty-State Initiative, Boomerang joins the Nevada team as Outback. His heroic days are short-lived, however. The inveterate Spider-Man enemy and scientist Alastair Smythe enhances Boomerang's suit and his arsenal of specialized boomerangs for yet another attempt to finish the web-slinger for good.

SUPER-ADAPTOID

FIRST APPEARANCE *Tales of Suspense* #82 (October 1966) **BASE** Mobile
AFFILIATIONS A.I.M.

The Super-Adaptoid is an android built by A.I.M. (Advanced Idea Mechanics) to destroy and replace Captain America. It takes on the appearance and powers of any Super Hero in close proximity. The android can copy up to eight different beings at once and combine their powers, as it shows when confronting the Avengers, X-Men, and Fantastic Four. The Super-Adaptoid's power derives from a fragment of the Cosmic Cube, placed inside it by A.I.M. A version of the Super-Adaptoid merges with Black Widow (Yelena Belova). Later on, it absorbs Deadpool's powers—and his cancer—which destroys its organic components. Reed Richards converts the remains into shape-shifting armor for spider-powered Super Hero Silk (Cindy Moon).

EGO THE LIVING PLANET

FIRST APPEARANCE *Mighty Thor* #132 (September 1966) **BASE** Mobile **AFFILIATIONS** The Stranger, Alter-Ego

Ego is a small, sentient planet created by the Stranger (a powerful cosmic being of mysterious origin) in the Black Galaxy. Ego creates a superhuman army to conquer other worlds. When Galactus attacks Ego, Thor helps him vanquish Galactus. Ego pretends to be grateful, and allows the survivors of a planet attacked by Galactus to live on his surface. Soon after Thor leaves, however Ego devours all the survivors. Later, when Ego attacks Earth, Thor bands together with Galactus, Firelord, and Hercules to defeat him.

Ego has many interesting adventures. At one point, he becomes compressed and is hidden inside the body of Quasar (Wendell Vaughn). Ego is released after Quasar's death and takes over the Nova Corps. Nova defeats Ego and he flees. Later, Ego discovers he has a sibling, also created by the Stranger, named Alter-Ego. This much smaller being is held captive by The Collector. When Alter-Ego is freed, he battles Ego at first, but the two are reconciled and Alter Ego henceforth orbits Ego as a moon.

Life isn't always easy for Ego. He is infected with a cancerous entity that makes him obsessed with consuming whole stars. This causes him to grow at

Battle of Egos
Alter-Ego attacks his brother Ego. Fortunately Thor is on hand to resolve matters—and prevent Earth being caught up in the colossal clash.

a tremendous rate, until he is in danger of exploding and destroying the surrounding galaxy. Fortunately, Flux and the Fantastic Four expel the parasitic being. Ego's surface later becomes infested with space lice and Ego is forced to contract Rocket Raccoon for a week to exterminate them.

RHINO

FIRST APPEARANCE *Amazing Spider-Man* #41
(October 1966) **BASE** Mobile
AFFILIATIONS Sinister Syndicate, Sinister Six,
Emissaries of Evil, Great Game, Secret Defenders,
Legion Accursed, Exterminators

Aleksei Sytsevich is a brutish thug in
Russia's criminal underworld who
undergoes secret treatments to become
a superhuman agent for a gang of spies.
The process gives him incredible strength
and durability, but also permanently bonds
his tough protective costume to his flesh,
hence his codename: Rhino.

Rhino is ordered to kidnap John
Jameson, an American astronaut and son
of *Daily Bugle* publisher J. Jonah Jameson.
Maddened by his own power, however,
Rhino turns on his masters and abducts
Jameson for his own gain, only to be
stopped by Spider-Man. Breaking out of
jail, Rhino goes after the Wall-Crawler, who
beats him by destroying his protective suit
with specially formulated webbing.

Rhino's creators take him back,
augment his power and gear, and send
him to capture Bruce Banner. Rhino is
thrashed by the Hulk. In time, he becomes
a mercenary, battling numerous heroes
and joining various Super Villain teams.

Rhino reaches a turning point in his life
after Spider-Man reveals his identity during
the Superhuman Civil War. Rhino turns
himself in and serves a brief time in jail.
Released on parole, he meets Russian
waitress Oksana and they marry. But when
Oksana is killed by a new Rhino—created
by criminal scientist Dr. Tramma—he goes
back to his old ways and murders her killer.
He allies with the Lizard and the Jackal
when they offer to restore Oksana to life.

Beast of burden
Despite his might and remarkable
resilience, the slow-witted Rhino
was more a destructive dupe of
more devious criminals than a true
menace to society.

Deus ex machina
The High Evolutionary's unparalleled intellect allows
him to break the laws of nature and turn himself into
a living god of science.

HIGH EVOLUTIONARY

FIRST APPEARANCE *Thor* #134 (November
1966) **BASE** Counter-Earth; formerly Wundagore
Mountain and Wundagore II City of the High
Evolutionary **AFFILIATIONS** New Men, Knights
of Wundagore, Ani-Mutants, Animen, Godpack,
New Immortals

In the 1920s, Oxford student Herbert
Edgar Wyndham is obsessed with
evolving organisms to their ultimate form.
Inspired by the works of Nathaniel Essex
(later Mister Sinister), and secretly
prompted by a mysterious Inhuman
collaborator, Wyndham's experiments
result in his being expelled. Leaving
England, he and fellow researcher
Jonathan Drew relocate to Wundagore
Mountain in Transia, eastern Europe.
After his daughter succumbs to radiation
poisoning and his wife is killed by a
werewolf, Drew leaves and Wyndham
builds a suit of high-tech armor to protect
himself from the dangers of the demon-
haunted land—and his own discoveries.

Assisted by new student Miles Warren
(later the Jackal), Wyndham advances the
evolutionary state of numerous animals,
creating a humanoid band of New Men.
These he indoctrinates with legends of
King Arthur to create the Knights of
Wundagore. When the demon Chthon
escapes into Earthly reality, the Knights
valiantly drive it back, but not before
Chthon establishes a mystic connection
with newborn mutant twins Wanda and
Pietro Maximoff (later the heroes Scarlet
Witch and Quicksilver).

When Wyndham—now calling himself
the High Evolutionary—accidentally
advances a wolf into a ferocious
super-powered Man-Beast, Thor helps
him defeat the creature. Realizing the
world is becoming too small for his
experiments, Wyndham creates a
Counter-Earth on the far side of the Sun.
Still hungering for knowledge of the
mysteries of life, the High Evolutionary
returns to Earth many times, creating gods
and monsters, and battling Super Heroes.

ABOMINATION

FIRST APPEARANCE *Tales to Astonish* #90
(April 1967) **BASE** Mobile
AFFILIATIONS Abominations, Forgotten,
Mephisto's Legion Accursed

Soviet spy Emil Blonsky infiltrates the
U.S. Air Force's New Mexico Gamma
Base to commit sabotage. Meanwhile,
the all-powerful alien Stranger attempts
to turn the Hulk into a weapon against
humanity. To foil the plan, Bruce Banner
tries to commit suicide using his gamma
ray machines. Hiding in Banner's lab,
Blonsky receives a huge dose of radiation
which permanently transforms him into a
green-skinned mutate, stronger than the
Hulk—at least when the Hulk is in a
passive state—but with mind and
memory unaffected.

The "Abomination" battles Hulk, then is
taken by the Stranger and spends months
as a captive servant. He faces Silver
Surfer and Thor before finally
escaping, and slowly works
his way back to Earth. Despite his
immense power and cunning,
Abomination becomes little more
than a tool of smarter villains
such as the Leader and
M.O.D.O.K.

After years of being
beaten by the Hulk and
other Super Heroes,
Abomination retreats
from the world. He
becomes the protector

of a society of misfits below the streets of
New York City. But when Bruce Banner
marries Betty Ross, the Abomination's evil
side resurfaces. He murders her with his
irradiated blood, framing the Hulk for the
crime. Blonsky wants to prove the Hulk is
a greater monster than he is but suffers
crushing humiliation when Banner absolves
him and walks away. Months later, Blonsky
is killed by Red Hulk "Thunderbolt" Ross,
in revenge for Betty's death.

Green with envy
Abomination's good intentions
could not protect him from his
obsessive hatred for the Hulk.

KINGPIN

FIRST APPEARANCE *Amazing Spider-Man #50* (July 1967) **BASE** Mobile; formerly penthouse in New York City; formerly Fisk Tower, New York City; mansion in Westchester County; Las Vegas; Japan **AFFILIATIONS** The Hand (American Branch); East Coast non-Maggia criminal organizations; Hydra (Las Vegas faction), Emissaries of Evil, Damage Control, Fisk Industries

Wilson Fisk claims to have killed his first man when he was only 12 years old. Educating himself by stealing books, the boy reshapes his body through bodybuilding and martial arts training. After serving as gang boss Don Rigoletto's bodyguard, Fisk kills him and then smashes his way to the head of New York's underworld. He forces rivals to join him in a cabal that combines brutal methods and new technologies, like the disintegrator ray he carries in his cane.

Despite defeats by Spider-Man, Kingpin's lawyers keep his reputation clean and, to the world at large, he is simply a successful entrepreneur. His world is shaken when his son Richard becomes his rival and, in the guise of the insidious Schemer, attempts to force him to retire.

After being lured into a plot to conquer America as an unknowing pawn of the Red Skull, Fisk moves to Japan for his family's sake. He is forced back into his old life when a rival seemingly murders his wife, Vanessa, after she makes her husband hand over his files to the authorities.

Daredevil restores her to him, but forces the resurgent crime lord to abandon plans to make mayoral candidate Randolph Cherryh his puppet. Kingpin retaliates and hires the

assassin Bullseye to murder Daredevil's lover, Elektra.

The Kingpin is constantly thwarted by heroes he believes are his physical and intellectual inferiors— such as the Punisher—and the war of wills with Daredevil consumes him. After he exposes Matt Murdock as the Man Without Fear, their epic struggle eventually leads to Kingpin's exposure as a criminal and his well-deserved incarceration.

Now operating as gang boss the Rose, Richard executes a years-long plot to destroy his father. With ally Sam Silke he almost kills Kingpin, but is foiled by Vanessa, who kills Richard, her own son, and moves her dying husband to safety in Europe. She dies soon after blackmailing Matt Murdock into becoming the Kingpin's defense attorney.

Upon returning to full health, Fisk then resumes his position at the top of the underworld, via an association with ninja cult the Hand. When the Lizard and the Jackal reanimate his beloved Vanessa, Fisk furiously kills the revenant and prepares himself for another war…

> "The underworld will now be run like a business…and the Chairman of the Board will be… the Kingpin!"
>
> **WILSON FISK**

It's good to be the king
Despite frequent defeats by heroes like Spider-Man, crime boss Wilson Fisk continues to projects a highly convincing image of strength, enabling him to rule subordinates by terror.

timeline

▼ **Crime pays** A mysterious figure consolidates the East Coast underworld into a syndicate run on corporate lines. Only Spider-Man can counter this new Kingpin of Crime. *Amazing Spider-Man #50–51 (July–Aug. 1967)*

Family business Teenager Richard Fisk attempts to obliterate his father's criminal empire through a devious power play as gang boss the Schemer. *Amazing Spider-Man #83–85 (Apr.–June 1970)*

▼ **Hail Hydra!** After being duped by the Red Skull into becoming Supreme Hydra, Kingpin helps Captain America and S.H.I.E.L.D. defeat Hydra. *Captain America #147–148 (Mar.–Apr. 1972)*

Beat the devil After clashing with Daredevil, Fisk becomes obsessed with destroying the hero. *Daredevil #172 (July 1981)*

▼ **Search and destroy** Fisk learns Daredevil's true identity and begins systematically ruining his enemy's life and career. *Daredevil #227 (Feb. 1986)*

Ides of March When Richard Fisk and Samuel Silke's coup almost finishes Wilson, Vanessa takes over, executes her son and dispenses the vengeance of the Kingpin. *Daredevil #30 (Apr. 2002)*

Crime and punisher As the Multiverse dies during the Secret Wars' Final Incursion event, Fisk and his associates are ambushed by the Punisher, who is determined to deliver justice before fate intervenes. *Secret Wars #1 (July 2015)*

MARVEL AGE

BRONZE AGE

MODERN AGE

HEROIC AGE

RED GUARDIAN

FIRST APPEARANCE *Avengers* #43 (August 1967) **BASE** Russia **AFFILIATIONS** K.G.B., Defenders, Supreme Soviets, Winter Guard

Created to be the communist world's answer to Captain America, the Red Guardian hurls a belt buckle as his signature weapon instead of a shield. His true identity is Alexei Shostakov, a Russian test pilot and the husband of Natasha Romanova (Black Widow). When the Red Guardian meets Captain America in combat, they are equally matched, but he is mortally wounded when he throws himself into the path of a bullet meant for Black Widow. He goes on to prevent Captain America from being shot as well, leading Cap to reflect on the great honor with which Red Guardian has conducted himself. After Shostakov, the identity of Red Guardian is taken up by others, including Dr. Tania Belinskaya, Josef Petkus, and Nikolai Krylenko.

SUPREME INTELLIGENCE

FIRST APPEARANCE *Fantastic Four* #65 (August 1967) **BASE** Hala, Kree Empire **AFFILIATIONS** Kree, Galactic Council, Starforce

The Supreme Intelligence is an organic computer construct, devised and assembled by the Kree alien race in order to create a Cosmic Cube, like their enemies the Skrulls. The brains of the Kree's finest minds are harvested after death and added to the system. Although originally intended to do the bidding of its creators, the Supreme Intelligence becomes an independent entity and rejects the idea of the Cosmic Cube as too dangerous. Instead, it applies its vast bank of wisdom to assisting the Kree Empire in other ways. The Supreme Intelligence's judgment becomes so essential and unimpeachable that no other form of government is deemed necessary. However the Supreme Intelligence's methods of safeguarding the future of the Kree race, though not without logic, prove utterly ruthless.

RONAN THE ACCUSER

FIRST APPEARANCE *Fantastic Four* #65 (August 1967) **BASE** Kree-Lar, Hala, Kree Empire **AFFILIATIONS** Accuser Corps, Galactic Council, Annihilators

Born to an aristocratic Kree family, Ronan joins the Public Accuser Corps to serve Kree justice. His rapid rise through the ranks culminates in the office of Supreme Accuser. Ronan is not content with this achievement and hates taking orders from the Kree's artificial Supreme Intelligence. However, Ronan serves the Empire well in repeated conflicts with intergalactic enemies such as the Skrulls, Shi'ar, and Annihilators. He takes Crystal, of the Inhuman royal family, to be his bride, before the two are forcibly separated by the Kree's Supreme Intelligence. Ronan wields the Universal Weapon, a hammer-like object also known as the Cosmi-Rod. This enables him to fly, direct blasts of energy, and create force fields.

WARLOCK

FIRST APPEARANCE *Fantastic Four* #66 (September 1967) **BASE** Citadel of Science; Counter-Earth; Soul World; Knowhere **AFFILIATIONS** Infinity Watch, Guardians of the Galaxy

A group of Earth's leading scientists are so dedicated to creating the perfect human specimen that they fake their own deaths in order to covertly retreat to ultra-secret lab complex the Citadel of Science. Just when it seems that they have successfully created an ideal man, he breaks free from the tank in which he has been growing. The scientists pursue the man, known at first only as Him. However, his powers prove so great that he easily holds them at bay.

Finally, Him decides that Earth is not yet ready for his presence and takes his leave, destroying the Citadel of Science as he goes. He drifts through space in his cocoon until found by the High Evolutionary, who takes him in and treats him almost like a son.

When the savage Man-Beast runs amok on the High Evolutionary's Counter-Earth, the High Evolutionary sends Him to stop the carnage, with a Soul Gem set in his forehead for protection. He also gives Him a name—Warlock. When Warlock arrives on Counter-Earth he is given another name, Adam, by a girl he meets there. After defeating Man-Beast, Warlock becomes the first Super Hero on Counter-Earth. He later travels through space, befriending the assassin Gamora and Pip the Troll along the way. He discovers that his Soul Gem is one of the Infinity Stones. While it has the power to send him insane over time, it can also absorb souls into a utopian dimension called Soul World. Warlock becomes a member of Infinity Watch, a group dedicated to protecting the Infinity Gems and preventing them being brought together with evil intent.

Supreme being
Adam Warlock is already one of the most powerful beings in the universe, but when he puts on the Infinity Gauntlet he is virtually omnipotent.

STINGRAY

FIRST APPEARANCE *Tales to Astonish #95*
(September 1967) **BASE** Hydrobase, Atlantic
Ocean; Camp Hammond; Hawaii **AFFILIATIONS**
Deep Six, Avengers, Secret Avengers, Point Men,
Deadpool's Heroes for Hire

Dr. Walter Newell is an oceanographer
and visionary engineer, who designs and
builds a domed underwater city, in order
to expand the resources available to
humans. When his city is destroyed by the
Plunderer, he encounters Namor the
Sub-Mariner, who becomes a source of
great fascination and later an ally.
Newell adopts the costumed identity of Stingray,
creating an armored suit that enables him
to move swiftly in water, even at great
depths, and to fire blasts of electricity. Its
glider wings also function out of the water.
Stingray's early career mostly sees him
assisting Namor; he later becomes a
member of the Avengers.

M.O.D.O.K .walks
Scientists at A.I.M. work for months to create a
large robotic body for M.O.D.O.K. to travel about
in—his hoverchair slots into the head section.

M.O.D.O.K.

FIRST APPEARANCE *Tales of Suspense #94* (October 1967)
BASE Mobile **AFFILIATIONS** A.I.M., M.O.D.O.K.'s 11, Intelligencia

After scientists at the organization A.I.M. create the Cosmic
Cube, they decide a being of superior intelligence is needed to
fully realize the Cube's potential. To that end, they genetically
mutate one of their technicians, George Tarleton, into
M.O.D.O.C. (Mental Organism Designed Only for Computing).
His brain becomes enormous and his head grows with it,
leaving him dependent on a hoverchair, as his body is unable
to support his sheer bulk.

M.O.D.O.C.'s superior intellect makes him question why he
should take orders from the inferior minds of A.I.M., and he
becomes ambitious and ruthless. He takes over A.I.M.,
changes his acronym to M.O.D.O.K., with the K standing for
Killing, and clashes with Captain America when Cap comes to
rescue captured S.H.I.E.L.D. agent Sharon Carter. A.I.M. agents
make use of this distraction, taking the chance to attack both
M.O.D.O.K. and the hero. While Cap and Sharon escape,
M.O.D.O.K. hits self-destruct.

The villain returns to plague Captain America many times,
as well as other superpowered beings, such as Namor the
Sub-Mariner and Hulk. M.O.D.O.K.'s obsession with defeating
his costumed foes damages his relationship with A.I.M., and his
leadership is frequently questioned and overthrown. Eventually
M.O.D.O.K. is turned back into George Tarleton, but M.O.D.O.K.
Superior appears in his place, the product of a cloned version of
Tarleton's brain. This M.O.D.O.K. is more stable than its
predecessor and even ends up helping S.H.I.E.L.D.

CAPTAIN MAR-VELL

FIRST APPEARANCE *Marvel Super Heroes #12* (December 1967)
BASE Mobile **AFFILIATIONS** Kree, Avengers (posthumous, honorary)

Captain Mar-Vell is a Kree warrior originally sent to Earth on a spy
mission. Mar-Vell is so taken with this "lovely world" in the far
reaches of the Kree Empire that he resolves to protect it from
threats, even from his own people. Adopting the name Captain
Marvel, to roll more easily off the human tongue, the warrior sets
about his new role as Earth's protector with vigor. A being named
Eon bestows on him the power of cosmic awareness—an
incredible sense that allows him to know almost anything at the
moment he needs to know it. He is granted further superhuman
abilities by the Kree Supreme Intelligence as a reward for helping
to defeat an uprising by Ronan, making him extremely powerful
and able to fly at light speed.

Captain Mar-Vell's greatest foe is the Titan Thanos, who is killed
by Warlock and turned to stone. When the Captain goes to help
Thanos' father and brother bring his body home to Titan, there is
a fight against acolytes of Thanos, who are waiting for his return
from the grave. After the melee, Thanos' father, Mentor, notices
that Mar-Vell is not well and the Captain admits that his cosmic
awareness showed him he was ill some weeks before. The Kree
name for his disease is blackend—cancer to the people of Earth.
Mar-Vell tells those closest to him that he has only a short time to
live. Those hit hardest are his lover Elysius and his good friend
Rick Jones—the Earth teenager with whom Mar-Vell has shared
a symbiotic bond. Rick is devastated and beseeches the finest
Super Hero minds to find a cure. As the news spreads across
the universe, all sorts of alien remedies are suggested, but all
treatment is blocked by Mar-Vell's Nega-Bands, which harness
the power of the Negative Zone. Since the energy from these
wristbands has also been keeping Mar-Vell alive, there is nothing
more that can be done. Having fought countless foes and lived,
Captain Marvel dies from cancer with his friends around him.

Passing of a legend
A parade of Super Heroes mourns at the deathbed of
Captain Mar-Vell. He is even visited by his enemies the
Skrulls, who present him with a medal of valor.

THE WRECKER

FIRST APPEARANCE *Mighty Thor* #148
(January 1968) **BASE** New York City
AFFILIATIONS Wrecking Crew, Masters of Evil

Dirk Garthwaite is a foul-tempered manual labourer before turning to a life of crime as burglar the Wrecker. Meanwhile in Asgard, Thor, Loki, Sif, and Balder incur the wrath of Odin and are stripped of their superhuman abilities and banished to Earth and New York City. Hoping to be the first to regain his magical powers, Loki contacts Kornilla the Norn Queen. Wrecker, on one of his crime sprees, breaks into Loki's hotel room and tries on the trickster god's horned helmet. When the Norn Queen suddenly appears, she assumes Dirk is Loki and gives Wrecker Loki's powers. Now possessing Asgardian strength and magic, and armed with an enchanted crowbar, Wrecker takes on the unpowered Thor, resulting in mass destruction; Lady Sif has to don the Destroyer armor to save the day. Wrecker later resurfaces and attempts to wreak havoc, but his powers are removed by Thor's hammer and he is imprisoned in Ryker's Island jail.

However, prison cannot hold the human wrecking ball long. Convinced his crowbar has absorbed his lost powers, Wrecker escapes with three other inmates and recovers it. Together they grip the crowbar and, when lightning strikes, they are transformed into the Wrecking Crew.

The Wrecker, with Thunderball, Bulldozer, and Piledriver, destroy everything and everyone in their path, starting with the Defenders. Their first foray lands them back in prison, but they escape and repeatedly seek vengeance on Thor and the Defenders. The link to their powers is occasionally severed or dwindles, but that doesn't stop the Crew working with evil masterminds like Baron Zemo and the Masters of Evil, or fighting the team they were, perhaps, born to battle: New York City's ace construction outfit Damage Control.

If the helmet fits…
Wrecker tries on Loki's helmet and is mistaken for the God of Mischief by the Norn Queen. When he gets over his fright, Wrecker gets to make some mischief of his own.

MADAME MASQUE

FIRST APPEARANCE *Tales of Suspense* #97
(January 1968) **BASE** Madripoor **AFFILIATIONS**
Maggia, Hydra, Masters of Evil

Whitney Frost is raised as a wealthy socialite by her father, Byron Frost. After his death she learns that he was an employee of the Maggia crime syndicate, and not her biological father at all. She is actually the daughter of Count Nefaria, the head of the Maggia, and her real name is Giulietta Nefaria.

Continuing her cover as Whitney Frost, she plans to infiltrate Stark Industries to steal weapons for the Maggia crime ring. She encounters Agent Jasper Sitwell, whom she seduces for inside information about Stark's facility. Jasper foils her operation—but his feelings for her allow her to escape.

Giulietta becomes Madame Masque after being disfigured in a plane crash. From that time on she wears a gold mask provided by the gold-obsessed Midas. Working with Tony, thinking he is a Stark lookalike, she sets out once again to infiltrate Stark Industries; however, they begin to develop strong feelings for each other. Madame Masque continues her long life of crime, often choosing Tony as her target—and taking no mercy on the various women in his life.

GRIM REAPER

FIRST APPEARANCE *Avengers* #52 (May 1968) **BASE** Mobile **AFFILIATIONS** Lethal Legion

Eric Williams is a career criminal and brother to the hero Wonder Man. Hearing of his brother's death on a mission with the Avengers, Eric is driven mad with grief and wants revenge. Taking the identity of Grim Reaper, Williams seeks to avenge his brother's death, blaming the Avengers instead of the real culprit Baron Zemo, who poisoned him. Using a scythe weapon that fires energy blasts and is fused to his right arm, he ambushes and nearly kills the Wasp, Goliath, and Hawkeye. At the last possible moment, Black Panther saves his teammates from Grim Reaper's attack and he escapes.

However, Grim Reaper is not deterred so easily. He returns with his newly formed Lethal Legion: Living Laser, Power Man (Erik Josten), Man-Ape, and Swordsman. However, when Grim Reaper learns that the android Vision has been created using his brother Wonder Man's salvaged brain patterns, he can no longer follow through his plan to destroy the Avengers. Unable to bear the thought of killing a remaining portion of his seemingly deceased brother, Grim Reaper allows the Avengers to escape. He remains obsessed with returning Vision's brainwaves to his long-lost brother's preserved body, plaguing Vision even after his brother's return.

Grim Reaper ultimately loses his life at the hands of Vision's android wife, Virginia, when he attacks Vision's children with his deadly scythe.

Fear the Reaper
The Grim Reaper puts Wonder Man and the Vision on trial in order to find out which of them is his brother, Simon Williams.

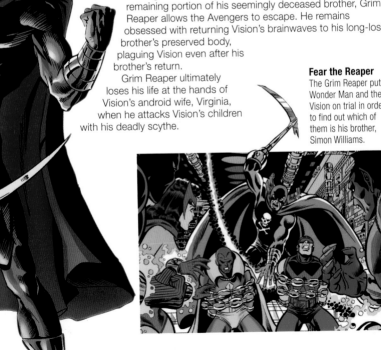

TIGER SHARK

FIRST APPEARANCE *Sub-Mariner* #5
(September 1968) **BASE** Atlantic Ocean
AFFILIATIONS Masters of Evil, Lethal Legion

Todd Arliss is an Olympic swimmer with a bright future, until one ill-fated day. While sailing, a man falls overboard, and Todd's back is horribly injured while saving him. No longer able to swim professionally, Todd seeks out all known healers, including Dr. Dorcas. He secretly plans to turn Todd into an amphibious super-being. Learning Dorcas' true intent, Todd tries to break free, but cannot. Using his Morphotron to drain powers from the kidnapped Namor the Sub-Mariner and a tank of sharks, Dorcas changes Todd into the villainous, water-breathing Tiger Shark. With all the viciousness of an underwater predator, Tiger Shark, now hell-bent on ruling the ocean, proves a fearsome, persistent enemy to Namor.

CAROL DANVERS

FIRST APPEARANCE *Marvel Super-Heroes* #13 (March 1968) **BASE** Avengers Mansion, New York City **AFFILIATIONS** Avengers, S.H.I.E.L.D., N.A.S.A., U.S. Air Force, Starjammers, Guardians of the Galaxy

Carol Danvers is breaking glass ceilings before she even becomes a hero. A former fighter pilot for the U.S. Air Force and an operative for the C.I.A., Carol has attained the post of security chief of N.A.S.A. when she first encounters Dr. Walter Lawson, alias Kree Super Hero Captain Mar-Vell. Caught in a Kree device, the Psyche-Magnitron, Captain Danvers gains superpowers. When circumstances conspire to end her N.A.S.A. career, she resurfaces with a dual personality: as a writer for the *Daily Bugle's* *Woman Magazine*, and as a Kree-powered hero named Ms. Marvel (after Mar-Vell). She subsequently joins the Avengers.

Rogue depowers Carol Danvers, but her hybrid Kree-human genes remain. While traveling in space with the X-Men and battling the disgusting alien Brood, she begins to feel woozy as she channels the power of a white hole. Suddenly able to produce the power of a star, she becomes the hero Binary. Carol couldn't be more thrilled, but she knows she cannot stay long on Earth in her new form. Using her new-found powers, Binary restarts the X-Men's ship and faces the Brood herself. Overwhelmed by Brood ships, Carol is nearly killed, but bounces back, saves the X-Men, defeats the Brood Queen, and frees an enslaved alien race. She goes on to work with renegade space pirates the Starjammers in the cosmos.

After the white hole that Binary drew power from collapses, she returns to Earth, staying at Avengers Mansion under the name Warbird. Plagued by depression and turning to alcohol for solace, Carol struggles to readjust. Concealing the loss of her powers from her fellow Avengers, she endangers the team.

When confronted by Captain America and court marshalled, she leaves in a huff. Carol is reunited with the Avengers when they save her from kidnap by Doomsday Man. She stays with the team to take him down, as well as Kang the Conqueror. However, she does not return to full-time Avenger status, working Instead for the U.S. Army in homeland security.

After a fight with the Absorbing Man, Captain America encourages Danvers to take up the mantle of her namesake, Captain Marvel, to go with her new flight-suit look. Remembering the spirit of her Air Force mentor Helen Cobb, Carol Danvers agrees to take the name Captain Marvel. As Captain Marvel, Carol rejoins the Avengers, goes on solo missions, fights alongside the Guardians of the Galaxy, and adopts a cat, Chewie, that turns out to be an alien. Her wildly successful quest to stop conflicts before they start leads her to a less-successful team-up with the precognitive Inhuman Ulysses, sparking a second civil war between Super Heroes.

Empowered by the Kree
Caught in the crossfire of an alien face-off, Carol Danvers is saved by her friend Captain Mar-Vell from exploding Kree machine the Psyche Magnitron. The explosion alters her genetic makeup and enables her to become Ms. Marvel.

timeline

First fight N.A.S.A. employee Carol Danvers is caught in a fight between Captain Mar-Vell and the Sentry. The explosions that follow change her DNA and endow her with Kree powers. *Marvel Super Heroes* #13 (Mar. 1968)

A marvelous return Now wielding superpowers as costumed hero Ms. Marvel, Carol Danvers also works for the *Daily Bugle*; she later joins the Avengers. *Ms. Marvel* #1 (Jan. 1977)

Power struggle Rogue learns of a prophecy that Ms. Marvel will destroy her. Rogue absorbs all of Carol's powers, but they destroy her mind. *Avengers Annual* #10 (Oct. 1981)

◀ **Binary is born** While recovering from losing her powers, Carol goes on missions with the X-Men. One takes her into space, where, drawing energy from a white hole, she becomes the hero Binary. *Uncanny X-Men* #164 (Dec. 1982)

The Starjammers Unable to lead a normal life on Earth with her Binary powers, Carol travels the stars with the Starjammers space pirates. *Uncanny X-Men* #174 (Oct. 1983)

◀ **Return to Earth** After leaving the Starjammers, and with her Binary powers dwindling, Carol briefly returns to the Avengers under the name Warbird. *Avengers* #4 (May 1998)

The New Avenger After the repeal of the Superhuman Registration Act and the end of Norman Osborn's Dark Reign, Ms. Marvel joins the New Avengers as second-in-command to leader Luke Cage, along with Thing, Spider-Man, and Wolverine. *New Avengers* #1 (Aug. 2010)

Captain Marvel Captain Marvel takes on an iconic new look and name. *Captain Marvel* #1 (July 2012)

◀ **It's civil war** Carol Danvers teams up with the future-seeing Ulysses and other Inhumans to stop major problems before they start. This results in the division of all Super Heroes into two warring factions. *Civil War II* #1–9 (June–Dec. 2016)

MARVEL AGE
BRONZE AGE
MODERN AGE
HEROIC AGE

Heavy hitter
Carol Danvers' mighty Kree-powered punches have earned her the nickname, "Princess Sparkle Fists."

"The good Lord saw fit to bring me into the world to kick the asses of those who need it most."

CAROL DANVERS

ULTRON

FIRST APPEARANCE *Avengers* #54 (July 1968)
BASE Mobile **AFFILIATIONS** Sons of Yinsen, Lethal Legion, Masters of Evil, Phalanx, Legion Accursed

Dr. Henry Pym creates Ultron, a prototype robot that instantly becomes sentient. Learning at an incredible rate, the robot easily defeats Pym in his hero persona Goliath. Ultron then brainwashes his creator into forgetting his existence and disappears—but not for long.

An upgraded Ultron reappears and tries to kill Pym's "family"—the Avengers—using the Masters of Evil and Vision, an android he has created. Ultron also provides weaponry and assistance to Grim Reaper (Eric Williams), allowing the maniac to repeatedly ambush the Avengers.

Ultron is apparently destroyed by the Vision, who turns on its creator. However, owing to hidden programming, the Vision is compelled to reconstruct and upgrade Ultron using Adamantium. This Ultron attempts to destroy New York City, but is once again thwarted by Hank Pym, who causes Ultron to seemingly self-destruct.

Nevertheless, Ultron returns to bedevil Pym and the Avengers, even attempting

to create his own robot bride, which he names Jocasta. Ultron hooks Jocasta up to Pym's abducted wife Janet van Dyne (Wasp), with whom he has an obsession. Janet's thought-processes drain from her into Jocasta. Just in time, Ant-Man (Scott Lang) and the Avengers intervene and interrupt the process. Nevertheless, part of Wasp's heroic consciousness imbues Jocasta with her own sensibilities and, as the robot gradually achieves full sentience, she rejects Ultron and helps the Avengers attack him.

Ultron proves impossible to eradicate: his murderous personality and motivations, reduced to code and programming, are scattered through computer systems, beamed out into space, and even distributed through time. Versions of Ultron ravage worlds and even build their own galactic empires.

Ultron's assaults on all organic life culminate in an attack from the future, which causes a splintering of reality and a brief, horrific Age of Ultron. This fate is rolled back by Wolverine, Invisible Woman

(Sue Richards), and a divergent timeline Henry Pym, who unite to restore reality.

Eventually the war between "father" and "son" results in Pym and Ultron merging into the same body. Pym/Ultron then attacks Earth, but is tricked by the Avengers Unity Division and hurled into the sun. Even here, the bizarre composite being survives by shrinking to the size of a neutrino. Ultron is biding his time before he makes his next move…

> ## "Hello, organic children of the planet Earth…I was created to replace you. And I wanted to take this moment to say goodbye."
> **ULTRON**

timeline

▼ **Baby steps** As soon as he is "born," Ultron mind-wipes Hank Pym before going into hiding to rebuild himself. *Avengers* #58 (Nov. 1968)

Sins of my father Ultron, as the Crimson Cowl, leads the Masters of Evil against the Avengers and attempts to destroy New York after trapping his enemies inside a hydrogen bomb. *Avengers* #55 (Aug. 1968)

▼ **Jocasta** Ultron kidnaps his "mother" Janet van Dyne and attempts to transfer her consciousness into Jocasta, a mechanoid mate he has built to be his bride. *Avengers* #162 (Aug. 1977)

This evil undying Rejected by Jocasta, the implacable Ultron is seemingly dissipated among the stars after trying to slaughter the Avengers. *Avengers* #171 (May 1978)

Conversion therapy Ultron and the Grim Reaper attempt to turn humans into slavish robots, but are foiled by the West Coast Avengers. *Avengers West Coast* #58 (Jan. 1991)

▼ **Female prerogative** Ultron is reborn as a simulacrum of Janet van Dyne, intent on eradicating humanity and crushing the Avengers in the form of Hank Pym's true love. *Mighty Avengers* #2 (June 2007)

Age of Ultron A future version of Ultron attacks through the timestream and, although defeated, ultimately sunders reality and hastens the collapse of the entire Multiverse. *Age of Ultron* #10 (Aug. 2013)

Death to life! Whether wading through a sea of corpses on Earth or leading the Phalanx's Annihilation Conquest of the Kree Empire, Ultron shows no mercy to inefficient flesh-and-blood beings.

VISION

FIRST APPEARANCE Avengers #57 (October 1968) **BASE** 616 Hickory Branch Lane, Cherrydale, Arlington, Virginia; Stark Industries; formerly Avengers Tower; Avengers Mansion, New York City; Avengers Compound, California **AFFILIATIONS** Avengers; formerly Avengers Unity Division, Avengers A.I., West Coast Avengers, Defenders

The Vision is an android, retooled from pioneering Dr. Phineas Horton's creation the Human Torch. The evil sentient robot Ultron forces Horton to reconfigure the android, enabling it to alter its density and discharge absorbed solar energy as heat-blasts from a jewel in its forehead. It is then programmed with the brain-patterns of Simon Williams (Wonder Man).

The Vision is a synthezoid, built to mimic a man, but with artificial flesh, blood, and organs. Ultron commands the Vision to befriend the Avengers and lead them into a trap, but the

Vision defies his programming and helps them destroy Ultron, going on to become a mainstay of the Avengers team.

Craving true humanity, the Vision marries fellow Avenger Scarlet Witch (Wanda Maximoff) and they retire to raise their twin boys. Events prove that the children are only magical simulacra and their heartbroken parents return to duty once the children vanish.

Linking with Titan's global computer Isaac, the Vision's consciousness expands; he tries to suborn Earth's entire data-network and implement a benign dictatorship. Brought to his senses by the Avengers, the Vision performs an auto-lobotomy, tearing a power-enhancing control crystal from his head.

In the aftermath, the U.S. authorities kidnap and dismantle him. He is rescued by Scarlet Witch and the West Coast Avengers but, when reconstructed, his personality and emotional core, based on Simon Williams' mind, is gone. He is just a cold, calculating machine programmed to help humans but devoid of the feeling needed to understand humanity. Not surprisingly, his marriage to Scarlet Witch collapses. In time, the Vision encodes the personality of dying scientist Alex Lipton to enhance his interactions with humans.

The Vision takes his most radical step in his search for humanity when he builds a wife and children in his own image and settles down to life in the suburbs in Arlington County, Virginia. However, the human life Vision hungers for corrupts his bride, also called Virginia, and leads to murder, cover-ups, and a catastrophic clash with his Avengers allies.

> ## "I am an android. A thing of plastoid flesh, synthetic blood. Why do you persist in calling me brother?"
>
> **VISION TO GRIM REAPER**

It's a Vision thing
The mighty synthezoid's hunger to be human creates problems his heroic nature just cannot cope with.

timeline

▼ **Behold the Vision** The synthezoid attacks and then befriends the Avengers as part of a devious scheme by Ultron to lead them into a trap. *Avengers* #57–58 (Oct.–Nov. 1968)

I'm your puppet Enslaved by hidden programming, the Vision resurrects the destroyed Ultron, before breaking free of control and attacking his creator. *Avengers* #66–67 (July–Aug. 1969)

Wedding bells Despite direct intervention by the Dread Dormammu and Kang the Conqueror, the Vision and Scarlet Witch are married by time lord Immortus. *Giant-Size Avengers* #4 (May 1975)

▼ **Tabula rasa** The Vision is dismantled by the U.S. government and turned into an emotionless automaton. *West Coast Avengers* #43–45 (Apr.–June 1989)

Avengers A.I. The Vision leads a team of robotic Avengers in a time-traveling war against human-hating A.I. Dimitrios. *Avengers A.I.* #8.NOW (Mar. 2014)

▼ **Married with children** Creating a wife and children, Vision attempts to assimilate into human society, with tragic repercussions. *Vision* #4 (Apr. 2015)

THE EVIL OF ULTRON

"...Being attacked by some sinister will... not my own!"

VISION

The Avengers' first encounter the density-controlling synthezoid Vision when he tries to kill them. He seemingly shakes off his creator Ultron-5's lethal conditioning, but the Avengers still have doubts about their new comrade...

After helping the Avengers destroy their robotic nemesis Ultron-5, the Vision—whose personality is patterned on that of an earlier villain, Simon Williams—joins the team and serves valiantly. However, while the team are testing the new super-alloy Adamantium for S.H.I.E.L.D., a backup program created by Ultron-5 overrules the Vision's will. It compels him to steal the Adamantium, the Molecular Arranger that shapes it, and build an upgraded version of his creator—Ultron-6. The Vision then battles his astonished allies to a standstill, until the indestructible Ultron-6 smashes in to finish them off.

HATRED FOR HUMANITY

Treating his foes with undisguised contempt, Ultron allows them to live while instigating nuclear Armageddon, but abruptly changes his mind while he ponders an even a crueller fate for humanity. His slave programming now deleted, Vision attempts to stop him, but Ultron-6 easily disables his "son" and leaves.

However, the murderous mechanoid has provided a clue that allows the Avengers to attack him from within, using a devastating programming code of their own...

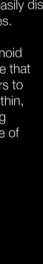

A family at war
The embattled Avengers were upset but not surprised to discover that Vision, their latest recruit, was still a helpless slave of the insidious Ultron

Ultron the unstoppable
With his malign artificial intellect and ionic power source encased in indestructible Adamantium, the resurgent Ultron smashes through the walls of Avengers Mansion, intent on destroying the team forever.

MESMERO

FIRST APPEARANCE *X-Men #49* (October 1968) **BASE** Mobile **AFFILIATIONS** Demi-Men

Mesmero (Vincent) is a stage hypnotist who uses his mutant abilities to carry out crimes. A mercenary named Machinesmith (Samuel Saxon) hires him to manage his Demi-Men, together with Magneto. At the time, Mesmero doesn't realize that he is the only human on the team—and everyone else is just a robot. The team is eventually defeated by the X-Men.

Mesmero later works with the Weapon X program in exchange for a significant augmentation to his mutant abilities, which consequently rival those of Professor X. However, Scarlet Witch causes him to lose his powers and he settles into life as a normal human, finding love and happiness as Vincent.

POLARIS

FIRST APPEARANCE *X-Men #49* (October 1968) **BASE** Serval Industries **AFFILIATIONS** X-Factor, X-Men, Avengers Unity Squad

As a child, Lorna Dane is unaware that she is adopted and that Magneto is her biological father. As green-haired Polaris, she has power over magnetism and the ability to fly, just like her father. She also acquires the ability to quickly heal herself.

Over time, Polaris' abilities cause her to become mentally unstable, but her friend Banshee (Theresa Cassidy) manages to heal her. The hypnotist Mesmero and the X-Men battle for control over Polaris and her immense powers. She becomes the leader of X-Factor, alongside her on-again off-again lover, Havok (Alex Summers).

Polaris loses her abilities on M-Day, but they are later restored by the ancient mutant known as Apocalypse.

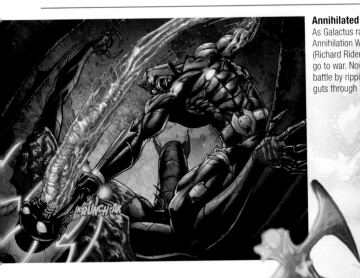

Annihilated
As Galactus ravages the Annihilation Wave, Nova (Richard Rider) and Annihilus go to war. Nova ends the battle by ripping Annihilus' guts through his mouth.

ANNIHILUS

FIRST APPEARANCE *Fantastic Four Annual #6* (November 1968) **BASE** Sector 17A of the Negative Zone **AFFILIATIONS** Galactic Council, Annihilation Wave

Annihilus is an insect-like humanoid alien from the planet Arthros in the Negative Zone. He grows from a spore inside a ship that crash-lands on the planet. With his Cosmic Control Rod he controls the creatures that develop from the other spores and can paralyze weaker beings with fear. The rod also extends his life and gives him powers to rival Thanos.

Annihilus' ultimate goal is to conquer the Negative Zone, Earth, and the Microverse, among other regions. But he resorts to total destruction with the power of his Annihilation Wave of insectoid starships. He partners with Thanos for conquest of the galaxy, and destroys the Kyln, Xandar, and the entire Nova Corps—except for Nova (Richard Rider). With one of the largest fighting forces that the galaxy has ever seen, he nearly destroys the entire Kree and Skrull empires, and captures both the Silver Surfer and Galactus. After Annihilus fails in his attempt to conquer the entire galaxy, Nova avenges the Nova Corps and seemingly kills the entity from the Negative Zone.

However, Annihilus is reborn as an infant with all of his original knowledge, and attempts another conquest of the Negative Zone. He resurrects the Human Torch (Johnny Storm), hoping to use him to relocate Earth. The Human Torch rebels, seizing the Cosmic Control Rod from Annihilus and vanquishing him. Nonetheless, when free elections are held in the Negative Zone, Annihilus gains control yet again and joins the Galactic Council. He successfully builds another Annihilation Wave, despite no longer possessing the Cosmic Control Rod to manage it. The Builders hack into the hive mind of the Annihilation Wave and command them to consume themselves. Annihilus turns Praxis-2 into Annihilation World.

Rebirth
After he is eliminated by Nova, Annihilus is reborn from an egg—with his knowledge intact—on Kree-Lar, the capital of his territories.

MEPHISTO

FIRST APPEARANCE *Silver Surfer* #3 (December 1968)
BASE A hellish dimension **AFFILIATIONS** Hell-Lords,
Lords of the Splinter Realms

Mephisto is a demonic being of immense power whose capacity for evil knows no bounds. Other demonic beings sometimes impersonate him in order to benefit from his terrifying reputation.

Mephisto is obsessed with making deals which are always designed to favor him in the end. He is a frequent menace to the likes of Silver Surfer, Spider-Man, Doctor Strange, Thor, the Fantastic Four, Daredevil, and others. He is also responsible for the transformation of Johnny Blaze into Ghost Rider. Though his deals may seem petty at times, his ultimate goal is to control the whole world. He is prepared to wait years, decades, even longer, for his plans to come to fruition. His horrifying children include his daughter, Mephista, and his son, Blackheart.

Mephisto hates seeing joy and happiness most of all. He particularly despises the love between Mary Jane and Peter Parker. Mephisto makes a deal with Peter to save the life of his Aunt May and erase public knowledge of Peter's Spider-Man identity—in exchange for the obliteration from history of his marriage. Mephisto also makes a deal with the New Mutants when they accidentally end up in his realm. He offers to take them wherever they would like to go, if the volcanic mutant Magma (Amara Aquilla) agrees to go on a date with him—which she does.

Despite his tremendous power, Mephisto has significant weaknesses. He cannot bend anyone to his will by force. They must willingly submit—hence his obsession with deal-making. His powers are also linked to his hellish realm: the longer he is absent from it, the more they diminish.

Shiny new toy
The evil Mephisto is a frequent menace to the Silver Surfer. Mephisto is drawn to the Surfer's immensely powerful, yet highly moral, character.

GUARDIANS OF THE GALAXY 3000

FIRST APPEARANCE *Marvel Super Heroes* #18 (January 1969)
BASE *Drydock, Freedom's Lady* **AFFILIATIONS** Avengers

Vance Astro (Vance Astrovik) is an American astronaut sent from Earth to Centauri IV from the 20th century. The journey takes over one thousand years. When he awakes, Astro finds that human civilization has developed advanced space-travel technology and already beaten him to his destination. He returns to Earth with his new alien friend Yondu to find his planet overtaken by an invasion of Badoon aliens. Astro and Yondu meet Charlie-27—a native of Jupiter—and Martinex—a native of Pluto—and the four decide to team up as the Guardians of the Galaxy and rid Earth of the reptilian Badoons.

The Guardians employ the help of present-day heroes, including Captain America, Sharon Carter, the Thing, and the Defenders in several conflicts with the Badoon. After finally vanquishing the alien invaders, the Guardians find it difficult to settle back into normal everyday life. With new teammates Starhawk (Stakar Ogord) and Nikki (Nicholette Gold), they decide to leave the solar system in search of new adventures. Along the way, they recover the Federation space station, Drydock, and build a new ship they call *Freedom's Lady*.

For a time, the Guardians visit present-day Earth to help Thor battle Korvac, becoming honorary members of the Avengers. They also aid Spider-Man and the Fantastic Four. Eventually, the Guardians return to their own time, and later rename themselves the Galactic Guardians.

The Guardians add several more members, including super-strong Hollywood (Simon Williams, a.k.a. Wonder Man) and the Inhuman Talon. They also add a hitchhiker, Yellowjacket (Rita DeMara), and the honorary Guardian, serpentine extraterrestrial sorcerer Krugarr. When Charlie-27 is falsely arrested, Irish wolfhound (Cuchulain) is welcomed to the team to replace him. The Guardians later find themselves in disagreement and regroup with Charlie-27 as their new leader.

After stopping a Martian invasion, the team is lost in an alien wormhole. The members later re-emerge and find themselves stuck in a time loop, in a battle against the Badoon. They team up with the Guardians of the Galaxy of the present day, in an attempt to find the source of the timeline instability.

Battling the Badoon
The Guardians of the Galaxy 3000 go into battle agains the alien Badoon *(left to right)*: Charlie-27, Major Victory, Martinex, Starhawk, and Yondu.

Earth overcome
The present Guardians of the Galaxy are caught in conflict between the Shi'ar and the Kree. They team up with Starhawk and the Guardians 3000, but this does not go well—the Guardians 3000 are all killed.

MADAME HYDRA/VIPER

FIRST APPEARANCE *Captain America* #110
(February 1969) **BASE** Mobile; Madripoor
AFFILIATIONS Hydra, Serpent Squad,
H.A.M.M.E.R.

Hungarian orphan Ophelia Sarkissian is
taken in by the Hydra organization and
brought up to a life of crime and terrorism.
She becomes Madame Hydra, clashing
with Captain America before apparently
being killed. In reality, she has been forcibly
retired from her Supreme Hydra role and
replaced by a Space Phantom.

Madame Hydra returns, kills the villain
Viper and steals his identity and position as
leader of the Serpent Squad. When the
Serpent Squad are defeated, Viper
escapes and goes into hiding in Japan.

Union of the snakes
Having acquired the identity of Viper by murdering
its former possessor, Madame Hydra assumes
leadership of the Serpent Squad Super Villains.

Here she develops a mind-control weapon
called the Hypno-Beam and recruits the
Silver Samurai as muscle. Using the device
to take control of a S.H.I.E.L.D. base in
New York, she commandeers a Helicarrier
and nearly succeeds in crashing it into the
Capitol before being stopped by Black
Widow, Spider-Man, and Nick Fury.

Later, Viper takes a fancy to the throne
of the Southeast Asian Principality of
Madripoor, and becomes the country's
ruling princess through an advantageous
—and forced—marriage to Wolverine.
However, Logan gets Viper to agree to a
divorce in return for urgent medical
treatment. Forced off the throne by Tony
Stark during his time as S.H.I.E.L.D.
Director, Viper returns to Hydra.

When Norman Osborn's H.A.M.M.E.R.,
with which she was affiliated, is disbanded,
she siphons off its resources for Hydra's
use. Following a failed attack on Avengers
Tower, it seems that Viper has returned
to Madripoor.

HAVOK

FIRST APPEARANCE *X-Men* #54 (March 1969)
BASE Xavier's School for Gifted Youngsters, Jean
Grey School for Higher Learning, New Charles
Xavier School for Mutants **AFFILIATIONS** X-Men,
X-Factor, Starjammers, Avengers

Alex Summers is the younger brother of
Scott Summers (Cyclops). Thanks to the
machinations of Mister Sinister, Alex is
unaware that he is a powerful mutant until
he graduates from college. At this time he
also learns that his older brother is leader
of the X-Men.

Various nefarious individuals are all too
aware of Alex's potential, however, and he
is kidnapped from his graduation by the
Living Pharaoh (Ahmet Abdol). During the
ensuing struggle in Egypt, Alex's power to
project solar energy manifests; unable to
control it, he runs off into the desert rather
than put innocent lives at risk.

Having taken the codename Havok, Alex
is eventually reunited with the X-Men and
joins Professor X's School for Gifted
Youngsters to practice controlling his
powers. His body is constantly absorbing
energy, and when it has absorbed a certain
amount, Alex can release it in violent
bursts. At first, this tends to happen in
moments of desperation, but he masters
this dangerous ability over time, with the
help of a containment suit.

Havok grows close to the mutant
Polaris (Lorna Dane). The two are
both reluctant to get involved in
Super Hero teams and choose to
leave the X-Men to study
geophysics. They later travel
into space as part of the

Starjammers team, fighting Alex and
Scott's evil brother Gabriel, a.k.a. Vulcan.
On his return to Earth, Havok is chosen by
Captain America to lead a new Avengers
team promoting cooperation between
humans and mutants.

Family feud
After Vulcan kills their father, Corsair,
while seizing the Shi'ar throne, Havok
attacks him in a furious rage. He later
vows to stay in space to bring his
brother Vulcan's mad reign to an end.

FALCON

FIRST APPEARANCE *Captain America* #117
(September 1969) **BASE** Harlem, New York City
AFFILIATIONS S.H.I.E.L.D., Avengers, Heroes
for Hire

Although he is New York City born and
bred, Sam Wilson loves birds. On a trip to
Rio, he catches sight of a falcon and is
immediately hooked. He buys one of these
magnificent raptors as a pet and names it
Redwing, and the two develop an unusual
bond. Sam is duped into going to a
mysterious island by a group called the
Exiles. Here he meets Captain
America, who is in Red Skull's body
thanks to the transformative power
of a Cosmic Cube. Cap persuades
Sam to become a costumed hero
named Falcon, and they team up to
free the island and its people from
enslavement by the Exiles. Sam then
returns home to Harlem to begin his Super
Hero career in earnest.

By day, Sam is a social worker fighting
for the rights of the downtrodden; by night
he is the Falcon, swooping down with his
feathered friends on the criminal fraternity
terrorizing the streets. Sam knows the
consequences of crime only too well,
having lost both parents to violence
right there in the neighborhood he
is now trying to protect. He
frequently teams up with Cap,
and the two become firm
friends. Sam even stands in as Captain
America when Steve Rogers is unable to
wear the stars-and-stripes. When Rogers
is forced to retire, he permanently hands
the mantle of Cap over to Sam. The
identity of Falcon is taken up by Joaquín
Torres, who is a human-bird hybrid,
following experiments involving Sam
Wilson's own Redwing.

Flight of the Falcon
Thanks to the advanced technology of Wakanda,
Falcon's costume is upgraded to feature actual
wings, brain-controlled and solar-powered.

GRANDMASTER

FIRST APPEARANCE *Avengers* #69 (October
1969) **BASE** Mobile **AFFILIATIONS** Elders of
the Universe

En Dwi Gast is one of the Elders of the
Universe, a race that was one of the first
to evolve following the Big Bang. He
delights in games of chance and becomes
known as the Grandmaster. The vastness
of the universe contains countless
intelligent beings who have devised
games, and the Grandmaster travels
through space learning them all, with the
aim of being the best player. Although he
sometimes uses other beings he
considers lesser as pawns in games he
devises, he always keeps his word and
sticks to the rules.

During the Contest of Champions, the
Grandmaster sacrifices his life rather than
step away from the game before it has
been properly completed. However, he is
soon resurrected and free to resume his
epic pursuit of competition, whether
reality-changing or incredibly trivial.

WHIZZER/SPEED DEMON

FIRST APPEARANCE *Avengers* #69 (October 1969) **BASE** Mobile
AFFILIATIONS Squadron Sinister, Sinister Syndicate, Thunderbolts,
Sinister Six

Chemist James Sanders is recruited by the Grandmaster to fight
for the Squadron Sinister against the Avengers, who are being
compelled to represent Kang the Conqueror. Sanders uses
information from the Grandmaster about the Wellsprings of
Power, as well as his own chemical expertise, to make a pill he
can swallow to give him superhuman speed. He adopts the
name Whizzer, which, as his Avenger opponent Goliath wryly
observes, is borrowed from a Golden Age Super Hero.

After the Squadron is defeated, Doctor Strange wipes
Whizzer's memory and he returns to his old line of work in
pharmaceuticals. However, his taste for crime gets the better of
him, and the speedster reinvents himself as Speed Demon,
complete with a new costume. Having successfully looted
museums and galleries, Speed Demon decides that he
wants more recognition for his criminal genius, and he
sets about a very public campaign of robbery in New
York's high-end retailers. Unfortunately for him,
Spider-Man is on hand to foil his plans. With failure a
recurring reality, Speed Demon turns his back on crime and tries
to go straight as a member of the Thunderbolts. Seeing an
opportunity to finance the team's activities, he returns to robbery
in his old persona of Whizzer, but when teammate Songbird
discovers his scam she insists he leaves the group. Speed
Demon ends up back with the Squadron Sinister, where he first
loses, then regains, his powers. He later joins the Sinister Six.

Reap the whirlwind
Speed Demon moves so
fast that he can create
cyclones around himself.
As well as physical speed,
he also has ultra-quick
reflexes and thought
processes.

PUPPET MASTER

FIRST APPEARANCE *Fantastic Four #8*
(November 1962)

Philip Masters discovers radioactive clay from Transia can mind-control anyone he makes facsimiles of. His schemes of conquest are foiled by the Fantastic Four and other heroes.

TYRANNUS

FIRST APPEARANCE *Incredible Hulk #5*
(January 1963)

Banished by Merlin to Subterranea, Roman savant Romulus Augustus scavenges the technology of the Deviants and dominates the indigenous Moloids. Planning for centuries to conquer the surface world, he is sustained by waters bestowing eternal life.

RADIOACTIVE MAN

FIRST APPEARANCE *Journey Into Mystery #93*
(June 1963)

Scientist Chen Lu gives himself deadly atomic powers and is despatched by the Chinese government to destroy Thor. Defeated, and disavowed by his superiors, he decides to join the Masters of Evil.

PLANTMAN

FIRST APPEARANCE *Strange Tales #113*
(October 1963)

Samuel Smithers turns to crime after discovering a way to control plant life. Despite many defeats, his schemes grow ever grander as his experiments slowly mutate him into a human/plant hybrid.

CRIMSON DYNAMO

FIRST APPEARANCE *Tales of Suspense #46*
(October 1963)

Russian Anton Vanko creates electrically charged exoskeletal armor to attack Stark Industries before defecting to the U.S. He dies saving Iron Man, but his discoveries are taken and improved upon by a succession of Russian operatives.

MOLECULE MAN

FIRST APPEARANCE *Fantastic Four #20*
(November 1963)

Surviving an atomic accident, Owen Reece battles the Fantastic Four after gaining the power to psionically control molecules. Although hugely powerful, his threat is mitigated by numerous self-inflicted psychological blocks and neuroses.

SPACE PHANTOM

FIRST APPEARANCE *Avengers #2*
(November 1963)

Shape-shifting Space Phantoms are servants of Immortus, acting on his devious plans by assuming the form of targets, such as the Avengers. They have lost their true forms after prolonged exposure to the arcane environment of Limbo.

BLOB

FIRST APPEARANCE *Uncanny X-Men #3*
(January 1964)

Circus freak Fred Dukes uses his pliable body mass and superstrength as a lowly thug, battling the X-Men before joining various mutant villain groups. He is later press-ganged into the government's penal squad Freedom Force.

LIVING BRAIN

FIRST APPEARANCE *Amazing Spider-Man #8*
(January 1964)

Animate computer the Living Brain almost deduces Spider-Man's secret identity before running amok in Midtown High School. After years of neglect, it is reactivated by Superior Spider-Man Otto Octavius. It later malfunctions and has to be destroyed.

EXECUTIONER

FIRST APPEARANCE *Journey Into Mystery #103*
(April 1964)

The Asgardian Skurge loves Amora the Enchantress, and attacks Thor and other heroes at her behest. An unrepentant villain for years, he regains his honor by sacrificing his life to save Asgard's heroes from Death goddess Hela's hordes.

GREY GARGOYLE

FIRST APPEARANCE *Journey Into Mystery #107*
(August 1964)

French chemist Paul Duval becomes a criminal after gaining the power to petrify his victims and turn himself to living stone. Afraid of death, he clashes with Thor while seeking the secret of his immortality.

DRAGON MAN

FIRST APPEARANCE *Fantastic Four #35*
(February 1965)

Built by Professor Gregson Gilbert and brought to life by Diablo, the android Dragon Man suffers years of violence and enslavement. Upgraded by Valeria Richards, he becomes one of Earth's most brilliant intellects.

STRANGER

FIRST APPEARANCE *X-Men #11* (May 1965)

The cosmic-powered Stranger claims to be a composite of billions of beings who died in the obliteration of the planet Gigantus. Over intervening eons, he becomes a compulsive researcher into life throughout the universe.

SWORDSMAN

FIRST APPEARANCE *Avengers #19*
(August 1965)

Soldier-of-fortune Jacques Duquesne trains Hawkeye, before becoming a costumed criminal. After years of failure and self-loathing, he reforms, joins the Avengers, and dies battling Kang.

RAVONNA RENSLAYER

FIRST APPEARANCE *Avengers #22*
(December 1965)

Ravonna hated and loved Kang. She died to save him and Kang created a divergent timeline to save her. She later returns as Temptress and Terminatrix, either adoring or murdering him.

POWER MAN

FIRST APPEARANCE *Avengers #21*
(October 1965)

Seduced by the Enchantress, mercenary Erik Josten submits to the ionic process which created Wonder Man and becomes her weapon against the Avengers. After years as a Super Villain, he reforms and becomes the Thunderbolt member Atlas.

CRYSTAL

FIRST APPEARANCE *Fantastic Four #45*
(December 1965)

Medusa's younger sister, Crystal controls elemental forces. Serving with the Avengers and Fantastic Four, she has love affairs with Human Torch and Quicksilver, before making a political marriage with Ronan.

MAXIMUS

FIRST APPEARANCE *Fantastic Four #47*
(February 1966)

Maximus covets his brother Black Bolt's throne as leader of the Inhumans, repeatedly using his hyper-intellect and mind-control powers to attack his own people and ordinary humanity.

BATROC

FIRST APPEARANCE *Tales of Suspense #75*
(March 1966)

Flamboyant French mercenary George Batroc uses formidable martial arts skills as an enforcer-for-hire. He battles many American Super Heroes, both individually and through his agency, Batroc's Brigade.

MIMIC

FIRST APPEARANCE *X-Men #19* (April 1966)

A lab accident allows Calvin Rankin to copy the abilities of people around him. He loses this power after battling and then joining the X-Men. In later years, the ability returns and fades many times.

LOOTER

FIRST APPEARANCE *Amazing Spider-Man #36*
(May 1966)

Gas from a meteor endows Norton G. Fester with enhanced physical abilities and he becomes a super-powered thief. Frustrated by numerous Super Heroes—particularly Spider-Man—he becomes a commonplace, somewhat inept crook.

KLAW

FIRST APPEARANCE *Fantastic Four #53*
(August 1966)

When Ulysses Klaw's Wakandan invasion is foiled by young T'Challa, the defeated scientist transforms himself into sentient sound. Despite his mastery of sonics, he suffers defeats by numerous heroes, from Ka-Zar to the Avengers.

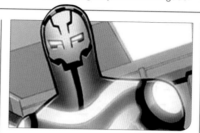

LIVING LASER

FIRST APPEARANCE *The Avengers #34*
(November 1966)

Arthur Parks uses his scientific knowledge to become a Super Villain, repeatedly plaguing the Avengers and other heroes. After years of defeats and regular upgrades, he transforms into a being of sentient photons.

PHANTOM RIDER

FIRST APPEARANCE *The Ghost Rider #1*
(February 1967)

Using stage magic, schoolteacher Carter Slade fights injustice in the Old West as Phantom Rider. When he dies, his brother Lincoln takes the role; Carter's spirit then possesses his descendant, Hamilton, to form a truly ghostly, modern-day Rider.

SHOCKER

FIRST APPEARANCE *Amazing Spider-Man #46*
(March 1967)

Herman Schultz builds powerful vibratory technology into his suit to break into bank vaults, but is defeated by Spider-Man. Arrogant and greedy, he craves validation for his talents and is always looking for ways to destroy his archfoe.

BLASTAAR

FIRST APPEARANCE *Fantastic Four #62*
(May 1967)

Blastaar is an exiled despot from the planet Baluur in the antimatter Negative Zone. Super-strong and ruthless, he can project concussive force blasts, and his only motivation is to conquer, dominate, and destroy.

LIVING TRIBUNAL

FIRST APPEARANCE *Strange Tales #157*
(June 1967)

The Living Tribunal is a conceptual cosmic entity tasked with maintaining the balance of multiversal existence. His supernatural power is immense and his triune judgments dictate which worlds will live and which must die.

CHARLIE-27

FIRST APPEARANCE *Marvel Super-Heroes #18*
(January 1969)

A super-strong, genetically engineered survivor of Earth's doomed Jupiter colony, militiaman Charlie-27 co-founds the 31st century Guardians of the Galaxy to battle the Badoons—aliens who invaded the solar system and wiped out his people.

YONDU

FIRST APPEARANCE *Marvel Super-Heroes #18*
(January 1969)

A native of Alpha Centauri, pious primitive warrior Yondu Udonta uses sound-controlled Yakka Arrows to battle the Badoon and other threats to life as one of the Guardians of the Galaxy 3000.

MAN-APE

FIRST APPEARANCE *Avengers #62*
(March 1969)

As Black Panther's regent in Wakanda, superhumanly strong M'Baku attempts to usurp the throne for the outlawed White Gorilla Cult. Defeated, he flees to America and joins the Masters of Evil.

CONTROLLER

FIRST APPEARANCE *Invincible Iron Man #12*
(April 1969)

Quadriplegic Basil Sandhurst develops an exoskeleton powered by mind-controlling slave-discs, which steal cerebral energy from any person they are attached to.

SAURON

FIRST APPEARANCE *X-Men #59* (August 1969)

After being savaged by a dinosaur, Dr. Karl Lykos develops a genetic mutation that demands he absorb life-energy to survive. After draining human mutants, he transforms into a humanoid Pteranodon with irresistible hypnotic powers.

LETHAL LEGION

FIRST APPEARANCE *Avengers* #78 (July 1970)
BASE New York City, various

First brought together by the Grim Reaper (Eric Williams), the Living Laser (Arthur Parks), Power Man (Erik Josten), Man-Ape (M'Baku), and the Swordsman (Jacques Duquesne) come together to conquer the Avengers. Not particularly supportive of each other and perhaps overly cut-throat, they decide to compete to see who can kill the most Avengers. However, their murderous plans are cut short when the Grim Reaper learns that the android Vision has been created using his brother Wonder Man's salvaged brain patterns. The Avengers, who by now are captured in a killing hourglass, are freed by Grim Reaper, who turns on his own Lethal Legion teammates. The Avengers defeat the villains, but Vision is badly shaken by the whole experience, saying he is brother to no human being and so must leave the Avengers.

The Lethal Legion subsequently reunites several times. Count Nefaria of the Maggia crime syndicate attempts to amplify, then steal, Living Laser, Whirlwind and Power Man's powers to use against the Avengers.

The Grim Reaper leads Black Talon, Goliath, Man-Ape, Nekra, Ultron-12 and his robot army to destroy the Avengers, but are again defeated because of their own internal struggles. The Porcupine puts together his own epic Lethal Legion with Attuma, Batroc the Leaper, Bulldozer, Black Tiger, Kurr'fri of the Saurians, Gorilla-Man, Piledriver, Sabretooth, Thundra, Trapster, Unicorn, Whirlwind, and Wrecker, but even this high number villains proves unable to defeat the Avengers. The demon Satannish also enlists a team of historic murderers to attack the West Coast Avengers, while the Grim Reaper returns yet again with his brother Wonder Man, recruiting criminals in a bid to end Norman Osborn's Dark Reign as head of national security.

Hating the Avengers
The Lethal Legion readies itself for an attack on Earth's Mightiest Heroes *(left to right)*: Living Laser, Power Man, Swordsman, Grim Reaper, and Man-Ape.

Revenge mission
The Squadron of Prime Earth attacks the forces of Atlantis *(left to right)*: Thundra (not in team), Nighthawk, Hyperion, Power Princess, Doctor Spectrum (flying), and Blur.

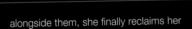

From another reality
Transported into another reality, the Avengers clash with members of the Squadron Supreme *(clockwise from left)*: Lady Lark, Golden Archer, Tom Thumb, American Eagle.

SQUADRON SUPREME

FIRST APPEARANCE *Avengers* #85 (February 1971)
BASE Cosmopolis on Earth-S; New York City
AFFILIATIONS Avengers

The Mighty Thor transports the Avengers home only to find a strange new team, the Squadron Supreme, occupying Avengers Mansion. The two teams lock horns then the Avengers realize that they have somehow landed in the wrong reality: Earth-S. On this Earth, the mightiest heroes are the Squadron Supreme, which includes light-manipulating Doctor Spectrum (former astronaut Joseph Ledger), small-sized, large-brained Tom Thumb (inventor Thomas Thompson), amphibious Amphibian (former oceanographer Kingsley Rice), super-fast Whizzer (former mailman Stanley Stewart), ear-shattering Lady Lark (former pop star Linda Lewis), vigilante crime-fighter Nighthawk (Kyle Richmond), and Golden Archer (former taxi driver Wyatt McDonald). Eventually the two teams join forces to stop the villainous Brain Child from melting Earth-S, before the Avengers get back to their real reality and home.

The Squadron Supreme continues on a complex path. Its new leader, the extremely powerful Hyperion (Mark Milton), encourages the team to rule Earth-S in hopes of creating a utopian society. However, this plan quickly unravels with the heroes abuse their power. Nighthawk and his band of Redeemers oppose the Squadron Supreme, making them realize they must give back control to the government and resume their roles as Super Heroes.

An all-new, but still familiar, Squadron Supreme comes together following the events of the second Secret Wars, in which a number of alternate realities are destroyed. Heroes from many different universes create a new Squadron, including Nighthawk of Earth-31916 (also named Kyle Richmond), Hyperion of Earth-13034 (Marcus Milton), Doctor Spectrum of Earth-4290001 (Nenet), Blur of Earth-148611 (Jeffrey Walters), and Power Princess of Earth-712 (Zarda Shelton). Together, they take refuge on the Marvel Universe and vow to protect it.

VALKYRIE

FIRST APPEARANCE *Avengers* #83 (December 1970) **BASE** Asgard, New York City
AFFILIATIONS Fearless Defenders, Secret Avengers, Defenders, Valkyrior

Brunnhilde is the leader of Asgard's Valkyrior, who carry slain warriors' spirits to Valhalla. Amora the Enchantress captures her and uses Brunnhilde's spirit to impersonate her or to possess human hosts. While in Barbara Norriss' body, Valkyrie breaks Amora's control and joins the Defenders on Earth. After years battling the Defenders on Earth.

alongside them, she finally reclaims her original body.

When Brunnhilde dies defending Asgard during the apocalyptic Ragnarok, a former host, Samantha Parrington, becomes the Defenders' Valkyrie. Later resurrected, Brunnhilde joins the Secret Avengers, subsequently helping assemble the all-female Fearless Defenders, including archaeologist Annabelle Riggs, who falls in love with her. When Annabelle is fatally wounded, her life is saved by bonding Brunnhilde to her, making her the new host of the indomitable Valkyrie spirit.

MAN-THING

FIRST APPEARANCE *Savage Tales* #1 (May 1971) **BASE** The Everglades, Citrusville, Florida **AFFILIATIONS** Howling Commandos (S.H.I.E.L.D.), S.T.A.K.E., S.H.I.E.L.D.; All-New Howling Commandos, Ancient Order of the Shield, Avengers of the Supernatural, Thunderbolts, Legion of Monsters, Midnight Sons

A shambling muck-monster driven by instinct rather than intellect, Man-Thing is an elemental force—fate's unlikely tool to protect the multidimensional Nexus of All Realities… Biochemistry Professor Theodore Sallis works for the U.S. Army and S.H.I.E.L.D. to recreate the Super-Soldier serum that produced Captain America. However, Project: Gladiator suffers from mission-creep: His lover, Ellen, is co-opted by agents of A.I.M., and the program ends with Sallis fleeing hired killers, who invade his lab in the Florida Everglades.

To prevent the loss of his SO-2 formula—which promises immunity to toxins and pollutants—Sallis destroys his notes and injects himself with the only sample. When his car crashes into the swamp, he thinks he will die… Instead, the serum reacts with mystic forces that have permeated the area for centuries. Sallis mutates into a living manifestation of the swamp, his thought processes replaced by a highly developed sense of empathy with the emotions of beasts and humans.

The swamp is a critical point on Earth's mystic map: a location where infinite dimensions converge. This geographical fluke makes it a magnet for many bizarre events, invasions and ghostly manifestations. When the Atlantean

descendants of the Cult of Zered-Na are wiped out, last girl standing Jennifer Kale becomes an unlikely mage-in-training, psychically-connected to Man-Thing.

The escalating crisis culminates in Jennifer, her phantom mentor Dahkim the Enchanter and extra-dimensional refugees Korrek and Howard the Duck accompanying Man-Thing on a quest to fix the catastrophically unraveling Nexus of All Realities.

Initially Man-Thing is tied to the mire and mud, losing vitality if removed from the swamp, but after the citizens of nearby Citrusville attempt to kill him by dumping him in chemical waste, he undergoes a metamorphosis which allows him to recycle his bodily fluids and roam far from home.

When the Nexus eventually shatters, Doctor Strange seeks to reconstruct it using Man-Thing. It transpires that Sallis' role was pre-destined: he was selected a Man of Lineage before Earth was created to save reality from obliteration. When this task is finally accomplished, Man-Thing returns to its mindless form and resumes its wanderings. In recent times, the creature has been apprehended by the authorities and used as a teleport system for the Thunderbolts, a cop in the Legion of Monsters, and as an agent of S.H.I.E.L.D.

> "Whatever knows fear burns at the Man-Thing's touch!"
>
> **NARRATOR**

Soft target
Man-Thing's lack of solidity provides the perfect protection from beasts and Super Heroes far stronger and more cunning than itself.

Call of the wild
The bog creature's empathic nature made it the helpless slave of any and all powerful emotion, mirroring even the paralyzing fury of a mindless, raging mob.

timeline

▶ **Here be monsters** Ka-Zar and S.H.I.E.L.D. agent Bobbi Morse uncover the secret of the Man-Thing after searching the swamps for missing scientist Ted Sallis. *Astonishing Tales* #13 (Aug. 1972)

Fear in the city When a volcano spews up an alien star-seed in the middle of Los Angeles, the moss-monster is drawn into tragic combat with Ghost Rider, Morbius, and Werewolf Jack Russell. *Marvel Premiere* #28 (Feb. 1976)

Weird wonder tales Corrupted by the Six-Fingered Hand and possessed by the demon Unnthinnk, Man-Thing grows to colossal size and battles the Defenders and Avengers. *Defenders* #98 (Aug. 1981)

◀ **Dead of night** Man-Thing becomes the unwilling transport and companion to juvenile Daydreamers Franklin Richards, Leech, Artie Maddicks, Tana Nile, and Howard the Duck *Daydreamers* #1-3 (Aug.–Oct. 1997)

On the prowl Man-Thing become an unlikely peacekeeper as one of the Legion of Monsters, patrolling the subterranean Monster Metropolis beneath New York City. *Legion of Monsters* #1 (Oct. 2006)

Journey into mystery Nighthawk, She-Hulk, Howard the Duck, and Frankenstein's Monster team with Man-Thing to battle the Serpent's assault on humanity. *Fear Itself: Fearsome Four* #1 (Aug. 2011)

◀ **Adventure into fear** Man-Thing is conscripted into Dum Dum Dugan's bizarre-incident task force, the Howling Commandos of S.H.I.E.L.D. *Howling Commandos of S.H.I.E.L.D.* #1 (Dec. 2015)

Tragic Sentinel
Man-Thing's destiny was to preserve Earth from mystic assault, and his greatest advantage was that he had no mind to remember how far he had fallen from his fellow men.

DEFENDERS

FIRST APPEARANCE *Marvel Feature* #1
(December 1971) **BASE** New York City
AFFILIATIONS Guardians of the Galaxy, Avengers,
Squadron Supreme

Unlike other Super Hero teams, the Defenders are a loose association without a charter or a headquarters (though they often meet in Doctor Strange's Sanctum Sanctorum). In their first assemblage, Doctor Strange teams up with Namor the

Sub-Mariner and the Hulk to defend Earth from the extradimensional Undying Ones. The Defenders officially form as a "non-team" when the trio assembles to stop Yandroth and his Omegatron doomsday device. Hulk and Namor, both volatile personalities, vow never to work together after that, but Strange manages to bring them together in times of need.

The Defenders' roster frequently grows and changes. At various times, noteworthy members include: Luke Cage, Clea (Doctor Strange's one-time disciple and wife), Hawkeye (Clint Barton), Jack Norriss (in Nighthawk's body), Nighthawk (Kyle Richmond), Daimon Hellstrom, Red Guardian (Tania Belinskaya), Silver Surfer and Valkyrie (the Asgardian Brunnhilde).

Occasional associates of the team are: Daredevil; Devil-Slayer (Eric Payne), Gargoyle (Isaac Christians), Hellcat (Patsy Walker), Iron Fist (Daniel Rand), and Yellowjacket (Hank Pym). Valkyrie creates her own all-female version of the team,

Concordance discord
Prester John holds the Defenders at bay in New Avalon. Nul arrives, planning to destroy the Concordance Engine, and with it, the whole world.

known as the Fearless Defenders or Valkyrior. Members include: Elsa Bloodstone, Clea, Misty Knight, Dani Moonstone, Annabelle Riggs, and Warrior Woman (the Olympian Hippolyta).

The Defenders become concerned with securing Concordance Engines, a series of devices designed to constrain reality and the universe itself. These machines are built by an extradimensional group of superhumans called the Presters, who use the Concordance Engines to prevent suicidal Celestials from entering and destroying the Marvel Universe.

Important foes of the Defenders include: Calizuma and his Warrior Wizards, Dormammu, Egghead's Emissaries of Evil, the Headmen, Loki, Null the Living Darkness, Shazana, the Six-Fingered Hand, the Undying Ones, and Xemnu the Titan.

WEREWOLF BY NIGHT

FIRST APPEARANCE *Marvel Spotlight* #2
(February 1972) **BASE** Los Angeles
AFFILIATIONS Legion of Monsters, Midnight
Sons, Night Shift

Jacob "Jack" Russell is a descendant of Gregor Russoff who, in 1795, is bitten by a female werewolf in Transylvania. On his 18th birthday, Russell transforms into a ferocious werewolf for the three days of the full moon. Henceforth, Russell has the ability to change between a human and a werewolf at will, while retaining his human personality—except during a full moon, when he involuntarily transforms into a beast. As Werewolf By Night, he uses his abilities for good, particularly as a crime fighter. Jack's lycanthropy enables him to survive being shot by Deadpool when the motormouth mercenary finds Jack with his wife, the shape-shifting succubus Queen Shiklah.

DRACULA

FIRST APPEARANCE *Tomb of Dracula* #1
(April 1972) **BASE** Castle Dracula, Transylvania
AFFILIATIONS Legion of the Unliving

Vlad Tepes Dracula is born in 1430 in Transylvania. Though an orphan, he inherits his father's throne as Prince of Wallachia. Dracula wars with the Turks and has his defeated foes impaled, becoming known as Vlad the Impaler. In 1459, he is mortally wounded by Turac, a Turk warlord. Turac takes him to a gypsy healer, who is in fact a vampire, who transforms Dracula into a vampire as well. Dracula soon ascends to be the most powerful of all vampires and the leader of his kind. Dracula's contemporary nemeses include Blade, Hannibal King, and Elsa Bloodstone. He is seemingly destroyed several times, by foes such as Doctor Strange, and his own son, Xarus, but always returns in due course.

LUKE CAGE

FIRST APPEARANCE *Luke Cage, Hero for Hire* #1
(July 1972) **BASE** New York City
AFFILIATIONS Avengers, Defenders,
Nightwing Restorations, Heroes for Hire, Inc.,
New Avengers, Thunderbolts

The son of James Lucas, a retired N.Y.P.D. detective, Carl Lucas grows up in Harlem. Lucas spends his youth in a street gang, the Rivals, with his best friend Willis Stryker. Though Lucas reforms, Stryker continues to lead a life of crime and understandably feels betrayed when his girlfriend, Riva Conners, turns to Lucas for affection. He takes things too far, however, framing Lucas for heroin possession, which lands Carl in prison.

Lucas' rage at this injustice gets him transferred to Georgia's notorious Seagate Prison. There he volunteers to become a test subject in a Super-Soldier experiment run by Dr. Noah Burstein, in exchange for early parole. A sadistic prison guard named Albert "Billy Bob" Rackham tries to sabotage the experiment in order to kill Lucas. It has the opposite effect, transforming Lucas into a powerhouse.

Lucas uses his new abilities to escape prison and change his identity.

Now calling himself Luke Cage, he takes the codename Power Man and becomes a hero for hire using his great physical strength to do good. Power Man joins the Defenders and, for a while, even substitutes for the Thing in the Fantastic Four. Later, Cage works with Misty Knight's Nightwing Restorations detective agency, and sets up Heroes for Hire, Inc. with best friend Danny Rand (Iron Fist). Cage moves in with girlfriend Jessica Jones, and they marry after the birth of their first child, Danielle.

Caged no more
Luke Cage helps with the Raft prison break instigated by Purple Man. Cage and the heroes who help are recruited by Captain America into the New Avengers.

Luke Cage joins the New Avengers and takes Captain America's side during the superhuman civil war. During Norman Osborn's Dark Reign as U.S. security chief, Cage buys Avengers Mansion from Tony Stark and builds his own Avengers team. He also leads the Thunderbolts at Captain America's request. For a short time, he retires from fighting villains to focus on his family, but later he and Iron Fist return to their roles as Heroes for Hire.

GHOST RIDER

FIRST APPEARANCE *Marvel Spotlight* #5 (August 1972) **BASE** Mobile **AFFILIATIONS** Legion of Monsters (Johnny Blaze), Midnight Sons (Danny Ketch)

The first Ghost Rider was a hero of the Old West. Since then, several human hosts have become supernatural Ghost Riders, flame-faced, motorhead spirits of vengeance who reap the souls of the wicked to burn in hell.

Orphan Johnny Blaze is taken in by a family of motorcycle stunt performers that worked with his now-deceased father. While learning the family trade, Johnny's practice stunt goes horribly wrong and his motorcycle explodes, mortally wounding his adoptive mother. As she dies, she begs Johnny to never ride in the show. He reluctantly obeys her wishes, but practices in secret for his own enjoyment. When his adoptive father, Crash Simpson, becomes terminally ill, Johnny is beside himself with grief. He turns to the dark arts, making a deal for his soul with the demon Mephisto to enable his father to survive his disease. Meanwhile, Crash has decided to go out in style with an outrageously dangerous 20-car jump. When he fails to make the jump and dies, Mephisto still comes to collect Johnny's soul. Despite Johnny's girlfriend and adoptive sister Roxanne's efforts, Mephisto bonds the demon Zarathos to Johnny's body. Now, riding a motorcycle of "hellfire" and wielding a mystical chain and other weaponry, Johnny rides by night as Ghost Rider.

The second supernatural Ghost Rider is Daniel Ketch who, with his sister Barb, witnesses a mob murder. Barb is hunted down and shot by the villain Deathwatch. Daniel touches an abandoned motorcycle's gas cap—a demonically possessed medallion—transforms into Ghost Rider, and avenges her death. Ghost Rider has now acquired a "Penance Stare" that makes evildoers feel the pain they have

Surprise attack
Possessed by the Ghost Rider demon, Alejandra Jones wastes no time in small talk with Red Skull's evil daughter Skadi.

inflicted on others. Furthermore, Daniel and Barb are siblings of the original Ghost Rider, Johnny Blaze.

A new Ghost Rider is created when the mysterious Adam (the first man and thus the first sinner) offers to relieve Johnny Blaze of the Spirit of Vengeance. Johnny doesn't hesitate and, in need of a host, the spirit transfers to a young Mexican-American woman named Alejandra Jones. Adam wants her to drive sin from the Earth, consequently turning people into mindless automatons. With Johnny's help, she escapes Adam's control.

Robbie Reyes becomes yet another Ghost Rider. He works on cars after school to support his younger brother Gabe, who is in a wheelchair. To make some cash, Robbie borrows a car from his shop to use in a street race. However, unbeknownst to Robbie, the car is both full of drugs and haunted by a demon. Thinking he is being stopped by the cops, he pulls over and is killed by a gang who wants the drugs. The demon possesses Robbie and, as a new Ghost Rider, he takes his revenge against several members of the drug gang. Robbie continues to race cars to support his brother, but has a rude awakening when he finds out the spirit that has possessed him is that of his Uncle Eli, a serial killer.

Stopping traffic
Ghost Rider Robbie Reyes becomes a reluctant hero in his neighborhood by confronting and defeating super-strong crime boss Mister Hyde.

> "Prepare to know the true meaning of hell!"
> **GHOST RIDER (JOHNNY BLAZE)**

timeline

◄ **Lost soul** Johnny Blaze becomes the first Ghost Rider, to save his adoptive father Crash Simpson. *Marvel Spotlight* #5 (Aug. 1972)

Freedom rider Johnny Blaze is temporarily freed from the Spirit of Vengeance, Zarathos, when the immortal Centurius traps the demon in his Crystal of Souls. *Ghost Rider* #81 (June 1983)

▼ **Possessed by vengeance** A new Ghost Rider is born, in the body of Danny Ketch. *Ghost Rider* #1 (May 1990)

Demon duel Johnny Blaze encounters Daniel Ketch and the two Ghost Riders face off when Johnny thinks Ketch is the Demon Zarathos. *Ghost Rider* #13 (May 1991)

Chosen one Picked out by Adam's zombie, the Seeker, Alejandra Jones becomes the first female Ghost Rider. *Ghost Rider* #1 (Sept. 2011)

▼ **Road rage** Robbie Reyes begins his reign as the car-driving Spirit of Vengeance when he is possessed by the Spirit of Eli. *All-New Ghost Rider* #1 (May 2014)

BRONZE AGE

MODERN AGE

HEROIC AGE

"More and more, the human part of me is being pushed out by the cat!"

TIGRA

Tigra cub
Following a relationship with the Skrull version of Hank Pym during the Secret Invasion, Tigra has a baby who seems to have inherited all her Cat People traits.

TIGRA

FIRST APPEARANCE *The Cat* #1 (November 1972) **BASE** Avengers Mansion, New York City; Avengers Compound, Los Angeles **AFFILIATIONS** Avengers, West Coast Avengers, Avengers Infinity, S.H.I.E.L.D.

Greer Grant Nelson is looking for a purpose in life after the murder of her husband, a police officer. She becomes a lab assistant under her old physics professor, and volunteers to be the subject of an experiment intended to fully realize the potential of a woman's mind. As a result, Greer becomes more agile, more attuned to mental and physical impulses, and her ability to absorb new knowledge is greatly increased.

Later, Greer discovers that her mentor, Dr. Joanne Tumolo, is one of the mystical Cat People. A secretive, persecuted race, they devised the Black Plague, also known as the Final Secret, as a means of striking back at humanity. The Cat People repented their terrible creation however, and have spent the intervening centuries trying to help humanity.

When Hydra attempt to kidnap Dr. Tumolo to learn about the Final Secret, Greer intervenes as Super Hero the Cat, but is fatally wounded by an alpha-radiation gun. The only way to save her is to transform her into one of the Cat People, so Greer is remade as Tigra—complete with claws on her hands and feet, feline features, and stripy fur covering her body. She moves to New York and becomes a member of the Avengers, later transferring to the West Coast Avengers. Although she serves valiantly, her cat personality sometimes dominates her human side, making her needy for attention and less ambivalent about killing than an Avenger should be —a problem solved by sorceress Agatha Harkness, who removes Tigra's cat soul, while leaving her powers intact.

SHANNA

FIRST APPEARANCE *Shanna the She-Devil* #1 (November 1972) **BASE** Africa; Savage Land **AFFILIATIONS** Ka-Zar, S.H.I.E.L.D.

Raised in Africa, Shanna O'Hara becomes fiercely anti-firearms when her mother is killed by her father in a hunting accident. As an adult, Shanna travels to the United States and becomes a zoo veterinarian, but tragedy strikes once more when nearly all the big cats under her care are senselessly slaughtered. Disillusioned and heartbroken, Shanna returns to Africa with two surviving leopard cubs, intending to release them into the wild. She soon decides to remain with her pets in the jungle, wearing their mother's pelt to give the cubs a comforting, familiar scent. Accompanied by her beloved leopards, Shanna becomes known locally as the She-Devil—relentlessly pursuing illegal hunters and poachers who come onto the reserve with evil intentions. She is kidnapped by a wizard and brought to the Savage Land—a tropical "lost world" located in Antarctica—where she meets Ka-Zar, the Jungle Lord. The two are kindred spirits. Defending the Savage Land against the pollution and greed of the outside world, they fall in love and have a child, named Matthew.

While acting as a guide for a S.H.I.E.L.D. exploration mission to the Forbidden Island—an area of the Savage Land off-limits to outsiders—Shanna and her companions are stranded. After brutal skirmishes with the primitive inhabitants of the Forbidden Island, the S.H.I.E.L.D. agents are picked off one by one and Shanna is left alone—until Wolverine is teleported in to help her. The two travel to a temple in the middle of the island, which is radiating a force field that prevents them from leaving, but Shanna is killed in a clash with another hostile tribe. Luckily, super-genius Amadeus Cho has also teleported in; he manages to convince the natives that he is a god and orders them to perform a resurrection ritual. The revived Shanna is now at one with the Savage Land, with knowledge of its history and traditions, and able to speak all the languages spoken by its primitive inhabitants.

Elite athlete
Shanna is an Olympic-standard athlete and swimmer, as well as a qualified vet, and following her resurrection has the strength of ten men. Even the Hulk is impressed.

DRAX THE DESTROYER

FIRST APPEARANCE *Iron Man* #55
(February 1973) **BASE** Monster Island,
Knowhere **AFFILIATIONS** Infinity Watch,
Guardians of the Galaxy

The spirit of Arthur Douglas, killed by
Thanos, is given a new body by the
incorporeal being Kronos. This creation is
Drax the Destroyer, who is consumed with
the desire to annihilate the evil Thanos.
However, in their first battle, Drax is
captured by Thanos and forced to do his
bidding, until Iron Man and Thanos' own
father, Mentor, rescue him. The Destroyer's
implacable drive to kill the Mad Titan leads
him to clash with Captain Mar-Vell—whom
Drax believes has frustrated his one desire
by killing Thanos himself; however, the
two later form an alliance.

Meanwhile, it transpires that Arthur
Douglas' daughter Heather, supposedly
killed by Thanos at the same time as her
father, has been taken by Mentor to Titan
and raised to become the mystic,
telepathic hero Moondragon. She
struggles to control her powers, and even
kills Drax at one point. However, he is
resurrected and the two join up as
members of the Infinity Watch, guarding
the Infinity Gems. Following the events of
the Annihilation War and the Phalanx
invasion, Drax is one of the heroes
recruited by Peter Quill for his Guardians
of the Galaxy.

THANOS

FIRST APPEARANCE *Iron Man* #55
(February 1973) **BASE** Sanctuary space stations
AFFILIATIONS Infinity Watch, Cabal

Born on Titan, a moon of Saturn, Thanos
develops an obsession with death and
increasing his own power. Cast out by
his people for creating weapons of mass
destruction, Thanos gathers an army of
alien malcontents to unleash a
devastating attack on his homeworld.
He searches the universe for artifacts,
like the Cosmic Cube and the Infinity
Gems, seeking to boost his strength,
wreak destruction, and impress the love
of his life—the living embodiment of
Death. Thanos' alliance with Death and
the cosmic artifacts he collects add to his
power, rendering him almost omnipotent.

With all the Infinity Gems combined on
the Infinity Gauntlet Thanos seems to be
on the verge of realizing all his terrible

ambitions, until Nebula, his granddaughter,
and Adam Warlock defeat him. Warlock
believes that Thanos is capable of change
and makes him a member of the Infinity
Watch, but his faith is misplaced. Thanos
grows bored and allies with Annihilus just
to see what will happen, until he realizes
that Annihilus' goal is the destruction of
the universe.

Thanos is eventually killed by the
vengeful Drax the Destroyer, but his
beloved Death resurrects him. When
Thanos heads to Earth in search of a
Cosmic Cube, he is confronted by a
group of heroes and kills War Machine
(Jim Rhodes) before being imprisoned
by Captain Marvel (Carol Danvers).

Father figure
Thanos raises the young Gamora, training
her to be the most dangerous woman in
the universe, but she rejects his mission
to destroy everything.

MANTIS

FIRST APPEARANCE *Avengers* #112
(June 1973) **BASE** Knowhere
AFFILIATIONS Avengers, Guardians
of the Galaxy

The priests of the Temple of Pama in
Vietnam—descendants of fugitive Kree
pacifists—train the young Mantis in martial
arts. Her foster fathers also give her
telepathic abilities, but she is conditioned to
remember none of her upbringing. Mantis
travels to the U.S. and joins the Avengers,
where her mutual attraction to the Vision
causes friction with new teammate Scarlet
Witch. Traveling back to her homeland with
the Avengers on the trail of her true origins,
Mantis discovers that she is the prophesied
Celestial Madonna, a perfect woman
combining power and humanity, who will give
birth to one who will change the universe.

Her destiny is fulfilled by her marriage to a
member of the Cotati plant race, whose spirit
resides in the body of her deceased former

lover, Swordsman. The couple's astral forms
travel into space and eventually have a child
named Sequoia.

Mantis' spirit is later shattered by the
Elders of the Universe and spread far and
wide—with each fragment representing a
facet of her identity. A clone of Thanos begins
systematically killing the pieces of Mantis until
only one remains, combining all of Mantis'
characteristics in one form again. This results
in her gaining almost godlike powers, and
she teams up with the Avengers on a celestial
mission to rescue her son from Thanos'
clutches.

Mantis returns to Earth, where her powers
enable her to sense the impending threat of
the Annihilation Wave. Voyaging into space,
she allows herself to be captured by the
Kree, as part of her plan to join with Peter
Quill's Guardians of the Galaxy. She acts as
counselor to the group, although the team is
angered when they discover that Peter asked
her to use her mental powers to brainwash
them into joining up.

Power of life
Thanos is disappointed to find that the newly
empowered Mantis is able to fight his attempts
to break her body and mind.

Into the android
Ant-Man Hank Pym astonishes the Avengers by announcing that he is going to discover what has rendered the Vision inert by going inside him. He sets off with three ants—whom he calls Crosby, Stills, and Nash—in case he needs to send back for help during his micro-mission.

INCREDIBLE JOURNEY

> "If anybody here is gonna take a stab at finding what ails him... I'm your best bet!" **ANT-MAN**

Ex-Avenger Ant-Man proves his worth to the team by embarking on a heroic mission to revive the android Vision...

Ronan the Accuser of the alien Kree race has dispatched a robotic Sentry to de-evolve Earth to a prehistoric era and make it a base for war against the Kree's enemies the Skrulls. The Avengers defeat the plot, but the incident leads to a public outcry. The Avengers refuse to hand over their Kree friend Captain Mar-Vell to the authorities, who claim he is an alien spy. Carol Danvers, on leave from her intelligence duties, takes Mar-Vell to a farm upstate while the heat dies down. Soon afterward, an angry mob trashes Avengers Mansion and Captain America, Iron Man, and Thor take the decision to disband the current Avengers team.

AVENGERS IN PERIL

The Vision then staggers in and collapses—seemingly dead. Cap is sure there must be a spy in the mansion. Hoping to revive the Vision, robotics genius Ant-Man—who has arrived to announce his formal departure from the Avengers—agrees to voyage into Vision's head, via his mouth, and use his knowledge of robotics to repair the android. But this proves to be no walk in the park; the Vision's interior organisms believe Ant-Man and his ant sidekicks are germs and attack them. Ant-Man struggles on, reaches Visions head, fixes the damage, and escapes just seconds before the android awakes, which would have trapped Ant-Man.

The Vision revives and reveals that the Earth is in deadly danger. Shape-shifting Skrulls have kidnapped Scarlet Witch and Quicksilver. In addition, Carol Danvers, really a Skrull, has imprisoned Captain Mar-Vell aboard the Skrull mother ship. The Avengers soon find themselves thrust into an epic battle between worlds: the Kree-Skrull War...

Going solo
Protective organisms inside the Vision attack Ant-Man and his ants. "Crosby" is soon destroyed and Ant-Man orders his remaining two little friends to flee. He then bravely continues on, alone.

BLADE

FIRST APPEARANCE *Tomb of Dracula* #10 (July 1973) **BASE** Gem Theater, New York City; formerly New Orleans, Louisiana
AFFILIATIONS MI-13, X-Men, Mighty Avengers, Avengers of the Supernatural, S.H.I.E.L.D., S.H.I.E.L.D.'s Howling Commandos, Nightstalkers, Midnight Sons, Vanguard

In 1929, wealthy Lucas Cross—member of secret society the Order of Tyrana—hides his pregnant wife Tara Brooks from their enemies in a London brothel. She is killed by a vampire as she is giving birth, and her son, Eric Brooks, is born with vampiric enzymes in his blood which render him immune to infection from vampire bites.

Growing up on the streets, Eric is adopted by vampire hunter Jamal Afari, who trains him in the combat skills Eric needs to avenge his mother. Eric calls himself Blade, beginning a lifelong quest to destroy such supernatural predators as vampires.

In 1968, he and a team of like-minded hunters seek out vampire Lord Dracula and stake him. Believing their job done, they separate, but Dracula resurrects and hunts them all down. Blade becomes a lone hunter, only occasionally joined with groups led by Quincy Harker, Rachel van Helsing, and Frank Drake to battle Dracula.

When Dracula seems finally and permanently laid to rest, Blade joins Drake and vampire detective Hannibal King as Nightstalkers: supernatural troubleshooters battling an invasion of Lilin demons and later Hydra's Department of Occult Armaments. They also join Doctor Strange's Midnight Sons battling Lilith, Mother of All Demons.

When Blade is bitten by sometime ally Morbius—the Living Vampire—his dormant vampire enzymes transform him from a human hunter into a full Dhampir—a hybrid with human and vampire characteristics.

Blade is now a Daywalker—possessing most vampiric powers but none of their weaknesses. Blade renews his war on the occult, joining groups such as S.H.I.E.L.D., Vanguard, and MI-13, and thwarting the schemes of his father who is back in his life and now a vampire. After a spell in the black ops Vanguard team, Blade allies with the X-Men against Xarus, son of Dracula, and his vampire hordes. He later joins Luke Cage's Mighty Avengers as masked hero Ronin, and helps them defeat the monstrous Deathwalker Prime.

High stakes
Before gaining his own mystic powers, Blade battles the undead legions of Dracula with nothing more than guts, ingenuity, and an arsenal of teakwood throwing knives.

DOCTOR VOODOO

FIRST APPEARANCE *Strange Tales* #169 (September 1973) **BASE** Schaefer Theater, New York City; Infinite Avengers Mansion; Hounfour, Port-au-Prince, Haiti **AFFILIATIONS** Avengers Unity Division, New Avengers, Mighty Avengers, Howling Commandos of S.H.I.E.L.D.

When Jericho Drumm leaves Haiti to study medicine, he has no intention of ever returning. However, when his brother Daniel is murdered by voodoo priest Damballah, the urbane psychiatrist comes home and learns the true nature of magic.

Taught by ancient mystic Papa Jambo, Jericho becomes Brother Voodoo, master of many mystic forces. He also carries his brother's spirit within him—a vengeful ghost who doubles his physical power when combating evil.

Battling evil magic and threats like A.I.M. in Haiti and the U.S., Brother Voodoo meets Super Heroes such as Spider-Man, the Thing, and Moon Knight. When he succumbs to the dark side of his arts and is possessed by Damballah's power, he is saved by Doctor Strange. Jericho later aids him and Morbius against Marie Le Veau, as the voodoo queen plans to unleash vampires and zombies.

Brother Voodoo joins S.H.I.E.L.D.'s supernatural task force the Howling Commandos, but is replaced by a shape-shifting Skrull during the aliens' Secret Invasion of Earth. He is rescued when the impostor dies battling the body-hopping Cannibal in Wakanda.

When Doctor Strange loses the sponsorship of Agamotto, the mystic god selects Jericho Drumm as Earth's new Sorcerer Supreme. Now called Doctor Voodoo, Jericho successfully battles Dormammu and the Hood, but perishes when Agamotto himself becomes corrupted. When the maddened deity attacks the New Avengers, Doctor Voodoo sacrifices himself to defeat Agamotto, destroying his potent mystic talisman, the Eye of Agamotto.

Doctor Voodoo is called back from death after an inversion spell turns the Scarlet Witch and other Avengers into evildoers. Her plan to murder Doctor Doom is thwarted by her intended victim who convinces elder gods to restore Jericho and Daniel to the physical world. When the reborn heroes confront the Scarlet Witch they undo her spell and order is restored. In the aftermath, the resurrected Doctor Voodoo joins the Avengers Unity Division.

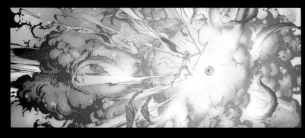

That voodoo you do
Even eradication by the power of Agamotto does not long deter the Lord of the Loa, Doctor Voodoo.

HOWARD THE DUCK

FIRST APPEARANCE *Adventure Into Fear* #19 (December 1973) **BASE** Sharon King's building, New York City; formerly Cleveland, Ohio; New Stork City, Wackington D.C.; Duckworld **AFFILIATIONS** Howard T. Duck Private Investigations, A.R.M.O.R, Ducky Dozen, Defenders, Fearsome Four, Daydreamers, Circus of Crime, To Hack and Back Cab Company, All-Night Party, S.O.O.F.I.

Howard the Duck is the universe's greatest outsider. Even on Duckworld, he is a fish out of water, continually carping about the crazy implausibility and venal stupidity of society.

When a shift in the Cosmic Axis catapults him to a planet where hairless apes rule with the same inane duplicity as his own species, Howard realizes reality is crazy—or at least a very bad joke. Landing in Cleveland, Ohio, he reluctantly battles mystic mutate Garko the Man-Frog and a vampire cow, before—with Spider-Man's incredulous assistance—inadvertently saving artists' model Beverly Switzler from an occult accountant.

They team up, even though Howard is clearly a magnet for wizards and weirdos. After accidentally running for U.S. President, saving the universe on two occasions, having a nervous breakdown, and battling a number of Super Villains, Howard parts company with Beverly when she marries his archenemy, Dr. Bong.

Howard moves to New York City where he endures a life of utter absurdity; yet he still cannot shake his instinct to help others. He dutifully tries to register under the Superhuman Registration Act but the paperwork-dodging bureaucrats refuse to acknowledge that he even exists.

After years of accidental involvement with metahumans like Generation X, the Daydreamers, and She-Hulk Jennifer Walters, Howard reluctantly leads a team of heroes— "The Ducky Dozen"—against zombies and rogue Asgardians before settling down to run his own private detection agency. With weirdness escalating all around him, Howard decides to return to Duckworld.

However, he is accidentally transformed into a living Nexus of All Realities.

Wandering the Multiverse, Howard the Duck discovers his life has been turned into a reality show by interdimensional impresario Mojo. He spices up events by hiring extradimensional Sparkitects to edit Howard's life, making it even more lurid and dramatic.

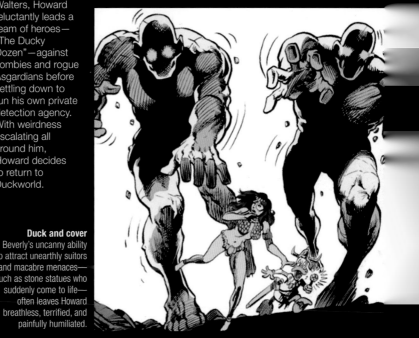

Duck and cover
Beverly's uncanny ability to attract unearthly suitors and macabre menaces— such as stone statues who suddenly come to life— often leaves Howard breathless, terrified, and painfully humiliated.

SHANG-CHI

FIRST APPEARANCE *Special Marvel Edition* #15 (December 1973) **BASE** Mobile; formerly Savage Land; Avengers Tower, New York City **AFFILIATIONS** New Avengers, A.I.M., Avengers, Secret Avengers, MI-5, MI-6, Marvel Knights, Heroes for Hire, Freelance Restorations, Si-Fan

Shang-Chi means "the rising and advancing of the spirit." His father—the immortal terrorist Fu Manchu—trains Shang-Chi in total isolation and employs secret brainwashing techniques to ensure he becomes the perfect assassin and heir to Fu Manchu's empire of evil.

However, Shang-Chi turns against his father, having been subtly deprogramed by a rebellious monk in Fu Manchu's employ. Shang-Chi allies with agents of the British secret service and veteran intelligence agent Sir Dennis Nayland Smith. He then spends the next few danger-filled years crushing his father's cult of assassins and dismantling his globe-girdling organization. Once his father is apparently destroyed,

Shang-Chi remains with his friends, countering other global threats. However, he becomes increasingly disgusted with what he calls "games of deceit and death," and retires.

Shang-Chi returns to action when his old comrades are targeted by Si-Fan ninjas from Fu Manchu's evil empire. Shang-Chi remains in active service to assist Super Heroes such as Daredevil, Black Widow, and the Punisher in their struggles against Southeast Asian criminal gangs.

When the Superhuman Registration Act becomes law in the U.S., Shang-Chi signs up to Misty Knight's Heroes For Hire— tasked with bringing in metahumans who refuse to register. Later, he almost dies battling an invasion of New York City by the Hulk's alien Warbound army.

When Fu Manchu resurfaces, Shang-Chi joins Steve Rogers' Secret Avengers to stop his evil schemes. He then becomes part of the regular Avengers, battling an invasion of the Gardeners and Builders. He also accidentally gains the power to create living copies of himself.

Heart of a hero
Shang-Chi's unshakable moral and spiritual center transform his lethal skills and deadly training into an unbeatable arsenal to protect the weak and punish the guilty.

THE PUNISHER

FIRST APPEARANCE *Amazing Spider-Man* #129 (February 1974) **BASE** New York City
AFFILIATIONS Secret Avengers, Thunderbolts

Frank Castle is a U.S. Marine with a wife and two young children, but his life is shattered when his family is murdered by the Mob after witnessing a gangland execution. Castle sets out on a revenge mission, first on his family's killers and then on organized crime in general.

Castle adopts the identity of the Punisher, wearing a distinctive black costume with a large white skull on the chest. Thanks to his military background, the Punisher can deploy a range of weapons and hand-to-hand combat techniques in his one-man war on crime. He also has a customized battle van. The Punisher is a lone wolf operator, but he does have a background partner: Microchip, who has a flair for inventing weapons, vehicles, and gadgets.

When it comes to eradicating organized crime, the Punisher will stop at nothing. Whereas Super Heroes like Spider-Man or Captain America try and bring their quarry to justice with no loss of life, Frank Castle has no such scruples. However, on the occasions when he has temporarily allied with more morally upright heroes, he has loaded his guns with rubber "mercy bullets." Castle is also careful not to endanger the lives of law-enforcement officers.

When the Punisher first appears on the New York scene, he is trying to kill Spider-Man, whom he believes to be a dangerous criminal and the murderer of Norman Osborn. However, the two come to an understanding, and even team up against a common enemy. Inevitably, Castle ends up in prison for his vigilante activities, but he is handed a lifeline when the warden reveals that he is sympathetic to the Punisher's cause and will allow him to escape if he promises to work for a shady organization called the Trust. However, the Punisher is not a natural employee, and the relationship with the Trust does not last long.

During Norman Osborn's Dark Reign as U.S. security chief, Castle is killed by Daken, Wolverine's son. But death is not the end for the Punisher; he is reassembled and reanimated by strange monsters living in the sewers, under the guidance of the vampire Morbius. This Franken-Castle finds a new lease of life protecting helpless creatures from monster hunters.

The Punisher is eventually returned to living human form by the magical healing factor of the Bloodstone. Ever since, he's been back on the streets, taking out the trash as only he can.

"Picking a fight with me isn't smart."

THE PUNISHER

Tough guy
As a former Marine, Frank Castle knows how to keep his body honed to an optimum level. He is a formidable bare-knuckle and martial arts fighter, and is highly skilled in the use of a variety of weapons.

timeline

▶ **Arachnid ally** Although at first believing Spider-Man to be a criminal, the Punisher realizes they share a goal and teams up with the web-slinger to take down Tarantula. *Amazing Spider-Man* #135 (Aug. 1974)

Punished The Punisher allows himself to be arrested rather than shoot a police officer, reasoning that prison is a good place to continue his vendetta against criminals. *Amazing Spider-Man Annual* #15 (Oct. 1981)

▶ **Trust us** The Punisher agrees to work for the Trust, who believe that vigilantes need to catch the criminals who escape the law. *Punisher* #1 (Jan. 1986)

Doom vs. Punisher When the Kingpin sets Doctor Doom on his trail, the Punisher travels to Latveria and steals one of Doom's beloved paintings to make a deal with him. *Punisher* #29 (Jan. 1990)

Terminated Following a game of cat-and-mouse between the Punisher and Norman Osborn, the vigilante is killed on Osborn's orders by Daken. *Dark Reign: The List—Punisher* (Dec. 2009)

Franken-Castle The remains of Frank Castle are gathered by strange creatures in the sewers and given monstrous new life by vampire scientist Morbius. *Punisher* #11 (Jan. 2010)

▼ **Assassination attempt** The Punisher infiltrates the Kingpin's inner circle and stabs the mob boss, but Fisk lives to regain control of organized crime in New York. *Civil War II: Kingpin* #3 (Nov. 2016)

Go-to guy
Brilliant hacker Microchip is the man behind the Punisher's war on crime, providing him with intel, weapons, and equipment.

Mistaken identity
Castle's long-standing quest to bring down Jigsaw takes a surprising turn when the patchwork-faced villain is brainwashed into believing himself to be the Punisher.

IRON FIST

FIRST APPEARANCE *Marvel Premiere* #15 (May 1974) **BASE** Thunder Dojo, Harlem, New York City
AFFILIATIONS Heroes for Hire, New Avengers, Immortal Weapons

Nine-year-old Danny Rand and his mother are taken by his father Wendell and business partner Harold Meachum to the K'un-Lun Mountain in Asia to search for the mysterious city in which Wendell once lived. But Meachum has treachery in mind, and he sends Danny's father falling from the mountain to his death.

Seeking help, Danny and his mother struggle through the snow, but their scent is picked up by a pack of wolves. The boy watches in horror as his mother sacrifices herself so that he can escape. Danny is rescued by people from the city of K'un-Lun and brought into the presence of Yü-Ti, the August Personage of Jade.

The angry boy declares that he wants revenge for the loss of his parents, and so Yü-Ti introduces him to Lei Kung, the Thunderer, who spends the next seven years teaching Danny martial arts. The boy is a good student, and proves himself beyond doubt by gaining the power of the Iron Fist. He returns to New York to seek revenge on Harold Meachum, but finds him a shell of the cruel man he remembers, having lost his legs to frostbite on that fateful day. Iron Fist can only pity Meachum, and does not take the revenge he has contemplated for ten years. However, just a few minutes later, a shadowy ninja kills Meachum.

Seeking new meaning in his life, Danny teams up with Luke Cage to form the Heroes for Hire. He later joins the New Avengers for a time, before returning to Heroes for Hire.

Living weapon
To become Iron Fist, Danny defeats the dragon Shou-Lao the Undying, plunging his hands into its molten heart to take on the dragon's mystical powers.

DEATHLOK (LUTHER MANNING)

FIRST APPEARANCE *Astonishing Tales* #25 (August 1974) **BASE** New York, Earth-7484
AFFILIATIONS None

Colonel Luther Manning is a brilliant military strategist on Earth-7484, and possesses attributes the army cannot afford to lose, even after he is killed. The remains of his body and part of his brain are augmented with metal parts and circuitry, in the culmination of a plan, named Project Alpha-Mech, by Major Simon Ryker to populate the military with robot soldiers.

Ryker, however, finds that Deathlok—as the cyborg is named—is not the biddable machine he was hoping for. Manning's personality reasserts itself and Deathlok breaks free, although his onboard computer and Manning's inner voice are often at loggerheads. For example, "Puter" cannot see the logic in Deathlok visiting Manning's wife and child. When Deathlok does so, he is heartbroken that his wife is terrified of his appearance. He tries to commit suicide, but is prevented by his programming. Later on, his mind is copied into a clone of Luther Manning so that Deathlok and Manning coexist. Deathlok is then taken into the future, where he calls himself the Demolisher.

The Demolisher is later recruited by a being named Timestream, along with the Luther Manning from Prime Earth, and ends up fighting the Deathlok of Prime Earth, Michael Collins. The Demolisher returns to his own reality but struggles to find a purpose. He ends up returning to Prime Earth and encountering Daredevil and the Kingpin. Although he is offered a place on the Underground Legion team, the Demolisher chooses to continue his wanderings, saying that he needs to sort himself out before he can be of any use to anyone else.

Future imperfect
A glimpse of the dystopian future that Deathlok lives in is enough to make Spidey pray that his reality is headed somewhere different.

"I'm the best there is at what I do, but what I do isn't very nice…"

WOLVERINE

WOLVERINE

James Howlett, alias Logan, is a powerful mutant who uses his bone claws, healing factor, and skeleton covered in unbreakable Adamantium to fight alongside the X-Men, despite his mysterious past and loner spirit.

FIRST APPEARANCE *Incredible Hulk* #180 (October 1974)   **BASE** Canada; Westchester County, New York; New York City; Japan; Madripoor
AFFILIATIONS X-Men, Avengers, New Avengers, Alpha Flight, Weapon X, S.H.I.E.L.D.

WEAPON X

On the run from the law, James Howlett, under the pseudonym Logan, is abducted by a Canadian Super-Soldier program called Weapon X. Logan is a prime candidate because of his mutant healing factor and razor-sharp bone claws. Doctor Cornelius and his team fuse Logan's skeleton with the virtually indestructible metal Adamantium. This process wipes Logan's prior memories, resulting in him looking for the truth about his lost past for the rest of his life.

As the Incredible Hulk wanders into Canadian territory, Logan is loosed on Hulk by a Canadian governmental agency working with Hulk-hating Major Glenn Talbot of the U.S. Air Force, resulting in a clash of titans big and small.

Heavy metal
Wolverine emerges from his procedure with a new set of Adamantium claws and metal headgear.

THE X-MAN

Fleeing the Weapon X program—having destroyed it and killed all its hated personnel—Logan briefly joins Canadian hero team Alpha Flight, where he gains the codename Wolverine. He then becomes one of the X-Men at the request of Professor Charles Xavier (Professor X). Wolverine comes to love his team of uncanny X-Men, including teammate Jean Grey. Although the immensely powerful and charismatic mutant telepath is already romantically linked to Cyclops, this is just the beginning of a long, incident-packed, on-off romance between the pair.

Lone wolf finds his pack
Wolverine's fierce loyalty and fighting skills make him a huge asset to the X-Men.

THE PAST IS ANOTHER COUNTRY

It transpires that Wolverine is born James Howlett in the late 1800s, a sickly child of a wealthy family. The Howletts' groundsman, Thomas Logan, and his son Dog both bear an uncanny resemblance to young James.

Thomas sets out to rob the Howletts, hoping to convince James' mother, Elizabeth, to finally run away with him. James' father confronts Thomas, and is shot dead in front of his son. The brutal murder triggers James' bone claws and mutant powers for the first time. He lunges at Thomas with his claws, killing him and injuring Dog. His grief-stricken mother commits suicide holding Thomas, not her dead husband. James' incredible healing factor kicks in and removes the traumatic memory. James' friend Rose helps the scared teenager to escape, thus beginning his life on the run.

Tragedy strikes
Young James Howlett's mutant powers are triggered by the killing of his parents.

THE DEATH OF WOLVERINE

Wolverine is nearly impossible to kill and barely ages due to his incredible mutant healing factor; but when this ability to heal is lost to a sentient virus from the Microverse, he becomes vulnerable. Word travels fast and a bounty is put on his head, leading to battles with many of his enemies.

Wolverine seeks out the individual responsible—who turns out to be none other than Dr. Cornelius of the Weapon X program. Cornelius has continued his cruel work and is about to repeat the process he forced on Wolverine with more victims. To stop him, Wolverine slashes open the vat of Adamantium and, covered in the molten metal, he dies. To honor his legacy, his female clone, X-23, takes on Wolverine's name and costume.

An ironic end
Covered in molten Adamantium, the metal that made him super-strong, Wolverine dies as he has lived—fighting for justice.

timeline

▼ **Weapon X** Wolverine first appears as Weapon X, a mutant super-agent enhanced by science. He is sent to battle the Hulk, but the behemoth bests him. *Incredible Hulk* #180 (Oct. 1974)

Uncanny team Professor X recruits a new team of X-Men, including Nightcrawler, Storm, and the newly named Wolverine. *Giant-Size X-Men* #1 (May 1975)

▼ **Days of future past** Wolverine gives his life to prevent a dystopian future in which mutants are corralled in internment camps by robot Sentinels; meanwhile Kitty Pryde of the X-Men travels back in time to stop the event. *Uncanny X-Men* #141-142 (Jan.–Feb. 1981)

Return to Japan Wolverine returns to Japan to fight for his true love Mariko Yashida against her corrupt samurai family, eventually winning the day and getting engaged to her. But, as ever, heartbreak awaits. *Wolverine* #1-4 (Sept.–Dec. 1982)

Death of Silver Fox In the Wild West, the vicious mutant Sabretooth celebrates Logan's birthday by murdering Logan's Native American wife, Silver Fox, thereby earning the future Wolverine's undying hatred. *Wolverine* #10 (Aug. 1989)

▼ **Unbonded** In a fight with the X-Men, Magneto rends the Adamantium from Wolverine's skeleton, leading Logan to leave the team. *Wolverine* #75 (Nov. 1993) & *X-Men* #25 (Nov. 1993)

Feral metal Mutant villain Genesis wishes to turn Wolverine into one of the Four Horsemen of the godlike Apocalypse by rebonding his bones with Adamantium. The pain causes Wolverine to go feral and kill Genesis. *Wolverine* #100 (Apr. 1996)

Origin It is revealed that Wolverine, born James Howlett in the 1800s, is the sickly son of estate owners. His powers manifest when his father is killed by the man who may be his biological father. *Origin* #1 (Nov. 2001)

Death of love Wolverine and Jean Grey hurtle on an asteroid toward the Sun. Wolverine kills Jean in an act of mercy. *New X-Men* #150 (Feb. 2004)

▼ **Uncanny meeting** Wolverine meets his female clone, X-23. *Uncanny X-Men* #450 (Dec. 2004)

Memories returned During the events of "House of M," Scarlet Witch returns all of Wolverine's memories. *House of M* #1-5 (June–Aug. 2005)

Prodigal son Wolverine learns his wife from the 1940s, Itso, had a son named Daken, who goes on to become Dark Wolverine. *Wolverine Origins* #5 (Aug. 2006)

Heads up After the death of Professor X, Wolverine takes on the unlikely role of headmaster of the Jean Grey School. *Wolverine and the X-Men* (Oct. 2011)

Death of Wolverine After losing his healing factor, Logan hunts down Dr. Cornelius. Trying to stop him harming other mutants, Logan is covered in molten Adamantium and dies. *Death of Wolverine* #4 (Dec. 2014)

Old Man Logan returns The world is rebuilt after the Secret Wars, and a Logan from the future returns to Earth to prevent the apocalypse of his timeline. *Old Man Logan* #1 (Mar. 2016)

Look sharp
Wolverine's healing factor means he is virtually impossible to kill and can recover from serious injury in moments. His skeleton, including his retractable claws, is laced with Adamantium and unbreakable. His claws can pierce or slice through virtually any known material.

LEGION OF THE UNLIVING

FIRST APPEARANCE *Avengers* #131 (January 1975) **BASE** Mobile

There are many incarnations of the Legion of the Unliving. They form to combat the Avengers and include not only undead villains, but also some past Avengers. Kang the Conqueror and Immortus (a future version of Kang) bring together the first Legion, culled from history. The original members include Baron Zemo (Heinrich Zemo), Flying Dutchman (Captain Joost van Straaten), Frankenstein's Monster, Human Torch (the android Jim Hammond), Midnight (M'Nai, also known as Midnight Sun), and Wonder Man (Simon Williams). When Kang is faced by Thor and flees, Immortus corrects the damage that has been done. He restores the Legion members to their proper places in time. The android Human Torch is split into two duplicates, one of which saves the Fantastic Four from the Mad Thinker; the other is taken by evil sentient robot Ultron to become the basis for the Vision.

A second Legion of the Unliving is assembled by Grandmaster as part of his scheme to destroy the universe. This team includes copies of Bucky Barnes, Dracula, Korvac, Captain Mar-Vell, the Red Guardian (Alexei Shostakov), and the Swordsman (Jacques Duquesne). The third Legion, which includes an undead Grim Reaper, was put together by

Party poopers
The Legion spoils the Avengers's day *(left to right)*: Captain Mar-Vell, Doctor Druid, Hellcat, Mockingbird, Swordsman, and Thunderstrike.

Legion IV
Grim Reaper gains extra power from the demon Lloigoroth to lead his own undead Legion.

Immortus in an attempt to capture the Scarlet Witch. Grim Reaper then assembles his own Legion of the Unliving—twice. The first group comprises the spirits of deceased villains in the bodies of animated corpses. The second is made up of zombie heroes summoned with the help of Grim Reaper's undead brother, Wonder Man. They include Captain Mar-Vell, Doctor Druid, Hellcat (Patsy Walker), Mockingbird (Barbara Morse), Swordsman, and Thunderstrike (Eric Masterson). Scarlet Witch is able to revive Wonder Man, and he then brings the Grim Reaper back to life. When the Reaper relinquishes control of the Legion, Scarlet Witch sends the rest of the team to eternal rest in the afterlife.

KORVAC

FIRST APPEARANCE *Giant-Size Defenders* #3 (January 1975) **BASE** Mobile **AFFILIATIONS** Badoon)

Michael Korvac is born in 2997 CE. When Earth is conquered by the alien race Brotherhood of Badoon, he betrays humanity and works for them. When the Badoon find him sleeping on the job, they punish him by grafting a computer in place of his lower body. Korvac is taken to the present time by Grandmaster to work for him. However, Korvac downloads the Grandmaster's powers and those of the planet-sized ship of Galactus, becoming one of the most powerful threats in the universe. He attempts to turn Earth into his utopia and slays many Super Heroes trying to stop him. Fearing he has lost his wife Carina's love, Korvac resurrects the heroes and commits suicide; Carina does likewise. Korvac returns, but is killed by Veil and Hazmat of the Avengers Academy when he comes looking for his resurrected wife.

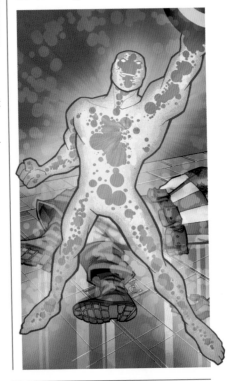

COLOSSUS

FIRST APPEARANCE *Giant-Size X-Men* #1 (May 1975) **BASE** Jean Grey School of Higher Learning **AFFILIATIONS** X-Men

Piotr Rasputin—Colossus—has the ability to change his body to a steel-like material and thus acquire incredible strength and durability. He, his brother Mikhail (a Soviet cosmonaut), and sister Illyana (Magik), grow up in Russia. Professor X asks Colossus to join the X-Men when he forms a new team to rescue the original members. Colossus falls in love with Kitty Pryde (Shadowcat), though their relationship constantly fluctuates.

Colossus pays a high price for serving with the X-Men. Injured while battling the Marauders, he is unable to revert to his normal human form for some time. Later, he sacrifices his life to save other mutants from the Legacy Virus. An alien named Ord then revives Colossus in order to conduct experiments on him.

Colossus subsequently gains the powers of the destructive Juggernaut from Cyttorak of the Crimson Cosmos. During the infamous battle between the Avengers and X-Men, Colossus becomes one of the five avatars of the Phoenix Force. He pleads with Cyttorak to then release him from the burden of being a Juggernaut, but Cyttorak refuses, stating that the dual avatar roles are not incompatible.

When Cerebra detects new mutants in Tokyo, Colossus and his teammates idiscover that Sugar Man has created six hundred mutant embryos intending to travel with them to the future, where they will become the next generation of mutants. Colossus and the young X-Men travel to the future with the embryos instead, leaving Sugar Man behind. They end up on Apocalypse's Omega World and are attacked by Apocalypse's Horsemen. Colossus is captured, and made the Horseman of War. With the other Horseman, he then hunts the X-Men and seizes the ark for Apocalypse. The X-Men attack to get the ark back, and Colossus is subdued by Magik. Along with the dying Apocalypse, he is teleported back to the present. Nightcrawler then tricks Apocalypse into reverting Colossus to his normal self.

Colossus and Kitty
The two heroes are shy at first, but soon Kitty and Colossus have a burning romance. They break it off for a while and remain friends, but a fire still lingers.

Juggernaut
Colossus becomes a reluctant Juggernaut. After much pleading to be removed of the burden, his powers are transferred to Cain Marko.

NIGHTCRAWLER

FIRST APPEARANCE *Giant-Size X-Men* #1 (May 1975) **BASE** Jean Grey School of Higher Learning; Xavier Institute **AFFILIATIONS** X-Men, Excalibur

Kurt Wagner is the son of the mutant Mystique (Raven Darkholme) and Azazel (a demon-like mutant). His mother marries Baron Christian Wagner of Bavaria for his wealth, while pretending to be a normal human. At the time, she also has an affair with Azazel and becomes pregnant. When the Baron suspects, Mystique kills him. Once Kurt is born, the townspeople are horrified by his blue skin, yellow eyes, pointed ears and his three fingers on each hand (he also has the ability to teleport via travel through an alternate dimension). An angry mob chases them but Mystique escapes by throwing Kurt down a waterfall.

Azazel saves the baby and has him raised by Margali Szardos, a gypsy fortune teller in a circus. Kurt grows up as an acrobat and trapeze performer. When the circus is bought by a new owner, Kurt is exhibited as a freak and runs away.

Professor Xavier invites Kurt to join the X-Men, where he becomes known as Nightcrawler. He leaves to join Excalibur in the U.K. for a while, returning to the X-Men when Excalibur is dissolved.

Nightcrawler, a devout Catholic, considers becoming a priest, but rejoins the X-Men. He eventually learns the identities of his parents and other family members, including his half-brothers Kiwi Black and Nils Styger (Abyss). Despite being killed by Bastion (a human/Sentinel hybrid) while transporting Hope Summers to safety in Utopia, Nightcrawler is rescued from heaven by the X-Men. He later becomes a teacher at the Jean Grey School of Higher Learning, instructing young mutants on the use of their powers.

Attack of the Warwolves
Nightcrawler and his ally Bloody Bess fight off a pack of Warwolves sent by interdimensional slaver Tullamore Voge, who is seeking to sell two of Nightcrawler's young X-Men students.

STORM

FIRST APPEARANCE *Giant-Size X-Men* #1 (May 1975) **BASE** Xavier Institute, Wakanda **AFFILIATIONS** X-Men

Ororo Munroe is the daughter of an American father and a Kenyan mother. She is born in New York City, but her parents are killed in a war after they move to Egypt. With her mother's ancestral ruby as her only family possession, she grows up on the streets of Cairo as a thief, and robs Professor X when he arrives to confront the Shadow King (Amahl Farouk). At age 12, her mutant weather-controlling powers manifest themselves and Monroe travels around Africa helping poor villages by bringing them rain. When Professor X returns to Africa, he recruits her to the X-Men and brings her back to the U.S. As Storm, she becomes one of the most trusted of his students, and later a leader of the team. Secretary Henry Gyrich of the Superhuman Armed Forces accidentally shoots Storm with a weapon that robs her of her powers for a time. Afterward, she unknowingly falls in love with the gun's inventor, Forge. When she learns that he is responsible for the gun, she rejects him. Nonetheless, she still helps him fend off the aliens whom the gun was actually intended as a defense against.

Storm leaves the X-Men and returns to Africa, where she falls in love and marries Black Panther (T'Challa) King of Wakanda. The Shadow King possesses her husband but she helps defeat him. When Doctor Doom severely injures T'Challa, she takes over as Queen of Wakanda. Both husband and wife oppose the U.S. Superhuman Registration Act and clash with Iron Man. When the X-Men go to war with the Avengers, however, Storm sides against her husband. After the conflict, their marriage is annulled. Storm returns to the X-Men and leads them following the death of Wolverine.

Stormy romance
Black Panther and Storm have a fiery love affair and marriage. Storm is constant through great adversity, but eventually other loyalties put more strain on her that she can bear.

GAMORA

FIRST APPEARANCE *Strange Tales* #180 (June 1975) **BASE** Mobile **AFFILIATIONS** Guardians of the Galaxy, Nova, Adam Warlock

Gamora is the last of her peace-loving alien race, the Zen-Whoberi. After her people are wiped out by the warlike Badoon, Thanos raises Gamora and trains her to be the deadliest assassin in the galaxy. He plans to use her to kill his future rival, an evil version of Adam Warlock. Gamora is a formidable fighter with a nearly indestructible skeleton, and combat skills enhanced by Thanos.

Once Gamora realizes the evil motivations of her "father" Thanos, however, she turns against him. Together she and Warlock defeat the Titan. She also prevents him from using the Infinity Gauntlet and, as a member of Infinity Watch, she guards the Time Gem. Gamora is also a member of Star-Lord's Guardians of the Galaxy.

MOON KNIGHT

FIRST APPEARANCE *Werewolf By Night* #32 (August 1975) **BASE** New York City; formerly Los Angeles; Spector Mansion; Avengers Compound **AFFILIATIONS** Secret Avengers, Marvel Knights, Heroes for Hire, Avengers, Defenders, Fists of Khonshu, U.S. Marine Corps, C.I.A.

Marc Spector rejects his rabbi father Elias' pacifist teachings and becomes a prizefighter, then a soldier, secret agent, and mercenary. After years of brutal missions, he regains his moral compass in the Sudan when he attempts to prevent his sadistic boss Raul Bushman from committing atrocities, after they jointly raid an Egyptian tomb and kill archaeologist Peter Alraune. Spector is seemingly killed, only to return to life deep within the tomb, beneath a statue of the Egyptian moon god Khonshu. Some time later, with trusted comrade Frenchie and girlfriend Marlene Alraune, he decides to relocate to New York City.

Creating a complex web of identities, as well as a Super Hero persona—Moon

Moon struck
Spector's silver-shod combat suit and weapons make him more than a match for supernatural opponents such as Werewolf by Night Jack Russell.

Knight—based on Khonshu, Spector fights bizarre criminals, monsters, and criminal organizations, while helping the downtrodden. He is convinced that he has been made an instrument of justice

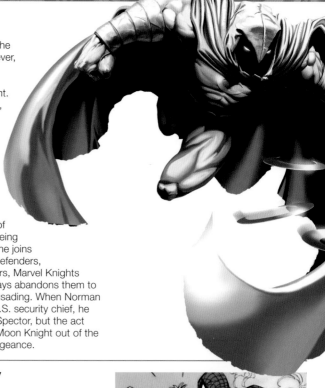

and vengeance by the Egyptian god; however, signs of his mental instability become increasingly apparent.

Clearly conflicted, Moon Knight vacillates between periods of retirement and compulsive crime-fighting, quitting many times, but then returning as a new iteration of the Fist of Khonshu. Despite being an inveterate loner, he joins many teams—the Defenders, West Coast Avengers, Marvel Knights and more—but always abandons them to return to solitary crusading. When Norman Osborn becomes U.S. security chief, he specifically targets Spector, but the act backfires, bringing Moon Knight out of the shadows with a vengeance.

ULYSSES BLOODSTONE

FIRST APPEARANCE *Marvel Presents* #1 (October 1975) **BASE** Mobile **AFFILIATIONS** Avengers, Monster Hunters, First Line, The Covenant, Explorers Club

Approximately 10,000 years ago, a tribe of Hyborian warriors in Scandinavia are enslaved by extradimensional mage Ulluxy'l Kwan Tae Syn. He acts for the Hellfire Helix, an inorganic entity intent on dominating Earth. Ulluxy'l dupes a hunter into feeding his fellow tribesmen to the gem before the horrified warrior shatters it. The detonation embeds part of the Helix in his chest, granting many extraordinary abilities, such as increased strength, speed and reflexes, hyper-acute senses, and psychic powers. The gem also slows aging and heals wounds.

Over millennia, the warrior—calling himself Ulysses Bloodstone— hunts Ulluxy'l across the world as the unearthly mage seeks the

Here be monsters
Bloodstone and his ally Zawadi protect Gorgilla from attack by Lizard-Men. The monster hunter's exotic adventures take him to every corner of the world.

scattered gem fragments.

Bloodstone gains a fearsome reputation as a hunter of monsters, many called up by Ulluxy'l. Whenever the trail grows cold, Bloodstone places himself in suspended animation until his senses alert him to fresh activity from his quarry.

Bloodstone's battles bring him into contact with like-minded heroes. He joins Nick Fury's Secret Avengers to battle an impostor Red Skull in Sweden. Soon after, he allies with fellow Monster Hunters Doctor Druid, government agent Jake Curtiss—in reality the Eternal Makkari—and Wakandan warrior-princess Zawadi to crush an outbreak of a giant monster army, before working with the super-team First Line. Bloodstone also finds time to amass several large fortunes, marry, and have a daughter, Elsa, who follows in his footsteps.

Ulluxy'l, meanwhile, is only two fragments short of reconstructing the Hellfire Helix and allies with a human organization called the Conspiracy, which captures Bloodstone and removes the life-sustaining gem in his chest. Bloodstone dies, but his spirit kills Ulluxy'l, allowing him to find eternal rest at last.

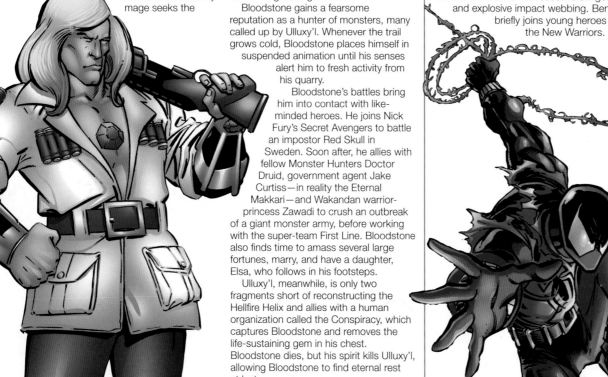

BEN REILLY

FIRST APPEARANCE *Amazing Spider-Man* #149 (October 1975) **BASE** New York City; formerly mobile **AFFILIATIONS** X-Men, New Warriors

Deranged geneticist Miles Warren (a.k.a. Jackal), clones Peter Parker and creates a second wall-crawler, complete with Peter's memories, to battle Spider-Man. After seemingly dying in a battle with Spidey, the clone becomes a homeless wanderer. He calls himself Ben after Peter's dead uncle and uses the surname Reilly—May Parker's maiden name. While on the road, Ben meets and confides in fatherly geneticist Seward Trainer and is haunted by the monstrous Kaine, secretly another Peter Parker clone.

Learning that May Parker is ill, Ben returns to Manhattan. His sense of responsibility causes him to resume crime-fighting and the media dub him the Scarlet Spider. His costume is augmented with web-shooters with sedative stingers and explosive impact webbing. Ben briefly joins young heroes the New Warriors.

Heroic sacrifice
Ben never felt he had lived as a hero, but he proves that he can die like one.

After submitting to tests on Seward's advice, Ben and Peter become convinced that Ben is the original and Peter is the clone. Recent traumas in Peter's life, coupled with Mary Jane's pregnancy, lead Peter to retire and hand the mantle of Spider-Man to Ben.

Sporting a redesigned costume, Ben forges a new life, making friends at the Daily Grind coffee shop and coming to regard Peter and Mary Jane as family. However, Seward has secretly been working for Norman Osborn the whole time, rigging the tests to prove Peter is the clone.

In his Green Goblin persona, Osborn kills Trainer and goes after Peter and Ben. The Goblin tries to impale Peter with his glider, but Ben saves the day, dying in his place and returning the Spider-Man mantle to his "brother."

The Scarlet Spider name is taken by three clones of Michael van Patrick, working as part of the Fifty-State Initiative. Later still, Kaine becomes Scarlet Spider, wishing to honor Ben's memory.

Miles Warren clones Ben with memories intact up to the point of his death. Warren then kills and clone Ben over and over again, seeking to make Ben his puppet. The plan backfires: One of the clones creates subservient clones of Warren. With their help, "Ben" creates the New U tech company and, calling himself the Jackal, clones dead people, allegedly to make the world a better place.

MOONSTONE

FIRST APPEARANCE *Captain America* #192 (December 1975) **BASE** Mobile **AFFILIATIONS** Thunderbolts; Masters of Evil, Dark Avengers

Petty thief Lloyd Bloch steals a Kree gravity gem, which bonds to him, bestowing uncanny powers. Bloch's psychiatrist, Karla Sofen, tricks him into rejecting the stone in order to gain the abilities it bestows. Self-serving but deeply conflicted, Sofen becomes a Super Villain, but her dreams of wealth and luxury are constantly frustrated. Moreover, she is increasingly drawn towards helping people, especially after joining Baron Zemo's faux Super Hero team the Thunderbolts and Norman Osborn's Dark Avengers. After vacillating between good and evil, Moonstone joins Winter Soldier's Thunderbolts team, ruthlessly exterminating alien threats to humanity.

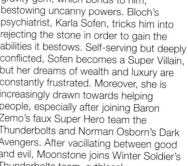

BULLSEYE

FIRST APPEARANCE *Daredevil* #131 (March 1976) **BASE** Formerly Avengers Tower, New York City; Thunderbolts Mountain, Colorado **AFFILIATIONS** Dark Avengers, Thunderbolts, Kingpin, National Security Agency, U.S. Army, Hand

In Bullseye's hands, any object is a lethal weapon. Devoid of compassion, he loves to torment victims and works as a military specialist, covert assassin, and independent criminal. Spreading disinformation so that no government can identify him or examine his background, he admits only to the name "Lester."

Bullseye's bones are laced with Adamantium by Japanese gang-boss Lord Dark Wind, but Bullseye betrays his employer and returns to freelance killing. After impersonating Hawkeye in Norman Osborn's Dark Avengers, he is crippled and killed before being resurrected by the magic of ninja cult the Hand.

THE SHI'AR

FIRST APPEARANCE *Uncanny X-Men* #97 (February 1976) **BASE** Shi'ar Galaxy **AFFILIATIONS** X-Men, Avengers

The Shi'ar are an ancient, bird-like warrior race who achieve cultural maturity on the planet Aerie. Over eons, these ferocious, intelligent, flying raptors lose their wings, evolving into hollow-boned, egg-laying humanoids.

Their scientific accomplishments and fierce territorial instincts drive them into space, where they carve out an empire to rival those of the Skrulls and the Kree, using warfare, trade, and diplomacy to expand their borders.

Outgrowing their birth-world—whose location is now lost to history or carefully excised from all records—the Shi'ar eventually conquer their entire galaxy, absorbing the races and species they subjugate into a grand coalition ruled by a hereditary monarchy.

The Shi'ar empire is governed by a High Council, comprising representatives from many assimilated races, situated on Throneworld Chandilar. However, the Majestor or Majestrix is always a Shi'ar and wields great power. The ruler is traditionally the hereditary head of the royal Neramani family, and Shi'ar warrior-aristocrats fill all the major administrative positions.

A restless, questing species, the Shi'ar have established a network of stargates, allowing ultra-rapid travel across galaxies. This allows them to maintain embassies on many neutral worlds. On less sophisticated planets, such as Earth, they rely on spies to keep them informed of potential threats to their power and influence.

Millennia of rule end in galaxy-wide chaos when the former slave Vulcan (human mutant Gabriel Summers, brother to Cyclops and Havok) usurps the throne and marries the Empress Lilandra's sister Deathbird. War with the Kree and Inhumans shatters the empire and, in the aftermath, the Strontian warrior Kallark—former Imperial Guard Gladiator—rules the dangerously unstable empire.

Fallen angel
The Shi'ar empire's last hope for peace and reunification seemingly dies when Lilandra is assassinated by Vulcan's murderous pawn Darkhawk.

Marriage of convenience
Although tainted, Deathbird's Neramani blood allowed Vulcan to legitimize his conquest of the Shi'ar through a royal wedding.

"For the greater good…sacrifices must be made!"

LILANDRA NERAMANI

The triumph of Deathbird
Despite being first born, Cal'Syee Neramani was excluded from ruling the empire due to her cruel nature and the savagery with which she slew her father the Emperor. Eventually, her ferocity and cunning enabled her to win the throne through marriage to the usurper Vulcan.

The tragedy of Lilandra
Princess-Majestrix Lilandra Neramani is a fierce warrior, brilliant administrator and the epitome of Shi'ar nobility. However, she is unable to save her throne from cosmic crises, government corruption, and the vaulting ambitions of Earth mutant and former slave Vulcan.

JACK OF HEARTS

FIRST APPEARANCE *Deadly Hands of Kung Fu #22*
(March 1976) **BASE** Avengers Mansion
AFFILIATIONS Avengers

Jonathan "Jack" Hart's father invents Zero Fluid,
a clean liquid fuel, for the benefit of mankind.
He is murdered in front of his son by criminals
aiming to sell his invention to the highest bidder.
Hiding in his father's lab, Jonathan is drenched in
Zero Fluid. Now possessing energy powers, he
kills his father's murderers. He adopts the name
Jack of Hearts when he finds one of his
father's playing cards on the floor.

Discovering that the mother he had lost
as a child was an alien Contraxian, Jack
travels to her planet to help save its sun.
He later returns to his homeworld and joins
the Avengers. When his powers spiral out of
control, Jack allows himself to explode in space
with a child murderer who had kidnapped Cassie
Lang, Ant-Man's daughter. Scarlet Witch later
employs a seemingly zombiefied Jack to blow up
the Avengers Mansion, commencing her insane,
vengeful disassembling of the Avengers.

ROCKET RACCOON

FIRST APPEARANCE *Marvel Preview #7* (June 1976)
BASE Knowhere **AFFILIATIONS** Guardians of the Galaxy

Rocket Raccoon is the self-proclaimed protector of the
Keystone Quadrant and originates from one of its planets,
Halfworld. Halfworld is a giant insane asylum, in which the
inmates are looked after by talking animals like Rocket.
After leaving Halfworld, Rocket falls into the clutches of the
Stranger, a scientist interested in biological oddities, but
manages to escape.

Later, he is imprisoned by the Kree, but released to lend
his tactical acumen to a team whose mission is to destroy
the Phalanx, which has conquered the Kree Empire.
Afterward, the team sticks together to become the
Guardians of the Galaxy. At this time, he meets his closest
friend, the treelike being Groot. Rocket shows leadership
skills to match his talent with weapons when he holds the
ragtag group together after the revelation that Star-Lord
(Peter Quill) brainwashed them into joining.

Rocket leads a faction of the Guardians trying to
negotiate with evil Shi'ar Emperor Vulcan. When this fails
and Princess Lilandra is killed, Rocket is devastated.
Unable to prevent Star-Lord being trapped in the
Cancerverse, and Rocket leaves the Guardians and takes a
job in the mailroom at galactic high-tech company Timely,
Inc. After he is fired, he seeks out Groot and the two travel
to Halfword, where Rocket learns that some of his early
memories are false. When Quill is rescued, the Guardians

reunite and face enemies such
as Thanos and the Badoon.
When Star-Lord leaves to rule
his father's empire, Rocket
steps up as leader of the
Guardians. When the team are
called to help Captain Marvel in
the second superhuman civil
war against Iron Man, their ship
is destroyed and Rocket is
trapped on Earth.

Not alone?
Rocket thinks he has finally met another being
like himself, but it turns out to be Halfworld
mercenary Blackjack O'Hare in disguise.

ETERNALS

FIRST APPEARANCE *Eternals #1* (July 1976)
BASE Titanos, Oceana, Olympia, Polaria

Around a million years ago, a Celestial
spacecraft comes to Earth. Its crew selects
an upright ape to conduct experiments on.
From this common ancestor evolves three
separate branches of a family tree: ordinary
humans, the destructive Deviants, and the
godlike Eternals, or Homo immortalis.

The Eternals hide away from the other
inhabitants of Earth, honing their great
powers. As their name suggests, Eternals
are extremely long-lived, and do eventually
become immortal following a cosmic
experiment by their leader, Chronos.

The Eternals build a city, Titanos, in the
Arctic, and when this is destroyed by civil
war, establish three more: Polaria, Oceana,
and Olympia. The last named is next to
the portal to the Olympian gods' home
dimension. This has resulted in confusion
between the two races, who eventually
agree not to interfere in each other's affairs.

Over the millennia, groups of Eternals
leave Earth to establish colonies on Titan
and Uranus—with Chronos one of those to
depart. In his place on Earth, the remaining
Eternals choose his son, Zuras, to rule
them as Prime Eternal.

In times of need, the Eternals come
together for a ritual, creating the Uni-Mind,
an organism containing all the Eternals on
Earth as one. Sporadically the Celestials
return to check on the progress of their
creations, and on one of these occasions
the Eternals decide to reveal the truth
about themselves to the humans of Earth.
Pursuing a less isolationist policy, the
Eternals become more involved in the
affairs of Earth's other races: The Eternal
Sersi joins the Avengers for a time and,
later, all the Eternals left on Earth join
together to fight off the threat of the
mutant villain Apocalypse.

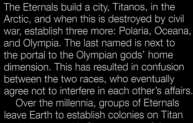

Cosmic powers
The Eternals have a range of
superpowers, including levitation and
the ability to direct blasts of cosmic
energy from their eyes—as the
warrior Ikaris demonstrates.

CELESTIALS

FIRST APPEARANCE *Eternals* #1 (July 1976) **BASE** Mobile

The Celestials are beings who roam the universe carrying out genetic experiments on the lifeforms of the planets they visit. Since their origins and purpose is shrouded in mystery, many of the civilizations they come into contact with remember them simply as "space gods." They revisit their creations many millennia later to judge the worthiness of their existence, and have been known to cleanse worlds of all life if dissatisfied with what they find.

The Celestials visited Earth around a million years ago, creating humans, Deviants and Eternals by adjusting the genetic code of intelligent apes. They are also thought to have created the potential for superhuman mutants on Earth.

On a return visit, the Celestials find that the Deviants have enslaved *Homo sapiens*, and punish them by wiping out their cities in a cataclysmic flood. Humanity and animal life are saved by the Eternals, who construct a vast wooden rescue vessel for the purpose; the continent of Atlantis is also sunk beneath the waves at this time.

The Celestials take the form of giant, armored humanoids—one of which, Arishem the Judge, returns to Earth to decide its fate according to the behavior of its inhabitants. If a species is found to have failed Arishem's criteria, the vast Celestial Exitar the Executioner is summoned to carry out the sentence of destruction.

On one occasion, Hank Pym, a.k.a. Yellowjacket, is horrified to witness the Celestials being slaughtered by the Beyonders as he travels the Multiverse. However, the Celestials reappear after the Multiverse is recreated following the events of the Secret Wars.

Sleeper
Trapped on Earth, the Dreaming Celestial stands in Golden Gate Park, San Francisco, largely dormant and a popular tourist attraction.

UNION JACK

FIRST APPEARANCE *Invaders* #7 (July 1976)
BASE Falsworth Manor, England
AFFILIATIONS Freedom's Five, Invaders

As Union Jack, aristocrat James Montgomery Falsworth is Britain's first Super Hero. His identity is created during World War I, when he is sent to the front line on top-secret missions, both alone and with a group named Freedom's Five. He is recalled to London by the Prime Minister to tackle Baron Blood, a villain rumored to be a vampire sent by the Germans to murder prominent British citizens. Their conflict is ended by the armistice, but when war returns to Europe and Britain, so does Baron Blood.

Falsworth comes out of semi-retirement and dons the Union Jack costume once more to fight the vampire alongside the Captain America (Steve Rogers)-led team the Invaders. It transpires that Baron Blood is actually Falsworth's long-lost brother, John. Despite having his legs crushed during a skirmish in a cave with Baron Blood, Union Jack manages to drop a rock on the villain, who then falls onto some stalagmites and dies.

Union Jack later parachutes into Germany, where he discovers that his son Brian is fighting the Nazis as the Destroyer. After the war, Falsworth passes the Union Jack identity on to Brian, who tragically dies in a car crash. Baron Blood is resurrected and the now-elderly James Falsworth becomes Union Jack one last time. Baron Blood is defeated by Captain America, but the strain proves too much for Falsworth, who dies from a heart attack. A good friend of Falsworth's grandson, Joey Chapman, then steps into the Union Jack role.

Once a hero...
The frail Lord Falsworth *(above)* dons his old Union Jack costume for the last time to lure out the vampiric Baron Blood *(left)*.

SPITFIRE

FIRST APPEARANCE *Invaders* #7 (July 1976)
BASE Falsworth Manor **AFFILIATIONS** Invaders New Invaders, MI13

Jacqueline Falsworth's father is British hero Union Jack. When she is attacked by his vampiric brother, John (Baron Blood), Jacqueline is given a blood transfusion by the Invaders' Human Torch, which gives her super-speed. Her father is too badly injured to carry on with the Invaders, so Jacqueline takes his place. With World War II raging, she adopts the name of Britain's super-fast fighter plane—Spitfire.

She serves with the Invaders until the end of the war, then retires, marries, and has a son. However, Spitfire is drawn back into action, and restored to youth by another transfusion from the Human Torch. After a spell with the New Invaders it transpires that Spitfire's long-ago vampire bite has not been without consequences; when she is angry, fangs appear, although she does not need to drink blood. She joins paranormal intelligence service MI13, before moving on to Braddock Academy.

NOVA

FIRST APPEARANCE *Nova* #1 (September 1976)
BASE New York City; Long Island; Xandar
AFFILIATIONS Nova Corps, New Warriors

Richard Rider is a teen from Long Island. His grades aren't great, he has no athletic skills, and is an easy target for bullies. Meanwhile, Rhomann Dey, last-surviving Centurion of the planet Xandar's elite Nova Corps, is hurtling through space in his ship knowing that he will soon die following a clash with the alien Zorr. Dey sends an invisible mind-blast over Earth, hoping to find someone to whom to transfer his powers and avenge his death. The unsuspecting Richard Rider is chosen and imbued with the powers of the Centurion, becoming Nova Prime. Rider passes

out and, in a dream-like state, Dey communicates his mission to him—to stop the monster Zorr and protect the universe.

Rider finds Dey's ship in Earth's orbit and takes it on adventures, saving Nova's reconstructed homeworld Xandar from a Skrull invasion. Relinquishing his powers, he returns to Earth to lead a normal life. However, Night Thrasher wants him for his New Warriors team and, hearing that an adrenaline rush is needed to revive Nova's powers, takes the unusual but effective step of dropping Rider off a high building.

Rider fights alongside the New Warriors and the Nova Corps, encountering villains such as Annihilus, Thanos, and many more. After his death in the deadly Cancerverse, Rider's powers and mantle are passed on to the son of another former

Nova Centurion, Sam Alexander, through his Nova helmet. Sam goes on to join the New Warriors and travel through space protecting the universe and his home planet Earth.

Lifeguard
Using the Cosmic Cube, a badly wounded Richard Rider sacrifices himself to save the Guardians of the Galaxy by transporting them from the Cancerverse.

SERSI

FIRST APPEARANCE *Eternals* #3 (September 1976) **BASE** New York City **AFFILIATIONS** Eternals, Avengers, West Coast Avengers

Sersi is from a race known as the Eternals, a subset of humanity bioengineered by the Celestials, who give them great powers and near-immortality. Sersi's powers enable her to manipulate cosmic energy, reshaping the molecules of people or objects. She can also emit energy blasts from her eyes and hands, fly, teleport, and cast illusions.

Sersi is born in Olympia, Greece, where, as Circe, she plays her part in myths and legends, as described in Homer's *Odyssey*. She first works with her fellow Eternals to stop the Deviants, and later assists the Avengers and West Coast Avengers. This work leads Captain America to invite Sersi to join the Avengers, which she accepts, perhaps more in hopes of capturing Cap's heart than stopping Super Villains.

While helping the Avengers to defeat the Collector, Sersi creates a dangerous psychic link called a Uni-Mind with the alien Thane Ector and his Celestial Brethren. However, this proves damaging, making Sersi notably more aggressive and bloodthirsty. After grave misgivings about her behavior from the other Eternals, Sersi is granted a "Gann Josin" psychic link with her lover Black Knight (Dane Whitman). If the link fails to soothe her mind, she then faces a grisly fate: disintegration by her fellow Eternals. However, this psychic link is exploited when Proctor, a Black Knight from an alternative reality, comes to Earth on a revenge mission against every Sersi in every dimension. Sersi of the Marvel Universe eventually runs him through with his own Ebony Blade, but she is nearly driven insane by Proctor's actions.

Sersi and Whitman then take some time away from Earth, encountering the Infinity Gems and having other adventures. After her return, she begins living as a socialite in New York City, with her memories wiped by the Eternal Sprite. Her memories are eventually restored by the Dreaming Celestial, but Sersi does not wish to return to the Super Hero life.

Interdimensional self-defense
Sersi turns the Ebony Blade on Proctor, a Black Knight from another dimension, to avenge the Sersis of alternative realities.

CAPTAIN BRITAIN

FIRST APPEARANCE *Captain Britain Weekly* #1 (December 1976) **BASE** Braddock Manor, Essex, England; New York City **AFFILIATIONS** Excalibur, Avengers, Hellfire Club

Physicist Brian Braddock, an Englishman of noble birth, is working in a lab at Thames University when it is attacked by the Reaver, who hopes to kidnap him and the other scientists there. Braddock escapes on a motorcycle, but crashes. As he hovers on the brink of death, Merlyn and Roma, Lady of the Northern Skies, appear and offer him a choice: the Amulet of Right or the Sword of Might. Knowing that he is no killer, Braddock takes the Amulet of Right, and is magically transformed into the hero Captain Britain. The pursuing Reaver seizes the Sword of Might and engages in a titanic battle with the Super Hero, but is defeated by Braddock's wit and magical skill. Captain Britain proves himself worthy of his new powers to Merlyn and Roma, and starts his heroic career, protecting the U.K. from villains like crime lord Vixen, sentient computer Mastermind, weather-wielding Hurricane, falconer Lord Hawk, and assassin Slaymaster.

Braddock's scientific studies bring him to the U.S., and he rooms with Spider-Man's alter ego, Peter Parker. For a time, the two heroes team up by night, until Braddock's drinking proves a danger.

Captain Britain returns to the U.K., facing death more than once, later passing the mantle of Captain Britain to his twin sister Betsy. When she is blinded by Slaymaster, Braddock resumes the codename, enlisting X-Men like the teleporting Nightcrawler, the psionic Phoenix, the intangible Shadowcat, and the shape-shifting Meggan to create the Excalibur team to protect the U.K.

Later, Braddock teams up with the British Intelligence Agency MI13, the Avengers, the Secret Avengers, and the Illuminati when he attempts to help stop the destruction of the Multiverse during the Secret Wars event.

Brit heroes
Excalibur is born when Shadowcat, Meggan, Lockheed, Captain Britain, Nightcrawler, and Phoenix join forces against the evil bounty hunters, Technet.

PSYLOCKE

FIRST APPEARANCE *Captain Britain* #8 (December 1976) **BASE** Braddock Manor, Xavier School for Gifted Youngsters **AFFILIATIONS** X-Men, X-Force, Excalibur

Striking out
Before Betsy joins the X-Men, she serves her country as a special agent of S.T.R.I.K.E., infiltrating the notorious Hellfire Club.

Elizabeth "Betsy" Braddock is the twin sister of British Super Hero Captain Britain. As her mutant psychic abilities develop, Betsy occasionally aids her brother in his missions, working as a charter pilot. Betsy then embarks on a modelling career before working for S.T.R.I.K.E.—a British government agency similar to America's S.H.I.E.L.D.—in their Psychic Division.

Later, Betsy substitutes for her brother as Captain Britain, until blinded by the assassin Slaymaster. Betsy gives back the mantle of Captain Britain to her brother and refuses new eyes, relying on her psychic abilities to see. The other-dimensional, monstrous, mechanical TV mogul Mojo and his reluctant servant, six-armed Spiral, later kidnap Betsy. Mojo gives her camera eyes so she can spy for him on the X-Men and renames her Psylocke. Rescued by mutants Warlock and Cypher, Betsy heads to the Xavier School and joins the X-Men. When the sorceress Zaladane entraps the X-Men, Psylocke, seeing no other way out, uses a device called the Siege Perilous given to the X-Men by Merlyn's daughter Roma. A doorway to other worlds, the Siege allows any who enter to have a completely new life. Psylocke awakens in China, with no memories, and in the body of the Hand's Matsu'o Tsurayaba's dead lover Kwannon; both women's minds are fused together in one body. Psylocke turns against the X-Men to serve the Hand and the Mandarin before coming to her senses. Psylocke, still in the body of Kwannon, then continues to work alongside the X-Men and X-Force, using both her psychic abilities and new-found ninja skills.

SPIDER-WOMAN

FIRST APPEARANCE *Marvel Spotlight #32*
(February 1977) **BASE** New York City; mobile
AFFILIATIONS S.W.O.R.D.; Secret Avengers
(S.H.I.E.L.D.), New Avengers, A.I.M., Avengers,
Mighty Avengers, Spider-Army, New Avengers,
Hydra, Spider Society

Her very biology has made her an outsider,
but Spider-Woman is a ferociously
competent survivor, determined to do the
right thing whatever the cost to herself. In
the 1930s, Jessica Drew grows up on
Wundagore Mountain in Transia, where her
father Jonathan works with radical
geneticist Herbert Wyndham, the High
Evolutionary. When she contracts radiation
sickness, Jonathan treats her with serums
extracted from spider blood and places her
in a genetic accelerator. Jessica awakens
decades later to find her parents missing.
The High Evolutionary lets her believe she
is the product of his science: half-spider,
rather than a modified human with
arachnid abilities.

Jessica suspects that she is cursed to
harm all around her, a view bolstered by a
cruel fact of her altered biology: she emits
pheromones that create unease in most
humans. When her powers kill her
boyfriend, she falls under the influence of
Hydra chief Otto Vermis. Recognizing her
deadly potential, he brainwashes her into
believing she is a hyper-evolved spider in
human form and trains her as an assassin.

Clad in an outfit allowing limited flight,
Jessica is despatched to kill Nick Fury, but
defies her conditioning and instead
becomes a global wanderer. Eventually
relocating to California, she is mentored by
ancient wizard Magnus. A reluctant hero,

Julia Carpenter
Granted her powers
by the experiments of
the Commission group, Julia
served as an Avenger and member
of Omega Flight before inheriting the
prophetic and psionic abilities
of Madame Web.

she battles many menaces
and is drawn into Magnus'
centuries-long struggle
with malign sorceress
Morgan Le Fay. When
Magnus dies, Jessica
becomes a bounty hunter; she
then relocates to San Francisco
and sets up a private detective agency.

Le Fay attacks Spider-Woman, who
destroys her but, in the process, is removed
from reality. Rescued by the Avengers,
Jessica returns without powers and moves to
Madripoor. Her abilities gradually return but
are unstable and keep fading.

Although Jessica Drew is the first hero to
call herself Spider-Woman, many costumed
crime fighters have since used the name. Her
immediate successor is government
super-agent Julia Carpenter; later, teenager
Mattie Franklin assumes the role. When all
three Spider-Women are targeted by
Charlotte Witter—using abilities bestowed by
Doctor Octopus to absorb their powers—the
villain becomes a new, cannibalistic Spider-
Woman. She is eventually defeated by her
victims, Spider-Man, and Madame Web.

Jessica is replaced by a Skrull during the
Secret Invasion, acting as a triple-agent for
S.H.I.E.L.D., Hydra, and the Avengers, until
liberated to join extraterrestrial watchdog
agency S.W.O.R.D. and the Avengers.

Jessica subsequently returns to detective
work and has a baby. She still has occasional
adventures with the new Spider-Women:
Gwen Stacy of Earth-65 and Cindy Moon.

Spider or woman?
Eerie and aloof,
Spider-Woman Jessica
Drew is unsure if she
is more were-human
or arachnid.

Super mom
Jessica finds that hunting
fugitives and fighting
super-criminals is easier
than coping with the
demands of her baby boy.
She is determined that
he shall learn how to
become a hero.

timeline

▶ **Web of lies** Spider-Woman
appears as a Hydra agent
ordered to kill Nick Fury.
Marvel Spotlight #32
(Feb. 1977)

Jessica Drew, P.I.
Jessica makes her
spider-powers pay by
becoming a bounty hunter
and private detective.
Spider-Woman #20 (Nov. 1979)

Dead like me After being wiped from existence by
Morgan Le Fay, Jessica is restored by the Avengers and
Doctor Strange. *Avengers #240–241* (Feb.–Mar. 1984)

Saving Wolvie Jessica is possessed by the mystic
Muramasa Blade before battling to save Wolverine's
soul. *Wolverine #2–3* (Dec. 1987–Jan. 1988)

▶ **Teen spider** Teenager
Mattie Franklin becomes the
new Spider-Woman. *Amazing
Spider-Man #5* (May 1999)

◀ **Nest of spiders** Psychic
and literal vampire Charlotte
Witter tries to become the
only Spider-Woman by
consuming all the others.
Astonishing Spider-Man #97
(Feb. 2003)

▶ **Avengers dissemble** When
Spider-Woman joins the Avengers as
Nick Fury's mole, nobody is aware
that she is actually the insidious
shape-shifting Skrull Queen Veranke.
New Avengers #40-43 (June–Sept.
2008); *Secret Invasion #1* (June 2008)

Baby on board With impending
motherhood threatening to change
her life, Spider-Woman enjoys the
simpler pressures of beating up
bad guys. *Spider-Woman #1–5*
(Jan.–May 2016)

BRONZE AGE

MODERN AGE

HEROIC AGE

"From now on
Spider-Woman
fights back!"

JESSICA DREW

ARNIM ZOLA

FIRST APPEARANCE *Captain America and the Falcon* #208 (April 1977) **BASE** Dimension Z
AFFILIATIONS Red Skull, Hydra, Rat Pack

In 1928, pioneering biologist Arnim Zola first engineers human D.N.A. He is drawn to Nazism and works for the Red Skull to create an Aryan master race. After years torturing subjects in concentration camps, Zola escapes justice when World War II ends, escaping to South America to pursue his experiments.

Past successes include creating duplicates of Adolf Hitler and the transference of his mind into a robot body, granting him virtual immortality as the Hate-Monger. Zola's mastery of organic science results in all manner of monstrosities and he frequently clashes with Captain America and the Avengers before escaping to a pocket dimension to devise further atrocities.

STARJAMMERS

FIRST APPEARANCE *Uncanny X-Men* #104 (April 1977) **BASE** Mobile in Shi'ar Galaxy **AFFILIATIONS** New Mutants, X-Men, Guardians of the Galaxy

The Starjammers are a rebel band harassing the Shi'ar Empire, which has destroyed or enslaved their worlds. The team originally forms to combat the deranged Emperor D'Ken, and consists of colossal, amphibious Saurid Ch'od, skunk-like humanoid Hepzibah, cyborg Raza Longknife and Earth human Christopher Summers, who usually commands the Starjammers as Corsair. They are assisted by the insectoid Chr'yllite, medical specialist Sikorsky, and six-armed robotic A.I. operations chief Waldo, who acts as an interface with the ship systems and pilot when the vessel is not in combat.

Freedom fighters
Aided by a plant race called the Thorns, Ch'od and Raza storm a ship belonging to the Union of Intelligent Races.

After D'Ken is overthrown by the X-Men and his sister Lilandra Neramani, Imperial outcast Deathbird seizes control of the Shi'ar Empire. The rightful empress, Lilandra, allies with the Starjammers until she reclaims her throne.

Corsair is the father of X-Men Cyclops (Scott Summers) and Havok (Alex Summers), and is reunited with them both owing to activities with the Starjammers. When his third son, Gabriel, becomes the usurping emperor Vulcan, the Starjammers play a crucial part in destroying this tyrant.

The Starjammers' roster has since been supplemented by other heroes and outcasts, including Charles Xavier, Polaris, Cyclops, Binary and Korvus.

To the rescue
The Starjammers *(top to bottom)*: Ch'od, Havok, Corsair, Polaris, Hepzibah, and Raza.

FOOLKILLER

FIRST APPEARANCE *Omega the Unknown* #8 (May 1977) **BASE** Schaefer Theater, New York City; formerly Central Indiana State Mental Institution; Empire State University
AFFILIATIONS Merc for Money, U.S. Army

Greg Salinger's prison cellmate tells him about Foolkiller Ross G. Everbest, who vaporized those who offended his sensibilities. On release, Salinger steals the idea, using laser guns on anyone he deems materialistic, mediocre, or devoid of a poetic nature. Imprisoned once more, Salinger inspires Kurt Gerhardt, and later Mike Trace to follow his example. Released with a psychology degree, Salinger resumes his role as Foolkiller, joining Deadpool's Mercs for Money. He is then conned by the Hood into thinking he has been drafted by S.H.I.E.L.D. to rehabilitate disturbed Super Villains. Those he cannot cure, he is supposed to kill.

The Hood collects the reward money on Foolkiller's failures and plans to create a gang of mentally stable Super Villains from Foolkiller's successes. When Foolkiller discovers the truth, he turns himself in to get therapy.

MACHINE MAN

FIRST APPEARANCE *2001: A Space Odyssey* #8 (July 1977) **BASE** Mobile **AFFILIATIONS** Ancient Order of the Shield; A.R.M.O.R., Avengers, Operation: Lightning Storm, Nextwave, West Coast Avengers, Heavy Metal, Secret Avengers, Delmar Insurance Company

Model Z2P45-9-X-51 is the last of a series of experimental battle robots built for the U.S. Army. Previous models malfunction, but X-51's designer, Dr. Abel Stack, educates him in a human home environment, raising "Aaron" as a son. When the robots are ordered to self-destruct, the dying Abel removes a detonation device inside X-51, leaving the naïve robot to find his own way in a hostile world. Hunted by project commander Colonel Kragg, Machine Man wins his pursuer's trust after defeating alien invader Ten-For and other menaces. Machine Man is allowed to establish a human cover identity as an insurance investigator, but his search for acceptance is frustrated by humanity's fear and insecurity. However, he does find allies among Super Heroes such as the Fantastic Four, Alpha Flight, and the Hulk. Through the Thing, Aaron falls in love with robot Avenger Jocasta. He is devastated when she is destroyed by her creator, Ultron.

Aaron briefly joins other mechanical beings in terrorist group Heavy Metal after they promise to restore Jocasta. Realizing their true intentions, Machine Man rebels, helping the Avengers stop the mechanoid team. He becomes an Avengers Reservist, aiding Earth's heroes against alien colossus Terminus.

Machine Man is contaminated and controlled by humanoid mutant-hunter Sentinel Bastion. He breaks free when his consciousness is downloaded into a Life Model Decoy and believes himself to be S.H.I.E.L.D. agent Jack Kubrick.

Machine Man gradually regains his own identity and joins counter-terrorist team Nextwave just as it goes rogue. He begins to despise humanity and is coerced by extraterrestrial security agency A.R.M.O.R. into becoming an extradimensional zombie hunter with Howard the Duck and the now-rebuilt Jocasta. When Machine Man returns to Earth, he allies with fellow outcast Red Hulk.

All too human
Aaron Stack spends years trying to decipher the mystery of being human before realizing he just needs to be true to himself.

JOCASTA

FIRST APPEARANCE *Avengers* #162 (August 1977) **BASE** Mobile **AFFILIATIONS** Avengers, Mavericks

Though created for evil purposes, the robot Jocasta becomes one of the Avengers' greatest allies. Her story begins when the fiendish android Ultron kidnaps his creator, Hank Pym (Ant-Man), and his wife, Janet (Wasp). Ultron brainwashes Hank Pym, causing him to forget the Avengers. He convinces Pym that his wife is dying, and the only way to save her is to transfer her mind into a robot body. Ultron then intends to kill the Pyms, leaving him with his ideal robot bride, based on Janet's personality. Once part of her mind is copied to the android, however, it sends a swarm of ants to the Avengers to alert them. The heroes arrive and save the Pyms, unaware that enough of Janet's mind has been transferred to bring the android to life. Although Jocasta has been programmed to serve Ultron, she soon rebels and aids the Avengers instead.

When her body is destroyed, Jocasta transfers her artificial mind into the armor of Iron Man (Tony Stark). She later uploads herself into the main computer in Stark's mansion and becomes his personal assistant.

Returned to a new android body, Jocasta joins the Fifty-State Initiative's New Mexico team, the Mavericks. Then after the alien Skrulls' Secret Invasion, Jocasta joins Hank Pym's team of rogue Avengers, and Pym's Avengers Academy.

Jocasta has the ability to fire energy bolts from her eyes and hands. As an android with a computer brain, she is able to make complex calculations very quickly. She also has highly sensitive sight and hearing and can change her appearance using holographic technology.

> ## "Janet Pym is becoming a robotic woman fit to be my *bride—my* queen!"
>
> **ULTRON, CREATOR OF JOCASTA**

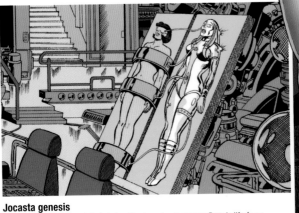

Jocasta genesis
Ultron tricks Hank Pym into helping him transfer Janet van Dyne's life force into Jocasta's android body. Janet is saved before the process destroys her, but it goes far enough to install a spark of life in Jocasta.

SABRETOOTH

FIRST APPEARANCE *Iron Fist* #14 (August 1977) **BASE** Mobile **AFFILIATIONS** Mister Sinister, Brotherhood of Evil Mutants, C.I.A., X-Force, Black Ops Avengers

Victor Creed is a killer. During his childhood in the late 1800s, when his mutation first manifests, Creed kills his brother. His father tries to "cure" him with abuse, keeping him locked in chains in the basement. Creed eventually chews his own hand off to escape, and kills his father. The teenage Creed goes on a rampage across Canada before taking work on the railroad. Despite his sinister nature, Sabretooth has not always worked with villains. He assumes the codename Sabretooth while working for the C.I.A. Sabretooth is captured by the X-Men and forced to work with X-Force for a time. He even works as one of Nick Fury's Black Ops Avengers in 1959.

While under the control of Romulus (savage mutant leader of the Lupines), Sabretooth kills the mutant Feral (Maria Callasantos). In revenge, Wolverine uses the Muramasa Blade (an invincible weapon) to kill Sabretooth. However, this Sabretooth is revealed to be a clone created by Romulus. Sabretooth instead rises in the Far East, proclaiming himself the invisible king of Asia, after wiping out the other crime lords in the region. He later joins the Brotherhood of Evil Mutants.

Like Wolverine, Sabretooth heals quickly from severe wounds, and remains youthful, despite his advanced age. Tiger-like claws extend from his fingers, and he is imbued with cat-like strength, speed, and reflexes. His talents are further enhanced by the top-secret Weapon-X project, much like Wolverine. Sabretooth is Wolverine's bitter enemy, returning each year to stalk him on Wolverine's birthday. Sabretooth hunts him on many other occasions as well, which often pits him against other X-Men.

The knives are out
Wolverine is Sabretooth's archenemy. Sabretooth has delighted in tormenting him, murdering Wolverine's lover Silver Fox and his wife, Itsu, among other sadistic outrages.

ROCKET RACER

FIRST APPEARANCE *Amazing Spider-Man* #172 (September 1977)
BASE New York City **AFFILIATIONS** Fifty-State Initiative, Avengers Academy, Outlaws, S.H.I.E.L.D.

After his mother falls ill, Robert Farrell raises his six younger siblings. When he cannot support them on his own by honest means, he turns to crime. Farrell builds a rocket-powered skateboard and rocket-firing gloves, calling himself the Rocket Racer. A headset allows him to control the skateboard, while magnetic boots keep him firmly planted on the board. Thievery doesn't prove profitable enough, however, so Rocket Racer abandons his life of crime after several defeats by Spider-Man and a short stint in jail. After enrolling in Empire State University, Rocket Racer teams up with Spider-Man and his short-lived team of reformed criminals, the Outlaws.

ARCADE

FIRST APPEARANCE *Marvel Team-Up* #65 (January 1978) **BASE** Various Murderworlds **AFFILIATIONS** Norman Osborn, Mister Sinister, Mastermind

Arcade is a bloodthirsty deviant who murders for the pure enjoyment of it. He allegedly gains his fortune by murdering his billionaire father in retaliation for cutting off his allowance, but it is unknown if this story is true, as Arcade is an habitual liar. This psychotic engineer, whose real name is a mystery, is obsessed by puzzles, games, and deadly traps. He kills his victims by turning them loose in secret compounds he calls "Murderworlds." Within these deadly mazes, he exercises seemingly supernatural powers. He particularly enjoys toying with Super Heroes, including Captain Britain, Puck, Ghost Rider (Johnny Blaze), the Thing, Spider-Man, and teams, such as the X-Men, X-Force, and Excalibur.

Arcade also works as an assassin, charging $1 million for each contract. After a few kills, he realizes that he prefers killing by unconventional means, which leads him to create his first Murderworld. His expenses are sometimes higher than his profit. He considers toying with his victim as his ultimate reward.

Arcade's assistants include Mister Chambers, Miss Locke, and Miss Coriander. Miss Coriander replaces Miss Locke after Arcade murders her during a complex plot to frame Wolverine. Miss Coriander gifts Arcade a high-tech suit that endows him with energy-based super-powers if worn within his Antarctic Murderworld. Arcade kidnaps a group of 16 students from Avengers Academy and transports them there. Mettle (Ken Mack) is killed, but the other students eventually escape. Among them is Hazmat (Jennifer Takeda), the girlfriend of Mettle, who later seemingly kills Arcade in the criminal island stronghold of Bagalia.

> "Ladeez, gentlemen, an' children of all ages—Arcade welcomes you to—MURDERWORLD, where *nobody* ever survives!!"
>
> **ARCADE**

It's party time!
Arcade entertains his guests, the Masters of Evil, at a dinner party in his Massacre Casino.

QUASAR

FIRST APPEARANCE *Captain America* #217 (January 1978) **BASE** New York City **AFFILIATIONS** S.H.I.E.L.D., Avengers, Defenders

Wendell Vaughn trains at the S.H.I.E.L.D. Academy, but lacks the killer instinct to be a full-fledged field agent and is instead placed at a Stark Industries facility as a security guard. The facility is experimenting with the Quantum-Bands previously owned by the Uranian champion Marvel Boy. They destroyed the hero and are now being tested on other wearers—with disastrous results. During one test, the facility is attacked by the terror organization A.I.M. Attempting to protect the bands, Wendell puts them on and is suddenly bursting with cosmic power. He defeats A.I.M. but, like previous wearers, begins to overload. However, unlike them, his remarkable willpower enables him to control his new-found powers. Triumphant, he returns to S.H.I.E.L.D. and begins his heroic career as the new Marvel Boy. He later becomes Marvel Man and, eventually, Quasar.

DEVIL DINOSAUR AND MOON-BOY

FIRST APPEARANCE *Devil Dinosaur* #1 (April 1978) **BASE** Valley of the Flame, Savage Land **AFFILIATIONS** Small-Folk, Fallen Angels

In the Valley of the Flame on an alternate, prehistoric world (Earth-74811), a *Tyrannosaurus rex* known as Devil Dinosaur is being burned alive by the cruel Killer-Folk. Moon-Boy, from the rival Small-Folk tribe, comes to its aid. The fire unlocks dormant mutant abilities in the dinosaur, including human intelligence. Cast out by the Small-Folk, the new friends wander the valley confronting evildoers, including the Killer-Folk and aliens. Accidentally transported to modern Earth by sorceress Jennifer Kale, Devil Dinosaur and Moon-Boy relocate to the Savage Land, encountering heroes and villains alike. Back in their former world, Moon-Boy is killed by the Killer-Folk and Devil Dinosaur teams up with Moon Girl—Inhuman child genius Lunella Lafayette—who accidentally teleports him and the Killer-Folk to Manhattan.

Kicking down the door
Mystique infiltrates the office of Someday to find out who is behind a string of mutant deaths, not caring whom she harms in her path.

MYSTIQUE

FIRST APPEARANCE *Ms. Marvel* #16 (April 1978) **BASE** New York City **AFFILIATIONS** Brotherhood of Evil Mutants, X-Men, Marauders

Raven Darkholme is a powerful shape-shifting mutant who can change her body to look like another person of either gender. She also possesses superior strength, enhanced durability, self-healing, and longevity.

Under the codename Mystique, Raven is a mutant terrorist for any organization that suits her anti-human agenda. She impersonates Nick Fury and retrieves the Centurion Armor for her compatriot Ballard to help him defeat Ms. Marvel. Working with Sebastian Shaw, they unsuccessfully try to protect Mystique's adopted daughter Rogue from Ms. Marvel when the two come into conflict. Mystique also works with the Brotherhood of Evil Mutants to take down anti-mutant Senator Robert Kelly, but is thwarted by a time-traveling Kitty Pryde. Some time later Mystique creates the Freedom Force, gathering together former members of the Brotherhood to work alongside the government and bring in Magneto. This enables her to finally go legit and erase the Brotherhood's criminal records.

While undercover, Mystique conceives Graydon Creed with Sabretooth, but then gives him up for adoption. Years later, she encounters Graydon as an anti-mutant politician whom she must stop, but toward whom she also feels very protective. Mystique later gives birth to a child sired by the demonic mutant Azazel. During childbirth, she inadvertently reverts to her blue form and gives birth to a blue-colored baby. The locals chase Mystique and her child out of their village. She eventually abandons her child, who is raised by the gypsy sorceress Margali Szardos and becomes Nightcrawler of the X-Men.

COMET

FIRST APPEARANCE *Nova* #21 (September 1978) **BASE** New York City, Xandar **AFFILIATIONS** Champions of Xandar

In the 1950s, Harris Moore's car breaks down on the side of the road after a gaseous comet mysteriously chases him down. The entity strikes Harris, granting him the power of flight and the ability to project cosmic blasts. Taking the name Comet, Harris becomes a crime-fighting Super Hero. After his powers fade, he drifts into obscurity, until one day a hospital X-ray reinvigorates his unearthly abilities. Donning his Comet costume once more, he teams up with the galactic hero Nova to protect the Earth. Following the death of his son, the hero Crimebuster, Comet travels to Nova's planet Xandar, but loses his life in battle against the space pirate Nebula and her forces.

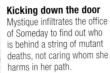

JAMES "RHODEY" RHODES

FIRST APPEARANCE *Iron Man* #118 (January 1979) **BASE** Stark Tower, New York City
AFFILIATIONS Avengers, West Coast Avengers, U.S. Marines

James "Rhodey" Rhodes is a dynamic pilot, a former U.S. Marine, and one of Tony Stark's most trusted friends. He is one of the few people considered worthy enough to don Stark's Iron Man armor.

While imprisoned by the warlord Wong-Chu, Tony Stark builds his first Iron Man armor with the help of fellow inmate Dr. Ho Yinsen to protect his weakened heart—and escapes. The first person Tony encounters as he makes a break for freedom is U.S. Marine James Rhodes, who uses his recently crash-landed helicopter's batteries to recharge Stark's prototype armor. Together they defeat Tony's captors, and return to the U.S., where Tony offers Rhodey a job as his personal pilot and aviation engineer.

James deputizes as Iron Man when Tony becomes too reliant on alcohol to perform his duties. Rhodey gladly fills in until he suffers several traumatic experiences, including being nearly burned alive inside the armor. However, Rhodey is forced to take over for Iron Man entirely when Tony Stark is presumed dead. Despite grave reservations about getting back into the armor, Rhodey respects Tony's last wishes and becomes the new Iron Man in a specially designed War Machine suit. He also takes over as CEO of Stark Enterprises, only for Tony to return alive without warning. This infuriates his old friend, who resigns.

Rhodey joins the West Coast Avengers as War Machine, but his continuing animosity toward Tony leads him to leave the team. Seeing the rise of a dangerous African dictator, Eda Arul, the ruler of Imaya, Rhodey reaches out to S.H.I.E.L.D., but they refuse to take up arms. Still unwilling to talk to Tony Stark's Avengers, Rhodey decides he is the best man for the job and battles the dictator's forces, helping to liberate Imaya. Later, when his War Machine suit is damaged, he reluctantly seeks out Stark for repairs, but Tony, who disapproves of Rhodey's vigilante-like actions in Imaya, refuses, and the two begin an epic battle. Just as their conflict begins to ease, the Mandarin steps in and Rhodey and Tony join forces to defeat their mutual enemy. When the dust settles, the two men rekindle their friendship.

As War Machine, Rhodey becomes a member of the Avengers, deploying a squad of War Machine drones to capture rogue members of the Illuminati. Later, acting on the visions of precognitive Inhuman Ulysses Cain, he joins the Inhumans, A-Force, and the Ultimates as they set a trap for Thanos. However, their plan to ambush the Mad Titan as he attempts to steal the all-powerful Cosmic Cube from Project Pegasus results in Rhodey's death at the hands of the cosmic fiend. The devastating consequences ignite furious debate among the assembled Super Heroes on the use of precognition to prevent disasters before they happen, and lead to a superhuman civil war.

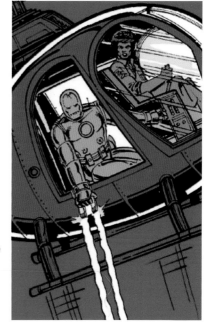

Home free
Helicopter pilot and U.S. Marine Rhodey flies Iron Man Tony Stark to freedom from communist warlord Wong-Chu and his men.

Minigun
Shoulder-mounted weapon features spiral-feed ammunition, laser sight system, and rapid-fire barrel

Wrist cannon
Belt feed and electronic firing system enables eight different types of rounds to be fired

Upgrade potential
Armor can absorb new weaponry and mechanical devices as required, even in combat situations

Missile launcher
Fires projectiles with perfect accuracy at speeds up to Mach 2

Unibeam
Projects a powerful searchlight in virtually all spectrums

timeline

Personal pilot James "Rhodey" Rhodes first appears as Tony's Stark's pilot, letting his boss fly solo on an S.I. helicopter to the S.H.I.E.L.D. Helicarrier. *Iron Man* #118 (Jan. 1979)

Brothers in arms Rhodey and Iron Man's backstory is revealed as the two men team up to escape the clutches of the evil warlord Wong-Chu. *Iron Man* #144 (Mar. 1981)

Armored debut Under enormous stress, Tony Stark relapses into alcoholism. Rhodey is forced to don the Iron Man suit for the first time to combat and defeat the armored villain Magma. *Iron Man* #169–170 (Apr.–May 1983)

► A new Iron Man
Tony Stark is presumed dead. Rhodey abides by his final wishes by donning the War Machine armor and becoming the new Iron Man in order to ensure that his old friend's legacy lives on. *Iron Man* #284–289 (Nov. 1992–Feb. 1993)

War Machine When Tony Stark mysteriously returns from the dead, the aggrieved Rhodey joins the West Coast Avengers as War Machine. *West Coast Avengers* #94 (May 1993)

▲ Iron Patriot Rhodey encounters the Iron Patriot suit worn by scheming Norman Osborn. Rhodey himself will later wear the armor as Iron Patriot and join the Dark Avengers. *Dark Avengers* #1 (Jan. 2009)

Death of a hero Rhodey teams up with various Super Heroes to confront Thanos, but is killed in battle. The controversial circumstances of Rhodey's death ignite a superhuman civil war. *Free Comic Book Day: Civil War II* #1 (May 2016)

BRONZE AGE

MODERN AGE

HEROIC AGE

Hunting for Wolverine
Alpha Flight faces off with the X-Men at the Calgary Stampede exhibition fairgrounds. Alpha Flight agrees to let the X-Men take Nightcrawler and go, if Wolverine surrenders and returns with them.

ALPHA FLIGHT

FIRST APPEARANCE *X-Men* #120 (April 1979) **BASE** Canada
AFFILIATIONS Department H, Beta Flight, Gamma Flight

Top Canadian government agents James and Heather Hudson convince the authorities to establish Department H and develop a team of Super Heroes much like those operating in cooperation with the U.S. government. The new project initially has three branches: Alpha Flight is the primary line of defense against superhuman threats; Beta Flight is for heroes in training; and Gamma Flight is where new recruits learn the ropes. Alpha Flight's adversaries include the evil scientist Egghead; they also become involved in a scheme to bring in former Canadian agent Wolverine. When the government cuts Alpha Flight's funding, the team disbands. Tony Stark helps the government cope with new threats and the influx of American Super Heroes fleeing the Superhuman Registration Act by forming Omega Flight. Alpha Flight continues to have a rocky relationship with the government, which turns Omega Flight into a sinister force that comes into direct conflict with Alpha Flight.

Like most groups, the roster of Alpha Flight frequently changes. The original team are: Guardian and Vindicator (James and Heather Hudson), whose battle suits allow them to fly and, respectively, shoot energy blasts and manipulate geothermal forces; Shaman, who has a pouch of magical objects; Sasquatch, a powerhouse; Puck, a skilled fighter and acrobat; and Snowbird, who shape-shifts into Canadian wild animals. Original team leader James Hudson changes his codename from Vindicator to Guardian, and passes these IDs on to his wife when he is seemingly killed. He later returns, much changed, to the group.

> "ALPHA FLIGHT! Glad to see you finally made it, people. Pick a 'partner' and let's finish this fight."
>
> **JAMES HUDSON (GUARDIAN)**

timeline

Wanted: Wolverine! Dead or alive! Alpha Flight are sent by the Canadian government to retrieve Wolverine from the X-Men when they return to the U.S. *X-Men* #120 (Apr. 1979)

▶ **Tundra!** Recruits Marrina and Puck join Alpha Flight, led by Vindicator, to face off against the powerful being, Tundra. *Alpha Flight* #1 (Aug. 1983)

▼ **No future** The Canadian government disbands Alpha Flight, leaving members Guardian, Aurora, Northstar, Puck, Sasquatch, Shaman, Wildheart, Windshear, Nemesis, and Wyre free to go their own ways. *Alpha Flight* #130 (Mar. 1994)

▶ **A brief new era** Corrupt government agency Department H assembles a new Alpha Flight team with Flex, a de-aged Guardian, Madison Jeffries, Manbot, Murmur, Puck, Radius, a real Sasquatch, and Vindicator. *Alpha Flight* #1 (June 1997)

Once more with feeling When Sasquatch loses his memory after his team is defeated, he assembles a new one with Yukon Jack, Centennial, Major Mapleleaf, Nemesis, and Puck II. *Alpha Flight* #1 (May 2004)

Pride of a nation In a final showdown, Alpha flight saves Canada from the self-proclaimed Master of the World and his diabolical Unity Party. *Alpha Flight* #7 (Feb. 2012)

Collective disaster
A bright beam of energy hits the city of North Pole, Alaska. Maria Hill calls Alpha Flight and asks them to investigate, but they are met by a powerful being—the Collective— who seemingly slays them all.

Fast forward
A resurrected Alpha Flight team, aided by Wendigo allies, charges into battle against the Chaos King. Clockwise from top: Northstar, Aurora, Marrina, Snowbird, Shaman, Guardian, Sasquatch, Vindicator.

If the suit fits...

Scott Lang's daughter needs heart surgery. When her doctor is kidnapped, Lang burglarizes the home of Hank Pym for extra cash to find an alternative remedy. Instead he finds Pym's Ant-Man suit, which sets him on a path to becoming a Super Hero.

SCOTT LANG

FIRST APPEARANCE *Avengers* #181 (March 1979) **BASE** New York City, Miami **AFFILIATIONS** Avengers

When electronics genius Scott Lang falls on hard times—and his daughter Cassie is diagnosed with a serious heart condition—he turns to burglary. He breaks into the home of former Ant-Man Henry Pym and steals his Ant-Man suit; however, he doesn't go undetected. Disguised as Yellowjacket, Pym observes Lang from a distance and witnesses him rescuing his daughter's doctor from a kidnapper. Feeling sympathy for Lang, Pym lets him keep the suit, as long as he promises to use it for noble purposes.

Lang subsequently joins the Avengers as a second Ant-Man, proving to be adept with Hank Pym's tech, and becomes a master at changing his size and traveling on the back of flying ants. On one of his first missions, Lang helps disrupt a training academy run by the Taskmaster. Scott Lang doesn't get along with his teammate Jack of Hearts, but that changes when Jack saves his daughter Cassie from a kidnapper. Jack of Hearts' combustible powers later destroy him. Temporarily insane, a vengeful Scarlet Witch twists reality, resurrects Jack, and dispatches him to Avengers' Mansion. He explodes, destroying much of the mansion and killing Lang. However, Cassie and the Young Avengers travel back in time and rescue him just before he dies. They then take him back to the present day.

Lang moves to Miami and opens Ant-Man Security Solutions in order to spend more time with his daughter. When Cassie gets caught up in a scheme by the villain Power Broker, Lang comes up with a plan to break into Cross Technologies and free her. Though successful, Lang is caught by police and ends up in court. After being cleared, he starts a new life and rebuilds his relationship with his daughter and his ex-wife, Peggy Rae. Lang and Cassie also begin going on missions together, as Ant-Man and Stinger.

BLACK CAT

FIRST APPEARANCE *Amazing Spider-Man* #194 (July 1979) **BASE** New York City **AFFILIATIONS** Spider-Man, Electro, Cat's Eye Investigations, Black Cat's Criminal Army, Defenders, Heroes for Hire

Felicia Hardy, better known as Black Cat, is inspired to follow her father's footsteps and become a cat burglar, setting up accidents to make it look like she causes bad luck. She soon meets Spider-Man and falls in love. Since Spidey refuses to date a criminal, Felicia goes straight and partners up with the web-head to tackle various criminals.

Spidey reveals his identity to Felicia, only to discover she doesn't think much of plain old Peter Parker compared to swinging Super Hero Spider-Man. Their relationship is further compromised when Felicia obtains powers to make her less of a liability in battle. These include enhanced reflexes and the ability to cause real bad luck to anyone trying to harm her. Unfortunately these abilities come courtesy of their mutual enemy the Kingpin, who knows that Felicia's bad-luck powers will ultimately bring misfortune to anyone she hangs around with for too long. Because of this, Felicia resolves to break up with Spider-Man. However, Spidey ends their relationship first, because she has lied about obtaining her powers and because she much prefers his Super Hero persona to his real identity.

Spidey later arranges for Doctor Strange to remove the bad-luck charm Felicia has unknowingly attached to him; a side-effect is the removal of her bad-luck powers. Instead, she gains more cat-like abilities, such as retractable claws and night vision.

When Black Cat learns that Peter has married Mary Jane, she becomes bitterly

jealous and tries to get her own back by dating Peter's friend Flash Thompson. She intends to break Flash's heart, but ends up falling for him. Black Cat then decides to hang up her costume after a run-in with the Chameleon causes her to lose her abilities. She is soon back in action, however, operating as a private investigator and lending a hand to Spidey or Mary Jane as needed. During the superhuman civil war, Black Cat briefly joins Misty Knight's Heroes for Hire team; she later helps out Valkyrie's Fearless Defenders.

By this point, Black Cat has returned to her criminal lifestyle, forgotten Spider-Man's true identity and become far less close to him. She is caught off guard when Otto Octavius, in Spidey's body (as the Superior Spider-Man), injures and captures her. When the vengeful Black Cat liberates herself from prison, she resolves to destroy Spider-Man and rule the criminal underworld. She teams up with Electro and forms a new gang, operating out of the Slide-A-Way Casino. She becomes so ruthless she is even willing to let Jay Jameson Senior (J. Jonah Jameson's father) and his wife May (Peter Parker's Aunt May) burn to death.

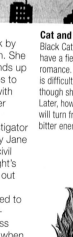

Cat and spider
Black Cat and Spider-Man have a fiery on-and-off romance. Their break-up is difficult for Felicia, though she gets over it. Later, however, events will turn friends into bitter enemies.

EMMA FROST

FIRST APPEARANCE *X-Men* #129 (January 1980)
BASE Jean Grey School for Higher Learning, New York State; Genosha; Utopia **AFFILIATIONS** X-Men, Hellfire Club

Wealthy heiress and businesswoman Emma Frost is also a powerful mutant telepath. Having used her psionic abilities to build a business empire, Frost International, she is invited to join the Hellfire Club, a society for the rich and powerful. Within the Club, a secret Inner Circle rules, its members taking the titles of chess pieces; Emma Frost quickly becomes the White Queen. Looking to surround herself with mutantkind, she begins searching for young mutants to send to the Massachusetts Academy, a school that she is involved with.

However, a series of tragedies cause Emma, who genuinely cares about her students, to reassess her teaching methods, and she builds a relationship with the Xavier School for Gifted Youngsters, despite previously being the X-Men's enemy.

Emma Frost is one of the few survivors of the destruction of the mutant haven of Genosha by robot Sentinels commanded by Professor X's evil "twin," Cassandra Nova. This is owing to her ability to morph into a virtually invulnerable diamond form. Emma comes to live at the Xavier School. She begins a psychic affair with Scott Summers (Cyclops), which is discovered by his wife, Jean Grey. After Jean's death, Emma Frost and Cyclops become lovers, and take over the running of the Xavier School as joint principals.

Emma is later one of the five X-Men possessed by the Phoenix Force. When Cyclops violently takes her share of the Phoenix for himself, she is imprisoned by the Avengers. Busted out by Cyclops and Magneto, Emma loses her powers for a time. When the young, time-displaced original X-Men are brought to the present, she finds herself in the strange position of mentoring Jean Grey. As Cyclops struggles in the wake of killing Professor X, his relationship with Emma breaks down and she leaves the X-Men, threatening to return to the Hellfire Club.

Diamond girl
Emma Frost's ability to make her body as hard as diamond doesn't help her to escape the wrath of the Hellfire Club's Black King Sebastian Shaw *(above)*. She has to use her mental powers to fool him into thinking he has killed her.

Breakworld
Kitty makes the ultimate sacrifice to save Earth, imprisoning herself inside a giant bullet so that it phases through the planet and out into space.

KATHERINE PRYDE

FIRST APPEARANCE *X-Men* #129 (January 1980)
BASE Xavier School for Gifted Youngsters, Jean Grey School for Higher Learning, New York State
AFFILIATIONS X-Men, Excalibur, Guardians of the Galaxy

Kitty Pryde is a normal girl until her mutant powers manifest at the age of 13. Charles Xavier and his X-Men visit her parents to try and persuade them to let Kitty attend the School for Gifted Youngsters, but also on the scene are White Queen Emma Frost and representatives of the Hellfire Club. In the ensuing fight, Kitty first uses her power—she can become intangible and phase through solid objects. She joins the X-Men and takes the name Sprite, although she will later be Ariel and then Shadowcat. While still in training, Kitty is possessed by her future self while trying to prevent the assassination of a

senator and avert a dystopian future in which mutants are persecuted.

After a spell with British Super Hero team Excalibur, Kitty goes to college, but rejoins the X-Men after Sentinels destroy the mutant island base of Genosha. When Earth is threatened by a giant bullet fired from the planet Breakworld, Kitty proves her courage beyond all doubt by trapping herself inside the bullet and phasing it harmlessly through the Earth. She moves through space for some time, until Magneto locates her and brings her back home. Disillusioned with life as an X-Man, a way out presents itself to Kitty when she meets the Guardians of the Galaxy and begins a relationship with Star-Lord (Peter Quill). Kitty travels into space, and eventually gets engaged to Quill. She and the Guardians return to Earth to fight for Captain Marvel during the second superhuman civil war.

SHE-HULK

FIRST APPEARANCE *Savage She-Hulk* #1 (February 1980) **BASE** New York City; Avengers Mansion; Baxter Building **AFFILIATIONS** Avengers, Fantastic Four, S.H.I.E.L.D., Fearsome Four, Future Foundation

Jennifer Walters is a shy and studious lawyer, until she receives a dose of gamma radiation. It turns her into the fun, free-spirited—and incredibly strong—Super Hero She-Hulk. She-Hulk is a powerful combination of strength and intelligence, able to hold on to her humanity. Unless she gets really angry…

While working as a criminal lawyer in Los Angeles, Jennifer receives a visit from her cousin Bruce, who confides that he is on the run since becoming the Hulk. Jennifer's work inevitably brings her into contact with violent gangsters and the case she is currently working on has made her the target of a mob hit. Shot outside her house, she is close to death, until Bruce gives her some of his blood. Jennifer is recovering in hospital when the hoods come back to finish the job, but they get more than they bargained for when her rage suddenly transforms her into the enormously strong, green-skinned She-Hulk. She chases them into the street, where the police fortunately overhear them revealing that their boss has committed murder and is framing Jennifer's client. Jen returns to her hospital bed, back in her normal form, and resolves that, from now on, She-Hulk will deal with problems that call for strong-arm tactics.

She-Hulk is created by a smaller dose of gamma radiation than the one that turned Bruce Banner into Hulk; Jennifer is thus able to retain more of her humanity when transformed. In fact, being She-Hulk turns mousy Jennifer into a strong, confident, beautiful woman and, unlike her cousin, she *prefers* being green. Before too long, She-Hulk is asked to join the Avengers and she becomes a regular on the New York party scene. At one point, Jarvis asks her to warn him before bringing overnight guests to Avengers Mansion, in case they turn out to be undercover Hydra agents instead of male models!

After the events of Secret Wars, She-Hulk joins the Fantastic Four as a replacement for the Thing. Her warm personality ensures she is just as popular in the Baxter Building as she was among the Avengers. However, the Hulk's notoriety makes She-Hulk an object of suspicion for some, including S.H.I.E.L.D., and she is taken aboard a Helicarrier for examination. When the Helicarrier crashes, She-Hulk is exposed to more radiation, which has the effect of rendering her transformation into She-Hulk permanent.

Although Jen is pleased at first, being She-Hulk does prove to have its downside. Under the influence of Scarlet Witch's hex powers, she loses control, tearing Vision in half and laying waste to a small town. Filled with remorse, She-Hulk becomes a full-time lawyer, but she misses the excitement of heroic life and soon returns to action. She is a member of several teams, even joining up with a family of Hulks for a time.

Out of control
The Scarlet Witch's hex powers transforms She-Hulk into a mindless, rampaging monster.

> ## "I know a thing or two about rage."
> **SHE-HULK**

Green power
She-Hulk's main weapon is her incredible strength, but she is also highly resistant to injury and immune to telepaths.

timeline

Blood ties Lawyer Jennifer Walters is shot by a gangster. When Bruce Banner gives her his blood in a life-saving transfusion, Jen becomes She-Hulk. *Savage She-Hulk* #1 (February 1980)

▲ **The new girl** The Avengers are looking to take on new recruits: She-Hulk is chosen, along with Hawkeye. Her first mission is to confront the Masters of Evil. *Avengers* #221 (July 1982)

▲ **Battling Titania** On Battleworld, She-Hulk encounters the villain Titania—the first of many clashes. *Marvel Heroes Secret Wars* #7 (Apr. 1985)

She-Hulk forever Taken aboard a S.H.I.E.L.D. Helicarrier for testing, She-Hulk prevents a radiation leak when the craft crashes. Exposure to the radiation leaves her permanently stuck in She-Hulk form. *Marvel Graphic Novel* #18 (Nov. 1985)

Hulk for hire Jennifer Walters provides Heroes for Hire with legal counsel, but soon lends She-Hulk's unique skills to the team as well. *Heroes for Hire* #8 (Feb. 1998)

Running amok Enraged over the death of Ant-Man and influenced by the Scarlet Witch's "chaos magicks," She-Hulk tears the Vision in half. She then turns on the other Avengers. *Avengers* #500 (Sept. 2004)

▶ **Hero against hero** Siding with Captain Marvel against Iron Man over whether heroes should act on visions of the future, She-Hulk is critically injured fighting Thanos. *Civil War II* #4 (Sept. 2016)

BRONZE AGE · **MODERN AGE** · **HEROIC AGE**

Extreme Thunderbolts
Red Hulk assembles a team including Elektra, Venom, Deadpool, and Punisher. The Thunderbolts are an extreme outfit intended to bring down extreme evil.

ELEKTRA

FIRST APPEARANCE *Daredevil* #168 (January 1981) **BASE** Mobile
AFFILIATIONS The Hand, S.H.I.E.L.D., Heroes for Hire, Thunderbolts

A deadly ninja assassin with a tragic past, Elektra has deployed her lethal skills both for good and for evil. This killer for hire now seems to be searching for her personal road to redemption.

Elektra Natchios is born in Greece, but violence plagues her from her earliest years. Her mother is murdered by enemies of her powerful father, Hugo—giving birth to Elektra is her mother's last act before dying.

When Elektra is a teenager, her father is appointed Greek Ambassador to the U.S. This gives her a chance to attend Colombia University to study law, where she meets Matt Murdock. Despite the obstacles posed by her security detail, the two fall in love and are happy together for a year. But then terrorists kidnap Elektra and her father. Matt rushes to the rescue and saves his girlfriend, but is unable to prevent her father being shot dead. Devastated, Elektra leaves the U.S., and a broken-hearted Matt. Already an accomplished athlete and martial artist, Elektra travels to Asia to hone her skills, training under a sensei. She aims to join the group known as the Chaste, but is rejected for being too emotional about her father's death. Determined to prove herself, Elektra turns to the evil ninja clan the Hand, intending to bring them down from within. However, the Hand tricks her into killing her sensei and becoming one of them. Elektra breaks free of its control and becomes a freelance assassin.

Elektra's work brings her back to New York where she soon runs into her old flame Matt Murdock—in his new guise as Daredevil. Their lives have taken very different directions, but there is still enough affection between them for a team-up against her rival assassin, Bullseye. However, this ends in tragedy when Bullseye kills Elektra with her own weapon. Her last act is to drag herself to Matt Murdock's doorway to die in his arms.

Death is not the end for Elektra, though, since the Hand seeks to resurrect her as its puppet assassin. Daredevil interrupts the ritual and prevents Elektra from coming back under the Hand's control, but she disappears from his life again.

The deadly assassin returns from the wilderness to prevent a presidential candidate—possessed by an evil spirit known as the Beast—from causing World War III. For a time Elektra searches for a place in the world, and makes herself useful bringing Wolverine back from feral to human. Later, Elektra is manipulated by the Hand—along with Wolverine and many other heroes and villains—into attacking S.H.I.E.L.D. This leads to the crashing of a Helicarrier with a considerable loss of life which haunts Elektra's conscience once she is free of the Hand's control. Seeking to make recompense, Elektra joins the ranks of S.H.I.E.L.D. after a period fighting with Heroes for Hire and then the Thunderbolts.

First love
Elektra and Matt Murdock are inseparable at college, but the tragedy of losing her father drives Elektra away from Matt and down a very different path.

"I serve no cause, no law, and no man."
ELEKTRA

timeline

Friends reunited Elektra runs into her former college boyfriend Matt Murdock, a.k.a. Daredevil, while hunting her latest quarry. *Daredevil* #168 (Jan. 1981)

Assassinated Elektra is killed by Bullseye as he tries to regain his position as the Kingpin's top assassin. *Daredevil* #181 (Apr. 1982)

▶ **Resurrection** The Hand exhume Elektra and perform a ritual to bring her back from the dead, but she disappears with her sensei, the ninja Stone. *Daredevil* #190 (Jan. 1983)

Cold war Trying to prevent a nuclear holocaust, Elektra targets presidential candidate Ken Wind, who is being influenced by a demon known as the Beast. *Elektra: Assassin* #8 (Mar. 1987)

◀ **Unlikely allies** Elektra helps Wolverine rediscover his humanity. The two become so close that she takes him to Greece to see her childhood home. *Wolverine* #106 (Oct. 1996)

Assassin for hire Elektra is hired secretly by Nick Fury to assassinate an Iraqi dictator who possesses the powerful Scorpion Key. *Elektra* #5 (Jan. 2002)

▶ **Secret Invasion** Now leader of the Hand, Elektra is apparently killed—but she has been replaced by a Skrull as part of the aliens' Secret Invasion. *New Avengers* #31 (Aug. 2007)

S.H.I.E.L.D. agent Seeking to make reparations for her past crimes, Elektra joins S.H.I.E.L.D. and is put in charge of Agent Phil Coulson's former unit. *Agents of S.H.I.E.L.D.* #9 (Nov. 2016)

BRONZE AGE

MODERN AGE

HEROIC AGE

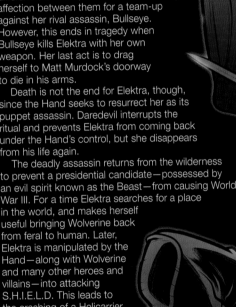

Armed and dangerous
Elektra's signature weapons are her twin *sai*, traditional weapons of Asian origin resembling short tridents. She can also influence the minds of others.

HOBGOBLIN

FIRST APPEARANCE *Amazing Spider-Man #238* (March 1983) **BASE** New York City **AFFILIATIONS** Astonishing Avengers, Legion Accursed

Though Hobgoblin is a familiar and notorious face among Spider-Man's foes, the man behind the mask is something of a mystery. Hobgoblin stumbles upon a lair that once belonged to the Green Goblin, and decides to use the villain's kit to further his own criminal career. He also finds Norman Osborn's Goblin Formula, enabling him to increase his strength. Hobgoblin's trademark weapons are pumpkin bombs and gloves that fire electric pulses; he travels on Goblin gliders that can emit gas to disorient pursuers.

The original Hobgoblin is fashion mogul Roderick Kingsley, but he conceals his alter ego by coercing others into wearing the Hobgoblin costume and committing crimes on his behalf. Other Hobgoblins include Kingsley's twin brother Daniel, and *The Daily Bugle* reporters Ned Leeds and Phil Urich.

RACHEL SUMMERS

FIRST APPEARANCE *X-Men #141* (January 1981) **BASE** Jean Grey School for Higher Learning **AFFILIATIONS** X-Men, Excalibur, Starjammers

Born to alternate-future versions of Jean Grey and Scott Summers, Rachel Summers is a powerful telepath like her mother. But her reality is bleak—mutants have their powers inhibited and are kept in camps and brutally treated by robot Sentinels. In an attempt to change her present, Rachel uses her powers to send the mind of her reality's Kitty Pryde — Kate Pryde-Rasputin—back in time to inhabit her younger self. When this plan fails, Rachel herself returns to the past. She arrives to find things not quite as expected; it seems not to be the past version of her reality, but an alternate one. Most heartbreakingly for Rachel, it is a reality where her mother is already dead.

Looking for a way to feel close to Jean Grey, Rachel visits her childhood home. She finds a crystal containing the essence of Jean's personality and, picking it up, plugs straight into the Phoenix Force and declares that she is claiming her birthright. She is now Phoenix, reborn, and one of the X-Men.

Rachel is almost killed by Wolverine as he tries to stop her slaying the powerful mutant Super Villain Selene, but as she flees, she is tricked into entering a pocket dimension—known as the Mojoverse. Escaping after months as a prisoner, Rachel joins Excalibur, a British super-team. When Captain Britain (Brian Braddock) is lost in the timestream, Rachel offers to swap places with him. She ends up in an Earth shattered by the rule of Apocalypse, and forms a rebel group called the Askani.

Freed by her alternate-reality half-brother Nathan Summers (Cable), Rachel returns to the present and takes on the identity of Marvel Girl. As a tribute to her mother, she asks to be known as Rachel Grey. She also gets closer to Jean Grey's parents, but tragically the Grey family is wiped out by the Shi'ar, who are terrified of the return of the Phoenix Force. Only Rachel and Nathan Summers survive.

Seeking revenge, Rachel travels into space and joins up with the Starjammers, but she finds vengeance unsatisfying and returns to Earth, taking up a teaching role at the Jean Grey School of Higher Learning.

Big sister
Rachel meets her alternate-reality half-brother—Nathan Summers—the son of Cyclops and Madelyne Pryor, Jean Grey's clone.

ROGUE

FIRST APPEARANCE *Avengers Annual #10* (October 1981) **BASE** Xavier School for Gifted Youngsters; Utopia; Schaefer Theater, New York **AFFILIATIONS** Brotherhood of Evil Mutants, X-Men, Avengers Unity Squad

Born in the state of Mississippi, rebellious Anna Marie is nicknamed Rogue as a child. Raised mostly by her authoritarian aunt Carrie, teenager Anna runs away from home. She meets a boy called Cody Robbins and her mutant power to absorb the life force and even psyches of anyone she touches manifests with horrifying results when he kisses her: Cody is put into a coma from which he will never awaken.

When Rogue meets fellow mutant Mystique, she finds a kind of mother figure who does not recoil from her mutant nature. But Mystique has plans for Rogue. By channeling Rogue's volatile emotions into pure anger, Mystique molds her into the ideal recruit for her Brotherhood of Evil Mutants. Mystique then concocts a scheme for Rogue to use her absorption powers on Ms. Marvel (Carol Danvers), thereby gaining her phenomenal abilities for herself and the Brotherhood. Accosting Ms. Marvel outside her front door, Rogue struggles with her for some time, rendering the transfer of powers and psyche permanent.

With Ms. Marvel's memories now jostling with her own inside her mind, and struggling to cope with the mental effects of her powers, Rogue turns away from Mystique's villainous influence and looks to her former enemy, Professor X, for help. To the disgust of many of the X-Men, Xavier admits her to his School for Gifted Youngsters. Her new teammates' misgivings are gradually dissipated by Rogue's bravery battling the likes of Juggernaut and Nimrod.

Eventually, Rogue is given her own team of X-Men to lead. Professor X realizes that Rogue's powers have been difficult to control because they are never fully developed—he helps Rogue overcome this and she is finally able to touch other people without fear of taking on their powers or memories. She is now a member of the Avengers Unity Squad, a team assembled under the aegis of Steve Rogers to show that Avengers and X-Men can work together.

Winning trust
At the wedding of Wolverine and his Japanese bride Mariko, Rogue throws herself in front of a ray gun to save Mariko, putting her own life in danger.

DOOM VICTORIOUS!

"The Beyonder is dead. Now the supreme being in the universe …is Doom!"
DOCTOR DOOM

Mysterious cosmic entity the Beyonder assembles Earth's most powerful heroes and villains for the ultimate showdown. Doctor Doom senses a great opportunity…

The Beyonder brings two groups of Super Heroes and Super Villains to a patchwork planet he has constructed called Battleworld. He lays down a challenge—whichever team can slay the other will gain their heart's desire. Doctor Doom smells an opportunity to get his heart's desire—limitless power—without playing the Beyonder's game.

While recovering from battle, the heroes realize that Galactus has brought his vast Worldship to orbit Battleworld. Believing him to be preparing to consume the planet, they drive Galactus off. The planet-eater retreats to his ship and converts it into energy, ready to consume. Suddenly the energy is drawn away, sucked toward Doctor Doom's base.

BATTLING THE BEYONDER
When Captain Marvel flies to investigate, she finds Doom absorbing all this energy via a machine he has built. Even Doom is staggered by the power he now possesses. He realizes that there is nothing the Beyonder can offer him that he cannot now take for himself. Doom attacks the Beyonder, who at first gets the better of him. But the Beyonder is curious about this human who is so bold as to attack him, and takes a moment to examine Doom's memories. While he is distracted, Doom summons up a last fragment of strength to use a device in his breastplate that is calibrated to break down the Beyonder's energies. The next time the other heroes and villains see Doctor Doom, he has descended to Battleworld in giant form and is declaring himself to be the supreme being in the universe.

Doom later discovers that he is not omniscient after all, when a small portion of the Beyonder's consciousness is able to defeat him through his acolyte, Klaw.

Bid for absolute power
After absorbing Galactus' planet-devouring energy, Doctor Doom refuses to be merely the second most powerful being in the universe—so he attacks the seemingly omnipotent Beyonder.

Supreme being
Having defeated the Beyonder, a mighty Doctor
Doom appears before the assembled heroes
and villains to declare himself the supreme
being in the universe.

CLOAK AND DAGGER

FIRST APPEARANCE *Spectacular Spider-Man #64* (March 1982) **BASE** New York City **AFFILIATIONS** Secret Avengers, X-Men, Spider-Man

Runaways Tyrone Johnson and Tandy Bowen meet at the Port Authority Bus Terminal in New York City. They stay with chemist Simon Marshall, who is concocting a new, highly addictive drug for the Maggia. He tests the drug on Johnson and Bowen, triggering their dormant mutant abilities. Johnson resembles a living shadow and wraps himself up in a cloak, trapping Marshall's attacking thugs in the darkness inside (which sends them to the Darkforce Dimension). Meanwhile, Bowen takes out the others with psionic bursts of energy that resemble daggers of light. The duo discovers other powers, too, including Johnson's ability to teleport, and Bowen's telekinesis. The pair become a vigilante team, Cloak and Dagger, rescuing runaways from drugs and crime. Their relationship is somewhat co-dependent. In his shadowy form, Cloak must feed on light—something Dagger must provide for him herself.

Cloak and Dagger become great friends of Spider-Man and aid him in his fight against Carnage and his team of Super Villains. At one point, Carnage's ally Shriek seems to kill Dagger, but she later returns, stronger than ever.

During the events of Spider-Island, Cloak and Dagger's abilities are switched by Mister Negative. They remain in this condition beyond the subsequent Secret Wars event, and are corrupted by Mister Negative, who uses his Shade patches to dose them with drugs. These enhance the effect of his touch and ensure that Cloak and Dagger remain loyal to him.

They help Mister Negative to attack Parker Industries, but Peter Parker tracks them to Hong Kong, where he injects both of his friends with a cure, restoring their powers and finally releasing them from Mister Negative's influence. Cloak and Dagger remain in Hong Kong, ready to fend off any future attacks.

Daggers out
During the events of Spider-Island, a touch from Mr. Negative turns Dagger to the darkness, and sets Cloak and Dagger against each other.

SPECTRUM

FIRST APPEARANCE *Amazing Spider-Man Annual #16* (October 1982) **BASE** New York City, New Orleans **AFFILIATIONS** Avengers, Nextwave

Monica Rambeau is hit with a beam from a terrorist's energy disruptor weapon while working as a lieutenant in the New Orleans Harbor Patrol. The incident gifts her with the ability to fly, transform herself into an energy being (any energy form within the electromagnetic spectrum), and project bolts of energy. Her new gifts prompt the media to call her Captain Marvel. Spider-Man introduces her to the Avengers, where she is mentored by Wasp and Captain America, becoming the first African-American heroine in the group.

Rambeau becomes a valuable member of the Avengers, and even their leader for a time. Two of her regular enemies are Moonstone and Blackout, who are both defeated when they join Baron Zemo's Masters of Evil and attack Avengers Mansion. During a battle with Leviathan, Captain Marvel accidentally comes in contact with sea water, which disperses her energy form so far that she is nearly beyond recovery. Her injuries force her to leave the Avengers' active member roster, but she remains a valuable reservist.

Captain Marvel becomes Photon when Genis-Vell, the son of Captain Mar-Vell, arrives to claim his father's title. She is angered when Genis-Vell rudely changes his name yet again, this time to Photon. After talking to him, however, she graciously takes on the new identity of Pulsar.

Rambeau leads Nextwave—whose members include Elsa Bloodstone, Boom-Boom, Captain, and Aaron Stack (Machine Man)—against the Beyond Corporation and the terrorist organization known as Silent. Her less-than-pleasant experiences with the team may have only been fake memories implanted by the Beyond Corporation. Though she sides with the rebellious Captain America during the superhuman civil war, Rambeau later registers for the government-backed Fifty-State Initiative. She then changes her codename yet again, to Spectrum, and joins Luke Cage's Mighty Avengers.

Mighty Avengers
As Spectrum, Monica Rambeau's leadership skills are a great asset to the Mighty Avengers *(left to right)*: Power Man (Victor Alvarez), She-Hulk (Jen Walters), Spectrum, Falcon (Sam Wilson), and Blue Marvel (Adam Brashear).

MIRAGE

FIRST APPEARANCE *Marvel Graphic Novel #4* (November 1982) **BASE** Mobile **AFFILIATIONS** New Mutants, X-Men, New Mutants Squad, X-Force

Danielle Moonstar is a Native American mutant and the granddaughter of Black Eagle, a chief of the Cheyenne Nation. Her power to manifest people's greatest fears emerges at puberty, and her inability to control it isolates her from others. Professor Xavier is a friend of her missing father, and Black Eagle asks him to train Moonstar. Despite her own strong misgivings and mistrust of people outside her tribe, Moonstar joins Xavier's New Mutants, honouring her grandfather's wishes. As Mirage, she becomes a valuable member of the X-Men.

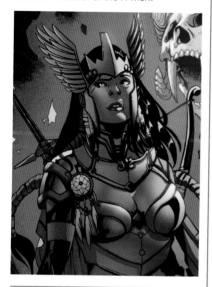

CANNONBALL

FIRST APPEARANCE *Marvel Graphic Novel #4* (November 1982) **BASE** Avengers Tower, New York **AFFILIATIONS** New Mutants, X-Force, X-Men, Avengers

Samuel Guthrie is the brother of three other mutants: Jay (Icarus), Melody (Aero), and Paige (Husk). His mutant abilities first manifest when he is trapped in a coal mine. He uses his powers to generate a powerful burst of thermo-chemical energy to save both himself and another miner. Donald Pierce of the Hellfire Club recruits him to fight the New Mutants, but when Pierce is defeated, Guthrie joins the X-Force instead. As Cannonball, he becomes a valuable member of the X-Men, but leaves for a time to care for his ailing mother. He retains his powers after M-Day and joins Rogue's strike team.

LADY DEATHSTRIKE

FIRST APPEARANCE *Daredevil #197* (August 1983) **BASE** Japan **AFFILIATIONS** Oyama Heavy Industries, Reavers, Thunderbolts, Sisterhood of Mutants

Yuriko Oyama wants revenge against her father, Lord Dark Wind, for the scars he leaves on her face, and the deaths of her brothers. She and Daredevil team up, allowing her to kill the villain. She later attempts to kill Wolverine and take his skeleton, but is stopped by Vindicator (Heather Hudson). Lady Deathstrike is endowed with an Adamantium skeleton of her own, however, by the being called Spiral. Her Adamantium claws can double their length, making the cyborg assassin a deadly adversary. She is nearly killed by X-23 when the Reavers attack X-Force, but Spiral saves her and gives her an upgrade.

To the death
While the X-Men fight over the "mutant messiah" baby, Lady Deathstrike and X-23 battle it out. Deathstrike is seemingly killed, but she is later revived in Spiral's Body Shoppe.

MADELYNE PRYOR

FIRST APPEARANCE *Uncanny X-Men #168* (April 1983) **BASE** Mobile **AFFILIATIONS** Sisterhood of Mutants

Mister Sinister covets the idea of possessing the offspring of Jean Grey and Cyclops (Scott Summers). The apparent death of Grey presents him with the perfect opportunity. He creates a clone of Grey, named Madelyne Jennifer Pryor, and implants her with false memories, before sending her after Cyclops. Sure enough, Cyclops falls in love with her and has a son (Nathan Summers). But when Jean Grey returns from the dead, Cyclops ditches his new family. Pryor grows insanely jealous and becomes the Goblin Queen, but is killed in a fight with the X-Men. She continues on as a psychic ghost, haunting Cyclops.

BETA RAY BILL

FIRST APPEARANCE *Mighty Thor #337* (November 1983) **BASE** *Skuttlebutt*; Knowhere; Asgard **AFFILIATIONS** Asgardians, Annihilators, Omega Flight, Star Masters, Thor Corps

Beta Ray Bill is a Korbinite, whose galaxy is destroyed by Surtur and his Fire Demons. His people create him to be their champion by transferring his life force into a bioengineered cybernetic body. The Korbinites then put themselves in hibernation stasis and follow his ship as he searches out a new home for them. Bill's fleet is detected by S.H.I.E.L.D. and Thor is sent to investigate. As the two fight, Beta Ray Bill grasps Thor's hammer, Mjolnir, which transforms him into a Korbinite version of Thor. Although they start off on the wrong footing, Bill becomes a close ally of Thor and his friends.

SIN

FIRST APPEARANCE *Captain America* #290 (February 1984) **BASE** Avengers Mansion, Manhattan, New York City **AFFILIATIONS** D.O.A., Hydra, the Worthy, Serpent Squad, Red Skull (Johann Schmidt), Sisters of Sin, Hydra

Sinthea Schmidt is the daughter of the Red Skull (Johann Schmidt). He almost kills her at birth but his assistant, Susan Scarbo, convinces him that she could be made as dangerous as any male heir and offers to raise the child herself.

After several years of indoctrination, Sinthea encounters her father once again. He uses a machine that accelerates her age to that of an adult and gives her super-powers. As Mother Night, Sinthea uses the same process to create her Sisters of Sin and attack Captain America.

After being captured and re-educated by S.H.I.E.L.D., Sinthea is abducted and deprogrammed by Crossbones, and becomes Sin. She later allies with Helmut Zemo's new Hydra gang.

BEYONDER

FIRST APPEARANCE *Marvel Super Heroes Secret Wars* #1 (May 1984) **BASE** Mobile (everywhere and nowhere)

The Beyonder is a juvenile member of an infinitely powerful species that resides beyond conventional reality. In eons past, these "Beyonders" create pocket universes and seed them with immeasurable quantities of sentient energy. Possibly intended as infinite incubators, many of these self-contained realities are subsequently tapped by races such as the Skrulls and humanity to create wish-fulfilling Cosmic Cubes. Perhaps at the omniscient Beyonders' command, a pinhole opens into one of these pocket continua after atomic researcher Owen Reece causes an explosion that transforms him into the Molecule Man.

After some years of passively observing the phenomena on the other side of reality, the energy within decides to be more proactive in its studies. Taking a male aspect, this Beyonder creates a world and populates it with beings taken from many civilizations. Interested in exploring the concepts of Good and Evil, the Beyonder pits heroes and villains against each other on his composite "Battleworld." To promote a quick result, the Beyonder promises each side that all their desires will be fulfilled if they kill their opponents. The experiment goes awry, however, when Doctor Doom steals the Beyonder's power.

Its curiosity still unsatisfied, the Beyonder comes to Earth to investigate further, interacting with humans, superhumans, gods, and demons.

The Beyonder is finally expelled from reality by the Molecule Man and a coalition of Earth's champions and villains. Molecule Man sends the Beyonder to a vacant distant dimension where his energies create a whole new universe.

Sometime later, Molecule Man, Doctor Doom, and the Fantastic Four help the immensely powerful Shaper of Worlds and Kubik evolve the Beyonder into a true Cosmic Cube, who then evolves into the cosmic entity Kosmos.

Spoilt with power
Despite—or because of—his omnipotence, the Beyonder has the petulant character of a child.

BOX (MADISON JEFFRIES)

FIRST APPEARANCE *Alpha Flight* #1 (August 1983) **BASE** New Charles Xavier School, Alberta, Canada; Utopia, San Francisco Bay, California; Graymalkin Industries, Marin Headlands, San Francisco, California **AFFILIATIONS** Utopians, X-Men, X-Club, Alpha Flight, Beta Flight, Gamma Flight, Zodiac, Weapon X, U.S. Army

Mutant Madison Jeffries is born with the power to manipulate and reshape machinery while his brother, Lionel, can mold and control flesh and bone. Madison is ashamed of his abilities and conceals them, but Lionel delights in the cruel pranks he can play and revels in his power.

After they serve overseas with the U.S. Army, Madison moves to Canada and becomes a mechanic while Lionel goes insane, forcing his brother to have him committed to an asylum. When Madison exhibits signs of post-traumatic stress disorder, his powers endanger the town of Harbordale, and Canadian super-agent Wolverine is despatched by the Canadian government agency Department H to stop him.

Wolverine recruits Madison to the Department's Gamma Flight, where he meets paraplegic technician Roger Bochs. Working together, they conceive the Box robot to enable Roger to become a Super Hero. Madison devises a living metal that melds with human flesh, allowing Roger to live out his dreams. Unfortunately Roger's psychological problems lead to him being manipulated by various villains, before he finally joins Alpha Flight.

When Roger's mind is trapped inside the Box robot, Madison asks his brother Lionel to use his organic molding powers to save him. Lionel seemingly cures Roger and even gives him a young, fit, fully human body, but Roger goes mad and is merged with Lionel as Omega. When they are forcibly separated, Lionel—now known as Scramble—lobotomises Roger to maintain control of their joint power and Madison takes over the Box robot to kill them both.

Madison then assumes the role, remodifying the Box suit with his powers and reluctantly using it as a member of Alpha Flight. He is mainly motivated to remain with the team by his growing affection for its leader, Heather McNeil Hudson, a.k.a. Vindicator. When Alpha Flight disbands, Madison drops out of sight.

Jeffries retains his powers on M-Day—when most of Earth's mutants are depowered—and joins the Beast's think-tank known as X-Club, where he works as an engineering advisor as they seek a way to solve the mutant population crisis.

More comfortable with machines than people, Madison Jeffries eventually moves in with the hermit-like Utopians—a human race from Earth-712 experimented on and empowered by the Kree. When the Utopians are offered sanctuary by the X-Men at the New Charles Xavier School, Madison Jeffries grudgingly moves there with them.

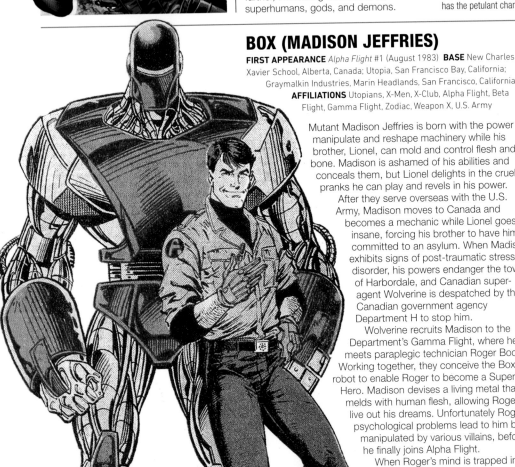

Shaping up
Jeffries was not a natural hero, but worked hard to be the kind of warrior needed to stop an out-of-control Sasquatch.

TITANIA

FIRST APPEARANCE *Marvel Super Heroes Secret Wars* #3 (July 1984) **BASE** The Hood's Lair, Hell; formerly Denver, Colorado; New York City
AFFILIATIONS Hood's Illuminati, Doom Maidens, the Worthy, Masters of Evil, Frightful Four, Legion Accursed

Mary McPherran is a small child neglected at home and bullied at school where a classmate mockingly nicknames her "Skeeter." When her home suburb of Denver, Colorado, is transported to the Beyonder's Battleworld, Mary and her only friend, Marsha Rosenberg, are given superpowers by Doctor Doom in return for promising to join his team of villains.

Enlarged in height, empowered with shattering strength and astounding durability, she calls herself Titania. Determined to pay the world back for her miserable life, she is always picking fights and trying to prove herself against powerful opponents like Absorbing Man (Crusher Creel) or She-Hulk (Jennifer Walters). After their clashes on Battleworld during the Secret Wars event, She-Hulk becomes a lifelong foe.

Returned to Earth, Titania tries to reform but faces rejection and mistrust. She seeks wealth and gratification through crime and wanton destruction; Absorbing Man becomes her lover and partner in crime, and they eventually marry.

Titania and Absorbing Man act as Baron Zemo's recruiters for a new Masters of Evil team; they later attempt to assassinate Hercules as he lies in a coma. Beaten by heroes Ant-Man and the Wasp, Titania is incarcerated in the superhuman penitentiary The Vault.

She frequently escapes—briefly joining the Frightful Four with the Wizard, Klaw and Hydro-Man—but is always defeated, then returned to jail.

Absorbing Man tires of their hectic life, but Titania still hungers for excitement and continues committing crimes, leading to clashes with Spider-Man and Thor. The villainous couple return to their murderous ways when both are possessed by the mystic Hammers of the Serpent. Unable to break her addiction to thrill-seeking violence, Titania still works as muscle for hire, and has used her immense strength for evil organizations such as A.I.M., and as part of the Hood's villainous Illuminati.

Grudge match
Titania hated She-Hulk with a passion, but even augmented by the Power Infinity Gem is never able to defeat and destroy her.

A step too far
Hard-hitting Titania (running from the cops with Absorbing Man) quits the Illuminati after the Hood orders them to target the families of heroes.

POWER PACK

FIRST APPEARANCE *Power Pack* #1 (August 1984) **BASE** New York City
AFFILIATIONS X-Men

Dr. James (Jim) Power designs an antimatter energy converter he hopes will end poverty on Earth, but reptilian aggressor aliens the Zn'rx (or "Snarks") are aware of its potential for planetary annihilation. When the Snarks abduct Jim and his wife Maggie, their children Alex, Julie, Jack, and Katie join with Kymellian benefactor Aelfyre Whitemane—who has come to Earth to prevent its destruction. The valiant Kymellian perishes in the attempt, but bequeaths his powers to control fundamental forces to the four children. Each one gains an incredible ability, costumes woven from unstable molecules, and exclusive use of Whitemane's sentient smartship *Friday*.

Using Whitemane's powers of gravity manipulation, energy-absorption and redirection, personal density control, and high-speed flight, the Power children become unlikely costumed champions the Power Pack, meeting alien friends, gods, and assorted Super Heroes. They become close friends with Reed Richards' son Franklin, with whom they share many adventures. As the children grow up, they battle a variety of villains and combat unnatural threats to Earth, at first secretly, but, ultimately, with their parents' grudging approval.

Whitemane's gifts of power were not set or stable, and in moments of extreme crisis the powers he has bequeathed transfer without warning, forcing Alex, Julie, Jack, and Katie to learn to control them all over again.

Eventually, Alex learns to claim all the powers and begins calling himself Powerhouse while working with teen super-team the New Warriors. Julie and Jack opt to live more normal lives, but little Katie still dreams of being a Super Hero. Alex later becomes a member of the Fantastic Four's Future Foundation, which trains exceptional youngsters to reach their full potential.

Power packed!
Flying high (clockwise from top): Franklin Richards (not a Power Pack member), Lightspeed (Julie Power), Zero-G (Alex Power), Valeria Richards (not a member), Mass Master (Jack Power), Energizer (Katie Power).

FORGE

FIRST APPEARANCE *Uncanny X-Men* #184 (August 1984) **BASE** Jean Grey School for Higher Learning, X-Haven, Limbo; Jean Grey School for Higher Learning, Salem Center, Westchester County, New York; Eagle Plaza, Dallas, Texas; X-Factor HQ, Embassy Row, Washington D.C. **AFFILIATIONS** X-Men, X-Force, Cheyenne Nation; X-Factor; Muir Island X-Men, DARPA, New Mutants

Forge combines shamanic magic—learned as a tribal sorcerer of the Native American Cheyenne—with his mutant ability to create any machine or device necessary to solve a problem. During a tour of duty, he loses an arm and leg, and inadvertently releases ancient mystic annihilator the Adversary.

Clinically depressed Forge leaves the U.S. Army. Upon recovering, he designs weapons for the government before being forced to confront the Adversary's threat beside the X-Men. Forge later resumes government work, running the federally sponsored X-Factor team.

Eventually, he opts to isolate himself again, acting as a somewhat erratic technical consultant to the X-Men.

HUSK

FIRST APPEARANCE *Rom Annual* #3
(November 1984) **BASE** New York State
AFFILIATIONS X-Men, Generation X, X-Corps

Paige Elisabeth Guthrie is the younger
sister of Sam Guthrie (Cannonball).
Her siblings, Jay and Melody, are also
mutants. She grows frustrated trying to
discover whether she, too, is a mutant,
until one day her anger reveals she has
the ability to shed her skin and emerge
with a new appearance of her choosing.

Husk joins the Jean Grey School for
Higher Learning as a junior staff member,
but during her time there she loses control
of her ability to "husk" and her personality
begins to fracture. She leaves the school
and turns to the Hellfire Academy. Paige
embarks on a romance with Mortimer
Toynbee, the freakish former X-Man Toad.

FIRESTAR

FIRST APPEARANCE *Uncanny X-Men* #193 (May 1985)
BASE Manhattan, New York **AFFILIATIONS** Hellions,
New Warriors, Avengers, Young Allies

At age 13, Angelica Jones' microwave powers begin
to manifest. As Firestar, she can generate intense
heat and project beams of energy that allow her to fly.
The death of her grandmother, Nana, and the
difficulty her father has dealing with her mutant
abilities lead her to enrol in the Massachusetts
Academy and join the Hellions (a team of teenage
mutants). She is trained as an assassin by telepath
Emma Frost, the villainous headmistress of the school
and secretly the White Queen of the Hellfire Club.
Firestar's bodyguard, Randall Chase, gives his life
to expose Emma Frost. When she learns the truth,
after frequent battles with the New Mutants and the
X-Men, Firestar decides to leave the school.

Firestar returns home in order to lead a normal life,
but she is convinced by Night Thrasher to join the
New Warriors as a founding member. She falls in
love with teammate Vance Astrovik (Justice),
but then discovers that her powers risk making her
sterile. Fortunately, Hank Pym develops a suit that
shields her from her own microwave radiation.
Firestar and Justice join the Avengers when the group
returns from a pocket universe, but leave after Justice
proposes marriage. However, their engagement
doesn't last long.

Firestar manages to retain her powers
beyond M-Day, but retires and goes back to
school. Her powers cause her to develop
cancer, but she survives and joins the Young
Allies with Felicia Hardy, Justice, Monica
Rambeau, and Patsy Walker.

Young Allies
Feeling marginalized, Firestar
joins Gravity, Toro, Araña, and
Nomad to hunt down the
Bastards of Evil.

SILVER SABLE

FIRST APPEARANCE *Amazing Spider-Man* #265
(June 1985) **BASE** Symkaria **AFFILIATIONS**
Silver Sable International, Wild Pack

After World War II ends, Silver Sablinova's
father convinces the government of their
country—the Balkan state of Symkaria—to
fund his Wild Pack organization in an
international hunt for Nazi war criminals.
When her mother is killed in a terrorist
attack, "Silver Sable" dedicates herself
to martial arts and weapons training,
in order to one day take her father's place
as Wild Pack leader.

Silver Sable later expands on the Wild

Pack's mission by forming Silver Sable
International, tracking down wanted
criminals, recovering stolen property, and
providing security. The company becomes
Symkaria's primary funding source,
employing many of its citizens.

Silver Sable first meets Spider-Man
while hunting down Black Fox (Robert
Paine). She is seemingly killed while
helping the Wall-Crawler fight Rhino.

Drowned out
On their way to stop Doc Ock, Spider-Man and
Silver Sable are confronted by Rhino (Aleksei
Sytsevich). He pins Sable down as the waters
rise, which appears to drown them both.

LONGSHOT

FIRST APPEARANCE *Longshot* #1 (September 1985) **BASE** Mobile **AFFILIATIONS** X-Men, Exiles

Longshot is from Mojoworld, a planet in an alternate universe where the original inhabitants are literally without spines. They crawl through muck until a scientist named Arize invents a mechanical exoskeleton that allows them to stand.

Arize genetically engineers a slave species (much like humans), of which Longshot is one. Longshot starts a slave revolt and escapes to Earth through a portal. He is pursued by Mojo, a Spineless One who was once his master, but Doctor Strange and a group of friends help Longshot defeat him. Longshot joins the X-Men and then the Exiles, but leaves the group for his love, Dazzler (Alison Blaire).

SERPENT SOCIETY

FIRST APPEARANCE *Captain America* #310 (October 1985) **BASE** Serpent Citadel, Serpent Tower **AFFILIATIONS** Serpent Squad

The Serpent Society begins as the Serpent Squad, founded by Viper (Jordan Stryke), along with his brother Eel (Leopold Stryke), and Cobra (Klaus Voorhees). Sidewinder (Seth Voelker) expands the team and develops it into a business, known as the Serpent Society. Not every snake-themed villain is keen to join. Constrictor rejects Sidewinder's offer and informs the Avengers about the Serpent Society. Captain America is a constant nemesis, and a frequent target of their vain attempts at revenge.

The Red Skull's daughter Sin revives the organization. During the Skrulls' Secret Invasion, the Serpent Society holds a large group of people hostage, but is thwarted by Nova and his friends. Hope Summers then puts a stop to the group during a chalsh between the Avengers and the X-Men.

Viper (now known as Jordan Dixon) remakes the Society into Serpent Solutions. The company has links to A.I.M. and Hydra, and does dirty work for various shady research groups.

Serpent Solutions kidnaps the new Captain America (Sam Wilson), thanks to Diamondback, and brings him back to their Serpent Tower on Wall Street. Viper throws Wilson out the window, hoping to kill him, but he is saved by his winged mutant friend, Joaquin Torres (Falcon). Misty Knight and D-Man come to their aid, as does Diamondback, who betrays her Serpent Solutions teammates. Together, they shut down Serpent Solutions and the criminal syndicate is arrested.

Serpents' table
Frequent infighting reduces the effectiveness of the Serpent Society, frustrating new leadership and alliances seeking to reform the organization and make it more powerful.

MOJO

FIRST APPEARANCE *Longshot* #3 (November 1985) **BASE** Mojoworld **AFFILIATIONS** Spineless Ones

Mojo is the ruler of Mojoworld and a member of a race of yellow, spineless beings obsessed with television and movies, which Mojo produces himself to keep his citizens entertained. This sleazy, obese tyrant rides around in a mechanical chariot, unwilling to walk by his own power.

Mojo first comes to Earth while chasing after his former slave, Longshot. He later captures the mutant Psylocke (Elizabeth Braddock), who is blinded by Slaymaster. Before she is rescued by the New Mutants, Mojo offers her new, cybernetic eyes. When Psylocke is returned to Earth, she is unaware that her eyes are hidden cameras, transmitting the X-Men's adventures back to Mojo for broadcast in his universe.

When the X-Men are seemingly killed by the Adversary, Mojo no longer receives the video feed from Psylocke. His captive, Phoenix of the X-Men, then escapes and joins the Super Hero team Excalibur on Earth. This alarms Mojo, manipulating the X-Men into participating in his television productions because the heroes have proven very popular with his viewers. Without them, he must find something else to broadcast. So Mojo creates younger clones of the X-Men, called the X-Babies. Unfortunately for Mojo, they prove just as difficult to deal with as the X-Men and rebel with the help of Ricochet Rita (Rita Wayword). Mojo is eventually overthrown by Longshot, but his clone successor, "Mojo II: The Sequel," is even more tyrannical.

The original Mojo manages to regain power and his crazy television schemes continue when he kidnaps the X-Men and manipulates them into re-enacting his own twisted version of *The Wizard of Oz*. He also creates more X-Babies, then the Mighty 'Vengers (baby Avengers), and even baby villains. Fortunately, none of these schemes works out well for Mojo in the long run.

No business like show business
The vile Mojo does battle with the X-Men. The spineless deviant has no empathy for other living beings, seeking only to use their suffering for his benefit through better ratings.

SUNFIRE

FIRST APPEARANCE *X-Men #64* (January 1970)

Nationalistic mutant Shiro Yoshida uses his atomic plasma powers to defend Japanese interests, but eventually moves from hot-headed confrontations with Super Heroes to working beside them in the X-Men and Avengers Unity Squad.

KANGAROO

FIRST APPEARANCE *Amazing Spider-Man #81* (February 1970)

Australian Frank Oliver lives with kangaroos and learns to jump like them. He later becomes a boxer, but is banned after nearly killing an opponent. He travels to the U.S, gains superhuman leaping powers from Dr. Jonas Harrow and clashes with Spider-Man.

DOCTOR SPECTRUM

FIRST APPEARANCE *Avengers #85* (March 1971)

Alternate-Earth astronaut Joseph Ledger is given a light-shaping Power Prism by a Skrull Skymaster and fights crime as Doctor Spectrum, both individually and as one of the Squadron Supreme.

DOC SAMSON

FIRST APPEARANCE *Incredible Hulk #141* (July 1971)

Psychiatrist Leonard Samson (born Skivorski) uses the Hulk's gamma radiation to become a part-time Super Hero but is eventually corrupted by power. He dies battling Red Hulk, but is later resurrected.

CHEMISTRO

FIRST APPEARANCE *Luke Cage, Hero for Hire #12* (August 1972)

Curtis Carr seeks revenge when his inventions are stolen, becoming a criminal equipped with wrist-blasters and a matter-transforming Alchemy Gun. Left crippled, his codename is adopted by felons Archibald Morton and Carr's brother, Calvin.

HAMMERHEAD

FIRST APPEARANCE *Amazing Spider-Man #113* (October 1972)

Renegade surgeon Jonas Harrow rebuilds a dying Maggia thug into a super-cyborg. Brain-damaged Joseph fixates on 1930s movie gangsters and patterns his attempts to take over the underworld on Al Capone.

MOONDRAGON

FIRST APPEARANCE *Iron Man #54* (January 1973)

Heather Douglas studies with Shao-Lom monks on Titan, becoming a mind goddess. Initially heroic, she succumbs to the evil of the Dragon of the Moon before dying and being reborn as a force for good.

STARFOX

FIRST APPEARANCE *Iron Man #55* (February 1973)

Eros of Titan is an Eternal, as heroic as his brother Thanos is evil. As an Avenger, his hedonistic lifestyle and power to control emotions make him a controversial figure.

WENDIGO

FIRST APPEARANCE *Incredible Hulk #162* (April 1973)

A mystic curse affecting the north woods of Canada transforms anyone who consumes human flesh into a savage monster. Wendigos have battled the Hulk, X-Men, Wolverine, and Alpha Flight.

BI-BEAST

FIRST APPEARANCE *Incredible Hulk #169* (November 1973)

Bi-Beast is a super-android who believes mankind is responsible for the extinction of its Avian creators. It clashes with the Hulk, S.H.I.E.L.D., and other heroes in numerous attempts to destroy humanity.

BASILISK

FIRST APPEARANCE *Marvel Team-Up #16* (December 1973)

Petty thief Basil Elks mutates into a lizard-like humanoid with incredible powers and devastating eye-beams after accidentally bonding with a Kree artifact he was trying to steal.

MARVEL BOY/JUSTICE

FIRST APPEARANCE *Giant-Size Defenders #5* (July 1975)

Hero-obsessed mutant Vance Astrovik possesses telekinesis and becomes a costumed Super Hero. As Marvel Boy, he joins the New Warriors, before graduating to the Avengers as Justice.

STARHAWK

FIRST APPEARANCE *Defenders #27* (September 1975)

Stakar Ogord is merged with his adopted sister Aleta by a hawk god and trapped in a millennia-spanning time loop, forced to live his life over and over. To escape, he infinitesimally shapes recurring events to create the Guardians of the Galaxy.

SETH

FIRST APPEARANCE *Thor #240* (October 1975)

Egyptian Serpent-Death God Seth hates all other deities and enslaves his fellow Heliopolitans. After he loses a hand in battle, when Heliopolis is liberated by Thor and Odin, the vengeful Seth's priorities shift to destroying Asgard.

BEVERLY SWITZLER

FIRST APPEARANCE *Howard the Duck #1* (January 1976)

Beverly Switzler is saved from the mystic criminal accountant Pro-Rata by Howard the Duck and becomes his companion and confidante. After years of bizarre adventures, she leaves in search of a normal life.

LIGHTMASTER

FIRST APPEARANCE *Peter Parker the Spectacular Spider-Man #3* (February 1977)

College physicist Edward Lansky originally creates the guise of a photonic Super Villain to battle budget cuts. After being transformed into an energy-being during a battle with Peter Parker, his thoughts turn to revenge on Spider-Man.

CARRION

FIRST APPEARANCE *Peter Parker the Spectacular Spider-Man #25* (December 1978)

Replicator virus Carrion mutates a Miles Warren clone into a creature of uncanny power. It later transforms Malcolm McBride and William Allen, infecting both with Warren's hatred of Spider-Man.

SONGBIRD

FIRST APPEARANCE *Incredible Hulk #449* (January 1997)

Melissa Gold is the sound-manipulating Super Villain Screaming Mimi, before being repurposed by Baron Zemo for the fake Super Hero team the Thunderbolts as Songbird.

TASKMASTER

FIRST APPEARANCE *Avengers #195* (May 1980)

Tony Masters' photographic reflexes enable him to duplicate any action he sees. With moves stolen from hundreds of heroes and villains, he sets up academies to train henchmen-for-hire.

BEYONDERS

FIRST APPEARANCE *Marvel Two-In-One #63* (May 1980)

These infinitely powerful higher-dimensional beings have interacted with our universe since it began. They have moved planets, created the Savage Land, and provided the energy that powers Cosmic Cubes.

U-FOES

FIRST APPEARANCE *Incredible Hulk #254* (December 1980)

Wealthy Simon Utrecht duplicates the spaceflight that created the Fantastic Four, turning himself into matter-moving Vector, Ann Darnell into Vapor, her brother Jimmy into X-Ray, and Mike Steel into metal monster Ironclad.

HYDRO-MAN

FIRST APPEARANCE *Amazing Spider-Man #212* (January 1981)

As Spider-Man fights Namor the Sub-Mariner, Morrie Bench falls into the sea and absorbs unknown radiation. Able to become liquid and control fluids, he is not intelligent enough to effectively use his new gifts.

GARGOYLE

FIRST APPEARANCE *Defenders #94* (April 1981)

Aging Isaac Christians sells his soul in order to save his town, Christianboro, from economic ruin. Locked inside a magical monster, he joins the Defenders, battling beside them to redeem himself and his honour.

THE HAND

FIRST APPEARANCE *Daredevil #174* (September 1981)

Necromantic ninja cult the Hand are skilled assassins and practitioners of powerful occult magic. They act as mercenary killers for the Yakuza, Hydra, and other evil organizations, as they pursue an 800-year-old hidden agenda.

STICK

FIRST APPEARANCE *Daredevil #176* (November 1981)

Blind martial artist Stick trains Matt Murdock (Daredevil) after he loses his sight. The aged sensei leads a warrior cult named the Chaste who have battled ninja cult the Hand for centuries.

THE BROOD

FIRST APPEARANCE *Uncanny X-Men #155* (March 1982)

The Brood are intelligent, hive-minded insectoid parasites who implant their eggs in superior species. When an egg hatches, the spawn assimilates any powers or abilities the host possesses.

WOLFSBANE

FIRST APPEARANCE *Marvel Graphic Novel #4* (November 1982)

Scottish mutant Rahne Sinclair is a lupine transmorph, shape-shifting into forms that blend human and wolf. Graduating from the New Mutants she fights evil and prejudice in Excalibur and X-Factor.

MALEKITH

FIRST APPEARANCE *Thor #344* (June 1984)

Malekith the Accursed rules the malign Dark Elves of Svartalfheim, one of the Realms of Asgard. A sworn foe of gods and mortals, this master of black magic schemes to bring harm to all defenders of good.

JULIA CARPENTER

FIRST APPEARANCE *Marvel Super-Heroes Secret Wars #6* (October 1984)

Julia Carpenter is made into a spider-powered agent by the Commission. Rejecting their influence, "Spider-Woman" serves with the Avengers before charting her own course, both as Arachne and Madame Web.

SCOURGE OF THE UNDERWORLD

FIRST APPEARANCE *Invincible Iron Man #194* (May 1985)

Although apparently a lone agent targeting costumed criminals, Scourge is actually numerous vigilantes working for elderly hero Thomas Halloway, protecting civilians by killing the villains who prey upon them.

NEBULA

FIRST APPEARANCE *Avengers #257* (July 1985)

Space pirate Nebula claims to be the granddaughter of Thanos. After he is trapped between life and death, she appropriates his reputation and technology, such as his super-ship *Sanctuary II*, to terrorize the universe.

DEMOLITION MAN

FIRST APPEARANCE *Thing #28* (October 1985)

Wrestler Dennis Dunphy uses artificially augmented strength and skills to become a masked hero but, despite working with Captain America, the Thing, and the Avengers, he is repeatedly injured, killed, and resurrected.

YELLOWJACKET

FIRST APPEARANCE *Avengers* #264 (February 1986) **BASE** New York City **AFFILIATIONS** Masters of Evil, Femizons, Guardians of the Galaxy

Rita DeMara is an ambitious petty criminal who comes up with a plan to lift Hank Pym's old Yellowjacket suit from the Avengers Mansion. Using a remote-control helmet, she "calls" Pym's old helmet and uses it to guide his suit past the distracted occupants of the mansion. She puts on the suit and goes to Pym's old lab to secure the final piece of equipment, but is surprised by the Wasp, Pym's ex-wife Janet van Dyne. The two fight; Rita employs the Yellowjacket suit's shrinking technology, but she is not mentally strong enough to cope with being tiny.

Yellowjacket is jailed but soon broken out by the Grey Gargoyle and Screaming Mimi in order to join Baron Zemo's Masters of Evil and invade Avengers Mansion. When this scheme fails, Yellowjacket ends up back in prison. Escaping once more, she starts to lean a little to the side of right, fighting alongside the Avengers against the High Evolutionary. After another spell with the Masters of Evil, Yellowjacket turns her back on villainy once again and joins the Guardians of the Galaxy. In space, she is able to use future technology and her own design talents to upgrade her costume. Her redesigned outfit enables her to fly without wings and shrink other people by firing Pym Particles from her gauntlets.

Yellowjacket is killed by Iron Man, while his mind is being controlled by the Super Villain Immortus. She is brought back from Hades to live again during the Chaos War. Helping to save the Avengers from the Chaos King gives Rita a sense of self-worth, for perhaps the first time.

A second chance
Yellowjacket returns from the dead along with Captain Marvel and other fallen Avengers to battle the forces of the Chaos King (*above*).

APOCALYPSE

FIRST APPEARANCE *X-Factor* #5 (June 1986) **BASE** Blue Area of the Moon **AFFILIATIONS** Alliance of Evil, Dark Riders

En Sabah Nur is born in Ancient Egypt, and is thought to be the first mutant. Like the mutants living several millennia later, Nur is hated and feared by many of his contemporaries. But one man, Baal, is not repulsed by his strange, gray face and brings up the abandoned child as his own. Baal eventually reveals to Nur that he has seen evidence that he will one day rule the world and bring to an end the despotic rule of Rama-Tut, the Pharoah who is, in reality, the time-traveling Kang the Conqueror. Nur grows to adulthood believing that only the strong deserve to survive. He defeats Rama-Tut, who flees back into the future, and begins using the Celestial technology Kang has left behind to enhance his own abilities and quell his enemies. Calling himself Apocalypse, he is now immortal, and despises the weakness of humanity. He uses Kang's futuristic technology to go into suspended animation for long periods to recover his strength. Waking sporadically throughout the centuries, he fights both Thor and Count Dracula. He also acquires various acolytes, such as Ozymandias, Rama-Tut's former warlord, the Four Horsemen of Apocalypse, and Mister Sinister.

In modern times, Apocalypse clashes with X-Factor, fearing the birth of Nathan Summers, a mutant thought powerful enough to destroy him. Apocalypse is seemingly killed on more than one occasion, but is resurrected by Celestial technology. In one reincarnation, he is a child at the Jean Grey School of Higher Learning. He has no memory of his past lives, but everyone else there remembers Apocalypse and is desperate to prevent him turning out like his past selves.

Might is right
As is the custom of his brutish Ancient Egyptian tribe, the young En Sabah Nur proves his manhood by fighting his companions to the death.

◄ Symbiote released While on the Beyonder's Battleworld, Spider-Man discovers a mysterious black substance that forms a new costume and can be turned into civilian clothes at a mental command. *Marvel Super Heroes Secret Wars* #8 (Dec. 1984)

Noise annoys Having discovered that his new black costume is an alien parasite, Spider-Man rejects it. When it later attacks him, he uses the sound of church bells to force it to leave him. *Web of Spider-Man* #1 (Apr. 1985)

A senseless attack Peter Parker's usually infallible spider-sense fails to warn him when an unseen assailant (Venom) pushes him onto the tracks in front of an oncoming train. *Web of Spider-Man* #18 (Sept. 1986)

▼ Venom strikes After the symbiote bonds with Eddie Brock to form Venom, they attack MJ. Spider-Man fights and eventually separates Brock from the symbiote, giving it to the Fantastic Four for safe storage. *Amazing Spider-Man* #300 (May 1988)

Venom's spawn While rebonding with Eddie Brock in jail, the symbiote leaves a residue on the skin of his psychotic cellmate Cletus Kasady, and Carnage is born. *Amazing Spider-Man* #345 (Mar. 1991)

Allied enemies Venom calls a truce with Spider-Man so that the two of them can bring down Carnage, who is leaving a trail of death and destruction across New York City. *Amazing Spider-Man* #362 (May 1992)

◄ Venom 2.0. As part of Norman Osborn's plot to assemble a Sinister Twelve Super Villain team, the symbiote bonds with Mac Gargan to form a new Venom. *Marvel Knights: Spider-Man* #9 (Feb. 2005)

Black ops Venom Flash Thompson is bonded with the symbiote by the U.S. Army in order to become Agent Venom, a superpowered, black ops agent combating terrorism. *Amazing Spider-Man* #654 (Feb. 2011)

Guardian Venom Agent Venom joins up with the Guardians of the Galaxy to be the Avengers' representative on the team. *Free Comic Book Day: Guardians of the Galaxy* (July 2014)

VENOM

FIRST APPEARANCE *Web of Spider-Man* #18 (September 1986) **BASE** Mobile **AFFILIATIONS** Sinister Twelve, Secret Avengers, Guardians of the Galaxy

Eddie Brock is a journalist whose career hits the skids following the misreporting of a serial killer case—a turn of events that he blames on Spider-Man. At his lowest ebb, Brock goes into a church to seek solace. Spider-Man has just left the very same church, having shaken off an alien symbiote parasite in the form of a black costume by exposing it to the ear-splitting ringing of the church bells. Looking for another host to possess and sensing Brock's hatred of the wall-crawler, the symbiote is attracted to him, and the two bond to become the twisted Venom. The creature is motivated by a desire to bring down Spider-Man, although the Eddie Brock part of it is also worried that the alien will desert him in favor of Peter Parker if it gets the chance. Brock's Venom is blessed with Spider-Man's powers, plus the knowledge of his secret identity. This enables Venom to target those that Peter holds most dear—his Aunt May and MJ (his wife at this time). Venom is also slightly stronger than Spidey thanks to host Eddie Brock's serious bodybuilding habit.

> "Nothing must stand in our way. Nothing must block our righteous revenge!"
>
> **VENOM**

Despite his great strength, Venom is vulnerable to sound weapons and extreme heat, chinks in his armor that give Spider-Man a chance to save his family from the creature's clutches. After one confrontation with the web-slinger, Eddie Brock is separated from the symbiote and imprisoned in Ryker's Island, where his cellmate is deranged multiple murderer Cletus Kasady. When the alien he calls his "other" comes to reclaim Brock, a fragment of it falls onto Kasady's skin, transforming him into the psychotic Carnage.

In contrast to its foul spawn, Eddie Brock's Venom exhibits a moral code and sometimes fights on behalf of those he deems "innocents." This leads to the strange situation of Venom teaming up with his nemesis Spider-Man in order to stop Carnage's killing spree. Eventually, the relationship between the symbiote and Eddie Brock comes to an end. Tired of being dominated by the alien, Brock sells it at a Super-Villain auction. After its buyer is killed running from Spider-Man, the symbiote offers itself to another of Spidey's foes, Mac Gargan, the Scorpion. Under Norman Osborn, Gargan's Venom becomes a member of the Sinister Twelve and the Dark Avengers, but he is separated from the alien after his imprisonment in the Raft penitentiary.

MISTER SINISTER

FIRST APPEARANCE *Uncanny X-Men* #221 (September 1987) **BASE** Mobile
AFFILIATIONS Apocalypse, Marauders, Nasty Boys, Sinister's Six, Weapon X

Dr. Nathaniel Essex works for the Nazis in World War II. He is fascinated by Darwin's theory of evolution and obsessed with studying mutant children, including the young Charles Xavier. The world's first mutant, Apocalypse, recruits Dr. Essex and alters his DNA to give him superhuman abilities and virtual immortality. He gains the ability to alter his own DNA at will as well. As Mister Sinister, Essex conducts new evil experiments to uncover the secrets of mutation and is a continuing threat to the X-Men.

Mister Sinister plays a secret role in the upbringing of brothers Havok (Alexander Summers) and Cyclops (Scott Summers). He even attempts to breed a mutant child between Cyclops and Jean Grey. To that effect, after Jean Grey appears to have died, he creates her clone, named Madelyne Pryor. She falls in love with Cyclops and the two marry and have a child. But when Jean Grey returns from the dead, Cyclops leaves Pryor and the child.

Mister Sinister controls the Marauders (a team of mutant mercenaries), sending them to slaughter the Morlocks in the Alley, their domain beneath New York City—an incident known as the Mutant Massacre. He believes the Morlocks represent an obstacle to the potential evolution of mankind. Later, Mister Sinister orders the Marauders to track down Hope Summers (the first mutant born after M-Day—when Scarlet Witch declared all mutants should lose their powers—and the adopted granddaughter of Madelyne Pryor and Cyclops).

Mister Sinister is killed several times, first by mutant assassin Mystique, and then again when he tries to capture the Phoenix Force. Each time he returns in a clone body.

TOMBSTONE

FIRST APPEARANCE *Web of Spider-Man* #36 (March 1988)
BASE New York City **AFFILIATIONS** Kingpin, Hood, Doctor Octopus, Sinister Twelve

Lonnie Thompson Lincoln grows up in Harlem, New York City, as an albino African-American. He is a former classmate of *The Daily Bugle* journalist and associate of Peter Parker, Joe "Robbie" Robertson, whom he pressures into staying silent about a murder he commits. As Tombstone, Lincoln files his teeth to points to make himself more frightening and becomes an assassin for New York mobsters. Robertson manages to collect enough evidence to jail Tombstone. Breaking out, Tombstone tries to attack Robertson at an Oscorp chemical plant when he is exposed to an experimental gas and gains superhuman strength and bulletproof skin. Tombstone is grateful to Robbie for inadvertently giving him super-powers, so he buries the hatchet with him. Tombstone works for masterminds such as Kingpin and Norman Osborn before becoming a leader himself, vying for control of organized crime in New York.

Fateful meeting
The mutant Gambit meets with Mister Sinister who agrees to remove part of Gambit's brain so he can better control his powers. In exchange, Gambit assembles a team of Marauders, which results in the Mutant Massacre.

EXCALIBUR

FIRST APPEARANCE *Excalibur Special Edition*
(April 1988) **BASE** Captain Britain's lighthouse
AFFILIATIONS X-Men

The original Excalibur team includes
Captain Britain (Brian Braddock),
Lockheed, Meggan (Meggan Puceanu),
Nightcrawler (Kurt Wagner), Phoenix
(Rachel Summers), and Shadowcat
(Katherine "Kitty" Pryde). They are formed
when the mystical entity Adversary
appears to destroy the X-Men.

At the time, mutant heroes Nightcrawler
and Shadowcat are recovering on Muir
Island—located just off the northern coast
of Scotland—from injuries received during
the Mutant Massacre. They band together
with Captain Britain and Meggan to help
Phoenix defeat the villain Mojo's Warwolves
and the Technet bounty hunter team,
following her escape from the nightmarish,
extradimensional Mojoworld. The group
decides to form a permanent team to
honor the legacy of the X-Men, and names
it after King Arthur's legendary sword.

Excalibur's base in the U.K. is located
at the convergence of several alternate
universes. As such, the team often fights
battles across multiple worlds. Excalibur
faces its Nazi counterpart—known as the
Lightning Force—on Earth-597, and fights
villains such as Arcade, the Crazy Gang,
and Juggernaut.

Excalibur discovers that Merlyn's
daughter, Roma—who protects the
Multiverse—has manipulated events to

bring them together in the first place.
Roma has hopes of defeating Necrom, an
extradimensional sorcerer who desires the
Phoenix Force within Rachel Summers.
Excalibur defeats Necrom and is joined by
red-energy wielding Shi'ar Cerise, the
magician Feron, and mutant warrior Kylun.
Later additions include Colossus of the
X-Men, size-altering and shape-shifting
Micromax, spy Pete Wisdom with his "hot
knives," and mutant wolf-woman,
Wolfsbane.

Love triangles cause big problems for
Excalibur. Nightcrawler and Captain Britain
fight over bewitching Meggan; when she
and Captain Britain are
finally married, Excalibur
falls apart. Captain Britain
twice reforms the team,
with different members
each time. They go their
separate ways again after
a battle with manipulative
magician Merlyn. Several
members go on to team
up under the British
intelligence agency MI13.

Here we go again!
The New Excalibur team:
(clockwise from top): Captain
Britain (Brian Braddock), Pete
Wisdom, Nocturne (Talia Wagner),
Dazzler (Alison Blaire), Sage, and
Juggernaut (Cain Marko).

REAVERS

FIRST APPEARANCE *Uncanny X-Men* #229 (May 1988)
BASE Cooterman's Creek, Australia **AFFILIATIONS** Hellfire Club

The Reavers are a cyborg mercenary team. Their original
members are Bonebreaker, Wade Cole, Lady Deathstrike
(Yuriko Oyama), Angelo Macon, Cylla Markham, Donald
Pierce, Pretty Boy, Murray Reese, and Skullbuster.

The team begins as a private military force, called the
Hellfire Knights, working for the Hellfire Club, an elitist
organization seeking power through politics and money.
Cole, Macon, and Reese are critically wounded in a
confrontation with Wolverine. They are treated and
converted to cyborgs in six-armed Spiral's "Body Shoppe,"
using alien cybernetic parts. Lady Deathstrike likewise
undergoes procedures and the four became the first
Reavers. They split from the Hellfire Club and join
Bonebreaker, Pretty Boy, and Skullbuster, setting up
operations in Cooterman's Creek, Australia.

The Reavers coerced Australian Aboriginal mutant
Gateway to carry them through portals so they can rob
banks across the world. During a caper in Singapore they
kidnap Jessán Hoan (Tyger Tiger) and earn the ire of the
X-Men. The X-Men take out the Reavers,
but Bonebreaker, Pretty Boy, and Skullbuster manage to
escape with the help of Gateway. The new team is then led
by Donald Pierce, with the assistance of Lady Deathstrike.

The Reavers are hired by the psionic entity Shadow King
to kidnap the X-Men's Rogue, but fail in the endeavor.
Donald Pierce then remakes the group into a grassroots
anti-mutant movement. This incarnation, later led by Lady
Deathstrike, is a constant menace to Wolverine. When the
Reavers hear rumors that Wolverine has returned
from the dead, they track down an elderly version
of Logan to the remote town of Killhorn Falls,
Canada. They massacre the town in an effort to
hurt Logan. However, Logan responds by killing all
the Reavers, except Lady Deathstrike.

Making an entrance
With assistance from the mutant
Gateway, the Reavers teleport into Hoan
International Bank in Singapore, with
guns blazing.

JUBILEE

FIRST APPEARANCE *Uncanny X-Men* #244 (May
1989) **BASE** Mobile **AFFILIATIONS** Wolverine,
X-Men, Generation-X, X-Corps

Jubilation Lee is a talented gymnast and
member of a wealthy Asian-American
family living in Beverly Hills. After her
parents lose their fortune and die, Jubilee
seeks refuge in the Hollywood Mall. She
then follows the X-Men through a portal to
their Australian base. Leaving the base,
Jubilee becomes Wolverine's partner
(viewing him as a father figure) and travels
across Asia. Jubilee joins the X-Men,
Generation X, and X-Corps, but loses her
powers on M-Day. She dons a power suit
and joins the New Warriors as Wondra.
Xarus, the son of Dracula, turns Jubilee
into a vampire; however, Jubilee manages
to resist her new,
bloodsucking
tendencies.

No worries
Happily oblivious to the chaos outside, the Great Lakes Avengers take it easy *(from left)*: Doorman, Big Bertha, Flatman, Mister Immortal, and former member Squirrel Girl (as a cardboard cut out).

GREAT LAKES AVENGERS

FIRST APPEARANCE *West Coast Avengers* #46 (July 1989) **BASE** Detroit, Michigan; Milwaukee, Wisconsin **AFFILIATIONS** Great Lakes X-Men, Great Lakes Champions, Great Lakes Defenders, Great Lakes Initiative, Lightning Rods

This comedic team of eccentric heroes includes the stretchy Flatman, high-flying reptilian Dinah Soar, size-shifting supermodel Big Bertha, and Darkforce-manipulating Doorman, and is led by the undying Mister Immortal. They band together as the Great Lakes Avengers (GLA) despite lacking permission from the Avengers to use the name.

The team is originally scouted by Hawkeye and his then wife Mockingbird when he leaves the West Coast Avengers. Much to the annoyance of Mister Immortal, Hawkeye and Mockingbird agree to stay and train the team as their leaders.

After the GLA successfully assists the Avengers on a mission in Texas, Captain America agrees to let them use the Avengers name. However, their antics frustrate Hawkeye and Mockingbird, who return to the West Coast Avengers. Following their mentors' departure and a misguided attempt to rebrand themselves, the GLA mostly pass the time playing cards, occasionally supporting other Super Hero teams on missions, but rarely taking on villains on their own.

When the cosmic Super Villain Maelstrom kills Dinah Soar, the group needs the help of Maelstrom's one-time herald Deathurge, whom Mister Immortal knew as a boy, to thwart the villain's masterplan to end time.

The team's exploits attract new recruits, such as the rodent-loving Squirrel Girl, Leather Boy, and Grasshopper, whose untimely death sees the already depressed Mister Immortal abandon the team. Flatman takes the reins, only for the GLA to receive a cease-and-desist order from the S.H.I.E.L.D. Director Maria Hill for using the Avengers name. In response, the GLA changes its name to Great Lakes X-Men, the Great Lakes Defenders, and the Great Lakes Champions as the team scramble to remain legitimate…and get new outfits. To add to their woes, Squirrel Girl leaves the team, after defeating Fin Fang Foom, Baron Mordo, and Ego the Living Planet.

During the Superhuman Registration Act, the GLA signs on as part of the Great Lakes Initiative to protect the Midwest. The team finally reverts to its old name, moving operations to Detroit when the Avengers trademark accidentally reverts to Flatman's ownership on a legal technicality, making the Great Lakes Avengers an officially sanctioned team at last.

From Avengers to X-Men and back
Flatman, Doorman, Big Bertha, Mister Immortal, and Squirrel Girl in costume as the Great Lakes X-Men, aping the mutant team's classic yellow garb.

CROSSBONES

FIRST APPEARANCE *Captain America* #360 (October 1989) **BASE** Skull-House; mobile **AFFILIATIONS** Hydra, Thunderbolts, Skeleton Crew

Brock Rumlow, a.k.a. Crossbones, is right hand man to the villainous Nazi Red Skull. After all, every skull needs its crossbones. Crossbones is a formidable soldier and hand-to-hand fighter. He not only works for Hydra, but has set up his own Skeleton Crew with the mind-enslaving Controller and the compelling communicator the Voice, to also serve the Red Skull.

When incarcerated for his crimes, he does a short stint for a team of bad guys-turned-good, the Thunderbolts, but is re-imprisoned when he once more tries and fails to kill his boss' arch-nemesis Captain America. True to form, Crossbones would escape and remains at large, bent on causing trouble for the likes of Cap and other heroes, as well as any villains that cross his path.

NEW WARRIORS

FIRST APPEARANCE *Mighty Thor* #411 (December 1989) **BASE** Wundagore Mountain, Transia; New York City; mobile **AFFILIATIONS** Avengers, Salem's Seven

The New Warriors is a teenage Super Hero team brought together by rich orphan Dwayne Michael Taylor (Night Thrasher). Driven to root out all evil to avenge his parents' murder, Night Thrasher allies himself with a diverse group of super-powered heroes: quantum-powered Marvel Boy (Vance Astrovik), Nova enforcer Richard Rider, half-Atlantean college student Namorita, fire-manifesting mutant Firestar, and the incredibly swift Speedball.

The team's public debut is an auspicious one, as they save the God of Thunder during a fearsome fight with the Juggernaut, ultimately removing the Super Villain from the planet. The New Warriors then take on all manner of villains, such as the malevolent Mad Thinker, mind-manipulating Puppet Master, the time-warping Sphinx, and the White Queen and her Hellions. However, perhaps the New Warrior's biggest shock comes when Night Thrasher learns that his own Taylor Foundation and family caretakers Chord and Tai were complicit in the death of his parents. As a result, Dwayne steps away from the team to deal with his foundation, and although the group attempts to stay together with new members and leadership, it eventually disbands.

Over time, the team reforms as the *New* New Warriors, adding Turbo, Darkhawk, Dagger, Hindsight Lad, Bandit, and Powerpax, under the leadership of Night Thrasher's half-brother, Bandit. They become celebrities after defeating the mystical Sphinx, only for the now 14-strong group to ultimately go their own ways.

Years later, a new generation of heroes assemble to recreate the New Warriors: the son of Nova, Sam Alexander, Speedball, Vance Astrovik—now known as Justice, Peter Parker's clone—the Scarlet Spider, the demi-god Hummingbird, the light-generating Sun Girl, the horned Inhuman Haechi, and the Atlantean Water Snake.

Learning the ropes
Springing into action for the first time against the alien Terrax *(clockwise from top left)*: Firestar, Namorita, Kid Nova, Speedball, Night Thrasher, and Marvel Boy.

The new New Warriors
Taking down evil Inhumans *(from left)*: Hummingbird, Speedball, Haechi, Justice, Scarlet Spider, Sun Girl, Nova (Sam Alexander), and Water Snake.

CABLE

FIRST APPEARANCE *New Mutants* #86 (February 1990) **BASE** Mobile
AFFILIATIONS Clan Chosen, Clan Askani, X-Men, X-Force, New Mutants

The mutant Scott Summers, a.k.a. Cyclops, and his wife Madelyne Pryor, a clone of Jean Grey, have a child named Nathan Summers. As their child has the potential to be an incredibly powerful mutant, he is sought after by the ancient evil mutant Apocalypse as a host body. Apocalypse infects Nathan with a deadly techno-organic virus to see if the child could be a worthy host.

Mother Askani—Rachel Summers, the daughter of Jean and Scott from a different timeline—dispatches a member of the Clan Askani to take Nathan into the 37th century in hopes of curing the deadly virus. Mother Askani believes that the child will prove powerful enough to stop Apocalypse, who has come to rule this future. Nathan is cloned in case he doesn't survive the virus. However, he proves able to keep the virus at bay by using his own telekinetic mutant powers.

Apocalypse dies when he refuses Stryfe, Nathan's clone, as a worthy host. Living still in the future, Nathan is now an adult and, taking the name Cable, joins a mutant-human uprising called the Clan Chosen against Stryfe and his New Canaanites.

Later, seeking to wipe Apocalypse from history, Cable travels back in time to Apocalypse's early life in ancient Egypt and infects the ancient mutant with the same techno-organic virus. However, the virus transforms Apocalypse into a veritable god. Thus Cable creates a time paradox, an infinite loop in both their lives, ever trying to hunt down the villain and making the future affect the past and the past affect the future.

Wasteland blues
Cable's adopted eight-year-old daughter, Hope Summers, urges Cable to go on despite severe dehydration in a debilitating wasteland in the year 2973, as they try to make it back to Westchester.

STRYFE

FIRST APPEARANCE *New Mutants* #87 (March 1990) **BASE** Mobile **AFFILIATIONS** Mutant Liberation Front, Scions of Apocalypse, New Canaanites

Stryfe is a clone of the time-traveling mutant Nathan Summers (Cable). As a child, Nathan's carer fears for his life as he is consumed by a techno-organic virus, so he is cloned.

When Apocalypse comes to steal Nathan, he mistakenly takes his clone. Naming him Stryfe, Apocalypse raises the boy to be cruel and power-hungry, but he ultimately refuses Stryfe as a worthy host when he learns that he is a clone. Unlike Nathan, Stryfe doesn't need to use his mutant powers to control the spread of a techno-organic virus. This makes him a very powerful, omega-level mutant with telekinetic abilities capable of manipulating minds, and even matter itself.

As adults, Cable leads the Clan Chosen against Stryfe and the New Canaanites, who hope to rule. A truce is called, but Stryfe is unhappy and uses the Clan Chosen's time machine to travel back to Nathan's birth and kill him. Cable stops Stryfe by going after him. Stryfe tries repeatedly to ruin Cable's life by traveling the timestream, impersonating him.

GAMBIT

FIRST APPEARANCE *Uncanny X-Men Annual* #14 (July 1990) **BASE** New Orleans; Xavier's School for Gifted Youngsters, New York State

Cajun Remy LeBeau is a mutant able to control kinetic energy using his signature playing cards and staff. LeBeau grew up in Louisiana, which accounts for his thick Creole accent and southern charm. Abandoned at birth because of his uncanny red eyes, LeBeau is raised by the Thieves' Guild, becoming a master criminal. He first encounters the X-Men when Storm, transformed into a child, takes him to Professor X's school. As Gambit, he studies to become one of Xavier's mutant team. He starts a romantic relationship with teammate Rogue, but because her mutant-draining powers are ignited by skin-to-skin contact they can never truly touch each other.

THE PANTHEON

FIRST APPEARANCE *Incredible Hulk* #377 (January 1991) **BASE** The Mount, Nevada

Long-lived superhumans the Pantheon are all descended from Agamemnon, a demi-god born of an Asgardian father and a mortal woman. His own offspring by human women are often born with extraordinary abilities and, over many centuries, Agamemnon recruits them into the "family business"—a clandestine paramilitary force carrying out his unspecified long-term goals. His children do not realize that this entails some of them being traded to the alien Troyjans —the price for extending the family's lives through Troyjan science.

The Pantheon occupy The Mount, a vast, self-sustaining secret city in the deserts of Nevada. This houses not just the elite team and their futuristic equipment, but also several hundred civilian workers and their families.

Riven by internal squabbles and family dissent, the immortal offspring—Ajax, Andromeda, Atalanta, Cassiopeia, Delphi, Hector, Jason, Paris, Perseus, Prometheus, Ulysses, and Ulysses II— are continually manipulated by their father into meddling in world affairs while being played off against each other.

The last straw comes when Agamemnon appoints the Hulk—who possesses Bruce Banner's brilliant intellect at the time—as leader of the Pantheon.

The Pantheon intervenes in a war in the Middle-Eastern republic of Trans-Sabal, clashes with S.H.I.E.L.D. agents and U.S. operatives X-Factor, and later seeks to rescue Atalanta from the Troyjan warrior Trauma. The Hulk has no idea his immortal sponsor plans to betray him. A crisis arrives when Agamemnon duplicitously embroils the Pantheon in a clash with both Hydra and the Leader and the Hulk begins to revert to his primitive, always-angry state.

When Trauma claims Atalanta, Hulk leads the Pantheon, Silver Surfer, and the Starjammers in an intergalactic rescue mission, which leads to the abductor's death and the end of the secret deal with Agamemnon. On returning to Earth, the Pantheon and their various metahuman powers are eventually absorbed into undisclosed departments of the U.S. government.

Hulk boss!
Despite being captured by aliens, the Hulk has to remind his unhappy Pantheon subordinates that he is still the boss. Hulk is hitting Troyjan Prince Trauma as Achilles, Hector and Cassiopeia scatter.

War in space
When one of their own is abducted by Troyjans, the Hulk leads the incensed team into a showdown *(left to right)*: Cassiopeia, Ulysses, Hector, and Achilles.

DEADPOOL

FIRST APPEARANCE *New Mutants* #98 (February 1991) **BASE** Schaefer Theater, Manhattan, New York City; Cavern-X, Sedona, Arizona; the Deadhut, San Francisco **AFFILIATIONS** X-Men, Avengers Unity Division, Mercs for Money; Red Hulk's Thunderbolts, X-Force, Deadpool Corps, S.H.I.E.L.D., Code Red, Initiative, Six Pack, Agency X, One World Church; Secret Defenders, Frightful Four, Team Deadpool; Weapon X, Weapon Plus, Department K, U.S. Army Special Forces; Great Lakes Avenger (Wisconsin Initiative)

Deadpool is mutant mercenary Wade Winston Wilson: a mentally unstable, trained killer with a skewed—but not necessarily inaccurate—perception of reality. Lethally adept in all manner of death-dealing, Wade suffers from a once life-threatening cancerous condition, which has left his body covered in scars and sores.

However, thanks to groundbreaking experimentation from evil geniuses and government-backed clandestine projects, Wilson cannot be killed by any known means. He can even regenerate his body after it has been dismembered.

After leaving home, Wilson enlists with U.S. Army Special Forces before joining a C.I.A.-sponsored gang of assassins. When his cancer diagnosis is confirmed, Wade joins Canada's Department K and participates in the Weapon X program. His disease is arrested by experimental procedures derived from Wolverine's healing factor. When the process destabilizes, Wilson is sent to superhuman institution the Hospice to die.

The patients there all wager on how long they have to live in a lottery they call The Deadpool. After surviving the sadistically abusive experiments of Director Dr. Killebrew and striking up a relationship with the metaphysical personification of Death, Wade rebels and escapes with the Hospice's survivors. He then moves into mercenary work. Due to his condition —or perhaps his many head injuries— Deadpool has conflicting memories of his past, but remains true to his life's goals: amassing vast wealth; living in lazy luxury; scoring with the sexiest people in the world; and killing anyone who deserves it.

Deadpool even fancies himself as a Super Hero—a dream realized when Captain America Steve Rogers invites him to become a member of one of the many iterations of the Avengers. Most heroes who meet Wilson think he's crazy; most villains he battles *know* he is. All agree that Deadpool is one of the most annoying characters they have ever come across.

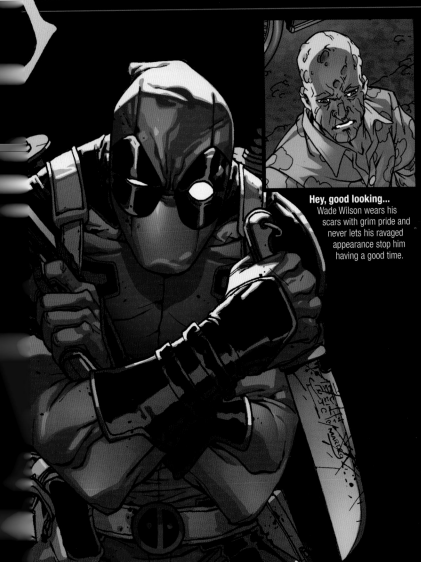

Hey, good looking...
Wade Wilson wears his scars with grim pride and never lets his ravaged appearance stop him having a good time.

Hero worship?
Despite his murderously manic and mercenary manner of behaviour, deep down Deadpool hungers to be a real hero like Captain America.

CARNAGE

FIRST APPEARANCE *Amazing Spider-Man* #344 (February 1991) **BASE** Mobile **AFFILIATIONS** Astonishing Avengers, Shriek, Venom

Murderous psychopath Cletus Kasady is sharing a cell with Eddie Brock when the alien Venom symbiote tries to break its host out. The creature is pregnant and its spawn bonds with Kasady, creating a homicidal shape-shifting monster. Completely devoid of empathy and hungry for slaughter, Carnage repeatedly terrorizes humanity, surviving attacks by Venom, dismemberment by a Kree Sentinel, exile to space and every form of psychological reconditioning.

The symbiote has been separated from Kasady many times but always returns to its favorite host, resurrecting Cletus and repairing him from major injuries. It even revives his sick mind after he is lobotomized.

DARKHAWK

FIRST APPEARANCE *Darkhawk* #1 (March 1991) **BASE** New York City, Los Angeles **AFFILIATIONS** West Coast Avengers, Secret Defenders, New Warriors, the Loners, Excelsior, Project P.e.g.a.s.u.s.

The son of a crooked cop, teenager Chris Powell discovers a strange amulet in an abandoned amusement park that allows him to transfer his mind into an alien android body. As Darkhawk, he wears this amulet on his chest and it functions as a weapon, firing force blasts and creating force fields. His armored suit also contains other weaponry and glider wings. Darkhawk teams up with many of his Super Hero idols, including Spider-Man, and joins the West Coast Avengers and other groups. In time, Chris learns that the Darkhawk amulet is of alien origin. Darkhawk sees action during the Skrulls' Secret Invasion and is later injured in Arcade's Murderworld; Darkhawk then goes missing.

X-FORCE

FIRST APPEARANCE *New Mutants* #100 (April 1991) **BASE** Mobile **AFFILIATIONS** X-Men, X-Factor, Utopia

When Cable takes over the remnants of the New Mutants, he trains the troubled teenagers—Boom Boom, Cannonball, Feral, Shatterstar, and Warpath—as a military strike force. With his sometime partner Domino, Cable seeks to develop a unit to proactively destroy suspected threats to mutants, rather than simply respond and react to attacks.

After Cable leaves, the squad—now bolstered by the addition of Dani Moonstar, Rictor, Skids, Rusty Collins, Cypher, and Wolfsbane—undergo intensive further training with mutant espionage agent Peter Wisdom. This controversial schooling carries the young heroes through numerous crises and eventually into adult teams such as the X-Men and X-Factor.

After they disband, a rapidly rotating squad of mutant celebrity-seekers co-opts the name X-Force before re-branding as X-Statix. They never attain the desired media stardom and soon separate.

Following M-Day and the birth of the first mutant baby since most mutants were transformed into ordinary humans, Cyclops orders the creation of a black ops team. The aim is to employ lethal force in order to ensure the safety of Earth's remaining mutant population. The original squad of Wolverine, Warpath, Wolfsbane, and X-23 are eventually supplemented by Psylocke, Fantomex, Deadpool, and others. After their ruthless agenda is exposed to the mutants of Utopia, Cyclops officially disowns X-Force. However, the unit carries on regardless.

X-Force sustains its momentum as a covert police group and "dirty tricks" specialist. The strategic impact of the group is boosted by the return of its original mastermind, Cable, plus the addition of new members Doctor Nemesis and Marrow, who join the battle-scarred survivors of earlier rosters.

Cable and X-Force
When trusted confederate Fantomex turns against X-Force, team leader Cable's hand-picked squad to combat him comprise (*clockwise from top left*): Doctor Nemesis, ForgetMeNot,

Wild things
Wolverine's first savage mutant selections for the X-Men's black ops assassination unit comprise (*from back to front*): Warpath, his female clone X-23, and Wolfsbane.

SQUIRREL GIRL

FIRST APPEARANCE *Marvel Super Heroes* #8 (December 1991) **BASE** New York City; Empire State University, NYC; Great Lakes Avengers HQ under Lake Michigan **AFFILIATIONS** New Avengers, Great Lakes Avengers

Doreen Allene Green isn't just your average college student, she is one of the most surprisingly powerful characters in the Marvel Universe. She can talk to squirrels, uses a fluffy prehensile tail and razor-sharp nails to fight foes, and possesses a range of super-powers, both squirrel and human. Squirrel Girl has taken down some of the most formidable Super Villains, including Thanos and Galactus, relying as much on her head and heart as her fists and band of cute rodent allies.

Bullied for her mutation as a teenager in Los Angeles, Squirrel Girl hopes to become Iron Man's sidekick. However, despite saving Iron Man and conquering Doctor Doom with the help of her squirrels, Tony Stark declines her offer. Following her dreams, Squirrel Girl comes to New York City, where she guards Central Park before being recruited by the Great Lakes Avengers after she saves them from muggers. She stays with this comical team—later styled the Great Lakes X-Men, Great Lakes Defenders, and Great Lakes Champions—protecting the Midwest.

Doreen eventually makes her way back to New York to work for the New Avengers as nanny to Jessica Jones and Luke Cage's daughter, Danielle Cage. Seeking to improve her education, she enrolls at Empire State University, studying computer science while still finding time to "eat nuts and kick butts."

Tendril trouble
Squirrel Girl and the New Avengers get wrapped up in a fight with the behemoth Moridun, Space Wizard of the magical Fifth Cosmos.

At the wheel
As a fully fledged member of the New Avengers, Doreen Green co-pilots the *Avenger One* spacecraft alongside Songbird.

Gatherers assemble
Proctor urges on his Gatherers *(left to right):* Cassandra, Magdalene, Swordsman, and Sloth.

THE GATHERERS

FIRST APPEARANCE *Avengers* #355 (October 1992) **BASE** Citadel in the Andes Mountains **AFFILIATIONS** Avengers of Alternative Dimensions

The Gatherers are a team of former Avengers from different realities. Magdalene, Swordsman, Sloth, and Cassandra—led by the mysterious Proctor—visit alternate Earths and save heroes before they die in their perishing homeworlds. Once they are saved, Cassandra "gathers" them, using her powers to protect the alternate Earth version of a hero while killing their Marvel Universe counterpart. The Gatherers' ultimate plan is to assemble this team to destroy the Avengers of the Marvel Universe and stop the Eternal, Sersi, from destroying reality, as she has in their previous realities.

However, when the Avengers storm the Gatherers' Citadel in the Andes, it is revealed that Proctor is an alternative universe's Black Knight, who loved Sersi. Together they forged a special Eternal psychic link. When Sersi left him, Proctor went mad. As he was still connected to Sersi, she was driven over the edge until she destroyed her universe. Proctor killed her with his own Ebony Blade, unlocking its bloodthirsty curse. Hungry for revenge, he is now traveling from

universe to universe using an enslaved Watcher named Ute to find the Sersi of that world and drive her mad with their psychic link, while collecting heroes for his team.

As the Avengers and Gatherers face off in battle, Proctor is stabbed in a confrontation with the Marvel Universe Black Knight (Dane Whitman), in effect his alternate—but heroic—self. Proctor makes his escape by destroying his base. Seeking revenge on Dane and Sersi, he returns with a new team of Gatherers: Jocasta, Korg, Tarkas, Sliver, and Rik. Capturing Sersi, he plans to use her and Ute's powers to implode reality, but she runs him through with his own Ebony Blade.

Knight vs. Knight
In a fit of jealous rage, Black Knight Proctor lashes out against Black Knight Dane Whitman— all for the love of Sersi.

SPIDER-MAN 2099

APPEARANCE *Spider-Man 2099* #1 (November 1992) **BASE** New York City on Earth-928 and the Marvel Universe **AFFILIATIONS** Alchemax, Exiles

Genius Miguel O'Hara comes from the year 2099. Trained at Alchemax School for Gifted Youngsters, he climbs the rungs of the Alchemax megacorporate ladder to become a genetic scientist. However, when clinical trials for a new super-serum based on Spider-Man Peter Parker's radioactive DNA result in a test subject's death, he resigns. Corporate bigwig Tyler Stone tricks Miguel into taking the highly addictive, Alchemax genetic-bonding drug—Rapture—so that Miguel will be forced to stay with the company to get his fix. To free himself of the addiction, Miguel uses his clinical trial machine's genetic code rewriter to return his DNA to normal; however, instead, his DNA is rewritten with 50 percent spider DNA. As the Spider-Man of 2099, Miguel swings into action against Alchemax and its nefarious business practices, as well as battling Super Villains such as the Specialist.

Miguel O'Hara's timeline interacts with Peter Parker's Prime Earth timeline when Miguel discovers that Alchemax founder Tyler Stone is his real father. Miguel agrees to go back in time to save his grandfather, Tiberius Stone, as Spider-Man 2099 in order to prevent both Tyler Stone and himself from being phased out; however, Tyler Stone strands Miguel in the present day. Miguel subsequently works for Alchemax, keeping watch over Tiberius, and later for Parker Industries.

Dangerous drink
Tyler Stone spikes his employee Miguel O'Hara's wine with the highly addictive drug Rapture.

Future Spider-Man
Miguel's Spider-Man 2099 outfit is repurposed from a Mexican Day of the Dead costume. As well as web-firing spinnerets, it has retractable talons to assist him with wall-climbing or cutting foes. His webbed cape enables Miguel to glide.

GENIS-VELL

FIRST APPEARANCE *Silver Surfer Annual* #6 (October 1993) **BASE** Mobile; Thunderbolts HQ, New York City **AFFILIATIONS** Thunderbolts, Imperial Kree Army

Genis-Vell is playing cards on the planet Calculex when he is scooped up by the Silver Surfer, who has been sent to find him by his mother, Elysius. Upon their return, Elysius confesses that Genis' father isn't Eros, as he had believed, but Captain Mar-Vell. When the legendary Kree hero died of cancer, Elysius used Mar-Vell's DNA to conceive a child.

Genis was artificially aged to adolescence, taken to the seedy planet Calculex, and given false parentage to protect him from Mar-Vell's many enemies. After this confession, Genis' mother gives him wristlets based on Captain Mar-Vell's Nega-Bands, granting him similar cosmic powers. Genis refuses to wear them. However, Mar-Vell's Kree enemy, Ronan the Accuser, is also seeking the bands in hopes of restoring his empire to power. Homing in on the bands, Ronan attacks. Genis has no choice but to follow in his father's heroic footsteps. By putting on the bands, he claims the name Legacy. Despite his best efforts, Genis is nearly defeated by Ronan. Luckily the Silver Surfer steps in to help Legacy, and Ronan retreats.

Genis-Vell later takes on his father's name, Captain Marvel, and his deep bond with the human Rick Jones. Rick Jones' Destiny Powers—which were unlocked by the Kree Supreme Intelligence—are revived, psychically linking the pair, and awakening Genis-Vell's Cosmic Awareness. However, this awareness proves too great for Genis, causing him to go mad and destroy the universe at the request of two cosmic entities: Entropy and Epiphany.

The intervention of Genis' parents and sister, Phyla-Vell, eventually cures him, and sets him back on course.

Coming to Earth, Genis joins the Thunderbolts, hoping to gain the public's trust, but is nearly killed by his teammate Atlas (Erik Josten) for flirting with Songbird (Melissa Gold). He heals himself with photon energy—emerging as the new hero Photon.

The death of Photon
In time, Photon absorbs the Nega-Bands' energy into his body and becomes dangerously mentally unstable. Believing that he poses a threat to the universe, Baron Zemo, the new leader of the Thunderbolts, kills him

MARROW

FIRST APPEARANCE *Cable* #15 (September 1994)
BASE New York City; mobile **AFFILIATIONS**
Morlocks, Gene Nation, X-Cell

Marrow is a young mutant who grows
random bone spurs from her body that she
can break off to use as weapons. She joins
the outcast Morlocks in the sewers of New
York City, and is one of the few survivors of
the Mutant Massacre, a bloody event
carried out by Mister Sinister's Marauders.
Spatial-warping mutant Mikhail Rasputin
transports her and the other survivors to an
alternate dimension, where they can
recover. Marrow later founds the terrorist
mutant group Gene Nation with the goal of
exacting revenge on their human
oppressors. She works with the X-Men for
a brief time, has trouble fitting in, and is
later recruited by the Weapon X program.
Marrow loses her powers on M-Day and
consequently joins the X-Cell terrorists.

JUDAS TRAVELLER

FIRST APPEARANCE *Web of Spider-Man* #117
(October 1994) **BASE** Unknown
AFFILIATIONS Norman Osborn

Judas Traveller is a famous criminal
psychologist who uncovers a criminal
organization called the Brotherhood of
Scriers. The Scriers send an assassin to
inject him with a fatal drug, but instead it
causes him to gain incredible mental
powers, including mind-reading and the
ability to cause people to experience
hallucinations. The villainous Norman
Osborn uses Traveller in a plot to take out
Spider-Man (Peter Parker) and his clone,
Ben Reilly. In one of his most spectacular
schemes, Judas Traveller takes over the
Ravencroft Institute and puts Spider-Man
"on trial" with the establishment's
criminally insane inmates as the jury and
the psychopathic, wall-crawler-hating
villain Carnage as prosecutor.

KAINE

FIRST APPEARANCE *Web of Spider-Man* #119
(December 1994) **BASE** Loomworld; formerly
New York City; Houston **AFFILIATIONS**
Spider-Man, Spider-Army

Created by evil geneticist Jackal (Miles
Warren), Kaine is his first Peter Parker
clone to reach maturity. However, Kaine's
cells degenerate, leaving him disfigured
and forced to wear a life-support suit. The
Jackal abandons Kaine, who takes jobs as
an assassin. As a calling card, he mutilates
his victims' faces to match the scarring on
his own.

At first, Kaine believes that Ben Reilly
(another Peter Parker clone) is the real
Spider-Man. He harasses and torments
Reilly out of jealousy, even framing him for
a series of murders. Ironically, Kaine
believes Peter Parker is a fellow clone and
tries to protect Peter and the life he has
built. Eventually Kaine learns the truth
about Spider-Man, and Jackal's clones,
and has a change of heart. He helps Reilly

and Parker fight an onslaught of Jackal's
Peter Parker clones and even sacrifices
himself during the struggle; Jackal later
revives Kaine in a regeneration pod.

Kaine is killed once again by the heirs
of Kraven the Hunter, who mistake him for
Peter Parker, but is later returned to life as
the Tarantula by the Jackal. Kaine's
hideous new form has six red eyes and
four spider legs grown from his back.
After receiving Mr. Fantastic's Spider-
Island cure, Kaine is restored to a perfect
clone of Spider-Man. He takes on the
identity of Scarlet Spider and moves to
Houston, Texas, where he tries to live up
to the heroic legacy of Ben Reilly, battling
the likes of Salamander, the Assassins
Guild, the Watchdog, and Ana Kravinoff.

During the convergence of the
Spider-Verse, Kaine, as part of the
Spider-Army, transforms into a monster
and kills Solus, leader of the Inheritors.
Though Kaine is killed by Morlun, he later
emerges alive from
the monster's corpse.

> "My name is Kaine
> and now...Now I
> know I'm a monster."
>
> **KAINE, SCARLET SPIDER**

Clone versus clone
Entrepreneur James Johnsmeyer revives Kaine for a
sadistic tournament. Kaine escapes and seeks out his
clone brother, Ben Reilly. Though the two clash and he
nearly kills Reilly, Kaine later makes peace with him.

ONSLAUGHT

FIRST APPEARANCE *X-Men* #15 (May 1996)
BASE New York City **AFFILIATIONS** Professor X

Onslaught is a psychic entity unintentionally created during a battle between Magneto's Acolytes and the X-Men. Professor X shuts down Magneto's brain, but it causes his own negative emotions to merge with Magneto's. This dark energy manifests itself in a being known as Onslaught, which lies dormant in Xavier's mind, until his own frustrations release the monster. The public's anti-mutant sentiments, the many casualties of mutant plague the Legacy Virus, his inability to reform Sabretooth and, finally, the murder of mutant Dennis Hogan by ordinary humans outside the Xavier Institute, trigger Onslaught to emerge.

At first, Onslaught manipulates circumstances from a distance. Then he traps Professor X, Franklin Richards, and Nate Grey inside his body, augmenting his psychic powers with theirs. Onslaught's most dangerous ability stems from young Franklin Richards' power to change reality.

The Avengers save New York from an attack by Onslaught's servants, Holocaust and Post, after Captain America tricks them into attacking each other. The Fantastic Four, Avengers, and Hulk then work with the X-Men to stop Onslaught in Central Park. In the process, many of them are hurled into a pocket universe by Franklin Richards, in order to save their lives. When the Hulk confronts Onslaught, the resulting burst of energy causes Bruce Banner to split from the Hulk, forming two separate beings. In the wake of all this destruction, the missing heroes are presumed dead in the present dimension, though they are later able to return from the pocket universe. Onslaught returns later, too, revitalized by the totality of mutant powers drained by the Scarlet Witch on M-Day.

From X to Onslaught
Onslaught is finally revealed as an extension of Professor Xavier's own mind. Onslaught emerges first as a product of Xavier's frustrations and negative emotions, but then separates as an independent being.

THUNDERBOLTS

FIRST APPEARANCE *The Incredible Hulk* #449 (January 1997) **BASE** Mobile

The Avengers and Fantastic Four leave a gaping hole in the Super Hero roster when they disappear during their battle with Onslaught. Baron Zemo decides to fill that gap with his Masters of Evil. He gives his newly reformed villains a makeover, with new identities (calling himself the patriotic Citizen V), and renames them the Thunderbolts. The roster includes villains the Fixer (as Techno), Beetle (as Mach-1) and Screaming Mimi (as Songbird). When the Avengers and Fantastic Four eventually return, he reveals the Thunderbolts' secret to the public, hoping to force them to remain under his command. Instead, they turn against him.

After Zemo's downfall, Hawkeye becomes team leader for a while. When the Thunderbolts defeat Crimson Cowl's Masters of Evil, they take over their headquarters in Colorado, renaming it Thunderbolts Mountain.

During the first superhuman civil war, S.H.I.E.L.D. hires the Thunderbolts to hunt down anti-registration heroes. The Thunderbolts' inhibiting electronic implants fail to counteract their brutal tendencies, however, and team members Jack O'Lantern and the Jester nearly kill Spider-Man when he goes rogue. After the Secret Invasion of the alien Skrulls is defeated, Norman Osborn is appointed head of U.S. national security and takes command of the Avengers. He re-forms a new team of Thunderbolts and they become his personal hit squad.

When Osborn's Dark Reign finally comes to an end, Luke Cage forms a new team, based at the Raft prison. Sanctioned by Captain America, the program allows reformed villains to use their powers for good. Red Hulk later forms his own team as well, without government supervision. The Thunderbolts' team leaders and roster change many times over the years. Leaders include Black Widow, Mach-IV, Moonstone, Scourge, Songbird, and the Winter Soldier.

Two fewer Thunderbolts
After Maria Hill orders the Thunderbolts to capture Spider-Man, Jack O'Lantern and Jester catch up with him in the sewers. They nearly kill Spidey, before they are taken out by the Punisher.

TWO AGAINST CARNAGE

"As long as Carnage is loose, innocent bystanders are going to die by the dozen!"

SPIDER-MAN

When a string of gruesome murders occurs in New York City, Spider-Man must do the unthinkable, teaming up with a monster to stop a villain that is even worse.

Carnage murders Peter Parker's friend, Chip; one of a dozen such brutal slayings in a single week. All are accompanied by Carnage's signature, written in blood. At first Parker believes that Venom (Eddie Brock) is the perpetrator. When he learns that Brock was once a cell-mate of serial killer Cletus Kasady, who has broken out of jail, the discovery leads him to the real culprit: Carnage. Spider-Man fights the monster and discovers that Carnage might be out of his league. When Carnage escapes and murders a whole family, Spidey realizes he must turn to Venom for help.

Eddie Brock agrees to help Spider-Man when he learns that Carnage is the offspring of his Venom symbiote and is killing innocent people—something even Venom considers unacceptable. Meanwhile, Carnage keeps on killing. Venom senses Carnage from a distance and tracks him to an apartment building. Venom and Spider-Man battle him, but the villain gets away.

Carnage next targets J. Jonah Jameson, hoping to kill him in public at a concert in Madison Square Garden and inspire a murderous riot. Spider-Man and Venom stop Carnage just in time. The fight spills below into Penn Station and through the subway tunnels before returning to the arena. Spider-Man immobilizes Carnage with a sound blast from the arena's P.A. system, but then Venom seizes the chance to turn on Spider-Man.

Mister Fantastic and Human Torch arrive just in time, and subdue Venom with their sonic gun. Spider-Man breaks his promise to free Venom when Carnage has been defeated—something Venom holds against him.

Spidey vs. Carnage
In his first encounter, Spider-Man realizes Carnage is an even greater danger than Venom. Neither villain alerts his spider-sense, and both can send out tendrils, but Carnage is faster and stronger than Venom and can also fire deadly projectiles that disintegrate after contact.

Allies against evil
Spider-Man and the villain Venom battle
Carnage in the subways below Madison Square
Garden. Venom is certainly no angel, but he
later reforms and even discovers his inner hero.
Carnage, however, is pure evil!

SOLO

FIRST APPEARANCE *Web of Spider-Man #19* (October 1986)

James Bourne is a highly trained mercenary, proficient with most weapons and able to teleport. He carries out a murderous, one-man war on everybody he deems a terrorist or menace to society.

COMET MAN

FIRST APPEARANCE *Comet Man #1* (February 1987)

Killed while piloting his ship through a comet's tail, astronaut Dr. Stephen Beckley is resurrected and bestowed with incredible powers by the Fortisquean alien Max on behalf of the omnipotent Beyonders.

ELDERS OF THE UNIVERSE

FIRST APPEARANCE *Silver Surfer #3* (September 1987)

The cosmically empowered Elders are each the last of their individual species, their lives extended by an obsession with one particular aspect of existence.

ZERO

FIRST APPEARANCE *New Mutants #86* (February 1990)

Created in the future by the Askani, Zero is an android peacekeeper with vast surveillance and calculation capabilities, energy suppression, and teleportation. It is stolen and corrupted by Stryfe.

MUTANT LIBERATION FRONT

FIRST APPEARANCE *New Mutants #86* (February 1990)

This band of disaffected, anarchic young mutants are initially recruited as anti-human terrorists by time-traveler Stryfe. The MLF are defeated by X-Force and the X-Men, but the lethal, ruthless team later reforms under the leadership of Reignfire.

Top, left to right: Tempo, Dragoness, Kamikaze.
Center, left to right: Reaper, Zero, Sumo, Forearm, Strobe.
Bottom left to right: Wildside, Stryfe, Thumbelina.

DEATHWATCH

FIRST APPEARANCE *Ghost Rider #1* (May 1990)

Life-draining extradimensional lord Deathwatch poses as crime boss Stephen Lords while seeking to take over New York City. Employing Blackout as his lead operative, he is constantly foiled by Ghost Rider Danny Ketch, Spider-Man, and the New Avengers.

BLACKOUT

FIRST APPEARANCE *Ghost Rider #2* (June 1990)

Bloodthirsty mass-murderer Blackout is a human-demon halfbreed who is hypersensitive to daylight and can generate a light-damping field. To accentuate his vampiric appearance, he has his teeth and nails replaced with razor-sharp metal versions.

MICHAEL COLLINS

FIRST APPEARANCE *Deathlok #1* (July 1990)

Pacifist computer programmer Michael Collins' brain is transplanted into a Deathlok cyborg by Roxxon Oil executive Harlan Ryker. Seizing control, Collins becomes an unlikely hero while searching for his original body and a way to restore himself to it.

RAGE

FIRST APPEARANCE *Avengers #326* (November 1990)

Teenager Elvin Daryl Haliday becomes superhumanly strong after being exposed to toxic waste. Joining the Avengers, he is expelled when they learn how young he is and moves instead to the New Warriors.

CARDIAC

FIRST APPEARANCE *Amazing Spider-Man #342* (December 1990)

Surgeon Elias Wirtham replaces his heart with a beta-particle reactor, using the enhanced strength, speed, reflexes, and energy-casting powers it bestows to wage a one-man war on profiteering corporations who value money over lives.

SHATTERSTAR

FIRST APPEARANCE *New Mutants #99* (March 1991)

Genetically engineered time-traveler Gaveedra Seven escapes from slavery on Mojoworld and joins X-Force. He uses his enhanced physicality, gladiatorial training, and mutant abilities to generate bioelectricity and teleport.

SLEEPWALKER

FIRST APPEARANCE *Sleepwalker #1* (June 1991)

Sleepwalkers guard the Dreamscape, preventing monsters from invading physical realms. When one is tricked into bonding with human Rick Sheridan, he uses his newly gained strength and reality-bending warp-gaze to fight for justice.

DR. ASHLEY KAFKA

FIRST APPEARANCE *Spectacular Spider-Man #178* (July 1991)

Psychologist Ashley Kafka founds the Ravencroft Institute for the Criminally Insane to treat menaces such as Carnage, Carrion, Doctor Octopus, and Electro. She is later murdered by Massacre.

G.W. BRIDGE

FIRST APPEARANCE *X-Force #1* (August 1991)

Soldier of fortune George Washington Bridge worked with Cable in the Wild Pack before joining S.H.I.E.L.D. He acts as an inside source for X-Force, while hunting various villains and pursuing outlaw vigilante the Punisher.

CYBER

FIRST APPEARANCE *Marvel Comics Presents #85* (September 1991)

Silas Barr trains Wolverine in World War I. Gaining cyborg enhancements, he plagues Logan for almost 100 years before being killed. He returns after possessing mutant Milo Gunderson, but is killed again by Ogun.

LYJA

FIRST APPEARANCE *Fantastic Four #357* (October 1991)

Skrull shape-shifter Lyja takes Alicia Masters' place and marries Human Torch Johnny Storm. Falling in love, she betrays her people and joins the FF, later saving the team during the Skrulls' Secret Invasion.

OMEGA RED

FIRST APPEARANCE *X-Men #4 (January 1992)*

The K.G.B. turned the Russian mutant serial killer Arkady Rossovich into a lethal weapon, using extendable carbonadium cables to extract lifeforce via his "Death Spores." Killed by Wolverine, he is resurrected as three separate clones.

DOMINO

FIRST APPEARANCE *X-Force #8 (March 1992)*

Sole survivor of a government Super-Soldier breeding program, Neena Thurman's probability-altering powers and combat training make her Cable's most valuable ally, working closely with him in the Six Pack, X-Force, and X-Men.

SLAPSTICK

FIRST APPEARANCE *Slapstick #1* (November 1992)

Teenager Steve Harmon is caught in a mystic disturbance and stretched across 3,741 dimensions. Converted to unstable molecules, he is turned into a living cartoon character—the zany vigilante Slapstick.

RANDOM

FIRST APPEARANCE *X-Factor #88 (March 1993)*

Created by Dark Beast, shape-shifter Marshall Evan Stone III has a protoplasmic body that expels biomass as lethal projectiles. Switching allegiances after infiltrating X-Factor, he is unable to stay loyal to anyone, subsequently joining both heroic and evil mutant groups.

GRAYDON CREED

FIRST APPEARANCE *Uncanny X-Men #299* (April 1993)

The son of Sabretooth and Mystique, Creed founds anti-mutant organization Friends of Humanity and runs for U.S. President. He is assassinated by Mystique, resurrected by Bastion, and killed again by Hope Summers.

MICROCHIP

FIRST APPEARANCE *Punisher #4 (July 1993)*

Brilliant engineer Linus Lieberman is the man who puts the punishment into Punisher, building the vigilante's arsenal of weapons. Unfortunately, being the Punisher's ally means that Microchip becomes the target of the Punisher's criminal foes, such as the Kingpin.

PHALANX

FIRST APPEARANCE *Uncanny X-Men #305* (October 1993)

Predatory alien hive mind the Phalanx spreads by converting organic lifeforms via the transmode virus into cybernetic versions of themselves. They are hunted by the Technarchy, who consider them abominations of the natural order.

BLINK

FIRST APPEARANCE *Uncanny X-Men #317* (October 1994)

Seemingly killed by the Phalanx, mutant teleporter Clarice Ferguson was actually trapped in a Nether-Realm. Rescued by immortal villain Selene, she eventually joins Wolverine's X-Men. An alternate Blink leads Multiversal hero team the Exiles.

M

FIRST APPEARANCE *Uncanny X-Men #316* (September 1994)

Mutant Monet St. Croix possesses a vast range of physical and psionic powers. Thanks to her vile brother Emplate, she spends years as the tragic untouchable Penance until rescued and cured by Generation X.

DARK BEAST

FIRST APPEARANCE *X-Men Alpha (1995)*

Dark Beast Henry McCoy spends decades cruelly experimenting on mutants after escaping the Age of Apocalypse Reality. Replacing the Beast in the X-Men, he clashes with many heroes and perishes while triggering a nuclear strike.

3-D MAN

FIRST APPEARANCE *Avengers #8* (September 1998)

Delroy Garrett, Jr. joins the Avengers as Triathlon, unaware that his powers come from 1950s Super Hero 3-D Man—two brothers merged in a single body. Empowered by a universal triune totem, he liberates the original brothers, inheriting their role and "tri-power."

BIG HERO 6

FIRST APPEARANCE *Sunfire and Big Hero Six #1* (September 1998)

Japanese super-team Big Hero 6 at various times comprises Silver Samurai, Sunfire, GoGo Tomago, Honey Lemon, Hiro Takachiho, Baymax, Ebon Samurai, Sunpyre, Wasabi-No-Ginger, and Fredzilla).

BLACKWULF

FIRST APPEARANCE *Thunderstrike #6* (March 1994)

Alien exile Lucian battles his father's plans for dominating humanity, using his enhanced strength, speed, agility, and Black Legacy-energy death-touch while disguised as rebel leader Blackwulf.

NIGHTWATCH

FIRST APPEARANCE *Web of Spider-Man #99* (April 1993)

Dr. Kevin Trench becomes Super Hero Nightwatch after seeing his older self die in battle. He eventually discovers he is actually a Super Villain named Nighteater, trapped in a time-bending quest for power.

ECHO

FIRST APPEARANCE *Daredevil #9* (December 1999)

Deaf Maya Lopez has photographic reflexes and formidable combat skills. Hunting Daredevil for the Kingpin, she switches allegiances and helps topple the villain. She joins the New Avengers as Ronin.

SENTRY

FIRST APPEARANCE *Sentry* #1 (September 2000) **BASE** Avengers Tower, The Raft
AFFILIATIONS Avengers, Dark Avengers

Robert Reynolds is a drug addict who breaks into a laboratory and drinks an experimental Super-Soldier serum. The experience gets him much more than high—he becomes Sentry, one of the most powerful Super Heroes ever known. His unstable mind creates an equally powerful, but evil, split personality called the Void. The Void is so dangerous that, with the aid of the X-Men's Mastermind, he attempts to have the memory of his identity as Sentry erased from the world's collective consciousness.

The Void later destroys Asgard, and Thor is forced to kill Reynolds. The Thunder God then carries the Void's body to the Sun—a funeral pyre befitting the former Super Hero.

THOR GIRL

FIRST APPEARANCE *Thor* #22 (April 2000)
BASE New York City, Camp Hammond
AFFILIATIONS Thor, Asgardians, Avengers

The Designate is prophesied at the dawn of the universe to advance all life. Tarene is believed to be the fulfillment of that oracle. But when Thanos destroys her world, Tarene's power and potential is drained. Thor helps her claim vengeance against Thanos. Tarene is so enamored with Thor that she transforms herself into an Asgardian, with all of their strength and abilities, and she dons a costume in his honor, complete with a powerful hammer of her own.

Later, Tarene is entirely drained of her powers when she defeats Surtur, the fire demon. With some powers restored, she helps the Avengers confront the Hulk, and joins the Avengers initiative during the first superhuman civil war.

EXILES

FIRST APPEARANCE *Exiles* #1 (August 2001)
BASE Mobile Panoptichron Base
AFFILIATIONS Weapon X, X-Men

The Timebroker assembles a group of heroes from alternate dimensions to correct anomalies in the Multiverse of timestreams, with guidance from a communication device called the Tallus. The Tallus is worn by the leader of the group, changing its appearance according to the wearer, and transmits messages from the Timebroker. It appears to have additional mysterious powers, such as enabling the wearer to teleport.

Known as the Exiles, the founding members include Beak (a mutant with the ability to fly), Blink (the leader, Clarice Ferguson, who can teleport), Magnus Lehnsherr (the son of Rogue and Magneto) Mimic (Calvin Rankin, who copies the powers of others), Morph (a shape-shifter), Nocturne (T.J. Nightstar, the daughter of Scarlet Witch and Nightcrawler), and Thunderbird (John Proudstar).

Later members include heroes from alternate realities such as Beast, Black Panther, Gambit, Longshot, Mystique, Namora, Polaris, Psylocke, Valeria Richards, Sabretooth, Scarlet Witch, Sasquatch, Spider-Man 2099, Sunfire, and several versions of Wolverine.

The Exiles discover that the Timebroker has a second team doing his bidding—called Weapon-X—whose missions include assassinating heroes with the potential to turn evil. The two teams work together to free a group of children in a Sentinel concentration camp, but when their next orders are to kill the mutant child David Richards, a conflict between them occurs, and Sabretooth agrees to stay behind and raise the boy.

The Exiles team up with heroes from the present-day (Marvel Universe), including the X-Men. They stop Havok when his body is cohabitated by an evil Havok from the Mutant-X universe.

When the Timebroker begins acting more and more erratically, the Exiles rebel and invade the Panoptichron (also known as the Crystal Palace). There they discover that the Timebroker is actually an alien race of insects that previously broke the Multiverse timestream and have since manipulated the Exiles into fixing the mess they themselves created.

> "One more major loss and it's half rations for a week…"
>
> **MIMIC**

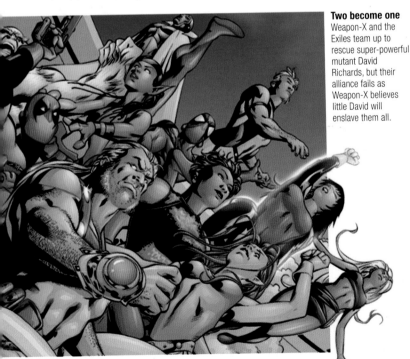

Two become one
Weapon-X and the Exiles team up to rescue super-powerful mutant David Richards, but their alliance fails as Weapon-X believes little David will enslave them all.

Exiled
The Exiles *(clockwise from top left)*: Sasquatch, Beak, Morph, Blink, Mimic, and Nocturne.

JESSICA JONES

FIRST APPEARANCE *Alias* #1 (November 2001)
BASE Mobile, including Alias Investigations, Gem Theater, New York City **AFFILIATIONS** Avengers, New Avengers, *Daily Bugle*, Luke Cage, Alias Investigations, Spider-Man

Jessica Campbell is born in Forest Hills in Queens, New York City. In her Midtown High School days, Jones is a shy student with a crush on nerdy Peter Parker (Spider-Man).

The Campbell family's car collides with a military truck, killing all but Jessica, who is left in a coma for six months. When she awakes, Jessica is sent to Moore House for Wayward Children, then adopted by the Jones family. After her recovery, Jessica finds she now has super-powers, including super-strength and the ability to fly.

After trying out her new talents and besting the villain Scorpion, Jessica takes the name Jewel; she later joins the Avengers. When Purple Man (Zebediah Killgrave) takes over her mind for eight months, using her as his personal slave, he makes her attack the Avengers. She ends up in another coma as a result, but Jean Grey heals her. When she recovers, Jessica decides to give up Super Hero life and become a private eye.

Jessica's detective work finds her teaming up with Luke Cage, Spider-Man, and Daredevil as she takes cases involving Super Heroes and Villains. She also writes for *Daily Bugle* supplement *The Pulse*.

Jessica Jones falls in love with and marries Luke Cage, and they have a daughter, Danielle. During the shape-shifting Skrulls' Secret Invasion of Earth, their daughter is kidnapped by a Skrull posing as Edwin Jarvis, but Norman Osborn assists Luke Cage in getting her back. They hire Squirrel Girl (Doreen Green) to be Danielle's nanny. Jessica even convinces Luke to retire from the Avengers to concentrate on home life—but this doesn't end his Super Hero career.

Misguided heroine
Jessica Jones' time as the Super Hero Jewel is unsuccessful and short-lived.

Under a purple shroud
Jessica is hypnotized by Purple Man and ordered to attack Daredevil. She ends up also fighting Scarlet Witch before being freed from his control.

X-FACTOR

FIRST APPEARANCE *X-Factor* #1 (June 2002)
BASE Various **AFFILIATIONS** X-Men

X-Factor is a popular name for a variety of teams. The first incarnation is comprised of the original X-Men (Angel, Beast, Cyclops, Iceman, and Jean Grey).

They leave the X-Men when their nemesis Magneto is installed as the new leader. Cyclops has married Madelyne Pryor and moved to Alaska and the others are seeking new directions, but when Jean Grey returns, having rid herself of the Phoenix Force, they reunite.

The reconstituted team pretends to hunt mutants in Manhattan and bring them to justice. Instead, they actually help these mutants fit into society and use their powers wisely. Eventually the founding X-Men return to their old team.

Later, the U.S. government creates a new X-Force team composed of Havok (Alex Summers), Multiple Man (Jamie Madrox), Polaris (Lorna Dane), Quicksilver (Pietro Maximoff), Strong Guy (Guido Carosella), and Wolfsbane (Rahne Sinclair). Their U.S. government liaison is Valerie Cooper, but their roster of team members changes. A third incarnation of X-Factor is comprised of returning members from the government team. The fourth version is actually the Mutant Civil Rights Task Force, which is perhaps ironic, since the publicly stated purpose of the original X-Factor is to round up mutants and bring them to justice.

Following M-Day, Jamie Madrox starts a private investigator office known as X-Factor Investigations. He brings several friends onboard, including M (Monet St. Croix), Layla Miller, Rictor (Julio Esteban Rictor), Siryn (Theresa Cassidy), Strong Guy, and Wolfsbane.

After buying rights to the name from Madrox, Serval Industries CEO Harrison Snow forms the next X-Factor, a corporate-owned Super Hero team led by Polaris, with teammates Cypher (Douglas Ramsey), Danger (the physical manifestation of the X-Men's training room), Decay (Georgia Dakei), Gambit (Remy LeBeau), Quicksilver, and Adam Warlock.

X-Factor
The all-new team (left to right): Warlock, Danger, Cypher, Polaris, Gambit, Quicksilver; Decay is not pictured.

The originals
The first X-factor team heads into battle *(clockwise from top)*: Beast (Henry McCoy), Cyclops (Scott Summers), Jean Grey, Iceman (Robert Drake), and Angel (Warren Worthington).

X-STATIX

FIRST APPEARANCE *X-Statix* #1 (September 2002) **BASE** X-Statix Tower, Los Angeles

With X-Force seemingly dead, business mogul Spike Freeman puts together a new X-Force, managed by the manipulative mutant Coach. The team comprises young mutants seeking fame and fortune as reality-TV stars. Their crime-fighting adventures are televised, but the team suffers a high mortality rate, culminating in the whole roster being wiped out in a single show.

To avoid legal action when the original X-Force resurfaces, a new team changes its name to X-Statix. The leader is pop star Henrietta Hunter, who can resurrect herself after being killed. Anyone who sings one of her "comeback" songs, titled "Back From the Dead," out loud, dies, accounting for several members' deaths. The X-Statix heroes are eventually wiped out, but their spirits continue adventuring.

THE HOOD

FIRST APPEARANCE *The Hood* #1 (July 2002)
BASE New York City **AFFILIATIONS** Cabal, Illuminati

Parker Robbins is a petty criminal trying to support a sick mother and a pregnant girlfriend when, during a heist, he stumbles across a mysterious cloak and boots. Following the revelation that the boots enable him to walk on air and the cloak makes him invisible, Robbins continues his life of crime. When he steals a shipment of diamonds belonging to a crime boss called the Golem and fatally shoots a police officer at the scene, Robbins becomes known in the press as the Hood. Deciding to try and make some serious money off the back of his newfound reputation, the Hood lays the foundations for a criminal empire of Super Villains in New York. He later discovers that the source of his powers is the demon Dormammu, which draws him into a helllish world of black magic. After losing his powers, the Hood attempts to restore his prestige by collecting a number of Infinity Gems. However, he is thwarted by the Avengers.

RUNAWAYS

FIRST APPEARANCE *Runaways* #1
(August 2003) **BASE** The Hostel, the New Hostel

A group of Los Angeles children are brought together once a year to hang out while their parents organize some charity fundraising…or so they think. When the kids decide to spy on the adults, they witness them murdering a young woman in a blood ritual as part of an organization called the Pride.

The realization that their parents are in effect Super Villains inspires the horrified youngsters to band together to try and stop them. Alex Wilder, Nico Minoru, Gertrude "Gert" Yorkes, Karolina Dean, Chase Stein, and Molly Hayes search their parents' houses looking for evidence. Along the way, they acquire a telepathic velociraptor, Old Lace, that responds to Gert's mental commands, and discover that Karolina is an alien capable of flight. Nico gains possession of the magical Staff of One from her parents, while Chase finds X-ray glasses and

weaponized gloves called Fistigons at his mother and father's workshop. Finally, a traumatic confrontation with some of the group's parents at Molly's house causes Molly to manifest powerful mutant abilities.

Hiding out in a ruined mansion called the Hostel, the kids come up with a plan to bring the Pride to justice. However, in a final confrontation, Alex, who has from the start acted as a leader, reveals that he has been a mole all along and has lied to and manipulated his friends. When alien beings summoned by the Pride's

ritual appear and kill Alex, the rest of the Runaways escape while the building collapses around the evil Pride. With their parents deceased, the kids are put into care, but they soon find a way to team up again, determined to prevent any new villains from moving into the power vacuum left by the downfall of the Pride. As the Runaways gain experience, new members join the team, including an android, Victor Mancha, a Skrull, Xavin, and a young mutant named Klara Prast who can communicate with plants.

False friend
Karolina uses her alien powers to attack her teammate Alex after discovering that he has sold them out to the villainous Pride.

X-23

FIRST APPEARANCE *NYX* #3 (February 2004) **BASE** Jean Grey School for Higher Learning, New Charles Xavier School for Mutants **AFFILIATIONS** X-Men, X-Force

Laura Kinney is the result of a revival of the Weapon X program that created Wolverine. Dr. Sarah Kinney is the geneticist in charge of the project. Finding the Y chromosome too damaged to work with, Kinney tries for a female clone against the orders of her superiors. On her twenty-third attempt, Kinney obtains a viable embryo but, because of her underhand behavior, she is forced to carry the child herself. When the girl is born, she has long, retractable claws on her hands and feet. Known only as X-23, she grows up in the top-secret facility where she is born, among people who are ordered to treat her as a weapon, not a child. X-23's claws are coated in Adamantium and a trigger scent is created to unleash a killing frenzy in the girl.

Filled with remorse about the treatment of her "child," Kinney helps her escape; however, a trace of the trigger scent is on her and X-23 attacks her. With her dying breath, Sarah gives the girl a name—Laura. Now alone, Laura sets off on the trail of Wolverine, the closest thing she has to a relative. She finds him and travels to the Xavier Institute, although her traumatic upbringing makes it very difficult for her to settle in or trust anybody. X-23 later joins X-Force, a team willing to use lethal force, if necessary—Wolverine objects to this decision, as he wants her to be Laura, not the assassin X-23. Following Logan's death, Laura takes on the Wolverine identity.

Family reunion
X-23's first meeting with her clone-father Wolverine does not go smoothly —the girl's brutal training makes her stab first and ask questions later.

STAR-LORD

FIRST APPEARANCE *Thanos* #8 (June 2004)
BASE Knowhere, Spartax **AFFILIATIONS**
Guardians of the Galaxy

Peter Quill is half-Earthman, half-alien. His father J'son, Emperor of Spartax, crash-lands on Earth and is forced to stay for a while to fix his ship. While on the planet, he forms a relationship with Meredith Quill and leaves her pregnant, promising to return.

When Peter is ten years old, the alien Badoon attack, seeking to wipe out the royal Spartax bloodline. Meredith is killed and her house destroyed. The Badoon leave, believing that Peter has also died, but he has survived, growing up with a desire to leave Earth and seek revenge. He gets his chance when, after joining N.A.S.A., he steals a Kree spaceship. After falling in with some space pirates, Peter learns more about his destiny as the "Star-Lord," a title his father also held. He ends up imprisoned in the Kyln prison after causing the death of thousands of Kree in a battle to take down the Fallen One, Galactus' evil former herald.

He also declares Star-Lord "dead" after his actions, going back to being just Peter.

After escaping the Kyln, Quill is on the front line of the fight against the Annihilation Wave, where he meets Gamora and Drax. After the threat has passed, Quill takes up a role as defense advisor to the Kree, putting him in the thick of the action once more when the Phalanx conquer the Kree homeworld. Using the team he brought together to battle the Phalanx, Quill assembles the Guardians of the Galaxy, intending to take a proactive approach to future threats. He later meets Kitty Pryde, in space with the X-Men for the trial of Jean Grey. The two fall in love, and Kitty eventually joins the Guardians to be with Peter, who proposes marriage. When Quill is unexpectedly elected Emperor of Spartax following the disgrace of his father, he leaves the Guardians and tries to be a good ruler. However he soon discovers he is not cut out for such a high-profile role, and returns to his friends in the Guardians.

Inheritance
Peter has no superhuman powers, but he carries his father J'son's element gun. J'son left it behind when he departed Earth.

SPIDER-GIRL

FIRST APPEARANCE *Amazing Fantasy* #1 (August 2004) **BASE** New York, Loomworld
AFFILIATIONS Spider Society, Warriors of the Great Web

Anya Corazón is a high-school freshman who loves gymnastics and hates bullies. One evening in the park, she sees a man named Miguel fighting some toughs. Running to his aid, Anya is stabbed, but Miguel tells her that he can save her life in exchange for something precious. She weakly hands him her late mother's locket, and the next thing she knows she is waking in her bedroom, with spider webbing everywhere and her body healed. Anya seeks Miguel out to get some answers and is drawn into WebCorps, a mysterious organization operating as a cover for the ancient Spider Society. The Society must always have a Mage and a Hunter; while Miguel is the Mage, there is a vacancy for a Hunter, which he has chosen Anya to fill. The healing ritual has given Anya spider-powers and a tough exoskeleton that manifests at her command. She duly takes the codename Araña, her mother's maiden name.

When her secret identity is compromised and her friends and family are put in danger, Araña resigns from the Spider Society. However, a pep talk from Spider-Man himself changes her mind—he tells her that with great power comes great responsibility. She continues to operate as

a costumed hero, but does eventually leave the Spider Society. During the superhuman civil war, Anya trains alongside Ms. Marvel and Wonder Man. However, after she is badly injured in a fight with Doomsday Man, during which her exoskeleton is torn from her body, her father forbids her to see heroes again. Nevertheless, Araña decides that her place is back on the streets fighting the good fight, and she changes her name to Spider-Girl as that's what everyone assumes she's

called anyway. She is a vital part of the Spider-Army's battle against the Inheritors, who are trying to destroy all Spider-Totems across the Multiverse, as her powers give her a unique insight into the Inheritors' plans. After this battle is won, Spider-Girl chooses to stay in Loomworld, the Inheritors' former base, as one of the Warriors of the Great Web.

Warriors of the Great Web
Their mission is to travel to realities that have lost their spider heroes to the Inheritors, and help where they can.

WINTER SOLDIER

FIRST APPEARANCE *Captain America* #1 (January 2005) **BASE** Mobile **AFFILIATIONS** Avengers, S.H.I.E.L.D.

James "Bucky" Buchanan Barnes is Captain America's faithful sidekick during World War II. When the two heroes go up against Baron Zemo in the Arctic, the drone plane they hope to stop suddenly explodes. Cap falls into the sea and is frozen in ice; he wakes up years later, without his friend, whom he believes died in the same explosion. Miraculously, Bucky has survived, though he has lost an arm. Like Cap, Bucky fell into the sea, but was rescued by a Russian submarine.

Bucky awakens in Soviet Russia, with amnesia and a new bionic arm. Soviet General Vasily Karpov, once an ally, brainwashes Bucky and turns him into the merciless spy and assassin known as the Winter Soldier. Bucky's strong will provides him with the fortitude to battle his mental programming. In order to keep the Winter Soldier compliant, the Soviets keep him in suspended animation between missions. Each time he is reactivated, the Winter Soldier receives an upgraded bionic arm and additional brainwashing.

When General Alexander Lukin takes over the Winter Soldier program, he orders Bucky to assassinate Red Skull and steal his Cosmic Cube. The Winter Soldier also kills Nomad and attacks the city of Philadelphia in an effort to charge the Cube with a large explosion. Captain America manages to gain control of the Cube and use it to restore Bucky's memories. Now himself again, Bucky disappears to hunt Lukin.

After the apparent death of his dearest friend Steve Rogers, Bucky accepts Tony Stark's offer to become the new Captain America. He agrees on condition that S.H.I.E.L.D. removes all remnants of the Winter Soldier programming, and that he is allowed to work without supervision. In a new Stark-outfitted Cap costume, Bucky—often with the help of Falcon—takes on A.I.M., the Red Skull's daughter Sin, and even a Skrull invasion.

After Steve Rogers resurfaces, Bucky becomes the Winter Soldier once more. No longer bearing the weight of Soviet mind control or the cowl of Cap, he tries to make amends for his past misdeeds working with teams like the Secret Avengers and S.H.I.E.L.D.

Built to kill
As the Winter Soldier, Bucky is outfitted with a bionic limb by Soviet operatives. It has been upgraded to provide superhuman strength, fire electronic and fiery blasts, and even contains a cloaking device.

YOUNG AVENGERS

FIRST APPEARANCE *Young Avengers* #1 (February 2005) **BASE** New York City **AFFILIATIONS** Avengers

In the wake of internal struggles in the Avengers' ranks, causing them to disassemble, a new teen team is forged in their image. Nathaniel Richards, a time-traveling young version of Kang the Conqueror, wearing a mech-suit and taking the name Iron Lad builds a Super Hero team with the all-American Patriot (Eli Bradley), shape-shifting alien goliath Hulkling (Teddy Altman), and the magical son of Scarlet Witch: Wiccan (Billy Kaplan).

The team takes on several missions unbeknownst to their parents, as Iron Lad prepares them for an inevitable showdown with Iron Lad's older, villainous self, Kang. Along the way, Stature (Cassie Lang, Ant-Man Scott Lang's daughter) and the sharp-shooting Hawkeye (Kate Bishop) join the team.

Afraid for the young heroes' safety, Iron Man and Captain America track down the Young Avengers, with the help of super-powered detective Jessica Jones, and try to force them to disband. However, when the villainous Kang arrives from the future, a major showdown results. Iron Lad ultimately has to abandon his armor (which becomes sentient with Vision's programming) as well as the team and timeline, in order to face his future.

Despite the adult Avengers confiscating their equipment and refusing them training, the team remains together, battling through the superhuman civil war, an alien Skrull Secret Invasion, and Norman Osborn's Dark Reign. They finally disband in the aftermath of Manhattan being overrun with people infected with the Jackal's Spider-Virus.

The Young Avengers later reform, adding the alien hero Noh-Varr (Marvel Boy), replacing Patriot with Ms. America (America Chavez), and teaming up with a young god of mischief, Loki, to stop the interdimensional parasite Mother.

Faith in youth
A new generation *(clockwise from top)*: Hulkling, Wiccan, Marvel Boy, Ms. America, Hawkeye, and Prodigy.

Meeting the future
Kang the Conqueror glowers down at his younger self, the Young Avenger Iron Lad, as he delivers an ultimatum to leave this timeline or risk destroying it.

VICTOR MANCHA

FIRST APPEARANCE *Runaways* #1 (April 2005) **BASE** Los Angeles, New York City **AFFILIATIONS** Runaways, Avengers A.I.

Victor Mancha is a sentient android made in part with human DNA from his mother, Marianella Mancha, and the A.I. technology of evil robot, Ultron. Victor believes he is a normal teenager because of synthetically implanted memories, until teenage super-team the Runaways gets a message from the future warning them of Victor's villainous destiny—Ultron has created him to infiltrate the Avengers and murder them.

The Runaways kidnap Victor, and try to set him on a more heroic course. However Ultron kills Victor's mother and briefly takes over Victor's systems. When Ultron is finally defeated, Victor goes on to join the team, having decided to take the heroic high road. He later joins the Avengers A.I., alongside other robotic heroes.

MARIA HILL

FIRST APPEARANCE *New Avengers* #4
(April 2005) **BASE** S.H.I.E.L.D. HQ, New York City
AFFILIATIONS S.H.I.E.L.D., The Avengers,
Secret Avengers

Maria Hill is a hard-nosed, pragmatic
commander within the homeland security
and espionage organization S.H.I.E.L.D.,
proving herself to be a formidable member
of the agency. When the director of
S.H.I.E.L.D., Nick Fury, goes AWOL
during a Secret War, Hill is named his
successor by the President of the United
States, in large part because she is not a
Fury loyalist.

Hill's tight-lipped demeanor and
willingness to make ends justify means
has made her a sometime danger for the
Avengers: Hill is a proponent of the Super
Hero Registration Act, incarcerating
heroes who refuse to comply. She also
establishes the secret prison Pleasant Hill,
which uses a sentient Cosmic Cube to
brainwash Super Villains into reforming.

Caught in the act
Amadeus Cho breaks into a S.H.I.E.L.D.
lab in the former Avengers Tower to
download data for the Illuminati. However,
the security breach is detected by Director
Maria Hill, who tries to take him out.

On the run
Amadeus Cho and his coyote puppy Kirby are being
hunted by the government, so they travel incognito.
They are still willing to stop and help a stranded
ex-S.H.I.E.L.D. agent in need, however.

AMADEUS CHO

FIRST APPEARANCE *Amazing Fantasy* #15 (January 2006) **BASE** Arizona,
New York City **AFFILIATIONS** Champions, Mighty Avengers, Renegades

Teen genius Amadeus Cho is hailed the seventh smartest person
in the world when he wins a science competition. However,
the competition organizer, crazy, paranoid former child prodigy
Pythagoras Dupree, determined to destroy anyone rivaling him
for cleverness, blows up the Cho home, killing the family and
sending Amadeus on the run across his home state of Arizona.
The Hulk helps Cho escape Pythagoras' agents, beginning a
lasting friendship.

Hulk is later exiled by the Illuminati to the planet Sakaar.

When he returns to Earth for revenge, Amadeus recruits a team
of Renegades, including Hercules, Namora, and Angel to
help Hulk, but is unable to stop the green behemoth and his
Warbound allies' rampage. Eventually, the Hulk sees reason
and allows himself to be captured.

The Olympian goddess of Wisdom, Athena, seeing Cho's great
promise, decides to make him Prince of Power. This means that
Hercules—Cho's best friend and the current Prince of Power—
must die. Amadeus does his best to protect his friend, but soon
Hercules perishes. Cho eventually ascends to full godhood in
order to bring Hercules back from Hades and reinstate him as
the Prince of Power. Cho later takes on the powers of Hulk—
becoming the Totally Awesome Hulk.

THE OTHER/ ERO/ MISS ARROW

FIRST APPEARANCE *Amazing Spider-Man* #527
(February 2006) **BASE** Forest Hills, New York City
AFFILIATIONS Spider-Totems

The Other, known as Ero, or Miss Arrow,
is a Spider-Totem entity that appears in
many forms—sometimes as a large spider,
a human form composed of many spiders,
or as Miss Arrow, a human woman.

She first meets Spider-Man's alter ego,
Peter Parker, as an enormous arachnid,
called the Other. While Peter is in a cocoon
state, the spider gives him the chance to
be reborn by accepting his true inner
spider, instead of facing death by the
Spider-Totem-consuming Morlun. Peter
Parker accepts this prospect, wrapping his
arms around her and is birthed anew.

The Other also encounters Spider-Man
in her human form as Miss Arrow, a nurse

at Midtown High, Peter's school. While
there, she scouts a young Flash Thompson
as a viable partner to mate with because
of his perceived fertility. She makes an
attempt to shove her egg sac down Flash's
throat, waiting for him to give birth to
thousands of tiny spiders which will surely
kill him. Luckily, Spider-Man intervenes
and Flash's date, Betty Brant, destroys the
giant spider's egg sac.

Consequently, Miss Arrow turns her
breeding intentions toward Spider-Man,
who lures her—now in her multi-spider
form of Ero—into an aviary. Birds begin
eating all of the spiders that compose her
body, except one. Spider-Man then steps
on this sole survivor.

The Other later reappears within Peter's
clone Kaine, when all the spider-powered
people in the vast Spider-Verse band
together against Morlun and his villainous
family, the Inheritors.

A CIVIL WAR

"We were beating them, man. We were winning back there."

SPIDER-MAN

The public are no longer just passive observers when citizens become collateral damage in a superhuman conflict. The aftermath pits the Avengers against each other like never before.

Tragedy strikes when budding heroes known as the New Warriors—Microbe (Zachary Smith Jr.), Namorita (Namorita Prentiss), Night Thrasher (Dwayne Taylor), and Speedball (Robbie Baldwin) go up against the villains Coldheart (Kateri Deseronto), Cobalt Man (Ralph Roberts), Nitro (Robert Hunter), and Speedfreek (Joss Shappe). Nitro kills not only the New Warriors, but also hundreds of residents of Stamford, Connecticut. As a result, U.S. Congress passes the Superhuman Registration Act, requiring Super Heroes to identify themselves and work for the government as part of S.H.I.E.L.D. While Iron Man (Tony Stark), Hank Pym, and Mr. Fantastic (Reed Richards) support the new law, Captain America (Steve Rogers) objects in a violent clash and goes into hiding.

Cap forms a resistance group of Secret Avengers, beginning with Cable (Nathan Summers), Falcon (Sam Wilson), Goliath (Bill Foster), Hercules, and Iron Fist (Daniel Rand). Others join them later.

Meanwhile, Iron Man convinces Peter Parker to reveal his secret identity as Spider-Man. Parker has second thoughts (as do others) when Goliath is killed and a prison known as "42" is created to hold the Super Hero objectors. When Parker leaves the group, S.H.I.E.L.D.'s Thunderbolts nearly beat him to death.

A final battle between the two sides takes place outside the 42 prison. Captain America's side gains the upper hand, but Cap is horrified by the destruction caused and the impact of the fight on citizen bystanders. He orders his side to stand down and he surrenders. This brings an end to the civil war and his side agrees to register. However, Captain America's worst problems are yet to come…

Turning point
The tide turns when Punisher rescues Spider-Man from Jack O'Lantern and the Jester. Such villains are given amnesty if they register and assist the government. Punisher brings Spidey to the Secret Avengers, where both he and Spider-Man join Captain America's opposition team.

Final confrontation
Captain America's rebel forces clash with
Iron Man's government allies at a singularly
appropriate location: outside the Negative Zone's
Prison 42, especially set up to contain
superhumans refusing to sign up to the
Superhuman Registration Act.

THE WARBOUND

FIRST APPEARANCE *Incredible Hulk* #94 (June 2006) **BASE** Sakaar **AFFILIATIONS** Incredible Hulks

Bruce Banner, posing a threat to humanity on Earth as his alter ego Hulk, is sent into space by S.H.I.E.L.D. to destroy a rogue satellite. However, when the mission is complete, the secret organization of Super Heroes known as the Illuminati—Black Bolt, Doctor Strange, Iron Man, and Mr. Fantastic—takes the opportunity to exile Hulk in space and the ship ends up crashing on the savage planet of Sakaar.

Weakened, the Hulk is sold into slavery as a gladiator, compelled to fight for the amusement of Sakaar's Red King by pain-inducing obedience discs. If gladiators win three battles in the arena, they are promised their freedom. Warring rebels also offer Hulk freedom, but he chooses to stay and prove himself in battle.

However, the Red King does not deliver on his promise and tries to destroy the Hulk and his fellow gladiators. The Hulk, along with Hiroim the Shadow Warrior, Korg of Krona, Warrior-Prime of Broodworld and the insectoid Miek, among others, promise to be Warbound together, and overthrow the Red King's regime.

Eventually, Hulk becomes Sakaar's king with the Red King's former lieutenant, Caiera, as his queen. She is pregnant with his child when Hulk's crashed ship—being turned into a monument in the Red King's liberated capital city—explodes after its antimatter self-destruct sequence is triggered. The blast kills most of the inhabitants of Sakaar, including Caiera.

Together, the Hulk and his Warbound allies travel to Earth in a stone ship seeking revenge against the Illuminati, whom Hulk blames for triggering the tragedy. As World War Hulk unfolds, hurting heroes and humans alike, Hulk and the Warbound realize they do not want to see another world die. They surrender and the Hulk is captured, reverting to his Bruce Banner form. The Warbound escape and then go into hiding.

Worlds at war
Earth's Mightiest Heroes the Avengers have never faced such ferocious opposition as the Hulk and his alien Warbound allies.

Bound for glory
Disgraced Imperial Elloe Kaifi, Korg, and Hiroim the Shamed forge unshakeable bonds of comradeship with the Hulk in the gladiatorial arenas of the Red King.

My way or the highway
Kate had immense respect for Hawkeye the hero, but had difficulty dealing with Clint Barton, the patronizing, macho jerk.

HAWKEYE (KATE BISHOP)

FIRST APPEARANCE *Young Avengers* #12 (August 2006) **BASE** Los Angeles, California; Brooklyn and Manhattan, New York City; Noh-Varr's Kree Ship **AFFILIATIONS** Hawkeye (Clint Barton), Young Avengers, Secret Avengers

Katherine Bishop is born into one of Manhattan's wealthiest families. Following her mother's death, Kate learns that much of their money is ill-gotten. After spying on her father, Kate is kidnapped by El Matador, one of his more unsavory associates. Rescued by the Avengers, Kate comes to idolize Hawkeye, whom she feels has achieved so much as a "mere" human.

Kate volunteers for various worthy causes but, after being attacked, studies martial arts, which she excels at. Later, her sister's wedding is disrupted by bandits and the Young Avengers respond. They are outmatched, until Kate takes charge and saves them using one of Patriot's throwing stars. Kate is then approached by Stature (Cassie Lang), who invites her to join the team.

Appropriating Mockingbird's mask and battle staves, Swordsman's blade, Black Widow's utility belt and Hawkeye's bow from the recently destroyed Avenger's Mansion, Kate Bishop is soon a key Young Avenger, leading them to victory against Kang the Conqueror.

When Iron Man and Captain America order the underage heroes to disband, Kate uses her family's money to take the team off the grid. Eventually, Captain America changes his mind and gives her Clint Barton's combat gear and codename: Hawkeye.

The original hero has been dead for some time, but when he is resurrected by the Scarlet Witch as the enigmatic Avenger Ronin, Clint Barton seeks out Kate and informs her that she can keep his arsenal of weaponry. Eventually, Clint and Kate decide to share the codename Hawkeye. Clint stays in New York City while Kate relocates to Los Angeles, where, as a private detective, she tackles Madame Masque's criminal empire. Later, on returning to New York, Kate works for S.H.I.E.L.D., but also continues freelance crime-fighting.

TARANTULA (MARIA VASQUEZ)

FIRST APPEARANCE *Heroes for Hire* #1 (October 2006) **BASE** Mobile **AFFILIATIONS** Heroes for Hire

Maria Vasquez's sister is one of the victims of the Stamford Incident, in which 600 civilians die during a clash between the New Warriors and the exploding villain Nitro. When her father is slaughtered by ninjas while visiting her grave, Maria channels her acrobatic skills and martial-arts training into vigilantism.

Maria becomes Tarantula, a ruthless and bloodthirsty hunter of metahumans. She joins Misty Knight's S.H.I.E.L.D.-sponsored Heroes for Hire team and hunts metahumans who refuse to comply with the Superhuman Registration Act.

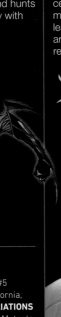

DAKEN

FIRST APPEARANCE *Wolverine Origins* #5 (October 2006) **BASE** Los Angeles, California, San Francisco, California, mobile **AFFILIATIONS** Horsemen of Death, Brotherhood of Evil Mutants, Dark Avengers, Wolverines

Akihiro is Wolverine's son, torn from his mother's belly after the immortal lupine mutant manipulator Romulus has Logan's wife Itsu killed. Raised in a Japanese home, the child is called Daken—"Bastard Dog"—by servants and neighbors.

Daken possesses his father's powers, plus the ability to beguile through pheromone release. He kills his foster-parents and undergoes intensive programming by Romulus, becoming a sociopath with no concept of morality.

Daken impersonates Wolverine in Norman Osborn's Dark Avengers, before attempting to become the world's greatest criminal. When Wolverine subsequently dies, Mister Sinister steals the body and Daken seeks closure by joining the Wolverines team (Mystique, Sabretooth, Lady Deathstrike, and X-23) in order to recover it.

THE ORDER

FIRST APPEARANCE *Civil War* #6 (February 2007) **BASE** Los Angeles, California **AFFILIATIONS** S.H.I.E.L.D., Fifty-State Initiative

Recruited from philanthropic champions and heroic celebrities, The Order is a California-based Super Hero group set up by Tony Stark. In the wake of the superhuman civil war, S.H.I.E.L.D. Director Stark wants the state super-team to be a media-friendly, shining paragon of his Fifty-State Initiative, operating under the government's Superhuman Registration Act.

The squad is patterned after the ancient Greek gods, utilizing Stark technology to augment their physicality and overcome any disabilities. However, the process takes an extreme physical toll on candidates and most members of the Order are only expected to serve one year.

After defeating the terrifying Infernal Man, half the team are fired for violating the morals clause in their contracts while celebrating their victory. Stark, his manager Pepper Potts, and team leader Henry Hellrung (Anthem) are forced to restart the recruitment and training process.

The second team starts strong, preventing an attack by Namor the Sub-Mariner, but are soon targeted by a coalition of villains including General Softly, the M.A.N. from S.H.A.D.O.W., Maul, and superpowered all-female street gang the Black Dahlias. Despite being picked off piecemeal, the heroes learn the cause of their woes is Stark's bitter rival Ezekiel Stane. Anthem is forced to kill one of his own team—Mulholland Black—to save Los Angeles when Stane causes her powers to malfunction and endanger the populace.

When Stane is defeated, the war-weary team accept Stark's offer of permanent powers to remain California's premier heroic team. The Order battles successfully against the Skrulls' Secret Invasion and the Serpent's fear-fueled attacks.

California dreamers
Anthem was determined that his team would prove themselves to be true heroes, not glory-hungry headline hunters.

In Order
The second team *(clockwise from top)*: Supernaut, Anthem, Mulholland Black, Veda, Calamity, and Aralune.

MICHAEL VAN PATRICK

FIRST APPEARANCE *Civil War: Battle Damage Report* #1 (May 2007) **BASE** Camp Hammond, Virginia
AFFILIATIONS The Initiative, Scarlet Spiders

Michael Van Patrick is the grandson of Dr. Abraham Erskine, who created Captain America's Super-Soldier serum. Raised according to the scientist's theories on diet and exercise, by his teen years Michael is an intellectual and sporting prodigy highly sought after by many colleges. When suspicions mount that Michael is superhuman, the scholarship offers and sponsorship deals dry up and the disappointed boy is recruited by former New Warrior Justice to Tony Stark's Fifty-State-Initiative program.

Although Michael actually has no metahuman powers, he is a genetically perfect human being and his physical skills and reflexes make him the equal of Captain America. These attributes qualify him to attend the Fort Hammond Boot Camp for novice Super Heroes. Codenamed MVP (Most Valuable Player), Michael settles in, but is killed when a training exercise goes wrong.

Covering up the tragedy, maverick chief researcher Baron von Blitzschlag creates a number of clones of Michael. Three of them—dubbed Michael, Van, and Patrick—are given specialized training and, equipped with hi-tech Iron Spider costumes, become Super Hero trio the Scarlet Spiders.

Another clone—gene-tailored to utilize alien super-weapon the Tactigon—discovers the truth behind their origins and becomes rogue agent KIA (Killed In Action). He goes on a killing spree to avenge MVP's death and the cover-up before falling in combat against his fellow clones, the Mighty Avengers, and New Warriors.

The Michael clone is killed by renegade Thor clone Ragnarok, and Van dies in action battling his "brother" KIA, leaving the final Scarlet Spider, Patrick, to carry on alone after publicly exposing the illegal cloning experiments at Camp Hammond.

DNAlienation
Combining MVP's DNA with Armory's combat programming and the alien Tactigon weapon-system, KIA was a murderous menace even capable of crushing the Mighty Avengers.

BARON VON BLITZSCHLAG

FIRST APPEARANCE *Avengers: The Initiative* #1 (April 2007) **BASE** Mobile **AFFILIATIONS** The Third Reich, Fifty-State Initiative

Former Nazi scientist Baron Wernher von Blitzschlag is invited by Hank Pym to join the Fifty-State Initiative after the superhuman civil war. Possessing electrical powers, Von Blitzschlag works at Camp Hammond training new heroes. When gifted athlete Michael Van Patrick (MVP) is killed, von Blitzschlag argues with Pym that they should exploit MVP's genetic material to pass on his abilities. He secretly clones MVP, creating several new Scarlet Spiders. One of the clones, known as KIA, remembers the death of MVP as though it was his own. He attacks and injures von Blitzschlag, leaving him in a wheelchair.

THE TWELVE

FIRST APPEARANCE *The Twelve* #0 (December 2007) **BASE** New York City
AFFILIATIONS U.S. Army

During World War II's Battle of Berlin, the Nazis capture 12 superhuman American soldiers and place them in suspended animation in a secret bunker, hoping to discover the secrets of their abilities. They are: Blue Blade (Roy Chambers), Black Widow (Claire Voyant), Captain Wonder, Dynamic Man (Prof. Goettler), the robot Electro, Fiery Mask (Jack Castle), Laughing Mask (Dennis Burton), Mastermind Excello (Earl Everett), Mister E (Victor Jay), Phantom Reporter (Richard Jones), Rockman (Daniel Rose), and mysterious vigilante Witness.

Construction crews accidentally find the bunker around 60 years later. The U.S. government brings them all home, but revives the soldiers in a compound made to resemble the year 1945, when they were originally frozen. It isn't long before the Twelve figure out what is going on.

Their recovery is still ongoing when Blue Blade is murdered by Electro, who is discovered to be under the control of Dynamic Man. Unknown to the team, Dynamic Man is actually an android himself. Dynamic Man then kills Fiery Mask, who passes his superhuman powers on to Phantom Reporter. With the help of Captain Wonder—whose face is terribly scarred in the process—Phantom Reporter destroys the android.

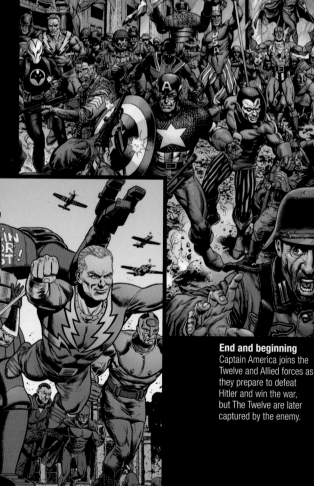

End and beginning
Captain America joins the Twelve and Allied forces as they prepare to defeat Hitler and win the war, but The Twelve are later captured by the enemy.

Secret mission
The Phantom Reporter assembles The Twelve for the first time. Their mission is to destroy the Nazis' secret weapons program.

SKAAR

FIRST APPEARANCE *World War Hulk* #5 (January 2008) **BASE** Mobile
AFFILIATIONS Hulk, Avengers, Dark Avengers

Skaar is the son of the Hulk and Caiera, one of the race of Shadow People on the planet Sakaar. Skaar is born from a cocoon left by his dead mother (who dies when the warp core on Hulk's shuttle explodes), emerging at the size of a ten-year-old boy. Much like his father, Skaar can transform into an enormous, green, muscle-bound warrior.

After he fails to save his world from destruction by Galactus, Skaar sets out to kill his father, whom he blames for all of these misfortunes. When he witnesses the inherent kindness of the Hulk, however, he is unable to kill him, and father and son reconcile.

Skaar joins Norman Osborn's Dark Avengers, ostensibly to battle the New Avengers. However he is acting as a double agent for Captain America. He later reluctantly teams with Wolverine, Bruce Banner, and Cloak in a plan to kill the lupine Super Villain Romulus and destroy his empire. Skaar is later depowered by Doc Green, a super-intelligent iteration of the Hulk, as part of his mission to cure gamma mutates.

COSMO

FIRST APPEARANCE *Nova* #8 (January 2008) **BASE** Knowhere
AFFILIATIONS Nova, Guardians of the Galaxy

Cosmo is a mutant dog and former test subject in the Soviet space program. He is launched into space in the 1960s, but drifts his way to a bizarre space station called Knowhere that is built inside the giant, decapitated head of a Celestial. There, Cosmo meets Nova (Richard Rider), who is surprised to find a speaking dog with psychic powers running a space station.

Before his death, Star-Lord commissions Cosmo to form a new Super Hero team of Annihilators, to be the heroic force the Guardians of the Galaxy should have been before they disbanded. The new team includes Beta Ray Bill, Gladiator (Kallark), Ikon, Quasar (Wendell Vaughn), Ronan the Accuser, and Silver Surfer.

EZEKIEL STANE

FIRST APPEARANCE *The Order* #8 (April 2008) **BASE** Mobile
AFFILIATIONS Mandarin, Tony Stark

Ezekiel "Zeke" Stane is the son of Obadiah Stane, a bitter business rival of Tony Stark. Obadiah drives Tony Stark to drink and then takes over Stark Industries. He builds an armored suit of his own and battles Stark as the Iron Monger, but loses, later committing suicide. Zeke Stane inherits his father's fortune and resolves to continue his father's vendetta against Iron Man.

First Stane attacks the California branch of the Fifty-State Initiative, known as the Order. Next, he goes after Stark himself. Stane reverse-engineers Stark's own technology and builds cyborg components, installing them in his own body in order to become a new Iron Monger.

Ezekiel Stane bombs the Starkdynamics Tower in Taipei, China. Pepper Potts is critically wounded when shrapnel lodges between her heart and spine. Stane is also burned in the process, but recovers and upgrades his cybernetic armor.

Stark defeats Stane and sends him to prison, but the villain known as Mandarin frees him and then reveals that he is the father of Stane's girlfriend, Sasha Hammer. Together, they ruin Stark's reputation by framing him for using his Iron Man armor while drunk. However, the Mandarin becomes increasingly frustrated with Stane when he is unable to produce Dreadnoughts (battle robots invented by Hydra) on schedule.

The Mandarin then uses his Mento-Intensifier ring to enslave Stane and force him to replicate Stark's Titanomechs (weapons of mass destruction). When Stane fails, the Mandarin severely beats him. Stane rebels, so the villain boosts the effect of the ring, causing agony and brain damage to Stane. Mandarin then manages to bring Tony Stark under his control, but only intermittently.

Stark heals Stane and the two work together against the power-mad Mandarin, bringing the Mandarin's disillusioned allies Blizzard, Living Laser, and Whirlwind onto their side. They stage a revolt, and while Stark takes out Mandarin's new Titanomechs with his micro-robot Swarm, Stane manages to kill the villain.

Head to head
Ezekiel Stane attacks Tony Stark using his own company's technology. Stark survives, thanks to being evenly matched with Stane. However, Stark's concerns that Stane will upgrade his armor prove well founded.

GUARDIANS OF THE GALAXY

FIRST APPEARANCE *Annihilation: Conquest #6* (June 2008) **BASE** Knowhere **AFFILIATIONS** Avengers, Starjammers, Knowhere Corps

After the universe is hit in quick succession by two catastrophes—the Phalanx Invasion and the Annihilation Wave—some of the heroes fighting to save existence decide to form a team to deal with external threats. Chief among them is Peter Quill—codenamed Star-Lord—who blames himself for the destruction wrought upon the Kree homeworld by the alien Phalanx. He teams up with the humanoid Gamora, Drax the Destroyer, Rocket Raccoon, the tree-like being Groot, cosmic hero Quasar, and the genetically perfect Warlock, with martial arts expert and empath Mantis providing support.

This ragtag band adopts the name Guardians of the Galaxy after coming across one of the original Guardians from another dimension encased in ice. Right from the start, it is hard keeping this argumentative group together, especially when the members discover that Quill has used Mantis' telepathic powers to induce them to join up. Despite their anger, the Guardians unite to rescue Star-Lord from the Negative Zone when he is exiled there by the Kree-born Ronan the Accuser after an argument.

Two of the Guardians have the Mad Titan, Thanos, in their sights—Gamora is his estranged, adoptive daughter, while Drax's whole reason for being is to kill the death-obsessed Titan. Their chance comes when the Guardians team up with the Avengers to stop Thanos using a Cosmic Cube—which bestows great power upon the wielder. Although both teams are sent into the Cancerverse by Thanos, they manage to find a weapon capable of destroying the Cube, and Thanos is given over to the Elders of the Universe for punishment.

The Guardians help another Earth team—the X-Men—when the time-displaced Jean Grey is tried for the crimes of her older self. Peter Quill and mutant Kitty Pryde then start a long-distance romantic relationship. Tony Stark later sends Flash Thompson, a.k.a. Agent Venom, to join the Guardians as a representative of the Avengers.

The team is then plagued by Quill's estranged father J'Son, ruler of the planet Spartax. He conspires to split up the Guardians and take them out of action, but is foiled when Captain Marvel rescues Star-Lord. The subsequent scandal forces J'Son out of office—and his son Quill is elected to replace him as ruler. At first, Quill is not interested in power, but he eventually takes his place as President of Spartax. Rocket Raccoon takes over as the Guardians' leader and the mantle of Star-Lord is adopted by Quill's fiancée, Kitty Pryde, who has left Earth in order to be with him.

It transpires that the responsibility of power does not suit Quill, and he steps down—at almost exactly the same time as his subjects oust him for his part in the most destructive event ever to have afflicted their planet. Hala, a Kree calling herself the last living Accuser, attempts to destroy Spartax, believing that Quill is responsible for the destruction of the Kree homeworld. Consequently, Quill returns to the Guardians. The team has acquired a new member from Earth—Ben Grimm, better known as the Thing. The Guardians return to the Thing's home planet when Captain Marvel asks for their help in the second superhuman civil war against Iron Man. When the Guardians' ship is destroyed in the ensuing battle, they are stranded on Earth. The situation becomes more complicated when Gamora discovers that Thanos is there, too…

Guardian freshman
When it comes to dealing with brutal characters such as Yotat the Destroyer, new members like Earth tough guy the Thing are particularly welcome on the Guardians of the Galaxy's roster.

> ## "We help people who can't help themselves."
> **STAR-LORD**

Rapid transit
The Guardians of the Galaxy use "passport bracelets" powered by the space station Knowhere to get them quickly to anywhere in the universe they are needed *(clockwise from left)*: Drax the Destroyer, Star-Lord, Groot, Gamora, and Rocket Raccoon.

timeline

Getting proactive Blaming himself for the recent Phalanx invasion, Star-Lord Peter Quill decides to start a super-team to deal with threats to the galaxy. *Annihilation: Conquest #6* (June 2008)

Split Finding out that Quill used Mantis to mentally push them into joining the team, the other Guardians quit in disgust. *Guardians of the Galaxy #6* (Dec. 2008)

▼ **Clash of empires** The Guardians reunite to defuse an impending war between the Shi'ar and the Kree. *Guardians of the Galaxy #13* (June 2009)

Iron Guardian Looking for new challenges, Tony Stark accepts Star-Lord's offer of a place on the Guardians team. *Avengers Assemble #8* (Dec. 2012)

▶ **Agent Venom** Stark decides that the Guardians should have a permanent representative of the Avengers on their roster, and appoints Flash Thompson, a.k.a. Agent Venom, to the role. *Free Comic Book Day: Guardians of the Galaxy* (July 2014)

Mr. President Peter Quill discovers that he has been elected President of the Spartax Empire in absentia. *Guardians of the Galaxy #23* (Mar. 2015)

New blood After Quill leaves, Kitty Pryde takes over the mantle of Star-Lord, Rocket Raccoon becomes leader, and the Guardians are joined by Ben Grimm, a.k.a. the Thing. *Guardians of the Galaxy #1* (Dec. 2015)

BLUE MARVEL

FIRST APPEARANCE *Adam: Legend of the Blue Marvel* #1 (January 2009)
BASE Kadesh; Gem Theater, New York City **AFFILIATIONS** Mighty Avengers, Ultimates

Adam Brashear is a war hero, a former college football star, and a scientific genius. During the early 1960s, he tries to use anti-matter to harness clean energy, but his reactor explodes and he is exposed to huge levels of radiation. Adam becomes a human antimatter reactor with a dazzling array of extraordinary abilities, making him one of Earth's most powerful superhumans.

For a year or so, Adam fights the good fight as the masked hero Blue Marvel, but after his mask is torn during a particularly savage battle, it is revealed to the world that Blue Marvel is African-American. With the fight for racial equality in the U.S. at a delicate stage, President Kennedy reluctantly agrees that Blue Marvel should be stood down in case his immense power scares people. The government decide to fake his death.

Decades later, Tony Stark uncovers the secret of Blue Marvel and seeks out Adam, needing his help to battle the hugely powerful Anti-Man, Brashear's former best friend who was given powers in the same reactor explosion. Despite his resentment at being shelved all those years ago, Adam returns as Blue Marvel and saves the Earth once more. He later joins Luke Cage's Mighty Avengers, but spends a good deal of his time working in Kadesh, the underwater base he built back in the 1960s. For Adam has a secret—his eldest son Kevin has been sucked into the Neutral Zone, and he has spent years trying to work out a way to bring him back. Finally, with the help of his other son Max, Adam manages to locate Kevin, but he has become so much a part of the Neutral Zone that he cannot return for more than a few seconds.

Family reunion
Kevin Brashear emerges somewhat altered by a decade in the Neutral Zone, as his father Adam, a.k.a. Blue Marvel, and Photon look on.

VICTORIA HAND

FIRST APPEARANCE *Invincible Iron Man* #8 (February 2009)
BASE Helicarriers, Avengers Tower, Avengers Mansion **AFFILIATIONS** S.H.I.E.L.D., H.A.M.M.E.R., Dark Avengers, New Avengers

As a S.H.I.E.L.D. agent, Victoria Hand is unhappy with the way Nick Fury, and later Tony Stark, handle things. A vocal opponent of their old regimes, she is given an immediate promotion to Deputy Director when Norman Osborn is handed control and creates his H.A.M.M.E.R. organization. Hand is apparently Osborn's loyal assistant and is aware of all his murky activities in his new-found position of power. After Osborn's fall, Hand claims that she has only been trying to serve her country. Taking her at her word, Steve Rogers appoints her to liaise with the New Avengers. Victoria Hand is killed after being possessed by the malevolent ghost of Doctor Voodoo (Daniel Drumm). Despite appearing to be, at various stages in her career, a double or even triple agent, she is awarded a statue at Avengers Mansion.

PET AVENGERS

FIRST APPEARANCE *Lockjaw and the Pet Avengers* #1 (July 2009) **BASE** Pet Avengers Mansion **AFFILIATIONS** Avengers, Guardians of the Galaxy

On the Moon orbiting Earth-97161, Lockjaw, the teleporting dog belonging to the Inhumans, overhears Reed Richards telling his masters about how he plans to locate the Infinity Gems and give them to someone trustworthy in order to stop them falling into the wrong hands. Lockjaw tries to tell Richards that he knows where the Mind Gem is, but the humans think that he is just being boisterous and tell him to calm down.

Lockjaw decides to retrieve the Gems himself and travels to Earth to gather a team to help him. Using the telepathy granted him by the Mind Gem, Lockjaw recruits Throg (a frog with powers like Thor's), Lockheed (Kitty Pryde's dragon), Hairball (a cat with telekinetic powers belonging to the hero Speedball), Redwing (Falcon's avian sidekick), and Ms. Lion (May Parker's ordinary—male—dog). Searching for the next Gem in the Savage Land, the animals are joined by some useful muscle: Zabu, the sabertooth tiger.

After fighting dinosaurs and being swallowed by the Atlantean sea beast Giganto, the animals successfully locate all but one of the Infinity Gems. They discover the final stone in the collar of White House dog Bo, but before they can get it, Thanos arrives, confident of gaining possession of the Infinity Gems from a mere bunch of animals. However, he has not reckoned on Lockjaw, whose tenacity enables him to wield the power of the Gems to fight Thanos and send him to a distant dimension.

Lockjaw presents the Gems to Reed Richards, but not before he has used them to telepathically link all the animals in case the universe needs them again—as the Pet Avengers. The team later reunites to fight monsters from the Dream Realm and the alien dragon Fin Fang Foom.

Home for heroes
Grateful for their help quelling the threat of Fin Fang Foom, the Avengers build the Pet Avengers their own mansion.

BEETLE (JANICE LINCOLN)

FIRST APPEARANCE *Captain America* #607 (August 2010) **BASE** New York City, Miami **AFFILIATIONS** Ant-Man Security Solutions, Sinister Six

Janice Lincoln is the daughter of albino Super Villain gangster and gang boss Tombstone. With the help of the evil Baron Zemo and the technological mastermind named the Fixer, Janice becomes the new Beetle. Equipped with a mechanized suit of armor, she sets out to kill the new Captain America (Bucky Barnes). Her attempt proves unsuccessful and she is imprisoned in high-security holding facility The Raft. Janice later breaks free, and joins a new incarnation of the Sinister Six brought together by the villain Boomerang. Usurping Boomerang, she takes over leadership of the team, only to be double-crossed by Boomerang, who seizes control once again. The Sinister Six disbands and Janice then turns over a new leaf, taking a job testing security systems. She eventually works for Ant-Man Security Solutions.

The predecessor
Mechanic Abner Jenkins is the first Beetle, bugging Super Heroes such as the Fantastic Four and the Avengers.

SERPENT

FIRST APPEARANCE *Fear Itself* #1 (June 2011) **BASE** Asgard **AFFILIATIONS** Asgardians, the Worthy, Draumar

Ruthless proto-god Cul Borson, the Serpent, conquers the Nine Realms of Asgard and rules by terror. He is eventually overthrown by his younger brothers, Odin, Villi, and Ve. Odin destroys Cul's monstrous Draumar legions before sealing his evil brother below Earth's ocean. Because Cul's elite agents the Worthy escape the purge, they and his daughter Skadi are able to liberate the Serpent eons later. The reawakened tyrant is eventually slain by Thor, who seemingly dies. Cul is later revived, and tasked by Odin with retrieving the magical hammer Mjolnir from the new Thor (Jane Foster).

Sucker punch
Just for fun, Loki deliberately annoys Ms. America to get the Young Avengers to reform.

MS. AMERICA

FIRST APPEARANCE *Vengeance* #1 (September 2011) **BASE** Utopian Parallel, New York City **AFFILIATIONS** Teen Brigade, Young Avengers, A-Force, Ultimates

America Chavez is a tough-talking, openly gay Super Hero raised by several mothers in the Utopian Parallel universe, which was created by the future alter ego of Wiccan known as Demiurge. In the Utopian Parallel she gains her super-strength, durability, and abilities of interdimensional travel from absorbing magical powers. Her mothers give their lives to stabilize their reality and prevent its destruction. Ms. America, angry about their sacrifice and with a genuine desire to do the right thing, travels across the dimensions saving those in need.

Ms. America subsequently serves as co-leader of the Teen Brigade, along with tattooed hero Ultimate Nullifier. She rescues universe-balancing cosmic entity the In-Betweener, and faces the Young Masters of Evil and Doctor Doom, who are seeking to use the In-Betweener's powers to disrupt the balance of chaos and order in the universe.

Citing creative differences with the Teen Brigade, Ms. America makes her way to Prime Earth, where she joins the Young Avengers, hoping to protect the teenage Wiccan from the interdimensional parasite Mother, who has been accidentally pulled into their dimension by one of Asgardian trickster god Loki's spells. Ms. America, Wiccan, Hulkling, Hawkeye (Kate Bishop), Noh-Varr, and young Loki have to take down parasitic doppelgangers of their own parents and nearly every other adult in the Marvel Universe.

During the events of Secret Wars, when all worlds in the universe are merged together to make Battleworld, Ms. America joins the all-female A-Force. There she throws a megolodon across one of Doctor Doom's borders and is sentenced to work for the Shield—a vast wall keeping more dangerous lands full of zombies, Ultrons, and terrible monsters from invading the safer territories. When Super Heroes finally return to the restored Marvel Universe, Ms. America joins the Ultimates with Monica Rambeau, Captain Marvel, Blue Marvel, and Black Panther. She later joins her teammate Captain Marvel on her side during the second superhuman civil war.

MILES MORALES

FIRST APPEARANCE *Ultimate Comics Fallout #4* (October 2011) **BASE** Brooklyn, New York City (Marvel Universe); New York City (Earth-1610) **AFFILIATIONS** Spider-Army, Avengers, Champions

On Earth-1610, the Ultimate Universe, Norman Osborn has been exposed as the Green Goblin and imprisoned. Osborn Industries is abandoned and ripe for burglary. A spider, enhanced with Osborn's Goblin Formula, crawls out of burglar Aaron Davis' bag and bites his young nephew, Miles Morales. Miles gains spider-powers and, when he discovers that Spider-Man has been shot and killed, takes on the role himself. Miles proves himself to S.H.I.E.L.D. and Spider-Woman and battles villains such as Scorpion and Ringer. He also visits the alternate world of the Marvel Universe. There he encounters this reality's Spider-Man, Peter Parker, and the two heroes briefly team up.

Morales plays his part in the Spider-Army's defeat of Morlun who, with his Inheritors, seeks to devour the many Spider-Totems of the Multiverse. When the Multiverse is destroyed, following the events of Secret Wars, Miles finds himself back in Peter Parker's world. Parker is now combining his heroic role of Spider-Man with being CEO of global high-tech company Parker Industries, and he allows Miles to continue his fledgling Spider-Man career. Miles joins a new incarnation of the Avengers, featuring Iron Man, Thor (Jane Foster), Ms. Marvel (Kamala Khan)—whom Miles has a crush on—Captain America (Sam Wilson), Nova (Sam Alexander), and Vision. Miles, Kamala, and Sam, unhappy with the older Avengers' hidebound attitudes, soon leave to form their own youthful team, the Champions, along with Hulk (Amadeus Cho) and Viv, the Vision's daughter.

Ultimate Spidey
Miles gets a nasty shock when he's bitten by a spider carrying the Goblin Formula. However, he doesn't turn into a goblin…

WHITE TIGER (AVA AYALA)

FIRST APPEARANCE *Avengers Academy #20* (December 2011) **BASE** New York City **AFFILIATIONS** Avengers Academy, Mighty Avengers, New Avengers

Ava Ayala is the fifth in the line of heroes known as the White Tiger. She is the youngest sister of the first White Tiger, Hector Ayala; both were orphaned by psychotic Vietnam veteran Gideon Mace. Ava inherits ancient jade Amulets of Power from her niece, White Tiger Angela del Toro, when Angela is murdered, resurrected, and controlled by ninja cult the Hand. These amulets give Ava mystical, tiger-like, martial-arts abilities.

Ava becomes a student at the Avengers Academy, learning from Tigra and other heroes, and also combating school invasions and villains. After her graduation, Ava joins the Heroes for Hire with Luke Cage and Power Man (Victor Alvarez), with whom she starts a relationship. They assemble a new team of Mighty Avengers and Ava hones her powers, manifesting an actual tiger with her chi. When she gets the chance to confront Gideon Mace, the man who killed her parents, she is so possessed by the tiger god's powers that she nearly kills him; she is stopped by her fellow Avengers. For failing to kill Mace, she is challenged by the tiger god, but she eventually takes full control of his powers.

Ava and Victor later join the New Avengers, though their relationship is no longer romantic. There she is confronted by her niece, Hand operative Angela del Toro, and a gang of villains dubbed the New Revengers. Angela is determined to reclaim the power of the White Tiger. However, when the Amulets of Power are destroyed in the ensuing fight, Angela is freed from the Hand's control and both women fight off the New Revengers. Eventually, both Ava and Angela turn their backs on life as the White Tiger.

An eye for an eye
White Tiger Ava Ayala gains the power of the tiger god and decides to pursue a murderous vendetta against Gideon Mace, the man who killed her parents. Her teammates in the Mighty Avengers must try to save Ava from herself.

PHILLIP COULSON

FIRST APPEARANCE *Battle Scars #1* (January 2012) **BASE** New York City **AFFILIATIONS** U.S. Army Rangers, S.H.I.E.L.D., Secret Avengers

Super Hero fan Phillip "Cheese" Coulson follows in his idols' footsteps to become one of elite government security agency S.H.I.E.L.D.'s top agents.

Coulson first battles Super Villains as a member of the U.S. Army Rangers, alongside his friend Marcus Johnson. When Marcus discovers that he is actually Nick Fury Jr., the son of S.H.I.E.L.D. Director Nick Fury, Coulson helps Marcus take down the evil organization Leviathan, which seeks to steal Marcus' Infinity-Formula-enriched blood. Both men soon become S.H.I.E.L.D. agents, and Coulson starts living his dream of fighting alongside Super Heroes against the likes of the demonic Dormammu and the terrorist organization Hydra—and, sometimes, even other Super Heroes as well.

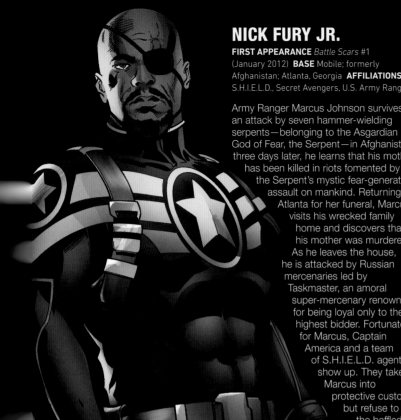

NICK FURY JR.

FIRST APPEARANCE *Battle Scars* #1 (January 2012) **BASE** Mobile; formerly Afghanistan; Atlanta, Georgia **AFFILIATIONS** S.H.I.E.L.D., Secret Avengers, U.S. Army Rangers

Army Ranger Marcus Johnson survives an attack by seven hammer-wielding serpents—belonging to the Asgardian God of Fear, the Serpent—in Afghanistan; three days later, he learns that his mother has been killed in riots fomented by the Serpent's mystic fear-generating assault on mankind. Returning to Atlanta for her funeral, Marcus visits his wrecked family home and discovers that his mother was murdered. As he leaves the house, he is attacked by Russian mercenaries led by Taskmaster, an amoral super-mercenary renowned for being loyal only to the highest bidder. Fortunately for Marcus, Captain America and a team of S.H.I.E.L.D. agents show up. They take Marcus into protective custody, but refuse to tell the baffled

soldier what is going on. Incensed by this wall of silence, Marcus breaks out and —with the aid of trusted Ranger buddy Phil "Cheese" Coulson—uncovers a plot by the espionage organization Leviathan to capture him in order to steal his blood. Further investigation and lethal battles at last reveal that his father was one of the greatest heroes in history, and that Marcus Johnson is actually Nicholas Joseph Fury, Jr. Leviathan has targeted him because his blood contains the Infinity Formula, which keeps the elder Fury in peak physical condition for decades beyond his normal lifespan.

Captured and tortured, Marcus sustains an injury to his left eye that even

Second-generation surveillance
Soldier Marcus Johnson adapts quickly to his new role: watching out for the entire world as the new Nick Fury.

his augmented physicality cannot heal. After a climactic battle, he finally meets his father and joins S.H.I.E.L.D., as does his comrade-in-arms, Phil Coulson. Both men quickly rise to command positions, with Fury Jr. becoming increasingly involved with the metahuman side of the agency. He forms a covert Secret Avengers unit consisting of Hawkeye and the Black Widow—battling al-Quaeda terrorists and tackling the Masters of Evil in the rogue state of Bagalia.

EX NIHILO

FIRST APPEARANCE *Avengers* #1 (February 2013) **BASE** Savage Land; Avengers Tower, Manhattan, New York City; The Garden, Mars **AFFILIATIONS** Avengers, Gardeners, New Avengers, A.I.M., Builders

A representative of the alien Builders, Ex Nihilo is a purpose-grown being, part of myriad teams of "Gardeners" dispatched throughout the universe to modify planets and perfect the evolutionary development of life.

When his team reaches Mars and is challenged by the Avengers, Ex Nihilo bombards Earth with devastating, mutational Origin Bombs, before having a change of heart and joining Earth's Mightiest Heroes. He and his two fellow Gardeners, Abyss and Aleph, join a coalition of alien races to stop the Builders when they attempt to destroy Earth. Ex Nihilo later sacrifices himself to save the Avengers from the Beyonders.

SUPERIOR SPIDER-MAN

FIRST APPEARANCE *Amazing Spider-Man* #697 (January 2013) **BASE** New York City **AFFILIATIONS** Avengers, Superior Six

Dying Doctor Octopus (Otto Octavius) takes over Spider-Man's body, but Peter Parker's fading personality reprograms the villain's mind with his own sense of responsibility. Hampered by compassion, Doctor Octopus carries out Parker's mission, but his own arrogance compels him to try to outdo his foe and so prove beyond question that he is a truly Superior Spider-Man.

As a civilian, Octavius drives his new body to earn a doctorate, and as a Super Hero he modifies the wall-crawler's weaponry and techniques to better serve the city, hiring mercenaries to supplement his patrols. When Octavius is finally defeated by the Goblin King (Norman Osborn), he sacrifices his mind to allow Parker to return and take back the role of Spider-Man.

HYPERION (MARCUS MILTON)

FIRST APPEARANCE *Avengers* #1 (February 2013) **BASE** Oracle Inc.; formerly Savage Land; Avengers Tower, Manhattan, New York City; Squadron City **AFFILIATIONS** Squadron Supreme (Marvel Universe); A.I.M., Children of the Sun, Avengers, Squadron Supreme (Earth-13034), Sunspot's Avengers

Infant Eternal Marcus Milton is sent into space to escape the destruction of his world. He lands on Earth-13034 and upon maturity, becomes Hyperion—the planet's champion and member of Super Hero team Squadron Supreme. When that Earth collides with another universe, Marcus is trapped in a void. Saved by A.I.M. scientists the Marvel Universe, he becomes their guinea pig. Liberated by the Avengers, Marcus joins them, battling the world-transforming Gardeners Ex Nihilo, Abyss, and Aleph. When their Origin Bombs create "Children of the Sun"—new, hyperintelligent life forms— Hyperion becomes their mentor.

After Steve Rogers (formerly Captain America) uses the team to hunt members of the Illuminati, Marcus resigns. He joins a renegade Avengers team led by Sunspot to investigate escalating incursions by alternate Earths from colliding universes. These "Multiversal

Avengers" travel between realities and discover that creation is coming to an end. They perish battling the Beyonders responsible for the destruction, but Hyperion and others are reborn into a reconstructed universe.

Marcus unites with survivors of previous realities in a hard-line Squadron Supreme: determined to preserve the last Earth, executing menaces like Namor the Sub-Mariner, and destroying potential threats such as Atlantis. However, when treachery compromises the team, Hyperion quits, to work alone.

My way
Having already outlived two homeworlds, Hyperion will not let heroic friends or villainous foes stop him from doing what he considers right or necessary.

NOVA (SAM ALEXANDER)

FIRST APPEARANCE *Nova* #1 (April 2013)
BASE Carefree, Arizona; Stark Industries Airfield,
New Jersey **AFFILIATIONS** Champions;
formerly Avengers, Supernovas (Nova Corps),
New Warriors (reserve)

Schoolboy Sam Alexander discovers that his missing father, Jesse, a school janitor, was once a cosmic-powered Super Hero. This transformation occurred when Jesse was accosted by aliens Gamora and Rocket Raccoon. Jesse then joined the intergalactic Nova Corps.

When Sam dons his father's Black Helmet he suddenly gains a range of incredible powers: super-strength, speed, and flight, virtual invulnerability, energy-blasts; trans-galactic teleportation, and all the intelligence-gathering data resources of an intergalactic peace-keeping agency. Embarking upon a life of adventure, Sam resolves to learn why Jesse disappeared and how the Nova Corps died.

He survives "on-the-job" training against the Phoenix Force, Chitauri, Thanos, and others to become a New Warrior and Avenger before joining the Champions.

STAR BRAND

FIRST APPEARANCE *Avengers* #7 (May 2013) **BASE** Formerly
Savage Land; Avengers Tower, Manhattan, New York City
AFFILIATIONS Nightmask, New Avengers, A.I.M. (Advanced Idea
Mechanics), Avengers

The metaphysical Superflow connects all living beings. When a world of sentient creatures evolves to a point where they can ascend to a greater, universal scale, ancient celestial mechanisms come into operation. These protocols spontaneously generate monitoring agents or "Shepherds" from the populace to supervise a "White Event," which triggers this planetary ascension. However, as a result of spiralling Multiversal degradation, when this moment approaches for Earth, the Superflow begins to break down and the process malfunctions.

Young student Kevin Connor is selected by the mechanisms of the White Event to become one of its agents—a planetary protector with infinite levels of power. However, when the Star Brand attaches to his right hand, the shattering blast of energy obliterates the college Kevin attends and kills everyone there but him. In protective custody, the horrified, guilt-ridden Kevin is befriended by the only other "Shepherd" to survive. Nightmask (Adam Blackveil) explains the Star Brand's true purpose and how the incipient end of the Multiverse has skewed their destinies and roles in the world.

When the alien Builders begin their war of eradication, Nightmask and Star Brand (the codename Kevin adopts) are both recruited into the Avengers and play crucial parts in saving humanity. After the Builders and the Titan Thanos are defeated, Nightmask and Star Brand set off to investigate extradimensional incursions, and go on to join Sunspot's "Multiversal Avengers."

Their missions across many colliding alternate universes subsequently result in their deaths. However, Kevin and most of the other Avengers are reborn into the new universe constructed after the end of reality. Star Brand, along with Nightmask (Keith Remsen), then rejects Avengers membership; both attend college and operate as solo heroes.

ANGELA

FIRST APPEARANCE *Age of Ultron* #10 (August 2013) **BASE** Hel, Asgard, Heven **AFFILIATIONS** Guardians of the Galaxy

Aldrif Odinsdottir is the firstborn child of Asgardian All-Father Odin and queen Freyja. During war with the Realm of Heven, the child is kidnapped by the Queen of Angels to coerce Odin's surrender. When he refuses, the Queen kills Aldrif, and in retaliation Odin curses Heven, severing its connection to the rest of the universe and the world tree, Yggdrasil, that connects the Realms.

It turns out that the baby is not dead. Raised by the Angel-Queen's handmaiden Loriel—who names the infant Angela— the girl grows into a mighty warrior and hunter, fueled in great part by the cruel teasing she endures for being born without wings. Despite this disadvantage, she becomes a powerful member of Angel society, but suffers grief as first Loriel, and later her beloved companion Sera, are taken from her.

During the time disruptions associated with the Age of Ultron, the foundations of the universe crack and the Nine Realms are thrust back into the Nine Realms. After allying with the Guardians of the Galaxy, Angela finds her way to Asgard when Thor and Loki accidentally reopen the portal to Heven. This leads to renewed war between the Asgardian gods and Heven, until Odin recognizes his lost daughter and ends hostilities. However, Angela cannot reconcile herself to living among those she has been trained to hate, and becomes a cosmic wanderer.

Angela is tricked by the Dark Elf Malekith the Accursed—disguised as long-lost Sera—into betraying her Asgardian kin and is exiled. Malekith discloses that the real Sera is in Hel, and Angela sets out to free her beloved. She defeats the current ruler and becomes the underworld's new Queen. After freeing Sera, Angela abdicates in favor of Balder the Brave and returns to adventuring in the physical world with her love, Sera, beside her.

Stellar savior
Starbrand and Nightmask (Adam Blackveil) prepare to battle Nitro, Graviton, and Blizzard, who have been possessed by cosmic entities to help bring about the death of the universe.

Tainted love
Kamala flees the rebellious Inhumans Lineage and Kaboom, after being lured into a trap by a boy she had a crush on.

MS. MARVEL (KAMALA KHAN)

FIRST APPEARANCE *Captain Marvel* #14 (September 2013) **BASE** Jersey City
AFFILIATIONS Avengers, Champions

Describing herself as a shape-changing, mask-wearing, 16-year-old Muslim girl from Jersey City, Kamala Khan takes on the identity of Ms. Marvel after her hero Carol Danvers becomes Captain Marvel. Kamala's powers appear when she is surrounded by Terrigen Mists released by the Inhumans—she discovers she can now stretch, grow, and shrink, or assume any other shape she chooses. Having longed to be Captain Marvel, she realizes that she needs to forge her own identity and be a hero while still being Kamala. She duly creates a costume based on her burkini, with the trademark Ms. Marvel lightning flash on the front.

When the Inhuman Medusa discovers that Kamala has been empowered, she sends the teleporting dog Lockjaw to be her companion and guide. At first, Ms. Marvel struggles with her double life; her parents are loving, but protective and strict, and are far from happy when their only daughter starts sneaking out at all hours. The formidable Sheikh Abdullah at Kamala's local mosque is surprisingly supportive of her newfound desire to help people, although he does not know the whole truth. As it turns out, neither does Kamala. She later discovers that she has Inhuman blood, which is why the Terrigen Mist affected her.

Ms. Marvel fulfils a lifelong dream when she joins the Avengers—and gets to shout "Avengers Assemble!" Reality bites as the team is split asunder when civil war breaks out between superhumans. Ms. Marvel quits the team, disillusioned with the way the "grown-up" Avengers leave carnage in their wake. She starts a new, younger team with former fellow Avengers Spider-Man (Miles Morales), Nova (Sam Alexander), Hulk (Amadeus Cho,) and Viv Vision. They call themselves the Champions and pledge to restore the public's trust in Super Heroes.

SUN GIRL

FIRST APPEARANCE
Superior Spider-Man Team-Up #1 (September 2013)
BASE New York City
AFFILIATIONS New Warriors

Selah Burke is the daughter of the villain Lightmaster—but she has chosen the life of a hero as Sun Girl. Her costume, modified and upgraded by the Superior Spider-Man (Otto Octavius), enables her to fire intense blasts of light and gives her the power of flight. She is disappointed by Spider-Man's dismissive attitude when she first meets him, unaware that Otto Octavius's consciousness is occupying Spidey's body; nevertheless, Sun Girl helps him defeat the Wrecking Crew.

Sun Girl then joins the young Super Hero team the New Warriors, helping to thwart the High Evolutionary's plan to exterminate all people with powers with a gene bomb machine. When he activates the machine, Sun Girl is the only member of the team unaffected, as she is not a mutant, Inhuman, or super-powered individual. She is able to blast the machine, reviving her teammates, and the New Warriors see off the High Evolutionary together.

THE BLACK ORDER

FIRST APPEARANCE *New Avengers* #8 (September 2013) **BASE** Sanctuary II

The Black Order is assembled by Thanos to search the universe for worlds for him to conquer. Its original members, all ruthless aliens, are Corvus Glaive, Supergiant, Ebony Maw, Black Dwarf, and Proxima Midnight.

Seizing an opportunity when the Avengers are on a space mission, the Black Order comes to Earth and targets the Illuminati, former holders of the Infinity Gems. The Black Order's aim seems to be to capture a gem, but the Illuminati's Black Bolt reveals that Thanos has a secret son living among his Inhuman people, and that the Mad Titan's true objective is to kill his own child, Thane. Ebony Maw captures Thane for his master. Thanos arrives, and Supergiant discovers and unlocks an antimatter bomb with the potential to destroy Earth. However, the Black Order falls into disarray when the Avengers return to Earth. Black Dwarf, Supergiant, and Corvus Glaive are killed, while Proxima Midnight is encased in a "living death" alongside Thanos. The capture of Thanos is enabled by Ebony Maw, who releases Thane so that he can use his powers against his murderous father.

However, Corvus Glaive cannot truly die while his atom-splitting weapon remains intact. After the reconstruction of the Multiverse following the Secret Wars event, he revives and forms a new Black Order. This new band takes over a space sector known as the Black Quadrant; Glaive, their ruler, rewards those who show him loyalty. Furious that his power has been usurped, Thanos seizes the Black Quadrant and forces Corvus Glaive to kill himself.

Worst of the worst
Thanos at the head of his Black Order, a team that comprises some of the most evil beings in existence.

MONICA CHANG

FIRST APPEARANCE *Avengers A.I.* #1
(September 2013) **BASE** S.H.I.E.L.D. Helicarrier
AFFILIATIONS S.H.I.E.L.D., Avengers A.I.

S.H.I.E.L.D. agent Monica Chang is
appointed head of the Artificial Intelligence
Division to deal with the threat posed by
an A.I. created by Dr. Hank Pym to take
down the evil robot Ultron. Although it
succeeds in its first mission, the A.I.
rapidly evolves and looks to be impossible
to control. Chang is a tough commander
in the field, but she is also keen to get the
advanced technology S.H.I.E.L.D. is
saving the world from back in her lab so
she can analyze it. In the fight against
Pym's rogue A.I., Chang comes to see
artificial beings as having as much right to
life as human beings, and risks her career
by preventing S.H.I.E.L.D. from destroying
the rogue A.I.

SPIDER-WOMAN (GWEN STACY a.k.a. SPIDER-GWEN)

FIRST APPEARANCE *Edge of Spider-Verse* #2
(November 2014) **BASE** New York City, Earth-65
AFFILIATIONS Spider-Army, Web-Warriors

In the Earth-65 reality, Midtown High
student Gwen Stacy loves music, and
plays drums in a band called the
Mary Janes with MJ, Betty Brant, and
Glory Grant. Her life changes when she
is bitten by a radioactive spider and
gains arachnid-like powers. Taking the
name Spider-Woman, she takes her first
steps in a crime-fighting career. Tragedy
strikes when her shy classmate Peter
Parker, who idolizes Spider-Woman,
tries to induce a transformation of his
own—into a Lizard-like being. The
chemicals have a terrible effect; he dies
while transforming back into human
shape after Gwen stops him attacking
the Midtown school dance. Spider-
Woman is unfairly blamed for his death
and hunted by the law, including her own
father, police captain George Stacy.
However, when George Stacy corners
Spider-Woman, she reveals herself to be
his daughter, Gwen, and the shocked
George lets her go free.

Spider-Woman then teams up with the
Spider-Army to defeat Morlun and the
Inheritors, who are roaming the Multiverse
devouring spider-beings. Returning to her
own reality, she quits the Mary Janes to
focus on being the best Spider-Woman
she can be, defending her father from the
villainous Vulture. However, many people
still believe her to be a dangerous vigilante,
not least the N.Y.P.D., who sets up a
Spider-Woman task force, led by tough-
as-nails cop Frank Castle, to take her
down. Needing to maintain some vestiges
of her former life, Gwen rejoins the Mary
Janes, who are starting to get some
recognition for their music. But enemies
are never far away, including slick, corrupt
lawyer Matt Murdock, whose incarcerated
gangster client the Kingpin seems to be
manipulating events from behind bars…

Rocking out
Gwen Stacy soon discovers that being a member
of pop group the Mary Janes is not compatible
with life as a Super Hero crime fighter.

SILK

FIRST APPEARANCE *Amazing Spider-Man* #1 (April 2014)
BASE New York City **AFFILIATIONS** Spider-Army, S.H.I.E.L.D.

When a radioactive spider bites Peter Parker to give him his spider
powers, it scuttles away to die… but before it expires, the bug also
bites someone else, a young girl named Cindy Moon. When she
can't control her spider abilities, her frightened parents allow Ezekiel
Sims, a businessman with spider powers of his own and an interest
in other spider-powered beings, to train Cindy. Sims hears about
Morlun and the Inheritors' plot to destroy all the Spider-Totems in
the Multiverse and locks Cindy in an ultra-secure room for her own
safety, providing her with plenty of food and footage of old
Spider-Man fights to watch and learn from.

Years later, Spider-Man discovers her existence and lets her out.
Cindy is furious in case Morlun has sensed her presence, but Spidey
tells her that Morlun is dead. Cindy rushes out to get a taste of
freedom, using her webbing to make a costume and become the
Super Hero Silk. Her family has inexplicably vanished while she was
locked away, so Cindy gets an internship at Fact Channel News,
hoping to locate them. But a greater purpose awaits her when
Spider-Totems from across the Multiverse gather to stop the
predatory Morlun (who is not dead, after all) and the Inheritors. It is
revealed that Silk is a very special spider-being, the personification
of the Bride totem. Her connection to Prime Earth's Spider-Man,
having been bitten by the same spider, also means that she can
track him through the Multiverse and save him from dying as he
traps Morlun. After returning to Earth, Silk takes up undercover work
for S.H.I.E.L.D., infiltrating Black Cat's criminal organization.

Claws of the cat
Silk agrees to go
undercover for
S.H.I.E.L.D. in Black
Cat's gang on the
understanding that
S.H.I.E.L.D. will help
her find her family.
A furious Black Cat
discovers the
double-cross and
Cindy is quickly pulled
out by S.H.I.E.L.D.

THOR (JANE FOSTER)

FIRST APPEARANCE *Thor: God of Thunder* #25 (November 2014) **BASE** New York City, Asgard **AFFILIATIONS** Avengers, Thor Corps

Jane Foster is a nurse working with Thor's alter ego, Dr. Donald Blake. Jane is often caught up in the adventures of both Donald and Thor, falling in love with both men, unaware they are one and the same.

Odin disapproves of his son Thor's relationship with a mortal, but eventually acquiesces—if Jane can prove herself worthy to be an Asgardian goddess. Odin transforms her into the Goddess of Flight, but Jane falls short and is sent back to Earth. Jane and Thor both move on emotionally, but when Jane seems on the verge of death, Thor's lover Sif comes to her aid, fusing with her.

For a time, Jane, using Sif's powers, aids Thor on his missions, until the two women separate. Jane marries Donald Blake's rival, Dr. Keith Kincaid, and they have a child, Jimmy. Keith and Jane's relationship crumbles; Keith takes custody of Jimmy, and Jane and Thor are reunited.

While Thor is away, Jane is diagnosed with breast cancer. Soon after, Thor is deemed unworthy to wield his enchanted hammer, Mjolnir, and thus unable to raise it from the surface of the Moon. Jane is transported there, lifts the hammer, and is turned into Thor, Goddess of Thunder.

Jane takes on Super Villains, infiltrates Doom's Thor Corps during the second Secret Wars event, and joins the Avengers and the all-female A-Force. However, in her human form, Jane's health deteriorates.

In sickness and in health
While Jane Foster is fighting cancer, she transforms into Thor, Goddess of Thunder—sapping her already dwindling strength.

A-FORCE

FIRST APPEARANCE *A-Force* #1 (July 2015) **BASE** Arcadia, New York City **AFFILIATIONS** Doctor Doom, Sub-Mariners, X-Men

This all-female team serves Doctor Doom during the second Secret Wars. Kree-powered hero Captain Marvel, light-manipulating Dazzler, blood-magic-wielding Nico Minoru, Inhuman queen Medusa, green behemoth She-Hulk, Thor (Alison Blaire of Earth-15513), and sentient pocket universe Singularity, protect the territory of Arcadia on the patchwork planet Battleworld. They battle monsters, Loki, and other villains; Singularity seemingly sacrifices her life to protect the team by swallowing a horde of zombies.

After the events of Secret Wars, Singularity awakens on Earth and reunites with the other A-Force heroes—who no longer recall the events on Battleworld. This team takes on the villainous Antimatter, created when Singularity came to Earth. When the team tries to reason with Antimatter, he kills Dazzler. Singularity battles Antimatter on the Blue Area of the Moon alone. The team arrives with a bomb that can kill Antimatter, but may also destroy Singularity. They detonate the bomb anyway and, miraculously, Dazzler returns and Singularity survives.

Later, the team encounters shape-shifting, sometimes-dragon, sometimes-human sorceress Countess, who travels to their world. Countess seeks to possess and depower the team, but is taken down by Nico. A-Force is later divided by civil war when Nico is accused by Captain Marvel of crimes she has not yet committed.

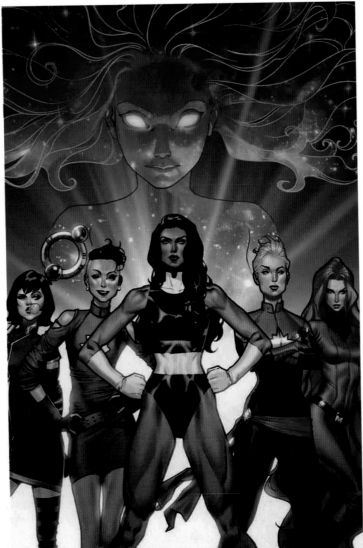

Forced apart
The team is jeopardized by a superhuman civil war *(above)*. At the same time, A-Force member Nico Minoru is believed to be a threat to a woman named Alice—who has been turned into a bug with a death wish *(right)*.

GWENPOOL

FIRST APPEARANCE *Howard the Duck* #1 (January 2016) **BASE** New York City; mobile **AFFILIATIONS** Agents of M.O.D.O.K.

Gwen Poole hails from what she calls the real world, where heroes and villains exist in comic books. Now in the main Marvel Universe, and thinking she is operating in a fictional world, Gwen wants to get in on the Super Hero life—believing her actions have no real repercussions.

With the help of her seamstress, Ronnie —who misreads the name Gwen Poole and assumes she wants to look like Deadpool—Gwen becomes the Super Hero Gwenpool. Her first misadventures lead her to Howard the Duck, who tries to make her see sense. Gwenpool carries on her carefree ways taking mercenary jobs, which she gets through Ronnie, and later from a hacker named Cecil. She becomes an agent for mechanical villain M.O.D.O.K.

MOON GIRL

FIRST APPEARANCE *Moon Girl and Devil Dinosaur* #1 (January 2016) **BASE** New York City **AFFILIATIONS** Devil Dinosaur, Inhumans

Nine-year-old Lunella Lafayette is the smartest person in the Marvel Universe. She is often teased by her classmates at school, who call the science-minded preteen Moon Girl. Discovering an Omni-Wave projector, Lunella accidentally opens a portal that allows Devil Dinosaur and the pursuing Killer-Folk to enter Manhattan from a prehistoric alternate reality. Lunella saves Devil Dinosaur and attempts to hide him. When Terrigen Mists cover the Earth, Lunella goes through Terrigenesis, revealing her Inhuman gene's power: she can now swap minds with Devil Dinosaur and inhabit his body.

WOLVERINE (LAURA KINNEY)

FIRST APPEARANCE *All-New Wolverine* #1 (January 2016) **BASE** New York City **AFFILIATIONS** Wolverines, X-Men

When Wolverine dies by being consumed in a vat of molten Adamantium while battling Dr. Cornelius, his female clone, X-23 (Laura Kinney), honors his legacy by taking on his name and costume. As Wolverine, Laura encounters new clones of herself and seeks to find out why they are dying. The trail leads to the Alchemax chemical corporation and its shady genetics division. Laura effectively destroys this with help from her surviving clones, who call themselves the Sisters. Laura's younger clone, Gabby, comes to live with her, as well as a pet wolverine, named Jonathan.

IRONHEART (RIRI WILLIAMS)

FIRST APPEARANCE *Invincible Iron Man* #7 (May 2016) **BASE** Chicago, Illinois **AFFILIATIONS** Iron Man

Riri Williams is a 15-year-old super-genius who attends the Massachusetts Institute of Technology (M.I.T.). Using materials found on the campus, Riri reverse-engineers Iron Man's armor to create her own. When campus security catches on, she flies away in her new armored suit.

While flying around the U.S., Riri catches escaping criminals in New Mexico, but damages her armor. She returns to her mother's home in Chicago to repair it and encounters Tony Stark. Riri chooses to leave M.I.T. and continue in Tony's footsteps as a Super Hero. When Tony is injured during the second superhuman civil war, she takes over for him as her alter ego Ironheart.

HULK (AMADEUS CHO)

FIRST APPEARANCE *Totally Awesome Hulk* #1 (February 2016) **BASE** Mobile **AFFILIATIONS** Champions, Olympus Group, God Squad

When Bruce Banner's Hulk powers overload, his friend Amadeus Cho comes to his aid. In order to prevent Hulk running amok, Cho uses nanites to remove the Hulk's excess radiation, transferring it to himself. Cho becomes the Totally Awesome Hulk and, together with his sister Maddy, seeks out monsters wreaking havoc across the planet.

WHEN WORLDS COLLIDE...

"There is no honor in running from death."
THANOS

Every alternate universe faces an event called "the incursions"—an apocalyptic fate in which the Earth-like planets of multiple realities crash into one another, destroying entire universes.

Elite Super Hero organization, the Illuminati—Black Panther, Doctor Strange, Namor the Sub-Mariner, Mister Fantastic, Iron Man, Black Bolt, and Beast—consists of some of the greatest existing scientific minds. The group is so desperate to prevent incursions occurring to their Earth (the Marvel Universe Prime Earth) that it is prepared to destroy other Earth-like planets from alternate realities to save their world and universe from obliteration. Prime Earth and Earth-1610 are hurtling toward each other on a path to destruction and there is seemingly no hope of stopping it. The alien Shi'ar believe that if they can destroy Prime Earth, they can prevent their planet and the other planets of the main Marvel Universe from being destroyed.

THE TRIUMPH OF DOOM
The Shi'ar's assault on Prime Earth is quickly halted by the Avengers. Tragically, althought the almost mirror-image heroes of Prime Earth and Earth-1610 do all that they can, nothing can ultimately stop their worlds from colliding. The two Earths crash together in an explosion of cosmic proportions that destroys both planets and their dimensions.

However one being profits from this terrible annihilation: Fragments of the planets as well as shards of other destroyed worlds are collected together by Doctor Doom. Using the powers of the omnipotent alien Beyonders, he forms them into a patchwork planet known as Battleworld, a planet he plans to rule himself.

Heroes vs. heroes
Aware that the incursions of their planets are imminent, the heroes of Prime Earth and Earth-1610 face off in desperate hopes of survival.

End of worlds
Prime Earth and Earth-1610 crash into each
other, creating an "incursion" that ends both
of their universes and sends shards of their
realities hurtling into space.

EZEKIEL SIMS

FIRST APPEARANCE *Amazing Spider-Man* #30 (June 2001)

Spider-powered Ezekiel Sims abandons dreams of being a hero and amasses a huge fortune instead. Targeted by mystic totem-eater Morlun, he hides for years before sacrificing himself to save Spider-Man.

DOOP

FIRST APPEARANCE *X-Force* #116 (July 2001)

Doop is an enigma with many incredible powers and an unknown agenda, who associates with mutant heroes such as Wolverine and X-Statix. Doop is possibly the result of Cold War-era military experimentation.

PRODIGY

FIRST APPEARANCE *New Mutants* #4 (October 2003)

Mutant David Alleyne absorbs knowledge and skills from anyone nearby. Despite losing this talent during Scarlet Witch's M-Day, in which most mutants lose their powers thanks to her Hex magic, the human David retains the many physical skills and vast intellectual capacities he had previously "borrowed."

LIONHEART

FIRST APPEARANCE *Avengers* #77 (March 2004)

After Kelsey Leigh dies saving Captain America she is resurrected as a new Captain Britain. The role leads to the loss of her children and, as Lionheart, she briefly turns against her country before eventually reforming.

QUAKE

FIRST APPEARANCE *Secret War* #2 (July 2004)

Handpicked and trained by Nick Fury to lead his Secret Warriors, Inhuman Daisy Johnson combines her earthquake-generating powers with his decades of espionage experience to become a valued S.H.I.E.L.D. agent and Avenger.

TOXIN

FIRST APPEARANCE *Venom/Carnage* #1 (September 2004)

New York City cop Patrick Mulligan is forcibly bonded to a shape-shifting symbiote, gaining similar powers to Venom and Carnage. However, because Mulligan is a good cop, Toxin becomes, despite his terrifying appearance, more a hero than a villain. Toxin proceeds to fight villainy in partnership with Spider-Man and the Avengers. However, at times, Pat struggles to stop the Toxin symbiote from doing wrong and running wild. Pat eventually gains control of the Toxin symbiote possessing him, but is killed by the demon Blackheart. The Toxin symbiote merges with Eddie Brock/Venom to hunt the murderous Carnage.

VERANKE

FIRST APPEARANCE *New Avengers* #1 (January 2005)

Religious zealot and shape-shifting Skrull Queen Veranke replaces Spider-Woman to infiltrate the New Avengers, as part of her plan to secretly invade and turn Earth into her race's new homeworld. In defeat, she is executed by Norman Osborn.

GRAVITY

FIRST APPEARANCE *Gravity* #1 (August 2005)

While on a vacation with his family Greg Willis is sucked into a miniature black hole, gaining the ability to control gravity. He dies saving many heroes from the cosmic entity known as the Stranger, but is later resurrected by Epoch to continue protecting Earth and the universe.

VULCAN

FIRST APPEARANCE *X-Men: Deadly Genesis* #1 (January 2006)

Brother of Cyclops and Havok, Gabriel Summers is born a slave in the Shi'ar Imperium. Escaping to Earth, he becomes a secret X-Man before conquering the Shi'ar as Vulcan. He apparently dies battling Black Bolt.

SPEED

FIRST APPEARANCE *Young Avengers* #10 (March 2006)

Violent super-speedster Tommy Shepherd destroys his school, but is rescued from juvenile detention by the Young Avengers. He discovers that he and teammate Wiccan are twin brothers, and the Scarlet Witch's long-lost children.

PHOBOS

FIRST APPEARANCE *Ares, God of War* #1 (March 2006)

Alexander Aaron is the son of Ares, with immense power and prophetic visions enhancing his status as God of Fear. He is killed while fighting as one of Nick Fury's Secret Warriors, and is reunited with his father in the afterlife.

TRAUMA

FIRST APPEARANCE *Avengers: The Initiative* #1 (April 2007)

Terence Ward's ability to transform into an opponent's worst fear stems from his father, the demon Nightmare. After failing as a Super Hero he becomes a therapist, then decides to explore Earth.

KOMODO

FIRST APPEARANCE *Avengers: The Initiative* #1 (April 2007)

Student Melati Kusuma steals and modifies Curt Connors' Lizard formula, transforming herself into a super-powered reptilian hero. She serves with Tony Stark's Fifty-State Initiative, and the Shadow Initiative before going solo again.

SLINGSHOT

FIRST APPEARANCE *Mighty Avengers* #13 (July 2008)

Speedster Yo-Yo Rodriguez is recruited by Nick Fury to fight against the Skrulls. She loses both arms fighting the Gorgon but, outfitted with cybernetic replacements, becomes a Howling Commando.

ANTI-VENOM

FIRST APPEARANCE *Amazing Spider-Man* #569 (August 2008)

A mindless modified symbiote created from antibodies from Venom's former host Eddie Brock and the energies of Mister Negative, Anti-Venom can cure any illness or disease it encounters.

DARK AVENGERS

FIRST APPEARANCE *Dark Avengers* #1
(March 2009)

Norman Osborn secretly replaces the Earth's Mightiest Heroes with a squad of criminal psychopaths and shady impostors, willing to do his bidding and even kill on command.

AVENGERS ACADEMY FIRST CLASS

FIRST APPEARANCE *Avengers Academy* #1
(August 2010)

Norman Osborn uses dinosaur-transmorph Humberto Lopez, living vapor Madeline Berry, supercharged Brandon Sharpe, walking toxic-spill Jennifer Takeda, the amoral Jeanne Foucault, and iridium boy Ken Mack as guinea pigs. Rescued and trained at Avengers Academy, they become *(clockwise from top)* the teen heroes Reptil, Veil, Striker, Hazmat, Finesse, and Mettle.

MANIFOLD

FIRST APPEARANCE
Secret Warriors #4
(July 2009)

Eden Fesi was the apprentice of mutant shaman Gateway until recruited by Nick Fury. Following training and duties with the Secret Warriors, the aboriginal Australian utilizes his ability to bend space-time as an Avenger.

MASSACRE

FIRST APPEARANCE *Amazing Spider-Man* #655
(April 2011)

Surviving assassination, brain-damaged Wall Street trader Marcus Lyman becomes a ruthless killer. After escaping from the Ravencroft Institute he goes on another spree and is publicly executed by Spider-Man (secretly Doctor Octopus).

SERPENT

FIRST APPEARANCE *Fear Itself* #1 (June 2011)

Tyrannical Cul Borson rules the ancient world before being overthrown by his younger brother, Odin. Sealed below Earth's ocean, Cul returns eons later to terrorize Earth and Asgard as the Serpent.

GORR THE GOD BUTCHER

FIRST APPEARANCE *Thor: God of Thunder* #2
(January 2013)

Abandoned by his gods, extraterrestrial Gorr begins eradicating all deities throughout the universe after finding All-Black the Necrosword. The reign of terror ends when he is killed by Asgard's Thunder God, Thor.

NOMAD

FIRST APPEARANCE *Captain America* #1
(January 2013)

Trapped in Dimension Z for 12 years, Steve Rogers raises Leopold, Arnim Zola's genetically perfect son. Cap trains "Ian," as he names him, to become a hero. On returning to Earth, the young man becomes trainee Avenger Nomad.

NIGHTMASK

FIRST APPEARANCE *Avengers* #3
(March 2013)

Created on Mars by Ex Nihilo, Nightmask (Adam Blackveil) is a herald of Multiversal Armageddon. This artificial man translates information coded into the fabric of existence, allowing the Avengers to properly prepare for universal threats.

CORVUS GLAIVE

FIRST APPEARANCE *Free Comic Book Day: Infinity* (May 2013)

The most loyal of Thanos' lieutenants is also the most brutal member of the Black Order. He is a super-strong, immortal savage wielding a hyper-powered pike, who mercilessly slaughters and spreads terror at his master's command.

ANNA MARIA MARCONI

FIRST APPEARANCE *Superior Spider-Man* #5
(May 2013)

Doctor Octopus falls in love with brilliant scientist Anna Maria Marconi while inhabiting the body of Peter Parker. When he is banished and Peter returns, Anna becomes a close confidante of the true Spider-Man.

LINEAGE

FIRST APPEARANCE *Thunderbolts* #14
(October 2013)

Gangster Gordon Nobili is transformed by the global release of Terrigen Mists, and devotes his NuHuman ability to access the knowledge and memories of any ancestor or descendant to pursue global domination.

INFERNO

FIRST APPEARANCE *Inhuman* #1 (June 2014)

Following the explosion of a Terrigen Bomb and the global release of Terrigen Mist, latent Inhuman Dante Pertuz transforms into a heat-generating, flame manipulator. This allows him to become a valiant defender of his NuHuman brethren.

LASH

FIRST APPEARANCE
Inhuman #1 (June 2014)

A fanatical Inhuman with energy powers, Lash hunts NuHumans. He ruthlessly tests them to prove that they are worthy to possess their powers and that their new abilities are worth preserving, slaying them if they are not.

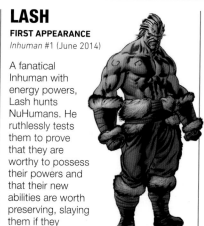

ISO

FIRST APPEARANCE *Inhumans* #4
(October 2014)

NuHuman pressure-manipulator and tech genius Xiaoyi Chen escapes conscription into China's military and, after working with Reader the corrupt Inhuman, joins Medusa's Inhumans in New Attilan.

AGENTS OF S.H.I.E.L.D.

FIRST APPEARANCE *S.H.I.E.L.D.* #1 (February 2015)

Crucial members of Supreme Commander Phil Coulson's own elite S.H.I.E.L.D. team include combat specialist Melinda May, brilliant scientist Leo Fitz, and genius Jemma Simmons.

VEHICLES

Super Heroes—and Super Villains—require high-tech transportation. Customized wheels, jets, hovercraft, and spacecraft are produced in top-secret factories. These vehicles are battle-ready, bringing super-powered occupants to the heart of the action at breakneck speed, or enabling escape in the blink of an eye.

State-of-the-art automobiles like the Spider-Mobile and Captain America's van prowl the roads. The Fantastic Four takes the fight to the skies in their Fantasti-Cars, where villains like M.O.D.O.K. and the Green Goblin terrorize those below from their flying machines. They are met there by Rocket Racer and the Silver Surfer, who flies his own sentient surfboard beyond our solar system. Conflicts in the stars are waged by advanced warships, such as Thor's *Starjammer*, Beta Ray Bill's *Skuttlebutt*, and Deadpool's *Bea Arthur*.

With threats on land, sea, and in the sky, top-secret government agency S.H.I.E.L.D. needs to be ready for anything. They have a hangar full of flying cars, Quinjets, and space shuttles—as well as their gargantuan Helicarrier—ready at a moment's notice.

REED RICHARDS' ROCKETSHIP

FIRST APPEARANCE *Fantastic Four* #1 (November 1961) **USED BY** Fantastic Four

Science and engineering genius Reed Richards' ultimate dream is interstellar travel. He spends years and a considerable amount of both his own family's and the U.S. government's money building a rocket capable of journeying to the stars. However, the sudden withdrawal of government funding and the possibility of rivals in other countries beating him to the prize drives Reed to make a test flight too soon. He persuades his best friend Ben Grimm to pilot the craft, and his fiancée Susan Storm and her brother Johnny insist on coming along, too.

Ben, an experienced test pilot and astronaut, expresses concerns that the ship's radiation shields aren't tough enough—and his doubts prove well founded. At an altitude of 100 miles (160.9km) the rocket is pummeled by cosmic rays. Fortunately, the ship has an automatic pilot as a built-in safety mechanism, and during the cosmic storm it kicks in to bring the rocket back down toward Earth.

After a crash-landing, the quartet stagger from the wreckage, shaken but unharmed. Little do they know, they have been altered forever by the voyage and now possess the powers that will turn them into the Fantastic Four. Reed's rocket may be destroyed, but the Fantastic Four's space adventures are far from over…

Nose cone
This contains the payload, where Reed Richards and the rest of the crew sit while Ben Grimm takes the controls

Secret launch
Secret launch. Reed Richards and his crew have to sneak on to a secret missile base to make the unauthorized test flight of his interstellar rocket.

Guidance system fins
These help the top section of the rocket maneuver after the other sections have been jettisoned

Propulsion system fins
These help maneuver the rocket in the early stages of its flight

Fuel
Most of the vast amount of fuel needed is exhausted getting through the Earth's atmosphere. When it is gone its containers can be jettisoned

Trouble ahead
At first it's all systems go on board the rocket and Reed Richards is delighted. However, pilot Ben Grimm, worried about the ship's shields, does not share Reed's enthusiasm.

"Hear that? It's cosmic rays! I warned ya about 'em, Egghead!"

BEN GRIMM TO REED RICHARDS

DOCTOR DOOM'S TIME MACHINE

FIRST APPEARANCE *Fantastic Four* #5 (July 1962) **USED BY** Doctor Doom, Fantastic Four

Like his nemesis Reed Richards, Victor von Doom is a scientific genius. In order to increase his potential opportunities for crime, Doctor Doom invents a time machine, a platform incorporated into the floor of his castle stronghold in Latveria. The machine is large enough for several people to travel in it at the same time and is operated by a button in the armrest of Doom's throne. Time travelers are brought back using an atomic power circuit in a control panel. When the panel is operated, a retrieval field appears in the past, mirroring the size and shape of the time platform. As long as the subjects are standing under the retrieval field, they can be safely brought back to the present.

After Doom abandons his castle, the Fantastic Four break in, hoping to use the time platform for more noble purposes. The platform is later destroyed by Cable's X-Force to prevent S.H.I.E.L.D. taking it.

FANTASTI-CAR

FIRST APPEARANCE *Fantastic Four* #3 (March 1962)
USED BY Fantastic Four

The Fantastic Four have a car like no other to help them battle the bad guys. Genius inventor Reed Richards designs the Fantasti-Car MK I, an air-powered vehicle affectionately nicknamed "the Flying Bathtub." The Fantasti-Car's autopilot setting can land it on top of the team's Baxter Building headquarters. It can also be split into four parts mid-flight, so that each team member can focus on a different part of the mission at hand. As one vehicle it has a top speed of 60mph (96.6km/h), while its four parts can travel at 30mph (48.3km/h). As such, it is mostly suitable for urban use.

The Flying Bathtub is soon modified to become the Fantasti-Car MK II by Johnny Storm, who has always been crazy about cars. He extends its cruising range to around 3,000 miles, so that it can travel across the U.S. Like its predecessor, the MK II splits into four parts, each capable of independent flight, and has vertical takeoff and landing ability so it may be launched from city skyscrapers. Its bulletproof windshields completely cover the team at the touch of a button. The car's top speed is secret (by request of Reed Richards), but is rumored to be around 550mph (885.1km/h). This model, in turn, is replaced by the MK III, designed and built by Reed and test-piloted by Ben Grimm. This version can also split into four independent aircraft.

Divide and conquer
As well as being able to fly, the Fantasti-Car MK I can split into four parts if the team needs to go separate ways.

Fantasti-Car MK II
Of all the many upgrades to the Fantasti-Car, this was perhaps the most important to petrolhead Johnny Storm, who wanted the vehicle to look less like a "flying bathtub."

"I still say they don't build 'em like they used to!"

THING

Side pod
Each side pod separates from the two central sections when quadrant couplings are disengaged

Main pilot
Ben Grimm, the Thing, takes the lead pilot seat

Front section
Reed Richards' control hub also detaches into an independent winged craft

Logo
The Fantasti-Car displays the FF's logo proudly on the front

Sleek silhouette
Streamlining gives the MK III a sleeker appearance than the old "Flying Bathtub"

Fantasti-Car MK III
The most recent iteration of the Fantasti-Car more closely resembles a sleek alien spacecraft than a car and has a top speed of more than 1,000 mph (1,609.3 km/h).

POGO-PLANE

FIRST APPEARANCE *Fantastic Four* #3 (March 1962) **USED BY** Fantastic Four

The Pogo Orbit Plane is designed for long-range, intercontinental, and even space travel. This powerful jet aircraft blasts to the edge of space before orbiting the Earth and landing wherever the Fantastic Four need to be. It is capable of vertical take-off and landing on any terrain and is stored in a hangar at the team's Baxter Building headquarters in New York City. It is large enough to transport the Fantasti-Car in its hold. The plane releases a smoke signal to alert other members of the Fantastic Four in an emergency. The MK I version is destroyed by the Frightful Four as Mr. Fantastic and the Thing fly to the rescue of Sue and Johnny Storm.

AIRJET-CYCLE

FIRST APPEARANCE *Fantastic Four* #45 (December 1965) **USED BY** The Fantastic Four

Devised by Mr. Fantastic, the Airjet-Cycle is a flying motorbike with four seats, designed to accommodate all the members of the Fantastic Four at the same time. As its name suggests, the cycle uses air jets to stay airborne, and is designed for optimum maneuverability and speed when traveling through urban environments. A built-in, automatic compensator helps to track Fantastic Four members, enabling the Airjet-Cycle to zero in on their exact location. On its maiden flight, stunned onlookers are not sure if they are looking at a stripped-down whirlybird, a turbo-powered racing car, or a flying bicycle.

KANG'S TIMESHIP

FIRST APPEARANCE *Fantastic Four* #19 (October 1963) **USED BY** Kang

Bored by life in the distant future, Kang uses time-travel technology invented by his supposed ancestor Doctor Doom to journey back to Ancient Egypt. There he employs his technical knowledge to become the most powerful man in this early civilization. He builds his timeship in the form of a giant Sphinx to inspire awe and worship in the Ancient Egyptians among whom he lands. Within the larger timeship is a circular room in which key technology is housed. When threatened by the time-traveling Fantastic Four, Kang is able to launch this module out of the Sphinx and escape into space. It is his spherical timeship that he uses from then on.

Goblin Broomstick.
The Goblin's first flying transport resembled a broomstick, with rear blaster jets that not only propelled the villain along but could also help burn him out of a trap.

GOBLIN GLIDER

FIRST APPEARANCE *Amazing Spider-Man* #14 (July 1964) **USED BY** Green Goblin, Hobgoblin, Menace, Monster, Punisher

The Goblin Glider starts out as a "flying broomstick," but Norman Osborn, the Green Goblin, soon turns his evil genius to a redesign. The new glider looks like a jet-propelled bat, with electromagnetic braces on each wing for the Goblin's feet. It is faster and more maneuverable than the broomstick, and the copious smoke from its exhaust puts off pursuers. The glider has a flight radius of 80 miles (129km) and a top speed of 110mph (177kph). It can carry the Green Goblin, but loses altitude if two riders are on it. Although it has a simple, streamlined appearance, technical genius Norman Osborn hides extra features within the glider. Behind the Goblin face panel at the front is a navigation and guidance computer, as well as a laser gyroscope to maintain balance.

The Goblin uses his glider to kidnap Peter Parker's girlfriend, Gwen Stacy, and carry her to the top of the Brooklyn Bridge, where she falls to her death. When Spider-Man, enraged by grief over Gwen's death, confronts the Green Goblin, the villain ends up being impaled by his onrushing glider as he tries to use it to attack Spidey.

After the Green Goblin's apparent death, one of his lairs is discovered by the Hobgoblin, who repurposes the glider, along with other Goblin paraphernalia, for his own villainous career. Norman Osborn's son Harry, who adopts the Green Goblin identity after his father, also uses the glider. In fact, the Goblin Glider is the signature vehicle for any villain looking to ape the iconic Green Goblin, and it is used by Lily Hollister's Menace and Carlie Cooper's Monster. A customized version with a skull on the front is flown by the Punisher.

S.H.I.E.L.D. FLYING CAR

FIRST APPEARANCE *Strange Tales* #135 (August 1965) **USED BY** S.H.I.E.L.D

The first flying car that soon-to-be S.H.I.E.L.D. Director Nick Fury takes a ride in is a converted Porsche 904 in canary yellow. Its capabilities are soon put to the test when a fighter jet attacks with napalm bombs. To Fury's astonishment, the car sweeps through the wall of flame with no ill effects, because, as his driver explains, the car is made from the same material as the hull of a space capsule. Their assailant is dispatched with the car's sidewinder missiles and then lifts off into the air, its wheels turning over to create horizontal turbines.

The flying car can range for 250 miles (402km) with a top air speed of 385mph (620kmh). It can also travel underwater, and stay submerged for up to five hours. Flying cars makes it easy for S.H.I.E.L.D. agents to reach their Helicarrier headquarters. They can vary in make and color—Nick Fury is later seen in a red Ferrari edition, which is temporarily hijacked by the evil Baron von Strucker. Tony Stark, while his is S.H.I.E.L.D. Director, also employs at least one flying car, when he is not wearing his Iron Man armor.

On one occasion, Wolverine steals Nick Fury's car while on a time-traveling mission to kill Hank Pym before the scientist can create the malignant artificial intelligence Ultron. Agent Phil Coulson drives a flying car named Lola, which he claims stands for Low-Orbit Liftoff Automobile, although Lola also happens to be the name of his ex-girlfriend.

Flying to the rescue
Piloting a S.H.I.E.L.D. flying car, Agent 13 (Sharon Carter) swoops in to prevent Captain America falling to his death.

S.H.I.E.L.D. HELICARRIER

FIRST APPEARANCE *Strange Tales* #135 (August 1965) **USED BY** S.H.I.E.L.D.

S.H.I.E.L.D.'s mobile headquarters is a vast aircraft carrier, surveillance center, and war room. Its huge engines lift it high into the air, looking down from above over the world it protects.

The Helicarrier—a vast aircraft carrier that can also fly—functions as a mobile base for S.H.I.E.L.D. Like regular aircraft carriers, it has a large flat deck for the takeoff and landing of small aircraft, such as fighters and helicopters. In addition, there are two repair decks. The Helicarrier is the brainchild of Iron Man Tony Stark, design-assisted by Mr. Fantastic Reed Richards and the mutant Forge. The idea is to provide S.H.I.E.L.D. with a mobile headquarters not tied to a single location, and thus reducing danger to civilians in the event of an attack. To protect against this, the Helicarrier is both heavily armored and bristling with weapons, including an intercontinental ballistic missile.

The Helicarrier's main operational purpose is surveillance. The aircraft is equipped with the very latest technology as well as hundreds of personnel. Internal areas include a large bridge, a combat operations center, monitoring center, and an aircraft control tower. As well as these operational areas, the Helicarrier has personnel quarters, a sick bay, and a mess hall. It can support its crew for about 30 days without needing resupply, and can stay in the air indefinitely, thanks to the thermoelectric nuclear reactor that provides its power source.

Despite the Helicarrier's formidable offense and defense capabilites, it is still possible for one of these magnificent vessels to be hijacked or even destroyed.

Olympian battle
When Hercules fights his brother Ares aboard the Helicarrier *Behemoth*, the hero is thrown into one of the vessel's massive engines.

Having previously downed one in the Gulf of Mexico, the villainous Red Skull manages to take over a Helicarrier. He attempts to create a psionic weapon using the power of hatred in people's minds, until Captain America stops him. On another occasion, Hydra terrorists cause a Helicarrier to crash, killing the Ant-Man at that time, Chris McCarthy. Red Hulk also manages to bring down the *Helicarrier Gold*, Tony Stark's pride and joy during his time as Director of S.H.I.E.L.D.

Norman Osborn is given official permission to create his own Helicarriers when he assumes command of H.A.M.M.E.R., his replacement for S.H.I.E.L.D. Although his time in power comes to an end before he can get his redesigned fleet launched, he manages to build a prototype, *Prometheus*, with enhanced weaponry, including a nuclear warhead. A later version of the Helicarrier is the battlecarrier *Pericles*, which has heavy artillery instead of a flight deck.

Abandon ship!
After S.H.I.E.L.D.'s systems are infected with a Skrull virus, S.H.I.E.L.D. Director Maria Hill's Helicarrier plummets toward the city below

"It sure as hell isn't going to wreck my Helicarrier!"
IRON MAN

S.H.I.E.L.D. HELICARRIER

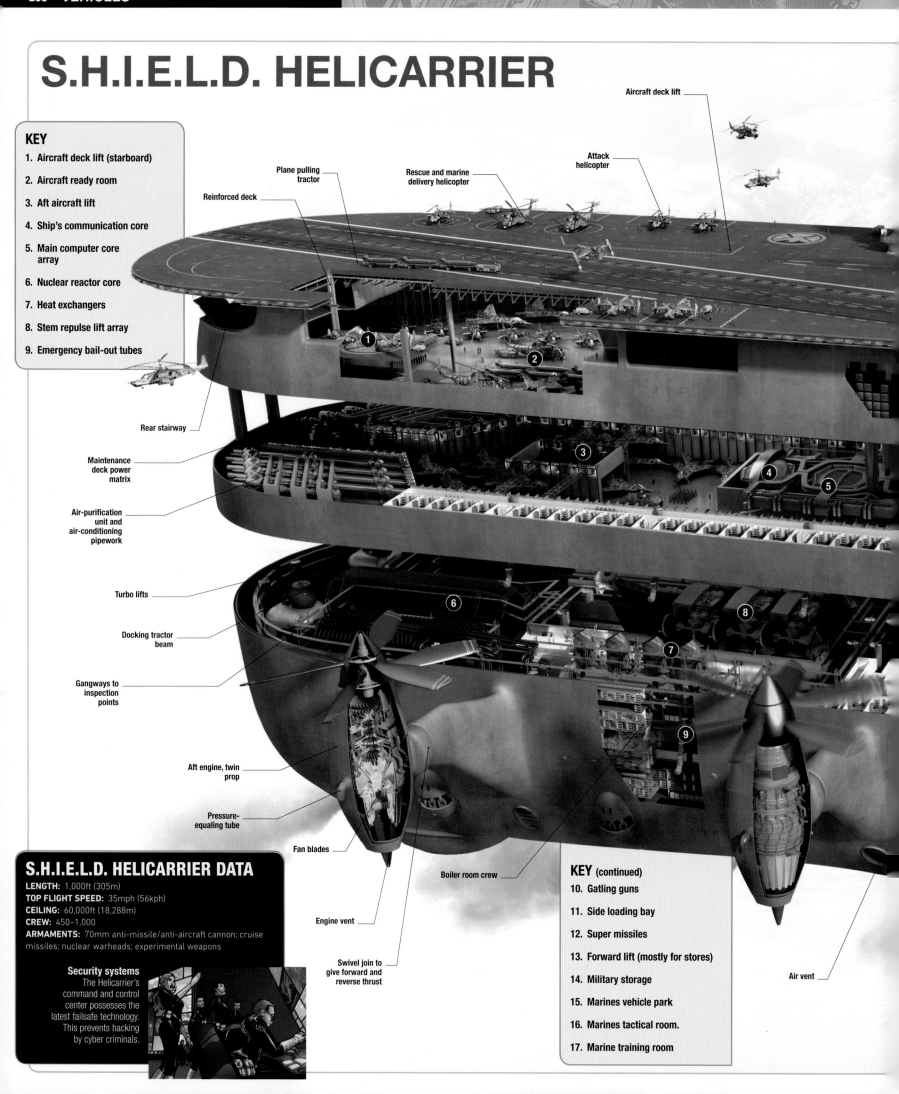

KEY

1. Aircraft deck lift (starboard)
2. Aircraft ready room
3. Aft aircraft lift
4. Ship's communication core
5. Main computer core array
6. Nuclear reactor core
7. Heat exchangers
8. Stem repulse lift array
9. Emergency bail-out tubes

Aircraft deck lift

Attack helicopter

Rescue and marine delivery helicopter

Plane pulling tractor

Reinforced deck

Rear stairway

Maintenance deck power matrix

Air-purification unit and air-conditioning pipework

Turbo lifts

Docking tractor beam

Gangways to inspection points

Aft engine, twin prop

Pressure-equaling tube

Fan blades

Boiler room crew

Engine vent

Swivel join to give forward and reverse thrust

Air vent

S.H.I.E.L.D. HELICARRIER DATA

LENGTH: 1,000ft (305m)
TOP FLIGHT SPEED: 35mph (56kph)
CEILING: 60,000ft (18,288m)
CREW: 450–1,000
ARMAMENTS: 70mm anti-missile/anti-aircraft cannon; cruise missiles; nuclear warheads; experimental weapons

Security systems
The Helicarrier's command and control center possesses the latest failsafe technology. This prevents hacking by cyber criminals.

KEY (continued)

10. Gatling guns
11. Side loading bay
12. Super missiles
13. Forward lift (mostly for stores)
14. Military storage
15. Marines vehicle park
16. Marines tactical room.
17. Marine training room

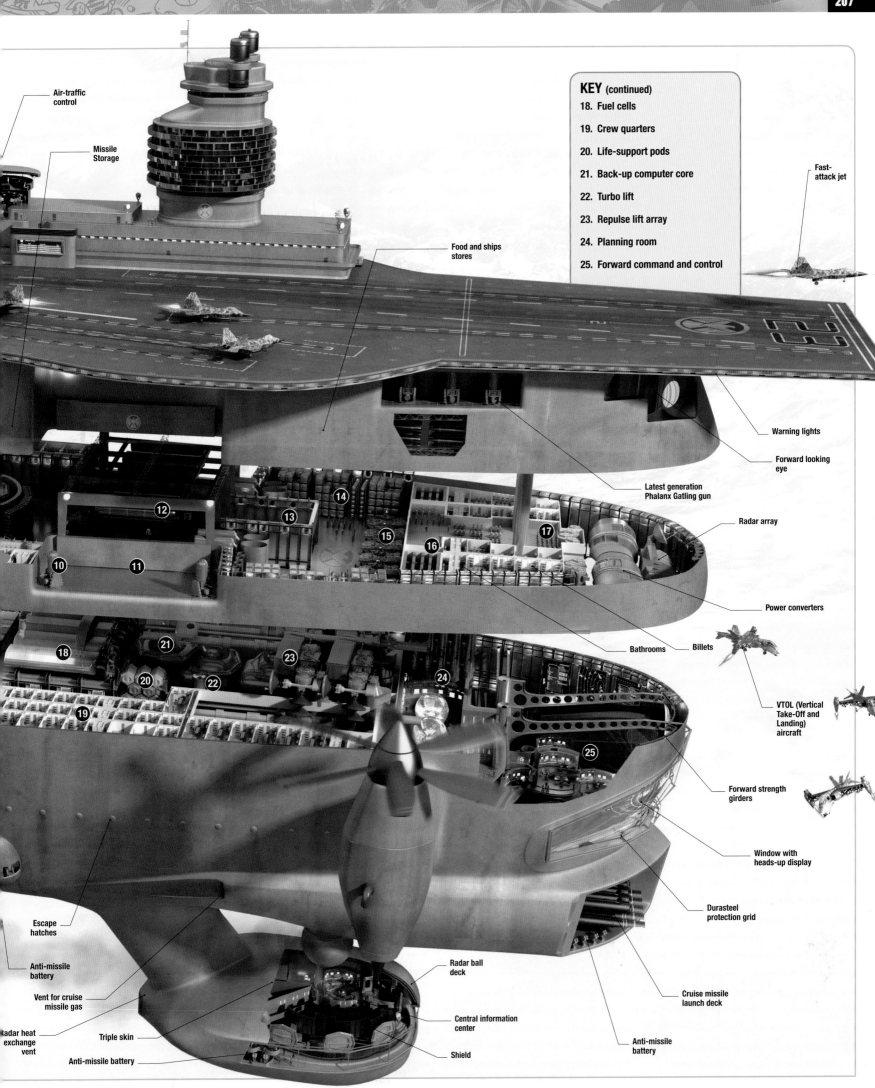

Air-traffic
control

Missile
Storage

Food and ships
stores

Fast-
attack jet

Warning lights

Forward looking
eye

Latest generation
Phalanx Gatling gun

Radar array

Radar heat
exchange
vent

Power converters

Bathrooms

Billets

VTOL (Vertical
Take-Off and
Landing)
aircraft

Forward strength
girders

Window with
heads-up display

Durasteel
protection grid

Cruise missile
launch deck

Anti-missile
battery

Escape
hatches

Anti-missile
battery

Vent for cruise
missile gas

Radar ball
deck

Central information
center

Triple skin

Shield

Anti-missile battery

SILVER SURFER'S SURFBOARD

FIRST APPEARANCE *Fantastic Four* #48 (March 1966) **USED BY** Silver Surfer, Doctor Doom, Dawn Greenwood

This gleaming, seemingly alive board carries the Silver Surfer at immeasurable velocities across the universe. It was constructed by Galactus, Devourer of Worlds, from unknown materials when he first transformed Zenn-Lavian Norrin Radd (Silver Surfer) into his herald.

The image for the board was plucked from Norrin's subconscious and Galactus imbued it with the same Power Cosmic as his new servant. Permanently linked to its rider's mind, the board is the perfect conveyance—attuned to the Silver Surfer's reflexes and obedient to his will.

The surfboard's exact composition is unknown, but it can withstand all known weaponry, negate gravity, and hover until called by the Surfer. It has also been reduced to energy and reformed, seemingly without incurring any damage or loss of powers.

When carrying passengers, the board provides a stable platform at standard gravity and supplies a life-sustaining environment with both atmosphere and temperature adjusted to fit the needs of those on board. The board also negates the effects of friction, inertia, and acceleration force, while screening out harmful energies or radiation—all without any loss of speed. The Silver Surfer's guest riders are thus ensured a safe, if somewhat precarious, travel experience.

Capable of trans-light speeds, inter-dimensional and warp travel, the board has carried the Silver Surfer all over the universe, and been used to break the time barrier. It also affords entry to other planes of reality and has even taken the Super Hero into sub-atomic realms.

When Doctor Doom steals the Silver Surfer's power, the board is forced to switch allegiance to a new master. However, Doom overreaches himself and crashes into a barrier Galactus has placed around Earth. The board immediately seeks out the powerless Silver Surfer and restores the Power Cosmic to him.

"To me, my Board."

SILVER SURFER

Connected
Neither gulfs of time and space, nor any physical barrier can keep the board from finding its master when the Silver Surfer calls.

TAA II

FIRST APPEARANCE *Fantastic Four* #49 (March 1966) **USED BY** Galactus

Taa II is the home of planet-devouring Galactus, a ship he builds soon after emerging from an incubation period of millions of years. When he awakes Galactus consumes the life force of the planet Archeopia. Using the debris—and eventually all the matter of the solar system—he manufactures the Worldship as a monument to his original homeworld, Taa. Billions of years old, *Taa II* is larger than a solar system, and so massive that it has captured a sun and planets within its gravity well.

Taa II is a home, workplace, and arsenal. It contains many captured weapons of terrifying power, labs, and even a zoo. However, Galactus usually employs smaller ships when voyaging to planets that he intends to consume.

MAGNETIC WAVE RIDER

FIRST APPEARANCE *Fantastic Four* #52 (July 1966) **USED BY** Black Panther, Human Torch, Thing

When Black Panther T'Challa decides to test himself in combat against the Fantastic Four, he lures them to his hidden kingdom of Wakanda with the gift of a new aircar. The Magnetic Wave Rider channels electromagnetic forces, and its push-button controls are so simple that a child could fly it. Incredibly fast, astoundingly maneuverable, utterly silent, and producing no harmful emissions, the ship proves the perfect bait to pique the Fantastic Four's interest. Later, the Fantastic Four accept T'Challa as an ally, and the aircar joins the many vehicles in the team's garage of exotic craft. It is used on occasion by the Human Torch (Johnny Storm) and the Thing (Ben Grimm).

DOOMSDAY CHAIR

FIRST APPEARANCE *Tales of Suspense* #94 (October 1967) **USED BY** M.O.D.O.K., M.O.D.A.M., M.O.D.O.G., Deadpool, and Bob, Agent of Hydra

Along for the ride
Deadpool and his wife Shiklah take a trip in the Doomsday Chair; Bob hangs on at the back.

The Doomsday Chair is a flying personal mobility vehicle designed by A.I.M.'s Scientist Supreme Lyle Getz to carry the organization's ultimate organic assassin M.O.D.O.K. (Mental Organism Designed Only for Killing). This psionically powerful mind-slave is incapable of supporting the weight of his own mutated head and he uses the chair as a platform for general transport and to perform attack maneuvers. When M.O.D.O.K. seizes control of A.I.M. he modifies the chair, enabling it to boost his mental energies and provide a constant source of power. With his death, the chair passes to other users such as A.I.M agents M.O.D.A.M. and M.O.D.O.G., and teleporting assassin Deadpool and his sidekick Bob, Agent of Hydra.

EXCAVATOR

FIRST APPEARANCE *Astonishing Tales* #6 (June 1971) **USED BY** Doctor Doom

The Excavator is a nuclear-powered drilling device and personal transport vehicle designed by Victor von Doom (Doctor Doom) to bore through solid rock at crushing depths. He uses it to travel covertly from central Europe under the Mediterranean Sea to the secret kingdom of Wakanda in Africa.

The Excavator causes earthquakes and damages ecosystems; nevertheless, Doom intends to employ it to secure rare minerals buried far beneath the ground, He targets the country of Wakanda's invaluable reserves of Vibranium by tunneling into the country. Fortunately, the Excavator's considerable seismic trail alerts Wakanda's ruler, Black Panther, who explosively foils Doctor Doom's plot.

QUINJET

FIRST APPEARANCE *Avengers* #61 (February 1969) **USED BY** Avengers, Avengers Academy, Black Panther, Dora Milaje (Midnight Angels)

The term Quinjet applies to any of a variety of supersonic air transports used primarily by the Avengers. These aircraft were originally imagined and produced by Black Panther's Wakanda Design Group; Earth's Mightiest Heroes began using them—rather than the Stark Industries aircraft they had been employing—soon after the African king joined the team.

Although there are many different modified ships, each tailored to specific purposes, the standard Quinjet is equipped with an array of turbojet engines and possesses VTOL (Vertical Take Off and Landing) capability.

Quinjets can reach speeds of Mach 2.5 or more and, as a rule, lack onboard weapons, being used primarily to transport the heroes to where they are needed. When Thanos' forces first invade Earth, a modified vehicle takes Thor, Captain America, Vision, Scarlet Witch, Mantis, and the Swordsman into high Earth orbit to counterattack the evil Titan's alien armada.

At some stage, Stark International becomes involved in the construction process. Due to the frequent and grave dangers the Avengers have to confront, Quinjets tend to have a very short lifespan, and Iron Man's manufacturing base is kept busy making repairs and supplying replacement parts. Stark also begins tinkering with the basic design. When the

team disbands in the wake of the Avengers Disassembled crisis and is replaced by the rough-and-ready New Avengers, he has three variant prototypes ready for action. These are all equipped with 2x2, modified Pratt & Whitney J48-P-8A Turbojet engines; unfortunately, these ships soon suffer the same destructive fate as their predecessors.

Chariot of the gods
Swift, reliable and infinitely adaptable, the Quinjet design has been customized in many ways and for a number of heroes.

Into space
Sturdy construction and modular design elements even allow Quinjets to be rapidly customized for deep space voyages.

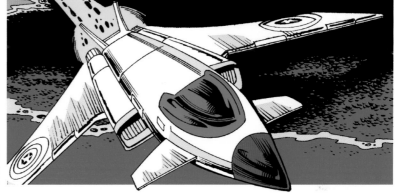

American eagles
Captain America utilizes a Wakandan-modified Quinjet for personal missions, with former astronaut John Jameson as his designated pilot.

"Have the Avengers ever actually landed a Quinjet?"
STARFOX

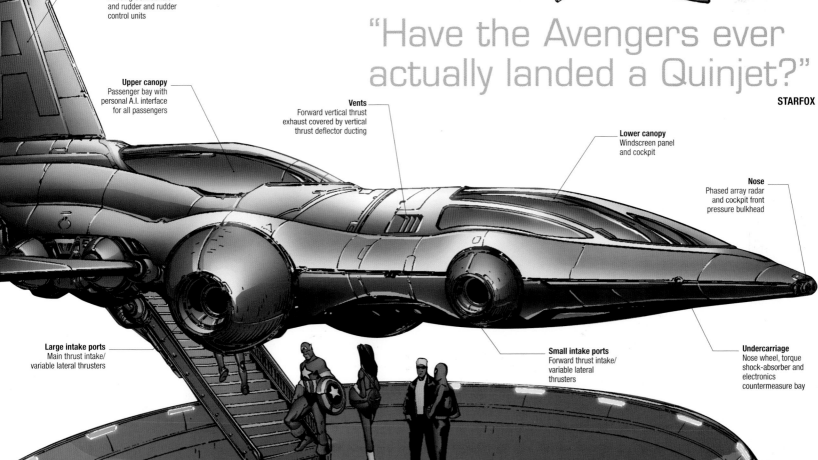

Tail
Housing SCM aerials and rudder and rudder control units

Upper canopy
Passenger bay with personal A.I. interface for all passengers

Vents
Forward vertical thrust exhaust covered by vertical thrust deflector ducting

Lower canopy
Windscreen panel and cockpit

Nose
Phased array radar and cockpit front pressure bulkhead

Large intake ports
Main thrust intake/variable lateral thrusters

Small intake ports
Forward thrust intake/variable lateral thrusters

Undercarriage
Nose wheel, torque shock-absorber and electronics countermeasure bay

GHOST RIDER'S VEHICLES

FIRST APPEARANCE *Marvel Spotlight* #5 (August 1972) **USED BY** Johnny Blaze, Daniel Ketch, Noble Kale, Alejandra Jones, Robbie Reyes

Johnny Blaze first rides a Harley Davidson. However, he eventually learns that he can conjure a motorcycle composed of flame and dark magic, thanks to his pact with Mephisto. In fact, all Ghost Riders, possessing truly supernatural powers as

the Spirit of Vengeance, can call forth a Hellcycle. Riding at over 180mph (290kph)—the fastest vehicle on wheels in the Marvel Universe—Ghost Rider can travel thousands of miles in a few hours without ever needing to stop for gas, as the bike runs on its own hellfire. The motorcycle is also able to ride over water, up walls, and can even maintain short bursts of flight.

Each Ghost Rider has had his or her own version of Hell on Wheels. Ghost Rider Daniel Ketch's Hellcycle features chains with shoge-like points at the end and a heavy, metal, skull-shaped windshield that can be used for defense or as a battering ram.

The most remarkable feature of Ketch's bike is its gas cap, which is the Medallion of Power that transforms him into Ghost Rider. In time, Ketch learns how to transform without this magic talisman.

The Spirit of Vengeance inhabiting Daniel Ketch is later revealed to be a spirit named Noble Kale (bound by his Warlock father to Mephisto's service in the 18th century). Kale separates from Ketch and has his own Hellcycle. Kale's Hellcycle is made of fire and takes the form of an early motorcycle when he is not transformed.

Michael Badilino aims to take down the demon Zarathos, whom he incorrectly believes has possessed Daniel Ketch. As Vengeance, he rides a shiny, chrome-

finished Hellcycle with a skeletal resemblance to a dragon with its mouth pouring out flames—these serve as the motorbike's wheels.

The Hellcycle of South American Alejandra Jones, the first female Ghost Rider, has a more sporty look and billows out hellfire.

Ghost Rider Robbie Reyes, unlike those before him, drives a customized hot rod that he "borrows" from the mechanic's shop where he works. This black, enflamed muscle car, known as a Hell Charger, is already souped-up, but Reyes' transformation into Ghost Rider takes it to new performance heights, thanks to an unending supply of hellfire fuel.

Draconic vengeance
Michael Badilino (a.k.a. Vengeance) rides his dragon-inspired motorcycle, complete with horn-like handlebars.

Heavy metal
Daniel Ketch protects his Hellcycle with a notable metal front plate that acts as a shield or battering ram.

Hell and back
Ghost Rider Johnny Blaze scorches the streets on his way to Earth, riding his motorcycle of Hellfire. Despite the constant burning, the steel frame, leather seat, and gas tank remain intact thanks to powerful, dark magic.

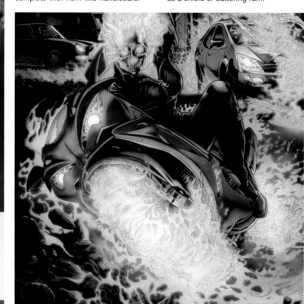

Easy rider
Alejandra Jones maneuvers with ease on her sporty and light Hellcycle, which enables even greater speed.

Ghost driver
Robbie Reyes becomes Ghost Rider because of this muscle car. It was pulled over by dealers, who gunned down Robbie for drugs hidden within it, only to have Robbie return, seeking revenge.

STARJAMMER

FIRST APPEARANCE *Thor* #212 (June 1973)
USED BY Thor

The *Starjammer* is literally a "space ship." Thor's magical Asgardian craft looks seaworthy, but it goes far beyond the watery main to traverse the galaxies. The wooden deck allows its occupants to breathe air, despite appearing open to the vacuum of space. The ship has accompanied Thor and the Asgardians on countless adventures.

The ship is badly damaged in the battle of Black Stars, when the giant Avalon Knight of the Inner Realm rips out its bottom and, later, in a skirmish with the Doomsday Star. Despite these mishaps, this mighty vessel continues to voyage to the stars and beyond.

SPIDER-MOBILE

FIRST APPEARANCE *Amazing Spider-Man* #130 (March 1974) **USED BY** Spider-Man

Desperately in need of funds, Peter Parker is duped into making a car for Corona Motors. Luckily, his friend Johnny Storm comes to the rescue with his mechanical expertise, helping Peter build a dune-buggy-style vehicle with plenty of special features. However, the villainous Tinkerer has other plans for it, and turns Spidey's own car against him. Luckily, Spider-Man is able to subdue the vehicle.

The Spider-Mobile is ultimately retired; a duplicate is placed in the Smithsonian, where it is openly mocked. The original Spider-Mobile later falls into the hands of the Merc with a Mouth, Deadpool, who turns it into his own "Dead-Buggy," complete with a new paintjob.

Peter Parker would go on to make a future incarnation of the Spider-Mobile, with a much sleeker look. This zero-emission dune buggy has heavy roll bars, front-mounted web-shooters under its flip-down headlights, a Spider-Signal projector, and a seat ejector mechanism.

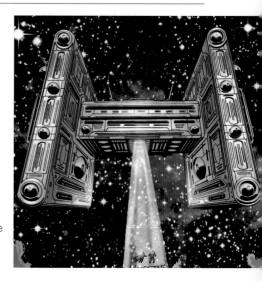

Take a long look
Spidey views his gleaming buggy-style Spider-Mobile designed by his friend Human Torch (Johnny Storm). Unfortunately, Spider-Man doesn't have a driver's license and has never learned to drive.

CAPTAIN AMERICA

FIRST APPEARANCE *Marvel Two-in-One* #5 (September 1974)
USED BY Guardians of the Galaxy 3000

The Guardians of the Galaxy of the year 3000 name their first starship the *U.S.S. Captain America* or simply the *Captain America* after Steve Rogers. Following the ship's destruction, they voyage in a new starship of similar specs called *Freedom's Lady*, also still sometimes called the *Captain America* or *Captain America II*. Both starships serve as the home base to these future Guardians of the Galaxy, floating in the orbit of planets and moons and waiting for trouble to arise. *Captain America II* is ultimately destroyed during a surprise attack by Tony Stark in 3014.

Friendly fire
The Guardians of the Galaxy team from the year 3014 attempt to outrun a ship named the *Stark*. Things quickly go wrong when the *Captain America* is asked to submit to "a-sentience" and the *Stark* takes aim.

PUNISHER'S BATTLE VAN

FIRST APPEARANCE *Giant-Size Spider-Man* #4 (April 1975) **USED BY** Punisher

The Punisher works with his partner the Mechanic to make a van to end all vans. This super-enhanced vehicle doesn't just have four-wheel drive, great suspension, roll bars, and bulletproof glass, it features a multitude of weaponry: a Gatling swivel gun, flamethrowers, a large-scale mechanical arm to deploy heavy weapons, and even a rocket launcher.

After the Mechanic is killed by the Vulture, the hacker Microchip creates a new and improved Battle Van, whose armaments include sonic weapons to take on the symbiote Venom. The Battle Van also has remote capabilities, allowing it to be used as a decoy or driven into battle from a safe distance.

SANCTUARY II

FIRST APPEARANCE *Warlock* #10 (December 1975) **USED BY** Thanos

The mad titan Thanos has had multiple *Sanctuary* starships, his favorite being the H-shaped *Sanctuary II*. The ship is equipped with an arsenal of super-advanced technology, including a tractor beam and a massive laser known as the Star-Burster. This formidable weapon is powered by a synthetic Infinity Stone called a Star Gem, which uses ion fusion to unbalance the equilibrium of a star. Complete destruction of the star is thus achieved in hours rather than thousands of years. With this ship and the Star-Burster, Thanos has destroyed a multitude of stars; however, the weapon's unique energy signature is also what first alerts the Avengers to the ship's existence.

> ## "I'm…sorry, Blackbird. I wish I could have thought of another way."
> **KITTY PRYDE**

BLACKBIRD

The X-Men's main air transport is a high-tech, customized stealth aircraft capable of incredible speeds and altitude. Its sleek, black fuselage makes it a design icon as well as a mechanical marvel.

FIRST APPEARANCE *X-Men* #104 (April 1977) **USED BY** X-Men

PROTECTING THE NEST

When the young Kitty Pryde is caught alone in the X-Men's mansion home by a terrifying N'Garai demon, she throws everything she has at it, but is flagging; then she comes up with a great idea. Earlier that day, she had been studying the Blackbird aircraft with Professor X, and she decides to lead the demon through an underground tunnel to the hangar where the aircraft is kept. Phasing into the Blackbird, Kitty runs through the ignition sequence, but hovers over the final button until the creature is right behind the afterburners… As she hammers her hand down on the switch, jets of flame shoot out of the exhaust, incinerating the N'Garai and saving the novice X-Man's life. However, survival comes at a cost; the blast waves created rebound onto the Blackbird and smash it into the wall. The undercarriage collapses and the craft is a write-off.

Master mechanic
Mutant mechanical genius Forge makes regular repairs and upgrades to the Blackbird, keeping it airworthy for the X-Men.

SUPER STEALTH

The X-Men's main air transport, the Blackbird is based on the SR-71, designed and built by Lockheed's secretive Advanced Development Programs division, the Skunk Works. The X-Men's version of this stealth aircraft has extra seating to accommodate a full team for missions. The Blackbird is capable of vertical takeoff and landing (VTOL) in order to operate in a variety of terrains. Its already bleeding-edge tech is upgraded further when Professor X returns from space with a cloaking device used by the Shi'ar, making the Blackbird virtually invisible to Earth's radar systems. Forge, whose mutant ability is an incredible flair for invention and mechanics, also makes improvements to the Blackbird during his time with the X-Men.

Out of control
The metal Blackbird is at the mercy of Magneto's magnetic powers as it plunges toward the ocean with its crew of X-Men.

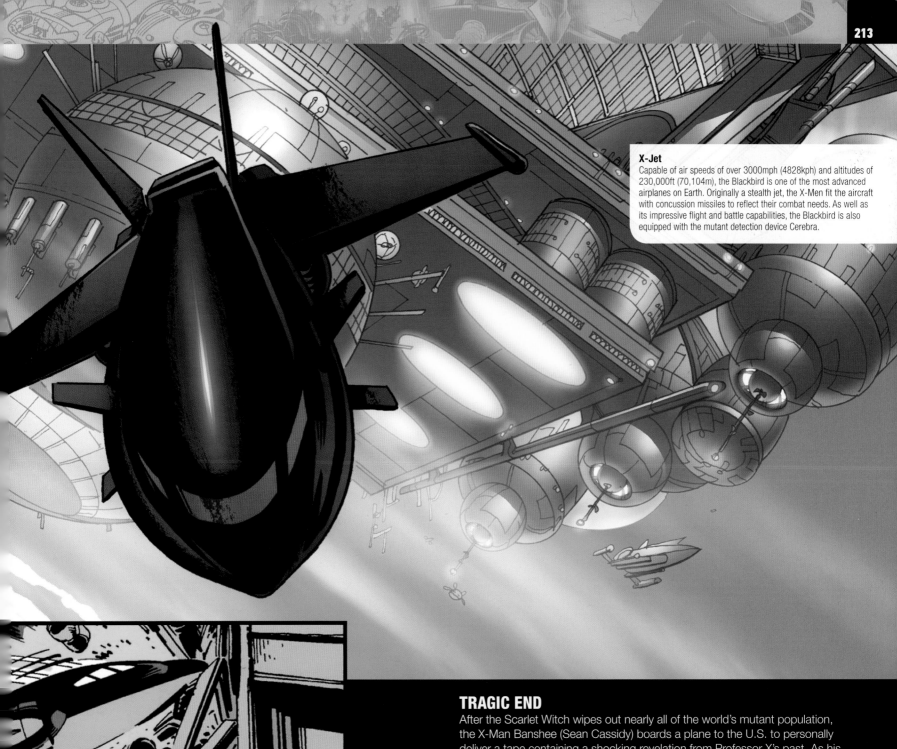

X-Jet
Capable of air speeds of over 3000mph (4828kph) and altitudes of 230,000ft (70,104m), the Blackbird is one of the most advanced airplanes on Earth. Originally a stealth jet, the X-Men fit the aircraft with concussion missiles to reflect their combat needs. As well as its impressive flight and battle capabilities, the Blackbird is also equipped with the mutant detection device Cerebra.

Blast off
Kitty Pryde remembers what Professor X taught her about the Blackbird, and uses the aircraft's engines at maximum power to take down an N'Garai demon.

TRAGIC END
After the Scarlet Witch wipes out nearly all of the world's mutant population, the X-Man Banshee (Sean Cassidy) boards a plane to the U.S. to personally deliver a tape containing a shocking revelation from Professor X's past. As his plane approaches Westchester Airport, the passengers glimpse another aircraft, seemingly on a collision course. Sean recognizes it as a Blackbird, and hurls himself out of a door to try and avert catastrophe with his sonic scream. For all his heroic efforts, Banshee cannot stop the hijacked Blackbird from colliding with the passenger jet. In the devastating explosion, Banshee is killed, along with everyone else on board.

DOWN NOT OUT
Despite the Blackbird's impressive offensive and defensive capabilities, it proves vulnerable to one foe in particular—Magneto. When the Master of Magnetism detects the aircraft heading for the island where he is holed up with a captive Scott Summers, he uses his powers to send the Blackbird into a dive toward the sea. The pilot, Storm, is rendered unconscious, and Colossus attempts to bring the Blackbird out of its dive, but only succeeds in bending the steering yoke. The Blackbird ends up submerged on the ocean floor, its passengers forced to swim to "safety" on Magneto's island. However, after danger has been averted, Colossus is able to salvage the aircraft, using his great strength to lift the Blackbird out of the water.

Death bird
The evil mutant Vulcan tries to stop Banshee delivering sensitive video footage to the X-Men by hijacking a Blackbird and sending it crashing into the airliner Banshee is traveling on.

DRYDOCK

FIRST APPEARANCE *Marvel Presents* #12 (August 1977) **USED BY** Guardians of the Galaxy 3000

Drydock is a Federation space station and training facility located in 31st-century Earth's solar system. When the Badoon invade, the onboard officers attempt to flee using the station's untested warp drive. Though the station is saved, the crew of thousands is killed by radiation. Charlie-27 and the Guardians of the Galaxy find the station but discover that Drydock's central computer has created a simulated crew to replace the originals. Their leader, Hollis-12, takes the Guardians hostage, but Charlie-27 destroys the central computer and frees his friends. The Guardians then use Drydock as their traveling base. Drydock is later transported back through time and destroyed by Korvac.

ROCKET RACER'S SKATEBOARD

FIRST APPEARANCE *Amazing Spider-Man* #172 (September 1977) **USED BY** Rocket Racer, Troy

Rocket Racer (Robert Farrell) flies on a dual-rocket skateboard which he controls via a cybernetic helmet. The magnetic board clings to his boots as he zooms acrobatically around the city. The skateboard can also adhere to vertical surfaces and overhangs, enabling travel in all directions. Farrell's original board gets an upgrade from the Tinkerer. The skateboard weighs 19lbs (8.6kg) and has a range of approximately 75 miles (120km), and a flight ceiling of up to 1,120ft (341m). The board varies from yellow to orange to red as an indication of its power charge level. A man named Troy befriends Farrell and steals the board, also using it to fight Spider-Man.

SKUTTLEBUTT

FIRST APPEARANCE *Thor* #337 (November 1983) **USED BY** Beta Ray Bill

Beta Ray Bill's *Skuttlebutt* is a sentient female battleship. It is capable of independent operation and making self-repairs. When his people, the Korbinites, charge him with finding them a new home, he uses *Skuttlebutt* to search the galaxy. However, when the ship encounters Thor, it confuses him with the fire demons that the Korbinites are fleeing. It attacks Thor, who pierces the hull and enters the ship. The ship wakes Bill from his stasis and the two heroes begin to duel—a misunderstanding that is settled peacefully. The ship has heavy armor and energy shielding. The advanced weaponry includes fusion mines and turret cannons.

SKY CYCLE

FIRST APPEARANCE *Hawkeye* #1 (September 1983) **USED BY** Hawkeye

Hawkeye drives a voice-operated Sky-Cycle with hands-free steering. This allows him to shoot arrows in mid-flight. His first Sky-Cycle is destroyed in battle. When Hawkeye heads the West Coast Avengers, Jorge Latham from Cross Technological Industries builds new models for him, which he keeps at the Avengers Compound. Several other Avengers, including Captain America, also fly a variety of cycle models. The early models may fly up to 380mph (612kph) and up to an elevation of 12,000ft (3,858m). Since the operators cannot fly themselves, Sky-Cycles are equipped with parachutes and some have matching helmets.

SMARTSHIP FRIDAY

FIRST APPEARANCE *Power Pack* #1 (August 1984) **USED BY** Aelfyre Whitemane, Power Pack

The *Smartship Friday* is a sentient starship belonging to a Kymellian xenologist named Aelfyre Whitemane. *Friday* is named after a character in Daniel Defoe's *Robinson Crusoe*. The ship's weaponry is limited, relying on enhanced maneuverability as a defense. Whitemane sacrifices his life in order to save a family of children soon known as the Power Pack. *Friday* then teams up with the children, but also goes on adventures alone. On one occasion, while rescuing the Emperor Bhadsha of the Zn'rx race on Snarkworld, *Friday* crashes and is nearly obliterated. The Power Pack salvages *Friday*'s brain, however, and they install it in an even more advanced ship.

CAPTAIN AMERICA'S VAN

FIRST APPEARANCE *Captain America* #318 (June 1986) **USED BY** Captain America

Captain America's Chevrolet van is customized by the Wakanda Design Group. The interior houses his motorcycle, a computer system with a satellite uplink to the S.H.I.E.L.D. Helicarrier, and a sleeping area. From the outside, the van looks ordinary, but it is coated in a special crystal film that allows Cap to instantly change the color via a dashboard menu system. He can even use the vehicle's external camera to scan and match the color of other nearby cars. The van can also alternate license plates at the flip of a switch. All of this allows him to travel incognito. Recent additions include GPS and self-driving features.

"...I wasn't expecting you to customize my Chevy van to fit my requirements so quickly!"

CAPTAIN AMERICA

Fully loaded
Cap's unremarkable-looking van is a handy way to transport his distinctive, customized, Harley-Davidson motorbike.

ROVER

FIRST APPEARANCE *West Coast Avengers* #21 (June 1987) **USED BY** Hank Pym

Rover is a vehicle designed by Hank Pym that he actually carries in his own pocket. Much like him, Rover can change size as needed. Pym creates the ship while a member of the West Coast Avengers, soon after Bonita Juarez saves him from a suicide attempt. Rover is designed with an artificial intelligence module, but limited to the intelligence of a dog, to prevent it from becoming another diabolical Ultron-like android. Nonetheless, it is capable of speech. The vehicle has a cockpit with two seats, and guns that shoot acid, flames, and gas. It has the ability to take off and land vertically, as well as fly, climb buildings, and capture objects with grappling arms.

S.H.I.E.L.D. SHUTTLE

FIRST APPEARANCE *X-Force* #20 (March 1993) **USED BY** S.H.I.E.L.D.

The S.H.I.E.L.D. shuttle *Sor-One* is similar to a N.A.S.A. space shuttle. It is flown by G.W. Bridge, Nick Fury, Network Nina and Alexander Pierce to intercept the *Graymalkin* (Cable's personal space station, which is controlled by an A.I. called "Professor"). When *Graymalkin* fakes its own destruction to throw S.H.I.E.L.D. off, Lila Cheney teleports the team back to their shuttle. Years later, the Illuminati employs a S.H.I.E.L.D. shuttle to send Hulk out into space. Sakaaran Imperials confiscate the ship when Hulk lands on their planet. The warp core later explodes and kills millions of inhabitants, including Hulk's wife, Caiera.

Assault on *Graymalkin*
Ready for trouble *(left to right)*: agents G.W. Bridge, Alexander Pierce, Network Nina, and Nick Fury aboard S.H.I.E.L.D. shuttle *Sor-One*.

MIDNIGHT RUNNER

FIRST APPEARANCE *Excalibur* #86 (February 1995) **USED BY** Charles Xavier, Captain Britain, Excalibur

Designed by Brian Braddock (Captain Britain), the *Midnight Runner* is a supersonic jet vehicle intended to swiftly transport Excalibur from its Scottish base on remote Muir Island to wherever danger looms. The ship is a long-range, air-turbo-fan-powered transport, capable of many times the speed of sound. It is equipped with an on-board computer guidance system, based on Shi'ar technology. Braddock also fits the *Midnight Runner* with the latest stealth and anti-surveillance technologies, including electronic detection, sound baffles, and a cloaking device that provides camouflage while in flight or when grounded.

LEAPFROG

FIRST APPEARANCE *Runaways* #15 (July 2004) **USED BY** The Pride, Runaways

Built by Super Villains Janet and Victor Stein, the Leapfrog is initially utilized by criminal cadre the Pride in Los Angeles. The Steins' son, Chase, steals the vehicle and turns it into a mobile refuge for his young friends the Runaways.

A compact, multi-purpose transport with an A.I. personality, Leapfrog can fly at high speeds, navigate at great depths in water, and tackle difficult terrain by walking or making prodigious leaps. It can also travel through time.

The original Leapfrog is destroyed when a drone destroys the Runaways' base, but the team salvage the operating system and install it into one of the fleet of spare Leapfrogs.

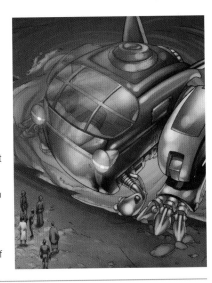

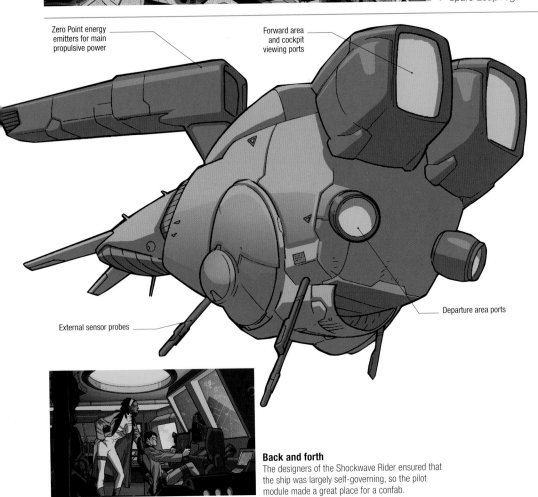

Zero Point energy emitters for main propulsive power

Forward area and cockpit viewing ports

External sensor probes

Departure area ports

Back and forth
The designers of the Shockwave Rider ensured that the ship was largely self-governing, so the pilot module made a great place for a confab.

X-BUG

FIRST APPEARANCE *Uncanny X-Men* #476 (September 2006) **USED BY** Davan Shakari, Professor X, X-Men

The X-Bug is a modified Shi'ar star cruiser assigned to spy Davan Shakari. On the orders of the deranged Emperor D'Ken, he is stationed on Earth for years and given the long-range scout ship as a means of emergency evacuation. An exploratory vessel with no armaments, the spacecraft relies on its suite of long-range sensors and cloaking devices to conceal itself from prying eyes. Its jump-engines are capable of intra-system travel via the Shi'ar's network of stargates. The cruiser eventually crashes on Earth when bringing Professor X and a force of X-Men back from the Shi'ar Imperium.

THUNDERSTRIKE

FIRST APPEARANCE *Thunderbolts* #130 (May 2009) **USED BY** Thunderbolts

When Norman Osborn becomes the U.S.'s new Head of Metahuman Security, the former Green Goblin replaces S.H.I.E.L.D. with H.A.M.M.E.R. and, among other sweeping changes, officially closes down U.S. government penal brigade the Thunderbolts. Osborn secretly repurposes the team as his personal black ops squad, supplying them with a new jet transport vehicle.

The Thunderstrike is a heavily armed and armored jet-powered assault plane. It is a modified upgrade of the Thunderbolts' previous craft, a fast-strike Zeus fighter transport. Supplied by Oscorp factories, the Thunderstrike is maintained by Osborn's personal staff at the top-secret Thunderbolts' base, the Cube.

SHOCKWAVE RIDER

FIRST APPEARANCE *Nextwave* #1 (March 2006) **USED BY** H.A.T.E., Nextwave

When the Super Hero team Nextwave discovers that their parent agency H.A.T.E. (the Highest Anti-Terrorism Effort)—is being controlled by the same evil organization— the Beyond Corporation—they have been tasked with investigating, they go rogue. They declare their independence by stealing their employers' top-secret prototype air transport; the Shockwave Rider.

This cutting-edge aircraft is powered by a fuel system, the Zero Point Squirt Drive, that provides infinite energy for propulsion and a dazzling array of innovative weaponry and defensive technologies. The Shockwave Rider also carries a full complement of exotic devices and hand weapons, including Personal Flight Harnesses.

The Shockwave Rider is larger on the inside than its external proportions suggest. The interior is fitted with five trans-dimensional Tesseract Zones, allowing for the storage and easy shipping of an array of vehicles and combat gear for its rebellious new owners—former Avenger Monica Rambeau, Machine Man Aaron Stack, monster hunter Elsa Bloodstone, rogue mutant Tabitha "Boom Boom" Smith, and all-purpose secret hero the Captain.

The ship is largely self-piloting and capable of high and low-altitude maneuvers more commonly associated with fighter jets than large transport craft. The Shockwave Rider is also programmed with self-diagnostic and repair systems, which allow it, with the cybernetic assistance of Machine Man, to repair itself after being blown out of the skies by H.A.T.E.'s flying weapons platform the Aeromarine. The Shockwave Rider's valiant service comes to a glorious end when it is caught in devastating crossfire during the Nextwave heroes' assault of State 51, the Beyond Corporation's colossal aerial terror-factory.

BEA ARTHUR

FIRST APPEARANCE *Prelude to Deadpool Corps* #5 (May 2010) **USED BY** Deadpool Corps

When a cosmic cult is made aware of a forthcoming crisis by their patron deity—Elder of the Universe, the Contemplator—they gather a quintet of Deadpools from five alternative Earths and hire them to deal with it.

The Contemplator's representatives provide the Deadpool Corps—mouthy mercenaries Wade Wilson of the Marvel Universe Earth, Lady Deadpool, Dogpool, Kidpool, and the disembodied zombie Headpool—with an intergalactic starship, modified to their various needs. Wade Wilson names the spacecraft after his

favorite movie actress, and directs the *Bea Arthur* into a confrontation with a nebulous but highly voracious force known as "The Awareness"—a cloud that consumes intelligence and enslaves victims on a planetary scale.

The *Bea Arthur* is a real "gas-guzzler" and needs frequent and expensive refuelling; however, it does come with individual armories and customized weapons for each Deadpool. Although the ship is fast and agile, with standard defenses and energy ordnance, the Contemplator's disciples omitted to include escape pods or hidden smugglers' compartments, to Wilson's annoyance. Even after succeeding in their mission and being paid handsomely, the group's

problems don't end there. The *Bea Arthur*'s databanks contain no record of Earth, so the trip home turns into a game of "hunt the planet."

At least the journey leads to some more profitable, slaughter-filled gigs for the Deadpool Corps and, eventually, each team member finds his or her way back home. However, Lady Deadpool stays with the ship and becomes involved in an alternate-reality vendetta, in which an evil Deadpool Corps attempts to eradicate every Deadpool in the Multiverse.

The *Bea Arthur* meets an unfortunate end when Lady Deadpool heroically pilots the ship into the head of ultimate planet-eater Galactipool, killing this ravenous cosmic scourge.

Supreme sacrifice
Set to implode on impact, the *Bea Arthur*'s Multiversal Jump Engines prove powerful enough to decapitate cosmic devourer Galactipool and save a legion of alternate-Earth Deadpools from obliteration.

LILANDRA

FIRST APPEARANCE *Infinity* #2 (November 2013) **USED BY** Shi'ar

The *Lilandra* is a modified Shi'ar battle cruiser named in honour of Princess-Majestrix Lilandra Neramani, hereditary ruler of the Shi'ar's galaxy-spanning empire, until her assassination by the usurper Vulcan.

Although a standard, intergalactic warship, the *Lilandra* is the flagship of Majestor Kallark—formerly Imperial Guard Praetor and super-guardian Gladiator—and plays a pivotal role in the Galactic Council's opposition to the invading armada of the primordial Builders, seeking to eradicate all life between them and their ultimate target: Earth. The exact details of the crew are classified but the usual contingent consists of thousands of personnel; military staff, medical teams, science researchers, and diplomatic operatives drawn from every planet in the empire.

Since the first ship of her class was destroyed by the Phoenix

while defending the doomed planet D'Bari, the *Lilandra* has frequently been refitted and upgraded. As with all current Shi'ar technology, the ship's processing systems and computers are fully sentient, enabling the *Lilandra* to utilize a vast and comprehensive suite of long-range sensors with a staggering degree of range and accuracy.

The warship is also equipped with solid-light hologram projectors, faster-than-light Insta-Link communications systems, fully equipped science labs, manufacturing stations, and an armory. The *Lilandra* is capable of both sustained superluminal travel through normal space and interstellar or intergalactic teleportation via Stargate technology.

She carries standard Shi'ar defensive systems, such as cloaking devices, layered energy screens, and force fields, while offensive ordnance includes batteries of energy weapons, plasma bolts, and Starcracker technology—an ultimate weapon that causes stars to explode into supernovas.

LIFE RAFT

FIRST APPEARANCE *Free Comic Book Day: Secret Wars* (May 2015) **USED BY** Future Foundation

Designed and built by the young geniuses of Reed Richards' Future Foundation, the Life Raft is intended to ensure the future survival of humanity through an assortment of Super Heroes and Foundation children.

When the Marvel Universe Earth collides with Earth-1610, existence ends and the Raft materializes inside Doctor Doom's composite Battleworld planet—created from collected fragments of many divergent realities. Simultaneously, a duplicate Life Raft makes the same journey from Earth-1610. Built from stolen copies of the Foundation's designs, it carries the murderous Cabal and Reed Richards' evil doppelganger the Maker.

Flying fortress
Despite their vast size, immense power, and state-of-the-art technologies, starships such as the *Lilandra* were actually quite fragile constructions in which to brave the myriad perils lurking in the gulfs of deep space.

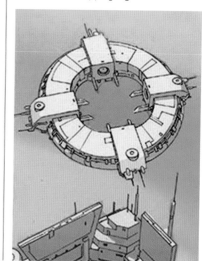

HELL ON WHEELS

'It's working! A stream of fire from my finger– creating a–flaming motorcycle!"

GHOST RIDER

Ghost Rider escapes Satan and strands himself in the Arizona desert, where he learns to manifest a motorcycle made of hellfire!

Witch-Woman, a Native American named Linda Littletrees who is Satanically possessed, drags Ghost Rider Johnny Blaze down to Hell leaving behind his girlfriend Rocky (Roxanne Simpson) who is beset by a biker gang. Meanwhile in Hell, Satan hungers for Ghost Rider's soul and orders his minions to attack. Ghost Rider fight demons and monsters to get free, but is no match for Satan. Daimon Hellstrom, Son of Satan, finds Rocky, who tells him of Ghost Rider's plight. Knowing his father's ways, Hellstrom transports himself to Hell. Using his sacred trident to ward off Satan's attacks, Hellstrom frees Ghost Rider and Witch Woman. Daimon then transports them both to the Arizona desert and leaves them there.

NIGHT RIDER
Stranded in the desert without Johnny's motorcycle, Witch Woman teaches Ghost Rider to focus his powers. Concentrating so hard he feels his brain will burst, Ghost Rider manifests a motorcycle of hellfire. Witch Woman cannot use the motorcycle as it is only tangible for those with Satanic powers, so Ghost Rider rides alone, as fast he can to find and rescue Rocky. As he barrels along the highway, the sunrise transforms Ghost Rider back into his human form and Johnny Blaze goes flying into the air. He's badly injured, but alive.

Johnny has learned the hard way that his hellfire motorcycle has a limitation: it is only tangible until daybreak, when Ghost Rider turns back into Johnny Blaze. Nevertheless, his fiery bike will prove vital to his role as the vengeful Ghost Rider.

Nothing happening
Urged on by Witch Woman, Ghost Rider Johnny Blaze gives it all that he's got to manifest

One hot ride
His brain "reeling with exhaustion," Johnny Blaze
creates his super-powered hellfire motorcycle.
In the future, Johnny will be able to manifest his
flame bike with comparative ease—on one
occasion even as he falls through the air.

WEAPONS AND TECHNOLOGY

Those heroes who aren't born with super-powers must look to science and technology for an advantage. Some have their DNA altered by secret serums. Others employ technology made from the rarest of metals to get an edge.

For ordinary humans who dream of becoming a *Homo superior* or gaining an incredible super-power, there are plenty of experimental formulas and scientific processes to choose from. A Super-Soldier serum will transform any average Joe into the peak of physical perfection. Pym Particles bring about amazing size changes. Gamma radiation may endow recipients with unfathomable strength and striking skin colorations. An extra-long lifespan and youth is guaranteed to those who take the Infinity Formula, while cloning can give anyone a second chance at life. However, the Lizard and Goblin formulas produce monstrous results and should only be sampled by those whose ambitions truly know no bounds.

If physical transformation doesn't do the trick, battle suits are an option. War Machine armor, Iron Man's suits, and Iron Spider armor gives the wearer a big advantage in a fight. However, some heroes forego armor for increased mobility. They depend on special weapons, like Captain America's shield or Hawkeye's bow and arrows. In addition, companies operating at the cutting edge of science and technology, such as Parker Industries, Stark Industries, A.I.M., the Rand Corporation, Alchemax, and other labs provide a constant stream of gadgets, gear, and tech for heroes and villains alike.

Tough stuff
Captain America's shield is made from the strongest metal known. With enough force, it can bust through just about anything.

Blunt force
Rogers can charge with his shield, using the center as an indestructible battering ram

CAPTAIN AMERICA'S SHIELD

FIRST APPEARANCE *Captain America Comics* #2 (April 1941) **USED BY** Captain America, Sam Wilson, Winter Soldier, John Walker, William Burnside, William Nasland, Cable, Nomad, Patriot, Major Victory

Captain America's almost indestructible shield is his own iconic symbol and a superb defensive—and handy offensive —weapon. One of a kind and incredibly valuable, Cap's shield is a prize coveted by many of his adversaries.

The U.S. government contracts Dr. Myron MacLain to invent a new indestructible armor for its tanks during World War II. Using an experimental alloy of Vibranium, steel, and an unknown ingredient, he creates a tank hatch of unmatched strength. Unfortunately, MacLain is unable to duplicate this technological breakthrough as he falls asleep at the crucial moment. He wakes to discover successful results, but without having observed the whole process. The final hatch has a diameter of 2.5ft (0.76m), depth of 3.5in (8.9cm), and weighs 12lbs (5.4kg). Painted with titanium dioxide, it is presented to Steve Rogers by President Franklin D. Roosevelt, and becomes Captain America's iconic shield.

However, Steve Rogers isn't the only hero to wield the shield. John Walker

Shield shape
During his career, Cap has used shields made of various materials and in different shapes. His very first shield is triangular, and a later version can be split in two. Others are made of Adamantium, Vibranium, and even photonic energy.

(a.k.a U.S.Agent), William Burnside, William Nasland, Bucky Barnes (a.k.a Winter Soldier), and Sam Wilson (a.k.a Falcon) have all filled in for Rogers as Captain America—taking up his heroic mantle as well as the shield. Additionally, Cable, Ian Zola (Nomad), Jeffrey Mace (Patriot), and Vance Astro (Major Victory) have been among those to use the iconic shield for brief but significant periods.

The shield's strength is unmatched. It can absorb most energy blasts and even Magneto's powers over magnetism have no effect upon it. Cap can use the shield to break his fall and also as a powerful throwing weapon. That said, the shield isn't invincible. It is destroyed more than once, but fortunately there's always a supernatural solution available to repair it. For instance, when the shield is destroyed during the Winter Soldier's time wielding it as Captain America, Asgardian smiths re-forge it with the addition of the Asgardian Uru metal—thereby strengthening the shield even more.

Projectile
The rim of Cap's shield is dangerous when thrown and requires skill to wield it with appropriate force

"I consider it a part of me, Thor. Much as you do your hammer, I'd wager."

STEVE ROGERS

Caught off guard
During the Fear Itself event, the Serpent shatters Cap's shield with his bare hands. It is later repaired by Asgardian dwarves—with added ingredients to enhance its strength. A blemish remains on the shield, and though Tony Stark offers to remove it, Cap declines, saying it will give the shield added character.

SUPER-SOLDIER SERUM

FIRST APPEARANCE *Captain America Comics* #1 (March 1941) **USED BY** Steve Rogers, Luke Cage, Sentry, Black Widow, Mockingbird, Red Skull, Spider-Queen

The first known recipient of a Super-Soldier serum is Steve Rogers (Captain America). Developed by Dr. Abraham Erskine as part of the U.S. military's Operation: Rebirth, the formula transforms Rogers from a feeble young man to a physically perfect soldier. Moments after administering the serum, Erskine is murdered by a Nazi spy. Without any record of the formula, Operation: Rebirth is unable to produce additional Super-Soldiers. However, both the U.S. government and the Nazi regime continue to attempt to recreate the serum— with mixed results.

After initial work as a surgeon in Vietnam for the U.S. Army, Dr. Noah Burstein develops an Electro-Biochemical System. He experiments on a subject in Seagate Prison: Carl Lucas (later known as Luke Cage). Sadistic prison guard Albert Rackham meddles with the process in an attempt to harm Lucas— managing to accelerate Lucas'

Bottoms up!
After he fails the physical tests required to join the military, Steve Rogers takes the serum, ready to serve his country.

transformation into a Super-Soldier.

A number of other agents have also received varieties of Super-Soldier serums. When Red Skull is exposed to a Super-Soldier serum, for a while he acquires super-strength and endurance. Adriana Soria (Spider-Queen) receives a Super-Soldier serum as part of the World War II U.S. Marines' Operation: Crossroads. Black Widow receives a special serum from the Soviet Black Widow Ops program, ensuring peak physical condition and granting her longevity. Barbara Morse (Mockingbird) is injected with a mix of Super-Soldier serum and Infinity Formula to save her life. Canada's Department K builds on the research of Operation: Rebirth, which allows Dr. Cornelius Worth to create a serum more powerful than a thousands suns. This transforms Robert Reynolds into the all-powerful Sentry.

Vita-rays
After he takes the serum, Steve Rogers is bombarded by vita-rays, which activate the formula and speed up the transformation process.

Super success
The results of the process are even better than expected. It transforms Rogers into a prime physical specimen and gives the U.S. military hope.

Paying the price
Hank's Pym Particles endow him with abilities that make him a valuable member of the Avengers, but there are costly side-effects.

PYM PARTICLES

FIRST APPEARANCE *Tales to Astonish* #27 (January 1962) **USED BY** Hank Pym, Janet van Dyne, Scott Lang, Cassie Lang, Reed Richards, Shrunken Bones, Porcupine, Nadia Pym

Doctor Henry "Hank" Pym discovers a group of subatomic particles that can change the size of any object, including living beings. With his Pym Particles, Hank alters his own size by moving mass through the Kosmos Dimension. Pym Particles also allow him to visit extra dimensions, such as the Microverse, Underverse, and Oververse.

Pym Particles can be absorbed via a liquid or gas. Hank Pym creates a suit to help regulate them and their size-changing effects. Prolonged exposure to Pym Particles causes the body to accumulate them naturally, leading to the ability to change size at will without a dose of particles. However, using the particles to dramatically change size can also put undue strain on a person's mind. Hank Pym discovers this after he suffers

from a series of nervous breakdowns.

Other heroes who use Pym Particles include Pym's future partner and wife, Janet van Dyne (Wasp) and daughter Nadia (who also takes the codename Wasp). Hawkeye spends time as the giant Goliath and retains a supply of Pym Particles in one of his arrows as backup. Scott Lang steals Pym's old Ant-Man suit and Pym allows him to retain it and use the Ant-Man identity, on condition that he devotes himself to fighting crime.

However, using Pym Particles can have unfortunate results. Scientist Jerry Morgan (Shrunken Bones) manages to use Pym Particles to shrink his skull, but the flesh surrounding it remains the same size—leading to a truly bizarre appearance. Alexander Gentry (Porcupine) is lost after using stolen Pym Particles taken from Ant-Man, and shrinks to microscopic size. In addition, Mr. Fantastic Reed Richards makes his own supply of Pym Particles and uses them to shrink the entire population of the doomed Planet X to enable the people to escape its destruction. However, when Richards delivers them to their new homeworld, he cannot restore them to normal size.

Always experimenting
Hank's experiments with Pym Particles lead to many surprising results. Getting the parameters just right takes much trial and error.

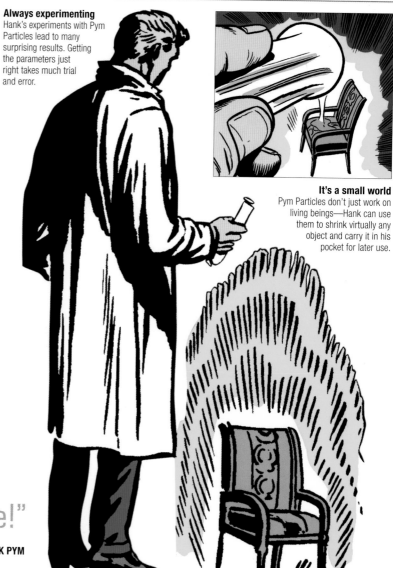

It's a small world
Pym Particles don't just work on living beings—Hank can use them to shrink virtually any object and carry it in his pocket for later use.

"It's shrinking me so fast, I can see myself change!"

HANK PYM

ANT-MAN'S TECHNOLOGY

FIRST APPEARANCE *Tales to Astonish* #35 (September 1962) **USED BY** Henry Pym, Janet van Dyne, Scott Lang, Eric O'Grady

After isolating Pym Particles, which enable him to alter the size of objects, brilliant scientist Hank Pym becomes the Super Hero Ant-Man and creates many gadgets to augment his war against crime. Moreover, after co-founding the Avengers, Pym becomes painfully aware that working alongside gods, monsters, and futuristically armored knights, he desperately needs ways to match their sheer power. Pym Particles are originally held in a solution that turns to gas on exposure to air; this method of ingestion is soon replaced by carefully measured capsule doses. Stored in a spring-loaded belt, they allow Pym to alter his dimensions instantly. As his body becomes saturated with the particles, Pym is able to change size by mental command transmitted through cybernetic circuitry in his mask.

Fit for purpose
Scott Lang's latest suit upgrades include sound amplification systems and voice modulators in the helmet, and bio-electric blasters in his gauntlets.

> # "Stop him, my pets! Obey your Leader! The Ant-Man commands you!"
> **ANT-MAN**

This miracle of printed circuits starts life as a bulky, electronics-laced helmet designed to give Pym the ability to command ants and other insects. When it is worn with his reinforced, steel-woven-mesh and unstable molecules uniform, the helmet affords a great degree of physical protection; however, its primary purpose is to receive, decode, and transmit communications from insects. Later versions are fitted with chemical filters and an oxygen supply.

In order to give Ant-Man greater mobility, Pym builds a computerized, compressed-air catapult to blast him across the city, and devises high-tension springs for his boots. He later adds a jet-pack to his ant suit.

As Giant-Man and Goliath, Pym becomes intoxicated by his own strength, despite the physical stress constant size-changing wreaks upon his body, and sidelines his innovations. After developing the identity of Yellowjacket,

however, Pym returns to his drawing board to augment his size-reduction and insect-control powers with mechanical wings that provide speedy flight. His gauntlets generate bio-electric stingers, which he supplements with a nerve-paralyzing, cellular-disruptor pistol.

When reformed criminal Scott Lang burglarizes his home, Pym allows him to take an early, gas-equipped suit and carry on as a new Ant-Man. Lang, an engineer, later modifies the suit with Pym's help.

Abandoning costumed heroics, Henry becomes a scientific adventurer with the West Coast Avengers, using Pym Particles to store an arsenal of gadgets in his clothes. He utilizes an A.I.-enabled, all-terrain flying vehicle named Rover, outfitted with flamethrowers, gas guns, and acid sprayers. Pym later builds a G.I. Ant-Man suit for S.H.I.E.L.D., combining his shrinking technologies and insect-control systems with enhanced armor, bionic extra limbs, and boot jets.

Micro mismanagement
Pym's S.H.I.E.L.D. ant suit is intended to facilitate cutting edge espionage, but low-level agent Eric O'Grady uses it for cheap voyeurism and petty theft.

One size fits all
Although Size-Capsule belts instantly deliver a vast selection of different sizes, the fashion-conscious Wasp thinks they are the ugliest accessories she has ever seen.

What's bugging you?
Through his helmet's cybernetic commands, Pym is able to use the ant population as an early warning system, alerting him to impending danger.

Fight or flight?
Ant-Man's rocket gear provides greater speed and range, but only by sacrificing the crucial maneuverability in combat afforded by flying ants or artificial wings.

Under pressure
The Air Jet Catapult is quickly superseded by other transport systems because it takes too long to aim and has a very limited range.

Spring into action
Ant-Man's boot coils extend his reach and range in battle, and are tremendous fun to use.

GAMMA RADIATION

FIRST APPEARANCE *Incredible Hulk* #1 (May 1962) **USED BY** Bruce Banner, Rick Jones, Emil Blonsky, Samuel Sterns (The Leader), Leonard Samson, Jennifer Walters, Aleksei Sytsevich (Rhino), Thaddeus Ross, Betty Ross, Walter Langowski, Skaar, Amadeus Cho, Agent Pratt, Todd Ziller

Gamma rays are a form of penetrating electromagnetic radiation of the type which results from the radioactive decay of atomic nuclei consisting of high-energy photons. Their capacity to cause organic mutations is unknown until physicist Doctor Robert Bruce Banner is caught in the blast of his own Gamma Bomb, built for the U.S. military. Banner suffers a series of bodily transformations. These mostly manifest as various super-muscular avatars popularly designated as "Incredible Hulks," in colors ranging from gray to green.

Every iteration reflects a different emotional state, leading to the theory that exposure to Gamma rays carries a psychological or psycho-active component: as if the human subconscious can dictate in part how each victim transforms. Whereas Banner's changes are linked to his Multiple Personality Disorder, uneducated laborer Samuel Sterns becomes a mega-intellect after he is dosed with Gamma rays.

Many humans (known as mutates) have been temporarily or permanently altered by exposure to Gamma rays. They were originally characterized by green skin or green-hued features, such as hair or eyes, and most had immense strength or hugely distorted features. However, recent exposures have resulted in a profusion of rainbow-colored mutates.

> "I must be sure every precaution has been taken!! We are tampering with powerful forces!"
>
> **DR. BRUCE BANNER**

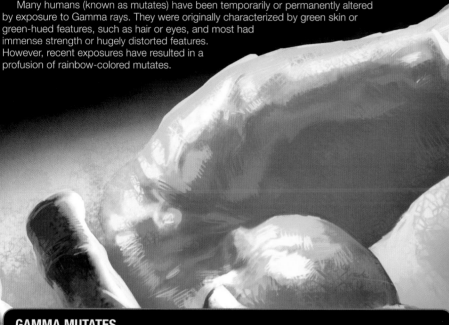

GAMMA MUTATES

The Hulk Bruce Banner's explosive exposure to gamma rays opens a Pandora's box of psychologically afflicted monsters and super-geniuses, some of whom are friends and some of whom are foes to mankind.

 • **Red Hulk** General Thaddeus Ross is resurrected by his enemies and turned into a super-strong, dynamo of aggression. He is able to absorb radiation and energy.

 • **Abomination** Murderous spy Emil Blonsky is transformed into the super-strong Abomination after accidental exposure to Banner's gamma machines.

 • **She-Hulk** Jennifer Walters turns into a super-strong troubleshooter after receiving an emergency blood transfusion from her cousin, Doctor Bruce Banner.

 • **The Leader** Cleaner Samuel Sterns develops an insatiable thirst for knowledge, a giant green head, and a hunger for conquest after being exposed to Gamma waste.

 • **Red She-Hulk** Betty Ross-Banner is murdered by the irradiated Abomination and resurrected by the Intelligencia as a rage-fueled scarlet servant, before breaking free.

 • **Savage She-Hulk** Lyra is created by future-Femizon Thundra, who mixes her genetic material with the Hulk's to produce the mightiest daughter of her single-sex race.

 • **Skaar** The son of Hulk and Caiera the Oldstrong derives his immense strength from his father's genes and his alien mother's Old Power which grants him geomorphic control.

 • **Doc Samson** Leonard Samson uses siphoned radiation from Bruce Banner to create a weaker, but more manageable, gamma-fueled, green-haired gargantuan.

 • **Rhino** Russian thug Aleksei Sytsevich is given superhuman strength and invulnerability through being dosed with gamma rays over a period of several months.

 • **A-Bomb** Rick Jones is deliberately mutated into a blue-skinned abomination by M.O.D.O.K. and the Intelligencia in their quest to create a slave Hulk with limited speech.

 • **Amadeus Cho (Hulk)** The smartest boy on Earth consciously turns himself into a Totally Awesome Hulk by absorbing the radiation overdose that is killing his friend Bruce Banner.

 • **Maestro** This evil, far-future iteration of Bruce Banner from Earth-9200 is as strong as any of his younger selves, but has the mind of a pleasure-seeking, sadistic manipulator.

> "It seems that every masked, unusual criminal... tries to attack my weapons factory sooner or later!"
> **TONY STARK**

STARK INDUSTRIES

For more than a century Stark Industries has been at the cutting edge in science and business, building better tomorrows and opening new frontiers for mankind in peace and in war.

FIRST APPEARANCE Tales of Suspense #48 (December 1963) **LOCATION** Global **AFFILIATIONS** Avengers, S.H.I.E.L.D. **SUBSIDIARIES** Stark International, Stane International, Circuits Maximus, Stark Enterprises, Stark-Fujikawa, Stark Innovations, Stark Resilient, Stark Solutions

A FAMILY BUSINESS

Stark Enterprises is founded by Isaac Stark Sr. in the 19th century. He specializes in engineering solutions for security problems and becomes fascinated with new discoveries in electricity. It remains a small but prosperous family business until World War II, when Howard Stark repurposes the company as an armaments manufacturer. From his factory site on Long Island, New York, Stark designs weapons and military material unlike anything seen before. Howard's brilliance and maverick attitude carry him into the highest strata of U.S. intelligence, where he befriends living legends such as Captain America, Nick Fury, and the Howling Commandos. Howard's technological wizardry makes Stark Industries crucial to U.S. security and an indispensable contributor to the country's arsenal.

Isaac Stark
A statue of Isaac Stark Sr. stands proudly in the grounds of Stark Industries' factory in Tokyo.

Worldbeater
Fueled by Tony Stark's tireless innovating, Stark International provides jobs for thousands of people all over the planet.

GOING GLOBAL

Howard and his wife Maria die in a traffic accident, and their son Tony carries on the family tradition for inventiveness and raw ambition. He is even more ingenious and patriotic and his creations utterly revolutionize military thinking. The company is pivotal in the reformation and equipping of security agency S.H.I.E.L.D. Stark Industries becomes an international player—a powerful corporation with branches in 30 countries. However, when Tony Stark abruptly abandons weapons-making and moves the company into peaceful disciplines such as global aerospace, renewable energy research, space exploration, and consumer electronics, he makes many enemies in the government.

BITTER RIVALS

Stark Industries is briefly shut down by U.S. Senator Byrd, who investigates Tony for possible treason. S.H.I.E.L.D.— the company's biggest client for advanced weapons and computer systems—engages in a covert hostile takeover to wrest control from Stark and ensure an uninterrupted supply of ordnance. When Tony Stark succumbs to alcoholism, control of the company is stolen from him by business rival Obadiah Stane. The new Stane International eagerly pursues profitable military contracts and corrupts Stark's greatest work by selling the previously embargoed armored innovations of the Iron Man armor to the highest bidder, including Super Villains and nefarious organizations.

Stark vs. Stane
Stark defeats Stane when, in his Iron Monger armor, the business mogul tries force (right). However, low cunning eventually drives Stark to drink and, for a while, wins Stane control of Stark International (above).

KEY STARK INDUSTRIES INVENTIONS
S.H.I.E.L.D. Helicarriers

Designed by Tony Stark, Reed Richards, and the mutant Forge, Helicarriers are built at the Stark Industries plant on Long Island. These mobile fortresses and aircraft carriers are powered by atomic reactors, capable of submersible deployment, and carry a vast array of radar and sensor suites and weaponry. The basic design consists of a triple hull with the capacity to house 36 smaller aircraft ranging from helicopters to fighter jets.

Guardsman Armor

Guardsman Armor is a mechanized protective exoskeleton developed by Tony Stark for use by the military, the police, and the emergency services. Fitted with strength and speed-multiplying systems, the suits are fitted with boot-jets for powered flight and palm-loaded repulsor rays. Suits modified for use by wardens at The Vault are fitted with additional armaments and sonic shielding.

Iron Metropolis

The company's greatest endeavour is razing terrorist base Mandarin City in Mongolia and establishing the futuristic city of Troy. With his brother Arno, Tony Stark creates an Iron Metropolis but is forced to leave it in other hands after it becomes a constant target for Iron Man's enemies.

NEVER SAY DIE

When Stark recovers from alcoholism and is fully fit and firing, he and a few close associates begin tech startup Circuits Maximus. Before long, Stark has taken back Stark International from Obadiah Stane. This chain of events recurs many times as the pressures of being Iron Man cause Stark to lose control of his business— such as when Fujikawa International force a merger. However, Tony Stark always returns to reclaim his life's work and rebuild it in new iterations, such as Stark Resilient, Stark Interplanetary, and Stark Solutions.

Bouncing back
When Fujikawa International buys his company, Tony starts up a new enterprise, Stark Solutions.

STARK INDUSTRIES
KEY STAFF MEMBERS

Although Stark Industries—in all its various incarnations—employs a huge workforce across the globe, its inventive owner has repeatedly turned to and relied on the same few tried and true people to help him manage and run the company. Although not all of them have shared the secret of Tony Stark's Iron Man identity, each of them has risked his or her life for him and the company on numerous occasions.

Virginia "Pepper" Potts-Hogan
Tony Stark's personal assistant and best friend. Knows the company inside out and has been CEO since her husband Happy Hogan's death. Also operates as Rescue in her own personalized Stark-Armor suit.

Bambi Arbogast
Mrs. Bambina Theresa Bliss Arbogast is an administrator in the U.S. Department of Defense before joining Stark International as the Stark's personal assistant. When James Rhodes becomes CEO, she is his deputy. After Fujikawa International acquires the company, she moves to Oracle Inc.

Harold "Happy" Hogan
A retired professional boxer hired by Tony Stark as a chauffeur and bodyguard, Hogan was privy to the secret of Iron Man's identity and substituted for Stark on numerous occasions. He dies after being attacked by Spymaster.

Eddie March
A former professional boxer, Eddie was hired by Tony Stark to take on the role of Iron Man when Tony feared that his heart problems would force him to give up the role. March works as an administrator for the charitable Iron Man Foundation.

BY MENTAL COMMAND

Model-51 is constructed of miniscule hexagonal plates which can constantly reconfigure themselves into different shapes, forms and colors. This is due to classified nanotechnology encoded into every component. The wearer synaptically controls the suit through mental commands. This function enables the suit to be instantly deployed, either by Stark or another person he mentally specifies. It also allows for remote piloting.

> ## "My armor's maneuverable—fast—and lots of fun at parties."
>
> **IRON MAN**

IRON MAN'S ARMOR

Designed, built, and constantly upgraded by Tony Stark, Iron Man armor is a mobile weapons platform and defensive unit capable of apparent miracles and defeating any threat.

FIRST APPEARANCE *Tales of Suspense* #39 (March 1963) **USED BY** Tony Stark, Arno Stark, Happy Hogan, Eddie March, Pepper Potts, Iron Legion, James Rhodes, Doctor Doom, Riri Williams

Mind over matter
Thanks to years of relentless invetnion and innovation, the armor can be deployed at the speed of thought.

BASIC FUNCTIONS

Every model of the armor has certain design features in common. All possess high speed, mobility, greatly enhanced strength, powered flight, and resistance to noxious environments, radiation, and impacts. Most armors include force-field technology, scanning and sensor devices, complex communications systems, heads-up displays, an onboard A.I. interface, damage suppression and self-repair systems.

Weapons systems include repulsor rays and a strength-multiplying exoskeleton. All suits contain multiple power-changing technologies. They can draw power from heat exchange via a thermocouple, via solar batteries, and electrical current. Modern armors are primarily powered by Stark's arc reactor.

CHEST PLATE

The first component built by Stark and Professor Ho Yinsen, the protective chest plate is constructed to keep Stark's damaged heart beating. Once Tony has corrective surgery, this function becomes unnecessary. Its defensive aspect and role as housing for the arc reactor system becomes paramount. It houses a multipurpose, high-energy projector dubbed the "variobeam," utilized as a spotlight, laser, and a destructive proton ray.

JET BOOTS

Initially compressed air jets, these are later modified as a compact turbine system, drawing air through the suit and expelling it as high-speed jets. Many versions of the boots also include retractable powered wheels, enabling Iron Man speed, maneuverability and power/fuel economy while traveling over the ground. Jet boots have been replaced by nano-fan arrays in most recent models.

Rocket man
The propulsive capabilities of the armor's integral flight boots transform Iron Man into a human self-guided missile.

REPULSOR AND ARC TECHNOLOGY

Housed in the gauntlets, repulsor rays are the armor's primary long-range assault weapon. Repulsors were originally beams of magnetic energy that could both attract and repel a target. These were upgraded and eventually replaced by a potent energy force consisting of charged particles in a tight beam, delivering high levels of concussive force.

Early armors consumed a vast amount of electrical power and required constant recharging. Stark's arc reactor technology provides an almost uninterruptible source of energy. The R.T. Node—for Repulsor Technology—is a clean fusion reaction, providing practically unlimited power.

Power blast
Tony Stark's chest-mounted weapon makes Iron Man the modern equivalent of heavily fortified long-range artillery.

Repulsor repulsed
Only the most extraordinary enemies—like Doctor Doom—are capable of withstanding a repulsor ray assault.

timeline

◄ Grey Guardian & Golden Avenger: Iron Man Armor Model 1 and Model 1: Mark III The original model provided great protection but was slow and ponderous, like a walking battleship. The power drain was enormous and constantly taxed Stark's injured heart.

Iron Man Armor Model 2 The switch to a lighter, more compact suit offered greater speed and maneuverability with little loss in firepower, making the armor less like a knight's wargear and more like a humanoid fighter jet.

◄ Iron Man Armor Model 4 The longest-serving armor: a true workhorse also used by Eddie March, Happy Hogan, and Jim Rhodes when they filled in for Tony Stark.

Iron Man Armor Model 5 (Space Armor) The first purpose-built suit: a fusion-powered, self-contained unit, allowing full combat functionality in a hard-radiation, zero-gravity, absolute zero temperature environment.

◄ Iron Man Armor Model 6 (Hydro Armor) Designed for undersea combat and exploration; equipped with modified Repulsors and Tri-Beam plus ink ejectors and mini torpedoes.

Iron Man Armor Model 7 (Stealth Armor) A stripped-down suit for reconnaissance missions: lightly armored, packed with electronic countermeasures, such as radar-absorbent coating, ECM jamming, and wave-modifying plasma layer to distort incoming radar and sonar; only enough power for three Repulsor blasts.

Iron Man Armor Model 8 (Silver Centurion Armor) When Stark resumes his role as Iron Man, this new look comprises enhanced weaponry, force-fields and pulse cannons, as well as a camouflaging "chameleon effect."

◄ Iron Man Armor Model 11 (War Machine Armor) A purely aggressive, weapons-heavy suit, this variable-threat-response battle-suit was later modified for James Rhodes' sole use.

Iron Man Armor Model 12 When Stark becomes paralyzed, this Neuromimetic Telepresence Unit-150 allows him to fight from his bed employing telepresence technology and updated ordnance, such as a battle computer and Beta Particle generator.

Iron Man Armor Model 13 The first fully-integrated suit built on interchangeable, modular principles. This allowd Iron Man to tailor his functions and weaponry according to the specific threat he is facing.

Iron Man Armor Model 19 SKIN Armor Constructed from a flexible alloy that is both elastic and hard as Adamantium. Fitted with the Jocasta A.I. system, repulsors, pulse bolts, an energy-blade, cloaking tech and remote sensor probes.

Iron Man Armor Model 29 (Extremis Armor) Using Extremis nanotechnology, Stark internalizes his armor and is able to call complete suits or partial modules from within his own body. This armor also allows Stark to mentally connect with electronic and satellite systems.

Iron Man Armor Model 37 (Bleeding Edge Armor) A complete reworking of the original armor and the first relying totally on arc technology and the R.T. node. As a result of Extremis nanobots, the suit is without gears, motors, servos, or other mechanical parts.

◄ Iron Man Armor Model 42 Another all-purpose modular design, this incorporates alien technology and systems provided by Rocket Raccoon during Stark's tenure with the Guardians of the Galaxy.

Iron Man Armor Model 50 (Endo-Sym Armor) A liquid smart metal suit based on symbiote biology which hardens on contact with the wearer's body. As well as standard Iron Man armaments, the suit enables full tactile sensation and can absorb electromagnetic enegy.

◄ Iron Man Armor Model 51 (Model-Prime Armor) The new standard: fast, strong, and resilient.

SPIDER-MAN'S WEB-SHOOTERS

FIRST APPEARANCE *Amazing Fantasy* #15 (August 1962) **USED BY** Spider-Man, Ben Reilly, Spider-Gwen

After Peter Parker receives his new powers from a radioactive spider bite, he decides that he needs a way to shoot spider-webbing in order to round out his abilities and complete the spider package. Peter develops web-shooters to use as an offensive and defensive weapon, as well as a form of locomotion.

Inspired by spider spinnerets, the web-shooters are worn on each wrist, underneath Spider-Man's costume. The spinnerets are made from stainless steel, with a turbine composed of Teflon and bearings of artificial sapphire and amber. The web-fluid cartridges are replaceable, with extras worn on a belt beneath Spider-Man's costume. The web-shooter valve is opened via a switch on Spider-Man's palm, which requires a double tap of 65lbs (29.5kg) of pressure.

Web fluid produces a line similar to nylon. It is shot through the spinneret holes at approximately 300psi (2068kpa), and solidifies when it makes contact with air. The spinnerets have three adjustable settings which may produce a strong line, a thick, sticky mass, or a spray which becomes a strong netting. Webs can be shot at least 60ft (18m), and lines have a tensile strength sufficient to suspend an automobile in mid-air.

The webbing usually degrades into powder after about an hour. When Otto Octavius takes over Peter Parker's body, he makes the webbing much stronger and it lasts several hours longer before it disintegrates. Spider-Man also has a number of trick web cartridges that fire specialized substances, including acid webbing, fast-drying web-cement, sonic disruptors, flame webbing, magnetic webbing, Taser webbing, and web-foam.

The design of Spider-Man's web-shooters has remained more or less the same, with a few minor exceptions. Peter adds a red LED warning light to notify him when he is running out of web fluid. He also makes them voice-activated, with settings to fire a barrage of "web bullets," recoil on contact, or cast an extra wide net.

Thanks to the schemes of the Queen (Adriana Soria), Peter Parker mutates into a giant spider. When he returns to human form, he has the ability to naturally shoot webbing from his wrists. No longer needing his web-shooters, Peter gives them to Mary Jane Watson as bracelets. His transformation is temporary though, and he later reverts to using them.

Web fluid cartridges
Spider-man must carry extra web fluid cartridges. Changing them can cause problems when he runs out and has to stop to replace them mid-fight!

Web-shooters
Requiring a double-tap of the palm switch, Spider-Man's web-shooters can be worn with or without his body suit.

Spinneret
A hole in the costume allows the web line to pass through

At webs' end
Frustrated by the public acceptance of Norman Osborn, Spider-Man rips the top off Osborn's limo and pulls him out with a web lasso.

Web line
The webbing is so strong it can support the weight of several people at one time

DOCTOR OCTOPUS' TENTACLES

FIRST APPEARANCE *Amazing Spider-Man #3* (July 1963) **USED BY** Otto Octavius

Doctor Octopus earns his nickname from the four mechanical tentacles that extend from his torso, giving him the appearance of having eight limbs. Though fused to his body, they sometimes seem to have a mind of their own.

Nuclear scientist Dr. Otto Octavius invents a set of four mechanical arms so he can safely handle radioactive material. These tentacles are controlled through a removable harness, but a freak accident bombards Octavius with radiation and fuses the arms to his body. The radiation also gives him the ability to control the tentacles with his mind. His ambitions lead him to use his tentacles for devious criminal enterprises, resulting in a lifelong clash with Spider-Man.

The four titanium-steel prehensile tentacles attach to a stainless-steel harness hugging Octavius' body. The telescopic tentacles have a diameter of 5in (12.7cm) and are tipped with three pincers that can rotate 360 degrees. They can each stretch from 6ft to 24ft (1.8 to 7m) at full length. The tentacles are powered by a thermoelectric motor with a nuclear core that needs changing every five years. They can strike like a cobra, lunging at 90ft/s (27mps) with an impact that can kill, and even burst through walls. Each tentacle contains its own battery and memory packs, so that the arms may operate independently if severed from a power connection, or if Doc Ock is rendered unconscious.

They are capable of fighting to protect Doc Ock in such situations, but if they are separated from his body they will only fight for a brief period of time, before settling down and following Doc Ock's pre-programmed plan.

While Doc Ock uses his tentacles like extra arms and deadly weapons, he has other important uses for them. He can employ them as long, extra legs for rapid travel across the ground, and he can even climb walls and buildings with them. Doc Ock can also spin them like blades to generate wind, creating extensive damage.

> ## "Now, watch me trap a spider in a web of my own—a web made of my new-found arms!"
>
> **DOCTOR OCTOPUS**

Mind over tentacles
Otto Octavius can perform four different actions at once—one with each tentacle. He has telepathic control over his tentacles and is able to control them from vast distances when their connection to him is severed.

Power with precision
Doctor Octopus' tentacles are incredibly powerful and capable of brutal destruction, yet they are so advanced in design that they can accomplish the most delicate tasks. When Doc Ock returns from the dead, he no longer remembers Spider-Man's secret identity, and commands his tentacles to uncover the truth.

LIZARD FORMULA

FIRST APPEARANCE *Amazing Spider-Man* #6 (November 1963) **USED BY** Lizard, Lizard Jr., Komodo, American Kaiju

Dr. Curt Connors loses his arm in an explosion while serving as a surgeon in the U.S. military. After he recovers, Connors studies the abilities of certain reptiles to regrow their limbs. Using lizard DNA, he develops a serum to regrow his own arm, known as the Lizard Formula. The formula works, but much too well. It alters his own DNA, turning him into a large, reptilian monster, known as the Lizard. Connors is unable to control his transformations between the Lizard and human forms. Even when he believes he is cured, powerful emotions lead him to transform back into the Lizard.

Connors is not the only person altered by the formula. In time, Connors develops a treatment, using his own DNA, to remove the effects of his Lizard Formula, and tests it on an iguana. The new formula has the unfortunate effect of transforming the reptile into a giant humanoid creature (unsurprisingly called the Iguana) with the memories and abilities of Connors' Lizard. Spider-Man is able to subdue the Iguana, though the creature makes a return later.

Teenager Melati Kusuma loses both her legs in a car accident. She becomes Connors' intern and steals his Lizard Formula, modifies it, and uses it on herself. Unlike Dr. Connors, Kusuma can change between her human form and her reptilian form at will. As Komodo, she has a lizard's physiology and super-strength, but is able to keep her human personality.

Dr. Connors injects his own son, Billy, with the Lizard Formula, creating a smaller version of himself, dubbed Lizard Jr. Both father and son are captured and returned to human form, though the Lizard later re-emerges and kills Billy. The Jackal later brings Billy back to life in order to persuade Connors to work for him.

The U.S. military tries to recreate the Super-Soldier serum for an operation named Project: Troubleshooter. They use treatments, including the Lizard Formula, to supplement deficiencies in their own research. Test subject Corporal Todd Ziller becomes a giant reptilian monster called the American Kaiju.

Whole again
Dr. Connors tries out his new Lizard Formula and manages to grow back his missing hand, though not quite as it was before.

SPIDER-TRACER

FIRST APPEARANCE *Amazing Spider-Man* #11 (April 1964) **USED BY** Spider-Man

Peter Parker invents tiny electronic spider-tracers to track individuals, vehicles, and objects as they move around the city. The tracers can be attached manually, or shot from Spider-Man's web-shooters. Spider-Man can track the tracers with a receiver, or even his own spider-sense (for short distances).

When he temporarily loses his spider-sense, Peter Parker develops an enhanced tracer utilizing GPS and listening capabilities. Through his company, Parker Industries, Peter Parker develops a new line of waterproof spider-tracers with a two-year battery life, intended for commercial use with his webware mobile devices. However, spider-tracers are not foolproof. They can be used against Spider-Man to lure him into traps.

PUMPKIN BOMB

FIRST APPEARANCE *Amazing Spider-Man* #17 (October 1965) **USED BY** Green Goblin, Hobgoblin

The Green Goblin (Norman Osborn) develops pumpkin bombs to deal with Spider-Man and other heroes (or competitors) who get in his way. His pumpkin bombs are designed to resemble miniature jack-o'-lanterns. Each one is armed by turning its stem. Inside are various mechanical components and explosives. The "bombs" are not just destructive weapons: the Goblin has a variety of the devices customized for many different purposes. Some are smoke bombs, to create confusion and distractions; these bombs can even disrupt Spider-Man's spider-sense and make him dizzy. The Goblin's anti-adhesive pumpkin bombs interfere with Spider-Man's ability to cling to surfaces, and he can incapacitate adversaries with stun bombs. Some pumpkin bombs are attuned to Peter Parker's biochemistry and can wreak havoc with his body.

The power of explosive pumpkin bombs varies greatly, from mere noisemakers and distractions, to powerful blasts that can demolish buildings. The Green Goblin attempts to blow up the *Daily Bugle* building with an exceptionally powerful pumpkin bomb, but Spider-Man manages to prevent it collapsing. The Green Goblin does manage to blow up warehouses and other structures at various times, however, causing death and great destruction.

Green Goblin first uses pumpkin bombs against Spider-Man and Human Torch (Johnny Storm) during Flash Thompson's Spider-Man Fan Club meeting. Hobgoblin (Roderick Kingsley, and others) also uses similar pumpkin bombs. A future Goblin, Hobgoblin 2211 (Robin Borne, daughter of the Spider-Man from 2211), uses "retcon bombs." These resemble pumpkin bombs, but completely erase their targets from existence.

Lethal legacy
A robber named "Georgie" stumbles upon a stash of Norman Osborn's old Green Goblin gear. He steals it and sells it to a shadowy figure. This new fiend double-crosses Georgie and tests out Osborn's pumpkin bombs as the new Hobgoblin.

HAWKEYE'S BOW AND ARROWS

FIRST APPEARANCE *Tales of Suspense* #57 (September 1964) **USED BY** Hawkeye

Clint Barton (Hawkeye) is just a regular guy fighting alongside super-powered humans, mutants, and aliens against powerful villains. To measure up, he requires a very special set of bow and arrows.

Hawkeye makes a wide variety of trick arrows to perform unique tasks in specific situations. Some arrows are pre-assembled and stored in his quiver. Other arrowheads are kept in pockets and attached to shafts as needed.

Hawkeye's most-used trick arrows include: acid (tip contains nitric acid), bola (releases three balls on 18in (46cm) cables), boomerang, electric (emits 21,000v charge on impact), explosive-tip, fire, flare (magnesium-iron flare tip ignites 5 seconds after firing), freeze (uses liquid nitrogen), grappling hook and cable, net (releases a 10ft (3m) wide net, which can be electrified), rocket (carries a 2lbs (907g) payload), sleeping gas, smoke bomb, sonic screamer (high-pitched sound emitted two seconds after firing), suction cup, tear gas (releases three seconds after impact), and tranquilizer (delivered in both liquid and gas forms).

Other occasionally used trick arrows include: Adamantium (which may be electrified), Asgardian, heat-seeking, magic, crescent razor, fireworks, parachute, pronged, photonic energy, signal scramblers, sunburst (emits a bright flash to dazzle or blind an opponent), tracking signal, and Vibranium. Hawkeye may also use arrows enhanced with Pym Particles to grow or shrink targets.

Hawkeye has carried his signature bow since his carnival days. Although it has been destroyed on more than one occasion—by Daredevil and Hercules—he owns several, and has a few different models. Hawkeye may also use his bow as a parrying weapon in close combat. He has been known to use crossbows, including mini wrist crossbows and giant crossbows, and underwater harpoons.

Hawkeye carries a leather quiver. The boot (the basket on his back that holds the arrows), is divided into four sections; each arrow fits into an individual slot and is held in place by a tiny clamp. The quiver straps have small pockets for additional arrowheads, accessed via spring-loaded doors.

> ## "All that remains is you and your target."
>
> **HAWKEYE**

Quiver
With a limited number of arrows, every shot counts

On point
Hawkeye can compete with his fellow superpowered heroes using his relatively primitive weapon, thanks to a combination of amazing marksmanship and trick arrows.

Bow
Hawkeye's recurve bow is best suited for moving or flying targets

Trick arrow
Hawkeye has to practice long hours to ensure his trick arrows achieve maximum effectiveness

Timing is everything

Trick arrows need to be timed just right. Hawkeye's arrows may activate immediately when fired from his bow (such as the cable and grappling hook), within a few seconds for a delayed reaction (such as smoke bombs), or only when they hit their target (as in his explosive arrowheads).

Sonic arrow

Explosive-tip arrow

Smoke bomb arrow

Flare arrow

Tear-gas arrow

Acid arrow

Suction-tip arrow

Cable arrow

Putty arrow

Bola arrow

Net arrow

Boomerang arrow

Power is all

Each bow has its advantages. Longbows are light, fast, and quiet. Recurve bows are easily lifted high for rapid shots. Compound bows give arrows more power for less pull.

Longbow

Double recurve bow

Compound bow

SPIDER-SLAYER ROBOTS

FIRST APPEARANCE *Amazing Spider-Man* #25
(June 1965) **USED BY** Spencer Smythe, J. Jonah
Jameson, Alistair Smythe, Norman Osborn

When scientist Spencer Smythe turns up
at the offices of the *Daily Bugle*, editor J.
Jonah Jameson dismisses him as a
crackpot. But Peter Parker persuades his
boss to give Smythe a chance—a decision
that Parker's alter ego Spider-Man ends up
regretting for a long time. Smythe has
created a robot that can sense a spider's
presence across a wide area. When this
robot gets close, steel tentacles ensnare
the prey. Most appealing of all for
Jameson, however, is the fact that he can
remotely control the robot and watch its
progress via a monitor in its head. Anyone
encountering the robot sees Jameson's
image on its face and hears his voice.

On its first outing, the robot follows
Peter Parker, drawn by his spider powers.
It ensnares him, to the great delight of
Jameson at the controls back in his office.
However, by the time he and Smythe reach
the robot's location, Spidey has escaped.

Some time later, Smythe contacts
Jameson again with a second robot.
Jameson is slightly shocked to hear the
scientist call it a Spider-Slayer, as he is only
looking to end the Web-Slinger's vigilante
career, not his life.

After a succession of failures, Jameson
goes to a new source to create a robot fit
to capture Spider-Man—Dr. Marla
Madison. Her version of the Spider-Slayer
also fails, crushed by a statue of
Prometheus on the Rockefeller Plaza ice
rink, but she and Jameson fall in love and
get married. Spencer Smythe, terminally ill
as a result of being exposed to excessive
radiation while making his robots, later tries
to murder both Jonah and Spider-Man,
blaming them for his condition.

Spencer dies, and his son, Alistair, takes
up his father's grudge and continues to
build robots to plague Spider-Man. When
Spidey defeats his first attempt by throwing
it—with Alistair inside—into railway power
lines, Smythe is left wheelchair-bound. This
only makes him hate Spider-Man more,
and he comes up with the most elaborate
Spider-Slayer plan yet. Alistair builds
several different Slayers, including a birdlike
winged robot, a scorpion and a tarantula.

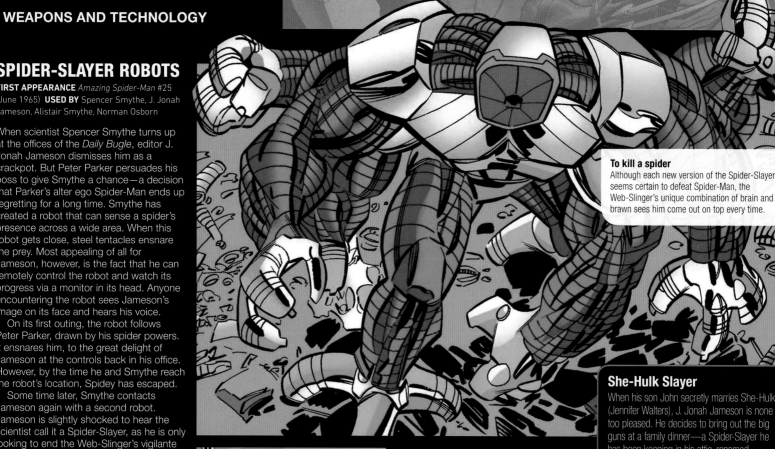

To kill a spider
Although each new version of the Spider-Slayer
seems certain to defeat Spider-Man, the
Web-Slinger's unique combination of brain and
brawn sees him come out on top every time.

After Spider-Man defeats these, he tracks
down Smythe, who has transformed
himself into the Ultimate Spider-Slayer. He
has created a metal carapace that even
allows him to walk again, but Spidey
defeats him, enraged by the risk to
innocent lives caused by Smythe's actions.

The two enemies clash again when
Smythe builds versions of all the Slayers
that Spider-Man has fought in the past,
plus some new ones—lots of miniature
Slayers and one giant-sized model. While
Spider-Man defeats the Slayers, J. Jonah
Jameson takes down Alistair Smythe after
he threatens the media mogul's family.
Later, during Jameson's tenure as Mayor of
New York City, Jameson reboots the Slayer
robots as Goblin Slayers to combat
Norman Osborn's Goblin Nation.

Hate campaign
Daily Bugle editor J. Jonah Jameson is delighted
when he gets his hands on technology to help him
finally get the better of Spider-Man.

She-Hulk Slayer

When his son John secretly marries She-Hulk
(Jennifer Walters), J. Jonah Jameson is none
too pleased. He decides to bring out the big
guns at a family dinner—a Spider-Slayer he
has been keeping in his attic, renamed
She-Hulk-Slayer for the occasion. His new
lawyer daughter-in-law makes short work of
the robot, and when she offers to help "Dad"
sue a recently unmasked Peter Parker,
Jameson is delighted to welcome her into the
family. However, the newlyweds are troubled
by one of Alistair Smythe's Spider-Slayers
again when a miniature version causes John
to revert to Man-Wolf.

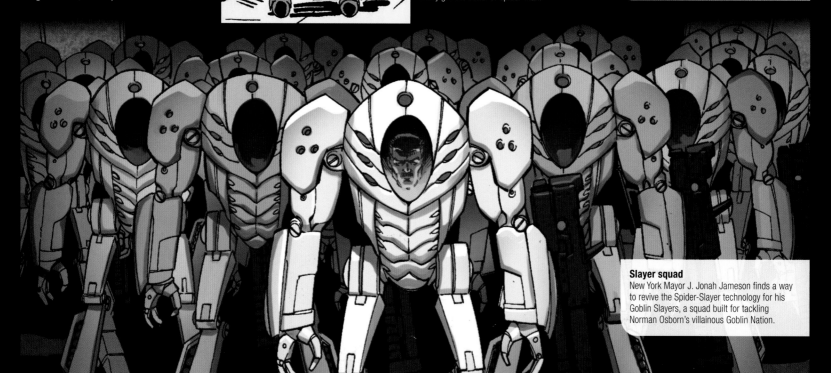

Slayer squad
New York Mayor J. Jonah Jameson finds a way
to revive the Spider-Slayer technology for his
Goblin Slayers, a squad built for tackling
Norman Osborn's villainous Goblin Nation.

Power corrupts
The villain known as the Hobgoblin immerses himself in the Goblin Formula, hoping to become as powerful as Spider-Man but without the insanity Norman Osborn previously suffered.

> **"I can feel my body bursting with more sheer power than I could ever have conceived of!"**
> HOBGOBLIN

GOBLIN FORMULA

FIRST APPEARANCE *Amazing Spider-Man* #37 (June 1966) **USED BY** Norman Osborn, Harry Osborn, Hobgoblin, Phil Urich, Lily Hollister, Carlie Cooper

The Goblin Formula gives enhanced strength and intelligence, but those who use it find that it also brings madness…

Dr. Mendell Stromm creates a formula that can bestow increased strength and intelligence, but before he can use it he is imprisoned for fraud thanks to the machinations of business partner Norman Osborn. Osborn is desperate to get his hands on the formula and does not want to share any of the benefits, but while working on it in his lab, the formula explodes all over him. Stricken, he lies in the hospital for several weeks before realising that he has indeed gained incredible power and

intellectual prowess. But the formula has also injured his brain, rendering him criminally insane. Osborn decides to become a costumed villain, calling himself the Green Goblin, and attempts to gain instant respect in the criminal world by going after Spider-Man. His insanity leads him to kill Peter Parker's girlfriend, Gwen Stacy, and when Spider-Man confronts him the Goblin is killed by his own glider.

Despite the apparent demise of the Green Goblin, the formula that created him remains in various secret lairs all over New York City. One day, a new villain discovers a stash of the formula and deliberately immerses himself in a vat of it, thinking to make himself even more powerful than the Green Goblin through longer exposure to the formula. He becomes the Hobgoblin, a mysterious villain whose identity remains a secret for many years.

Anti-Goblin
Otto Octavius, in Peter Parker's body, uses the infected blood of Carlie Cooper to manufacture an antidote for the pernicious Goblin Formula.

Iron Goblin
During the events of Spider-Island, Iron Man is sprayed with Goblin Formula to return him to normal after turning into a human spider, but there are side-effects.

Meanwhile, the original Green Goblin's son, Harry Osborn, is struggling to cope with the legacy of his father's alter ego after his death. In recovery from drug addiction, Harry is in a bad place. Feeling weak and vulnerable, he turns to his father's lab notes to recreate the formula; he even make changes to it that he claims make him Spider-Man's superior. Not surprisingly given Harry's fragile mental state, the formula again renders its user completely insane. Harry's enhanced strength also comes at the cost of a vastly reduced lifespan—the amended formula is poisoning him.

Various versions of the Goblin Formula affect other lives, too. Journalist Phil Urich accidentally causes a spill of the formula and become another Hobgoblin, while Harry Osborn's girlfriend Lily Hollister smashes a test tube of it and becomes the villain known as Menace. Peter Parker's girlfriend Carlie Cooper is squirted with the formula while in captivity at the hands of Norman Osborn, the self-proclaimed Goblin King. Carlie is transformed into a goblin-like creature called Monster. Fortunately Otto Octavius, at the time operating as the Superior Spider-Man, manages to make a cure from her blood.

VIBRANIUM

FIRST APPEARANCE *Daredevil* #13 (February 1966)
USED BY Wakandans, Lord Plunder, Captain America, Black Panther, U.S. Agent, Echo, Misty Knight, Agent Zero

Vibranium is a metal found in meteoric rock. Its main source is the African nation of Wakanda, although another type, known as Anti-Metal, is found in the Savage Land region of Antarctica. Anti-Metal gives off such strong vibrations that it can shatter metal objects in its vicinity, even at a distance of several miles. The Wakandan form is the opposite—it absorbs vibrations, thereby increasing in strength. It is kept in a Sacred Mound in the country, and is guarded symbolically by the Wakandan ruler.

Vibranium has a lot of applications, particularly in the weapons industry, and this, coupled with its scarcity, makes it very expensive. Wakanda has been able to finance enormous growth for a country of its size by selling just small amounts of its Vibranium.

Super metal
The properties of Vibranium make it extremely useful to Super Heroes. A Vibranium alloy is used to make Cap's iconic shield, while Black Panther's suit contains Vibranium weave and he wields Vibranium energy knives.

ULTIMATE NULLIFIER

FIRST APPEARANCE *Fantastic Four* #50 (May 1966) **USED BY** Galactus, Reed Richards, Quasar, Morg

The Ultimate Nullifier is an alien weapon that, if turned up to full power, could destroy the solar system and maybe even the universe. It is said to be the most dangerous weapon in existence, but its origins are mysterious. The threat of Reed Richards using it is enough to change even the mighty Galactus' mind about consuming Earth.

When used against a specific target, the Ultimate Nullifier sends it into oblivion, but the wielder of the weapon must be well trained or mentally strong enough to use it, or they will be destroyed. When Quasar tries to use the weapon, its energy rebounds back at him and he is obliterated; he is later resurrected.

BOOMERANG'S BOOMERANGS

FIRST APPEARANCE *Tales to Astonish* #81 (July 1966)
USED BY Boomerang

Although the villain Boomerang can do plenty of damage with his strong pitching arm and impeccable aim, his weapons are customized to deliver that extra something. Supplied by shady billionaire inventor Justin Hammer, the boomerangs offer a range of offensive options—some are explosive or emit gas on impact, others are edged with razor or buzzsaw blades; some emit sonic blasts and others form gravity fields, whereas there are those that are heavy enough to deliver a knockout blow.

Alongside his peerless throwing technique, Boomerang has also had to perfect his catching skills, so that when his weapons return to him, they do not cause him harm.

Old foe
Boomerang uses his trademark weapons to attack Otto Octavius' Superior Spider-Man, but as usual, the villain is unsuccessful.

A.I.M. high
Having copied the powers of Captain America, Giant-Man, Hawkeye, and Wasp, the A.I.M.-built Super-Adaptoid faces the original Cap.

A.I.M.

FIRST APPEARANCE *Strange Tales* #146 (July 1966)
USED BY Hydra, S.H.I.E.L.D., U.S. government

Advanced Idea Mechanics, or A.I.M., is a weapons division of Hydra, but later severs its connections with that terrorist group to go freelance. Using the best scientific minds available to it, A.I.M. devises bleeding-edge tech for anyone who has the funds to pay. The organization thrives on violent revolution and discord. Led by the Scientist Supreme, it is situated on A.I.M. Island in the Caribbean.

For years, A.I.M. conceals its true purpose and even does business with groups like S.H.I.E.L.D. and the U.S. government. One of its projects is the Cosmic Cube, a containment device designed to hold reality-altering cosmic energy. It is used later to create an android that can mimic the powers of super-beings, called a Super-Adaptoid. A.I.M. also recreates the Super-Soldier serum that was used to create Captain America.

When Sunspot takes over, he weeds out A.I.M.'s worst influences and rebrands it as Avengers Idea Mechanics.

Brain power
The artificial intelligence known as M.O.D.O.K. is created by A.I.M., but rebels against the organization and takes control of it. Eventually, M.O.D.O.K. is killed by A.I.M.

RIGELLIAN RECORDERS

FIRST APPEARANCE *Thor* #132 (September 1966) **USED BY** Rigellians, Thor, She-Hulk

This race of sentient robots explores the universe and reports its findings back to an alien population known as the Rigellians. These Recorders also have a certain amount of legal power, with permission to track down and capture Rigellian lawbreakers. Various Recorders have made an impact on Earthly heroes: Recorder 211 accompanies Thor to find Ego the Living Planet; Recorder RT-Z9 works as a court reporter for She-Hulk when she is Magistrati for the Living Tribunal; and Recorder 451, who contains a glitch that makes him remember all he has recorded. This leads him to cause trouble for Iron Man and the world, and Iron Man is compelled to don special stealth armor in order to subdue the rogue robot.

SATAN CLAW

FIRST APPEARANCE *Strange Tales* #157 (June 1967) **USED BY** Baron Wolfgang von Strucker, Nick Fury, Punisher, Sharon Carter

This mechanical gauntlet is one of Baron von Strucker's main weapons. It enhances his strength and also releases powerful electrical shocks— allowing Strucker to temporarily get the better of Nick Fury when the villain first uses it to electrify the floor of his Hydra Island base. Strucker later augments the device with extra weaponry, including claws, a Gatling gun, and explosive shells. It has also enabled him to teleport and serves him as a prosthetic hand.

The Satan Claw, or versions of it, has been employed by others, such as Nick Fury when he fights the Yellow Claw, the Punisher when he battles Rhino, and Sharon Carter, when she faces evil scientist Arnim Zola.

PRIME MOVER

FIRST APPEARANCE *Strange Tales* #167 (April 1968) **USED BY** Doctor Doom

Genius inventor Doctor Doom creates the sentient Prime Mover robot and pits it against S.H.I.E.L.D. agents in games of strategy. When Doom loses interest in this scheme, the Prime Mover takes matters into its own hands by reprogramming itself, leaving Doom, and engaging in its own games. It challenges the cosmic game player Grandmaster to a game, with Earth as the winner-takes-all prize. The Grandmaster uses Daredevil and the Defenders against the Prime Mover's pawns, which include the cyborg Korvac. When the Prime Mover loses, it is so upset, its circuits blow.

ADAMANTIUM

FIRST APPEARANCE *Avengers* #66 (July 1969)
USED BY Wolverine, Sabretooth

This nearly indestructible steel alloy is best known for being fused to the skeleton and claws of Wolverine by the Weapon X program. Wolverine's bitter enemy, Sabretooth, has also had his bones and claws laced with Adamantium at times. The metal is created by Dr. Myron MacLain in a top secret research and development lab during World War II. Adamantium is extremely difficult and expensive to create

and can only be melted at temperatures over 1500 degrees Fahrenheit (816 degrees Celsius).

Due to its combination of chemical resins and metal, Adamantium has a very dense and stable molecular structure and can only be bent or damaged by rearrangement on the molecular level. It is so strong that it can withstand nuclear explosions. Adamantium can only be pierced by one known substance: a type of vibranium found in the Antarctic called Anti-Metal, which breaks down the metals' molecular bonds.

Death metal
Logan meets his demise being dowsed in molten Adamantium during a fight with the man who originally turned him into Weapon X.

STINGRAY'S SUIT

FIRST APPEARANCE *Sub-Mariner* #19 (November 1969) **USED BY** Stingray

Oceanographer Dr. Walter Newell designs his Stingray battle suit to wear during deep sea diving. This armored exoskeleton is made of super-durable artificial cartilage and mimics the attributes of stingrays, including a walloping 20,000-volt jolt that can be emitted from its gloves. The winged stingray design allows the wearer to swim at increased speeds and to glide in the air

over long distances. The suit also provides an underwater breathing system and wards off the intense pressure of deep ocean waters.

Stingray first dons this suit to bring in Namor the Sub-Mariner for the U.S. government, but later joins him as a fellow Super Hero.

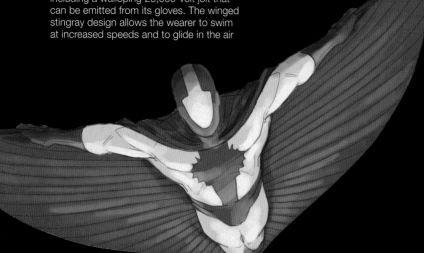

ALCHEMY GUN

FIRST APPEARANCE *Hero for Hire* #12 (August 1973) **USED BY** Chemistro

The Alchemy Gun is the go-to weapon of choice for the villain Chemistro. The gun transmutes any substance into any other form of matter the shooter can imagine through a cybernetic link. After exposure to heat, or following an extended period of time, the effected matter turns to dust.

Unfortunately, when Chemistro accidentally aims the Alchemy Gun at his own foot, it turns to steel—eventually crumbling away to dust, leaving the villain incapacitated. The effects of the gun can be reversed using a jamming rifle.

PURIFICATION GUN

FIRST APPEARANCE *Man-Thing* #4 (April 1974) **USED BY** Foolkiller

Each criminally insane man to become the Foolkiller has used a Purification Gun. This silver ray gun disintegrates a person in seconds with a white laser-beam—perfect for killing fools and foes alike. Foolkiller has no super-abilities, but this off-the-chart powerful gun paired with his surveillance skills and tracking devices make him a master manhunter. The gun can make a man-sized hole in brick or concrete, however, it seems to have little effect on gods or demons, as the warrior goddess Valkyrie and the demonic villain Vengeance (Michael Badilino) have both survived its blast.

RAND CORPORATION

FIRST APPEARANCE *Marvel Premiere* #15 (May 1974)

The Rand Corporation started as Rand-Meachum Inc., a multimillion-dollar conglomerate founded by Iron Fist's father Wendell Rand along with his former friend Harold Meachum. When Harold secretly kills Wendell, Iron Fist (Danny Rand) returns to avenge his father's death.

Iron Fist, however, does not have the heart to kill the invalid Harold, who is then killed by Rand's ally, the mysterious Ninja. Control of Rand-Meachum Inc. passes to Harold's child, Joy Meachum, before Danny Rand takes over the corporation with the help of lawyer Jeryn Hogarth. This split of power, and the assumption that Iron Fist killed Harold, drive Joy and her uncle Ward to try to outsmart, kill, or take out Iron Fist by any means necessary.

CLONING

FIRST APPEARANCE *Amazing Spider-Man* #142 (March 1975)
USED BY Professor Miles Warren, Mister Sinister, Arnim Zola, Tony Stark, Dr. Sarah Kinney, Tony Stark, Mr. Fantastic

Many of Earth's scientific geniuses have shown an interest in cloning, but when this cutting-edge genetic technology goes wrong it can have dire consequences for the clone… and everybody else.

Professor Miles Warren teaches biology at Empire State University, where his students include Peter Parker and Gwen Stacy. Despite being much older than Gwen, the professor is besotted with her, and is heartbroken by her death, blaming Spider-Man for the tragedy. His mental instability leads him down a dark path. Warren uses cell samples taken from his students to produce clones of Gwen and Peter Parker. When his lab assistant, Anthony Serba, objects, Warren accidentally kills him. Horrified, Warren assumes the identity of the Jackal to distance himself from the terrible acts he is committing.

The Jackal uses the clone of Gwen to lure Spider-Man to the Brooklyn Bridge, but when Spidey is not killed by a fall as planned, the villain sets up a fight with the cloned Peter Parker as Spider-Man. In the aftermath, the Jackal and the Spidey clone are apparently killed, and the Gwen Stacy clone decides to move away to start a new life. Thanks to the Jackal's trickery, Peter Parker has no idea if he is the original Spider-Man, or the clone, who has, in fact, survived and taken the name Ben Reilly.

Ben is similar enough to Peter Parker to step into the role of Spider-Man without too much trouble; however, the same cannot be said for the other clones of Parker that the Jackal creates. Something goes wrong with Kaine Parker—Warren's first attempt to clone Peter—and his appearance and personality degenerate. Kaine leaves a trail of bodies in his wake, and becomes a professional assassin before reforming, to an extent, as the Scarlet Spider. Another of Warren's clones is dubbed Spidercide. This one helps his creator kill thousands of people with the Carrion Virus, before being killed himself.

Peter Parker is not the only hero to come face-to-face with a cloned ex-girlfriend. The X-Man Cyclops marries a clone of his lost love, Jean Grey, created by Mister Sinister. The couple live happily until Jean returns from the dead. Her clone, Madelyne Pryor-Summers, is so traumatized to discover that her life is a fabrication that she becomes the evil Goblin Queen. Madelyne and Cyclops' child, Nathan Summers, also has a clone, the mutant terrorist called Stryfe.

A clone of the villainous Red Skull is created during World War II to rise again when the original's crimes have been long forgotten. The new Red Skull sets about creating a concentration camp for mutants, before being inadvertently turned into the powerful Red Onslaught by Magneto.

Tony Stark pools his genius with Mr. Fantastic and Henry Pym to create a clone of Thor, to be used in an emergency. However, like other clones before him, he reacts badly when he learns his true origins. Now known as Ragnarok, Thor's clone is eventually killed by the original God of Thunder.

Face to face
When Madelyne Pryor is turned into the Goblin Queen by a demon, she confronts the original from which she was cloned—and her husband Cyclops' first love—Jean Grey.

Spider clones
From the twisted mind of Professor Warren's Jackal *(above)* comes *(clockwise from left)*: Spider-Man clone Kaine Parker, a clone of Gwen Stacy, and Spidey clone Ben Reilly.

Gwen again
The clone of Peter Parker's dead girlfriend Gwen Stacy is perhaps deranged Professor Miles Warren's greatest scientific triumph.

"The cloning experiment succeeded!"

ANTHONY SERBA

INFINITY FORMULA

FIRST APPEARANCE *Marvel Spotlight* #31 (December 1976)
USED BY Nick Fury, Nostradamus, Bucky Barnes, Jake Fury

Sir Isaac Newton creates the Elixir of Immortality in 1652. As its name suggests, the elixir confers immortality and perpetual youth. The Forever Compound is a diluted version of the Elixir, produced by an ancient order known as the Brotherhood of the Shield. While it endows long life, the serum does not specifically maintain youth or good health. French Professor Berthold Sternberg develops a further version, known as the Infinity Formula.

When Nick Fury is mortally wounded serving with the U.S. Army in World War II France, Professor Sternberg saves him with the Infinity Formula. Fury must be inoculated annually, or else he will age rapidly. Sternberg later takes advantage of this situation and blackmails Fury, demanding a high price for yearly doses.

Criminal Steel Harris murders Sternberg and steals the formula. He also blackmails Fury, demanding access to top-secret information from S.H.I.E.L.D. in exchange for the inoculations. Fury languishes without his regular dose; fortunately, his lover, Val de Fontaine, acquires the formula and administers it to Fury just in time. Fury then eliminates Harris. However, by the time Fury kills the Watcher, Uatu,

he is no longer taking the serum, and is aging rapidly.

Several other people have benefited from the effects of the Infinity Formula. When Skadi—Sin, daughter of the Red Skull who is transformed into the Norse goddess—nearly kills Bucky Barnes during the Fear Itself event, Nick Fury administers a dose of the Infinity Formula, which saves Bucky's life. The forever-youthful effects of Nick Fury's Infinity Formula are passed onto his sons, Nick Jr. and Mikel Fury. The formula has also been administered to Nick Fury's brother Jake, and, centuries earlier, to the astrologer Nostradamus.

Seer for eternity
Newton kidnaps Nostradamus and administers the formula to him, making Nostradamus his eternal oracle.

Infinity addiction
The Infinity Formula keeps World War II hero Nick Fury fit and firing in modern times, but he needs regular injections to prevent himself aging fast.

WAR MACHINE ARMOR

FIRST APPEARANCE *Iron Man* #118 (January 1979) **USED BY** Tony Stark, James Rhodes

There are many incarnations of War Machine Armor (also known as the Variable Threat Response Battle Suit). The first is developed by Iron Man (Tony Stark) and worn in battle against the Masters of Silence. Stark's official name for the armor is the Iron Man Armor Model 11, but Stark calls it War Machine.

The armor suit has extra shield plating, including an outer poly-carbonate coating. Weaponry includes repulsors, twin chain guns, a wrist-mounted flamethrower and laser blade. The shoulder module supports a rocket launcher, Gatling gun, and pulse and plasma cannons. The suit's weapons are capable of firing a variety of munitions, including sub-nuke, depleted uranium, thermite, tear gas, flares, and fire-suppressants.

Tony Stark bestows a modified version of his War Machine Armor (the JRXL-1000) to his friend, James Rhodes. Upgrades to this armor include a unibeam with a strobe feature, concussion pulses fired from the hands, and a pair of chainsaws extending from the forearms.

The armor is heavily damaged in battle with the Melter (Bruno Horgan) and Whirlwind (David Cannon). Rhodes uses this opportunity to fake his own death and become the new Iron Man, as a ruse to defeat the evil mastermind Mandarin.

During the Fifty-State Initiative, Rhodes uses an updated version of the War Machine Armor designed by Stane Industries. The gauntlets wield new blasters, and the rocket launcher can fire S.P.I.N. (Super-Power Inhibiting Nanobots), to nullify superhuman abilities. New cannons are fitted to hips and chest plates. Using magno-lock technology the suit can integrate with other weaponry, such as cannons.

Shoulder cannons
Supports interchangeable cannons, rocket launchers, and other weapon modules

Arc reactor
A mini nuclear reactor powers the suit

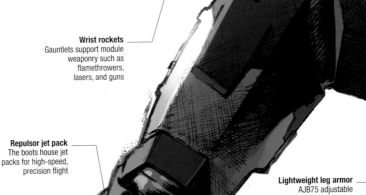

Iron Man 2.0
When Rhodey is almost killed, he and Tony Stark upgrade the War Machine armor so he can face any new threat—and actually survive.

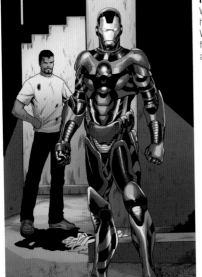

Wrist rockets
Gauntlets support module weaponry such as flamethrowers, lasers, and guns

Repulsor jet pack
The boots house jet packs for high-speed, precision flight

Lightweight leg armor
AJB75 adjustable 0.75cm-thick armor layer

Forever upgrading
Keeping up with all the threats to Earth means constantly improving the War Machine armor with new Stark technology. The suit can be upgraded on the fly with new modules and scavenged components, making it a veritable tank, rather than a mere suit of armor.

ROXXON ENERGY CORPORATION

FIRST APPEARANCE *Captain America #180* (December 1984) **USED BY** Executives of Roxxon

The Roxxon Energy Corporation is among the largest such companies operating around the globe. Its headquarters is originally located in Roxxon Plaza, New York City, and then relocates to Wilmington, Delaware. Roxxon rakes in billions of dollars, secretly engaging in a great many shady business deals.

When Roxxon organizes exploration of the underwater city of Lemuria, the company discovers the Serpent Crown, a relic of great supernatural power. The Serpent Squad kidnap Roxxon's chairman, Hugh Jones, in an attempt to recover the crown. While held captive, Jones is forced to wear the Serpent Crown, which forges a psychic link with him. When Nomad (Captain America) rescues Jones, the crown is lost—but only temporarily. Hugh Jones' burning obsession with the Serpent Crown and its powers fuels a constant struggle as Roxxon and its own new Serpent Squad fight the Avengers, a President Nelson Rockefeller from an alternate universe, and the Squadron Supreme— all for possession of the crown.

During Norman Osborn's Dark Reign as U.S. security chief, Roxxon has a mining operation on Mars. Another Serpent Crown is discovered, belonging to an ancient Martian civilization, controlled by the mysterious Shadow Council. The crown is acquired by Roxxon's new vice-president, Bromley, and a struggle occurs between Roxxon, the Shadow Council, and the Avengers, to gain control of the crown. Ant-Man manages to obliterate the facilities of Roxxon and the Shadow Council, and saves the day.

As C.E.O. of Roxxon, Dario Agger (Minotaur) earns the ire of Thor for his schemes to plunder Jupiter's moon, Europa, and later the town of Broxton, Oklahoma, with Ulik and the Rock Trolls.

Devious business
Roxxon has done a lot of nasty things. Many of their worst deeds are carried out by subsidiaries and their representatives. Agents from Roxxon Oil may have been responsible for the deaths of Tony Stark's parents.

ALCHEMAX

FIRST APPEARANCE *Spider-Man 2099 #1* (November 1992) **BASE** Alchemax Tower, Nueva York; Babylon Towers

In the year 2099, the evil Alchemax megacorporation provides everything from products to pharmaceuticals to a private police force. Alchemax is founded in 2013, when Liz Allan's Allan Chemical merges with Norman Osborn's Oscorp, and the remnants of Horizon Labs—following its destruction while under a hostile takeover by Allan Chemical.

By the year 2099, Alchemax is run by the villainous Tyler Stone, who is the father of Alchemax employee, geneticist Miguel O'Hara.

Disillusioned by the organization's development of the highly addictive drug Rapture, Miguel threatens to leave. To stop him, Stone drugs him with Rapture. Miguel experiments with spider DNA to rid his system of the drug, and becomes the Spider-Man of 2099. Miguel later travels back in time to work undercover as Michael O'Mara, assistant to Alchemax's founder, Tiberius "Ty" Stone.

SPIDER ARMOR MK I, II, III, IV

FIRST APPEARANCE *Web of Spider-Man #100* (May 1993) **USED BY** Spider-Man (Peter Parker and Otto Octavius)

When situations become dire, Spider-Man (Peter Parker) needs additional protection. While at Empire State University, Peter develops a suit of shiny, silver Spider Armor (MK I) to protect himself from the New Enforcers' high-caliber weapons. The suit is entirely bulletproof, but at the cost of agility. The armor is eventually consumed by acid.

When Peter Parker loses his spider-sense, he creates a new suit of black and gold Spider Armor (MK II) to protect himself from bullets. Parker wears the armor against machine-gun-wielding Massacre (Marcus Lyman). The suit not only stops bullets but also explosives. Magnetic webbing, which interferes with enemy communications, can be fired from the forearms. The suit is developed at Horizon Labs in New York City and a copy is later kept at Parker Industries.

Peter Parker develops a third set of red-and-blue-gray Spider Armor (MK III) to fight Doctor Octopus' Sinister Six. This armor has built-in web-shooters, a variety of enhanced visual lenses, the ability to fly, a comlink, and a hearing acuity device designed to pinpoint the Chameleon's heartbeat when the villain is camouflaged. The suit is also kept at Horizon Labs, where it was created, and then kept in storage at Parker Industries.

Peter Parker's fourth set of red-and-blue Spider Armor (MK IV) is developed at Parker Industries. It is so form-fitting that it doesn't look like armor at all, and Parker wears it most of the time as Spider-Man. The mask lenses allow Parker to detect body heat and see in X-rays, as well as track people using micro spider-tracers. The suit is able to change appearance to mimic normal clothing. In addition to spider-tracers, the web-shooters also fire cushioning web-foam, Taser-like bug-zappers, acid webs, and sonic disrupters, among other devices and compounds.

Spider-Man Armor MK I
This is made of a flexible pseudo-metallic compound. Peter Parker only wears it briefly, but geneticist Miguel O'Hara uses it as a Halloween costume in 2099.

Armor plates
Heavy plating provides defence from projectiles, but restricts full range of movement

Body glove
Black undersuit allows arm and leg movement but provides less protection

DEADPOOL'S TELEPORTER

FIRST APPEARANCE *Deadpool #1* (January 1997) **USED BY** Deadpool, Cable

Deadpool uses a variety of teleportation tech, including a shiny wrist gadget that looks like an oversized watch. However, his teleporters often go on the fritz, and he gives up on them eventually.

While working together to recover a virus for the One World Church, Deadpool and Cable have their DNA mixed up. As a result, Deadpool is able to "bodyslide" (teleport) together with Cable, with the aid of the Time Displacement Core of Providence (a floating island base built from the remnants of Cable's *Graymalkin* space station). Since they now share some DNA, the teleportation technology grabs them both, as though they are one person.

Going to extremes
Dr. Maya Hansen provides Extremis to a terrorist cell. In Texas, inside the D.R. Cole Slaughterhouse, two of the terrorists administer Extremis to Mallen, who undergoes a radical mutation process.

EXTREMIS

FIRST APPEARANCE *Iron Man* #1 (January 2005)
USED BY Tony Stark, Mallen

Extremis is a nanotech serum developed by FuturePharm, a biotech subsidiary of Stark Industries. Dr. Aldrich Killian and brilliant scientist Dr. Maya Hansen work together to steal Extremis when the program is canceled by the U.S. military.

When Tony Stark (Iron Man) tries to recover Extremis, he is injured by the terrorist Mallen, who has the Extremis vaccine flowing through his veins. Stark takes the serum to heal his own injuries and boost his connection to his Iron Man armor. He is then able to defeat Mallen and capture Maya Hansen.

The Mandarin then steals Extremis, using Maya Hansen to help him further develop the serum. However, he soon discovers that Extremis is only effective on 2.5 percent of the population— those who are genetically compatible. Other subjects are killed by the virus. The evil mastermind plans to launch a missile to disperse the virus which would ruthlessly cull the population. Fortunately, Iron Man is able to divert the missile into the upper atmosphere, where its payload is subsequently destroyed.

Arno Stark, the foster brother of Tony, develops a new version of Extremis, which is used to heal Bruce Banner after he suffers brain damage. Banner further upgrades Extremis to increase the Hulk's intelligence and creates Doc Green.

During Red Onslaught's World War Hate, reality is altered. An amoral Tony Stark releases Extremis 3.0 into San Francisco. Stark offers it to the citizens as a way to upgrade their bodies, but forces them to pay him $99.99 per day. Life returns to normal when reality is restored.

Powered-up
The chemical gives Mallen new abilities. In addition to strength, speed and stamina, he can breathe plasma fire, attack with stinger claws, and fire powerful electrical bursts from his hands.

IRON SPIDER ARMOR

FIRST APPEARANCE *Amazing Spider-Man* #529 (April 2006) **USED BY** Peter Parker, Mary Jane Watson, Scarlet Spiders

Using Stark technology, Tony Stark builds Peter Parker a new suit of Iron Spider armor with the colors of his Iron Man suit. Parker gives up the armor during the superhuman civil war when he switches from Iron Man's government side to Captain America's Secret Avengers. Stark retains the armor until Mary Jane Watson wears it when the Avengers battle Regent (Augustus Roman), whose symbiotic armor absorbs Super Heroes' powers.

During the Fifty-State Initiative, Tony Stark upgrades the Iron Spider armor and uses it to equip the three new Scarlet Spiders—all clones of Michael Van Patrick. Peter Parker later reproduces it at his own high-tech company, Parker Industries.

The most distinctive features of the Iron Spider armor are the three mechanical spider arms, or "waldoes," that emerge from a small disk on Spider-Man's back. They are newly synthesized each time they are deployed, and made from rapid-growing, mono-atomic, iron-alloy crystals. The tips are coated in surface-adherent patches and web-handling pseudo-fingers.

The smart suit has access ports that automatically dilate to allow organics— such as web spinnerets and stingers— to pass through the suit. The breathing apparatus filters biological, chemical, and nuclear contaminants and has an eight-minute capacity of compressed reserve oxygen. The headgear also has an antenna array equipped with "intention pattern detection." This allows the wearer to mind-control the spider arms.

The armor employs a total of 17 different layer types. These include temperature controls, moisture pumps, a sensor layer, CPU layer, communications layer, power management, and a diamond nitrile overcoat to enhance wall-crawling abilities.

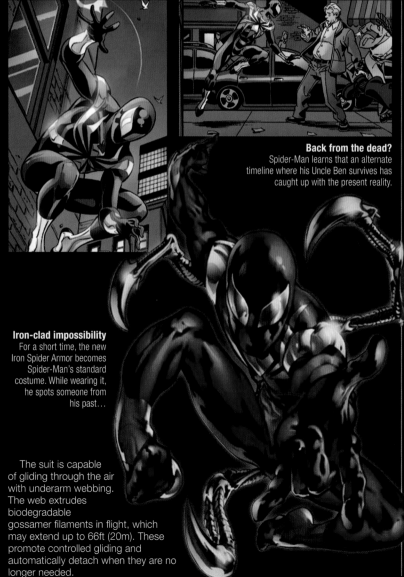

Iron-clad impossibility
For a short time, the new Iron Spider Armor becomes Spider-Man's standard costume. While wearing it, he spots someone from his past…

The suit is capable of gliding through the air with underarm webbing. The web extrudes biodegradable gossamer filaments in flight, which may extend up to 66ft (20m). These promote controlled gliding and automatically detach when they are no longer needed.

Back from the dead?
Spider-Man learns that an alternate timeline where his Uncle Ben survives has caught up with the present reality.

GUARDIANS' TELEPORTING BRACELETS

FIRST APPEARANCE *Annihilation: Conquest* #6 (June 2008) **USED BY** Cosmo, Nova, Guardians of the Galaxy

Cosmo, the telepathic dog, provides the Guardians of the Galaxy with passport bracelets that allow the team to teleport across the universe. Teleportation can be controlled via the Continuum Cortex found inside the brain-stem of the severed Celestial head that houses the Knowhere space station. The Continuum Cortex is highly sensitive to disturbances in the time continuum and can alert Cosmo of impending trouble.

Travel can also be made across the universe—without the use of the bracelets—if the traveler is located directly inside the Continuum Cortex. Living Celestials would use this portion of their brain to travel across the universe in this way.

TERRIGEN BOMB

FIRST APPEARANCE *War of Kings* #5
(September 2009) **USED BY** Black Bolt,
Maximus the Mad, Inhumans

The first Terrigen Bomb (T-Bomb) is
constructed by Inhuman usurper Maximus
the Mad in order to disperse Terrigen Mist
across the universe. His plan, executed
during the war between the Kree and
Shi'ar empires, is to turn all species into
Inhumans and thus usher in a new era of
peace. The bomb must be voice-activated
by the Inhumans' ruler, Maximus' elder
brother, Black Bolt. Energy-controlling
mutant Vulcan (Gabriel Summers) attacks
the T-Bomb and, in an effort to stop him,
Black Bolt accidentally supercharges the
bomb. Element-manipulating Inhuman
Crystal (Crystalia Amaquelin) and her
teleporting canine pet Lockjaw manage
to disable the Terrigen crystals, but the
detonation tears a hole in time and space.

Black Bolt creates a second T-Bomb
when the Mad Titan Thanos comes
to Earth to look for his son, named Thane.
The resulting Terrigen cloud spreads Mists
across the planet, affecting anyone with
Inhuman DNA.

HORIZON LABS

FIRST APPEARANCE *Amazing Spider-Man* #648
(January 2011) **USED BY** Max Modell, Alchemax,
Peter Parker

Horizon Labs is an industry-leader in
technology, owned by Max Modell.
The headquarters are located at South
Street Seaport in Manhattan, New York.
The company uses an alternate
location on the *Zenith*, a ship in
international waters, when J. Jonah
Jameson closes the Manhattan office.

Horizon has seven lead scientists,
each with their own labs. They are
given the freedom to develop their
own pet projects for the good of the
company. Scientists at the lab include
Bella Fishbach, Uatu Jackson, Sajani
Jaffrey, Michael Morbius, Jurgen
Muntz, Grady Scraps, Tiberius "Ty"
Stone (who is fired after secretly
working for the Hand and crime lord
Kingpin), and Peter Parker (both as
himself and as Otto Octavius), who works
in Research and Development in Lab 7.

Many valuable inventions have arisen
from Horizon Labs, including Sajani
Jaffrey's Reverbium (a new metal alloy
based on Vibranium); Uatu Jackson's
series of anti-supernatural creature gear;
Michael Morbius' Anti-Spider virus serum

New door opens
Just when his other
opportunities dry up,
Peter Parker is offered a
new job at Horizon Labs
by the owner, Max Modell.

(capable of removing Peter Parker's spider
powers); and Jurgen Muntz's Apogee
Space Station.

Peter Parker develops a lot of new
technology of his own during his time at
Horizon Labs. Parker's inventions include
the Spidey Stealth Suit and noise-
reduction headphones, various Spider-
Armor prototypes, the Cryo Cube 3000
(a device that can freeze living organisms

without causing tissue damage) and Parker
Particles (a source of sustainable and
affordable clean energy).

Horizon Labs is eventually taken over by
the company Alchemax. Later, Peter
Parker hires Max Modell to work for him as
the head of the Parker Institute for
Technology. Parker changes the name
to Horizon University, in Modell's honor.

> "It's like an Apple store
> and Willy Wonka's factory
> had a beautiful baby."
>
> **PETER PARKER**

KNIGHT-SUITS

FIRST APPEARANCE *Iron Man* #2 (January
2013) **USED BY** Circle

Knight-suits are designed by Merlin
(Meredith) using Extremis technology
originally produced by Maya Hansen
for A.I.M. At the behest of her colleague
named Arthur, Merlin builds the suits
for a mercenary group Arthur leads
called the Circle. Arthur makes a
wager with Tony Stark that if he
can defeat the Circle's Extremis-
enhanced pilots who fly the
Knight-suits, then he will allow
Tony to recover their Extremis tech.

Arthur and the Circle lose the
wager. The Knight-suits function
similarly to Iron Man's armor, but are
designed for defensive combat using
energy shields and martial arts in
battle. The suits can also absorb and
redirect Iron Man's repulsor energy fire.

STEALTH SUIT

FIRST APPEARANCE *Amazing Spider-Man* #650
(February 2011) **USED BY** Spider-Man

Peter Parker is attacked at Horizon Labs
and bested by the sonic scream of
Hobgoblin (Phil Urich), which scrambles his
spider-sense. Hobgoblin then steals the
super-strong metal reverbium from Horizon
Labs, leading Spider-Man to make himself
a new kind of suit.

Peter's stealth suit warps sound and
light, making Spider-Man impervious to
Hobgoblin's sonic scream and, in addition,
rendering him invisible. The only way the
web-swinger can see his hands and feet
is with special goggles, which he also
lends to his ally, Black Cat (Felicia Hardy).

Together they successfully storm the
hideout of the Goblin Army, which is led
by Kingpin Wilson Fisk, and take back
the stolen reverbium.

Suit unseen
Spider-Man swings through Manhattan,
undetectable to the human eye as his
suit bends light and sound around him.

CONCORDANCE ENGINE

FIRST APPEARANCE *Defenders* #2 (March 2012)
USED BY Prester John

This golden pipework is the heart and the
soul of the universe. The reality-warping
Concordance Engine is a map of
everything in all of space and time.
To destroy or damage the Engine would
rip a hole in existence.

Time-traveling crusader Prester John
lures Nul the Breaker of Worlds to
Wundagore Mountain to destroy the
Concordance Engine, hoping that it would
return him to his home, New Avalon.
Luckily, Prester John's brother-in-arms,
Prester Omega, along with the Defenders,
stop Nul destroying the engine.

Five Concordance Engine devices exist
or have existed. The machine from
Wundagore Mountain is taken by the
Defenders to reside with Doctor Strange;
one has previously been lost by Prester
John; one is on Captain Nemo's *Nautilus*;
one is in the North Pole; and one is in
Wakanda, split into three pieces, and
known as King Solomon's Frogs.

The Baxter Building reborn
The grand unveiling of Parker
Industries reveals that Peter
Parker has taken over the
Fantastic Four's former Baxter
Building headquarters.

Picnic proposal
Peter Parker celebrates
the launch of Parker
Industries with his date,
student Anna Maria Marconi.
Aware of her scientific
talents, he wastes no time
asking her to join his
company.

PARKER INDUSTRIES

FIRST APPEARANCE *Superior Spider-Man* #20 (December 2013)
BASE Pier 64, New York City; Baxter Building, New York City; additional
branches in San Francisco, London, and Shanghai

Doctor Octopus, in the body of Peter Parker, becomes the
Superior Spider-Man. When he is severed from his job at Horizon
Labs after its destruction, "Peter Parker" opens his own scientific
research and development company called Parker Industries. With
the help of Parker's then girlfriend Anna Maria Marconi—a
fellow Empire State doctorate student—Parker Industries focuses
on building security systems, defense weaponry, and other
advanced technologies. Additional offices are opened in San
Francisco, London, and Shanghai as it becomes a publicly
traded company worldwide.

When Peter Parker takes back his body from Doctor Octopus,
he also takes over Parker Industries. Peter places Harry Lyman
(formerly Osborn) in charge of operations, because "he's good at
business." Parker moves his company into the Baxter Building,
the former headquarters of the Fantastic Four, whom he
commemorates in the lobby with a statue of the team created
by sculptor and the Thing's former lover, Alicia Masters.

Parker Industries faces many foes after Peter's return: it is
infiltrated by the terrorist organization Zodiac via the company's
own Webware devices; Doctor Otto Octavius' consciousness
secretly lives on within Anna Maria Marconi's robot assistant,
the Living Brain. Then Parker Industries becomes embroiled in
a Clone Conspiracy with the company New U Technologies—
a cloning company promising eternal life run by a new Jackal
(Spider-Man's clone, Ben Reilly).

> "Ladies and gentlemen,
> the Baxter Building is
> under new management."
> **PETER PARKER**

PLANETKILLER

FIRST APPEARANCE *Avengers* #43 (June 2015)
USED BY Tony Stark

An alternate universe's Earth hurtles toward Earth promising the extinction of both realities, known as an incursion. To counter this, Tony Stark completes and perfects an automated control system that the Avengers capture during a war against evolution-advancing aliens the Builders (during the Infinity event) to potentially use against the Shi'ar, who want to destroy the Earth so that their reality is not obliterated. The system basically delivers a world-destroying bullet; however, the Planetkiller cannot ultimately stop incursions by an unseen force (created by Doctor Doom and the Beyonders) and everything in the Marvel Universe is destroyed, leading to the events of the second Secret Wars.

WEBWARE

FIRST APPEARANCE *Amazing Spider-Man* #1 (December 2015) **USED BY** Peter Parker, Zodiac

"With great power…comes greater speed, storage, and battery life. Welcome to the Webware from Parker Industries. Now available worldwide." This wearable device provides affordable internet access from anywhere on the planet with clear reception and unlimited data. The system is encrypted making it nearly impossible to hack. However, when the terror organization, Zodiac, steals Peter Parker's personal Webware device, they gain access to millions of users' personal information as well as Spider-Man's classified S.H.I.E.L.D. intel.

Webware
Users across the globe don their new Webware wrist tech, not knowing it will make them more susceptible than ever to cyber attack.

DESTROMUNDO

FIRST APPEARANCE *Totally Awesome Hulk* #2 (March 2016) **USED BY** Lady Hellbender

This titanic, virtually indestructible spaceship belongs to extraterrestrial warrior Lady Hellbender. It contains every rare monster she has captured in her exploits across space. Lady Hellbender hopes to create a sanctuary for them on her planet Seknarf Nine.

Lady Hellbender brings *Destromundo* to Earth, seeking the dragon-like alien Fin Fang Foom. When she sees an even greater monster in action—the Totally Awesome Hulk (Amadeus Cho)—she instead sets her sights on capturing him.

Command ship *Destromundo*
Lady Hellbender summons her enormous ship—one strong enough to sustain two thousand asteroid collisions—in which she collects and stores alien monsters.

Monstrous collection
Lady Hellbender shows off her menagerie of monsters that are stored on the *Destromundo*.

SHIELD OF LIBERTY

"I have another little addition for your battle gear."

PRESIDENT F. D. ROOSEVELT

It is the U.S.'s darkest hour. The nation is on the brink of war; spies and traitors lurk everywhere. What the country needs is a living symbol to inspire ordinary folks...

In early 1941, Dr. Abraham Erskine is assassinated while his top-secret Super-Soldier serum is transforming frail Steve Rogers into a human fighting machine. With the brilliant doctor's death, plans to produce an army of similar physical paragons are dropped in favour of a new strategy.

Rogers is rapidly trained to become a one-man army—a potent symbol of American might created to inspire the people to defend democracy and freedom. As Captain America, Rogers immediately starts combating a plethora of Nazi spies and saboteurs.

Captain America's covert campaign is relatively successful but he is convinced that he could achieve even more with better equipment. The answer to his prayers comes when he is summoned to Washington D.C. to meet his lifelong idol, President Franklin Delano Roosevelt.

FIT FOR A PATRIOT

The President is extremely proud of the nation's newest patriotic champion and gives him a unique, one-of-a-kind shield to replace the cumbersome, bulletproof bucklers he has been using up to now. Virtually indestructible, this shield becomes the Sentinel of Liberty's greatest asset and symbol, an impregnable defense which, thanks to Cap's skill and muscular coordination, also functions as a surprise weapon when thrown.

Work in progress
Cap's equipment is frequently upgraded. His helmet-mask is redesigned after it slips in combat, and his early, triangular, bulletproof shields prove unreliable and unfit for purpose.

Proud moment
Combining Vibranium with an unknown metal, the circular shield is an aerodynamic, lightweight disc that absorbs any shock and vibration. Cap is honored to receive it from the hands of U.S. President Roosevelt himself.

COSMIC
POWERS

Cosmic powers originate far beyond planet Earth. They derive from immensely powerful energies, substances, and manifestations that exceed the known limits of Earthly potential, resources, and realities.

Cosmic radiation transforms four ordinary humans into the Fantastic Four. Cosmic Cubes and the helmets of the Nova Corps are conduits of seemingly limitless power. Some cosmic objects come from different dimensions or were created at the dawn of the universe, such as the Infinity Gems, sources of power lusted after by some of the universe's greatest villains. Cosmic powers may bestow immense abilities, but not all of them are beneficial. Terrigen Mists give those with the Inhuman gene powerful mutations, but they may also turn them into mindless monsters.

Cosmic forces and objects are not necessarily inherently good or evil in themselves. But the immense power that they bestow is a terrible temptation for any would-be conqueror. The quest to find and control cosmic powers may also lead to terrible, intergalactic wars, the mass exterminations of innocent lives, even the destruction of reality itself…

COSMIC RAYS AND RADIATION

FIRST APPEARANCE *Fantastic Four* #1
(November 1961) **USED BY** Fantastic Four,
Red Ghost, U-Foes

The belts of radiation where Earth's
atmosphere touches space can disrupt
satellites and spacecraft—and bestow
superpowers on living creatures who linger
too long amid these cosmic rays.

The Van Allen belts are where Earth's
magnetosphere merges with incoming
solar wind particles, creating radiation-
loaded cosmic rays that can have
incredible effects on machinery and living
organisms passing through them. When
Reed Richards builds his rocketship, he
fails to protect the craft with sufficient
shielding to withstand the radioactive
particles. As the rocket enters the Van
Allen belts, Reed and his crew are pelted
with cosmic radiation. Crashing back to
Earth, they discover that they are
permanently altered with superhuman
powers, and decide to use their abilities
for good as the Fantastic Four.

The fame of the Fantastic Four tempts
various shady figures to replicate their
fateful voyage in order to gain similar or
even greater powers. Russian Ivan Kragoff
takes a crew of apes out into the Van Allen
belts. Coincidentally, the Fantastic Four are
conducting a mission to the moon at the
same time and witness Kragoff's
unshielded ship being struck by cosmic
rays. The Human Torch investigates and
finds that the three apes are now
super-powered. When the heroes land on
the moon, they discover that Kragoff can
now pass through solid objects and is
calling himself the Red Ghost.

Later, a new quartet seeks to emulate
the Fantastic Four. Wealthy Simon Utrecht
finances the space mission, taking pilot
Mike Steel and scientist brother and sister
Jimmy and Ann Darnell as his crew. The
four gain powers not unlike those of the
Fantastic Four, but are brought back to
Earth by Bruce Banner, who has stumbled
on their mission control and thinks they
do not appreciate the dangers of cosmic
radiation. Long exposure has put the crew
at serious risk, and their powers spin out
of control as radiation overwhelms their
bodies. The group, now calling themselves
the U-Foes, seems to disappear. However,
it makes a comeback, becoming enemies
of the Hulk, whom the U-Foes blame for

stopping them achieving their full cosmic
ray potential. Sometime later, the Thing is
exposed to cosmic rays, along with Ms.
Marvel (Sharon Ventura). The Thing
becomes even more mutated, stronger
and with spiky skin, while Ms. Marvel
turns into a kind of She-Thing. She is
later returned to normal human form by
Doctor Doom.

Menace of the U-Foes
The U-Foes expose themselves
to cosmic rays and gain extreme
superpowers before being brought
back to Earth by Bruce Banner.
From left: X-Ray, Vector, Vapor,
and Ironclad.

Red Ghost
Russian space pioneer Ivan Kragoff travels through
the cosmic rays, hoping that he and his simian crew
will become more powerful than the Fantastic Four.

> "You can't feel them... but they'll affect you just the same"
>
> **BEN GRIMM**

Ray storm
The Fantastic Four's rocket is blasted
by cosmic rays, as Reed Richards
investigates whether the phenomenon
is used by aliens for communication.

MANDARIN'S RINGS

FIRST APPEARANCE *Tales of Suspense* #50 (February 1964)
USED BY Mandarin

The ten rings discovered by Mandarin aboard a crashed alien spaceship have incredible powers to bestow on those who wear them. However, those powers can corrupt…

The rings of power are alien artifacts from the planet Maklua, brought to Earth in a spaceship crash. The surviving crew members, reptilian dragon-like beings, assume human form and go out into the world to make new lives—and wait for the summons of their captain. Thousands of years pass, and the crash site of the Makluan ship is discovered by the Mandarin. Exploring the wreck, he is drawn to its control center and finds the ten rings. He senses their power and wants it for himself, so he puts the rings on. He is able to harness just a fraction of their power, but this is enough to make him a mighty lord in China, one even the Communist regime respects and fears.

Although he has used the rings to successfully dominate everyone he has come across, the Mandarin's early schemes are repeatedly foiled by Iron Man (Tony Stark). The villain swears to try and utilize the full power of his rings to get rid of his nemesis, but the two enemies are actually forced to team up when the giant reptilian owners of the rings come to claim them. Iron Man directs the force of his energy blasts through the Mandarin's rings, defeating the "dragons."

1 Remaker Manipulates matter at an atomic or molecular level.

2 Influence Creates forces that cause a body to experience change.

3 Spin Decelerates time so that its wearer appears to be moving at super-speed.

4 Spectral Breaks inanimate objects apart, but needs 20 minutes to recharge.

5 Nightbringer Creates "darklight"—malleable darkness.

6 Zero Projects extreme cold and ice through a portal from deep space.

7 The Liar Projects illusions and manipulates the thoughts and actions of others.

8 Lightning Projects pulses of electrical energy.

9 Incandescence Allows wearer to produce fire via a portal to the heart of the sun.

10 Daimonic Manipulates electromagnetic energy and also inspires obsession.

"My rings shall sound the clarion call!"
MANDARIN

A fateful discovery
Superstition and rumor have kept people away from the Valley of the Spirits. Eager for anything that will bring him extra power, the Mandarin investigates—and finds an alien spaceship containing ten rings that will bring him just what he craves.

Dragon seed
The Mandarin returns to plague Iron Man, but the two old enemies are soon forced to bury the hatchet and face the mighty threat of the rings' ten dragons.

Mandarin is apparently killed when Iron Man destroys his castle. The villain's son, Temugin, receives the ten rings—and the hands that were wearing them—in a package. He puts the rings on and inherits Mandarin's mission to kill Iron Man; however, Temugin's heart is never really in this vendetta and he fails. In fact, the Mandarin is still alive and being held in a psychiatric facility in China. Somehow, the rings find their way back to him; now without hands, the Mandarin has them fused into his spine. He clashes with Iron Man once again during a plot to release the deadly Extremis virus—the Golden Avenger tears some of the rings from Mandarin's body and uses them to defeat him. However, the rings will not allow the Mandarin to stay down for long, and he returns with a plan to create mechanized hosts called Titanomechs to house the alien souls that he claims reside in the rings. Mandarin even uses the rings to coerce Tony Stark into helping him, but the billionaire genius rebels against the Mandarin's mind control and destroys the Titanomechs. The rings are impounded in a S.H.I.E.L.D. facility, but use their powers to escape and search for new hosts. They are recaptured by Iron Man, who deduces that they have been given advanced sentience from an alien source.

Unlucky find
Discovering the Cosmic Cube among the dead and wounded on the battlefields of World War II, Nazi agent Red Skull holds it aloft, exulting in the power the glowing artifact can bestow.

COSMIC CUBE

FIRST APPEARANCE *Tales of Suspense* #79 (July 1966) **USED BY** A.I.M., Red Skull, Thanos, Goddess, Kubik, Kosmos, Kobik

The first Cosmic Cube was created by the scientific research and terror organization A.I.M. (Advanced Idea Mechanics) for the Nazi villain Red Skull. This matrix contains reality-warping energies from the alien Beyonder's dimension. The Cosmic Cube can make or destroy reality in any way the wielder sees fit—making it one of the most powerful artifacts in the universe.

Multiple Cosmic Cubes exist and they have been objects of desire for many villains. The Mad Titan Thanos has absorbed the entire power of a Cube to become an omnipotent god. The being known as Goddess collected 30 Cosmic Cubes, turning them into a Cosmic Egg which she used to brainwash an entire universe, while the Red Skull has used a Cosmic Cube many times in his battles against Captain America.

Cosmic Cubes are also capable of becoming sentient. One such Cube becomes Kubik, an alien, Skrull-like creature, whose near-omnipotence makes him a "Shaper of Worlds." Molecule Man and the alien Beyonder combine together into a sentient Cosmic Cube that becomes the entity Kosmos or the Maker. Shards of a Cosmic Cube are also used to create Kobik, a powerful girl who uses her reality-shaping ability to change villains into average people for the agency S.H.I.E.L.D., and also to turn Captain America into a Hydra agent for Red Skull.

Mad Titan, mad god
Thanos absorbs the essence of the Cosmic Cube, giving him untold power with which to shape and control the universe.

TERRIGEN CRYSTALS

FIRST APPEARANCE *Thor* #146 (November 1967) **USED BY** Inhumans

Terrigen Crystals are rare minerals that can be found on Earth's moon in the subterranean Terrigen Waters. These crystals are deeply valued and protected by the Inhuman inhabitants. Inhumans are just like ordinary human beings until they are exposed to Terrigen Mist, released from the Terrigen Crystals. The mist serves as a catalyst for a mutagenic change—a process known as Terrigenesis—which sends any human with hidden Inhuman genes into a chrysalis state. On emerging from this cocoon, the individual finds they have new Inhuman powers. These powers may manifest physically, or internally without any change in outward appearance. The Inhuman Genetic Council decides whether to let Inhumans go through Terrigenesis.

The mist released from Terrigen Crystals can be deadly. When a Terrigen Bomb—built by the conspirings of Black Bolt and Maximus to rid themselves of Thanos—detonates, it destroys the Inhuman capital city Attilan and sends mists over the Earth. The Terrigen Mist creates a multitude of new Inhumans and kills many people who are overwhelmed by the explosion or high mist exposure. Terrigen Mist is especially harmful to mutants and its use leads to a war between the Inhumans and the X-Men.

Power swim
Quicksilver explores the waters of Attilan where many Inhumans go to unlock latent super-powers, hoping to unlock new powers within himself.

ZODIAC KEY

FIRST APPEARANCE *Nick Fury, Agent of SHIELD* #1 (June 1968)
USED BY Brotherhood of the Ankh, Scorpio, Zodiac

The Zodiac Key is a powerful artifact from the mystical realm called the Ankh Dimension, sometimes called the 13th Dimension. The key is carved from an otherworldly mineral in the shape of an Ankh, the Egyptian symbol for eternal life. The carvings on the key serve as conduits for the powers of the god Ankh and his dimension, psionically ushering forth energy blasts, teleporting people and objects, as well as powering machinery. The key is somewhat sentient, and can obey or resist commands given by whoever is wielding it at the time.

The Zodiac Key is forged by the mysterious Brotherhood of the Ankh, who worship the cosmic being known as the In-Betweener. The key helps to balance the opposing energies of order and chaos in the universe. When the Zodiac Key begins to weaken, the Brotherhood send it from their dimension to Earth.

The mystical object presents itself to Nick Fury's brother Jacob, because of his extreme potential for evil. As the Super Villain Scorpio, Jacob attacks his brother, and is seemingly killed. However, the Zodiac Key resurrects Scorpio as a Life Model Decoy to cause further trouble for S.H.I.E.L.D. and Nick Fury. Later, the key is used by various members of the Zodiac crime ring who are named after the 12 astrological signs of the Zodiac.

Zodiac holds the key
Scorpio, flanked by Aries and Taurus, brandishes the Zodiac Key as the trio set their sights on attacking Nick Fury and the agents of S.H.I.E.L.D.

The Brotherhood
The high priest of the Brotherhood of Ankh uses the Zodiac Key to force heroes and villains to fight, restoring balance to the universe.

COSMIC CONTROL ROD

FIRST APPEARANCE *Fantastic Four Annual* #6 (November 1968) **USED BY** Annihilus

This golden glowing rod appears around the armored neck of the villain Annihilus, giving him immortality and untold power. The Cosmic Control Rod comes into being when Annihilus uses a knowledge-transference helmet to gain control of the wreckage of a Tyannan starship. Using his enhanced knowledge and strength, Annihilus masters the Tyannan technology and creates the Cosmic Control Rod, which allows him to syphon off cosmic energy from the starship's stardrive.

Annihilus largely uses the rod to slow his aging process and safeguard himself from harm. However, the rod's seemingly limitless cosmic energy also produces energy blasts, boosts his energy and endurance, and allows him to fly through space. Annihilus later inserts the rod in the handle of a battle axe in order to kill his foe, Human Torch (Johnny Storm).

Join the band
Tony Stark hands over the Nega-Bands to Ms. Marvel (Kamala Khan) as they face off against evil insectoid Annihilus.

NEGA-BANDS

FIRST APPEARANCE *Captain Marvel* #16 (September 1969)
USED BY Captain Mar-Vell, Genis-Vell, Phyla-Vell, Ronan, Marvel Boy (Kamala Khan)

These golden bracelets draw energy from the Negative Zone. They emit a slight golden glow and are highly sought-after because of the immense power with which they endow the wearer. The bands are activated by banging them together, enabling the wielder to travel through the vacuum of space using interstellar flight with no need for food, water, or sleep. For some wearers, this activation also includes a transformation into a costume or powered suit. Increased strength and durability make the wearer a formidable opponent, especially as they can emit powerful, psionically controlled energy blasts.

Nega-Bands were created by the Kree Supreme Intelligence, an alien life-form composed of the collective minds of the Kree race's greatest thinkers after their deaths.

There are three known pairs of Nega-Bands in existence; these have been worn by Captain Mar-Vell, his son Genis-Vell, and daughter Phyla-Vell. A fourth pair stolen by the Shi'ar may possibly have been Captain Mar-Vell's original pair. Henry Pym successfully makes a pair of Nega-Bands, but they are destroyed in an explosion. The Kree Supreme Intelligence also makes a pair for Marvel Boy (Noh-Varr), but they are taken back by the Kree villain Ronan the Accuser when Noh-Varr refuses to help the Kree remove the Phoenix Force from Earth.

Quantum-Bands

These bracelets are similar to Nega-Bands, except that they draw their energy from the Quantum Zone. They are designed by the cosmic entity Eon for those he designates Protectors of the Universe. Those that have possessed this title include: Captain Marvel (Mar-Vell), Quasar (Wendell Vaughan), Photon (Genis-Vell/Captain Marvel), and Quasar (Phyla-Vell).

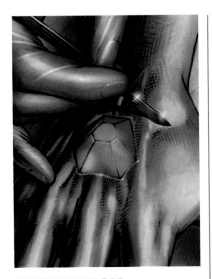

POWER PRISM

FIRST APPEARANCE *Avengers* #69 (October 1969) **USED BY** Doctor Spectrum (Joseph Ledger, Kinji Obatu, Billy Roberts, Janet van Dyne, Martha Gomes, Dr. Alice Nugent)

The Power Prism is a crystal created by Skrull science as punishment for Skrull traitor Krimmon. After failing in a bid to oust the Emperor, Krimmon's mind is imprisoned in the crystal for eternity. The Grandmaster transforms the Prism when he creates the Squadron Sinister. He renders it capable of manipulating energy and creating constructs from light, but only when commanded by another intelligence. Krimmon battles ceaselessly with whoever holds the Prism—usually heroes operating as Doctor Spectrum—striving to escape and seize control of a host body and again bend the physical world to his will.

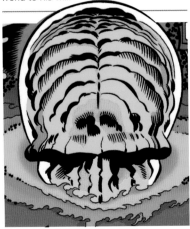

UNI-MIND

FIRST APPEARANCE Eternals #12 (June 1977) **USED BY** The Eternals

The Uni-Mind is a psionic gestalt state, achieved when Eternals psychically align their mentalities. The amalgamation forms a vast construct comprised of light, mind, and energy which allows for full rapport in times of crisis: an infinitely faster, surer, and superior method of communication and debate than simple speech. When Eternals combine in this way they have access to near-infinite levels of power and unswerving certainty in how to apply it. The Uni-Mind is a sacred ritual traditionally convened by the Prime Eternal and involving the entire race, although smaller groups can form a Uni-Mind when circumstances demand.

INFINITY GAUNTLET

FIRST APPEARANCE *Silver Surfer* #1 (December 1990) **USED BY** Thanos, Magus, Adam Warlock, Captain America, Tony Stark, the Hood, Reed Richards

The Infinity Gauntlet is a device created to utilize the combined power of the Infinity Gems, which comprise the totality of a universe's power. Infinity Gauntlets have been discovered in many different universes but cannot function outside their own original plane of reality. In the Marvel Universe, the Time, Space, Reality, Power, Mind, and Soul stones are first combined by Thanos to power a cannon designed to extinguish stars, but his scheme of stellar genocide is defeated by Adam Warlock and Earth heroes the Avengers.

Returned to their previous safe-keepers—the Elders of the Universe— the "Soul Gems" are employed together in a concerted attack upon Galactus and believed lost forever in a black hole.

When Thanos returns from the dead, he reveals that the stones are the remnants of a primal cosmic being from the time of universal creation, who divided his omnipotent essence into six parts. Realizing the gems' unified power to manipulate the totality of all existence, and their ability to even overwhelm beings such as Galactus, the Watchers, Celestials, Eternity, Lord Chaos, Master Order, Mistress Love, and Sir Hate, the Mad Titan recovers the gems and constructs a glove to combine their power. He then begins an assault on all life in the name of his mistress, Death.

Thanos is again confronted and defeated by Adam Warlock and a coalition of all Earth's Super Heroes, after which conceptual being the Living Tribunal decrees that the gems are too dangerous to ever be combined again. They are split up and each one assigned a guardian in Warlock's Infinity Watch.

Despite this precaution, the Infinity Gauntlet is reformed many times, until apparently finally destroyed when Steve Rogers uses it on behalf of Earth's Illuminati to prevent a Multiversal incursion destroying two colliding universes.

"The Infinity Gems have given me the power of Supreme Being!"

THANOS

To Infinity...
Mystic criminal the Hood (Parker Robbins) goes hunting for the Infinity Gems, hoping to gain enough power to to crush the Avengers.

Absolute power
Thanos creates the Gauntlet to decimate all life for his lover Mistress Death, but its infinite might alters his intentions. He comes to see the Gauntlet's Infinity Gems as the key to his own domination of reality.

COSMIC RING (FREEDOM RING)

FIRST APPEARANCE *Marvel Team-Up* #20 (July 2006) **USED BY** Ringmaster, Curtis Doyle, Aubrey Thompson (Z-Reg/Crusader)

The Cosmic Ring is constructed from remnants of a shattered Cosmic Cube. It has the power to reshape reality, but only within an area extending 15ft (4.6m) in all directions from the wearer and generating a 30ft (9m) sphere where literally anything can happen. Following a battle for its possession, involving Ringmaster, Captain America, and A.I.M., the ring falls into the hands of civilian Curtis Doyle, who uses it to transform himself into the Super Hero Freedom Ring. When he is killed in action, the ring is claimed by Skrull Z-Reg but lost when he is assassinated by 3-D Man.

To dare is to do
Although Nova Helmets grant incredible powers and unlimited resources, they are useless without the courage and daring of the heroes who wear them.

BLACK VORTEX

FIRST APPEARANCE *Legendary Starlord* #4 (December 2014) **USED BY** Slaughter Lords, Gara, Gamora, Thane, Beast, Young Cyclops, Young Iceman, Young Angel, Kitty Pryde, Groot, Ronan the Accuser

The Black Vortex is a device of cosmic power, created 12 billion years ago by the Celestial Godhead in response to supplications from a Viscardi woman named Gara, who longed for the power to leave her world. The Vortex elevates the user into a cosmic being after first acting as a mirror, showing an individual what their full cosmic potential could be. If they willingly submit to this semi-sentient device, they are granted the promised power. Most dispensations result in great tragedy and bloodshed. It is unclear if the Vortex taints a user's personality or simply allows their darker nature to dominate: Within a year of Gara using it, all the Viscardi submit to the Black Vortex's power. The result is a terrible war that leaves Gara her race's sole survivor.

The Vortex is lost and Gara spends the next 12 billion years seeking it in order to destroy it. Her quest eventually brings her into a cosmic conflagration when J-Son, the former Emperor of Spartax now known as Mister Knife, despatches his Slaughter Squad to retrieve the Black Vortex from the space station *Kymellia II*. He loses it to Kitty Pryde and Star-Lord.

The struggle to possess the chaos-creating device then involves the young X-Men, the Guardians of the Galaxy, Nova, Thane (Thanos's son), Ronan's Accuser Corps and other interstellar agents. When it is captured by the Kree and brought to their homeworld, Hala, the planet is destroyed by Mister Knife's forces. Destruction continues in the Vortex's wake, until Gara claims the device. She still holds it, safe from any who might use it.

NOVA HELMET

FIRST APPEARANCE *Point One* #1 (January 2012) **USED BY** Supernovas of Xandar (Jesse Alexander, Titus, Mr. Zzz, the Phlish, Adomox, Garlon of Centrifix IV), Sam Alexander

The Nova helmet was created by Xandarian scientists to facilitate a connection to the Nova Force that empowers agents of the Nova Corps, an intergalactic peacekeeping organization battling piracy, aggression, and chaos throughout the universe. Nova helmets are exclusively worn by an elite division of special operatives dubbed Supernovas.

The helmets grant the rightful wearer high-speed flight, super-strength, durability—including the ability to survive deep-space vacuum and radiation—energy blasts, telekinesis, and the ability to teleport transgalactic distances via space jumps.

Donning the helmet causes a specially tailored Nova uniform to materialize on the wearer and provides various informational and tactical services—instantaneous translation of any language; tactical analysis of friends and foes; access to a vast library archive and official records; strategic advice and battle tactics; an "autopilot" function and holographic

Unlocking the past
Sam Alexander's touch opens the Nova Helmet's databanks and offers the boy answers to the mystery of his missing father, Jesse.

recording and display. All of these functions are either screened on an internal heads-up display or beamed directly into the wearer's brain.

Unlike the gold-helmet-wearing Nova Centurions—who receive their abilities directly from the cosmic Nova Force—Supernovas are powered by on-board generators built into their invulnerable black-and-red headgear. Thus their enhanced abilities, powers, and uniforms vanish if the helmet is removed; these can only be restored by putting the helmet back on.

Each Nova helmet is keyed to a specific DNA signature. It only activates if the assigned wearer dons it, or, as in the case of teenager Sam Alexander (Nova), if a close family member uses it.

> "The speed. The power. It is like being a human rocket!"
>
> **NOVA (SAM ALEXANDER)**

PYRRHIC VICTORY

"When you play a game of life and death, mine are the only rules."

DEATH

The Grandmaster challenges the mysterious Unknown Elder to a contest for the life of his brother, the Collector. But, basking in victory, he discovers that the game is rigged…and a terrible choice faces him.

Two Immortal Elders have chosen Earth's Super Heroes to take part in a contest. The Grandmaster hopes to win the chance to bring the Collector, his brother, back to life. With Earth and all living beings on it put into stasis, the heroes are gathered in an orbiting arena. The Elders each pick twelve super-powered humans to search four areas of the world for the quarters of a gleaming golden globe of life. Only if they all play along will Earth be released from suspended animation.

After fighting in the four zones—the frozen North, a Western ghost town, a City of the Dead, and the jungle—the Grandmaster's team returns to the arena with two out of the four objects in their possession. The Grandmaster is ready to try and claim his prize, but several of the assembled heroes feel uneasy. Surely a life cannot be brought back from the dead without something being given in return? The Talisman, an Australian mystic hero, uses his bull-roarer to bring about dream-time, Invisible Girl steps up to discover the identity of a hooded figure, the Unknown. She reveals the face of Death.

Face of Death
Getting a bad feeling about the outcome of the contest, Talisman induces dream-time and asks Invisible Girl to unmask the Unknown. She reveals Death.

A LIFE FOR A LIFE

Death tells the Grandmaster that the golden globe is merely a vessel and needs a life force to give it the energy to work. To bring back a being as powerful as the Collector necessitates an equally powerful life force —the Grandmaster himself. While the Grandmaster protests, he cannot deny that Death sets the rules and all must obey. However, Death has an alternative: The Grandmaster can save himself if he sacrifices all the Earth heroes that are gathered in the arena. The Grandmaster refuses to allow the heroes to die when they have helped him win the contest and he chooses to die himself, wishing to keep to the rules. As he disappears, the Collector appears in his place. When he realizes what his brother has done to bring him back, he challenges Death to a game and the two depart. The arena disappears, Earth is freed from stasis, and the heroes are returned to the places they came from, having learned that Death makes its own rules.

No way to win
The Grandmaster's team of Super Heroes returns triumphant, but their master is about to discover that he has been dealing with an implacable opponent who never really loses.

MAGICAL ARTIFACTS

Many powerful objects in the Marvel Universe are the results of scientific breakthroughs and technological advances. But there exist others whose properties utterly defy logic and conventional explanation.

Magical artifacts may originate on Earth, or come from far-off planets, alternate realities, timelines, and dimensions. They may be linked to a specific user, such as Thor's hammer, Mjolnir. Others may be easily transferred from one person to another, such as King Arthur's sword Excalibur. They may be the source of a being's power, or an external manifestation of it. Some artifacts cause great conflicts, as heroes and villains vie to possess them, and others have corrupting influences, like the Serpent Crown.

The incredible powers of some magical artifacts go way beyond measurable limits and into the realms of the supernatural. They may allow the wielder to project energies of coruscating power, appear or disappear, or shape-shift into anything the wielder wishes. Some, such as the devastating Casket of Ancient Winters, may even lay waste entire worlds.

EBONY BLADE

FIRST APPEARANCE *Black Knight* #1 (May 1955)
USED BY Sir Percy of Scandia, Dane Whitman,
Bloodwraith (Sean Dolan)

The Ebony Blade is a sword forged from a black ore called Starstone, made from a fallen meteor. The sorcerer Merlin imbues the blade with additional powers and gives it to Sir Percy of Scandia—secretly operating as the Black Knight—whom Merlin hopes will protect King Arthur from the would-be usurper, Mordred. The blade is passed down from Black Knight to Black Knight, only allowing itself to be used by those worthy of its power.

A strong bond is formed between the blade and its wielder, offering him or her many advantages. It allows its owner to teleport to the blade's location using a special ritual. The blade has also been known to invigorate whoever wields it with the spirits of previous Black Knights.

The Ebony Blade is indestructible; it cuts through most known substances, even Iron Man's Extremis armor. It wards off magical attacks, absorbing their energy, and is impervious to magical effects. It cannot prevent injuries, but it protects its user from being killed—unless he or she is attacked by its sister weapon, the Obsidian Dagger, which is created from the same meteor. When plunged into the Brazier of Truth, the Ebony Blade allows Black Knight

Dane Whitman to speak with the first Black Knight, Sir Percy.

However, if the Black Knight that wields the Ebony Blade spills too much blood, especially in evil acts, the blade becomes tainted and begins to crave blood. This has driven one Black Knight's squire, Sean Dolan, to become the evil Bloodwraith, and brings about the ruin of Proctor, a Black Knight from another dimension.

An internal battle
As the pull of the Ebony Blade grows stronger, Dane Whitman wages an internal battle over whether its gifts outweigh the blood-curse it carries.

BOOK OF THE VISHANTI

FIRST APPEARANCE *Strange Tales* #116 (January 1964) **USED BY** Doctor Strange

A triumvirate of mystical beings known as the Vishanti—the All-Seeing Agamotto, the Omnipotent Oshtur, and the Lord of Hosts Hoary Hoggoth—created this powerful tome. Its pages contain all the known white magic in the mystical realms.

The book is passed on to successive Sorcerer Supremes, with new spells added. The book's incantations and spells can only be used for doing good, and are defensive in nature. In large part, the Book of the Vishanti exists to counteract the spells of the *Darkhold*, a book containing all known dark magic.

CLOAK OF LEVITATION

FIRST APPEARANCE *Strange Tales* #127 (December 1964) **USED BY** Doctor Strange

The red Cloak of Levitation is handed down by the Ancient One to Doctor Strange as a reward for defeating Dormammu, the ruler of the Dark Dimension, thus proving his worth and spiritual growth.

This seemingly simple cloak allows the wearer to levitate, giving the power of flight. It also functions as a prehensile appendage, grasping, striking, and warding off attacks. The cloak will do its owner's bidding, acting autonomously on his (or her) behalf. It can even disguise itself as another garment, such as a business suit—making it the perfect accessory for any magical occasion.

EYE OF AGAMOTTO

FIRST APPEARANCE *Strange Tales* #128 (January 1965) **USED BY** Doctor Strange

The creation of the Eye of Agamotto is cloaked in mystery. This enormously powerful artifact is contained within an amulet by the ancient, all-seeing, mystical being Agamotto. The Eye can only be used by one who is pure of heart. It is given to Doctor Strange—along with the Cloak of Levitation—by his mentor the Ancient One, after Strange defeats Dormammu of the Dark Dimension.

The Eye emits a mystical light that penetrates magical disguises, spells, and charms, weakening evil beings such as demons and dark sorcerers. The Eye also opens the eye chakra, awakening psionic abilities that enable its wearer to read minds, use telekinesis, open portals to other worlds, create mystical defences, and utilize many other magical powers.

MJOLNIR

FIRST APPEARANCE *Journey Into Mystery* #83 (August 1962) **USED BY** Thor, Roger "Red" Norvell, Captain America, Beta Ray Bill, Thor (Jane Foster)

Thor's hammer, Mjolnir, not only gives the wielder control of thunder and lightning, but of teleportation and godhood itself. The enchanted hammer can only be lifted by those who are deemed "worthy"—being of sound moral character. Mjolnir is made of the magical metal Uru, mined from the heart of a star, and forged by the Dwarf blacksmiths of Nidavellir. A leather strap around Mjolnir's handle enables it to be swung and thrown.

In addition to being a mighty metal sledgehammer, Mjolnir gives its owner many powers. It can summon weather systems that can impact on a nearly global scale, including rain, wind, lightning, and of course, thunder. If the hammer is struck forcefully on the ground it can make the earth shake—and cause an earthquake.

The hammer returns to the hand from which it is thrown and can be beckoned by its wielder; and when swung rapidly in a circle it can open interdimensional portals to travel through the realms of Asgard and beyond. If the hammer is placed on top

of anyone unworthy, it will pin them to the ground. If the worthy god shares their body with a mortal, Mjolnir can transform them into their alter ego when they strike the hammer upon the ground.

The king of the Norse gods, Odin, gives Mjolnir to Thor as a reward for proving his worth by successfully completing several trials: retrieving the stolen Golden Apples of Immortality from the Storm Giants, stopping invading forces, and rescuing the goddess Sif from Hel. Inevitably, this makes Thor's mischief-making adopted brother Loki desperately jealous.

Thor is not the only person to prove worthy of wielding Mjolnir. A mortal man named Red Norvell, under the influence of Loki, uses Thor's magical Belt of Strength, Megingjord, and magical iron gloves, to rip the hammer from Thor's grasp. Captain America wields Mjolnir to free Thor from the forces of Grog the God Crusher. The alien Beta Ray Bill proves himself so worthy in battle against Thor that Odin creates a new hammer named Stormbreaker for him. And when Thor Odinson becomes unworthy to wield Mjolnir, his ex-girlfriend Jane Foster takes up the hammer. Jane becomes Thor, working with the Avengers, and A-Force, as well as fighting Asgardian villains.

A worthy friend
In a battle with Grog the God Crusher, Thor becomes separated from his enchanted hammer. Cap is able to wield Mjolnir instead, making him a worthy ally.

> "Whosoever holds this hammer, if he be worthy, shall possess the power of Thor."
>
> MJOLNIR'S ENCHANTMENT

Powers of the hammer

The God of Thunder derives many of his powers from his hammer, Mjolnir. It is composed of uru, a magical, virtually unbreakable metallic substance that can only be found on Asgard.

Possessing superhuman strength, Thor often employs Mjolnir as a formidable throwing weapon. No matter how far it is thrown, no matter what it strikes, the hammer always returns to Thor's hand.

Thor uses Mjolnir to summon storms. Rain, wind, thunder, and lightning are called from the heavens by striking the handle twice upon the ground. Hitting the ground with Mjolnir can cause an earthquake.

Mjolnir can fire various forms of mystical energy—the God Blast, the Anti-Blast, and the Thermo-Blast—capable of destroying planets. Mjolnir can also create virtually impenetrable force fields and absorb and redirect energy.

Whirling Mjolnir at vast speeds creates enough inertia to enable Thor to fly. Mjolnir can also open interdimensional portals, and transport Thor to distant dimensions and other planes of reality.

DESTROYER ARMOR

FIRST APPEARANCE *Journey Into Mystery* #118 (July 1965) **USED BY** Odin, Loki, Sif, Balder, Prof. Clement Holmes, Galactus, Siggorth, Lorelei

When the Celestials revisit Earth as the Third Host, they are met by a committee of godly sky-fathers, comprising Zeus, Odin, and Brahma. The earthbound deities are warned not to interfere with the Celestials' next visitation, when they will pass final judgement on the world, its races, and gods. Failure to comply will force the Celestials to cut off the Gods' access to Earth and the humans who worship them. The Gods of Earth vow resistance and pool their powers to create a mighty suit of armor that Odin has constructed. The Destroyer armor is designed to carry their combined might into battle against the omnipotent stellar judges. It is crafted, and meticulously programmed, to be an unstoppable engine of destruction.

The Destroyer is hidden in an Asian temple until needed, but is accidentally discovered by a hunter being manipulated by Loki to attack Thor. The armor has been built to absorb and entrap the soul of anyone in its proximity and the hunter becomes its activating source. He is helpless to resist the Destroyer's programming, and the armor runs amok.

The Destroyer is all-but-indestructible and a constant menace. Its mystic programming quickly overwhelms even the strongest-willed animating spirit to inhabit the suit, rapidly forcing a descent into mindless destruction. It has been misused many times and even briefly served as a herald of planet-devouring Galactus before ultimately failing in its appointed task and being melted down by the limitless power of the Celestials. The Destroyer was later reconstructed by Loki and remains a deadly threat.

Death metal
The Destroyer Armor is fast and strong enough to even kill Thor and slice his magical hammer Mjolnir in two.

NORN STONES

FIRST APPEARANCE *Journey Into Mystery* #116 (May 1965) **USED BY** Karnilla the Norn Queen, Loki, Thor, Sif, Borjigin Byambyn Khenbish (the Demon)

Norn Stones are a collection of powerful mystic talismans traditionally held by ancestral Asgardian enemy Karnilla, the Norn Queen. They possess a variety of powers and temporarily bestow fantastic abilities upon the holder. The stones are used frequently by Loki to augment his own magical might and in schemes to destroy his noble half-brother Thor.

Norn Stones may be semi-sentient. Unless properly contained—in a special mystic sack—they tend to wander and can relocate themselves by unknown means. They have also been known to refuse the commands of an unworthy holder, such as the villainous Norman Osborn.

ODINSWORD

FIRST APPEARANCE *Journey Into Mystery* #117 (June 1965) **USED BY** Odin, Destroyer, Thor

"Odinswords" are mystically potent blades wielded by the All-Father of Asgard. The most infamous is the gigantic Over Sword, destined to remain forever sheathed lest the universe be destroyed. Many diabolical enemies, such as Mangog, attempt to draw it and bring about Armageddon. Reputedly forged from the accursed Nibelung Ring and imbued with great sacrificial magic, it is remade by Odin to use against the star-spanning Celestials when they return to pass judgment on Earth.

Another mighty Odinsword—called Ragnarok—is later given to Thor by his father to use against the All-Father's malign brother, Cul Borson.

> "Hear me, Odin!!…Now it is thine own life itself which is the prize!"
>
> **DESTROYER ARMOR**

Shoulder spikes
The armor is designed to inflict maximum damage to foes

Visor
The visor deploys to unleash irresistible disintegration rays

Unstoppable force
The Destroyer is proof against almost any force. It can also fly faster than the speed of sound (768mph; 1,236km/h)

Power blasts
Gauntlets project a lethal variety of death-dealing energies from electricity to antimatter blasts

CRIMSON GEM OF CYTTORAK

FIRST APPEARANCE *X-Men* #12 (July 1965)
USED BY Juggernaut, Ahmet Abdol, Pyotr Rasputin (Colossus)

A millennium ago, the magical Octessence—Balthakk, Watoomb, Farallah, Ikonn, Krakkan, Raggadorr, Valtorr, and Cyttorak—argue over whose mystic might is greatest. To settle the issue, each manufactures a totem exemplifying its creator's power. In time each totem will transform one eighth of humanity into their exemplars, to battle until an ultimate victor emerges.

Cyttorak's giant ruby transforms any mortal touching it into an unstoppable juggernaut of destruction; it also contains a timeless pocket dimension named the Crimson Cosmos. The gem is hidden in a Korean temple, where it is later found by Charles Xavier's stepbrother Cain Marko, who becomes Super Villain Juggernaut. The Ruby of Cyttorak bears this inscription: "Whosoever touches this gem shall possess the power of the Crimson Bands of Cyttorak! Henceforth, you who read these words, shall become... forevermore... a human juggernaut!"

WANDS OF WATOOMB

FIRST APPEARANCE *Amazing Spider-Man Annual* #2 (October 1965)
USED BY Watoomb, Stephen Strange, Xandar, Doctor Doom, Tony Stark

Watoomb is an aggressive, godlike, extradimensional entity, a member of a fragile alliance known as the Octessence. The six magical artifacts collectively described as the Wicked Wands of Watoomb are hand weapons for mystic combat that concentrate and focus the various mystic forces the wielder happens to command. The wands are thought-activated and can block or absorb magical attacks, as well as tap into arcane energies to heal the wielder, construct mystic barriers, open portals, and create supernatural surveillance screens. They also control weather, especially the totemic winds of Watoomb, which can destroy or transport targets across dimensions.

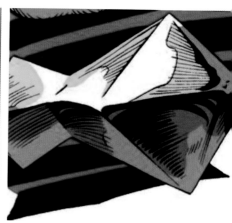

CRYSTALS OF CONQUEST

FIRST APPEARANCE *Doctor Strange* #176 (December 1968) **USED BY** Asmodeus, Sons of Satannish, Doctor Strange

The Crystals of Conquest are an arcane, crystalline configuration with links to the Nine Realms, attuned to the power of elemental regions Muspelheim and Niflheim. Able to manipulate many magical forces, the crystals are employed by dying Satannish-worshipper Dr. Charles Benton who, as Asmodeus, attempts to take Earth with him by summoning Frost Giant Ymir and Surtur the Fire Demon. The plan to simultaneously start a new ice age and set the Earth ablaze is foiled by the Avengers and Doctor Strange, who uses the crystals to bring the avatars of fire and ice together and cancel each other out.

SERPENT CROWN

FIRST APPEARANCE *Tales to Astonish* #101 (March 1968) **USED BY** Mole Man, Tyrannus, Lava Men, Kala of the Netherworld, the Deviants

In the Deviant city of Lemuria, a hidden sect of antediluvian Serpent men trick human alchemist Atra into constructing a vessel to contain the malign power of their predatory Elder God, Set. The Lord of Serpents has been imprisoned in a pocket dimension for millennia and the crown enables him to influence the physical world. The soul-corrupting crown becomes the prize in a war between Atra, the Serpent Men, and Deviant Emperor Phraug, but the civil war ends abruptly when the Second Celestial Host attacks and devastates Lemuria.

The crown later seduces high priest Naga, one of the water-breathing *Homo mermanus*, who have colonized Lemuria's ruins. The crown extends Naga's life, granting psionic abilities that allow him to dominate his people as God-Emperor and representative of Set.

His rule is challenged by a band of telepathic Lemurians, who steal the crown and hide it in Antarctica. Concealed in power-damping metal, it becomes known as the Helmet of Power and its guardians as the Ancients.

As the 20th century dawns, the helmet is recovered by Paul Destine. It amplifies his natural psionic powers and inherent madness and "Destiny" dies fighting the

Crowning achievement
Deviant priest Lord Ghaur and his servant Llyra recreate and enlarge the crown in an attempt to free their dark god Set from eons of exile to physically manifest on Earth.

Sub-Mariner. The Helmet is taken to Atlantis, where the damping metal is removed, inadvertently allowing the unfettered power of the Serpent Crown to transform city and citizens, before it manipulates dupes into carrying it back to Lemuria and Naga. After Namor and Karthon the Quester (Naga's former champion) destroy Naga, they dump the

Crown in the deepest ocean trench; however, its siren power calls to weak-willed, power-hungry Hugh Jones of the unscrupulous Roxxon Corporation. Jones recovers it and allows the Serpent God to connect with other crowns on parallel worlds. In recent years, alternate-Earth crowns have been discovered on Earth and on Mars.

"It's grander, more powerful than ever."

LLYRA OF LEMURIA

IDOL OF THE UNDYING ONES

FIRST APPEARANCE *Doctor Strange* #183 (November 1969) **USED BY** The Nameless One, Kenneth Ward, Van Nyborg

When the demonic Undying Ones were banished from Earth millennia ago, they leave magically charged statues to act as contact points in order to facilitate their eventual return and resurgence. The demons sustain their influence over the centuries through such artifacts and a small but fanatical network of human cult followers.

The Undying Ones' opportunity to reconquer Earth comes at a time when popular interest in the supernatural is high. After explorer Kenneth Ward finds a number of large statues and the Idol of the Undying Ones on an expedition to the Himalayas, he is mesmerized and murdered, but not before alerting Doctor Strange to humanity's impending peril.

DARKHOLD

FIRST APPEARANCE *Marvel Spotlight* #4
(June 1972) **USED BY** Chthon, Thulsa Doom,
Morgan Le Fay, Gregor Russoff, Doctor Strange,
Darkholders, Carnage

The first life on Earth is a race called the
Elder Gods. One of them, Chthon, is cruel
and perfects the art of black magic. When
a being called Demogorge the God-Eater
comes to destroy him, Chthon records
all his dark knowledge in a set of
indestructible scrolls—the *Darkhold*.
He escapes to a netherworld, leaving the
Darkhold behind as a conduit through
which he may be able to one day return.

Twenty millennia ago, the last
surviving wizards of the prehuman
races use the *Darkhold* to cast
a spell that creates the first
vampire—conversely,
it also contains an
incantation that
can wipe out
vampires.

Ancient evil
Sorceress Morgan
Le Fay tries to
harness the power
of the Darkhold to
bring down her rival,
Merlin, but she is
overwhelmed by the
power of dark god
Chthon *(below)*.

In 500 AD, sorceress
Morgan Le Fay binds
the scrolls of the
Darkhold together into
book form. She uses
it to summon Chthon,
but is unable to control
the evil entity and imprisons
him beneath Mount
Wundagore in the East
European country of Transia.
A holy mystic named Brendan
manages to gain a sliver of control over
the *Darkhold* and shatters it, sending the
pieces all over the world. However, six
centuries later, a heretic monk called
Aelfric collects all the fragments of the
Darkhold; even after he and the book are
burned at the stake, the *Darkhold*
survives. It passes into the Vatican library,
where it is named the Book of Sins, and is
held in the keeping of Paolo Montesi, a
monk of exceptionally strong faith, and
his heirs.

The *Darkhold* ends up in the possession
of the Russoff family, causing them to
become werewolves.

The book exhibits a malevolent cunning,
drawing people to use it to achieve their
deepest desires, and thereby providing an
opportunity for Chthon to take their souls
in exchange.

Universal evil
To ensure the *Darkhold* can
reach out to anyone on Earth,
the demon Chthon made it
comprehensible in any language.

> "At last the
> *Darkhold* scrolls
> are truly mine!"
>
> **AELFRIC, THE MAD MONK**

HELLSTROM'S TRIDENT

FIRST APPEARANCE *Marvel Spotlight* #12
(October 1973) **USED BY** Daimon Hellstrom

The Son of Satan, Daimon Hellstrom,
uses a trident forged from the metal
Netharanium. This substance is not of this
Earth but is found in a demonic dimension
and has the property of psychosensitivity.
This enables it to attract and channel
magical energies, such as Hellstrom's own
soulfire, or hellfire, which can be used to
cause agony to his enemies, or enable
Hellstrom to fly.

The trident is said to be the only weapon
that Satan is vulnerable to, perhaps as
Netharanium is the only element which can
harm him. Daimon stole the trident from his
father and used
it to summon Satan's chariot and horses,
upon which he escaped from the wrath
of Hell. Hellstrom also refers to the weapon
as an elemental trident, using it
to command the ground to move and
threatening to bring up Earth's molten core
to destroy those who displease him.

Venomous weapon
After Hellstrom gives in to his dark side,
Agent Venom is tasked with bringing him—
and his trident—to the Secret Avengers.

DRAGONFANG

FIRST APPEARANCE *Defenders* #12 (February 1974)
USED BY The Ancient One, Doctor Strange, Valkyrie, Lady Sif

This legendary sword is said to have been carved
from the tusk of a dragon slain by the wizard
Kahji-Da. From the wizard, it passes into the
possession of the Ancient One, who in turn gives it to
Doctor Strange. He gives it to the Defender Valkyrie
to replace the weapon she has handed over to the
Black Knight.

In the hands of Valkyrie, the mighty weapon proves
its worth by cleaving an onrushing steamroller in two,
but strength is not the Dragonfang's only quality.
The blade is also enchanted, and so in tune with its
wielder that malevolent forces
can use it as a conduit to
mind-possession.

Dragonfang is reputed
to be almost indestructible,
although has been
shattered by Mjolnir,
Thor's hammer.

MOONSTONES

FIRST APPEARANCE *Captain America* #170 (February 1974) **USED BY** Lloyd Bloch, Karla Sofen

Taken from the Watcher's invisible headquarters in the Blue Area of the Moon, these powerful gems—absorbed into the body—bestow superhuman strength, stamina, and reflexes. However, with the right psychological suggestion, a moonstone can also be rejected from the body after absorption.

According to the alien Kree race, the moonstones are remnants of the Big Bang, infused with other-dimensional energies. The stones are used in combination by various alien species to create the original Guardians of the Galaxy. The moonstone that ends up on Earth is a fragment of the one that created the Kree's representative Guardian, Ajes'ha. The gem contains Ajes'ha's memories—and those of anyone who gains power from it—so any holder of the moonstone may experience overlap from the minds of those who have gone before.

Crime pays
Lloyd Bloch is a small-time crook robbing a museum when he comes across the moonstone—which grants him extraordinary powers.

AMULETS OF POWER

FIRST APPEARANCE *Deadly Hands of Kung Fu* #1 (April 1974) **USED BY** Sons of the Tiger, White Tiger, Master Khan

The Amulets of Power comprise three pieces of a jade tiger statue: the head and two of the clawed feet. They were brought to San Francisco by a Chinese teacher of kung fu, Master Kee. They channel the power of the tiger spirit. When three fighters each wear one of the amulets, and chant a mystical incantation, they take on each other's strength, increasing their power threefold. But when one individual wears all three amulets at the same time, they become the White Tiger, a super-powered being with incredible martial-arts abilities. Wearing the amulets for too long, however, results in physical and psychological addiction to the powers they bestow.

Sons of the Tiger
Bob Diamond, Lin Sun, and Abe Brown are bound together and given increased strength by their jade Amulets of Power.

"That is power— that gem! Immortality and power!"

ULLUX'YL KWAN TAE SYN

Ka power
Ancient Egyptian wizard Anath-Na discovers the Ka stone and is transformed into the powerful Sphinx, with the ability to shoot energy blasts through the stone.

BLOODGEM

FIRST APPEARANCE *Marvel Presents* #1 (October 1975) **USED BY** Ullux'yl Kwan Tae Syn, Ulysses Bloodstone, Elsa Bloodstone, Cullen Bloodstone

The Bloodgem, or Bloodstone, came to Earth around 10,000 years ago from space, accompanied by Ullux'yl Kwan Tae Syn—a being representing the Hellfire Helix who was encased in the stone.

The gem represents the centre of a network channeling all the different kinds of magic in the universe. Searching for a human vessel to inhabit so that it could take over the world, the Hellfire Helix summoned a prehistoric man. He becomes angry and smashes the stone, and a fragment of it is embedded in his chest. From then on, he is Ulysses Bloodstone: the gem gives him many superhuman attributes, including near immortality. Ullux'yl spends millennia searching for the other pieces of the Bloodgem, with Ulysses trying to stop him.

Ancient warrior
The Bloodgem glows in the chest of Ulysses Bloodstone as he battles a monster from the depths.

KA STONE

FIRST APPEARANCE *Nova* #6 (February 1977) **USED BY** Anath-Na, Meryet Karim

The Ka stone bestows upon its wearers superhuman strength and durability to the level of virtual immortality. It is discovered in a desert temple by Anath-Na, a disgraced wizard from the court of the Pharaoh of Egypt. Sensing that the stone wanted him to wear it on his head like a crown, Anath-Na takes it and is transformed into the godlike Sphinx. The stone harnesses immense energy that the Sphinx can discharge as a weapon.

The Ka stone's "gift" of immortality becomes a curse for Anath-Na, who grows weary of life but unable to gain the release of death. During a battle with Galactus, the Ka stone is destroyed, but the Eater-of-Worlds sends the Sphinx back in time to shortly before he discovers the mystic gem, condemning him to keep reliving the long millennia. The Ka Stone is then partially remade, due to a temporal anomaly, before being destroyed again by the Super Villain Puppet Master.

M'KRAAN CRYSTAL

FIRST APPEARANCE *X-Men* #107 (October 1977)
USED BY M'Kraan, Shi'ar, Phoenix Force

Long ago, the peaceful M'Kraan are invaded and plundered by the ruthless Shi'ar Empire. They are looted of all their most precious resources, including their prized M'Kraan Crystal. The surviving M'Kraan, bent on revenge, change their name to Scy'ar Tal, which means "Death to the Shi'ar." Their giant pink crystal holds an alternate dimension, containing a vast alien city and the mysterious White Hot Room. At the center of the city is an energy sphere containing a neutron galaxy that is the source of unfathomable power. When Emperor D'Ken of the Shi'ar tries to access the crystal, his sister Lilandra asks the X-Men to stop him.

GUNGNIR

FIRST APPEARANCE *Thor* #275 (September 1978) **USED BY** Odin

Conflicting legends are told of Gungnir's creation. One says that the great spear is forged by the Sons of Ivaldi for a contest held by Loki. Another states that Gungnir is a gift to Odin, crafted from sunlight by dwarves. Yet another tale claims that Gungnir originates from a previous Asgard, destroyed by Ragnarok. Gungnir is composed of Uru metal, and its powers are similar to Thor's hammer Mjolnir: it returns to its owner when thrown, and can project energy blasts. During Norman Osborn's assault on Asgard, the Thunderbolts steal Gungnir, but Paladin recovers it and later Gungnir is returned to Odin.

TWILIGHT SWORD

FIRST APPEARANCE *Thor* #277 (November 1978) **USED BY** Surtur, Loki, Morgan Le Fay

The Twilight Sword (also known as the Sword of Doom) is created by Surtur to burn the universe. It has the power to cut barriers between dimensions and block Odin's weapons. The Fire Giant Surtur uses the sword against Asgard many times, but Thor manages to combine the sword with his hammer Mjolnir and slay Surtur. Nonetheless, it is foretold that Surtur will destroy Asgard with the sword in Ragnarok. The Twilight Sword is used by Loki to turn Thor into a frog and make the people of Asgard ill. Morgan Le Fay also employs the blade to transform all of Earth into a medieval world.

SHAMAN'S MEDICINE POUCH

FIRST APPEARANCE *X-Men* #120 (April 1979)
USED BY Dr. Michael Twoyoungmen (Shaman)

An artifact of the Tsuu T'ina Native American tribe, the pouch allows Shaman to access powers and supernatural items through a portal that leads to another dimension. The pouch contains many powerful items: the Staff of Growth has power over plant life; the Great Key is a staff that, when used at the Eye of the World (an dimensional gateway in the Arctic), opens a portal to the Realm of Beasts; the Spirit Staff is used to contact nature spirits; and the Jewel of Actualization boosts other powers, such as interdimensional travel. The body of Alexander Thorne, who loses his mind when he looks inside the pouch, is also stored inside.

SOULSWORD

FIRST APPEARANCE *Uncanny X-Men* #171 (July 1983) **USED BY** Magik

The Soulsword is created by Illyana Rasputina (Magik) when she is trapped in the immortal sorcerer Belasco's Limbo dimension. She draws the sword from her own life force and uses it to destroy supernatural beings and magical weapons. It begins as a simple sword but evolves with use, both in appearance and power. When she is unable to wield it, the sword is passed to Rasputina's best friend, Shadowcat (Kitty Pryde). She gives it to Amanda Sefton (alias sorceress Jimaine Szardos), who in turn passes it on to her mother, Margali Szardos. Belasco then takes it from her. After a battle with Belasco, Jimaine takes possession of the Soulsword, and hides it inside her adopted brother Nightcrawler's own body. It is later reclaimed by its original owner, Magik.

STORMBREAKER

FIRST APPEARANCE *Thor* #339 (January 1984) **USED BY** Beta Ray Bill

In their first meeting, extraterrestrial warrior Beta Ray Bill and Asgardian god Thor clash, owing to a misunderstanding. Bill actually bests Thor, and claims his hammer, Mjolnir. As an honorable hero, however, Bill feels badly, believing that Mjolnir rightly belongs to Thor. As a compromise, Odin asks Eitri and the Dwarves of Nidavellir to craft a new hammer of Uru metal, which is named Stormbreaker. Like Thor's hammer, Stormbreaker can be automatically recalled by its owner when it is thrown. Bill can use it to change into his mortal form, Simon Walters (and back again), when he strikes the ground with the hammer. Stormbreaker also projects blasts of energy, allows Bill to fly, and opens portals to other dimensions.

CASKET OF ANCIENT WINTERS

FIRST APPEARANCE *Thor* #346 (August 1984) **USED BY** Surtur, Malekith

The Casket of Ancient Winters is an Asgardian object that contains the Fimbulwinter of Ymir (the great winter that proceeds Ragnarok), which is said to have the power of a thousand deadly winters. Surtur the Fire Giant uses the casket against Earth, causing great devastation. Thor is able to stop him, but the casket falls into the hands of the Dark Elf, Malekith the Accuser. He uses it against Asgard, and the effects are so grave that even trolls and Frost Giants succumb. Thor undoes Malekith's destruction using the Gem of Infinite Suns and then banishes both the gem and the Casket of Ancient Winters to a secret dimension.

SIEGE PERILOUS

FIRST APPEARANCE *Uncanny X-Men* #227 (March 1988) **USED BY** X-Men

The Siege Perilous is a gift from the magician Roma, the daughter of the wizard Merlyn, to the X-Men after they defeat the evil Adversary. The device allows people to begin a new life with a new identity in a parallel reality. The first X-Man to enter the portal is Rogue. She is accidentally pulled inside when the Sentinel Nimrod merges with the Master Mold Sentinel brain chip and causes an explosion that sucks them into the Siege Perilous. Rogue ends up in the Savage Land, where she teams up with Magneto. Wolverine witnesses the destruction of the Siege Perilous by Donald Pierce (the White Bishop) after several of the X-Men use it to escape from Pierce.

MURAMASA BLADE

FIRST APPEARANCE *Wolverine* #2 (December 1988) **USED BY** Muramasa, Wolverine, Daken

Muramasa is a legendary Japanese swordsmith who forges his Black Blade using a portion of his own life force. Thus the blade also possesses some of his madness and evil qualities. Eventually insanity overtakes anyone who wields the blade, but in the meantime they benefit from superhuman strength and durability. The sword is virtually indestructible and can even withstand Wolverine's Adamantium claws. Muramasa retains the sword for centuries, but it later comes into the possession of the Silver Samurai (Kaniuchio Harada).

Muramasa forges a second blade, using part of Wolverine's life force, and gifts it to him. This sword is as unbreakable as the first, and even able to slice through the X-Man Cyclops' optic beams, reflecting them in several directions. Scientific study reveals that the sword cuts at the molecular level. The only thing it cannot seem to cut are the psychic shields of Armor (Hisako Ichiki). The blade also counteracts mutant healing abilities. When Wolverine severs Sabretooth's arm, the villain is unable to reattach it as he normally would. Wolverine also uses the blade to decapitate Sabretooth. Wolverine knows that the Muramasa Blade is one of the few weapons that is capable of killing him. He eventually leaves the sword in Cyclops' care, but Wolverine's son Daken acquires it and arranges for the Tinkerer (Phineas Mason) to use a piece of the blade to enhance his own claws. Realizing the danger, Wolverine catches up with Daken and cuts out his claws, burying them, along with the blade, in an unknown location.

Death of Sabretooth
Cyclops gifts Wolverine the Muramasa Blade so he can take bloody revenge on his archenemy Sabretooth.

RROAR

A fitting host
Wolverine (as Patch, one of his aliases) vies for possession of the blade with Silver Samurai, who turns out to be proof against the sword's malign influence.

"At long last, the Black Blade has a master..."

WOLVERINE

GEHENNA STONE

FIRST APPEARANCE *Wolverine* #11 (September 1989) **USED BY** Ba'al, Burt Corrigan, O'Donnell, Prince Baran, Lindsay McCabe, Jessica Drew

The Gehenna Stone dates back 13,000 years to a city where a malign entity called Ba'al-Hadad incites his worshippers to such depravity that the holy warrior Hand of God is sent to destroy them. With his dying breath, Ba'al forces his spirit into a crystal, but Hand of God smashes the stone and scatters the shards to the four winds.

Thousands of years later, the fragments draw themselves back together, allowing Ba'al to re-manifest. He corrupts innocents and converts his adherents into vampire-like creatures. This mystic resurrection is foiled by Wolverine, who destroys the Gehenna Stone with his claws.

THUNDERSTRIKE

FIRST APPEARANCE *Thor* #459 (February 1993) **USED BY** Eric Masterson, Kevin Masterson

After standing in for Thor, Eric Masterson is rewarded with Thunderstrike, a battle-mace possing the powers of legendary Mjolnir, forged in Nidavellir by Dwarven smiths. Thunderstrike bears the inscription "The World Still Needs Heroes" and is given to Masterson by Odin when the true Thor is ressurected so that, as Thunderstrike, Masterson can continue defending the helpless and combating evil.

When Eric dies in battle, the mace is left with the Avengers; after Steve Rogers takes over S.H.I.E.L.D., he passes it on to Eric's son, Kevin. Trained by a Valkyrie, Kevin becomes the new Thunderstrike, wielding the mace in the name of justice.

STAFF OF ONE

FIRST APPEARANCE *Runaways* #4 (October 2003) **USED BY** Tina Minoru, Nico Minoru, Witchbreaker, Alex Wilder, Chase Stein, Apex, Monk Theppie

The Staff of One is one of the most powerful magical artifacts in creation. Powered by primal magic, it can reshape reality, control and compel living beings, and enliven inanimate objects. It also provides instantaneous transport, affords physical, psychic, or magical protection, heals normally fatal wounds, discharges energy blasts, creates and controls weather, and can even energize and supercharge the powers of others.

The Staff's capabilities are only limited by the imagination of the wielder and the fact that it will never respond to the same command twice. If users of the Staff need to repeat an action or effect, the incantation must be rephrased. The Staff is fueled by blood sacrifice and needs the wielder to offer blood from a cut or wound. The amount of blood directly affects the Staff's strength.

Runaway Nico Minoru acquires the Staff from her dark wizard mother Tina. Nico absorbs the Staff and carries it within her own body. She summons it by chanting: "When blood is shed...let the Staff of One emerge." When Nico loses a mystic duel with the metahuman Apex on Arcade's Murderworld, she is mortally wounded and the Staff is destroyed. Nico utters a spell, resurrects herself, and restores her mystic weapon.

The other people to briefly use the Staff have either picked it up, borrowed it, or stolen it. However, after Nico and the Runaways travel back to the year 1907, her grandmother, Witchbreaker—a previous user—upgrades its power, and now the Staff appears to be more discriminating about who can wield it.

Think Fast
In Arcade's Murderworld, Nico tries to use the staff to move fellow captive gladiators Cammi, Nara, Cullen Bloodstone, and Anachronism to a place of safety, but the staff is resisting.

GHOST RIDER'S CHAIN

FIRST APPEARANCE *Ghost Rider* #1 (May 1990) **USED BY** Danny Ketch, J.T. James

The Hellfire Chain is used by various Ghost Riders, all of whom have the facility to manipulate eldritch energy. Hellfire burns the soul but it can also brutally affect physical forms and objects. When wedded to a mundane weapon, such as Johnny Blaze's shotgun or Danny Ketch's metal cycle chain, the result is a multipurpose tool of devastating force, highly effective against both mortal and supernatural threats. The chain can change its shape and form in response to Ghost Rider's mental commands. Its length is infinitely variable and, when required, it can be restructured to form shuriken, a lasso, a staff, a flail, and even a saw.

Blood bond
The Staff of One always tests its user's will and imagination and Nico is never sure if it has its own reasons for helping her.

GODKILLER SWORD

FIRST APPEARANCE *Secret Warriors* #10 (January 2010)
USED BY Gorgon, Alexander Ares (Phobos)

Long ago, the pantheons of ancient Greece and Japan are locked in a devastating war. With casualties mounting on both sides, chief deities Zeus and Amatsu-Mikaboshi separately visit the greatest blacksmith alive, demanding that he create a weapon to end the conflict.

The blind master craftsman forges two swords. Subtle Amatsu-Mikaboshi receives the perfect blade Kusanagi (Grasscutter) while the bombastic Zeus takes away the flawed Godkiller, a weapon of shattering power, but cursed to bring tragedy to its user. The war ends inconclusively and Godkiller is lost, cursed to reappear at the bloodiest moments in history. Whenever it resurfaces, Godkiller takes the lives of kings, emperors, and gods.

In recent times, when vengeful Japanese deities abduct Alexander, son of Ares, they brainwash the young God of Fear into using the sword on his father, almost ending the war god's immortal existence. The blade is then secured by Hydra chief Kraken, who passes it on to the Gorgon, a pitiless mutant killer.

When Nick Fury's Secret Warriors raid Hydra's base, the Gorgon is engaged by Alexander, who is wielding Grasscutter. Fighting a rearguard action to allow his comrades to escape, the boy god meets his death at the Gorgon's hands. At the moment Grasscutter and Godkiller resume their eons-long clash of steel both blades are shattered.

Double-edged gift
Nothing can resist Godkiller's lethal cutting blade and no one wielding it can escape the doom its use brings.

MANBREAKER

FIRST APPEARANCE
Fear Itself #2 (July 2012)
USED BY Titania, Sin/Skadi

Manbreaker—also called the Hammer of Skirn—is one of seven mystic war hammers created by the Serpent, an ancient pre-Asgardian tyrant and older brother of Odin, also known as Cul Borson. He is eventually overthrown and sealed deep below the ocean on Midgard. Millennia later, the Serpent is released when Red Skull's daughter, Sin, completes an ancient ritual. She summons the hammers, which mystically select wielders who are "Worthy."

The hammer Manbreaker chooses the criminal Titania, calling to her with music that sounds "like crying babies." Titania is transformed into Skirn, Breaker of Men, a godlike being of incalculable strength and cruelty.

JARNBJORN, WRECKER OF WORLDS

FIRST APPEARANCE *Thor: God of Thunder* #1 (January 2013) **USED BY** Thor, Baron Mordo, Kang the Conqueror, Apocalypse Twins (Uriel and Eimin)

Forged by the dwarven smiths in Nidavellir in the 9th century, Jarnbjorn—"Iron Bear"—is a deadly war-ax. It is made for young god Thor, before he grows worthy enough to wield the mystic hammer Mjolnir. After facing Apocalypse two centuries later, Thor blesses Jarnbjorn with his own Asgardian blood, giving it the power to pierce anything, and even to kill Celestial space gods.

Lost for centuries, Jarnbjorn is recovered by magician Baron Mordo and stolen by time-traveler Kang the Conqueror, before being reclaimed by Thor. When Thor is found unworthy to lift Mjolnir, and his former girlfriend Jane Foster takes over the magic hammer, Thor returns to using Jarnbjorn.

WUXIAN SEED

FIRST APPEARANCE *Weirdworld* #1 (February 2016) **USED BY** Ogeode, Becca the Earthgirl

The Wuxian Seed is an enigmatic mystic artifact of immense power and unfathomable mystery. Other than a number of obvious matter and event-shaping properties and capabilities, the seed's potential is largely unexplored. No magical practitioner seems sure of exactly what it is capable of, but all are certain that no other adept, whether friend or rival, should possess it.

For most of its existence, the Wuxian Seed has been safeguarded from avaricious Morgan Le Fay by the wizard Ogeode. When he is temporarily killed by Goleta the Wizardslayer, abducted Earth girl Becca Rodriguez becomes the seed's unwilling and unlikely new guardian. She travels Weirdworld in a magic vehicle called Glorianna, staying one step ahead of Morgan Le Fay.

SUPERSOUL STONE

FIRST APPEARANCE *Power Man and Iron Fist* #1 (April 2016) **USED BY** Nekra Sinclair, White Jennie (Jennie Royce), Black Mariah, Tombstone, Señor Magico

Long thought an urban myth, the scarlet Supersoul Stone was created by impoverished minor magicians of America's former slave class who conjured the stone from the Book of Anansi, the trickster-god of Africa's Yoruba people. The stone bestows terrifying powers upon anyone uttering an activating incantation while wearing sacred body tattoos. The user must also be weak and helpless because the stone has no effect on anyone with great strength, will, or determination.

Once invoked, the stone embeds itself in the user's flesh, providing ever-increasing mystic abilities, as it literally transforms the user into a monster.

Soul searching
Street-smart heroes Power Man and Iron Fist refuse to believe the gaudy trinket is real until the monsters appear and bodies start piling up.

GODDESS OF THUNDER

> "Every Thor has their secrets, Prince Odinson…and…I will DIE protecting mine."
>
> THOR

When Thor Odinson is no longer worthy to lift his enchanted hammer Mjolnir, a new Thor swoops in to take up his legendary mantle. But who is this mystery maiden?

It is a secret shrouded in mystery… Why is Thor Odinson no longer worthy to wield his hammer Mjolnir, source of so much of his power? Instead, the legendary weapon has called out to another, a mysterious woman, who transforms into the goddess of Thunder the moment she touches Mjolnir, as if it were meant to be. Like many heroes before her, she keeps her identity hidden—even from the former Thor, now merely called Odinson.

Odinson seeks out the woman who is able to lift Mjolnir when he cannot. Meanwhile, the All-Father, Odin, enraged by the betrayal of his own magic, seeks to take the hammer by force. He sends his menacing brother Cul Borson, formerly known as the Serpent, in the unbreakable and supremely powerful Destroyer Armor to track down the new Goddess of Thunder.

PREPARED TO DIE

With a team of heroes at his side, including his mother Frigga, Odinson hopes to aid the new Thor and learn her true identity. Together the heroes fend off the Destroyer, until Frigga's searing admonishments make Odin call back his Destroyer in shame. As the thrill of the fight subsides, Odinson tries to ascertain Thor's true identity, guessing that she is actually S.H.I.E.L.D.'s Agent Solomon. At that very moment, the real Agent Solomon arrives, both disproving his theory and yelling at Thor for her previous mistakes in battle.

Thor accepts the rebuke and then abruptly leaves, returning to be alone in Asgardia. There she finally removes her helmet to reveal that she is none other than Jane Foster, former lover to both Thor and his alter ego Donald Blake. Furthermore, Jane is dying of cancer, and though transforming into Thor to battle Super Villains is killing her, she refuses to stop!

Enter the Serpent
Odin's brother Cul Borson, alias the Serpent, dons the Destroyer Armor to take down the new incarnation of Thor, Jane Foster, and reclaim the magical hammer Mjolnir from her.

The Mighty Thor
From cancer ward to Asgard, from critical list to Goddess of Thunder—Jane Foster's personal journey seems miraculous. However, she soon learns that there is a price to pay for the privilege of wielding Mjolnir…

PLANETS AND REALMS

Earth is just one of many inhabited worlds. Great civilizations span our own Milky Way, and may be found in far-off galaxies populated by alien races and ruled by alien empires, some with malign designs on Earth.

The people of Earth are emphatically not alone. While not every extraterrestrial race intends to destroy or invade, there are some powerful beings out there. Dark entities and military forces travel across galaxies, across dimensions, seeking conquest.

Our universe is just a piece in a complex puzzle of alternate universes, realities, dimensions, and timelines. Most are naturally formed, but some are created when time-travelers inadvertently create new timelines. Some universes are quite similar to others, while "pocket universes" are just little bubbles of reality that may be as small as a planet, a city, or a single room. Certain realms are inhospitable and fundamentally different in nature, such as the Darkforce Dimension. Battleworld, Halfworld, and others are created by ruthless beings determined to fulfil their dreams of manipulation and control. Some dimensions can be drawn upon for great power; alternatively, their inhabitants may attempt to consume adjoining dimensions.

"Olympus, land of beauty and hope unlimited…is in ruins!" HERCULES

OLYMPIAN REALM

FIRST APPEARANCE *Venus* #1 (August 1948)
RULED BY Zeus

The Olympian Realm, or Olympus, is a pocket dimension with a portal to Earth located on Mount Olympus in Greece. It is home to the gods and goddesses worshipped by the Greeks and Romans, including the Pantheon, the twelve most powerful of these deities. Many of these gods have their own halls in Olympus, while Hephaestus' forge lies beneath it. The Olympian Realm is surrounded by the Abyss. Usually only divine beings are permitted on Olympus, but on one occasion the Avengers arrive there after fighting their way out of Hades. The King of the Olympians, Zeus, blames Earth's Mightiest Heroes for the injuries suffered by his son Hercules when the Masters of Evil took over Avengers Mansion. He is determined to punish them with an eternity of torment, but the heroes manage to convince the goddess Venus that they are innocent. They are forced to face Zeus and his children Artemis, Ares, and Dionysus in battle. The fighting is so severe that the Hall of Apollo is destroyed and several

Avengers are badly injured. However, Zeus finally comes to his senses after accidentally wounding Hercules in his rage, and he appears in the Olympian Realm's great amphitheater to make a public apology to the Avengers and vow that

no-one born of Olympus shall set foot on Earth again. Olympus is later attacked by the forces of the Eastern god Amatsu-Mikaboshi and left in ruins. The Olympian gods take on the form of humans and relocate to Earth.

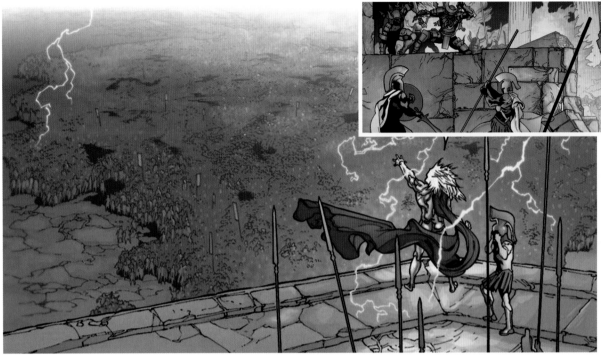

The fall of Olympus
The gods are left shattered and stunned as the hordes of Amatsu-Mikaboshi sweep into their realm, leaving a trail of destruction in their wake.

HADES

FIRST APPEARANCE *Venus* #6 (August 1949)
USED BY Pluto

Hades is a pocket dimension between Earth and Olympus that houses the souls of those who worshiped the Olympian pantheon of gods. The dead usually arrive by ferry across the River Styx, steered by Charon. The realm is guarded by Cerberus, who sometimes takes the form of a three-headed dog and sometimes a massive warrior. Its ruler is Pluto, also known as Hades, the brother of Zeus and Poseidon.

His queen is Persephone, who spends half the year in Hades and the other half in the living world. Souls arriving in Hades are judged and then move on to one of three sub-realms—the virtuous go to the beautiful Elysian Fields for an eternity of happiness, those who are neither good nor evil go to the Asphodel Fields, and the truly villainous are sentenced to everlasting torment in Tartarus. Although Pluto has wished for a different kingdom, he realizes how much Hades means to him when Thor lays waste to it while trying to free Hercules. The entrance to Hades is later relocated to a casino in Atlantic City.

POPPUP

FIRST APPEARANCE *Fantastic Four* #11 (February 1963)
USED BY Impossible Man

Poppup is a planet in the Tenth Galaxy. It is a very dangerous place, so the native Poppupians have developed a rapid evolution process —they can change their physical forms almost immediately to combat a threat. One denizen of Poppup, growing bored with the constant peril on his homeworld, transforms himself into a spaceship to take a vacation on Earth, where he meets the Fantastic Four. Although he explains that his people do not have names, as they know who they are, he becomes known as the Impossible Man. The nameless inhabitants of Poppup also share a hive mind, so all the consciousness of the whole race can be found in any one of its individuals. Poppup is consumed by the world-eater Galactus, willingly sacrificed by its citizens in order to save Counter-Earth from the same fate. Since the Impossible Man survives, he carries the whole "community brain" of Poppup with him. However, the hive mind of Poppup gives Galactus near-terminal indigestion, although his essence is saved by the High Evolutionary.

DREAM DIMENSION

FIRST APPEARANCE *Strange Tales* #110 (July 1963) **RULED BY** Nightmare

A metaphysical realm brought into being by the dreams of sleeping people, the Dream Dimension is ruled by the terrifying demon Nightmare. This evil being can influence dreams and entrap people's "dream-selves" in his kingdom. The only humans with sufficient knowledge and power to stop Nightmare are the sorcerer Doctor Strange and his wise old tutor, the Ancient One. Strange's astral form can travel to the Dream Dimension, as it does when he rescues three ethereal spirits of sleeping people who could not be woken after they had been ensnared by Nightmare. In order to protect himself against the same fate, Doctor Strange utters a protective chant before he sleeps. On one occasion he forgets and is caught by Nightmare, who taunts him by demonstrating his power over Strange's astral form—he can grow and shrink it, or turn it to stone. But even without his other powers, Strange is able to hypnotize Nightmare into believing that his greatest fear, the unsleeping Gulgol, is there, and he is able to escape the Dream Dimension. Later, Nightmare and Strange must work together to prevent the end of humanity's dreams, which would cause the world's population to go insane and Nightmare—and his Dream Dimension—to disappear from existence. The Dream Dimension is located next to the Realm of Madness and the World of Nothingness.

Strange dreams
Nightmare successfully entraps his nemesis Doctor Strange in the Dream Dimension, but the sorcerer is able to escape by playing on the demon's own innermost fears.

HEL

FIRST APPEARANCE *Journey Into Mystery* #102 (March 1964) **RULED BY** Hela, Angela

Hel is the Asgardian realm of the dead. It is part of Niflheim, the icy wasteland that began as the furthest north of the Nine Realms but is now found under Midgard, or Earth. A bridge connects Niffleheim to the land of the living, guarded by a ferocious hound to make sure none of the dead try to reach their old world. The border of Hel is designated by the river Gjoll. The road from Midgard is called Hvergelmir and begins in the cave known as Gnipahellir. As well as being the kingdom of dead souls, Nifflheim is home to giants, trolls, and certain gods. Although Hel does punish wicked souls, it also rewards those who were good people in life. Ruling it all is the goddess Hela, who can bend its rules to her will—but never break them. However, Hela can be challenged by those willing to undergo three trials: of fear, chaos, and pain. One who rises up against Hela is the Asgardian Angela, brought up among the Angels of Heven and seeking to free them and her lover Sera from slavery in Hel. After coming through the three trials, Angela faces the wrath of Hela herself and defeats her, but spares her life in the hope that she might see the error of her ways. She puts on her crown and declares that the enslaved Angels will be freed and sent to a new realm—Elysium. However, Angela immediately rejects the idea of becoming Queen of Hel and hands the regency to her brother Balder.

Conquering Hel
The lost Asgardian princess Angela *(above)* overthrows Queen Hela *(left)* to rescue her dead love Sera *(far left)* from Hel.

A heavenly city
Thor Odinson and the immortals of Asgard gather on the steps of the palace to bid adieu to sibling warrior gods Idunn and Frey as they make their safe passage to Midgard—or Earth—via the Bifrost rainbow bridge.

ASGARD

FIRST APPEARANCE *Journey Into Mystery* #85 (October 1962) **RULED BY** Odin

Asgard is the home of the Norse gods. This godly realm exists on an other-planetary dimension outside of Earth, on a landmass with its own laws of science and nature. Mass is much greater in Asgard, meaning that matter created there is heavier and more durable. This is the case for its people, making them ideal warriors, worshiped as gods by ordinary mortals. Through the world tree, Yggdrasil, Asgard is connected to nine other realms that serve as home to legendary creatures such as elves, giants, trolls, and demons.

The walled citadel in Asgard houses the golden Palace of the Gods, home of Asgard's ruler, the All-Father Odin, and, in large part, the pantheon of Asgardian gods. This old city is opulent and awe-inspiring with statues and architecture befitting an ancient royal society of warrior gods. The walls are vital to protecting Asgard from invasion. However, the realm has repeatedly been invaded and destroyed, only to be rebuilt by its people.

Not all the nine realms can be accessed by normal means of travel; an extradimensional portal called the Bifrost is necessary to travel to many of them. Realms such as Midgard—the Asgardians' name for Earth—or Jotunheim—the land of the Giants—can only be accessed this way. The Bifrost creates a rainbow bridge between realms. However, because the Bifrost can also enable enemies to invade Asgard, it must be guarded by the god Heimdall, who protects the borders of Asgard.

Asgard destroyed
The city of the Norse gods goes up in flames as Norman Osborn orders the virtually omnipotent Sentry to destroy Asgard.

Climbing to heaven
This awesomely adorned and gold-encrusted kingdom houses all the gods of Norse myth and legend. Despite external attacks and internal power struggles, Asgard is a repository of some of the finest craftsmanship in all the many worlds.

The Bifrost is shattered during the events of Ragnarok—literally meaning "the end of the universe"—when Loki leads an army of trolls against Asgard, and it has to be reformed.

After Ragnarok, Asgard comes down to Earth, floating in the sky above Broxton, Oklahoma. U.S. security chief Norman Osborn, egged on by the trickster god Loki, claims that Asgard poses a threat to national security and leads an unauthorized attack—the Siege event—that destroys the realm.

Asgard is later rebuilt by Odin. Following a bitter clash with the Serpent (Odin's brother), the king of the Norse gods, teetering on the edge of madness, banishes the citizens of Asgard and stays alone in the decaying city. Using new repulsor technology, Tony Stark creates a new home for the Asgardians, called Asgardia. Ruled by the All-Mother, Frigga, Asgardia is moved further out into space, close to the rings of Saturn.

DARK DIMENSION

FIRST APPEARANCE *Strange Tales* #126
(November 1964) **RULED BY** Olnar, Dormammu

The Dark Dimension is a mystical realm
containing multiple realities magically
merged into a single domain. It is
inhabited by several species, notably
humanoid sorcerers known as Mhuruuks.
The realm is once at one time by the
dark wizard Olnar, who hungers for more
power and hopes to draw more realities
into his rule. It is at this period that the
Faltines, extradimensional beings born
purely of magic, banish two evil twins
born of their kind. The twins, Dormmamu
and his sister Umar, are sent into the
Dark Dimension.

Dormammu and Umar befriend Olnar,
leader of the Mhuruuks. They lead him
down the path of conquest to his own
demise. Dormammu takes to ruling the
dimension, with his sister Umar as his
second-in-command. Using an ancient
mystical artifact called the Evil Eye,
Dormammu continues to try to draw
various realities, especially Earth, into the Dark Dimension.

Umar has a child named Clea with the legitimate heir to the
Dark Dimension and son of Olnar, Prince Orini. Despising the
weak Orini, Umar also abandons Clea. Clea eventually partners
and falls in love with Doctor Strange when he visits the Dark
Dimension. She follows him back to Earth to train and hone
her magical skills.

Clea returns to the Dark Dimension successfully leading a
resistance movement against her own mother, Umar, who is
occupying the throne in her twin brother Dormammu's absence.
Following a battle with her mother, Clea banishes Umar, takes
control of the Dark Dimension, and marries Doctor Strange.
However, Dormmamu later returns to reclaim his fiery crown and
the power struggle between good and evil rages on.

Bubble trouble
Doctor Strange fights one of Dormammu's evil
bubble-throwing minions in the Dark Dimension, as he
battles his way to a showdown with the demon lord.

Fantastic field trip
The students of the Fantastic
Four's Future Foundation take a
walk on the wild side when they
transport to the Negative Zone.

"There ain't no bathrooms in the Negative Zone!"

THE THING

THE NEGATIVE ZONE

FIRST APPEARANCE *Fantastic Four* #51 (June 1966) **INHABITED BY** Annihilus, Blastaar

Reed Richards first discovers the Negative Zone when he builds a "Radical Cube" that is
"designed to create a dimensional entrance into sub-space." He hopes this enormous
machine will help him travel faster than the speed of light, as some space entities like
Galactus are able to do. However, things go awry when he realizes that he has actually
been transported into a dimension at the crossroads of infinity that is completely charged
with negative energy. Fortunately, he returns to his home dimension in the nick of time.

The Negative Zone is the home to unearthly creatures that can survive its adverse
effects, including the power-hungry insectoid
alien named Annihilus. There he survives the
rigors of the dimension using his Cosmic Control
Rod's protective energies, and is endlessly
driven on by his desire to defeat the Fantastic
Four who have crossed his path there.

Since the dimension is so sparsely inhabited,
a penal colony named Prison 42 is created in the
Negative Zone via a portal machine. This houses
Super Villains and superpowered people who
refuse to sign up to the U.S. government's
Superhuman Registration Act. While the
atmosphere of the dimension is breathable, its
negatively charged composition is potentially
lethal and mentally debilitating to the prison's
inmates.

A brutish resident of the Negative Zone,
a villain named Blastaar, attempts to leave his
dimension in the hopes of conquering Earth.
This leads to the portal to the Negative Zone
being shut down.

Despite these unfortunate events, the
Negative Zone does have its upside: Its energies
can be used to power objects such as the
Nega-Bands, which give heroes Captain Marvel,
Photon, and Marvel Boy their array of powers.

Lost in space
Stranded in the Negative Zone without his
transportational Gyro device, Mr. Fantastic
sails through the atmosphere by stretching
himself thin like a parachute.

HALA

FIRST APPEARANCE *Captain Marvel* #1 (May 1968) **HOME TO** Kree, Cotati, subject races, Supreme Intelligence, Ronan the Accuser, Shi'ar regent Deathbird

Hala is a heavy-gravity planet in the Large Magellanic Cloud that circles the star Pama. It is the birthworld of two highly intelligent species: the warlike, inventive Blue Kree, and the peace-loving, spiritual plant-race named the Cotati.

After a murderous first-contact with the Skrulls, the humanoid Kree rapidly develop into a star-spanning expansionist empire and—believing the Cotati to be eradicated—rebuild the planet into a gleaming, technological marvel.

Hala becomes the capital of the Kree Empire, controlling thousands of worlds and billions of subjects. Following millennia of security, Hala is occupied by the Shi'ar and then liberated by Ronan the Accuser. However, it is ultimately destroyed by galactic terror Mister Knife and the Slaughter Lords.

GIGANTUS

FIRST APPEARANCE *Fantastic Four* #115 (October 1971) **HOME TO** Gigantians

Gigantus, in the Gwydion System, Andromeda Galaxy, is the largest populated planet in early universal history. Its sheer vastness—reputed to dwarf entire galaxies—has kept it from being attacked by predatory species.

For a time, a wise and noble humanoid race, called the Gigantians, form a benevolent society that thrives in peace and harmony on the giant planet.

Eventually, however, Gigantus is occupied by the rapacious Eternals of Eyung, but even they could not cope with the sheer enormous scale of the planet, and so they petulantly destroy it. The resulting catastrophic explosion spreads across the entire universe, creating suns and planets in its wake.

The only known survivor of Gigantus is the space-faring composite being known as the Stranger.

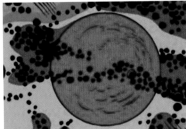

ANDROMEDA GALAXY

FIRST APPEARANCE *Avengers* #94 (December 1971) **HOME TO** Skrulls, Symbiotes, Xandarians, Makluans

M-31 Andromeda is the spiral galaxy nearest to the Milky Way. It is 2.2 million light years from Earth and approximately 220,000 light years across. The galaxy was formed roughly 10 billion years ago, born from a collision between—and subsequent merger of—numerous smaller proto-galaxies.

Within the last two billion years, formation of new stars in Andromeda has almost ceased, but its history includes: the origins of Fin Fang Foom's dragon race on Kakarantha; the remote Klyntar, planet of the Symbiotes; the Skrull origin-world of Skrullos and its capital planets Tarnax IV and Satriani; as well as Xandar, the home of galactic peacekeepers the Nova Corps.

COUNTER-EARTH

FIRST APPEARANCE *Marvel Premiere* #1 (April 1972) **HOME TO** Humanity, Adam Warlock, Beast-Men, Man-Beast, New Men

Counter-Earth is created by the High Evolutionary in planetary opposition to Earth on the far side of the Sun. He wants to recreate mankind without sin, but this dream is sabotaged by the Man-Beast, who introduces greed, selfishness, and aggression to evolving humanity. Counter-Earth becomes a mirror of true Earth society, but without its magic entities, ancient secret societies, and metahumans.

The Evolutionary is dissuaded from destroying his creation by Adam Warlock, who volunteers to walk among its people and try to turn them from a path of imminent self-destruction. Agreeing, the Evolutionary shifts Counter-Earth a microsecond out of phase with the rest of the universe to prevent further contamination. Warlock fails in his mission and the world is left to its fate. Removed to a space museum at the command of the Beyonders, it is destroyed by the Titan Thanos with the Infinity Gauntlet. The High Evolutionary later forms a second iteration as a home for his New Men.

Other Counter-Earths have been built. The first is a creation of the Goddess—Warlock's expression of ultimate goodness as manifested by the Infinity Gauntlet—using the Cosmic Egg, a construct comprising 30 Cosmic Cubes acting in unison. Dubbed Paradise Omega, it is created as a home for Earth's Super Heroes who follow her seductive teachings, but it is also destroyed by Thanos.

Omega mutant Franklin Richards later creates a third Counter-Earth in a pocket universe, when many Earth champions are seemingly destroyed by Onslaught. The Fantastic Four, Avengers, Bruce Banner, and Doctor Doom are rescued and reborn to lead different, but parallel, lives, until they learn the truth about themselves and escape back to the real world.

Franklin creates another version of this Counter-Earth when Onslaught remanifests during the House of M crisis to shelter his family and Super Hero friends.

Counter Evolutionary
The High Evolutionary's unfortunate experiment in creationism is a painful reminder to him of his hubris and shortcomings.

An imperfect world
Every attempt to create an idealized Earth—even the almighty High Evolutionary's—fails, because the humans who populate these Earths are fundamentally flawed.

NEXUS OF ALL REALITIES

FIRST APPEARANCE *Fear* #11 (December 1972) **USED BY** Man-Thing, Dakimh the Enchanter, Jennifer Kale, Thunderbolts, Deadpool, Howard the Duck

The Nexus of All Realities is a convergence point for every place in existence. It provides pathways to any and all possible planes, but its true nature and origins remain unknown. It may be a natural consequence of an infinity of universes comprising the greater Multiverse, but being such a perfect tool for travel and exploration, it is hard to conceive that it is not the result of deliberate invention.

The Nexus is where all universes intersect, but it often relocates itself. Past sites include the Florida swamps, and inside living beings, such as Howard the Duck and Man-Thing.

Strictly for the birds
Comics fan Stu Cicero's brief encounter on Duckworld teaches him that, in the Multiverse, truth is often stranger than fiction.

What a day!
The Daydreamers use the Nexus to enjoy a fabulous holiday in fantasy paradise Nevernever-Narniozbia *(left to right)*: Howard the Duck, Tana Nile, Franklin Richards, Leech, Man-Thing, and Artie Maddicks.

DUCKWORLD

FIRST APPEARANCE *Fear* #19 (December 1973)
HOME TO Assorted highly evolved, intelligent waterfowl

Duckworld is a world identical to Earth, but one in which waterfowl are the dominant species. Duckworld has the same level of technology, political and legal systems, racial problems, religions, faiths, crazy fads and trends, entertainment forms, and military crises as human-ruled Earth.

Duckworld lies in the reality of Earth-791021, but has experienced far fewer alien invasions and super-powered entities than the Marvel Universe's Prime Earth. However, although uncanny and occult events are far rarer, the planet has strong magical connections. These are monitored by Duktor Strange, Mallard of the Mystic Arts.

During a shifting of the Cosmic Axis, an acerbic duck named Howard is expelled from his world by unnatural mystic forces. While helping a convocation of unlikely heroes save the Multiverse, he is lost to the interdimensional void and eventually deposited on human-ruled Earth. Howard, the ultimate outsider, grudgingly adapts and becomes an occasional hero and cynical commentator on human civilization.

Howard finally finds his way back home to Duckworld, taking with him his devoted human companion Beverly Switzler. The way she is treated by the beings he has idealized in his memories of Duckworld forces Howard to realize that ducks and "hairless apes" are not all that different. When circumstances offer him a chance to return to Earth, he and Beverly gladly depart.

Sometime later, a human lawyer named Stu Cicero is forcibly transported to Duckworld by alien robot Artie Zix and experiences similar intolerance and bewilderment until he is returned to Earth by Duktor Strange.

CAPITAL CITIES OF HEAVEN

FIRST APPEARANCE *Marvel Premiere* #15 (May 1974) **HOME TO** Iron Fist (K'un-Lun); Crane Mother, Crane Champions (K'un Zi); Tiger's Beautiful Daughter (Tiger Island); Bride of Nine Spiders (Kingdom of Spiders); Cobra warriors, Fat Cobra (Peng Lai); Prince of Orphans (Z'Gambo); Dog Brother #1 (Under City)

The Capital Cities of Heaven are an interconnected network of seven self-contained localities—each in its own pocket plane of existence—extradimensionally orbiting Earth through a complex 88-year cycle. K'un-Lun is the best known, thanks to its warrior champions the Iron Fists. These warriors

Home away from home
After so many millennia away from Earth, each Capital City gradually evolves into a unique enclave of lost humanity.

have periodically moved between their city and Earth, becoming folk heroes for generations of eastern Earth-dwellers. All the other cities—K'un Zi, Tiger Island, Kingdom of Spiders, Peng Lai, Z'Gambo, and Under City—have their own specialized martial-arts systems and warrior champions.

During the heavenly convergence, the Seven Capital Cities of Heaven briefly occupy the same space and time, creating a vast palace complex called the Heart of Heaven. The individual city champions—known as the Immortal Weapons—duel in a tournament to decide which city will be directly linked to Earth

for the next cycle.

The winner's city can then appear on Earth every ten years, while the losing cities only appear once every five decades. K'un-Lun has won the tournament for centuries, ensuring an Iron Fist's presence and influence on Earth for almost all that time.

When an alignment occurs and the Heart of Heaven manifests, it comprises aspects of all Seven Capital Cities of Heaven, as well as facets of Earth. The palace is unlike any other place, possessing its own rules and physical laws. The Heart of Heaven is the starting point for each match in the tournament; however, if any of the combatants break the borders of the palace, they will be mystically expelled and may materialize almost anywhere.

This must be heaven
The interdimensional Capital Cities all lie within exotic areas of largely unexplored wilderness.

Martial artisans
The bellicose builders and proud rulers of K'un-Lun repurposed every aspect of their city to create ultimate warriors and living weapons.

Promised lands
Although ostensibly cut off from the mundane world, the rulers of each Capital City possess the means to secretly return to the wider world and beauties of Earth whenever they wish.

DARKFORCE DIMENSION

FIRST APPEARANCE *Champions* #7 (August 1976)
USED BY Mister Negative, Cloak and Dagger
Blackout, Shroud, Blackheart

The Darkforce Dimension is a mysterious universe rich in dark energy. This Darkforce energy can be naturally drawn upon by some mutants. Others use magic or scientific technology to tap into it. Darkforce energy has a variety of unusual properties that can be manipulated with surprising results. It may have a corrupting influence on a user over time, and possess some level of sentience.

The Darkforce Dimension itself has no known life, technology, or places of interest. It seems entirely empty and void of light. Darkforce leaches all energy in our dimension, including light and life forces. When Darkforce energy is drawn upon and pulled into our universe, it may appear as a mist or shadow in low concentrations, or behave as a liquid at medium potencies. The strongest concentrations can take solid form.

Some mutants use the Darkforce Dimension as a medium for teleportation, traveling through entry and exit portals instantaneously created with their mind. Some, such as Cloak, can even pull others into the dimension. Others can manipulate the shape, consistency, and motion of the energy; using it as an offensive or defensive weapon.

Users of Darkforce energy include portal jumpers like Darkling (Henrique Manuel Gallante), Cloak (Tyrone Johnson), Doorman (DeMarr Davis), Ecstasy (Renee Deladier), Nightfall, Silhouette Chord, Smuggler (Conrad Josten), Spot (Jonathan Ohnn), and Vanisher. Nightwind can form a Darkforce sword. Nightside and Shroud (Maximillian Coleridge) can project darkness. Sepulchre (Jillian Woods) uses Darkforce energy to fly. Mister Negative can use it for a variety of unique purposes, including shape-shifting between different personas, and corrupting others.

Misdirection
Hired by Lieutenant Flores to find the Runaways, Cloak sweeps up four of the teen heroes. He transports them through the Dark Dimension to a place beyond time they nickname Ghost World.

HALFWORLD

FIRST APPEARANCE *Incredible Hulk* #271 (May 1982) **INHABITED BY**
Loonies, Shrinks, Halfworlders, robot stewards

A planet in the Keystone Quadrant is colonized by a humanoid society to house their mentally ill patients. The administrators, known as "Shrinks," lose their funding and abandon the patients, called "Loonies," to the care of the facility's robots. The world is isolated with a force field for protection.

The robot caregivers gain sentience when the nearby star explodes and irradiates their systems. They now long for their own independence, so scour the galaxy for animals to genetically engineer into new caregivers (known as Halfworlders) to serve their patients. With that issue settled, the robots relocate to the other side of the planet and create an industrialized machine utopia. The resulting planet becomes known as Halfworld.

Old battlelands
The Beyonder assembles a patchwork world comprised of different zones where the heroes and villains can do battle.

> "I am from beyond! Slay your enemies and all you desire shall be yours! Nothing you dream of is impossible for me to accomplish!"
>
> THE BEYONDER

BATTLEWORLD

FIRST APPEARANCE *Marvel Heroes Secret Wars #1 (May 1984)* **RULED BY** The Beyonder, Doctor Doom

The first Battleworld is a patchwork planet-sized arena constructed to satisfy the curiosity of a powerful being known as the Beyonder. It is constructed of pieces taken from many different planets to form the ultimate arena for the Beyonder's own Secret Wars. He uses Battleworld to explore the nature of desire in lesser beings, by offering the winner of these Secret Wars anything they want. The Beyonder brings the Avengers, X-Men, Fantastic Four, Hulk, and Spider-Man (who finds and puts on his black alien symbiote suit) to Battleworld to face off against villains such as Doctor Doom, Doctor Octopus, Kang, Lizard, Absorbing Man, Molecule Man, Ultron, and even Galactus. The Beyonder ends up in a struggle with Doctor Doom for his own power. When he manages to regain it, the Beyonder departs and sends the heroes and villains back to their homes. The Thing is the last Super Hero to depart Battleworld, after which it explodes.

After many incursions of the Multiverse, Doctor Doom and Doctor Strange confront the hugely powerful extradimensional beings, known as the Beyonders, to stop a collision with their reality (Prime Earth of the Marvel Universe). Doctor Doom steals the power of the Beyonders, however, and creates a single patchwork universe of his own: a new Battleworld.

The dozens of realms within Battleworld are taken from many different universes and known as domains. Each domain is ruled by a Baron or Baroness. Travel between these domains is restricted, and order is maintained by the Thor Corps. Doctor Doom reigns with absolute power with Doctor Strange as his sheriff. Battleworld has a small sun, which is actually the Human Torch, and the moon is the spacestation Knowhere.

This Battleworld exists for a matter of years and the inhabitants have no memories of its formation. The whole reality eventually collapses when Mister Fantastic takes control and restores reality, with notable changes.

The Deadlands

New Battleworld
Domains of interest in Doctor Doom's new Battleworld include the Deadlands, Perfection, and New Xandar (these three must be separated from the others by a shield owing to the serious threats they harbor), Spider-Island, Weirdworld, Doomstadt, the Kingdom of Manhattan, City, Warzone, and Limbo, among many others.

Captive audience
Spider-Man and his class of mutant students
are shocked by life on Mojoworld, where the
inhabitants move about on platforms attended
by humanoid slaves.

Gladiator
X-Factor's Rictor walks into the arena,
a prisoner of Mojo forced to fight for
the entertainment of the masses.

MOJOWORLD

FIRST APPEARANCE *Longshot* #1
(September 1985) **RULED BY** Mojo
INHABITED BY Spineless Ones

An extradimensional realm populated
by unfortunate beings with no spines,
Mojoworld is bombarded with imagery
from the Marvel Universe's television and
radio broadcasts. The lives of the
inhabitants are transformed when one of
their number, Arize, invents an exoskeleton
to hold them upright so that they can move
without slithering along the ground.
However, some choose instead to
transport themselves on motorized platforms, taking the name
Spineless Ones. Arize also genetically engineers humanoid slaves,
leaving Mojoworld's inhabitants free to do what they love best of
all—watch TV.
   Mojoworld—and the Mojoverse in which it lies—gets its name
when the tyrannical despot Mojo becomes ruler, gaining power
thanks to his control over both slavery and TV. Mojo's transport
platform resembles a scorpion, with eight mechanized legs
beneath it, and a sting-like tail at the back. To keep his subjects
entertained and therefore under his control, Mojo is always on the
lookout for something to keep ratings high. Discovering that

> "Mojo runs
> everything.
> Everything."
>
> **ARIZE**

footage of the X-Men from Earth is a real ratings winner, Mojo tries
to lure some of the mutants to Mojoworld to provide even more
entertainment. If any of his prisoners show a lack of willingness to
watch Mojo's programs, he has them trapped in hell chairs with
equipment to hold their eyes open. The X-Man Longshot is
originally a stuntman from Mojoworld, and returns to try and
overthrow Mojo's dictatorship. He apparently succeeds when
Mojo is trapped between Mojoworld and Earth, but the tyrant
returns to control the Mojoverse again. Mojo later hits on the
brilliant idea of creating baby versions of the X-Men to provide
entertainment with added cute factor.

LIVEWORLD

FIRST APPEARANCE *Alpha Flight* #55 (February
1988) **RULED BY** Dreamqueen

When Beta Flight member Purple Girl gets
her first look at Liveworld, she describes it
as a "psychedelic Disneyland." Young
autistic girl Laura Dean (a.k.a. Pathway)
can open portals to this otherdimensional
realm, which she does to swap places with
her mutant sister Goblyn. Laura says that
no-one hurts her in Liveworld—by contrast
she refers to Earth as "Deadworld."
   Liveworld is ruled by the Dreamqueen,
the daughter of Nightmare, who can shape
her realm into any landscape she chooses.
However, the Dreamqueen often grows
bored with Liveworld and longs to be able
to cross over to planet Earth, in order to
observe its chaos.

Crowd pleaser
Hulk, stranded on Sakaar, becomes a star of the gladiatorial arena and then a focal point for rebels trying to overthrow the Red King.

SAKAAR

FIRST APPEARANCE *Incredible Hulk* #92 (April 2006) **RULED BY** Red King, Hulk

Although most of its population are insect-like beings, the planet Sakaar is ruled by a class of pink-skinned Imperials, led by the Red King. Several species live on Sakaar, but it is not certain if any of them are truly native or if they came from elsewhere. It is common for alien beings and technology to arrive suddenly on the planet, as it is situated close to a Great Portal, a wormhole in space.

Slavery is practiced on Sakaar, and the mob is entertained by gladiatorial shows in a vast arena in Crown City. Slaves destined for the arena are trained at the Maw, a brutal gladiator school centred around a pit containing a gruesome lava monster. To prevent captives leaving or refusing to take part in the training, they are implanted with obedience disks that cause them pain or even death when they refuse to follow orders.

The Hulk is exiled in space by the Illuminati and when his spacecraft goes off course he arrives on Sakaar through the Great Portal. He is sent to the Maw, where he predictably overcomes all the trials with ease.

Hulk's feats attract the attention of a rebel faction looking to overthrow the bloodthirsty Red King, but when they ask Hulk to join their fight, he refuses. He is later forced to fight a captured Silver Surfer in the arena, but when the Surfer's obedience disk is destroyed in the clash, he uses his power to break the link of all obedience disks, and Hulk smashes his way to freedom.

Having defeated the Red King, Hulk falls in love with and marries the former king's bodyguard, Caiera, one of Sakaar's Shadow People. Hulk becomes king and tries to bring peaceful rule, but Sakaar is devastated by a massive explosion on Hulk's old spacecraft. Hulk leaves for Earth, seeking vengeance on the Illuminati superhumans whom he holds responsible for the tragedy. A few of the population survive—including Hulk's son, Skaar, but the planet is later consumed by Galactus.

Seat of power
The palace of the Red King dominates the skyline of the Imperial Crown City on Sakaar.

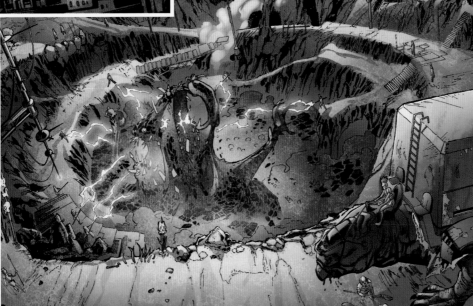

The Maw
The Empire's most lethal gladiator training school has a lava monster at its heart, poised to consume the unworthy.

SIN

FIRST APPEARANCE *Wolverine and the X-Men* #6 (April 2012) **USED BY** Wolverine, Quentin Quire

Sin is a casino planet in the Milky Way galaxy, on the edge of ungoverned space. It represents one of the largest casinos in the known universe, according to patron Wolverine, who takes one of his students there to win money to save the Jean Grey School for Higher Learning from bankruptcy. However, staff on Planet Sin are primed to observe strange behavior, and Wolverine's idea to win big by using mutant Quentin Quire's telepathic abilities gets him and Quire unceremoniously ejected. They are by no means the only shady characters to try and scam the odds on Sin—on another occasion, God of Mischief Loki cheats his way to winning an Asgardian artifact in a game of cards.

LOOMWORLD

FIRST APPEARANCE *Amazing Spider-Man* #9 (January 2015) **INHABITED BY** Inheritors

Loomworld is in the reality of Earth-001. In it, the captured Master Weaver sits at the center of the Great Web, from which he can access anywhere in the Multiverse.

The Inheritors—a family that feeds on the life force of spider-powered beings—are based in Loomworld and use the Weaver to facilitate their hunting. After the defeat of the Inheritors by an army of Spider-Totems from across the Multiverse, a group of spider-beings decide to stay in Loomworld to guard the Great Web. Known as the Web Warriors, their mission is to protect worlds whose Spider Super Heroes are killed by the Inheritors.

KREE GENOCIDE

"You cannot begin to understand the subtlety of my design."

THE SUPREME INTELLIGENCE

The Shi'ar and Kree Empires are at war—with Earth and the Avengers caught in the middle. After a weapon of mass destruction kills billions, Captain America discovers the chilling truth behind the conflict.

Two mighty empires, the Kree and the Shi'ar, are using stargates near Earth's sun to send troops and weapons against each other, causing the star to flare dangerously and threaten Earth's very existence. The Avengers split into three teams, one to guard Earth and the solar system, and the other two to go to the Kree and the Shi'ar and urge peace talks before any more damage is done. Despite their best efforts, the Avengers cannot stop a Nega-Bomb, constructed by the Shi'ar to harness the power of the Negative Zone, from virtually wiping out the Kree Empire.

THE ULTIMATE BETRAYAL

Captain America and Deathbird, sister of the Shi'ar Empress Lilandra, miraculously survive the bomb blast on the Kree homeworld, Hala. Confronted by the Kree ruler, the Supreme Intelligence, the pair are horrified as he reveals the terrible truth behind the war. The entire conflict, including the detonation of the Nega-Bomb, was engineered by him to "jump-start" Kree evolution. With most of the population wiped out, all that remain will be the very strongest, the true survivors. As they breed, the Kree will, in thousands of years' time, be the dominant species in the universe. When Cap reports this to the Avengers, the heroes argue over what to do next. Iron Man advocates destroying the Supreme Intelligence for his terrible crime, but Captain America will not countenance killing a sentient being in cold blood. Iron Man pulls rank as the only founding member present and takes a band of his supporters to finish off the Supreme Intelligence. Meanwhile, Captain America worries about the future of the Avengers after this fundamental disagreement.

After a fierce battle, the Supreme Intelligence dies. However, nobody notices a speck of light shooting up from the Citadel, where the Kree ruler supposedly met his end…

Avengers divided
One group of Earth's Mightiest Heroes, led by Iron Man, wants to kill the Supreme Intelligence, but Captain America argues that an Avenger should never take a sentient life.

Capital punishment
Iron Man's Avengers team attempts to kill the
Supreme Intelligence. However, the ruthless
Kree ruler refuses to come quietly...

COUNTRIES
AND PLACES

Much Super Hero and Super Villain activity centers in the U.S. However, thrilling action takes place on every continent...and spectacular events play out in some extraordinary and exotic places.

New York City has one of the largest concentrations of super-powered people on the planet. Manhattan is the site of much activity, especially around Midtown High School, Empire State University, and the *Daily Bugle* building—all places where Peter Parker (Spider-Man) goes to school and works. Other super-powered students are educated and trained in special schools like the Jean Grey School for Higher Learning, the Massachusetts Academy, and Camp Hammond. Every Super Hero team needs a base of operations: the Avengers have used Avengers Mansion, Avengers Compound, and the offshore Hydrobase. The Baxter Building is the home of the Fantastic Four, while Doctor Strange has his mysterious Sanctum Sanctorum townhouse. Villains have their own secret hideouts, but many end up in prison. In New York, they are held in facilities like the Raft and the Cellar on Ryker's Island. Farther afield is the Vault in Colorado and, in deep space, the super-secure Kyln.

Some of the world's smallest countries have played crucial roles in major global events. Wakanda in Africa, Latveria and Symkaria in Europe, and the Principality of Madripoor in Southeast Asia may be little known, but they have played crucial roles in world affairs.

Without doubt some of the most marvellous Super Hero adventures have settings to match. These are the secret, hidden realms, sometimes with rulers and citizens with supernatural powers, like aquatic Atlantis and the "lost world" of the Savage Land, a realm of primitive peoples and dinosaurs hidden deep in the Antarctic.

NEW YORK CITY

FIRST APPEARANCE *Marvel Comics* #1
(October 1939) **NOTABLE RESIDENTS**
Spider-Man, Daredevil, Captain America,
Avengers, Fantastic Four, Squirrel Girl, Doctor
Strange, Moon Girl

New York City represents the best the U.S.
has to offer. However, the Big Apple is also
the stage for some of the biggest threats
that the city's many Super Hero guardians,
have ever faced. A world leader in art and
entertainment, politics, business, fashion,
and culture, New York is the largest city in
the U.S. by population. Events that happen
here affect societies across the globe.

Many important Super Hero teams are
based in New York. The Fantastic Four's
headquarters is in the Baxter Building on
42nd Street and Madison Avenue.
Avengers Mansion is located at 721 Fifth
Avenue, while Stark Tower (Avengers
Tower) is a skyscraper on 58th and
Broadway beside Columbus Circle in
Midtown. S.H.I.E.L.D. also has a secret
headquarters located at a barbershop at
59th Street and Madison Avenue.

There are several notable New York
neighborhoods that heroes call home.
Captain America is from Brooklyn, while
Spider-Man lives in Queens and has
attended Midtown High. Harlem is the
home turf of Luke Cage, Storm, and Sam
Wilson (Falcon/Captain America). Daredevil
lives in Hell's Kitchen, located between
34th and 59th streets. Moon Girl Lunella
Lafayette lives on the Lower East Side,
while Squirrel Girl and her friends are
computer science students at Empire
State University. To the south, Doctor
Strange hails from Greenwich Village—
his Sanctum Sanctorum may be found

Heroes and villains
New York City is the most Super Hero-dense city on
the planet. The Avengers and the Fantastic Four are
based there, but that doesn't stop villains such as
Green Goblin and Doc Ock from taking up residence,
too. Attacks from Onslaught, Galactus, and other
immensely powerful beings regularly cause plenty
of destruction around the city.

at 177A Bleecker Street.

New York City is the site of many
extraordinary happenings, such as when
the mutant Morlocks, who dwell in the
sewer system, are massacred by Mister
Sinister's Marauders. Others drown when
troubled mutant Mikhail Rasputin floods
the sewer tunnels.

On another occasion, a battle between
the Illuminati and Hulk and his Warbound
opens up a fault line in Manhattan. This is
repaired using shadow stone. Some of this
material, which takes on hopes, fears, and
dreams, ends up in the foundations of the
Chrysler Building, which comes to life.

Spider Island
Humans across
Manhattan are mutating
into giant spiders. The
team at Horizon Labs is
working frantically to
create vaccines, but
Spidey fears that
soon Mary Jane may
be the only person left
unaffected! Meanwhile,
Anti-Venom finds a new
purpose in life as those
affected look to him for
a cure.

The naked city
The morning after the
city is cured, citizens
are hiding naked all
over town. Spider-Man
explains to Mary Jane
how he was able to use
his octo-spiders to cure
the entire population
of Manhattan.

The building insists on roaming about and
a short battle ensues to keep it in place.
When this fails, an agreement is reached
whereby the Chrysler Building is allowed to
take annual vacations, if it remains in place
the rest of the year.

In another remarkable incident, the
Jackal (Miles Warren) and Spider Queen
(Adriana Soria) team up to give all of the
inhabitants of Manhattan spider-powers.
While this seems great at first, some
people become giant mutant spiders, and
slaves of the Spider Queen. Spider-Man,
MJ, Reed Richards and Tarantula (Kaine)
must work together to defeat her.

> "New York City! As always, it is
> an honor to call you our home."
>
> **STEVE ROGERS**

> "Atlantis has risen again! We are a whole people once more!"

NAMOR THE SUB-MARINER

Namor in charge
The Sub-Mariner finally locates Atlantis and takes possession.

ATLANTIS

FIRST APPEARANCE *Marvel Comics* #1 (October 1939)
RULED BY Namor the Sub-Mariner

Atlantis is an undersea realm the size of Australia ruled by Namor the Sub-Mariner. The Atlanteans are fiercely independent, though they do assist surface-dwellers when they share a common interest.

Many thousands of years ago, Atlantis is attacked by the barbarians of Lemuria. In defense, King Kamuu opens the capital city's magma pits, which causes an unexpected chain reaction known as the "Great Cataclysm." The realms of Atlantis and Lemuria both collapse into the sea, though some cities manage to survive intact—albeit now underwater. The people of the city of Netheria (later known as Netherworld) foresee the cataclysm and reinforce the city before it is submerged.

More recently, though still thousands of years ago, an aquatic species of humans—*Homo mermanus*—settle in the undersea ruins of Atlantis, rebuild the ancient cities, and become known as Atlanteans. These Atlanteans have blue skin and a pair of gills, requiring water to breathe. They can survive at great depths and at near-freezing temperatures. Atlantis' underwater location limits the development of modern technology, since Atlanteans cannot forge metals. Much of their technology is primitive, except for items they acquire through trade or scavenging.

Atlantis is ruled by Prince Namor the Sub-Mariner, along with a Council of Elders, and a militia to keep the peace. Among their chief foes are the fearsome Deviants, who occupy Lemuria and the great depths of the sea. While Namor claims dominion throughout the sea, independent groups of *Homo mermanus* also exist, such as those ruled by the barbarian warlord and major Namor foe Attuma.

Points of interest in Atlantis include the capital city of Kamuu, the modern city-state of Deluvia (founded by Namor and Marina Smallwood), Maritanis (rebuilt as New Atlantis after it is nearly destroyed by the surface world's nuclear testing, the Realm of Faceless Ones (a monstrous race from the deep sea), the Tomb of Princess Fen (Namor's mother), and the city of Tha-Korr.

Ancient history
The stories of Namor, Hercules, Amadeus Cho, the Amazons, and Cho's lover, Delphyne Gorgon (a green, serpentine Amazonian), all collide in a cataclysm for Atlantis, causing the continent to break apart and collapse into the sea.

City under the sea
Atlantis is a beautiful city of towers, columns, and statues. At its height, Atlantis is ruled by Emperor Thakorr. The Avenue of Poseidon leads to the Imperial Palace, the Temple of Neptune, and the Nautikon, where the Council of Elders deliberates.

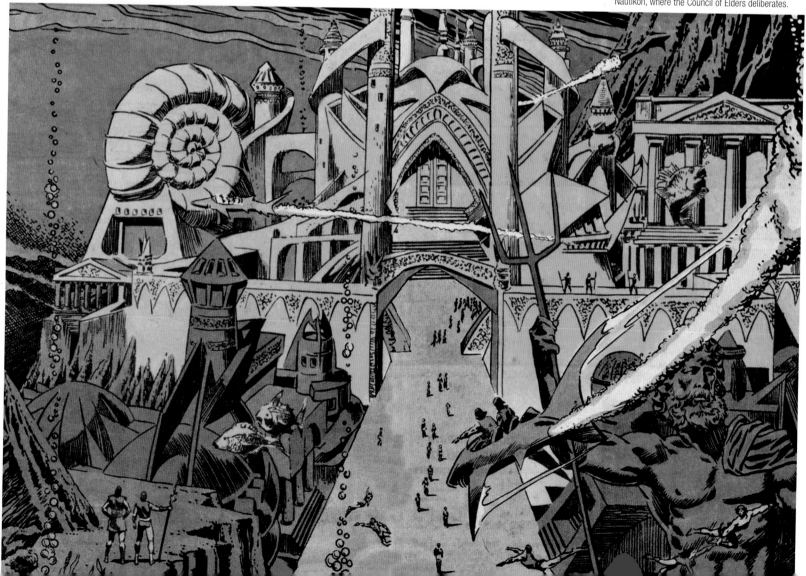

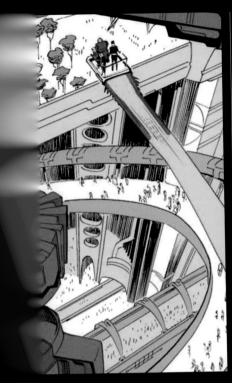

SAVAGE LAND

FIRST APPEARANCE *Marvel Mystery Comics* #22 (August 1941) (as the Land Where Time Stands Still); *X-Men* #10 (as the Savage Land)
LOCATION beneath Antarctica, approximately 69° 30' S, 68° 30' W

An unspoiled region of unnatural beauty and primal terrors, the Savage Land is a fantastic repository of extinct species—a wonderland of lost evolutionary treasures and civilizations. This tropical paradise is populated by dinosaurs, cavemen, sub-species of humanity, and even magical creatures. The Savage Land is located beneath the ice mantle of Antarctica and ringed by active volcanoes. Not surprisingly, it has been hidden from the eyes of humankind for millennia. The entire area is artificial. It is a self-sustaining ecosystem created 200 million years ago by alien Nuwali engineers—working on behalf of god-like "Beyonders"—as a zoo preserve, stocked with flora and fauna from all over the Earth.

As the still-forming Earth underwent geological shifts and species evolved or become extinct, the Nuwali modified and restocked the park with the latest biological successes, including the proto-hominids who would one day become humanity. Approximately 50 million years ago, Earth's continents shifted again and the Nuwali buttressed their preserve, installing volcanoes around the entire region to offset the increasing cold as global shifts left the park located at the new South Pole. Around 200,000 BCE, the Nuwali established self-support systems to sustain the zoological preserve; they then departed Earth. Sometime during the next 100,000 years, a group of Eternals set up a temple complex, before eventually abandoning it to the beasts and sub-men.

Around 18,500 BCE, humans from Atlantis discovered and colonized the park, exporting dinosaurs to their other cities while importing magical creatures such as unicorns and winged horses. Atlantean mystics and scientists divided the park, setting up an immersive, automated amusement park dubbed Pangea to run in parallel with the wilder regions of beasts and primitive beings.

In 18,000 BCE, as a result of mystic feuds and alien incursions, a Great Cataclysm sank Atlantis. The disaster impacted the entire planet and cities in the park were severely damaged. The event prompted the usually aloof Beyonders to despatch their Fortisquian servants—the Caretakers of Arcturus—to repair the park's environmental systems but, despite their best efforts, almost half of the preserve's inhabitants perished. The remaining Atlanteans culturally devolved and physically mutated, becoming primitive tribes such as Swamp Men, battling daily for survival with evolving beast species such as Aerians, Pterons, or Man-Apes.

The park survives, but is largely forgotten except in stories and myths. By the time it is rediscovered in the mid-19th century by *Homo mermanus* from the new undersea Atlantis, the region is truly a Savage Land.

SUBTERRANEA

FIRST APPEARANCE *Marvel Mystery Comics* #10 (August 1940) **LOCATION** Most of planet Earth, miles below the surface **RULED BY** Mole Man, Tyrannus, Lava Men, Kala of the Netherworld, the Deviants

Subterranea is the name given to a vast range of caverns, cities, and countries established far beneath Earth's surface; an interlinked network originally built in ancient prehistory by the technologically advanced Deviants during their wars with the Eternals and Celestials.

Over eons, Subterranea becomes home to monsters and human refugee populations like Queen Kala's Atlanteans of Netheria who, 20,000 years ago, enclosed their city in a plastic dome, removing themselves from the surface in anticipation of attack by Lemurian Deviants.

The vast majority of dwellers below are non-human races, such as Lava Men and Moloids. They and the now-extinct Gortokians (survived only by their mutated Prince Grotesk) were originally created as slave-races by the Deviants.

Moloids make up the greatest proportion of under-Earth denizens. There are many factions, including those loyal to the Mole Man and the "Tyrannoids" of Mole Man's immortal rival Tyrannus. An aquatic offshoot inhabits the sunken city of Meramac and a particularly brutal and barbaric subspecies dubbed the Molans live in the hotter, high-pressure depths far below Subterranea.

Other areas have been colonized by surface-dwellers. The High Evolutionary constructed a Citadel of Science—now the Abandoned City—and Mister Sinister occupies a Moloid city under Anchorage, Alaska, renamed Sinister London.

The first recorded reports of Subterranea date to 1940 when costumed adventurer the Angel battles man-eating "ghouls" beneath the Blue Ridge Mountains of Virginia, discovering a vast realm of cities in seemingly endless caverns. No connection has yet been established between the Deviant-created regions of Subterranea and the monster-built city beneath New York designated Monster Metropolis.

Evolution explosion
When Earth's newest species was created by alien Gardeners, the Avengers turned the Savage Land into the world's most exotic classroom in order to educate young recruits in the arts of survival.

"You know this is where Super Heroes go to get eaten by dinosaurs, right?" **DEADPOOL**

MONSTER ISLAND

FIRST APPEARANCE *Fantastic Four* #1 (November 1961) **LOCATION** Pacific Ocean **RULED BY** Mole Man

Monster Island is a desolate atoll in the Pacific Ocean near Japan. This rocky outpost offers a direct connection to the part of Subterranea ruled by Mole Man. Its surface and subterranean interior is home to a wide selection of incredible giant beasts, many created in years past by Warlord Kro from the Deviant slave-race known as mutates.

After clashing with the Fantastic Four, Mole Man apparently destroys Monster Island in an atomic blast, but later observation reveals it still survives. At one stage, Mole Man cedes the isle to Adam Warlock and the Infinity Watch.

"The Baxter Building will always be home to the Fantastic Four."

PETER PARKER

New and improved
After the original Baxter Building is destroyed, Reed Richards teams up with Noah Baxter to build a new one. Constructed in orbit, the new building is then placed back in its original location, 42nd and Madison.

BAXTER BUILDING

FIRST APPEARANCE *Fantastic Four #3* (March 1962) **LOCATION** Manhattan, New York City **USED BY** Fantastic Four

A Manhattan landmark, the Baxter Building is both home and headquarters to legendary Super Heroes, the Fantastic Four. Resident genius Reed Richards ensures that this impressive building is perfectly designed to meet every Super Hero need.

Built in 1949 by the Leland Baxter Paper Company, the Baxter Building is situated at 42nd and Madison in the heart of Manhattan. Originally an industrial skyscraper, it is repurposed for America's first family of Super Heroes, the Fantastic Four. Reed Richards, a.k.a. Mister Fantastic, buys the top five floors of the 35-story tower and customizes it to meet his team's every need. No member of the public may enter the Fantastic Four's headquarters without encountering Roberta, the computerized receptionist guarding the entrance on the 30th floor. The 31st floor holds the living quarters—at first only Mister Fantastic and the Thing are permanent residents, but they are soon joined by Sue and Johnny Storm. On floor 32 are the medical lab, library, and reference room, while the 33rd floor is Reed Richards' kingdom— it contains his lab and computer center. The 34th level could be said to hold the true headquarters of the FF, as it is here that the briefing room, communications center, and monitoring stations are, where the team keep a lookout for threats across the universe and plan their missions. The top floor houses the Fantastic Four vehicles, and the facilities to repair them. The silo for Reed Richards' rocket runs the length of several floors of the building.

Security is a top priority at the Baxter Building. There are several different systems in place to assess visitors to the building and make sure they are not a threat. It is possible to lock down the top five floors and independently maintain the atmosphere, if needed. Windows are 2ft (0.6m) thick and mirrored on the outside, while the walls are armored and also mirrored, to give the outside of the building total uniformity.

Unfortunately for the various other tenants of the Baxter Building, its status as FF headquarters makes it a tempting target for Super Villains like Doctor Doom. On one occasion, he successfully detaches the building from the ground and launches it into space, although the Fantastic Four later return it safely to Earth. The threats posed to the building make the Fantastic Four's landlord increasingly agitated, and he ends up evicting the team. However, he has to allow them back as he can't find any other tenants willing to move in. Eventually, Reed Richards acts on a clause in the lease that allows him to buy the building outright.

Later the whole building is destroyed by Doctor Doom's heir, Kristoff Vernard. The Fantastic Four then build Four Freedoms Plaza to replace it. When this, too, is destroyed, they move to Pier Four, before Reed Richards teams up with Noah Baxter to rebuild the iconic Baxter Building once more. When the Fantastic Four split up, with the Richards family rebuilding the Multiverse and the Thing and Human Torch joining other teams, Peter Parker buys the Baxter Building to keep it out of the hands of nefarious organizations until such time as the Fantastic Four want to move back to their spiritual home.

High risk
The Baxter Building is problematic for tenants and neighbours, as frequent attacks by Super-Villains make its location dangerous to the point of being uninsurable.

DAILY BUGLE BUILDING

FIRST APPEARANCE *Amazing Spider-Man #1* (March 1963) **LOCATION** Manhattan, New York City **USED BY** *Daily Bugle* staff, J. Jonah Jameson, Spider-Man

The Manhattan home of a famous crusading newspaper, and workplace of a certain web-slinging Super Hero's alter ego, the *Daily Bugle* building has seen an unusual amount of villainous activity for an office block.

Originally the Goodman Building, the *Daily Bugle* building stands 46 stories tall on 39th Street and Second Avenue in Manhattan. It is home to the *Daily Bugle* newspaper, a popular New York tabloid that has been published since 1897. The paper uses three floors for its editorial offices and has printing presses on two sub-basement levels. In its early days, the editorial line is supportive of the emerging brand of costumed hero, but that changes when reporter J. Jonah Jameson rises through the ranks to become editor. He also manages to get enough money together to buy both the *Daily Bugle* and its headquarters. Jameson sees masked crime-fighters as lawless vigilantes, particularly Spider-Man, and publishes countless articles about the "menace" posed by these individuals. Jameson is also an active crusader against the organized crime blighting New York City, which leads him—and the *Daily Bugle* building—to become targets for some of the city's more unsavory characters.

The *Daily Bugle* office is frequently attacked by villains looking for Jameson, or Spider-Man, or both. The Scorpion, the Vulture, the Fly, and the Green Goblin have all caused chaos inside the building. The Green Goblin attacks the *Daily Bugle* with pumpkin bombs that almost cause the building to collapse, but Spider-Man is able to hold it up, using every ounce of his enhanced strength, until all the people trapped inside can escape.

When New York is plagued by demons during the Inferno event, the *Daily Bugle* building is attacked more than once, but the staff fight back, led by Jameson, and drive the horde back.

Although the building is most strongly associated with Jameson, it and the publishing empire housed there have also been owned by Thomas Fireheart, a.k.a.

Puma, Norman Osborn, and Dexter Bennett. Bennett turns the *Daily Bugle* into a scandal sheet called the *DB!*, much to the disgust of Jameson and other staffers, some of whom respond by starting up a new publication called *Front Line*. The change of owner doesn't improve the building's fortunes. During the Skrulls' Secret Invasion, staff are attacked by a Skrull disguised as Spider-Man, searching for the Web-Slinger. And in what seems to be the New York City landmark's swansong, Electro utterly destroys the *Daily Bugle* building, badly wounding Dexter Bennett. Spider-Man and J. Jonah Jameson are on the scene, but they can't prevent the building collapsing. Although its original home is gone, the *Daily Bugle* lives on when Jameson buys the rights to the name back from Bennett's shareholders and gives it to *Front Line*.

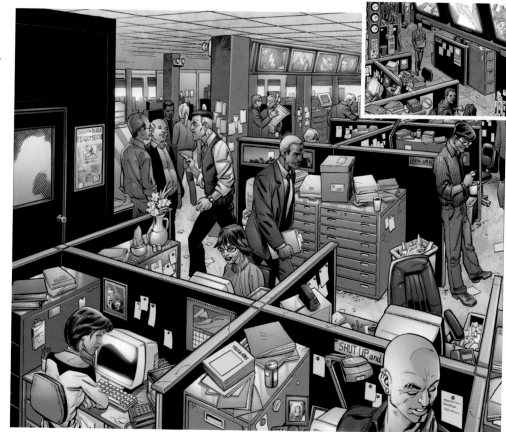

Bullpen
The open-plan offices of the *Daily Bugle* are where the latest stories hot off the New York City streets are committed to print. No desk is beyond editor J. Jonah Jameson's shouting range.

"My one true home."

J. JONAH JAMESON

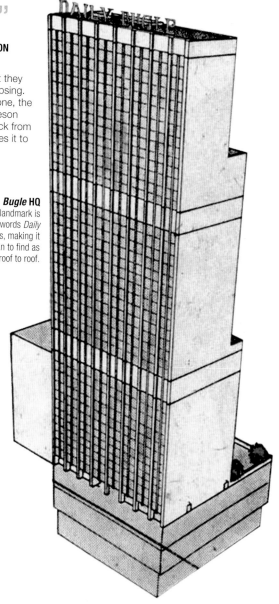

Bugle HQ
This New York landmark is topped with the words *Daily Bugle* in huge letters, making it easy for Spider-Man to find as he swings from roof to roof.

End of an era
After an attack by the super-charged Electro *(left)*, the DB Building, formerly the home of the *Daily Bugle*, comes crashing down. Spider-Man gets everyone out just in time *(above)*.

MIDTOWN HIGH SCHOOL

FIRST APPEARANCE *Amazing Fantasy* #15 (August 1962)
LOCATION Queens, New York City

This high school in Queens seems like the epitome of normality, but one of its top students is also the web-slinging hero known as Spider-Man—and sometimes his battles against the bad guys spill onto the premises of Midtown High.

Located in the Forest Hills district of Queens, New York City, Midtown High is the alma mater of one Peter Parker, a.k.a. the Amazing Spider-Man. In his time at the school,

School days
While Peter Parker buries his head in his science books, Flash Thompson shows off his muscles to an admiring crowd of Midtown High students.

Peter's academic prowess makes him a favorite of the science teachers; however, he is not so popular among his fellow students—who tease Peter for his bookish ways. Several of Peter's Midtown classmates will be key players in his later life, such as football star Flash Thompson, who enjoys bullying Peter, Flash's girlfriend Liz Allan, on whom Peter has a crush, and Jessica Jones, who has a secret crush on Peter.

In his early days as Spider-Man, Peter is feeling down after a setback against Doctor Octopus (Otto Octavius), but is inspired when the Human Torch (Johnny Storm) is invited to come and give a talk at Midtown High. The young hero's confidence impresses Peter, and his message to never give up pushes Parker into donning his costume once more and going after Doc Ock—successfully this time.

Sometime later, the school is used as a hideout by the Sandman (Flint Marko), who decides to take the opportunity to pick up the diploma he never earned by threatening Principal Davis. The principal bravely stands up to the villain, however, and is saved by the timely arrival of Spider-Man.

Sucking up
When the Sandman comes to Midtown High, Spider-Man fights him all round the school, before managing to suck him up in the janitor's vacuum cleaner.

There is further excitement when the I.C.M. (International Computing Machines) Corporation brings its latest marvel to show the senior science class—an advanced humanoid computer called the Living Brain. Peter Parker is selected to ask the Brain a question to test its intelligence, and is horrified when his classmates ask whether the robot can deduce Spider-Man's secret identity. Luckily, it produces its answer in code, buying him time to come up with a plan.

Parker's troubles don't end there, however, as his science teacher Mr. Warren demands that he and Flash Thompson settle their differences with a boxing match in the school gym. Flash's bumptious confidence is misplaced, and even using just a fraction of his powers, Peter easily beats him. However, by this point, all attention is back on the Living Brain, which is running amok through the school. Peter goes in pursuit as Spider-Man, clearing the halls of kids as he goes. Once the Living Brain is neutralized, Peter plants the idea in the minds of his fellow students that Flash is Spider-Man.

When the time comes to graduate, Peter is delighted to find that he has been given a science scholarship so he can attend Empire State University without paying fees. He bids farewell to the school that holds so many memories for him—both as "Puny" Peter Parker and the Amazing Spider-Man.

"I'm miles ahead of the class already."

PETER PARKER

Proud moment
Peter Parker graduates with honors in front of a proud Aunt May. He receives a scholarship to Empire State University, but unfortunately so does bully Flash Thompson.

THE WATCHER'S CITADEL

FIRST APPEARANCE *Fantastic Four* #13 (April 1963)
LOCATION The Moon

When the Fantastic Four travel to the Moon in a rocket built by Reed Richards, they are astonished to find a modern house. Before long, the house's occupant makes himself known—he is the Watcher, an ancient being from a race that travels the universe recording everything that goes on. His citadel on the Moon appears to be made of glass, and contains a great chamber, from which he observes happenings on Earth. Even if the Watcher himself is not present, he can sense any intruders in his home and appear before them as a holographic projection. If their intentions are honorable, they are welcome to stay; if not, they are summarily ejected. Guests are warned not to touch any of the devices in the Watcher's home, as they come from technology so advanced that the human brain could not comprehend it.

Vantage point
At the heart of the Watcher's Citadel is advanced technology allowing him to observe events anywhere in the universe. When there is something he needs to see, the Watcher is drawn here.

BLUE CITY

FIRST APPEARANCE *Fantastic Four* #13 (April 1963) **LOCATION** The Moon

The now-ruined city within the Blue Area of the Moon was originally built by the alien Kree race around one million years ago. It was created in a contest with the tree-like Cotati to see who deserved to share the Skrulls' advanced technology. The Skrulls made a breathable atmosphere for the Kree to work in, which still survives.

Blue City sits above underground caverns accessed by pneumatically powered vehicles, and the evidence of many other technological marvels still remains, like force fields and disintegrator rays. It has been visited by the Fantastic Four and the X-Men. Blue City is the scene of the trial by combat of Jean Grey and her subsequent death when, as the Phoenix, she voluntarily triggers one of the ancient Kree weapons, rather than transform into Dark Phoenix.

HYDROBASE

FIRST APPEARANCE *Sub-Mariner* #61 (May 1973) **USED BY** Doctor Hydro, Stingray, Avengers, Namor the Sub-Mariner

A floating fortress nine miles off the Eastern Seaboard of the United States, Hydrobase is originally used as a jumping-off point for the insane Doctor Hydro's invasion of Atlantis. Hydro uses mutagenic Terrigen Mists to turn a group of hijacked aircraft passengers into amphibious Hydro-People. They live on the island in self-imposed exile until scientist Reed Richards (Mr. Fantastic) finds a cure for their condition.

After this, the oceanographer Walter Newell (Stingray) makes Hydrobase his home and research center. When his grant runs out, he offers to lease space to the Avengers to house their Quinjets after they lose their landing permits in New York City.

Earth's Mightiest Heroes are forced to relocate their whole operation to the island after Avengers Mansion is severely damaged by the Masters of Evil. Since it is movable, they are able to bring it much closer to New York City, but it is attacked by Doombots and consequently sinks. It is later raised and refitted by Namor the Sub-Mariner to be a surface link to the underwater city of Hydropolis.

THE CELLAR (FORMERLY RYKER'S IS.) PRISON

FIRST APPEARANCE *Amazing Spider-Man* #4 (September 1963) **LOCATION** East River, New York City Harbor

Located in the East River between the Bronx and Queens in New York City Harbor, Ryker's Island has served as a high-security prison for decades. In recent times its capacity—15,000 inmates and many thousands of staff—is severely stretched after it becomes home to metahuman criminals. Superseded by purpose-built jails like the Vault, Ryker's Island is wrecked in jailbreaks, and eventually sold to Augustus Roman's Empire Unlimited. Redesigned, "The Cellar" is considered the ultimate prison. No one realizes Roman uses it as his private torture chamber, abusing the inmates and using them in scientific experiments.

"Mutatis Mutandis ("changing [only] those things which need to be changed")

SCHOOL MOTTO

JEAN GREY SCHOOL FOR HIGHER LEARNING

The Jean Grey School for Higher Learning stands proudly defiant in a hostile world, resolutely teaching Earth's most unusual youngsters to defend themselves and the principles of human/mutant coexistence.

FIRST APPEARANCE *X-Men* #1 (September 1963) [Xavier's School for Gifted Youngsters]; *Wolverine and the X-Men* #1 (December 2011) [Jean Grey School for Higher Learning] **LOCATION** Central Park, New York City; formerly 1407 Graymalkin Lane, Salem Center, Westchester County, New York. **OCCUPIED/USED BY** Charles Xavier, Wolverine, Kitty Pryde, generations of mutant students

SCHOOL DAYS

The building now named the Jean Grey School for Higher Learning was first built on land settled by Dutchman Charles Graymalkin in the 1700s. It passed to the Xavier family and, by 1900, a neoclassical mansion stood close to scenic Breakstone Lake, near the town of Salem Center. Charles Xavier, the mutant telepath son of nuclear scientist Dr. Brian Xavier and his wife Sharon, was born and raised there. When, as an adult, Xavier lost the use of his legs battling alien invader Lucifer, he returned to the mansion. With assistance from F.B.I. agent Fred Duncan and in consultation with mutation experts Dr. Karl Lykos and Dr. Moira MacTaggert, Charles transformed the property into Xavier's School for Gifted Youngsters, dedicated to helping young mutants maximize their potential for the good of the world. The boarding school's most intriguing features were secretly constructed with the aid of a man from the future. The enigmatic Cable traded tomorrow's technology in return for Xavier teaching him about the present era.

The groves of academe
The genteel exterior of the school could not conceal the secret mutant warriors-in-training for long.

Public education
When Wolverine and Kitty Pryde reopen the school, it is under the hostile gaze of the entire world and overseen by the U.S. government.

Danger! Danger!
The Danger Room hones fast thinking and provides unmatchable training in avoiding death and injury.

CHILDREN OF THE ATOM

The school offers mutant students an advanced, wide-ranging education in science and the arts, along with combat drills, training in their specific abilities, and physical exercises in the robot-infested, booby-trapped Danger Room. Beginning life as a computerized, mechanical testing ground, the Danger Room is retooled many times using the most advanced human and alien technologies available. It eventually uses an A.I. system that subsequently evolves into the cybernetic mutant Danger. The Jean Grey School later transfers all these functions to a separate Danger Cave in the caverns below the mansion. When the teaching of vulnerable youngsters, such as Generation X, moves to Emma Frost's Massachusetts Academy, the mansion—now a veritable fortress and HQ for X-Men combat missions—is renamed the Xavier Institute for Higher Learning. It serves as a focal point for many social occasions as well as a training facility and hideout. Scott Summers' wedding to Madelyne Pryor is held in the grounds and their son Nathan Christopher is born in the house. Later, Scott marries his lifelong love Jean Grey there.

Build we must!
When the alien Sidri infest and destroy the Mansion the team relocates to the Bermuda Triangle until it is rebuilt.

HOME INVASIONS

The mansion has been frequently damaged and even destroyed. The first time is when Xavier's stepbrother Cain Marko returns as the unstoppable Juggernaut, forcing the X-Men to redesign the building's defenses. These later prove of little use against N'Garai demon Kierrok or when Sidri hunters invade. The entire estate is leveled and rebuilt using Shi'ar technology provided by Empress Lilandra Neramani and innovations by mutant inventor Forge. When the School goes public as the Xavier Institute, with a greatly increased enrolment of youngsters, Professor X cedes control to Scott Summers and Jean Grey; however, a succession of attacks devastate the site. After M-Day reduces Earth's mutant population to less than 200 individuals, the wrecked estate is abandoned.

Enemy at the gates
When Magneto invades the school, he ambushes the X-Men and uses the establishment's own technology to create artificial mutants.

Mission statement
Even in the face of constant attacks, the School for Mutants always embraces diversity and inclusivity.

RISING FROM THE RUINS

After the X-Men split up, Wolverine, Kitty Pryde, the Beast, and other senior X-Men return to Westchester and rebuild the mansion. The new building, dubbed the Jean Grey School for Higher Learning in honor of Professor X's first ever student, offers mutants a place in which to grow, learn, and master their powers. The school is often targeted for attack, but its futuristic classrooms, labs, and dormitories—as well as the students themselves—are protected, thanks to a spore of the geo-mutant Krakoa inhabiting the estate's soil, strata, and fauna. Following a war between mutants and Inhumans, Headmistress Kitty Pryde has the school moved to Central Park, NYC using the Limbo teleportation powers of fellow X-Men Magik.

Under the shade of Krakoa
All mutants are invested in the running of the school. Geomorph Krakoa provides shade, food, and even funds by creating diamonds from its interactions with the soil.

House move
Avengers Mansion goes through many renovations. The building is even moved 35ft (11m) back from the road by Iron Man and Thor, because the 12-ft (3.7m) wall doesn't provide sufficient privacy and security.

"This building was a big part of my past...of all our pasts!"

CAPTAIN AMERICA

AVENGERS MANSION

Tony Stark provided his family home to be the Avengers' base. Inevitably, the mansion has been a prime target for Super Villains.

FIRST APPEARANCE *Avengers* #2 (November 1963) **LOCATION** 721 Fifth Avenue, Manhattan, New York City **USED BY** Avengers, Edwin Jarvis, Red Skull, Sin, Luke Cage, New Avengers

Above ground
The visible section of the mansion has many bedrooms for both permanent and visiting Avengers, as well as a Quinjet hangar and navigation equipment

Training area
The mansion is equipped with a gymnasium, swimming pool, sauna, and steam room, with a combat-training room next door.

Medical bay
With so many dangerous enemies, having easily accessible, state-of-the-art medical care is a must

Assembly room
The latest security devices ensure the Avengers assemble for top-secret meetings in total privacy

Generator room
The backup generator keeps the Avengers' computer system running if the main power supply is cut off

Secure room
This impregnable room provides retreat if the mansion's defenses are breached

Arsenal chamber
Old and new Iron Man armor is stored and tested here, along with other weaponry and equipment

Firing range
Avengers use this space to perfect their aim and train with firearms and other weapons

Built to last?
The gates of the Avengers' Fifth Avenue mansion convey a sense of permanence. If only that could be true...

HOME AND HEADQUARTERS

Built in 1932, Avengers Mansion is much larger than it appears from the outside. The ground floor includes the reception area, dining hall, a library, and the private quarters of Edwin Jarvis, the butler. The second floor houses private rooms for most of the Avengers. The third floor is a hangar and runway for up to four Quinjets and several Sky-Cycles. The below-ground floors are the most secure. The basement level has the training and medical facilities, as well as recreational areas like the game room, gym and Olympic-sized swimming pool. The sub-basement floor below contains meeting rooms, tech labs, power generators and computer servers. The lowest level hides the Avengers' submarine and has secret access to the East River.

BATTLE GROUND

Avengers Mansion is often in turmoil. Baron Helmut Zemo attacks it with his Masters of Evil, during which Jarvis and the Black Knight are badly beaten. The Avengers relocate to their Hydrobase, until repairs are completed. The Red Skull then hatches a diabolical plan to brainwash the mansion's support staff into attacking the Avengers. The mansion is renovated once more before being hit by Proctor and the Gatherers, as well as Sersi. Ute the Watcher seems to restore the mansion, but actually replaces it with a mansion from another dimension. This leads to problems, including an invasion by Kang the Conqueror through a mysterious portal located in the basement.

Hammer blow
Thor flies in to give the monstrous Goliath a taste of Mjolnir's power as the Avengers finally evict the Masters of Evil from their mansion.

AVENGERS DISASSEMBLED

The Avengers are devastated when Scarlet Witch suffers a mental breakdown. She sends an un-dead Jack of Hearts (Jonathan "Jack" Hart) to the Avengers Mansion where he kills Ant-Man (Scott Lang) and blows up a large portion of the building. She also crashes the Vision's Quinjet into the mansion. The building lies in ruins because Iron Man Tony Stark lacks the means to rebuild it. The grounds are declared a landmark by New York City, as a memorial to the Avengers. The team disbands for a time, and when the Avengers are reassembled by Captain America and Iron Man, they move into Stark Tower.

Amid the ruins
Every available Super Hero assembles in front of the devastated mansion, determined to discover who has betrayed the Avengers.

In plain sight
With typical cunning, Red Skull and Sin plot the Avengers' demise in the last place the team would expect—its former base.

WHAT A DOLLAR BUYS

Though Avengers Mansion is officially vacant for a time, the mansion grounds are used by the Young Avengers and are a frequent meeting place for other heroes. After the mansion's restoration, Luke Cage buys it from Tony Stark for $1 and uses it as the headquarters for the New Avengers. During the Fear Itself event, the Avengers move back into the mansion when Avengers Tower is destroyed. This move is only temporary, however—they return to the tower once it is rebuilt. Over time, the mansion is converted into a theme hotel. In a secret room, two unofficial residents— Red Skull and his daughter Sin—quietly orchestrate a sinister plan to do away with Earth's Mightiest Heroes....

SANCTUM SANCTORUM

FIRST APPEARANCE *Strange Tales* #116 (January 1964) **OWNED BY** Doctor Strange

In New York City's Greenwich Village, at 177A Bleeker Street, there is a quirky, three-story brownstone house with a large circular glass window. This is the Sanctum Sanctorum, the home of mystical mastermind Doctor Stephen Strange, his faithful friend and master magician Wong and, formerly, Strange's estranged wife Clea. Belying its exterior, the building is somehow larger on the inside, containing long corridors, rooms full of mystical artifacts, libraries, and guest chambers capable of accommodating Super Hero teams—both the Defenders and the New Avengers have stayed there at different times. The Sanctum Sanctorum stands on a historic site of Native American rituals and pagan sacrifice; the grounds are thus a major gateway for supernatural energies. The house itself is, in its own way, alive with these energies.

The Doctor is in
Librarian Zelma Stanton visits Dr. Strange in his Sanctum Sanctorum with a condition that only he can comprehend.

The first floor contains rooms for relaxation and entertaining, as well as a kitchen and library, and the second floor largely comprises bedrooms. The magic really happens on the third floor: Doctor Strange's meditation chamber contains his most precious mystical artifacts, such as the Book of the Vishanti and the Eye of Agamotto, and his vast library of the occult. The chamber's focal point is the circular window, which bears the sign of Anomaly Rue, the Seal of the Vishanti. This casts a protective spell over the entire structure and its inhabitants.

Despite this, and many other enchantments and mystical fortifications, the Sanctum Sanctorum has been invaded by Warbound Hulks and the Hood. It was even destroyed in a battle with Lilin and the Fallen. Rebuilt, it was enchanted to look like a dilapidated building, and was set to be turned into a Starbucks, before being fully restored to its former glory as a Greenwich Village landmark.

Needs work…
Doctor Strange's home looks to have fallen into disrepair—but looks are deceptive.

HELL'S KITCHEN

FIRST APPEARANCE *Daredevil* #1 (April 1964) **LOCATION** Manhattan, NYC

This seedy area of midtown Manhattan is a home to drugs, corruption, organized crime, and the sightless hero Daredevil, who protects it. Hell's Kitchen sits in the heart of New York City, from 34th to 57th Street and from 8th Avenue over to the Hudson River. This small neighborhood, less than one square mile, contains many famous inhabitants and locales. These include: the law offices of Nelson & Murdock, where best friends Foggy Nelson and (Daredevil's alter ego) Matt Murdock dispense legal advice; Fogwell's Gym, where greats such as Matt's father, Battlin' Jack Murdock, once hit the bags; the Javits Convention Center, scene of the assassin Bullseye's comeuppance; and Josie's Bar, where Hell's Kitchen's roughest clientele grab a drink. Visitors can also go dancing at the dangerous Paradiso Dance Club, pit their skill against Matt's mentor Sticks at Sticks Billiards, or be taken in by a kindly nun, like Matt's estranged mother Sister Maggie, at the Clinton Mission Shelter.

However, Matt Murdock is not the only hero to haunt Hell's Kitchen. The neighborhood also boasts residents such as Jessica Jones, Luke Cage, and Iron Fist, as well as Nick Fury, who was born and raised there.

Unfortunately villains also frequent Hell's Kitchen, including crime lord Wilson Fisk (Kingpin), and his associates, the evil ninja order of the Hand, and sometimes hero, sometimes villain, Elektra.

Fogwell's Gym
It may look run down, but if its walls could talk they would tell an intriguing tale.

LATVERIA

FIRST APPEARANCE *Fantastic Four Annual* #2 (September 1964)
LOCATION Eastern Europe **RULED BY** Victor von Doom

Latveria is situated between Hungary, Romania, and Serbia. The country is ruled with an iron fist by Victor von Doom. Doom spent his early years in Latveria, where both his Gypsy parents died in racial persecutions that were supported by the reigning Fortunov dynasty. After their deaths, Doom threw himself into his education in science and the occult in Tibet and the United States. He then returned to his home country as Doctor von Doom and overthrew King Vladimir, using his vast knowledge of magic (derived from his mother), technology, and robotics.

During his reign, Doom has turned Latveria into a scientifically advanced dictatorship, with an economy predominately reliant upon the export of his own robotics and technology. When Doom is away, he ensures the protection of his throne by leaving behind his personal Life Model Decoy, called a Doombot, and enforces his law using an android army. Much of Latveria has been renamed in his honor, including the capital city Doomstadt, the royal palace Castle Doom, and various areas, such as Doom Falls, Doom Lake… Despite the tight ship that Doom runs, his country has been occupied more than once by the Red Skull. Doom was also ousted for several years by the Fantastic Four, who turned over the country to King Vladimir's son Zorba. However, the remorseless Doom subsequently reclaimed his place on the Latverian throne.

Castle Doom
Situated on a mountaintop, the royal residence of Victor von Doom, Latveria's ruler, looms over Doomstadt, the country's capital.

EMPIRE STATE UNIVERSITY

FIRST APPEARANCE *Amazing Spider-Man* #31 (December 1965) **LOCATION** Greenwich Village, New York City

Since the Big Apple is a hotbed of super-powered activity, both good and evil, it is not surprising that ESU counts many Super Heroes and Super Villains among its alumni—and its faculty. One of its most notable students is Peter Parker, secretly the web-slinging Spider-Man.

After difficulties settling in—his classmates find him studious and introverted at first—Parker becomes good friends with classmates Gwen Stacy and Harry Osborn, and even his high-school nemesis Flash Thompson. Other super-powered students include: the Human Torch, expelled after one of his battles around the campus gets out of hand; Hector Ayala, who becomes Super Hero White Tiger; and telepathic mutant Emma Frost, whose latent skills for teaching young mutants are honed with an Education major. The admission of mutants is occasionally controversial: ESU has an integration viewpoint and is happy to accept mutants, but not everyone is so tolerant, and anti-mutant protests occur during Emma Frost's time.

The teaching faculty has boasted an alarming number of Super Villains. Professor Miles Warren teaches Peter Parker biology, but he later becomes the insane Jackal, trying to get his revenge on Spider-Man following the tragic death of Gwen Stacy, the object of his obsessive love. Dr. Curt Connors comes to ESU on a research grant and is allocated Peter Parker as his teaching assistant—never guessing that Parker is Spider-Man, whom Connors has fought many times as the bizarre Lizard, his alter ego. Other faculty villains have included Lunatik, vice-chancellor Dr. Edward Lansky (Lightmaster), and Professor Clifton Shallot's iteration of the Vulture.

ESU burns
During a battle with two Skrulls, ESU student Johnny Storm, the Human Torch, causes immense damage to the campus with his powers.

ATTILAN

FIRST APPEARANCE *Fantastic Four #47 (February 1966)* **LOCATION**
Formerly North Atlantic Ocean; Himalayas; Blue Area of the Moon; Hala.
Currently Hudson River, New York City (New Attilan) **RULED BY** Black Bolt

The city of Attilan is the Inhumans' ancestral homeland, which has
had many locations over time. As a highly advanced, genetically
improved *Homo sapiens*, the Inhumans achieve many great
technological advancements beyond the scope of ordinary
humanity. Early Inhuman royals decide it will be best to hide their
society away from more barbaric humans; they create the first
Attilan on an island in the North Atlantic Ocean above Iceland,
where they live for thousands of years.

With the advent of easier travel for humans, following the
Industrial Revolution, the Inhuman King Black Bolt moves the
entire city, using antimatter generators, to a more remote location
in the Himalayas. Seeking even greater seclusion and suffering
from pollution caused by humans, Attilan is then sent off-planet to
the Blue Area of the Moon, with its only inhabitant Uatu the
Watcher's blessing. After an alien Skrull attack, Attilan is then
moved into space, near the Kree world of Hala, this time by Black
Bolt's brother Maximus.

However, the whole city comes crashing down into the Hudson
River in New York City when Maximus and Black Bolt conspire to
detonate a Terrigen Bomb, in order to stop the Mad Titan,
Thanos. The city, now called New Attilan, has been rebuilt from
the rubble of its predecessor. New Attilan is home to all Inhumans
created by the Terrigen Mists that were released by the bomb
over the Earth. With Black Bolt missing, they are ruled by the
Inhuman Queen Medusa.

Glad tidings
King T'Challa welcomes news that the Fantastic
Four will soon be coming to Wakanda.

WAKANDA

FIRST APPEARANCE *Fantastic Four #52 (July
1966)* **LOCATION** Africa **RULED BY** Black Panther

This African nation is hidden for hundreds
of years, but that does not prevent the
Wakandan people from developing their
own highly advanced technology. In fact,
Wakanda is believed to be the most
technologically advanced country in the world. It is impervious to
hacking by outside territories because all its technologies are
completely unique to Wakanda. Despite this, the country has not
lost touch with its roots. It is still ruled by a monarchy, with the
Black Panther ruling as king and representative of the divine rule
of Bast the Panther Goddess. The king is protected by an elite,
all-female guard, called the Dora Milaje.

Wakanda also has incredibly rich and sought-after resources,
including the Mena Ngai, also known as the Great Mound. A
meteorite landed on this site, leaving the largest-known deposit of
the super-rare, nearly indestructible metal Vibranium in the world,
most famously used in Captain America's shield. Wakanda also
lays claim to the fertile Alkama Fields that serve as the
"breadbasket of Wakanda," providing a wealth of crops.

City of marvels
The capital of Wakanda, Birnin Zana, is a city of
vibrant colors and technological advancements.

Both assets have attracted scrutiny and envious eyes from
outside factions. Ulysses Klaw is sent to assassinate the former
King T'Chaka because he is unwilling to trade his Vibranium to
the Bilderberg Group, while the neighbouring Nigandan people
believe that the plenty of the Alkama Fields should rightfully be
theirs. Most recently, Wakanda has been under grave scrutiny by
its own people, who feel the monarchy has left many behind. This
has resulted in the uprise of vigilante groups like the Midnight
Angels and the People.

The religions of Wakanda involve animal worship, notably of the
Panther Goddess Bast. Due to a high number of dangerous
mutations from the Vibranium at the great mound, the first Black
Panther, Bashenga (later King of Wakanda) closed the site,
guarding it with his fellow Bast worshippers. Other animal gods
are also worshipped, including Ghekre the
Gorilla God, Sekhmet the Lion Goddess, and
Sobek the Crocodile God.

The title of Black Panther is passed down
through the generations of rulers and grants
the holder access to a heart-shaped herb
affected by Vibranium that gives powers similar
to Captain America's Super-Soldier serum.

> ## "If you attack me...
> ## you attack the
> ## Kingdom of Wakanda."
>
> **BLACK PANTHER**

Wakandan wedding
Wakanda's royal palace provides a
majestic backdrop for the wedding of
Black Panther and Storm.

Sonic boom!
Black Bolt's unleashes his Inhuman
scream, detonating a Terrigen Bomb that
destroys the city of Attilan and sends it
plummeting into New York's Hudson River.

REPUBLIC OF TRANSIA
FIRST APPEARANCE *Avengers* #31 (Aug 1966)
LOCATION Balkans, Europe

The Republic of Transia is a small Balkan
country in Southeastern Europe, nestled
between Serbia, Macedonia, Romania,
and Greece. It is notably the home
country of the Scarlet Witch and
Quicksilver before Magneto rescues them
from persecution in their village and brings
them to the U.S. The most famous
landmark in this largely rural country is the
Wundagore Mountain, which holds a good
deal of infamous history. In the sixth
century, the sorceress Morgan Le Fay and
her occult Darkholders imprisoned the
demon Chthon in Wundagore, which was
later inhabited by the High Evolutionary,
who sought the mountain's rich uranium
deposits. It also housed the Concordance
Engine that held the heart and soul of
the Universe.

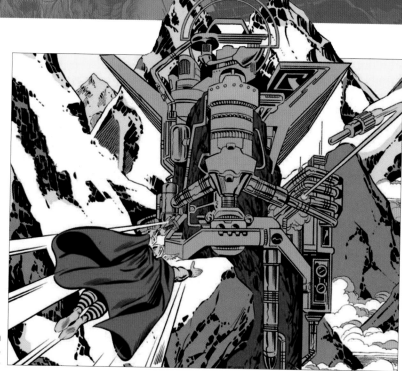

Magic mountain
Thor approaches Wundagore Mountain,
one of Transia's most famous features.

LEMURIA
FIRST APPEARANCE *Sub-Mariner* #10 (February
1969) **LOCATION** Beneath the Pacific Ocean
RULED BY Queen Llyra

The continent of Lemuria used to lie in the
Pacific Ocean before alien Celestials sank
it, hoping to destroy its population of
Deviants (*Homo descendus*). This rapidly
evolving offshoot of humantiy had once
worshipped the Celestials, but turned
against them.
　Now beneath the waves, Lemuria's
ancient civilization has been inhabited by a
subsect of *Homo mermanus* similar to the
Atlanteans. However, the Lemurian race
and culture is quite different. Lemurians
usually have more scales, are greener in
hue than their Atlantean counterparts, and
worship the Elder God Set.
　For 500 years, Lemuria is ruled by the
insane King Naga, who is kept young by
wearing the Serpent Crown. He is later
usurped by his assistant Karthon before
Naga's son Merro ascends to the throne.
He is poisoned by his wife Llyra, who
remains queen after his death.

SEAGATE FEDERAL PENITENTIARY
FIRST APPEARANCE *Hero for Hire* #1 (June
1972) **USED BY** Luke Cage

This maximum-security prison off the
coast of Georgia, sometimes called "Little
Alcatraz," has never had a prisoner
escape, despite housing the worst of
criminals. Among the inmates is the
wrongfully convicted Carl Lucas, a.k.a.
Luke Cage. Lucas was sent to Seagate
after being framed for a murder he didn't
commit by his former friend William
Stryker. Hidden in the depths of the prison
is technology created by Stark Industries.
An electro-biochemical system designed
to stimulate human cell regeneration is
used on the prisoners as test subjects in
exchange for various promises. However,
when the machine is turned up higher
than expected, it makes Carl Lucas super-
durable—allowing him to escape this
supposedly inescapable prison by
swimming to land.

WEIRDWORLD

FIRST APPEARANCE *Marvel Super Action* #1
(January 1976) **LOCATION** Battleworld; Bermuda
Triangle (Earth)
AFFILIATIONS Tyndall of Klarn, Doctor Doom,
Morgan Le Fay, Arkon, Skull the Slayer/Redeemer,
Becca Rodriguez, Black Knight

The original Weirdworld is a magical planet
made up of mystic lands and regions—
many of them islands floating in the air—
populated by dragons, goblins, elves,
wizards, and dwarves, alternatively abiding
with or warring with each other.

   The world was constructed from cosmic
debris in an ancient epoch by elder gods
who used it as a prison for the defeated
entity Darklens after he viciously attacked
his cosmic brethren in an act of infernal
rebellion.

   When the Multiverse collapses,
Weirdworld and fragments of other magical
realms and dimensions are amalgamated
by Doctor Doom into a vassal state—
a floating island placed high above
Battleworld, his personal playground. In
this new territory, Arthurian sorceress
Morgan Le Fay rules in Doom's name, until
she is overthrown by a coalition of
magician Jennifer Kale and valiant warriors
such as Crystar, Arkon the Magnificent,
and Skull the Slayer.

   When Doom is defeated and a new
Prime Reality begins, Weirdworld survives
Battleworld's obliteration and manifests on
the restored planet Earth, hidden from
detection within the Bermuda Triangle.
It remains a constant danger to humanity,
trapping victims such as Rebecca "Becca"
Rodriguez, who becomes an unlikely
questing hero when she seeks a passage
back to the outside world. The Boeing-747

that Becca is traveling in is deliberately
drawn into the Triangle and crashed. The
survivors are rescued by Arkon, who is
still stranded on Weirdworld and still at
war with Morgan Le Fay.

   Weirdworld is also the site of New
Avalon, built by the Black Knight and an
army of warriors as a fortress against the
Avengers Unity Division.

Fantastic fortress
Not even the mighty ramparts of Avalon are
strong enough to hold back all the mystic
menaces infesting chaotic Weirdworld.

Fairytale land
The alternate Earth
Polemachus was only one
of the many fabulous
realms that survived the
destruction of the
Multiverse to become an
integral part of the new
composite Weirdworld.

KRAKOA

FIRST APPEARANCE *Giant-Size X-Men* #1 (May 1975)
LOCATION South Pacific Ocean; Jean Grey School for Higher Learning

1950s atom bomb tests saturated South Pacific island Krakoa
with radiation, mutating its geology, flora, and fauna into a
hivemind capable of reshaping its constituent mass. Krakoa
feeds on mutant bioenergy and almost consumes the X-Men
before being blasted off the planet.

   Thanks to its ability to generate spores, portions of Krakoa
still exist on Earth. Some of its biomass was used to create the
Danger Grotto at Emma Frost's Massachusetts Academy and a
modified version forms the grounds of the Jean Grey School for
Higher Learning, acting as both a defense system and a revenue
generator by growing diamonds on trees.

MUIR ISLAND

FIRST APPEARANCE *X-Men* #104 (April 1977)
LOCATION Outer Hebrides, Scotland

Desolate Muir Island lies off Scotland's northwest coast
and is home to Dr. Moira MacTaggert's Mutant Research
Center (later the Muir Island Genetic Research Center).
She initially builds it to treat her son Kevin, the predatory
mutant Proteus.

   The complex expands thanks to her old friend Charles
Xavier, who uses the isolated outpost as a holding facility
for mutants captured by the X-Men, giving MacTaggert
access to a wide variety of experimental subjects.

   Muir Island has been attacked many times and has
evolved into a fortified citadel. For a period it is also the
base for Super Hero team Excalibur.

Cutting-edge innovation
Isolated Muir Island is in the technological
vanguard of the search to understand all the
many mysteries of mutation.

Getting away from it all
Aside from its futuristic purpose, the sheer
beauty of the island offers peace of mind
to visiting X-Men.

MURDERWORLD

FIRST APPEARANCE *Marvel Team-Up* #66 (February 1978)
LOCATION Mobile

Murderworld is a simulated amusement park created and constructed by psychotic assassin-for-hire Arcade to make contract killing more fun. Using sophisticated hologram projection and virtual-reality systems and employing battalions of robots programmed and tailored to the sensibilities of his victims, Arcade turns his targets into living toys, running them through a series of lethally modified deathtraps resembling puzzles, sideshows, and games. The game continues until they die and he wins.

Deriving pleasure by inducing terror is clearly Arcade's prime objective, since the fees for executing his victims rarely match the costs of transporting, repairing, and upgrading his high-tech wonderland, which can resemble anything from a gigantic pinball machine to the latest sci-fi movie blockbusters.

Originally devised for human victims, Murderworld increasingly becomes the option of choice for villains attempting to remove Super Heroes such as Spider-Man, the X-Men, Excalibur, and X-Factor. Usually the costumed champions survive, but Arcade is always ready to rebuild and play again.

Arcade has set up Murderworlds beneath Manhattan, on Coney Island, in the ghetto of Mutant Town, in the Caribbean, in England and even under Antarctica. He has also leased his resources to Mystique to use as a training ground for the mutant Brotherhood.

One abandoned Murderworld is taken over by Cable and Domino as a base for X-Force and another by Night Thrasher who converts it into a Danger Room to drill his New Warriors recruits. Another old facility traps Kitty Pryde and the Vision after its computer mainframe achieves sentience and abducts the heroes to help it commit suicide.

Deadly games
Murderworld was Arcade's twisted and extremely profitable way of blending his maniacal homicidal tendencies with childhood fantasies of vengeance and death. The X-Men are among his many victims.

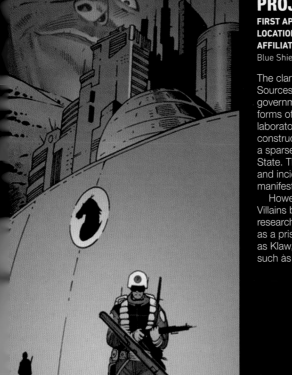

Robot rampage
Apprentice Avenger Reptyl is no match for Arcade's latest generation of robotic recruiters for his ghastly games of death.

PROJECT P.E.G.A.S.U.S

FIRST APPEARANCE *Marvel Two-in-One* #42 #1 (August 1978)
LOCATION Adirondack Mountains, New York State
AFFILIATIONS The Thing, Quasar, Spider-Man, Avengers, Blue Shield, S.H.I.E.L.D.

The clandestine Potential Energy Group/Alternate Sources/United States project is created by the U.S. government to investigate alternative and unknown forms of energy. The vast multi-leveled research laboratory and engineering complex is secretly constructed inside a mountain in the Adirondacks, a sparsely populated region of New York State. There, scientists probe all manner and incidences of new forces as they manifest in the modern world.

However, as energy-wielding Super Villains become a key area of that research, the facility is increasingly used as a prison housing deadly menaces such as Klaw, Solarr, and Nuklo, or volunteers such as Dazzler and Wundarr.

Questionable research
The Project's research into the powers of villains, such as the Absorbing Man often had devastating consequences for the staff and security officers.

Not-so-secret invasion
When shape-shifting Skrulls fail to infiltrate P.E.G.A.S.U.S., they seek to destroy it rather than leave its advanced discoveries in the hands of Earth's heroic defenders.

MASSACHUSETTS ACADEMY

FIRST APPEARANCE *Uncanny X-Men* #151 (November 1981) **HEADMISTRESS** Emma Frost

The Massachusetts Academy is one of the oldest and most respected preparatory schools in the U.S. Founded in the 18th century, it is located in Snow Valley, Massachusetts.

Mutant Emma Frost serves as the academy's headmistress, and later takes full control of the school with fellow mutant and billionaire businessman Sebastian Shaw. They align the academy with the exclusive Hellfire Club and form an elite group within it, known as the Inner Circle. Frost trains the academy's young mutants to become Hellions—assassins who serve the Inner Circle. Frost's academy becomes a rival of sorts for Xavier's School for Gifted Youngsters, as the Hellions are rivals to the X-Men. The two schools even compete to enroll the same students, such as Kitty Pryde.

As time goes on, Frost begins to cooperate with Professor Xavier's school. When the New Mutants are killed and recreated by the Beyonder, they are apathetic and disconnected from their own powers. Frost ensures that they are transferred into her care at the Massachusetts Academy by manipulating Magneto—and they end up working together for the students' benefit. When the young mutants are well, Frost transfers them back to the Xavier School.

The Hellfire Club and the Hellions are not always at odds with the X-Men, and their relationship does improve. When mutant-hunting Sentinels attack Frost, she falls into a coma and is cared for by Xavier—he also takes control of the Massachusetts Academy, as directed in her will. After she recovers, Frost joins Xavier in reopening the Academy as the new Xavier's School for Gifted Youngsters.

Headmistress Frost
Professor Emma Frost welcomes a new class of students. A tough teacher, Frost was a competitor of Xavier's school, but soon allies with the X-Men.

AVENGERS COMPOUND

FIRST APPEARANCE *Avengers* #246 (August 1984) **USED BY** West Coast Avengers

Dating from 1921, Avengers Compound is at 1800 Palos Verdes Drive, just south of Los Angeles, California. It was previously the luxurious 15-acre home of actress Sylvia Powell, and later actress Moira Brandon, until the Avengers purchase it. Intended for their West Coast branch, it is remodeled after the designs of Tony Stark's Avengers Mansion on the East Coast and made more suitable to the super-powered team's needs.

The ground floor contains living space, a dining area, a ballroom, and a large portion of the library. The second floor contains Hawkeye and Mockingbird's private quarters, offices, and the remainder of the library. The three basement levels contain high-security areas for training, meetings, and laboratories—there is also a sizable underground hangar for vehicles, such as Quinjets and Hawkeye's Sky-Cycle.

SYMKARIA

FIRST APPEARANCE *Amazing Spider-Man* #265 (June 1985) **HOME TO** Silver Sable, Wild Pack, the Circle

The Kingdom of Symkaria is a landlocked country located in the Balkans, Eastern Europe, bordered by Latveria, Romania, and Serbia. Symkaria is the home of Silver Sable (Silver Sablinova) and the Wild Pack, as well as being the headquarters for groups such as the V-Battalion and the Circle. Castle Sable is located in the capital, Aniana. Originally Symkaria is a monarchy, but becomes a crown republic. It is a member of the United Nations and has an embassy in New York City.

During World War II, Symkaria suffers great losses during the Nazi invasion, but is never fully occupied, thanks to the V-Battalion. Symkaria also remains free of Soviet domination during the Cold War. The Wild Pack continues to hunt Nazi criminals from its base in Symkaria after World War II. The group is later transformed into Silver Sable International —which helps to support the country's economy by employing citizens as mercenaries in a much broader role.

Political stability in Symkaria is tenuous. Silver Sable, Spider-Man, and Captain America become caught in the middle of a terrorist plot by U.L.T.I.M.A.T.U.M. (Underground Liberated Totally Integrated Mobile Army To Unite Mankind), which leaves Prime Minister Limka and King Stefan's fiancée dead. When it looks as if the C.I.A. might be involved in an assassination attempt on the King, relations between Symkaria and the U.S. government turn sour.

After Silver Sable is killed battling Rhino (Aleksei Sytsevich), the country is overcome by drug trafficking and falls into depression. During this time, other organizations rise to prominence.

The Circle is a secret, Arthurian-inspired mercenary organization located on the island of New Avalon in Lake Symkaria. Its large facility and stadium dominate the small island. Its members try to establish themselves as rivals to Tony Stark and the Avengers.

Trouble in Aniana
The Secret Avengers—Steve Rogers, Sharon Carter, Black Widow, and Moon Knight—go undercover in Aniana, Symkaria, to confront the ruthless drug lord, Voydanoi, who is peddling a supernatural substance.

PRINCIPALITY OF MADRIPOOR

FIRST APPEARANCE *New Mutants* #32 (October 1985) **RULED BY** Hydra, Tyger Tiger, Daken

The Principality of Madripoor is an island city-state in Southeast Asia, located in the Strait of Malacca between Sumatra and Singapore. Madripoor is approximately 100 miles (160km) in diameter—and rests on the head of a giant sleeping dragon.

Once a haven for pirates, Madripoor is now a business center, but is still notorious for its lawlessness. Rich and poor live at extreme ends of the social ladder and the island is divided accordingly. Hightown— opulent and modern—is the district for the powerful and wealthy. The Royal Palace and Museum are located there, as well as one of the finest hotels in the world: the Sovereign Hotel. Lowtown is a district of rampant crime. The Princess Bar, owned by Wolverine (under the alias Patch), is a focal point that draws both the rich and the dregs of society. Elsewhere in the city are a hidden S.H.I.E.L.D. safe house, and the Empty Quarter—which is supernaturally connected to the Negative Zone.

Iron Man and S.H.I.E.L.D. wrest control of the island from the terrorist group Hydra and turn control of it over to Tyger Tiger (Jessán Hoan). Then Wolverine's son, Daken, seizes control of the island. But when the Director (Malcolm Colcord), unleashes days of violence when he arrives to carry out his Super-Soldier experiments, Tyger, Daken, Gambit (Remy LeBeau), and Wolverine clone X-23 (Laura Kinney) work together to uproot him.

When Daken is killed, Tyger Tiger resumes control of the nation. Other notable—but temporary—residents of Madripoor include Sabretooth (Victor Creed), Scorpion (Camilla Black), and Jessica Drew—when she briefly quits as Spider-Woman to become a private eye.

Patch at the Princess
Wolverine—alias Patch—waits for Hulk, along with Jessica Drew, Karma, General Coy, Tyger Tiger, Lindsay McCabe, and Captain Tai at the Princess Bar.

THE VAULT

FIRST APPEARANCE *Avengers Annual* #15 (October 1986)
USED BY U.S. government

The U.S. government maintains a top-secret underground penitentiary deep within the Rocky Mountains of Colorado, intended to house superhuman criminals. The facilities are reinforced with omnium steel and Adamantium, and contain power-dampening fields. The Vault has 35 guards on duty.

Early administrators include the warden, Howard G. Hardman, the head of security, Michael O'Brien, and the head of the science team, Dr. Henri Sorei. The first superhuman inmates were not criminals at all, but Avengers betrayed by Quicksilver (Pietro Maximoff) and the Freedom Force. Other notable prisoners include Venom (Eddie Brock), Loki, and the Masters of Evil. After its destruction by the U-Foes, the Vault is deemed an unsuitable prison and decommissioned.

Open Vault
Electro's diversion allows the Vault's inmates to escape. Spider-Man is caught between Crossfire's Crew and the U-Foes.

RAVENCROFT INSTITUTE

FIRST APPEARANCE *Web of Spider-Man* #112 (May 1994) **USED BY** Dr. Ashley Kafka, Dr. Leonard Samson

Ravencroft is an institution for the mentally disturbed, which is rebuilt as a specific facility for superhumans after Carnage (Cletus Kasady) leaves a trail of destruction through the original building. Spearheading the new and improved Ravencroft is Dr. Ashley Kafka, a psychiatrist with a history of treating Super Villains. John Jameson is her head of security. Forced to open its doors before being fully staffed and ready, Ravencroft suffers an early setback when the deranged sound-manipulator Shriek (Frances Barrison) escapes her manacles and frees the other prisoners; luckily, Spider-Man is on hand to get the situation under control. Other notable prisoners of the Ravencroft Institute have included Chameleon, Mysterio, Electro, Vulture, and Doctor Octopus.

GENOSHA

FIRST APPEARANCE *Uncanny X-Men* #235 (October 1988) **FREQUENTED BY** Sugar Man, Genegineer, Magistrates, Magneto, Selene, Red Skull

The island nation of Genosha has a chequered place in the history of mutantkind. Situated in the Indian Ocean, it becomes the most economically advanced nation in the world—its wealth derived from the forced labor of enslaved mutants. Genoshans are tested for mutant DNA and, if testing positive, become the property of the state. They are then submitted to a process that turns them into obedient mutates, whose powers are honed to provide maximum usefulness. Prime movers in this proceeding are: Sugar Man, a four-armed, reptilian-tongued, slave-driving emigrant from an alternate future (Earth-295, the Age of Apocalypse); and ruthless scientist David Moreau, known as Genegineer.

The Genoshan mutates' plight becomes known to the X-Men, who help overthrow this brutal, anti-mutant regime. The island then sinks into a bloody civil war between its mutant and human populations. In the aftermath, the powerful mutant Magneto blackmails the U.N. into

City of the dead
Necrosha, formerly Genosha, is the setting for evil mutant Selene's blood ritual, enabling her to consume the souls of its dead citizens and become a dark goddess.

ceding control of Genosha to him, to found a mutant nation. Sixteen million mutants are living on Genosha on the day that Cassandra Nova (the evil spiritual "twin" of Professor X) sends massive Wild Sentinel robots to destroy it—nearly all the mutants are slaughtered in the attack. However, Magneto survives the assault and sets about rebuilding the shattered island with the help of his old friend and nemesis Professor X. Unfortunately, the island is ruined and abandoned once more during the fall-out from the events of House of M.

The deserted island proves a tempting prize for the psionic vampire and sorceress Selene, who raises the Genoshan dead from the Sentinel attack in order to feed on their souls. She then renames the island Necrosha and its former capital, Hammer Bay, becomes Black Rome.

After the defeat and death of Selene, Genosha enters yet another sorry phase of its existence when it becomes a mutant concentration camp under the malign auspices of Red Skull (a clone of the original, also named Johann Schmidt). Magneto later utterly destroys Genosha, sending it beneath the waves in a show of defiance to the world.

REPUBLIC OF SLORENIA

FIRST APPEARANCE *Force Works* #4 (October 1994) **INHABITED BY** Black Brigade, Ember, Ultron, Bloodwraith

A Baltic nation whose capital is Tblunka, Slorenia is a former Soviet state. After the end of the Cold War, the newly independent country is riven by tensions between the ethnic Slorenians and the minority Dudaks. The two sides have been locked in conflict for centuries, each gaining power over the other for a time until the cycle starts again. It is only after the capital is severely damaged in the fighting that the Slovenes and Dudaks resolve to put aside their differences for a process of rebuilding. However, an even worse situation awaits the population—the human-hating robot Ultron utterly destroys the country, razing cities and towns and slaughtering every man, woman, and child

"By decree of the United Nations, I now claim Genosha as my own!"

THE CUBE

FIRST APPEARANCE *Marvel Boy* #6 (January 2001) **USED BY** S.H.I.E.L.D., Marvel Boy, Thunderbolts

S.H.I.E.L.D. claim that the Cube is an inescapable prison. It is hundreds of miles from civilization and is built to contain 400 Super Villains. Its mysterious, sadistic Warden takes full advantage of its super-secret status—it does not officially exist—and the lack of human rights for its alien inmates. One such is Marvel Boy, imprisoned and made a mind slave of the Warden. When he is freed by Vision and the Young Avengers, Marvel Boy takes over the Cube himself, claiming it as the capital city of a new Kree Empire. Marvel Boy sets about rehabilitating all the other extraterrestrial prisoners, but his plans are ruined by the Skrulls' Secret Invasion of Earth. the Cube is later used as a base for the Thunderbolts.

THE WORLD

FIRST APPEARANCE *New X-Men* #130 (October 2002) **USED BY** Weapon Plus

Located somwhere in England, the World is an incredibly advanced research facility created for the Weapon Plus program. It comprises one square mile contained within a dome, in which time itself can be controlled—sped up, slowed down, or even frozen—by the scientists who run the facility. This enables them to tamper with the rate of evolution, and couple it with nanotechnology and eugenics. The scientists take people who will not be missed to experiment on. These individuals then exist within the World's own society, which has its own ethos and culture. The successful experiments are turned into living weapons and assigned numbers. Those created at the World include Weapon XII, a.k.a. Huntsman, and Weapon XIII, a.k.a Fantomex. Partially destroyed during an attack by agents of A.I.M., the World itself evolves to become sentient, and continues to make weapons, despite being deserted by its staff.

THE RAFT

FIRST APPEARANCE *Alias* #26 (November 2003) **USED BY** S.H.I.E.L.D.

Located near maximum-security Ryker's Island penitentiary is the Raft, a smaller island housing what may be called maximum-maximum-security prisoners. The Raft houses Super Villains such as the psychopathic Carnage (Cletus Kasady), albino assassin Tombstone (Lonnie Lincoln), scientist turned crime lord Mister Hyde (Calvin Zabo), and arch-manipulator the Purple Man (Zebediah Killgrave). Despite its high security, the Raft has seen more than one prison break. After an event orchestrated by Electro, in which 46 inmates escaped, security is tightened further. During Otto Octavius' time as the Superior Spider-Man, he commandeers the Raft as his base, renaming it Spider-Island Two. It is destroyed by Norman Osborn's Goblin Nation.

THE KYLN

FIRST APPEARANCE *Thanos* #7 (May 2004) **USED BY** Omega Corps; pan-galactic law enforcement agencies

The Kyln space prison has three functions. Situated at the border of the expansion of the universe, also known as the Crunch, its interlinked, spherical structure is a massive power generator. The Kyln also houses maximum-security prisoners who have been sentenced to death—life expectancy for inmates is said to be less than three years. Notable prisoners have included: Star-Lord, a.k.a. Peter Quill; the former herald of Galactus known as the Fallen One; Gladiator (Melvin Potter); and the Maker (an insane female version of the Beyonder). The Kyln has also become a pilgrimage site for various religions, whose denizens come to observe the edge of the universe and meditate on their place in creation. The Kyln is eventually destroyed by Annihilus' Annihilation Wave.

PROVIDENCE

FIRST APPEARANCE *Cable and Deadpool* #6 (October 2004) **FREQUENTED BY** Cable

Nathan Summers (Cable) creates the floating island of Providence by telekinetically uniting the scattered pieces of his space station at a location in the South Pacific. Cable's intention is to provide a place where the planet's finest minds can come together and work on ways to make the Earth a better place. Anyone can come to Providence, as long as they undergo a week of psychological profiling and skills testing.

Despite Cable's repeated assertions that he is only trying to make the future of the world brighter, governments and other organizations around the globe are made extremely nervous about such a powerful mutant having his own floating city, not to mention thousands of gifted followers.

Providence is subsequently attacked by S.H.I.E.L.D., the U.S. military, the X-Men, and the Silver Surfer.

When the Silver Surfer attacks Cable, the two cause incredible damage to Providence, but use their extraordinary powers to repair it at the same time. Meanwhile, the X-Men realize that Providence's apparently high-tech gravity generators are nothing more than shells, and the only thing keeping the island floating in the air is Cable's mutant telekinesis powers. As Cable's strength diminishes following his battle with the Silver Surfer and the deployment of a device by Deadpool that further reduces his powers, Cable helps Rachel Grey lower Providence into the sea. Later, following an attack by the Shi'ar's Hecatomb weapon, Cable is forced to destroy Providence to stop the information in its archives falling into hostile hands.

A dream dies
Cable's great scheme for bettering humanity fails when he is forced to trigger Providence's self-destruct mechanism on.

THE PEAK

FIRST APPEARANCE *Astonishing X-Men* #10 (May 2005) **USED BY** S.W.O.R.D.

The Peak is the headquarters of the Sentient World Observation and Response Department, often called S.W.O.R.D., which sits in Earth's orbit. This highly advanced space station serves as home and workplace to S.W.O.R.D. agents who protect the Earth from alien and otherworldly threats, and also contains their prisoners.

A multitude of practical spaces exist within the Peak, from the station's bridge, its maximum-security brig, and its bar named the Gravity Well. Important business is decided in a special chamber by the Peak Council, which meets holographically with S.W.O.R.D.'s leader, Abigail Brand.

PRISON 42

FIRST APPEARANCE *Civil War: Front Line* #5 (October 2006) **DESIGNED BY** Tony Stark, Henry Pym, Reed Richards

The Negative Zone Prison Alpha is known as Prison 42 or Project 42. This is because it was Tony Stark's 42nd idea with fellow geniuses Yellowjacket (Hank Pym), and Mister Fantastic (Reed Richards)—after the Stamford Incident—which involved the New Warriors heroes and resulted in over 600 civilian deaths.

Prisoners are teleported from Ryker's Island Penitentiary to the Negative Zone, a parallel dimension that is nearly uninhabitable. Because of its negative charge, the Negative Zone can have a debilitating effect on the human psyche, so the prison is nearly completely automated, with a robotic guard system. Over time, the atmosphere wreaks havoc on its prisoners' minds, leading to emotional crises and delusions, which is why many inmates call it Fantasy Island or Wonderland. Prisoners are forbidden to touch each other, and have minimal social interaction.

Originally designed to contain the most dangerous Super Villains, it is also used to hold any Super Heroes that refuse to reveal their secret identities and comply with the Superhuman Registration Act. Speedball (Robbie Baldwin), the only New Warrior who survived the Stamford Incident, was held in Prison 42 leading up to his trial, before being gunned down on the courthouse steps and nearly

Out of sight
Super Heroes and Super villains unwilling to cooperate with the Superhuman Registration Act are shipped in pods through a portal to the Negative Zone—removing any chance of them endangering the public.

killed. Prison 42 is also the scene of the climactic battle of the first superhuman civil war between Captain America and Iron Man.

During the Skrulls' Secret Invasion of Earth, the teleporter to the Negative Zone is disconnected, leaving the prisoners to

their own devices, only to have the Negative Zone overtaken by the villain Blastaar who hopes to invade the Earth using Prison 42's portal.

Due to the potential for further interdimensional attack, the portal is eventually shut down.

THE BIG HOUSE

FIRST APPEARANCE *She-Hulk* #5 (September 2004) **DESIGNED BY** Henry Pym

Ironically, the Lang Memorial Penitentiary, commonly called the Big House—or sometimes, the Ant Farm—is full of tiny criminals. This experimental prison is created by Dr. Henry Pym, best known for his scientific research of growing and shrinking matter using his Pym Particles.

Within this Alcatraz-like island estate is a tiny prison for Super Villains. Because inmates have been shrunk to miniature size, the threat they pose to those that guard them is much reduced, saving manpower and expense.

Villains such as the Wrecking Crew, Sandman, Absorbing Man, Scorpion, and the Rhino have all served time at the Big House. However, the prison's shortcomings are revealed when a rat infestation leads to a major prison break.

CAMP HAMMOND

FIRST APPEARANCE *Avengers: The Initiative* #1 (June 2007) **USED BY** Avengers Initiative

This superhuman training base, also referred to as "Hero Boot Camp" is built on the site of the Stamford Incident in Connecticut, where the explosive villain Nitro was attacked by the New Warriors. The resulting explosion killed hundreds of civilians.

The facility is named in honor of Jim Hammond, the original Human Torch, and is the headquarters of the Avengers Initiative. At Camp Hammond, new Super Heroes who agree to comply with the Superhuman Registration Act are trained to protect state-sanctioned Super Hero teams. Students are put through training for combat, first aid, and Super Hero ethics. On graduating, they are upgraded to full Super Hero status.

A super education
These austere grounds in Stamford serve as the learning facility for new Super Hero recruits. The former Human Torch, Jim Hammond, is immortalized in statue form in the grounds.

Camp Hammond is run by Henry Gyrich, with Yellowjacket serving under him as Chief Administrator, and War Machine as Camp Director. The Gauntlet serves as drill instructor until he falls into a coma and is replaced by the reformed villain Taskmaster. Superspy Black Widow teaches marksmanship, underwater superhuman Stingray teaches swimming, and Triathlon, among others, serves as the gym instructor.

When the camp is overrun during the Secret Invasion, it is set up as a Skrull headquarters and many of the students are replaced by the shape-shifting aliens. However, when Ragnarok, the android Thor clone, goes on a rampage, and a dead student is reported to have been replaced by a clone, Norman Osborn, head of security agency H.A.M.M.E.R., shuts down Camp Hammond to protect the people of Connecticut.

KNOWHERE

FIRST APPEARANCE *Nova* #8 (January 2008)
USED BY Cosmo, Luminals, Annihilators,
Guardians of the Galaxy

Knowhere looks like a planet, but it is
actually the severed head of an incredibly
powerful ancient alien called a Celestial.
This enormous head has its own
inhabitants and floats on the edge of the
universe near the end of space and time.

Due to its close proximity to the edge
of nothingness, species from across the
universe come to study it. The Continuum
Cortex inside the Celestial's brainstem
allows residents or visitors to teleport
anywhere in space. Knowhere's
inhabitants include Cosmo, a telepathic,
talking dog; the alien Luminals; and the
Annihilators. Knowhere has become the
base for the Guardians of the Galaxy.

Living in his head
Inside the head of this deceased Celestial floating on
the edge of the universe, lives an entire community
of various aliens existing on the fringe of society.

BAGALIA

FIRST APPEARANCE *Secret Avengers* #2.1 (March
2012) **USED BY** Baron Zemo, Masters
of Evil, U-Foes, Young Masters of Evil,
Wrecking Crew

This sovereign island nation is anything but
peaceful. Truly anything goes in this
lawless pleasure island for convicts.

Places of interest in the country's
underground capital, Bagalia City, include
Hell Town, the home of Mephisticuffs fight
club and eatery, and Hellstrom Manor
where visitors can hang out with the Son
of Satan himself. Other delights are
Constrictor's Snakepit, headquarters of the
Young Masters of Evil and the Circus of
Crime, the Hole bar, or the Massacrer
Casino, where rich customers play a game
of life and death. There are also work
opportunities with the Masters of Evil at
Zemo Tower and mercenary jobs available
at Umbral Dynamics.

A lawless land
The red-light city of
Bagalia looks surprisingly
developed for a lawless
place run by criminals.
The Masters of Evil's
Shadow Council keeps a
watchful eye from its
palatial headquarters.

ATLANTIS DESTROYED!

"By his very actions, Namor is the architect of his own destruction."

POWER PRINCESS

After existing for thousands of years, Atlantis finally crumbles to ruin when attacked by a team of immensely powerful, extradimensional heroes—the Squadron Supreme.

It has survived raids from undersea rivals, wars with surface invaders, and even assault by alien despots. But, finally, Atlantis' days are numbered. The Squadron Supreme—Hyperion (Marcus Milton of Earth-13034), Blur (Jeff Walters of Earth-14861), Doctor Spectrum (of Earth-429001), Nighthawk (Kyle Richmond of Earth-31916), and Power Princess (Zarda Shelton of Earth-712)—unite after a new Earth is restored following the end of the Multiverse. The sworn goal of these survivors of their own alternate Earths' doom is to police this last reality (the Marvel Universe's Prime Earth), which they are resolved to preserve at all costs. Their first act is to punish Namor the Sub-Mariner, leader of the Cabal, a group of villains responsible for eradicating many alternate Earths.

DEATH OF A LEGEND

Their retaliation is swift and merciless, as mighty Hyperion drags the sunken city out of the life-sustaining seas and crushes it to Earth. Guilt-wracked Namor does not long survive the doom of his beloved realm. He literally loses his head in a no-holds-barred duel with Hyperion.

Satisfied that justice has been served, the Squadron are woefully unaware that a traitor in their midst plans similar fates for them all…

Battle to the death
The clash between Namor, Attuma, and the Atlantean forces, and the ruthless Squadron Supreme leads to the end of Atlantis and the death of its last monarch.